Thomas Babington Macaulay

The complete works of Lord Macaulay

Thomas Babington Macaulay

The complete works of Lord Macaulay

ISBN/EAN: 9783741175954

Manufactured in Europe, USA, Canada, Australia, Japa

Cover: Foto ©Andreas Hilbeck / pixelio.de

Manufactured and distributed by brebook publishing software (www.brebook.com)

Thomas Babington Macaulay

The complete works of Lord Macaulay

THE WORKS

OF

LORD MACAULAY.

VOL. II.

THE WORKS

OF

LORD MACAULAY

COMPLETE.

EDITED BY HIS SISTER LADY TREVELYAN.

IN EIGHT VOLUMES.

VOL. II.

LONDON:
LONGMANS, GREEN, AND CO.
1871.

CONTENTS
OF
THE SECOND VOLUME.

CHAPTER VII.

	PAGE
William, Prince of Orange; His Appearance	1
His early Life and Education	2
His theological Opinions	3
His military Qualifications	4
His Love of Danger: his bad Health	6
Coldness of his Manners and Strength of his Emotions; His Friendship for Bentinck	7
Mary, Princess of Orange	10
Gilbert Burnet	11
He brings about a good Understanding between the Prince and Princess	15
Relations between William and English Parties	16
His Feelings towards England; His Feelings towards Holland and France	17
His Policy consistent throughout	21
Treaty of Augsburg; William becomes the Head of the English Opposition	24
Mordaunt proposes to William a Descent on England	25
William rejects the Advice	26
Discontent in England after the Fall of the Hydes; Conversions to Popery; Peterborough; Salisbury	27
Wycherley; Tindal; Haines	28
Dryden	29
The Hind and Panther	31
Change in the Policy of the Court towards the Puritans	33
Partial Toleration granted in Scotland	37
Closeting; It is unsuccessful	38
Admiral Herbert; Declaration of Indulgence	39
Feeling of the Protestant Dissenters	41
Feelings of the Church of England	42
The Court and the Church	43

	PAGE
Letter to a Dissenter; Conduct of the Dissenters	45
Some of the Dissenters side with the Court; Care	49
Alsop; Rosewell; Lobb	49
Penn; The Majority of the Puritans are against the Court; Baxter	50
Howe; Bunyan	51
Kiffin	53
The Prince and Princess of Orange hostile to the Declaration of Indulgence	58
Their Views respecting the English Roman Catholics vindicated	59
Enmity of James to Burnet	65
Mission of Dykvelt to England; Negotiations of Dykvelt with English Statesmen	67
Danby; Nottingham	68
Halifax	69
Devonshire	70
Edward Russell; Compton; Herbert	73
Churchill	74
Lady Churchill and the Princess Anne	75
Dykvelt returns to the Hague; with Letters from many eminent Englishmen	78
Zulestein's Mission; Growing Enmity between James and William	79
Influence of the Dutch Press; Correspondence of Stewart and Fagel	81
Castlemaine's Embassy to Rome	82

CHAPTER VIII.

Consecration of the Nuncio at St. James's Palace; His public Reception; The Duke of Somerset	87
Dissolution of the Parliament; Military Offences illegally punished	89
Proceedings of the High Commission; The Universities	91
Proceedings against the University of Cambridge	94
The Earl of Mulgrave	95
State of Oxford	97
Magdalene College, Oxford	99
Anthony Farmer recommended by the King for President	102
Election of the President; The Fellows of Magdalene cited before the High Commission	103
Parker recommended as President; The Charterhouse	104
The Royal Progress	105
The King at Oxford; He reprimands the Fellows of Magdalene	107
Penn attempts to mediate	108
Special Ecclesiastical Commissioners sent to Oxford	111
Protest of Hough; Parker	112
Ejection of the Fellows	114
Magdalene College turned into a Popish Seminary	115
Resentment of the Clergy	116
Schemes of the Jesuitical Cabal respecting the Succession	117
Scheme of James and Tyrconnel for preventing the Princess of Orange from succeeding to the Kingdom of Ireland	119

THE SECOND VOLUME.

	PAGE
The Queen pregnant; General Incredulity	120
Feeling of the Constituent Bodies, and of the Peers	122
James determines to pack a Parliament	124
The Board of Regulators	125
Many Lords Lieutenants dismissed; The Earl of Oxford	126
The Earl of Shrewsbury	127
The Earl of Dorset	128
Questions put to the Magistrates; Their Answers; Failure of the King's Plans	132
List of Sheriffs; Character of the Roman Catholic Country Gentlemen	136
Feeling of the Dissenters	138
Regulation of Corporations	139
Inquisition in all the Public Departments	142
Dismission of Sawyer	143
Williams Solicitor General	144
Second Declaration of Indulgence	145
The Clergy ordered to read it	146
They hesitate; Patriotism of the Protestant Nonconformists of London	147
Consultation of the London Clergy	148
Consultation at Lambeth Palace; Petition of the Seven Bishops presented to the King	150
The London Clergy disobey the Royal Order	153
Hesitation of the Government	154
It is determined to prosecute the Bishops for a Libel	156
They are examined by the Privy Council	157
They are committed to the Tower	158
Birth of the Pretender; He is generally believed to be suppositious	160
The Bishops brought before the King's Bench and bailed	164
Agitation of the Public Mind	166
Uneasiness of Sunderland	167
He professes himself a Roman Catholic; Trial of the Bishops	168
The Verdict; Joy of the People	177
Peculiar State of Public Feeling at this time	182

CHAPTER IX.

Change in the Opinion of the Tories concerning the lawfulness of Resistance	185
Russell proposes to the Prince of Orange a Descent on England; Henry Sydney	191
Devonshire	191
Shrewsbury; Halifax; Danby	191
Bishop Compton	193
Nottingham; Lumley; Invitation to William despatched	196
Conduct of Mary	193
Difficulties of William's Enterprise	193
Conduct of James after the Trial of the Bishops	203
Dismissions and Promotions	204
Proceedings of the High Commission. Sprat resigns his Seat	205
Discontent of the Clergy; Transactions at Oxford	206

	PAGE
Discontent of the Gentry	207
Discontent of the Army	208
Irish Troops brought over; Public Indignation	209
Lillibullero	214
Politics of the United Provinces; Errors of the French King	215
His Quarrel with the Pope concerning Franchises	217
The Archbishopric of Cologne	218
Skilful Management of William	219
His Military and Naval Preparations	220
He receives numerous Assurances of Support from England	222
Sunderland	223
Anxiety of William	226
Warnings conveyed to James	227
Exertions of Lewis to save James	228
James frustrates them	229
The French Armies invade Germany	231
William obtains the Sanction of the States General to his Expedition	232
Schomberg	233
British Adventurers at the Hague	234
William's Declaration	235
James roused to a Sense of his Danger	237
His Naval Means	238
His Military Means; He attempts to conciliate his subjects	239
He gives Audience to the Bishops	240
His Concessions ill received	242
Proofs of the Birth of the Prince of Wales submitted to the Privy Council	244
Disgrace of Sunderland	246
William takes leave of the States of Holland	247
He embarks and sails; He is driven back by a Storm; His Declaration arrives in England	248
James questions the Lords	249
William sets sail a second time	250
He passes the Straits	252
He lands at Torbay	253
He enters Exeter	257
Conversation of the King with the Bishops	261
Disturbances in London	263
Men of Rank begin to repair to the Prince	264
Lovelace	265
Colchester; Abingdon	266
Desertion of Cornbury	267
Petition of the Lords for a Parliament	270
The King goes to Salisbury	272
Seymour; Court of William at Exeter	273
Northern Insurrection	275
Skirmish at Wincanton	277
Desertion of Churchill and Grafton	279
Retreat of the Royal Army from Salisbury; Desertion of Prince George and Ormond	280
Flight of the Princess Anne	281
Council of Lords held by James	281

	PAGE
He appoints Commissioners to treat with William; the Negotiation a Feint	287
Dartmouth refuses to send the Prince of Wales into France	289
Agitation of London	290
Forged Proclamation	291
Rising in various Parts of the Country	292
Clarendon joins the Prince at Salisbury; Dissension in the Prince's Camp	294
The Prince reaches Hungerford; Skirmish at Reading	297
The King's Commissioners arrive at Hungerford; Negotiation	298
The Queen and the Prince of Wales sent to France; Lauzun	303
The King's Preparations for Flight	306
His Flight	307

CHAPTER X.

The Flight of James known; Great Agitation; The Lords meet at Guildhall	308
Riots in London	312
The Spanish Ambassador's House sacked	313
Arrest of Jeffreys	314
The Irish Night	316
The King detained near Sheerness	320
The Lords order him to be set at liberty	324
William's Embarrassment	325
Arrest of Feversham; Arrival of James in London	326
Consultation at Windsor	328
The Dutch Troops occupy Whitehall; Message from the Prince delivered to James	331
James sets out for Rochester; Arrival of William at St. James's	332
He is advised to assume the Crown by Right of Conquest	334
He calls together the Lords and the Members of the Parliaments of Charles II.	336
Flight of James from Rochester	339
Debates and Resolutions of the Lords	340
Debates and Resolutions of the Commoners summoned by the Prince; A Convention called; Exertions of the Prince to restore Order	341
His tolerant Policy	342
Satisfaction of Roman Catholic Powers; State of Feeling in France	344
Reception of the Queen of England in France	345
Arrival of James at Saint Germains	347
State of Feeling in the United Provinces	348
Election of Members to serve in the Convention	349
Affairs of Scotland	350
State of Parties in England	353
Sherlock's Plan	355
Sancroft's Plan	356
Danby's Plan	358
The Whig Plan	360

	PAGE
Meeting of the Convention; Leading Members of the House of Commons	361
Choice of a Speaker	363
Debate on the State of the Nation	365
Resolution declaring the Throne vacant	366
It is sent up to the Lords; Debate in the Lords on the Plan of Regency	368
Schism between the Whigs and the Followers of Danby	375
Meeting at the Earl of Devonshire's	376
Debate in the Lords on the Question whether the Throne was vacant; Majority for the Negative; Agitation in London	378
Letter of James to the Convention	379
Debates; Negotiations; Letter of the Princess of Orange to Danby; the Princess Anne acquiesces in the Whig Plan	380
William explains his Views	381
The Conference between the Houses	383
The Lords yield; New Laws proposed for the Security of Liberty	385
Disputes and Compromise	387
The Declaration of Right	389
Arrival of Mary	389
Tender and Acceptance of the Crown	390
William and Mary proclaimed	391
Peculiar Character of the English Revolution	392

CHAPTER XI.

William and Mary proclaimed in London	399
Rejoicings throughout England; Rejoicings in Holland	400
Discontent of the Clergy and of the Army	401
Reaction of Public Feeling	402
Temper of the Tories	403
Temper of the Whigs	406
Ministerial Arrangements	408
William his own Minister for Foreign Affairs	409
Danby	410
Halifax	411
Nottingham	412
Shrewsbury; The Board of Admiralty	413
The Board of Treasury; The Great Seal	414
The Judges	415
The Household	416
Subordinate Appointments	418
The Convention turned into a Parliament	419
The Members of the Two Houses required to take the Oaths	422
Questions relating to the Revenue	424
Abolition of the Hearth Money	426
Repayment of the Expenses of the United Provinces; Mutiny at Ipswich	427
The first Mutiny Bill	431
Suspension of the Habeas Corpus Act	435
Unpopularity of William	436

THE SECOND VOLUME.

	PAGE
Popularity of Mary	438
The Court removed from Whitehall to Hampton Court	440
The Court at Kensington	443
William's foreign Favourites	444
General Maladministration	445
Dissensions among Men in Office	447
Department of Foreign Affairs	450
Religious Disputes	452
The High Church Party	453
The Low Church Party	454
William's Views concerning Ecclesiastical Polity; Burnet, Bishop of Salisbury	456
Nottingham's Views concerning Ecclesiastical Polity	460
The Toleration Bill	461
The Comprehension Bill	468
The Bill for settling the Oaths of Allegiance and Supremacy	475
The Bill for settling the Coronation Oath	489
The Coronation	490
Promotions	492
The Coalition against France; The Devastation of the Palatinate	493
War declared against France	497

CHAPTER XII.

State of Ireland at the Time of the Revolution; The Civil Power in the hands of the Roman Catholics	499
The Military Power in the hands of the Roman Catholics	501
Mutual Enmity between the Englishry and the Irishry	502
Panic among the Englishry	503
History of the Town of Kenmare	504
Enniskillen	507
Londonderry	508
Closing of the Gates of Londonderry	510
Mountjoy sent to pacify Ulster	512
William opens a Negotiation with Tyrconnel	513
The Temples consulted	515
Richard Hamilton sent to Ireland on his Parole	516
Tyrconnel sends Mountjoy and Rice to France	517
Tyrconnel calls the Irish People to arms	518
Devastation of the Country	519
The Protestants in the South unable to resist	523
Enniskillen and Londonderry hold out	524
Richard Hamilton marches into Ulster with an Army	525
James determines to go to Ireland	526
Assistance furnished by Lewis to James	527
Choice of a French Ambassador to accompany James	528
The Count of Avaux	529
James lands at Kinsale; James enters Cork	531
Journey of James from Cork to Dublin	533
Discontent in England	535
Factions at Dublin Castle	536

	PAGE
James determines to go to Ulster; Journey of James to Ulster	541
The Fall of Londonderry expected	544
Succours arrive from England; Treachery of Lundy; The Inhabitants of Londonderry resolve to defend themselves	546
Their Character	548
Londonderry besieged	552
The Siege turned into a Blockade	554
Naval Skirmish in Bantry Bay	555
A Parliament summoned by James sits at Dublin	556
A Toleration Act passed	560
Acts passed for the Confiscation of the Property of Protestants	561
Issue of Base Money	565
The Great Act of Attainder	567
James prorogues his Parliament	569
Persecution of the Protestants in Ireland	570
Effect produced in England by the News from Ireland	572
Actions of the Enniskilleners	574
Distress of Londonderry	575
Expedition under Kirke arrives in Lough Foyle; Cruelty of Rosen	576
The Famine in Londonderry extreme	579
Attack on the Boom	581
The Siege of Londonderry raised	583
Operations against the Enniskilleners	586
Battle of Newton Butler	587
Consternation of the Irish	589

HISTORY OF ENGLAND.

CHAPTER VII.

THE place which William Henry, Prince of Orange Nassau, occupies in the history of England and of mankind is so great that it may be desirable to portray with some minuteness the strong lineaments of his character.*

He was now in his thirty-seventh year. But both in body and in mind he was older than other men of the same age. Indeed it might be said that he had never been young. His external appearance is almost as well known to us as to his own captains and counsellors. Sculptors, painters, and medallists exerted their utmost skill in the work of transmitting his features to posterity; and his features were such as no artist could fail to seize, and such as, once seen, could never be forgotten. His name at once calls up before us a slender and feeble frame, a lofty and ample forehead, a nose curved like the beak of an eagle, an eye rivalling that of an eagle in brightness and keenness, a thoughtful and somewhat sullen brow, a firm and somewhat peevish mouth, a cheek pale, thin, and deeply furrowed by sickness and by care. That pensive, severe, and solemn aspect could scarcely have belonged to a happy or a goodhumoured man. But it indicates in a manner not to be mistaken capacity equal to the most arduous enterprises, and fortitude not to be shaken by reverses or dangers.

Nature had largely endowed William with the qualities of

---

* The chief materials from which I have taken my description of the Prince of Orange will be found in Burnet's History, in Temple's and Courville's Memoirs, in the Negotiations of the Counts of Estrades and Avaux, in Sir George Downing's Letters to Lord Chancellor Clarendon, in Wagenaar's voluminous History, in Van Kampen's Karakterkunde der Vaderlandsche Geschiedenis, and, above all, in William's own confidential correspondence, of which the Duke of Portland permitted Sir James Mackintosh to take a copy.

CHAP.
VII.

His early
life and
education.

a great ruler; and education had developed those qualities in no common degree. With strong natural sense, and rare force of will, he found himself, when first his mind began to open, a fatherless and motherless child, the chief of a great but depressed and disheartened party, and the heir to vast and indefinite pretensions, which excited the dread and aversion of the oligarchy then supreme in the United Provinces. The common people, fondly attached during three generations to his house, indicated, whenever they saw him, in a manner not to be mistaken, that they regarded him as their rightful head. The able and experienced ministers of the republic, mortal enemies of his name, came every day to pay their feigned civilities to him, and to observe the progress of his mind. The first movements of his ambition were carefully watched; every unguarded word uttered by him was noted down; nor had he near him any adviser on whose judgment reliance could be placed. He was scarcely fifteen years old when all the domestics who were attached to his interest, or who enjoyed any share of his confidence, were removed from under his roof by the jealous government. He remonstrated with energy beyond his years, but in vain. Vigilant observers saw the tears more than once rise in the eyes of the young state prisoner. His health, naturally delicate, sank for a time under the emotions which his desolate situation had produced. Such situations bewilder and unnerve the weak, but call forth all the strength of the strong. Surrounded by snares in which an ordinary youth would have perished, William learned to tread at once warily and firmly. Long before he reached manhood he knew how to keep secrets, how to baffle curiosity by dry and guarded answers, how to conceal all passions under the same show of grave tranquillity. Meanwhile he made little proficiency in fashionable or literary accomplishments. The manners of the Dutch nobility of that age wanted the grace which was found in the highest perfection among the gentlemen of France, and which, in an inferior degree, embellished the Court of England; and his manners were altogether Dutch. Even his countrymen thought him blunt. To foreigners he often seemed churlish. In his intercourse with the world in general he appeared ignorant or negligent of those arts which double the value of a favour and take away the sting of a refusal. He was little interested in letters or science. The discoveries of Newton and Liebnitz, the poems of Dryden and Boileau, were unknown to him. Dramatic performances tired him, and he was glad to turn away from the stage and to talk about public affairs, while Orestes was raving, or while Tartuffe was pressing Elmira's hand. He had indeed some talent for sarcasm, and not seldom employed, quite unconsciously, a natural rhetoric, quaint, indeed, but vigorous, and original. He did not, however, in the least affect the character of a wit or of an orator. His attention had been confined to those studies which form strenuous and sagacious men of business. From a child he listened with interest when high questions of alliance, finance, and war were discussed. Of geometry he learned as much as was necessary for the construction of a ravelin or a hornwork. Of languages, by the help of a memory singularly powerful, he learned as much as was necessary to enable him to comprehend and answer without assistance everything that was said to him, and every letter which he received. The Dutch was his own tongue. With the French he was not less familiar. He understood Latin, Italian, and Spanish. He spoke and wrote English and German, inelegantly, it is true, and inexactly, but fluently and intelligibly. No qualification could be more important to a man whose life was to be passed in organising great alliances, and in commanding armies assembled from different countries.

One class of philosophical questions had been forced on his attention by circumstances, and seems to have interested him more than might have been expected from his general character. Among the Protestants of the United Provinces, as among the Protestants of our island, there were two great religious parties which almost exactly coincided with two great political parties. The chiefs of the municipal oligarchy were Arminians, and were commonly regarded by the multitude as little better than Papists. The princes of Orange had generally been the patrons of the Calvinistic divinity, and owed no small part of their popularity to their zeal for the doctrines of election and final perseverance, a zeal not always enlightened by knowledge or tempered by humanity. William had been carefully instructed from a child in the theological system to which his family was attached; and he regarded that system with even more than the partiality which men generally feel for a hereditary faith. He had ruminated on the great enigmas which had been discussed in the Synod of Dort, and had found in the austere and inflexible logic of the Genevese school something which suited his intellect and his temper. That example of intolerance indeed which some of his prede-

CHAP. VII.

censors had set he never imitated. For all persecution he felt a fixed aversion, which he avowed, not only where the avowal was obviously politic, but on occasions where it seemed that his interest would have been promoted by dissimulation or by silence. His theological opinions, however, were even more decided than those of his ancestors. The tenet of predestination was the keystone of his religion. He often declared that, if he were to abandon that tenet, he must abandon with it all belief in a superintending Providence, and must become a mere Epicurean. Except in this single instance, all the sap of his vigorous mind was early drawn away from the speculative to the practical. The faculties which are necessary for the conduct of important business ripened in him at a time of life when they have scarcely begun to blossom in ordinary men. Since Octavius the world had seen no such instance of precocious statesmanship. Skilful diplomatists were surprised to hear the weighty observations which at seventeen the Prince made on public affairs, and still more surprised to see a lad, in situations in which he might have been expected to betray strong passion, preserve a composure as imperturbable as their own. At eighteen he sate among the fathers of the commonwealth, grave, discreet, and judicious as the oldest among them. At twenty-one, in a day of gloom and terror, he was placed at the head of the administration. At twenty-three he was renowned throughout Europe as a soldier and a politician. He had put domestic factions under his feet: he was the soul of a mighty coalition; and he had contended with honour in the field against some of the greatest generals of the age.

His military qualifications.

His personal tastes were those rather of a warrior than of a statesman: but he, like his great-grandfather, the silent prince who founded the Batavian commonwealth, occupies a far higher place among statesmen than among warriors. The event of battles, indeed, is not an unfailing test of the abilities of a commander; and it would be peculiarly unjust to apply this test to William; for it was his fortune to be almost always opposed to captains who were consummate masters of their art, and to troops far superior in discipline to his own. Yet there is reason to believe that he was by no means equal, as a general in the field, to some who ranked far below him in intellectual powers. To those whom he trusted he spoke on this subject with the magnanimous frankness of a man who had done great things, and who could well afford to acknowledge some deficiencies. He had never, he said, served an apprenticeship to the military profession. He had been placed, while still a boy, at the head of an army. Among his officers there had been none competent to instruct him. His own blunders and their consequences had been his only lessons. "I would give," he once exclaimed, "a good part of my estates to have served a few campaigns under the Prince of Condé before I had to command against him." It is not improbable that the circumstance which prevented William from attaining any eminent dexterity in strategy may have been favourable to the general vigour of his intellect. If his battles were not those of a great tactician, they entitled him to be called a great man. No disaster could for one moment deprive him of his firmness or of the entire possession of all his faculties. His defeats were repaired with such marvellous celerity that, before his enemies had sung the Te Deum, he was again ready for conflict; nor did his adverse fortune ever deprive him of the respect and confidence of his soldiers. That respect and confidence he owed in no small measure to his personal courage. Courage, in the degree which is necessary to carry a soldier without disgrace through a campaign, is possessed, or might, under proper training, be acquired, by the great majority of men. But courage like that of William is rare indeed. He was proved by every test; by war, by wounds, by painful and depressing maladies, by raging seas, by the imminent and constant risk of assassination, a risk which has shaken very strong nerves, a risk which severely tried even the adamantine fortitude of Cromwell. Yet none could ever discover what that thing was which the Prince of Orange feared. His advisers could with difficulty induce him to take any precaution against the pistols and daggers of conspirators.* Old sailors were amazed at the composure which he preserved amidst roaring breakers on a perilous coast. In battle his bravery made him conspicuous even among tens of thousands of brave warriors, drew forth the generous applause of hostile armies, and was scarcely ever questioned even by the injustice of hostile factions. During his first campaigns he exposed himself like a

---

* William was earnestly entreated by his friends, after the peace of Ryswick, to speak seriously to the French ambassador about the schemes of assassination which the Jacobites of Saint Germain's were constantly contriving. The cold magnanimity with which these intimations of danger were received is singularly characteristic. To Bentinck, who had sent from Paris very alarming intelligence, William merely replied, at the end of a long letter of business.—"Pour les assassins je ne lay en ay pas voulu parler, cruiant que c'étuit un dessein de moy." May $\frac{1}{11}$, 1698. I keep the original orthography, if it is to be so called.

man who sought for death, was always foremost in the charge and last in the retreat, fought, sword in hand, in the thickest press, and, with a musket ball in his arm and the blood streaming over his cuirass, still stood his ground and waved his hat under the hottest fire. His friends adjured him to take more care of a life invaluable to his country; and his most illustrious antagonist, the great Condé, remarked, after the bloody day of Seneff, that the Prince of Orange had in all things borne himself like an old general, except in exposing himself like a young soldier. William denied that he was guilty of temerity. It was, he said, from a sense of duty, and on a cool calculation of what the public interest required, that he was always at the post of danger. The troops which he commanded had been little used to war, and shrunk from a close encounter with the veteran soldiery of France. It was necessary that their leader should show them how battles were to be won. And in truth more than one day which had seemed hopelessly lost was retrieved by the hardihood with which he rallied his broken battalions and cut down the cowards who set the example of flight. Sometimes, however, it seemed that he had a strange pleasure in venturing his person. It was remarked that his spirits were never so high and his manners never so gracious and easy as amidst the tumult and carnage of a battle. Even in his pastimes he liked the excitement of danger. Cards, chess, and billiards gave him no pleasure. The chase was his favourite recreation; and he loved it most when it was most hazardous. His leaps were sometimes such that his boldest companions did not like to follow him. He seems even to have thought the most hardy field sports of England effeminate, and to have pined in the great park of Windsor for the game which he had been used to drive to bay in the forests of Guelders, wolves, and wild boars, and huge stags with sixteen antlers.*

His love of danger: his bad health.

The audacity of his spirit was the more remarkable because his physical organisation was unusually delicate. From a child he had been weak and sickly. In the prime of manhood his complaints had been aggravated by a severe attack of

* From Windsor he wrote to Bentinck, then ambassador at Paris. "J'ay pris avant hier un cerf dans la forest avec les chains du Pr. de Denm. et ay fait un assez jolie chasse, autant que ce vilain païs le permest." March 29, April 1, 1698. The spelling is bad, but not worse than Napoleon's. William wrote in better humour from Loo. "Nous avons pris deux gros cerfs, le premier dans Dierewaert, qui est un des plus gros que je sache avoir jamais pris. Il porte seise." Oct. 14, Nov. 4, 1697.

smallpox. He was asthmatic and consumptive. His slender frame was shaken by a constant hoarse cough. He could not sleep unless his head was propped by several pillows, and could scarcely draw his breath in any but the purest air. Cruel headaches frequently tortured him. Exertion soon fatigued him. The physicians constantly kept up the hopes of his enemies by fixing some date beyond which, if there were anything certain in medical science, it was impossible that his broken constitution could hold out. Yet, through a life which was one long disease, the force of his mind never failed, on any great occasion, to bear up his suffering and languid body.

He was born with violent passions and quick sensibilities: but the strength of his emotions was not suspected by the world. From the multitude his joy and his grief, his affection and his resentment, were hidden by a phlegmatic serenity, which made him pass for the most coldblooded of mankind. Those who brought him good news could seldom detect any sign of pleasure. Those who saw him after a defeat looked in vain for any trace of vexation. He praised and reprimanded, rewarded and punished, with the stern tranquillity of a Mohawk chief: but those who knew him well and saw him near were aware that under all this ice a fierce fire was constantly burning. It was seldom that anger deprived him of power over himself. But when he was really enraged the first outbreak of his passion was terrible. It was indeed scarcely safe to approach him. On these rare occasions, however, as soon as he regained his selfcommand, he made such ample reparation to those whom he had wronged as tempted them to wish that he would go into a fury again. His affection was as impetuous as his wrath. Where he loved, he loved with the whole energy of his strong mind. When death separated him from what he loved, the few who witnessed his agonies trembled for his reason and his life. To a very small circle of intimate friends, on whose fidelity and secrecy he could absolutely depend, he was a different man from the reserved and stoical William whom the multitude supposed to be destitute of human feelings. He was kind, cordial, open, even convivial and jocose, would sit at table many hours, and would bear his full share in festive conversation. Highest in his favour stood a gentleman of his household named Bentinck, sprung from a noble Batavian race, and destined to be the founder of one of the great patrician houses of England. The fidelity of Bentinck had been tried by no common test. It was while the United Provinces were struggling for existence against the French power that the young Prince on whom all their hopes were fixed was seized by the smallpox. That disease had been fatal to many members of his family, and at first wore, in his case, a peculiarly malignant aspect. The public consternation was great. The streets of the Hague were crowded from daybreak to sunset by persons anxiously asking how His Highness was. At length his complaint took a favourable turn. His escape was attributed partly to his own singular equanimity, and partly to the intrepid and indefatigable friendship of Bentinck. From the hands of Bentinck alone William took food and medicine. By Bentinck alone William was lifted from his bed and laid down in it. "Whether Bentinck slept or not while I was ill," said William to Temple, with great tenderness, "I know not. But this 1 know, that, through sixteen days and nights, I never once called for anything but that Bentinck was instantly at my side." Before the faithful servant had entirely performed his task, he had himself caught the contagion. Still, however, he bore up against drowsiness and fever till his master was pronounced convalescent. Then, at length, Bentinck asked leave to go home. It was time: for his limbs would no longer support him. He was in great danger, but recovered, and, as soon as he left his bed, hastened to the army, where, during many sharp campaigns, he was ever found, as he had been in peril of a different kind, close to William's side.

Such was the origin of a friendship as warm and pure as any that ancient or modern history records. The descendants of Bentinck still preserve many letters written by William to their ancestor: and it is not too much to say that no person who has not studied those letters can form a correct notion of the Prince's character. He, whom even his admirers generally accounted the most distant and frigid of men, here forgets all distinctions of rank, and pours out all his thoughts with the ingenuousness of a schoolboy. He imparts without reserve secrets of the highest moment. He explains with perfect simplicity vast designs affecting all the governments of Europe. Mingled with his communications on such subjects are other communications of a very different, but perhaps not of a less interesting kind. All his adventures, all his personal feelings, his long runs after enormous stags, his carousals on Saint Hubert's day, the growth of his plantations, the failure of his melons, the state of his stud, his wish to procure an easy pad nag for his wife, his vexation at learning that one of his household, after ruining a girl of good family, refused to marry her, his fits of sea sickness, his coughs, his headaches, his devotional moods, his gratitude for the divine protection after a great escape, his struggles to submit himself to the divine will after a disaster, are described with an amiable garrulity hardly to have been expected from the most discreet and sedate statesman of the age. Still more remarkable is the careless effusion of his tenderness, and the brotherly interest which he takes in his friend's domestic felicity. When an heir is born to Bentinck, "he will live, I hope," says William, "to be as good a fellow as you are; and, if I should have a son, our children will love each other, I hope, as we have done."* Through life he continues to regard the little Bentincks with paternal kindness. He calls them by endearing diminutives; he takes charge of them in their father's absence, and though vexed at being forced to refuse them any pleasure, will not suffer them to go on a hunting party, where there would be risk of a push from a stag's horn, or to sit up late at a riotous supper.† When their mother is taken ill during her husband's absence, William, in the midst of business of the highest moment, finds time to send off several expresses in one day with short notes containing intelligence of her state.‡ On one occasion, when she is pronounced out of danger after a severe attack, the Prince breaks forth into fervent expressions of gratitude to God. "I write," he says, "with tears of joy in my eyes."§ There is a singular charm in such letters, penned by a man whose irresistible energy and inflexible firmness extorted the respect of his enemies, whose cold and ungracious demeanour repelled the attachment of almost all his partisans, and whose mind was occupied by gigantic schemes which have changed the face of the world.

His kindness was not misplaced. Bentinck was early pro-

---

* March 8. 1679.
† "Voilà ce peu de mal le détail de nostre St. Hubert. Et j'ay en soin que M. Woodstoc" (Bentinck's eldest son) "n'a point esté à la chasse, bien moins au souper, quoyqu'il fut icy. Vous pouvez pourtant croire que de s'avoir pas chassé l'a un peu mortifié, mais je ne l'ay pas aussi prendre sur moy, puisque vous m'avies dit que vous ne le souhaitiies pas." From Loo, Nov. 4. 1697.
‡ On the 16th of June, 1688.
§ September 6. 1679.

nounced by Temple to be the best and truest servant that ever prince had the good fortune to possess, and continued through life to merit that honourable character. The friends were indeed made for each other. William wanted neither a guide nor a flatterer. Having a firm and just reliance on his own judgment, he was not partial to counsellors who dealt much in suggestions and objections. At the same time he had too much discernment, and too much elevation of mind, to be gratified by sycophancy. The confidant of such a prince ought to be a man, not of inventive genius or commanding spirit, but brave and faithful, capable of executing orders punctually, of keeping secrets inviolably, of observing facts vigilantly, and of reporting them truly; and such a man was Bentinck.

William was not less fortunate in marriage than in friendship. Yet his marriage had not at first promised much domestic happiness. His choice had been determined chiefly by political considerations; nor did it seem likely that any strong affection would grow up between a handsome girl of sixteen, well disposed indeed, and naturally intelligent, but ignorant and simple, and a bridegroom who, though he had not completed his twenty-eighth year, was in constitution older than her father, whose manner was chilling, and whose head was constantly occupied by public business or by field sports. For a time William was a negligent husband. He was indeed drawn away from his wife by other women, particularly by one of her ladies, Elizabeth Villiers, who, though destitute of personal attractions, and disfigured by a hideous squint, possessed talents which well fitted her to partake his cares.* He was indeed ashamed of his errors, and spared no pains to conceal them: but, in spite of all his precautions, Mary well knew that he was not strictly faithful to her. Spies and talebearers, encouraged by her father, did their best to inflame her resentment. A man of a very different character, the excellent Ken, who was her chaplain at the Hague during some months, was so much incensed by her wrongs that he, with more zeal than discretion, threatened to reprimand her husband severely.† She, however, bore her injuries with a meekness and patience which deserved, and gradually obtained, William's esteem and gratitude. Yet

* See Swift's account of her in the Journal to Stella.
† Henry Sidney's Journal of March 31. 1680, is in Mr. Blencowe's interesting collection.

there still remained one cause of estrangement. A time would probably come when the Princess, who had been educated only to work embroidery, to play on the spinet and to read the Bible and the Whole Duty of Man, would be the chief of a great monarchy, and would hold the balance of Europe, while her lord, ambitious, versed in affairs, and bent on great enterprises, would find in the British government no place marked out for him, and would hold power only from her bounty and during her pleasure. It is not strange that a man so fond of authority as William, and so conscious of a genius for command, should have strongly felt that jealousy which, during a few hours of royalty, put dissension between Guildford Dudley and the Lady Jane, and which produced a rupture still more tragical between Darnley and the Queen of Scots. The Princess of Orange had not the faintest suspicion of her husband's feelings. Her preceptor, Bishop Compton, had instructed her carefully in religion, and had especially guarded her mind against the arts of Roman Catholic divines, but had left her profoundly ignorant of the English constitution and of her own position. She knew that her marriage vow bound her to obey her husband; and it had never occurred to her that the relation in which they stood to each other might one day be inverted. She had been nine years married before she discovered the cause of William's discontent; nor would she ever have learned it from himself. In general his temper inclined him rather to brood over his griefs than to give utterance to them; and in this particular case his lips were sealed by a very natural delicacy. At length a complete explanation and reconciliation were brought about by the agency of Gilbert Burnet.

The fame of Burnet has been attacked with singular malice and pertinacity. The attack began early in his life, and is still carried on with undiminished vigour, though he has now been more than a century and a quarter in his grave. He is indeed as fair a mark as factious animosity and petulant wit could desire. The faults of his understanding and temper lie on the surface, and cannot be missed. They were not the faults which are ordinarily considered as belonging to his country. Alone among the many Scotchmen who have raised themselves to distinction and prosperity in England, he had that character which satirists, novelists, and dramatists have agreed to ascribe to Irish adventurers. His high animal spirits, his boastfulness, his undissembled vanity,

CHAP. VII.

Gilbert Burnet.

CHAP. VII.

his propensity to blunder, his provoking indiscretion, his unabashed audacity, afforded inexhaustible subjects of ridicule to the Tories. Nor did his enemies omit to compliment him, sometimes with more pleasantry than delicacy, on the breadth of his shoulders, the thickness of his calves, and his success in matrimonial projects on amorous and opulent widows. Yet Burnet, though open in many respects to ridicule, and even to serious censure, was no contemptible man. His parts were quick, his industry unwearied, his reading various and most extensive. He was at once a historian, an antiquary, a theologian, a preacher, a pamphleteer, a debater, and an active political leader; and in every one of these characters he made himself conspicuous among able competitors. The many spirited tracts which he wrote on passing events are now known only to the curious: but his History of his own Times, his History of the Reformation, his Exposition of the Articles, his Discourse of Pastoral Care, his Life of Hale, his Life of Wilmot, are still reprinted, nor is any good private library without them. Against such a fact as this all the efforts of detractors are vain. A writer, whose voluminous works, in several branches of literature, find numerous readers a hundred and thirty years after his death, may have had great faults, but must also have had great merits: and Burnet had great merits, a fertile and vigorous mind, and a style, far indeed removed from faultless purity, but generally clear, often lively, and sometimes rising to solemn and fervid eloquence. In the pulpit the effect of his discourses, which were delivered without any note, was heightened by a noble figure and by pathetic action. He was often interrupted by the deep hum of his audience; and when, after preaching out the hourglass, which in those days was part of the furniture of the pulpit, he held it up in his hand, the congregation clamorously encouraged him to go on till the sand had run off once more.* In his moral character, as in his intellect, great blemishes were more than compensated by great excellence. Though often misled by prejudice and passion, he was emphatically an honest man. Though he was not secure from the seductions of vanity, his spirit was raised high above the influence both of cupidity and of fear. His nature was kind, generous, grateful, forgiving.† His re-

* Speaker Onslow's note on Burnet, L 590.; Johnson's Life of Sprat.
† No person has contradicted Burnet more frequently or with more asperity than Dartmouth. Yet Dartmouth wrote, "I do not think he designedly published

ligious zeal, though steady and ardent, was in general restrained by humanity, and by a respect for the rights of conscience. Strongly attached to what he regarded as the spirit of Christianity, he looked with indifference on rites, names, and forms of ecclesiastical polity, and was by no means disposed to be severe even on infidels and heretics whose lives were pure, and whose errors appeared to be the effect rather of some perversion of the understanding than of the depravity of the heart. But, like many other good men of that age, he regarded the case of the Church of Rome as an exception to all ordinary rules.

Burnet had during some years enjoyed an European reputation. His History of the Reformation had been received with loud applause by all Protestants, and had been felt by the Roman Catholics as a severe blow. The greatest Doctor that the Church of Rome has produced since the schism of the sixteenth century, Bossuet, Bishop of Meaux, was engaged in framing an elaborate reply. Burnet had been honoured by a vote of thanks from one of the zealous Parliaments which had sate during the excitement of the Popish plot, and had been exhorted, in the name of the Commons of England, to continue his historical researches. He had been admitted to familiar conversation both with Charles and James, had lived on terms of close intimacy with several distinguished statesmen, particularly with Halifax, and had been the spiritual guide of some persons of the highest note. He had reclaimed from atheism and from licentiousness one of the most brilliant libertines of the age, John Wilmot, Earl of Rochester. Lord Stafford, the victim of Oates, had, though a Roman Catholic, been edified in his last hours by Burnet's exhortations touching those points on which all Christians agree. A few years later a more illustrious sufferer, Lord Russell, had been accompanied by Burnet from the Tower to the scaffold in Lincoln's Inn Fields. The Court had neglected no means of gaining so active

CHAP. VII.

anything he believed to be false." At a later period Dartmouth, provoked by some remarks on himself in the second volume of the Bishop's history, retracted this praise; but to such a retractation little importance can be attached. Even Swift has the justice to say, "After all, he was a man of generosity and good nature."—Short Remarks on Bishop Burnet's History.

It is usual to censure Burnet as a singularly inaccurate historian; but I believe the charge to be altogether unjust. He appears to be singularly inaccurate only because his narrative has been subjected to a scrutiny singularly severe and unfriendly. If any Whig thought it worth while to subject Reresby's Memoirs, North's Examen, Mulgrave's Account of the Revolution, or the Life of James the Second, to a similar scrutiny, it would soon appear that Burnet was far indeed from being the most inexact writer of his time.

and able a divine. Neither royal blandishments nor promises of valuable preferment had been spared. But Burnet, though infected in early youth by those servile doctrines which were commonly held by the clergy of that age, had become on conviction a Whig; and he firmly adhered through all vicissitudes to his principles. He had, however, no part in that conspiracy which brought so much disgrace and calamity on the Whig party, and not only abhorred the murderous designs of Goodenough and Ferguson, but was of opinion that even his beloved and honoured friend Russell had gone to unjustifiable lengths against the government. A time at length arrived when innocence was not a sufficient protection. Burnet, though not guilty of any legal offence, was pursued by the vengeance of the Court. He retired to the Continent, and, after passing about a year in those wanderings through Switzerland, Italy, and Germany, of which he has left us an agreeable narrative, reached the Hague in the summer of 1686, and was received there with kindness and respect. He had many free conversations with the Princess on politics and religion, and soon became her spiritual director and confidential adviser. William proved a much more gracious host than could have been expected. Of all faults officiousness and indiscretion were the most offensive to him; and Burnet was allowed even by friends and admirers to be the most officious and indiscreet of mankind. But the sagacious Prince perceived that this pushing talkative divine, who was always blabbing secrets, putting impertinent questions, obtruding unasked advice, was nevertheless an upright, courageous and able man, well acquainted with the temper and the views of British sects and factions. The fame of Burnet's eloquence and erudition was also widely spread. William was not himself a reading man. But he had now been many years at the head of the Dutch administration, in an age when the Dutch press was one of the most formidable engines by which the public mind of Europe was moved, and, though he had no taste for literary pleasures, was far too wise and too observant to be ignorant of the value of literary assistance. He was aware that a popular pamphlet might sometimes be of as much service as a victory in the field. He also felt the importance of having always near him some person well informed as to the civil and ecclesiastical polity of our island; and Burnet was eminently qualified to be of use as a living dictionary of British affairs. For his knowledge, though not always accurate, was of immense extent; and there were in England and Scotland few eminent men of any political or religious party with whom he had not conversed. He was therefore admitted to as large a share of favour and confidence as was granted to any but those who composed the very small inmost knot of the Prince's private friends. When the Doctor took liberties, which was not seldom the case, his patron became more than usually cold and sullen, and sometimes uttered a short dry sarcasm which would have struck dumb any person of ordinary assurance. In spite of such occurrences, however, the amity between this singular pair continued, with some temporary interruptions, till it was dissolved by death. Indeed, it was not easy to wound Burnet's feelings. His selfcomplacency, his animal spirits, and his want of tact, were such that, though he frequently gave offence, he never took it.

All the peculiarities of his character fitted him to be the peacemaker between William and Mary. When persons who ought to esteem and love each other are kept asunder, as often happens, by some cause which three words of frank explanation would remove, they are fortunate if they possess an indiscreet friend who blurts out the whole truth. Burnet plainly told the Princess what the feeling was which preyed upon her husband's mind. She learned for the first time, with no small astonishment, that, when she became Queen of England, William would not share her throne. She warmly declared that there was no proof of conjugal submission and affection which she was not ready to give. Burnet, with many apologies and with solemn protestations that no human being had put words into his mouth, informed her that the remedy was in her own hands. She might easily, when the crown devolved on her, induce her Parliament not only to give the regal title to her husband, but even to transfer to him by a legislative act the administration of the government. "But," he added, "your Royal Highness ought to consider well before you announce any such resolution. For it is a resolution which, having once been announced, cannot safely or easily be retracted." "I want no time for consideration," answered Mary. "It is enough that I have an opportunity of showing my regard for the Prince. Tell him what I say; and bring him to me that he may hear it from my own lips." Burnet went in quest of William: but William was many miles off after a stag. It was not till the next day that the decisive interview took place. "I did not know till yesterday," said

CHAP. VII.

He brings about a good understanding between the Prince and Princess.

Mary, "that there was such a difference between the laws of England and the laws of God. But I now promise you that you shall always bear rule; and, in return, I ask only this, that, as I shall observe the precept which enjoins wives to obey their husbands, you will observe that which enjoins husbands to love their wives." Her generous affection completely gained the heart of William. From that time till the sad day when he was carried away in fits from her dying bed, there was entire friendship and confidence between them. Many of her letters to him are extant; and they contain abundant evidence that this man, unamiable as he was in the eyes of the multitude, had succeeded in inspiring a beautiful and virtuous woman, born his superior, with a passion fond even to idolatry.

The service which Burnet had rendered to his country was of high moment. A time had arrived at which it was important to the public safety that there should be entire concord between the Prince and Princess.

Relations between William and English parties.

Till after the suppression of the Western insurrection grave causes of dissension had separated William from both Whigs and Tories. He had seen with displeasure the attempts of the Whigs to strip the executive government of some powers which he thought necessary to its efficiency and dignity. He had seen with still deeper displeasure the countenance given by a large section of that party to the pretensions of Monmouth. The opposition, it seemed, wished first to make the crown of England not worth the wearing, and then to place it on the head of a bastard and impostor. At the same time the Prince's religious system differed widely from that which was the badge of the Tories. They were Arminians and Prelatists. They looked down on the Protestant Churches of the Continent, and regarded every line of their own liturgy and rubric as scarcely less sacred than the gospels. His opinions touching the metaphysics of theology were Calvinistic. His opinions touching ecclesiastical polity and modes of worship were latitudinarian. He owned that episcopacy was a lawful and convenient form of church government; but he spoke with sharpness and scorn of the bigotry of those who thought episcopal ordination essential to a Christian society. He had no scruple about the vestments and gestures prescribed by the Book of Common Prayer. But he avowed that he should like the rites of the Church of England better if they reminded him less of the rites of the Church of Rome. He had been heard to utter an ominous growl when first he saw, in his wife's private chapel, an altar decked after the Anglican fashion, and had not seemed well pleased at finding her with Hooker's Ecclesiastical Polity in her hands.*

CHAP. VII.

He therefore long observed the contest between the English factions attentively, but without feeling a strong predilection for either side. Nor in truth did he ever, to the end of his life, become either a Whig or a Tory. He wanted that which is the common groundwork of both characters; for he never became an Englishman. He saved England, it is true; but he never loved her; and he never obtained her love. To him she was always a land of exile, visited with reluctance and quitted with delight. Even when he rendered to her those services of which, at this day, we feel the happy effects, her welfare was not his chief object. Whatever patriotic feeling he had was for Holland. There was the stately tomb where slept the great politician whose blood, whose name, whose temperament, and whose genius he had inherited. There the very sound of his title was a spell which had, through three generations, called forth the affectionate enthusiasm of boors and artisans. The Dutch language was the language of his nursery. Among the Dutch gentry he had chosen his early friends. The amusements, the architecture, the landscape of his native country, had taken hold on his heart. To her he turned with constant fondness from a prouder and fairer rival. In the gallery of Whitehall he pined for the familiar House in the Wood at the Hague, and never was so happy as when he could quit the magnificence of Windsor for his far humbler seat at Loo. During his splendid banishment it was his consolation to create round him, by building, planting, and digging, a scene which might remind him of the formal piles of red brick, of the long canals, and of the symmetrical flower-beds among which his early life had been passed. Yet even his affection for the land of his birth was subordinate to another feeling which early became supreme in his soul, which mixed itself with all his passions, which impelled him to marvellous enterprises, which supported him when sinking under mortification, pain, sickness, and sorrow, which, towards the close of his career, seemed during a short time to languish, but which soon broke forth again fiercer than ever, and continued to animate him even while the prayer for the departing was read at his bedside. That feeling was enmity to

His feelings towards England.

His feelings towards Holland and France.

* Dr. Hooper's MS. narrative, published in the Appendix to Lord Dangannon's Life of William.

VOL. II.   C

France, and to the magnificent King who, in more than one sense, represented France, and who to virtues and accomplishments eminently French joined in large measure that unquiet, unscrupulous, and vainglorious ambition which has repeatedly drawn on France the resentment of Europe.

It is not difficult to trace the progress of the sentiment which gradually possessed itself of William's whole soul. When he was little more than a boy his country had been attacked by Lewis in ostentatious defiance of justice and public law, had been overrun, had been desolated, had been given up to every excess of rapacity, licentiousness, and cruelty. The Dutch had in dismay humbled themselves before the conqueror, and had implored mercy. They had been told in reply that, if they desired peace, they must resign their independence, and do annual homage to the House of Bourbon. The injured nation, driven to despair, had opened its dykes, and had called in the sea as an ally against the French tyranny. It was in the agony of that conflict, when peasants were flying in terror before the invaders, when hundreds of fair gardens and pleasure houses were buried beneath the waves, when the deliberations of the States were interrupted by the fainting and the loud weeping of ancient senators who could not bear the thought of surviving the freedom and glory of their native land, that William had been called to the head of affairs. For a time it seemed to him that resistance was hopeless. He looked round him for succour, and looked in vain. Spain was unnerved, Germany distracted, England corrupted. Nothing seemed left to the young Stadtholder but to perish sword in hand, or to be the Æneas of a great emigration, and to create another Holland in countries beyond the reach of the tyranny of France. No obstacle would then remain to check the progress of the House of Bourbon. A few years; and that House might add to its dominions Lorraine and Flanders, Castile and Aragon, Naples and Milan, Mexico and Peru. Lewis might wear the imperial crown, might place a prince of his family on the throne of Poland, might be sole master of Europe from the Scythian deserts to the Atlantic Ocean, and of America from regions north of the Tropic of Cancer to regions south of the Tropic of Capricorn. Such was the prospect which lay before William when first he entered on public life, and which never ceased to haunt him till his latest day. The French monarchy was to him what the Roman republic was to Hannibal, what the Ottoman power was to Scanderbeg, what the Southron domination was to Wallace. Religion gave her sanction to that intense and unquenchable animosity. Hundreds of Calvinistic preachers proclaimed that the same power which had set apart Samson from the womb to be the scourge of the Philistine, and which had called Gideon from the threshing floor to smite the Midianite, had raised up William of Orange to be the champion of all free nations and of all pure Churches; nor was this notion without influence on his own mind. To the confidence which the heroic fatalist placed in his high destiny and in his sacred cause is to be partly attributed his singular indifference to danger. He had a great work to do; and till it was done nothing could harm him. Therefore it was that, in spite of the prognostications of physicians, he recovered from maladies which seemed hopeless, that bands of assassins conspired in vain against his life, that the open skiff to which he trusted himself on a starless night, amidst raging waves, and near a treacherous shore, brought him safe to land, and that, on twenty fields of battle, the cannon balls passed him by to right and left. The ardour and perseverance with which he devoted himself to his mission have scarcely any parallel in history. In comparison with his great object he held the lives of other men as cheap as his own. It was but too much the habit even of the most humane and generous soldiers of that age to think very lightly of the bloodshed and devastation inseparable from great martial exploits; and the heart of William was steeled, not only by professional insensibility, but by that sterner insensibility which is the effect of a sense of duty. Three great coalitions, three long and bloody wars in which all Europe from the Vistula to the Western Ocean was in arms, are to be ascribed to his unconquerable energy. When in 1678 the States General, exhausted and disheartened, were desirous of repose, his voice was still against sheathing the sword. If peace was made, it was made only because he could not breathe into other men a spirit as fierce and determined as his own. At the very last moment, in the hope of breaking off the negotiation which he knew to be all but concluded, he fought one of the most bloody and obstinate battles of that age. From the day on which the treaty of Nimeguen was signed, he began to meditate a second coalition. His contest with Lewis, transferred from the field to the cabinet, was soon exasperated by a private feud. In talents, temper, manners, and opinions, the

CHAP. VII.

rivals were diametrically opposed to each other. Lewis, polite and dignified, profuse and voluptuous, fond of display and averse from danger, a munificent patron of arts and letters, and a cruel persecutor of Calvinists, presented a remarkable contrast to William, simple in tastes, ungracious in demeanour, indefatigable and intrepid in war, regardless of all the ornamental branches of knowledge, and firmly attached to the theology of Geneva. The enemies did not long observe those courtesies which men of their rank, even when opposed to each other at the head of armies, seldom neglect. William, indeed, went through the form of tendering his best services to Lewis. But this civility was rated at its true value, and requited with a dry reprimand. The great King affected contempt for the petty Prince who was the servant of a confederacy of trading towns; and to every mark of contempt the dauntless Stadtholder replied by a fresh defiance. William took his title, a title which the events of the preceding century had made one of the most illustrious in Europe, from a city which lies on the banks of the Rhone not far from Avignon, and which, like Avignon, though enclosed on every side by the French territory, was properly a fief not of the French but of the Imperial Crown. Lewis, with that ostentatious contempt of public law which was characteristic of him, occupied Orange, dismantled the fortifications, and confiscated the revenues. William declared aloud at his table before many persons that he would make the most Christian King repent the outrage, and when questioned about these words by Lewis's Ambassador, the Count of Avaux, positively refused either to retract them or to explain them away. The quarrel was carried so far that the French minister could not venture to present himself at the drawingroom of the Princess for fear of receiving some affront.*

The feeling with which William regarded France explains the whole of his policy towards England. His public spirit was an European public spirit. The chief object of his care was not our island, not even his native Holland, but the great community of nations threatened with subjugation by one too powerful member. Those who commit the error of considering him as an English statesman must necessarily see his whole life in a false light, and will be unable to discover any principle, good or bad, Whig or Tory, to which some of his most important acts can be referred. But, when we consider

* Avaux, Negotiations, Aug. 18., Sept. 12., Nov. 7., Dec. 7., 1682.

him as a man whose especial task was to join a crowd of feeble, divided and dispirited states in firm and energetic union against a common enemy, when we consider him as a man in whose eyes England was important chiefly because, without her, the great coalition which he projected must be incomplete, we shall be forced to admit that no long career recorded in history has been more uniform from the beginning to the close than that of this great Prince.*

The clue of which we are now possessed will enable us to track without difficulty the course, in reality consistent, though in appearance sometimes tortuous, which he pursued towards our domestic factions. He clearly saw what had not escaped persons far inferior to him in sagacity, that the enterprise on which his whole soul was intent would probably be successful if England were on his side, would be of uncertain issue if England were neutral, and would be hopeless if England acted as she had acted in the days of the Cabal. He saw not less clearly that between the foreign policy and the domestic policy of the English government there was a close connection; that the sovereign of this country, acting in harmony with the legislature, must always have a great sway in the affairs of Christendom, and must also have an obvious interest in opposing the undue aggrandisement of any Continental potentate; that, on the other hand, the sovereign distrusted and thwarted by the legislature, could be of little weight in European politics, and that the whole of that little weight would be thrown into the wrong scale. The Prince's first wish therefore was that there should be concord between the throne and the Parliament. How that concord should be established, and on which side concessions should be made, were, in his view, questions of secondary importance. He would have been best pleased, no doubt, to see a complete reconciliation effected without the sacrifice of one tittle of the prerogative. For in the integrity of that prerogative he had a reversionary interest; and he was, by nature, at least as covetous of power and as impatient of restraint as any of the

His policy consistent throughout.

* I cannot deny myself the pleasure of quoting Massillon's unfriendly, yet discriminating and noble, character of William. "Ce prince profond dans ses vues; habile à former des ligues et à réunir les esprits; plus heureux à exciter les guerres qu'à combattre; plus à craindre encore dans le secret du cabinet, qu'à la tête des armées; un ennemi que la haine du nom Français avoit rendu capable d'imaginer de grandes choses et de les exécuter; un de ces génies qui semblent être nés pour montrer à leur gré les peuples et les souverains; un grand homme, s'il n'avoit jamais voulu être roi."—Oraison Funèbre de M. le Dauphin.

Stuarts. But there was no flower of the crown which he was not prepared to sacrifice, even after the crown had been placed on his own head, if he could only be convinced that such a sacrifice was indispensably necessary to his great design. In the days of the Popish plot, therefore, though he disapproved of the violence with which the opposition attacked the royal authority, he exhorted the government to give way. The conduct of the Commons, he said, as respected domestic affairs, was most unreasonable; but while the Commons were discontented the liberties of Europe could never be safe; and to that paramount consideration every other consideration ought to yield. On these principles he acted when the Exclusion Bill had thrown the nation into convulsions. There is no reason to believe that he encouraged the opposition to bring forward that bill or to reject the offers of compromise which were repeatedly made from the throne. But when it became clear that, unless that bill were carried, there would be a serious breach between the Commons and the Court, he indicated very intelligibly, though with decorous reserve, his opinion that the representatives of the people ought to be conciliated at any price. When a violent and rapid reflux of public feeling had left the Whig party for a time utterly helpless, he attempted to attain his grand object by a new road perhaps more agreeable to his temper than that which he had previously tried. In the altered temper of the nation there was little chance that any Parliament disposed to cross the wishes of the sovereign would be elected. Charles was for a time master. To gain Charles, therefore, was the Prince's first wish. In the summer of 1683, almost at the moment at which the detection of the Rye House plot made the discomfiture of the Whigs and the triumph of the King complete, events took place elsewhere which William could not behold without extreme anxiety and alarm. The Turkish armies advanced to the suburbs of Vienna. The great Austrian monarchy, on the support of which the Prince had reckoned, seemed to be on the point of destruction. Bentinck was therefore sent in haste from the Hague to London, was charged to omit nothing which might be necessary to conciliate the English court, and was particularly instructed to express in the strongest terms the horror with which his master regarded the Whig conspiracy.

During the eighteen months which followed, there was some hope that the influence of Halifax would prevail, and that the court of Whitehall would return to the policy of the Triple Alliance. To that hope William fondly clung. He spared no effort to propitiate Charles. The hospitality which Monmouth found at the Hague is chiefly to be ascribed to the Prince's anxiety to gratify the real wishes of Monmouth's father. As soon as Charles died, William, still adhering unchangeably to his object, again changed his course. He had sheltered Monmouth, to please the late King. That the present King might have no reason to complain Monmouth was dismissed. We have seen that, when the Western insurrection broke out, the British regiments in the Dutch service were, by the active exertions of the Prince, sent over to their own country on the first requisition. Indeed William even offered to command in person against the rebels; and that the offer was made in perfect sincerity cannot be doubted by those who have perused his confidential letters to Bentinck.*

The Prince was evidently at this time inclined to hope that the great plan, to which in his mind everything else was subordinate, might obtain the approbation and support of his father in law. The high tone which James was then holding towards France, the readiness with which he consented to a defensive alliance with the United Provinces, the inclination which he showed to connect himself with the House of Austria, encouraged this expectation. But in a short time the prospect was darkened. The disgrace of Halifax, the breach between James and the Parliament, the prorogation, the announcement distinctly made by the King to the foreign ministers that Continental politics should no longer divert his attention from internal measures tending to strengthen his prerogative and to promote the interest of his Church, put an end to the delusion. It was plain that, when the European crisis came, England would, if James were her master, either remain inactive or act in conjunction with France. And the European crisis was drawing near. The House of Austria had, by a succession of victories, been secured from danger on the side of Turkey, and was no longer under the necessity of submitting patiently to the encroachments and insults of Lewis. Accord-

* For example, "Je crois M. Feversham un très brave et honnête homme. Mais je doute s'il a assez d'expérience à diriger une si grande affaire qu'il a sur le bras. Dieu lui donne un succès prompt et heureux! Mais je ne suis pas hors d'inquiétude." July 7/17, 1685. Again, after he had received the news of the battle of Sedgemoor. "Dieu soit loué du bon succès que les troupes du Roy ont en contre les rebelles. Je ne doute pas que cette affaire ne soit entièrement assoupie, et que le règne du Roy sera heureux, ce que Dieu veuille." July 13.

ingly, in July, 1686, a treaty was signed at Augsburg by which the Princes of the Empire bound themselves closely together for the purpose of mutual defence. The Kings of Spain and Sweden were parties to this compact, the King of Spain as sovereign of the provinces contained in the circle of Burgundy, and the King of Sweden as Duke of Pomerania. The confederates declared that they had no intention to attack and no wish to offend any power, but that they were determined to tolerate no infraction of those rights which the Germanic body held under the sanction of public law and public faith. They pledged themselves to stand by each other in case of need, and fixed the amount of force which each member of the league was to furnish if it should be necessary to repel aggression.* The name of William did not appear in this instrument: but all men knew that it was his work, and foresaw that he would in no long time be again the captain of a coalition against France. Between him and the vassal of France there could, in such circumstances, be no cordial good will. There was no open rupture, no interchange of menaces or reproaches. But the father in law and the son in law were separated completely and for ever.

At the very time at which the Prince was thus estranged from the English court, the causes which had hitherto produced a coolness between him and the two great sections of the English people disappeared. A large portion, perhaps a numerical majority, of the Whigs had favoured the pretensions of Monmouth: but Monmouth was now no more. The Tories, on the other hand, had entertained apprehensions that the interests of the Anglican Church might not be safe under the rule of a man bred among Dutch Presbyterians, and well known to hold latitudinarian opinions about robes, ceremonies, and Bishops; but since that beloved Church had been threatened by far more formidable dangers from a very different quarter, these apprehensions had lost almost all their power. Thus, at the same moment, both the great parties began to fix their hopes and their affections on the same leader. Old republicans could not refuse their confidence to one who had worthily filled, during many years, the highest magistracy of a republic. Old royalists conceived that they acted according to their principles in paying profound respect to a Prince so near to the throne. At this conjuncture it was of the highest moment that there should be entire union be-

* The treaty will be found in the Recueil des Traités. iv. No. 209.

tween William and Mary. A misunderstanding between the presumptive heiress of the crown and her husband must have produced a schism in that vast mass which was from all quarters gathering round one common rallying point. Happily all risk of such misunderstanding was averted in the critical instant by the interposition of Burnet; and the Prince became the unquestioned chief of the whole of that party which was opposed to the government, a party almost coextensive with the nation.

There is not the least reason to believe that he at this time meditated the great enterprise to which a stern necessity afterwards drove him. He was aware that the public mind of England, though heated by grievances, was by no means ripe for revolution. He would doubtless gladly have avoided the scandal which must be the effect of a mortal quarrel between persons bound together by the closest ties of consanguinity and affinity. Even his ambition made him unwilling to owe to violence that greatness which might soon be his in the ordinary course of nature and of law. For he well knew that, if the crown descended to his wife regularly, all its prerogatives would descend unimpaired with it, and that, if it were obtained by election, it must be taken subject to such conditions as the electors might think fit to impose. He meant, therefore, as it appears, to wait with patience for the day when he might govern by an undisputed title, and to content himself in the meantime with exercising a great influence on English affairs, as first Prince of the blood, and as head of the party which was decidedly preponderant in the nation, and which was certain, whenever a Parliament should meet, to be decidedly preponderant in both Houses.

Already, it is true, he had been urged by an adviser, less sagacious and more impetuous than himself, to try a bolder course. This adviser was the young Lord Mordaunt. That age had produced no more inventive genius, and no more daring spirit. But, if a design was splendid, Mordaunt seldom inquired whether it were practicable. His life was a wild romance made up of mysterious intrigues, both political and amorous, of violent and rapid changes of scene and fortune, and of victories resembling those of Amadis and Launcelot rather than those of Luxemburg and Eugene. The episodes interspersed in this strange story were of a piece with the main plot. Among them were midnight encounters with generous robbers, and rescues of noble and beautiful ladies

Mordaunt proposes to William a descent on England.

CHAP. VII.

William rejects the advice.

from ravishers. Mordaunt, having distinguished himself by the eloquence and audacity with which, in the House of Lords, he had opposed the court, repaired, soon after the prorogation, to the Hague, and strongly recommended an immediate descent on England. He had persuaded himself that it would be as easy to surprise three great kingdoms as he long afterwards found it to surprise Barcelona. William listened, meditated, and replied, in general terms, that he took a great interest in English affairs, and would keep his attention fixed on them.* Whatever his purpose had been, it is not likely that he would have chosen a rash and vainglorious knight errant for his confidant. Between the two men there was nothing in common except personal courage, which rose in both to the height of fabulous heroism. Mordaunt wanted merely to enjoy the excitement of conflict, and to make men stare. William had one great end ever before him. Towards that end he was impelled by a strong passion which appeared to him under the guise of a sacred duty. Towards that end he toiled with a patience resembling, as he once said, the patience with which he had seen a boatman on a canal strain against an adverse eddy, often swept back, but never ceasing to pull, and content if, by the labour of hours, a few yards could be gained.† Exploits which brought the Prince no nearer to his object, however glorious they might be in the estimation of the vulgar, were in his judgment boyish vanities, and no part of the real business of life.

He determined to reject Mordaunt's advice; and there can be no doubt that the determination was wise. Had William, in 1686, or even in 1687, attempted to do what he did with such signal success in 1688, it is probable that many Whigs would have risen in arms at his call. But he would have found that the nation was not yet prepared to welcome a deliverer from a foreign country, and that the Church had not yet been provoked and insulted into forgetfulness of the tenet which had long been her peculiar boast. The old Cavaliers would have flocked to the royal standard. There would probably have been in all the three kingdoms a civil war as long and fierce as that of the preceding generation. While that war was raging in the British Isles, what might not Lewis attempt on the Continent? And what hope would there be for Holland, drained of her troops, and abandoned by her Stadtholder?

* Burnet, i. 763.   † Temple's Memoirs.

William therefore contented himself for the present with taking measures to unite and animate that mighty opposition of which he had become the head. This was not difficult. The fall of the Hydes had excited throughout England extreme alarm and indignation. Men felt that the question now was, not whether Protestantism should be dominant, but whether it should be tolerated. The Treasurer had been succeeded by a board, of which a Papist was the head. The Privy Seal had been entrusted to a Papist. The Lord Lieutenant of Ireland had been succeeded by a man who had absolutely no claim to high place except that he was a Papist. The last person whom a government having in view the general interests of the empire would have sent to Dublin as Deputy was Tyrconnel. His brutal manners made him unfit to represent the majesty of the crown. The feebleness of his understanding and the violence of his temper made him unfit to conduct grave business of state. The deadly animosity which he felt towards the possessors of the greater part of the soil of Ireland made him especially unfit to rule that kingdom. But the intemperance of his bigotry was thought amply to atone for the intemperance of all his other passions; and, in consideration of the hatred which he bore to the reformed faith, he was suffered to indulge without restraint his hatred of the English name. This, then, was the real meaning of His Majesty's respect for the rights of conscience. He wished his Parliament to remove all the disabilities which had been imposed on Papists, merely in order that he might himself impose disabilities equally galling on Protestants. It was plain that, under such a prince, apostasy was the only road to greatness. It was a road, however, which few ventured to take. For the spirit of the nation was thoroughly roused; and every renegade had to endure such an amount of public scorn and detestation as cannot be altogether unfelt even by the most callous natures.

It is true that several remarkable conversions had recently taken place; but they were such as did little credit to the Church of Rome. Two men of high rank had joined her communion; Henry Mordaunt, Earl of Peterborough, and James Cecil, Earl of Salisbury. But Peterborough, who had been an active soldier, courtier, and negotiator, was now broken down by years and infirmities; and those who saw him totter about the galleries of Whitehall, leaning on a stick and swathed up in flannels and plasters, comforted themselves for his defection by remarking that he had not changed his religion till he had outlived his faculties.* Salisbury was foolish to a proverb. His figure was so bloated by sensual indulgence as to be almost incapable of moving; and this sluggish body was the abode of an equally sluggish mind. He was represented in popular lampoons as a man made to be duped, as a man who had hitherto been the prey of gamesters, and who might as well be the prey of friars. A pasquinade, which, about the time of Rochester's retirement, was fixed on the door of Salisbury House in the Strand, described in coarse terms the horror with which the wise Robert Cecil, if he could rise from his grave, would see to what a creature his honours had descended.†

These were the highest in station among the proselytes of James. There were other renegades of a very different kind, needy men of parts who were destitute of principle and of all sense of personal dignity. There is reason to believe that among these was William Wycherley, the most licentious and hardhearted writer of a singularly licentious and hardhearted school.‡ It is certain that Matthew Tindal, who, at a later period, acquired great notoriety by writing against Christianity, was at this time received into the bosom of the infallible Church, a fact which, as may easily be supposed, the divines with whom he was subsequently engaged in controversy did not suffer to sink into oblivion.§ A still more infamous apostate was Joseph Haines, whose name is now almost forgotten, but who was well known in his own time as an adventurer of versatile parts, sharper, coiner, false witness, sham bail, dancing master, buffoon, poet, comedian. Some of his prologues and epilogues were much admired by his contemporaries; and his merit as an actor was universally acknowledged. This man professed himself a Roman Catholic, and went to Italy in the retinue of Castelmaine, but was soon dismissed for misconduct. If any credit be due to a tradition which was long preserved in the green room, Haines had the impudence to affirm that the Virgin Mary had appeared to him and called him to repentance. After the Revolution, he attempted to make his peace with the town by a penance more

* See the poems entitled The Converts and The Delusion.
† The lines are in the Collection of State Poems.
‡ Our information about Wycherley is very scanty; but two things are certain, that in his later years he called himself a Papist, and that he received money from James. I have very little doubt that he was a hired convert.
§ See the article on him in the Biographia Britannica.

scandalous than his offence. One night, before he acted in a farce, he appeared on the stage in a white sheet with a torch in his hand, and recited some profane and indecent doggerel, which he called his recantation.*

With the name of Haines was joined, in many libels, the name of a more illustrious renegade, John Dryden. Dryden was now approaching the decline of life. After many successes and many failures, he had at length attained, by general consent, the first place among living English poets. His claims on the gratitude of James were superior to those of any man of letters in the kingdom. But James cared little for verses and much for money. From the day of his accession he set himself to make small economical reforms, such as bring on a government the reproach of meanness without producing any perceptible relief to the finances. One of the victims of this injudicious parsimony was Dryden. A pension of a hundred a year which had been given to him by Charles and had expired with Charles was not renewed. The demise of the Crown made it necessary that the Poet Laureate should have a new patent; and orders were given that, in this patent, the annual butt of sack, originally granted to Jonson, and continued to Jonson's successors, should be omitted.† This was the only notice which the King, during the first year of his reign, deigned to bestow on the mighty satirist who, in the very crisis of the great struggle of the Exclusion Bill, had spread terror through the Whig ranks. Dryden was poor and impatient of poverty. He knew little and cared little about religion. If any sentiment was deeply fixed in him, that sentiment was an aversion to priests of all persuasions, Levites, Augurs, Muftis, Roman Catholic divines, Presbyterian divines, divines of the Church of England. He was not naturally a man of high spirit; and his pursuits had been by no means such as were likely to give elevation or delicacy to his mind. He had, during many years, earned his daily bread by pandering to the vicious taste of the pit, and by grossly flattering rich and noble patrons. Selfrespect and a fine sense of the becoming were not to be expected from one who had led a life of mendicancy and adulation. Finding that, if he continued to call himself a Protestant,

CHAP. VII.

Dryden

* See James Quin's account of Haines in Davies's Miscellanies: Tom Brown's Works; Lives of Sharpers: Dryden's Epilogue to the Secular Masque.   † This fact, which escaped the minute researches of Malone, appears from the Treasury Letter Book of 1685.

his services would be overlooked, he declared himself a Papist. The King's parsimony speedily relaxed. Dryden's pension was restored: the arrears were paid up; and he was employed to defend his new religion both in prose and verse.*

Two eminent men, Samuel Johnson and Walter Scott, have done their best to persuade themselves and others that this memorable conversion was sincere. It was natural that they should be desirous to remove a disgraceful stain from the memory of one whose genius they justly admired, and with whose political feelings they strongly sympathised; but the impartial historian must with regret pronounce a very different judgment. There will always be a strong presumption against the sincerity of a conversion by which the convert is directly a gainer. In the case of Dryden there is nothing to countervail this presumption. His theological writings abundantly prove that he had never sought with diligence and anxiety to learn the truth, and that his knowledge both of the Church which he quitted and of the Church which he entered was of the most superficial kind. Nor was his subsequent conduct that of a man whom a strong sense of duty had constrained to take a step of awful importance. Had he been such a man, the same conviction which had led him to join the Church of Rome would surely have prevented him from violating grossly and habitually rules which that Church, in common with every other Christian society, recognises as binding. There would have been a marked distinction between his earlier and his later compositions. He would have looked back with remorse on a literary life of near thirty years, during which his rare powers of diction and versification had been systematically employed in spreading moral corruption. Not a line tending to make virtue contemptible, or to inflame licentious desire, would thenceforward have proceeded from his pen. The truth unhappily is that the dramas which he wrote after his pretended conversion are in no respect less impure or profane than those of his youth. Even when he professed to translate he constantly wandered from his originals in search of images which, if he had found them in his originals, he

* It has lately been asserted that Dryden's pension was restored long before he turned Papist, and that therefore it ought not to be considered as the price of his apostasy. But this is an entire mistake. Dryden's pension was restored by letters patent of the 4th of March 168¾; and his apostasy had been the talk of the town at least six weeks before. See Evelyn's Diary, January 19. 168⅘. (1857.)

ought to have shunned. What was bad became worse in his versions. What was innocent contracted a taint from passing through his mind. He made the grossest satires of Juvenal more gross, interpolated loose descriptions in the tales of Boccaccio, and polluted the sweet and limpid poetry of the Georgics with filth which would have moved the loathing of Virgil.

The help of Dryden was welcome to those Roman Catholic divines who were painfully sustaining a conflict against all that was most illustrious in the Established Church. They could not disguise from themselves the fact that their style, disfigured with foreign idioms which had been picked up at Rome and Douay, appeared to little advantage when compared with the eloquence of Tillotson and Sherlock. It seemed that it was no light thing to have secured the cooperation of the greatest living master of the English language. The first service which he was required to perform in return for his pension was to defend his Church in prose against Stillingfleet. But the art of saying things well is useless to a man who has nothing to say; and this was Dryden's case. He soon found himself unequally paired with an antagonist whose whole life had been one long training for controversy. The veteran gladiator disarmed the novice, inflicted a few contemptuous scratches, and turned away to encounter more formidable combatants. Dryden then betook himself to a weapon at which he was not likely to find his match. He retired for a time from the bustle of coffeehouses and theatres to a quiet retreat in Huntingdonshire, and there composed, with unwonted care and labour, his celebrated poem on the points in dispute between the Churches of Rome and England. The Church of Rome he represented under the similitude of a milkwhite hind, ever in peril of death, yet fated not to die. The beasts of the field were bent on her destruction. The quaking hare, indeed, observed a timorous neutrality: but the Socinian fox, the Presbyterian wolf, the Independent bear, the Anabaptist boar, glared fiercely at the spotless creature. Yet she could venture to drink with them at the common watering place under the protection of her friend, the kingly lion. The Church of England was typified by the panther, spotted indeed, but beautiful, too beautiful for a beast of prey. The hind and the panther, equally hated by the ferocious population of the forest, conferred apart on their common danger.

CHAP. VII.

The Hind and Panther.

They then proceeded to discuss the points on which they differed, and, while wagging their tails and licking their jaws, held a long dialogue touching the real presence, the authority of Popes and Councils, the penal laws, the Test Act, Oates's perjuries, Butler's unrequited services to the Cavalier party, Stillingfleet's pamphlets, and Burnet's broad shoulders and fortunate matrimonial speculations.

The absurdity of this plan is obvious. In truth the allegory could not be preserved unbroken through ten lines together. No art of execution could redeem the faults of such a design. Yet the Fable of the Hind and Panther is undoubtedly the most valuable addition which was made to English literature during the short and troubled reign of James the Second. In none of Dryden's works can be found passages more pathetic and magnificent, greater ductility and energy of language, or a more pleasing and various music.

The poem appeared with every advantage which royal patronage could give. A superb edition was printed for Scotland at the Roman Catholic press established in Holyrood House. But men were in no humour to be charmed by the transparent style and melodious numbers of the apostate. The disgust excited by his venality, the alarm excited by the policy of which he was the eulogist, were not to be sung to sleep. The just indignation of the public was inflamed by many who were smarting from his ridicule, and by many who were envious of his renown. In spite of all the restraints under which the press lay, attacks on his life and writings appeared daily. Sometimes he was Bayes, sometimes Poet Squab. He was reminded that in his youth he had paid to the House of Cromwell the same servile court which he was now paying to the House of Stuart. One set of his assailants maliciously reprinted the sarcastic verses which he had written against Popery in days when he could have got nothing by being a Papist. Of the many satirical pieces which appeared on this occasion, the most successful was the joint work of two young men who had lately completed their studies at Cambridge, and had been welcomed as promising novices in the literary coffeehouses of London, Charles Montague and Matthew Prior. Montague was of noble descent: the origin of Prior was so obscure that no biographer has been able to trace it: but both the adventurers were poor and aspiring: both had keen and vigorous minds: both afterwards climbed high; and both united in a remarkable degree the love of letters with skill in those departments of business for which men of letters generally have a strong distaste. Of the fifty poets whose lives Johnson has written, Montague and Prior were the only two who were distinguished by an intimate knowledge of trade and finance. Soon their paths diverged widely. Their early friendship was dissolved. One of them became the chief of the Whig party, and was impeached by the Tories. The other was entrusted with all the mysteries of Tory diplomacy, and was long kept close prisoner by the Whigs. At length, after many eventful years, the associates, so long parted, were reunited in Westminster Abbey.

Whoever has read the tale of the Hind and Panther with attention must have perceived that, while that work was in progress, a great alteration took place in the views of those who used Dryden as their interpreter. At first the Church of England is mentioned with tenderness and respect, and is exhorted to ally herself with the Roman Catholics against the Protestant Dissenters: but at the close of the poem, and in the preface, which was written after the poem had been finished, the Protestant Dissenters are invited to make common cause with the Roman Catholics against the Church of England.

This change in the language of the court poet was indicative of a great change in the policy of the court. The original purpose of James had been to obtain for the Church of which he was a member, not only complete immunity from all penalties and from all civil disabilities, but also an ample share of ecclesiastical and academical endowments, and at the same time to enforce with rigour the laws against the Puritan sects. All the special dispensations which he had granted had been granted to Roman Catholics. All the laws which bore hardest on the Presbyterians, Independents, and Baptists, had been executed by him with extraordinary rigour. While Hales commanded a regiment, while Powis sate at the Council board, while Massey held a deanery, while breviaries and mass books were printed at Oxford under a royal license, while the host was publicly exposed in London under the protection of the pikes and muskets of the foot-guards, while friars and monks walked the streets of London in their robes, Baxter was in gaol; Howe was in exile; the Five Mile Act and the Conventicle Act were in full vigour; Puritan writers were compelled to resort to foreign or to secret presses; Puritan congregations could meet only by night or in waste places; and Puritan ministers were forced to preach in the garb of colliers or of sailors. In Scotland the King, while he spared no exertion to extort from the Estates full relief for Roman Catholics, had demanded and obtained new statutes of unprecedented severity against Presbyterians. His conduct to the exiled Huguenots had not less clearly indicated his feelings. We have seen that, when the public munificence had placed in his hands a large sum for the relief of those unhappy men, he, in violation of every law of hospitality and good faith, required them to renounce the Calvinistic ritual to which they were strongly attached, and to conform to the Church of England, before he would dole out to them any portion of the alms which had been entrusted to his care.

Such had been his policy as long as he could cherish any hope that the Church of England would consent to share ascendency with the Church of Rome. That hope at one time amounted to confidence. The enthusiasm with which the Tories hailed his accession, the elections, the dutiful language and ample grants of his Parliament, the suppression of the Western insurrection, the complete prostration of the faction which had attempted to exclude him from the crown, elated him beyond the bounds of reason. He felt an assurance that every obstacle would give way before his power and his resolution. But he was disappointed. His Parliament withstood him. He tried the effects of frowns and menaces. Frowns and menaces failed. He tried the effect of prorogation. From the day of the prorogation the opposition to his designs had been growing stronger and stronger. It seemed clear that, if he effected his purpose, he must effect it in defiance of that great party which had given such signal proofs of fidelity to his office, to his family, and to his person. The whole Anglican priesthood, the whole Cavalier gentry, were against him. In vain had he, by virtue of his ecclesiastical supremacy, enjoined the clergy to abstain from discussing controverted points. Every parish in the nation was warned every Sunday against the errors of Rome; and these warnings were only the more effective, because they were accompanied by professions of reverence for the Sovereign, and of a determination to endure with patience whatever it might be his pleasure to inflict. The royalist knights and esquires who, through forty-five years of war and faction, had stood so manfully by the throne, now expressed, in no measured phrase, their resolution to stand as manfully by the Church. Dull as was the intellect of James, despotic as was his temper, he felt that he must change his course. He could not safely venture to outrage all his Protestant subjects at once. If he could bring himself to make concessions to the party which predominated in both Houses, if he could bring himself to leave to the established religion all its dignities, emoluments, and privileges unimpaired, he might still break up Presbyterian meetings, and fill the gaols with Baptist preachers. But, if he was determined to plunder the hierarchy, he must make up his mind to forego the luxury of persecuting the Dissenters. If he was henceforward to be at feud with his old friends, he must make a truce with his old enemies. He could overpower the Anglican Church only by forming against her an extensive coalition, including sects which, though they differed in doctrine and government far more widely from each other than from her, might yet be induced, by their common jealousy of her greatness, and by their common dread of her intolerance, to suspend their mutual animosities till she was no longer able to oppress them.

This plan seemed to him to have one strong recommendation. If he could only succeed in conciliating the Protestant Nonconformists he might flatter himself that he was secure against all chance of rebellion. According to the Anglican divines, no subject could by any provocation be justified in withstanding the Lord's anointed by force. The theory of the Puritan sectaries was very different. Those sectaries had no scruple about smiting tyrants with the sword of Gideon. Many of them did not shrink from using the dagger of Ehud. They were probably even now meditating another Western insurrection, or another Rye House plot. James, therefore, conceived that he might safely persecute the Church if he could only gain the Dissenters. The party whose principles afforded him no guarantee would be attached to him by interest. The party whose interests he attacked would be restrained from insurrection by principle.

Influenced by such considerations as these, James, from the time at which he parted in anger with his Parliament, began to meditate a general league of all Nonconformists, Catholic and Protestant, against the established religion. So early as Christmas 1685, the agents of the United Provinces informed the States General that the plan of a general toleration had been arranged and would soon be disclosed.* The reports which had reached the Dutch embassy proved to be premature. The separatists appear, however, to have been treated with more lenity during the year 1686 than during the year 1685. But it was only by slow degrees and after many struggles that the King could prevail on himself to form an alliance with all that he most abhorred. He had to overcome an animosity, not slight or capricious, not of recent origin or hasty growth, but hereditary in his line, strengthened by great wrongs inflicted and suffered through a hundred and twenty eventful years, and intertwined with all his feelings, religious, political, domestic, and personal. Four generations of Stuarts had waged a war to the death with four generations of Puritans; and, through that long war, there had been no Stuart who had hated the Puritans so much, or who had been so much hated by them, as himself. They had tried to blast his honour and to exclude him from his birthright: they had called him incendiary, cutthroat, poisoner: they had driven him from the Admiralty and the Privy Council: they had repeatedly chased him into banishment: they had plotted his assassination: they had risen against him in arms by thousands. He had avenged himself on them by havoc such as England had never before seen. Their heads and quarters were still rotting on poles in all the marketplaces of Somersetshire and Dorsetshire. Aged women, held in high honour among the sectaries for piety and charity, had, for offences which no good prince would have thought deserving even of a severe reprimand, been beheaded and burned alive. Such had been, even in England, the relations between the King and the Puritans; and in Scotland the tyranny of the King and the fury of the Puritans had been such as Englishmen could hardly conceive. To forget an enmity so long and so deadly was no light task for a nature singularly harsh and implacable.

The conflict in the royal mind did not escape the eye of Barillon. At the end of January, 1687, he sent a remarkable letter to Versailles. The King,—such was the substance of this document,—had almost convinced himself that he could not obtain entire liberty for Roman Catholics and yet maintain the laws against Protestant Dissenters. He leaned,

* Van Leeuwen, Jan. 14/24 1687.

therefore, to the plan of a general indulgence; but at heart he would be far better pleased if he could, even now, divide his protection and favour between the Church of Rome and the Church of England, to the exclusion of all other religious persuasions.*

A very few days after this despatch had been written, James made his first hesitating and ungracious advances towards the Puritans. He had determined to begin with Scotland, where his power to dispense with Acts of Parliament had been admitted by the obsequious Estates. On the twelfth of February, accordingly, was published at Edinburgh a proclamation granting relief to scrupulous consciences.† This proclamation fully proves the correctness of Barillon's judgment. Even in the very act of making concessions to the Presbyterians, James could not conceal the loathing with which he regarded them. The toleration given to the Catholics was complete. The Quakers had little reason to complain. But the indulgence vouchsafed to the Presbyterians, who constituted the great body of the Scottish people, was clogged by conditions which made it almost worthless. For the old test, which excluded Catholics and Presbyterians alike from office, was substituted a new test, which admitted the Catholics, but excluded most of the Presbyterians. The Catholics were allowed to build chapels, and even to carry the host in procession anywhere except in the high streets of royal burghs: the Quakers were suffered to assemble in public edifices: but the Presbyterians were interdicted from worshipping God anywhere but in private dwellings: they were not to presume to build meeting houses: they were not even to use a barn or an outhouse for religious exercises; and it was distinctly notified to them that, if they dared to hold conventicles in the open air, the law, which denounced death against both preachers and hearers, should be enforced without mercy. Any Catholic priest might say mass: any Quaker might harangue his brethren; but the Privy Council was directed to see that no Presbyterian minister presumed to preach without a special license from the government. Every line of this instrument, and of the letters by which it was accompanied, shows how much it cost the King to relax

* Barillon, Jan. 31/Feb. 10 1687. "Je crois que, dans le fond, il ne pourroit laisser que la religion Anglicane et la Catholiques établies par les loix, le Roy d'Angleterre en seroit bien plus content."
† It will be found in Wodrow, Appendix, vol. ii. No. 129.

in the smallest degree the rigour with which he had ever treated the old enemies of his house.*

There is reason, indeed, to believe that, when he published this proclamation, he had by no means fully made up his mind to a coalition with the Puritans, and that his object was to grant just so much favour to them as might suffice to frighten the Churchmen into submission. He therefore waited a month, in order to see what effect the edict put forth at Edinburgh would produce in England. That month he employed assiduously, by Petre's advice, in what was called closeting. London was very full. It was expected that the Parliament would shortly meet for the despatch of business; and many members were in town. The King set himself to canvass them man by man. He flattered himself that zealous Tories,—and of such, with few exceptions, the House of Commons consisted,—would find it difficult to resist his earnest request, addressed to them, not collectively, but separately, not from the throne, but in the familiarity of conversation. The members, therefore, who came to pay their duty at Whitehall, were taken aside, and honoured with long private interviews. The King pressed them, as they were loyal gentlemen, to gratify him in the one thing on which his heart was fixed. The question, he said, touched his personal honour. The laws enacted in the late reign by factions Parliaments against the Roman Catholics had really been aimed at himself. Those laws had put a stigma on him, had driven him from the Admiralty, had driven him from the Council Board. He had a right to expect that in the repeal of those laws all who loved and reverenced him would concur. When he found his hearers obdurate to exhortation, he resorted to intimidation and corruption. Those who refused to pleasure him in this matter were plainly told that they must not expect any mark of his favour. Penurious as he was, he opened and distributed his hoards. Several of those who had been invited to confer with him left his bedchamber carrying with them money received from the royal hand. The Judges, who were at this time on their spring circuits, were directed by the King to see those members who remained in the country, and to ascertain the intentions of each. The result of this investigation was that a great majority of the House of Commons seemed fully determined to oppose the measures

CHAP. VII.

Closeting.

It is unsuccessful.

* Wodrow, Appendix, vol. ii. Nos. 128, 129, 132.

of the Court." Among those whose firmness excited general admiration was Arthur Herbert, brother of the Chief Justice, member for Dover, Master of the Robes, and Rear Admiral of England. Arthur Herbert was much loved by the sailors, and was reputed one of the best of the aristocratical class of naval officers. It had been generally supposed that he would readily comply with the royal wishes: for he was heedless of religion: he was fond of pleasure and expense; he had no private estate: his places brought him in four thousand pounds a year; and he had long been reckoned among the most devoted personal adherents of James. When, however, the Rear Admiral was closeted, and required to promise that he would vote for the repeal of the Test Act, his answer was, that his honour and conscience would not permit him to give any such pledge. "Nobody doubts your honour," said the King; "but a man who lives as you do ought not to talk about his conscience." To this reproach, a reproach which came with a bad grace from the lover of Catharine Sedley, Herbert manfully replied, "I have my faults, sir; but I could name people who talk much more about conscience than I am in the habit of doing, and yet lead lives as loose as mine." He was dismissed from all his places; and the account of what he had disbursed and received as Master of the Robes was scrutinised with great and, as he complained, with unjust severity.†

It was now evident that all hope of an alliance between the Churches of England and of Rome, for the purpose of sharing offices and emoluments, and of crushing the Puritan sects, must be abandoned. Nothing remained but to try a coalition between the Church of Rome and the Puritan sects against the Church of England.

On the eighteenth of March the King informed the Privy Council that he had determined to prorogue the Parliament till the end of November, and to grant, by his own authority, entire liberty of conscience to all his subjects.‡ On the fourth of April appeared the memorable Declaration of Indulgence.

In this Declaration the King avowed that it was his earnest wish to see his people members of that Church to which he

---

* Barillon, Feb. 14/24 1687.; Van Citters, Feb. 11/21.; Reresby's Memoirs; Bonrepaux, May 10/20. 1687.
† Barillon, March 14/24. 1687; Lady Russell to Dr. Fitzwilliam, April 1.;
Burnet, i. 671. 762. The conversation is somewhat differently related in the Life of James II. 204. But that passage is not part of the King's own memoirs.
‡ London Gazette, Mar. 21. 1687.

himself belonged. But, since that could not be, he announced his intention to protect them in the free exercise of their religion. He repeated all those phrases which, eight years before, when he was himself an oppressed man, had been familiar to his lips, but which he had ceased to use from the day on which a turn of fortune had put it into his power to be an oppressor. He had long been convinced, he said, that conscience was not to be forced, that persecution was unfavourable to population and to trade, and that it never attained the ends which persecutors had in view. He repeated his promise, already often repeated and often violated, that he would protect the Established Church in the enjoyment of her legal rights. He then proceeded to annul, by his own sole authority, a long series of statutes. He suspended all penal laws against all classes of Nonconformists. He authorised both Roman Catholics and Protestant Dissenters to perform their worship publicly. He forbade his subjects, on pain of his highest displeasure, to molest any religious assembly. He also abrogated all those Acts which imposed any religious test as a qualification for any civil or military office.*

That the Declaration of Indulgence was unconstitutional is a point on which both the great English parties have always been entirely agreed. Every person capable of reasoning on a political question must perceive that a monarch who is competent to issue such a Declaration is nothing less than an absolute monarch. Nor is it possible to urge in defence of this act of James those pleas by which many arbitrary acts of the Stuarts have been vindicated or excused. It cannot be said that he mistook the bounds of his prerogative because they had not been accurately ascertained. For the truth is that he trespassed with a recent landmark full in his view. Fifteen years before that time, a Declaration of Indulgence had been put forth by his brother with the advice of the Cabal. That Declaration, when compared with the Declaration of James, might be called modest and cautious. The Declaration of Charles dispensed only with penal laws. The Declaration of James dispensed also with all religious tests. The Declaration of Charles permitted the Roman Catholics to celebrate their worship in private dwellings only. Under the Declaration of James they might build and decorate temples, and even walk in procession along Fleet Street with crosses, images, and censers. Yet the Declaration of

* London Gazette, April 7. 1687.

Charles had been pronounced illegal in the most formal manner. The Commons had resolved that the King had no power to dispense with statutes in matters ecclesiastical. Charles had ordered the obnoxious instrument to be cancelled in his presence, had torn off the seal with his own hand, and had, both by message under his sign manual, and with his own lips from his throne in full Parliament, distinctly promised the two Houses that the step which had given so much offence should never be drawn into precedent. The two Houses had then, without one dissentient voice, joined in thanking him for this compliance with their wishes. No constitutional question had ever been decided more deliberately, more clearly, or with more harmonious consent.

The defenders of James have frequently pleaded in his excuse the judgment of the Court of King's Bench, on the information collusively laid against Sir Edward Hales; but the plea is of no value. That judgment James had notoriously obtained by solicitation, by threats, by dismissing scrupulous magistrates, and by placing on the bench other magistrates more courtly. And yet that judgment, though generally regarded by the bar and by the nation as unconstitutional, went only to this extent, that the Sovereign might, for special reasons of state, grant to individuals by name exemptions from disabling statutes. That he could by one sweeping edict authorise all his subjects to disobey whole volumes of laws, no tribunal had ventured, in the face of the solemn parliamentary decision of 1673, to affirm.

Such, however, was the position of parties that James's Declaration of Indulgence, though the most audacious of all the attacks made by the Stuarts on public freedom, was well calculated to please that very portion of the community by which all the other attacks of the Stuarts on public freedom had been most strenuously resisted. It could scarcely be hoped that the Protestant Nonconformist, separated from his countrymen by a harsh code harshly enforced, would be inclined to dispute the validity of a decree which relieved him from intolerable grievances. A cool and philosophical observer would undoubtedly have pronounced that all the evil arising from all the intolerant laws which Parliaments had framed was not to be compared to the evil which would be produced by a transfer of the legislative power from the Parliament to the Sovereign. But such coolness and philosophy are not to be expected from men who are smarting under present

CHAP. VII.

Feeling of the Protestant Dissenters

CHAP. VII.

Feelings of the Church of England.

pain, and who are tempted by the offer of immediate ease. A Puritan divine might not indeed be able to deny that the dispensing power now claimed by the Crown was inconsistent with the fundamental principles of the constitution. But he might perhaps be excused if he asked, What was the constitution to him? The Act of Uniformity had ejected him, in spite of royal promises, from a benefice which was his freehold, and had reduced him to beggary and dependence. The Five Mile Act had banished him from his dwelling, from his relations, from his friends, from almost all places of public resort. Under the Conventicle Act his goods had been distrained; and he had been flung into one noisome gaol after another among highwaymen and housebreakers. Out of prison, he had constantly had the officers of justice on his track: he had been forced to pay hushmoney to informers: he had stolen, in ignominious disguises, through windows and trapdoors, to meet his flock, and had, while pouring the baptismal water, or distributing the eucharistic bread, been anxiously listening for the signal that the tipstaves were approaching. Was it not mockery to call on a man thus plundered and oppressed to suffer martyrdom for the property and liberty of his plunderers and oppressors? The Declaration, despotic as it might seem to his prosperous neighbours, brought deliverance to him. He was called upon to make his choice, not between freedom and slavery, but between two yokes; and he might not unnaturally think the yoke of the King lighter than that of the Church.

While thoughts like these were working in the minds of many Dissenters, the Anglican party was in amazement and terror. This new turn in affairs was indeed alarming. The House of Stuart leagued with republican and regicide sects against the old Cavaliers of England; Popery leagued with Puritanism against an ecclesiastical system with which the Puritans had no quarrel, except that it had retained too much that was Popish; these were portents which confounded all the calculations of statesmen. The Church was then to be attacked at once on every side; and the attack was to be under the direction of him who, by her constitution, was her head. She might well be struck with surprise and dismay. And mingled with surprise and dismay came other bitter feelings; resentment against the perjured Prince whom she had served too well, and remorse for the cruelties in which he had been her accomplice, and for which he was now, as it seemed, about to be her punisher. Her chastisement was just. She reaped that which she had sown. After the Restoration, when her power was at the height, she had breathed nothing but vengeance. She had encouraged, urged, almost compelled the Stuarts to requite with perfidious ingratitude the recent services of the Presbyterians. Had she, in that season of her prosperity, pleaded, as became her, for her enemies, she might now, in her distress, have found them her friends. Perhaps it was not yet too late. Perhaps she might still be able to turn the tactics of her faithless oppressor against himself. There was among the Anglican clergy a moderate party which had always felt kindly towards the Protestant Dissenters. That party was not large; but the abilities, acquirements, and virtues of those who belonged to it made it respectable. It had been regarded with little favour by the highest ecclesiastical dignitaries, and had been mercilessly reviled by bigots of the school of Laud: but, from the day on which the Declaration of Indulgence appeared to the day on which the power of James ceased to inspire terror, the whole Church seemed to be animated by the spirit, and guided by the counsels, of the calumniated Latitudinarians.

Then followed an auction, the strangest that history has recorded. On one side the King, on the other the Church, began to bid eagerly against each other for the favour of those whom up to that time King and Church had combined to oppress. The Protestant Dissenters, who, a few months before, had been a despised and proscribed class, now held the balance of power. The harshness with which they had been treated was universally condemned. The Court tried to throw all the blame on the hierarchy. The hierarchy flung it back on the Court. The King declared that he had unwillingly persecuted the separatists only because his affairs had been in such a state that he could not venture to disoblige the established clergy. The established clergy protested that they had borne a part in severity uncongenial to their feelings only from deference to the authority of the King. The King got together a collection of stories about rectors and vicars who had by threats of persecution wrung money out of Protestant Dissenters. He talked on this subject much and publicly; he threatened to institute an enquiry which would exhibit the persons in their true character to the whole world; and he actually issued several commissions empowering agents on whom he thought that he could depend to ascertain the amount of the sums extorted in different parts of the country by professors of the dominant religion from sectaries. The advocates of the Church, on the other hand, cited instances of honest parish priests who had been reprimanded and menaced by the Court for recommending toleration in the pulpit, and for refusing to spy out and hunt down little congregations of Nonconformists. The King asserted that some of the Churchmen whom he had closeted had offered to make large concessions to the Catholics, on condition that the persecution of the Puritans might go on. The accused Churchmen vehemently denied the truth of this charge, and alleged that, if they would have complied with what he demanded for his own religion, he would most gladly have suffered them to indemnify themselves by harassing and pillaging Protestant Dissenters.*

The Court had changed its face. The scarf and cassock could hardly appear there without calling forth sneers and malicious whispers. Maids of honour forebore to giggle, and Lords of the Bedchamber bowed low, when the Puritanical visage and the Puritanical garb, so long the favourite subjects of mockery in fashionable circles, were seen in the galleries. Taunton, which had been during two generations the stronghold of the Roundhead party in the West, which had twice resolutely repelled the armies of Charles the First, which had risen as one man to support Monmouth, and which had been turned into a shambles by Kirke and Jeffreys, seemed to have suddenly succeeded to the place which Oxford had once occupied in the royal favour.† The King constrained himself to show even fawning courtesy to eminent Dissenters. To some he offered money, to some municipal honours, to some pardons for their relations and friends, who, having been implicated in the Rye House plot, or having joined the standard of Monmouth, were now wandering on the Continent, or toiling among the sugar canes of Barbadoes. He affected even to sympathise with the kindness which the English Puritans felt for their foreign brethren. A second

---

* Warrant Book of the Treasury. See particularly the instructions dated March 9, 1687. Burnet, i. 715.; Reflections on His Majesty's Proclamation for a Toleration in Scotland; Letters containing some Reflections on His Majesty's Declaration for Liberty of Conscience; Apology for the Church of England with relation to the spirit of Persecution for which she is accused, 1688. But it is impossible for me to cite all the pamphlets from which I have formed my notion of the state of parties at this time.

† Letter to a Dissenter.

and a third proclamation were published at Edinburgh, which greatly extended the nugatory toleration granted to the Presbyterians by the edict of February.* The banished Huguenots, on whom the King had frowned during many months, and whom he had defrauded of the alms contributed by the nation, were now relieved and caressed. An Order in Council was issued, appealing again in their behalf to the public liberality. The rule which required them to qualify themselves for the receipt of charity, by conforming to the Anglican worship, seems to have been at this time silently abrogated; and the defenders of the King's policy had the effrontery to affirm that this rule, which, as we know from the best evidence, was really devised by himself in concert with Barillon, had been adopted at the instance of the prelates of the Established Church.†

While the King was thus courting his old adversaries, the friends of the Church were not less active. Of the acrimony and scorn with which prelates and priests had, since the Restoration, been in the habit of treating the sectaries scarcely a trace was discernible. Those who had lately been designated as schismatics and fanatics were now dear fellow Protestants, weak brethren it might be, but still brethren, whose scruples were entitled to tender regard. If they would but be true at this crisis to the cause of the English constitution and of the reformed religion, their generosity should be speedily and largely rewarded. They should have, instead of an indulgence which was of no legal validity, a real indulgence, secured by Act of Parliament. Nay, many churchmen, who had hitherto been distinguished by their inflexible attachment to every gesture and every word prescribed in the Book of Common Prayer, now declared themselves favourable, not only to toleration, but even to comprehension. The dispute, they said, about surplices and attitudes, had too long divided those who were agreed as to the essentials of religion. When the struggle for life and death against the common enemy was over, it would be found that the Anglican clergy would be ready to make every fair concession. If the Dissenters would demand only what was reasonable, not only civil but ecclesiastical dignities would be open to them; and

* Wodrow, Appendix, vol. ii. Nos. 132. 134.
† London Gazette, April 21. 1687; Animadversions on a late paper entituled A Letter to a Dissenter, by H. C. (Henry Care), 1687.

Baxter and Howe would be able, without any stain on their honour or their conscience, to sit on the episcopal bench. Of the numerous pamphlets in which the cause of the Court and the cause of the Church were at this time eagerly and anxiously pleaded before the Puritan, now, by a strange turn of fortune, the arbiter of the fate of his persecutors, one only is still remembered, the Letter to a Dissenter. In this masterly little tract, all the arguments which could convince a Nonconformist that it was his duty and his interest to prefer an alliance with the Church to an alliance with the Court, were condensed into the smallest compass, arranged in the most perspicuous order, illustrated with lively wit, and enforced by an eloquence earnest indeed, yet never in its utmost vehemence transgressing the limits of exact good sense and good breeding. The effect of this paper was immense; for, as it was only a single sheet, more than twenty thousand copies were circulated by the post; and there was no corner of the kingdom in which the effect was not felt. Twenty-four answers were published; but the town pronounced that they were all bad, and that Lestrange's was the worst of the twenty-four.[*] The government was greatly irritated, and spared no pains to discover the author of the Letter; but it was found impossible to procure legal evidence against him. Some imagined that they recognised the sentiments and diction of Temple.[†] But in truth that amplitude and acuteness of intellect, that vivacity of fancy, that terse and energetic style, that placid dignity, half courtly half philosophical, which the utmost excitement of conflict could not for a moment derange, belonged to Halifax, and to Halifax alone.

The Dissenters wavered; nor is it any reproach to them that they did so. They were suffering; and the King had given them relief. Some eminent pastors had emerged from confinement; and others had ventured to return from exile. Congregations, which had hitherto met only by stealth and in darkness, now assembled at noonday, and sang psalms aloud in the hearing of magistrates, churchwardens, and constables. Modest buildings for the worship of God after the Puritan fashion began to rise all over England. An

---

[*] Lestrange's Answer to a Letter to a Dissenter; Care's Animadversions on A Letter to a Dissenter; Dialogue between Harry and Roger; that is to say, Harry Care and Roger Lestrange.

[†] The letter was signed T. W. Care says, in his animadversions, "This Sir Politic T. W., or W. T.; for some critics think that the truer reading."

observant traveller will still remark the date of 1687 on some of the oldest meeting houses. Nevertheless the offers of the Church were, to a prudent Dissenter, far more attractive than those of the King. The Declaration was, in the eye of the law, a nullity. It suspended the penal statutes against nonconformity only for so long a time as the fundamental principles of the constitution and the rightful authority of the legislature should remain suspended. What was the value of privileges which must be held by a tenure at once so ignominious and so insecure? There might soon be a demise of the crown. A sovereign attached to the established religion might sit on the throne. A Parliament composed of Churchmen might be assembled. How deplorable would then be the situation of Dissenters who had been in league with Jesuits against the constitution! The Church offered an indulgence very different from that granted by James, an indulgence as valid and as sacred as the Great Charter. Both the contending parties promised religious liberty to the separatist: but one party required him to purchase it by sacrificing civil liberty; the other party invited him to enjoy civil and religious liberty together.

For these reasons, even if it could have been believed that the Court was sincere, a Dissenter might reasonably have determined to cast in his lot with the Church. But what guarantee was there for the sincerity of the Court? All men knew what the conduct of James had been up to that very time. It was not impossible, indeed, that a persecutor might be convinced by argument and by experience of the advantages of toleration. But James did not pretend to have been recently convinced. On the contrary, he omitted no opportunity of protesting that he had, during many years, been, on principle, adverse to all intolerance. Yet, within a few months, he had persecuted men, women, young girls, to the death for their religion. Had he been acting against light and against the convictions of his conscience then? Or was he uttering a deliberate falsehood now? From this dilemma there was no escape; and either of the two suppositions was fatal to the King's character for honesty. It was notorious also that he had been completely subjugated by the Jesuits. Only a few days before the publication of the Indulgence, that Order had been honoured, in spite of the well known wishes of the Holy See, with a new mark of his confidence and approbation. His confessor, Father Mansuete, a Franciscan, whose mild temper and irreproachable life commanded general respect, but who had long been hated by Tyrconnel and Petre, had been discarded. The vacant place had been filled by an Englishman named Warner, who had apostatised from the religion of his country and had turned Jesuit. To the moderate Roman Catholics and to the Nuncio this change was far from agreeable. By every Protestant it was regarded as a proof that the dominion of the Jesuits over the royal mind was absolute.* Whatever praises those fathers might justly claim, flattery itself could not ascribe to them either wide liberality or strict veracity. That they had never scrupled, when the interest of their Order was at stake, to call in the aid of the civil sword, or to violate the laws of truth and of good faith, had been proclaimed to the world not only by Protestant accusers, but by men whose virtue and genius were the glory of the Church of Rome. It was incredible that a devoted disciple of the Jesuits should be on principle zealous for freedom of conscience: but it was neither incredible nor improbable that he might think himself justified in disguising his real sentiments, in order to render a service to his religion. It was certain that the King at heart preferred the Churchmen to the Puritans. It was certain that, while he had any hope of gaining the Churchmen, he had never shown the smallest kindness to the Puritans. Could it then be doubted that, if the Churchmen would even now comply with his wishes, he would willingly sacrifice the Puritans? His word, repeatedly pledged, had not restrained him from invading the legal rights of that clergy which had given such signal proofs of affection and fidelity to his house. What security then could his word afford to sects divided from him by the recollection of a thousand inexpiable wounds inflicted and endured?

When the first agitation produced by the publication of the Indulgence had subsided, it appeared that a breach had taken place in the Puritan party. The minority, headed by a few busy men whose judgment was defective or was biassed by interest, supported the King. Henry Care, who had long been the bitterest and most active pamphleteer among the Nonconformists, and who had, in the days of the Popish plot, assailed James with the utmost fury in a weekly journal en-

* Ellis Correspondence, March 15. $\frac{4}{14}$. 1687; Ronquillo, March $\frac{7}{17}$. 1687, July 27. 1686; Barillon, $\frac{5-8}{5-18}$. March 14 the Mackintosh Collection.

titled the Packet of Advice from Rome, was now as loud in adulation as he had formerly been in calumny and insult.* The chief agent who was employed by the government to manage the Presbyterians was Vincent Alsop, a divine of some note both as a preacher and as a writer. His son, who had incurred the penalties of treason, received a pardon; and the whole influence of the father was thus engaged on the side of the Court.† With Alsop was joined Thomas Rosewell. Rosewell had, during that persecution of the Dissenters which followed the detection of the Rye House plot, been falsely accused of preaching against the government, had been tried for his life by Jeffreys, and had, in defiance of the clearest evidence, been convicted by a packed jury. The injustice of the verdict was so gross that the very courtiers cried shame. One Tory gentleman who had heard the trial went instantly to Charles, and declared that the neck of the most loyal subject in England would not be safe if Rosewell suffered. The jurymen themselves were stung by remorse when they thought over what they had done, and exerted themselves to save the life of the prisoner. At length a pardon was granted: but Rosewell remained bound under heavy recognisances to good behaviour during life, and to periodical appearance in the Court of King's Bench. His recognisances were now discharged by the royal command; and in this way his services were secured.‡

The business of gaining the Independents was principally entrusted to one of their ministers named Stephen Lobb. Lobb was a weak, violent, and ambitious man. He had gone such lengths in opposition to the government, that he had been by name proscribed in several proclamations. He now made his peace, and went as far in servility as he had ever done in faction. He joined the Jesuitical cabal, and eagerly recommended measures from which the wisest and most honest Roman Catholics recoiled. It was remarked that he was constantly at the palace and frequently in the closet, that he lived with a splendour to which the Puritan divines were little accustomed, and that he was perpetually surrounded

CHAP.
VII.

Alsop.

Rosewell.

Lobb.

---

* Wood's Athenæ Oxonienses; Observator; Heraclitus Ridens, passim. But Care's own writings furnish the best materials for an estimate of his character.
† Calamy's Account of the Ministers ejected or silenced after the Restoration in Northamptonshire; Wood's Athenæ Oxonienses; Biographia Britannica.
‡ State Trials; Samuel Rosewell's Life of Thomas Rosewell, 1718; Calamy's Account.

by suitors imploring his interest to procure them offices or pardons.*

With Lobb was closely connected William Penn. Penn had never been a strongheaded man: the life which he had been leading during two years had not a little impaired his moral sensibility; and if his conscience ever reproached him, he comforted himself by repeating that he had a good and noble end in view, and that he was not paid for his services in money.

By the influence of these men, and of others less conspicuous, addresses of thanks to the King were procured from several bodies of Dissenters. Tory writers have with justice remarked that the language of these compositions was as fulsomely servile as anything that could be found in the most florid eulogies pronounced by Bishops on the Stuarts. But, on close enquiry, it will appear that the disgrace belongs to but a small part of the Puritan party. There was scarcely a market town in England without at least a knot of separatists. No exertion was spared to induce them to express their gratitude for the Indulgence. Circular letters, imploring them to sign, were sent to every corner of the kingdom in such numbers that the mail bags, it was sportively said, were too heavy for the posthorses. Yet all the addresses which could be obtained from all the Presbyterians, Independents, and Baptists scattered over England did not in six months amount to sixty; nor is there any reason to believe that these addresses were numerously signed.† One of the most adulatory was that of the Quakers; and Penn presented it with a speech more adulatory still.‡

The great body of Protestant Nonconformists, firmly attached to civil liberty, and distrusting the promises of the King and of the Jesuits, steadily refused to return thanks for a favour, which, it might well be suspected, concealed a snare. This was the temper of all the most illustrious chiefs of the party. One of these was Baxter. He had, as we have seen, been brought to trial soon after the accession of James, had been brutally insulted by Jeffreys, and had been convicted by a jury, such as the courtly Sheriffs of those times were in the habit of selecting. Baxter had been about a year and a half in prison

* London Gazette, March 13, 1687; Nichols's Defence of the Church of England; Pierce's Vindication of the Dissenters.

† The Addresses will be found in the London Gazettes.

‡ London Gazette, May 26, 1687; Life of Penn prefixed to his Works, 1726.

when the Court began to think seriously of gaining the Nonconformists. He was not only set at liberty, but was informed that, if he chose to reside in London, he might do so without fearing that the Five Mile Act would be enforced against him. The government probably hoped that the recollection of past sufferings and the sense of present ease would produce the same effect on him as on Rosewell and Lobb. The hope was disappointed. Baxter was neither to be corrupted nor to be deceived. He refused to join in any address of thanks for the Indulgence, and exerted all his influence to promote good feeling between the Church and the Presbyterians.*

If any man stood higher than Baxter in the estimation of the Protestant Dissenters, that man was John Howe. Howe had, like Baxter, been personally a gainer by the recent change of policy. The same tyranny which had flung Baxter into gaol had driven Howe into banishment; and, soon after Baxter had been let out of the King's Bench Prison, Howe returned from Utrecht to England. It was expected at Whitehall that Howe would exert in favour of the Court all the authority which he possessed over his brethren. The King himself condescended to ask the help of the subject whom he had oppressed. Howe appears to have hesitated; but the influence of the Hampdens, with whom he was on terms of close intimacy, kept him steady to the cause of the constitution. A meeting of Presbyterian ministers was held at his house, to consider the state of affairs, and to determine on the course to be adopted. There was great anxiety at the palace to know the result. Two royal messengers were in attendance during the discussion. They returned with the unwelcome news that Howe had declared himself decidedly adverse to the dispensing power, and that he had, after long debate, carried with him the majority of the assembly.†

To the names of Baxter and Howe must be added the name of a man far below them in station and in acquired knowledge, but in virtue their equal, and in genius their superior, John Bunyan. Bunyan had been bred a tinker, and had served as a private soldier in the parliamentary army. Early in his life he had been fearfully tortured by remorse for his youthful sins, the worst of which seem, however, to have been such as the world thinks venial. His keen sensibility

---

* Calamy's Life of Baxter.
† Calamy's Life of Howe. The share which the Hampden family had in the matter I learned from a letter of Johnstone of Waristoun, dated June 12, 1688.

CHAP.
VII.

and his powerful imagination made his internal conflicts singularly terrible. He fancied that he was under sentence of reprobation, that he had committed blasphemy against the Holy Ghost, that he had sold Christ, that he was actually possessed by a demon. Sometimes loud voices from heaven cried out to warn him. Sometimes fiends whispered impious suggestions in his ear. He saw visions of distant mountain tops, on which the sun shone brightly, but from which he was separated by a waste of snow. He felt the Devil behind him pulling his clothes. He thought that the brand of Cain had been set upon him. He feared that he was about to burst asunder like Judas. His mental agony disordered his health. One day he shook like a man in the palsy. On another day he felt a fire within his breast. It is difficult to understand how he survived sufferings so intense, and so long continued. At length the clouds broke. From the depths of despair, the penitent passed to a state of serene felicity. An irresistible impulse now urged him to impart to others the blessing of which he was himself possessed.* He joined the Baptists, and became a preacher and writer. His education had been that of a mechanic. He knew no language but the English, as it was spoken by the common people. He had studied no great model of composition, with the exception, an important exception undoubtedly, of our noble translation of the Bible. His spelling was bad. He frequently transgressed the rules of grammar. Yet his native force of genius, and his experimental knowledge of all the religious passions, from despair to ecstasy, amply supplied in him the want of learning. His rude oratory roused and melted hearers who listened without interest to the laboured discourses of great logicians and Hebraists. His books were widely circulated among the humbler classes. One of them, the Pilgrim's Progress, was, in his own lifetime, translated into several foreign languages. It was, however, scarcely known to the learned and polite, and had been, during more than a century, the delight of pious cottagers and artisans before it took its proper place, as a classical work, in libraries. At length critics condescended to enquire where the secret of so wide and so durable a popularity lay. They were compelled to own that the ignorant multitude had judged more correctly than the learned, and that the despised little book was really a masterpiece. Bunyan is indeed as decidedly the first of allegorists as Demosthenes is the first of

* Bunyan's Grace Abounding.

orators, or Shakspeare the first of dramatists. Other allegorists have shown equal ingenuity; but no other allegorist has ever been able to touch the heart, and to make abstractions objects of terror, pity and of love.*

It may be doubted whether any English Dissenter had suffered more severely under the penal laws than John Bunyan. Of the twenty-seven years which had elapsed since the Restoration, he had passed twelve in confinement. He still persisted in preaching: but, that he might preach, he was under the necessity of disguising himself like a carter. He was often introduced into meetings through back doors, with a smock frock on his back, and a whip in his hand. If he had thought only of his own ease and safety, he would have hailed the Indulgence with delight. He was now, at length, free to pray and exhort in open day. His congregation rapidly increased: thousands hung upon his words; and at Bedford, where he ordinarily resided, money was plentifully contributed to build a meeting house for him. His influence among the common people was such that the government would willingly have bestowed on him some municipal office: but his vigorous understanding and his stout English heart were proof against all delusion and all temptation. He felt assured that the proffered toleration was merely a bait intended to lure the Puritan party to destruction; nor would he, by accepting a place for which he was not legally qualified, recognise the validity of the dispensing power. One of the last acts of his virtuous life was to decline an interview to which he was invited by an agent of the government.†

Great as was the authority of Bunyan over the Baptists, that of William Kiffin was still greater. Kiffin was the first man among them in wealth and station. He was in the habit of exercising his spiritual gifts at their meetings: but he did not live by preaching. He traded largely: his credit on the Exchange of London stood high; and he had accumulated an ample fortune. Perhaps no man could, at that conjuncture, have rendered more valuable services to the Court. But between him and the Court was interposed the remem-

CHAP. VII.

Kiffin.

---

* Young classes Bunyan's prose with Durfey's poetry. The people of fashion in the Spiritual Quixote rank the Pilgrim's Progress with Jack the Giantkiller. Late in the eighteenth century Cowper did not venture to do more than allude to the great allegorist:—

"I name thee not, lest so deserved a praise should move a sneer at thy deserved fame.

† The continuation of Bunyan's Life appended to his Grace Abounding.

brance of one terrible event. He was the grandfather of the two Hewlings, those gallant youths who, of all the victims of the Bloody Assizes, had been the most generally lamented. For the sad fate of one of them James was in a peculiar manner responsible. Jeffreys had respited the younger brother. The poor lad's sister had been ushered by Churchill into the royal presence, and had begged for mercy: but the King's heart had been obdurate. The misery of the whole family had been great: but Kiffin was most to be pitied. He was seventy years old when he was left desolate, the survivor of those who should have survived him. The heartless and venal sycophants of Whitehall, judging by themselves, thought that the old man would be easily propitiated by an Alderman's gown, and by some compensation in money for the property which his grandsons had forfeited. Penn was employed in the work of seduction, but to no purpose.* The King determined to try what effect his own civilities would produce. Kiffin was ordered to attend at the palace. He found a brilliant circle of noblemen and gentlemen assembled. James immediately came to him, spoke to him very graciously, and concluded by saying, "I have put you down, Mr. Kiffin, for an Alderman of London." The old man look fixedly at the King, burst into tears, and made answer, "Sir, I am worn out. I am unfit to serve Your Majesty or the City. And, sir, the death of my poor boys broke my heart. That wound is as fresh as ever. I shall carry it to my grave." The King stood silent for a minute in some confusion, and then said, "Mr. Kiffin, I will find a balsam for that sore." Assuredly James did not mean to say anything cruel or insolent: on the contrary, he seems to have been in an unusually gentle mood. Yet no speech that is recorded of him gives so unfavourable a notion of his

* An attempt has been made to vindicate Penn's conduct on this occasion, and to fasten on me the charge of having calumniated him. It is asserted that, instead of being engaged, on behalf of the government, in the work of seduction, he was really engaged, on behalf of Kiffin, in the work of intercession. In support of this view the following passage is triumphantly quoted from Kiffin's Memoirs of himself. "I used all the means I could to be excused both by some lords near the King, and also by Sir Nicholas Butler, and Mr. Penn. But it was all in vain ...." There the quotation ends, not at a full stop, but at a semicolon. The remainder of the sentence, which fully bears out all that I have said, is carefully suppressed. Kiffin proceeds thus:—"I was told that they (Nicholas and Penn) knew I had an interest that might serve the King, and although they knew my sufferings were great, in cutting off my two grandchildren, and losing their estates, yet it should be made up to me, both in their estates, and also in what honour or advantage I could reasonably desire for myself. But I thank the Lord, these proffers were no snare to me."

character as these few words. They are the words of a hard-hearted and lowminded man, unable to conceive any laceration of the affections for which a place or a pension would not be a full compensation.*

Since Kiffin could not be seduced by blandishments and fair promises, it was determined to try what persecution would effect. He was told that an information would be filed against him in the Crown Office, and he was threatened with a lodging in Newgate. He asked the advice of counsel; and the answer which he received was that, by accepting office without taking the sacrament according to the Anglican ritual, he would make himself legally liable to a fine of five hundred pounds, but that, by refusing office, he would make himself liable, not legally, but in fact, to whatever fine a servile bench of judges might, in direct defiance of the statutes, think fit to impose. He might be mulcted in ten, twenty, thirty, thousand pounds. His family, which had already suffered so cruelly from two confiscations, might be utterly ruined by this third calamity. After holding out many weeks, he so far submitted as to take the title of Alderman: but he abstained from acting either as a Justice of the Peace or as one of the Commission of Lieutenancy which commanded the militia of the City.†

That section of the dissenting body which was favourable to the King's new policy had from the first been a minority, and soon began to diminish. For the Nonconformists perceived in no long time that their spiritual privileges had been abridged rather than extended by the Indulgence. The chief characteristic of the Puritan was abhorrence of the peculiarities of the Church of Rome. He had quitted the Church of England only because he conceived that she too much resembled her superb and voluptuous sister, the sorceress of the golden cup and of the scarlet robe. He now found that one of the implied conditions of that alliance which some of his pastors had formed with the Court was that the religion of the Court should be respectfully and tenderly treated. He soon began to regret the days of persecution. While the penal laws were enforced, he had heard the words of life in secret and at his peril: but still he had heard them. When the brethren were assembled in the inner chamber, when the sentinels had been posted, when the doors had been locked,

* Kiffin's Memoirs; Lucas's Letter to Brooke, May 31. 1773, in the Hughes Correspondence.   † Kiffin's Memoirs.

when the preacher, in the garb of a butcher or a drayman, had come in over the tiles, then at least God was truly worshipped. No portion of divine truth was suppressed or softened down for any worldly object. All the distinctive doctrines of the Puritan theology were fully, and even coarsely, set forth. To the Church of Rome no quarter was given. The Beast, the Antichrist, the Man of Sin, the mystical Jezebel, the mystical Babylon, were the phrases ordinarily employed to describe that august and fascinating superstition. Such had been once the style of Alsop, of Lobb, of Rosewell, and of other ministers who had of late been well received at the palace: but such was now their style no longer. Divines who aspired to a high place in the King's favour and confidence could not venture to speak with asperity of the King's religion. Congregations therefore complained loudly that, since the appearance of the Declaration which purported to give them entire freedom of conscience, they had never once heard the Gospel boldly and faithfully preached. Formerly they had been forced to snatch their spiritual nutriment by stealth: but, when they had snatched it, they had found it seasoned exactly to their taste. They were now at liberty to feed: but their food had lost all its savour. They met by daylight, and in commodious edifices; but they heard discourses far less to their taste than they would have heard from the rector. At the parish church the will worship and idolatry of Rome were every Sunday attacked with energy: but, at the meeting house, the pastor, who had a few months before reviled the established clergy as little better than Papists, now carefully abstained from censuring Popery, or conveyed his censures in language too delicate to shock even the ears of Father Petre. Nor was it possible to assign any creditable reason for this change. The Roman Catholic doctrines had undergone no alteration. Within living memory, never had Roman Catholic priests been so active in the work of making proselytes: never had so many Roman Catholic publications issued from the press: never had the attention of all who cared about religion been so closely fixed on the disputes between the Roman Catholics and the Protestants. What could be thought of the sincerity of theologians who had never been weary of railing at Popery when Popery was comparatively harmless and helpless, and who now, when a time of real danger to the reformed faith had arrived, studiously avoided uttering one word which could give offence to a Jesuit? Their conduct was indeed easily explained. It was known that some of them had obtained pardons. It was suspected that others had obtained money. Their prototype might be found in that weak apostle who from fear denied the Master to whom he had boastfully professed the firmest attachment, or in that baser apostle who sold his Lord for a handful of silver.*

Thus the dissenting ministers who had been gained by the Court were rapidly losing the influence which they had once possessed over their brethren. On the other hand, the sectaries found themselves attracted by a strong religious sympathy towards those prelates and priests of the Church of England who, in spite of royal mandates, of threats, and of promises, were waging vigorous war with the Church of Rome. The Anglican body and the Puritan body, so long separated by a mortal enmity, were daily drawing nearer to each other, and every step which they made towards union increased the influence of him who was their common head. William was in all things fitted to be a mediator between these two great sections of the English nation. He could not be said to be a member of either. Yet neither, when in a reasonable mood, could refuse to regard him as a friend. His system of theology agreed with that of the Puritans. At the same time, he regarded episcopacy, not indeed as a divine institution, but as a perfectly lawful and an eminently useful form of church government. Questions respecting postures, robes, festivals, and liturgies, he considered as of no vital importance. A simple worship, such as that to which he had been early accustomed, would have been most to his personal taste. But he was prepared to conform to any ritual which might be acceptable to the nation, and insisted only that he should not be required to persecute his brother Protestants whose consciences did not permit them to follow his example. Two years earlier he would have been pronounced by numerous bigots on both sides a mere Laodicean, neither cold nor hot, and fit only to be spewed out. But the zeal which had inflamed Churchmen against Dissenters and Dissenters against Churchmen had been so tempered by common adversity and danger that the lukewarmness which had once been imputed to him as a crime was now reckoned among his chief virtues.

* See, among other contemporary of the threatening Dangers impending pamphlets, one entitled a Representation over Protestants.

CHAP.
VII.

The Prince
and
Princess of
Orange
hostile
to the
Declaration of
Indulgence.

All men were anxious to know what he thought of the Declaration of Indulgence. For a time hopes were entertained at Whitehall that his known respect for the rights of conscience would at least prevent him from publicly expressing disapprobation of a policy which had a specious show of liberality. Penn had visited Holland in the summer of 1686, confident that his eloquence, of which he had a high opinion, would prove irresistible. He had harangued on his favourite theme with a copiousness which tired his hearers out. He had assured them that a golden age of religious liberty was approaching: whoever lived three years longer would see strange things: he could not be mistaken; for he had it from a man who had it from an Angel. Penn also hinted that, though he had not come to the Hague with a royal commission, he knew the royal mind. There was nothing, he was confident, which the uncle would not do to gratify the nephew, if only the nephew would, in the matter of the Test Act, gratify the uncle. As oral exhortations and promises produced little effect, Penn returned to England, and thence wrote to the Hague that His Majesty seemed disposed to make large concessions, to live in close amity with the Prince, and to settle a handsome income on the Princess.* There can indeed be little doubt that James would gladly have purchased at a high price the support of his eldest daughter and of his son in law. But, on the subject of the Test, William's resolution was immutable. "You ask me," he said to one of the King's agents, "to countenance an attack on my own religion. I cannot with a safe conscience do it, and I will not, no, not for the crown of England, nor for the empire of the world." These words were reported to the King and disturbed him greatly.† He wrote urgent letters with his own hand. Sometimes he took the tone of an injured man. He was the head of the royal family: he was as such entitled to expect the obedience of the younger branches; and it was very hard that he was to be crossed in a matter on which his heart was set. At other times a bait which was

---

* Burnet, i. 693, 694.; Avaux, Jan. 10. 1687. Penn's letters were regularly put, by one of his Quaker friends who resided at the Hague, into the Prince's own hand.

† "Le Prince d'Orange, qui avoit étudié jusqu'alors de faire une réponse positive, dit . . . . . qu'il ne consentiroit jamais à la suppression de ces luix qui avoient été établies pour le maintien et la sureté de la religion Protestante, et que sa conscience ne le lui permettoit point, non seulement pour la succession du royaume d'Angleterre, mais même pour l'empire du monde; en sorte que le roi d'Angleterre est plus aigri contre lui qu'il n'a jamais été."—Bonrepaux, June 1687.

thought irresistible was offered. If William would but give way on this one point, the English government would, in return, cooperate with him strenuously against France. He was not to be so deluded. He knew that James, without the support of a Parliament, would, even if not unwilling, be unable to render effectual service to the common cause of Europe; and there could be no doubt that, if a Parliament were assembled, the first demand of both Houses would be that the Declaration should be cancelled.

CHAP. VII.

The Princess assented to all that was suggested by her husband. Their joint opinion was conveyed to the King in firm but temperate terms. They declared that they deeply regretted the course which His Majesty had adopted. They were convinced that he had usurped a prerogative which did not by law belong to him. Against that usurpation they protested, not only as friends to civil liberty, but as members of the royal house, who had a deep interest in maintaining the rights of that crown which they might one day wear. For experience had shown that in England arbitrary government could not fail to produce a reaction even more pernicious than itself; and it might reasonably be feared that the nation, alarmed and incensed by the prospect of despotism, might conceive a disgust even for constitutional monarchy. The advice, therefore, which they tendered to the King was that he would in all things govern according to law. They readily admitted that the law might with advantage be altered by competent authority, and that some part of his Declaration well deserved to be embodied in an Act of Parliament. They were not persecutors. They should with pleasure see Roman Catholics as well as Protestant Dissenters relieved in a proper manner from all penal statutes. They should with pleasure see Protestant Dissenters admitted in a proper manner to civil office. At that point their Highnesses must stop. They could not but entertain grave apprehensions that, if Roman Catholics were made capable of public trust, great evil would ensue; and it was intimated not obscurely that these apprehensions arose chiefly from the conduct of James.*

The opinion expressed by the Prince and Princess respecting the disabilities to which the Roman Catholics were subject was that of almost all the statesmen and philosophers who were then zealous for political and religious freedom. In our age, on the contrary, enlightened men have often pro-

Their views respecting the English Roman Catholics vindicated

* Burnet, i. 710.; Boarepaus, May 24/June 4, 1687.

nounced, with regret, that, on this one point, William appears to disadvantage when compared with his father in law. The truth is that some considerations which are necessary to the forming of a correct judgment seem to have escaped the notice of many writers of the nineteenth century.

There are two opposite errors into which those who study the annals of our country are in constant danger of falling, the error of judging the present by the past, and the error of judging the past by the present. The former is the error of minds prone to reverence whatever is old, the latter of minds readily attracted by whatever is new. The former error may perpetually be observed in the reasonings of conservative politicians on the questions of their own day. The latter error perpetually infects the speculations of writers of the liberal school when they discuss the transactions of an earlier age. The former error is the more pernicious in a statesman, and the latter in a historian.

It is not easy for any person who, in our time, undertakes to treat of the revolution which overthrew the Stuarts, to preserve with steadiness the happy mean between these two extremes. The question whether members of the Roman Catholic Church could be safely admitted to Parliament and to office convulsed our country during the reign of James the Second, was set at rest by his downfall, and, having slept during more than a century, was revived by that great stirring of the human mind which followed the meeting of the National Assembly of France. During thirty years the contest went on in both Houses of Parliament, in every constituent body, in every social circle. It destroyed administrations, broke up parties, made all government in one part of the empire impossible, and at length brought us to the verge of civil war. Even when the struggle had terminated, the passions to which it had given birth still continued to rage. It was scarcely possible for any man whose mind was under the influence of those passions to see the events of the years 1687 and 1688 in a perfectly correct light.

One class of politicians, starting from the true proposition that the Revolution had been a great blessing to our country, arrived at the false conclusion that no test which the statesmen of the Revolution had thought necessary for the protection of our religion and our freedom could be safely abolished. Another class, starting from the true proposition that the disabilities imposed on the Roman Catholics had long been productive of nothing but mischief, arrived at the false conclusion that there never could have been a time when those disabilities were useful and necessary. The former fallacy pervaded the speeches of the acute and learned Eldon. The latter was not altogether without influence even on an intellect so calm and philosophical as that of Mackintosh.

Perhaps, however, it will be found on examination that we may vindicate the course which was unanimously approved by all the great English statesmen of the seventeenth century, without questioning the wisdom of the course which was as unanimously approved by all the great English statesmen of our own time.

Undoubtedly it is an evil that any citizen should be excluded from civil employment on account of his religious opinions; but a choice between evils is sometimes all that is left to human wisdom. A nation may be placed in such a situation that the majority must either impose disabilities or submit to them, and that what would, under ordinary circumstances, be justly condemned as persecution, may fall within the bounds of legitimate selfdefence; and such was in the year 1687 the situation of England.

According to the constitution of the realm, James possessed the right of naming almost all public functionaries, political, judicial, ecclesiastical, military, and naval. In the exercise of this right he was not, as our sovereigns now are, under the necessity of acting in conformity with the advice of ministers approved by the House of Commons. It was evident therefore that, unless he were strictly bound by law to bestow office on none but Protestants, it would be in his power to bestow office on none but Roman Catholics. The Roman Catholics were few in number; and among them was not a single man whose services could be seriously missed by the commonwealth. The proportion which they bore to the population of England was very much smaller than at present. For at present a constant stream of emigration runs from Ireland to our great towns: but in the seventeenth century there was not even in London an Irish colony. More than forty-nine fiftieths of the inhabitants of the kingdom, more than forty-nine fiftieths of the property of the kingdom, almost all the political, legal, and military ability and knowledge to be found in the kingdom, were Protestant. Nevertheless the King, under a strong infatuation, had determined to use his vast patronage as a means of making proselytes. To be of his Church was, in his view, the first of all qualifications for office. To be of the national Church was a positive disqualification. He reprobated, it is true, in language which has been applauded by some credulous friends of religious liberty, the monstrous injustice of that test which excluded a small minority of the nation from public trust: but he was at the same time instituting a test which excluded the majority. He thought it hard that a man who was a good financier and a loyal subject should be excluded from the post of Lord Treasurer merely for being a Papist. But he had himself turned out a Lord Treasurer whom he admitted to be a good financier and a loyal subject merely for being a Protestant. He had repeatedly and distinctly declared his resolution never to put the white staff in the hands of any heretic. With many other great offices of state he had dealt in the same way. Already the Lord President, the Lord Privy Seal, the Lord Chamberlain, the Groom of the Stole, the First Lord of the Treasury, the Principal Secretary of State, the Lord High Commissioner of Scotland, the Chancellor of Scotland, the Secretary of Scotland, were, or pretended to be, Roman Catholics. Most of these functionaries had been bred Churchmen, and had been guilty of apostasy, open or secret, in order to obtain or to keep their high places. Every Protestant who still held an important post in the government held it in constant uncertainty and fear. It would be endless to recount the situations of a lower rank which were filled by the favoured class. Roman Catholics already swarmed in every department of the public service. They were Lords Lieutenants, Deputy Lieutenants, Judges, Justices of the Peace, Commissioners of the Customs, Envoys to foreign courts, Colonels of regiments, Governors of fortresses. The share which in a few months they had obtained of the temporal patronage of the crown was much more than ten times as great as they would have had under an impartial system. Yet this was not the worst. They were made rulers of the Church of England. Men who had assured the King that they held his faith sate in the High Commission, and exercised supreme jurisdiction in spiritual things over all the prelates and priests of the established religion. Ecclesiastical benefices of great dignity had been bestowed, some on avowed Papists, and some on half concealed Papists. And all this had been done while the laws against Popery were still unrepealed, and while James had still a strong interest in affecting respect for the rights of conscience. What then was his conduct likely to be, if his subjects consented to free him, by a legislative act, from even the shadow of restraint? Is it possible to doubt that Protestants would have been as effectually excluded from employment, by a strictly legal use of the royal prerogative, as ever Roman Catholics had been by Act of Parliament?

How obstinately James was determined to bestow on the members of his own Church a share of patronage altogether out of proportion to their numbers and importance is proved by the instructions which, in exile and old age, he drew up for the guidance of his son. It is impossible to read without mingled pity and derision those effusions of a mind on which all the discipline of experience and adversity had been exhausted in vain. The Pretender is advised, if ever he should reign in England, to make a partition of offices, and carefully to reserve for the members of the Church of Rome a portion which might have sufficed for them if they had been one half instead of one fiftieth part of the nation. One Secretary of State, one Commissioner of the Treasury, the Secretary at War, the majority of the great dignitaries of the household, the majority of the officers of the army, are always to be Catholics. Such were the designs of James after his perverse bigotry had drawn on him a punishment which had appalled the whole world. Is it then possible to doubt what his conduct would have been if his people, deluded by the empty name of religious liberty, had suffered him to proceed without any check?

Even Penn, intemperate and undiscerning as was his zeal for the Declaration, seems to have felt that the partiality with which honours and emoluments were heaped on Roman Catholics might not unnaturally excite the jealousy of the nation. He owned that, if the Test Act were repealed, the Protestants were entitled to an equivalent, and went so far as to suggest several equivalents. During some weeks the word equivalent, then lately imported from France, was in the mouths of all the coffeehouse orators; but at length a few pages of keen logic and polished sarcasm written by Halifax put an end to these idle projects. One of Penn's schemes was that a law should be passed dividing the patronage of the crown into three equal parts, and that to one only of those parts members of the Church of Rome should be admitted. Even under such an arrangement the members of the Church of Rome would have obtained near twenty times their fair portion of official appointments; and yet there is no reason to believe that even to such an arrangement the King would have consented. But, had he consented, what guarantee could he give that he would adhere to his bargain? The dilemma propounded by Halifax was unanswerable. If laws are binding on you, observe the law which now exists. If laws are not binding on you, it is idle to offer us a law as a security.*

It is clear, therefore, that the point at issue was not whether secular offices should be thrown open to all sects indifferently. While James was King it was inevitable that there should be exclusion; and the only question was who should be excluded, Papists or Protestants, the few or the many, a hundred thousand Englishmen or five millions.

Such are the weighty arguments by which the conduct of the Prince of Orange towards the English Roman Catholics may be reconciled with the principles of religious liberty. These arguments, it will be observed, have no reference to any part of the Roman Catholic theology. It will also be observed that they ceased to have any force when the crown had been settled on a race of Protestant sovereigns, and when the power of the House of Commons in the state had become so decidedly preponderant that no sovereign, whatever might have been his opinions or his inclinations, could have imitated the example of James. The nation, however, after its terrors, its struggles, its narrow escape, was in a suspicious and vindictive mood. Means of defence therefore which necessity had once justified, and which necessity alone could justify, were obstinately used long after the necessity had ceased to exist, and were not abandoned till vulgar prejudice had maintained a contest of many years against reason. But in the time of James reason and vulgar prejudice were on the same side. The fanatical and ignorant wished to exclude the Roman Catholic from office because he worshipped stocks and stones, because he had the mark of the beast, because he had burned down London, because he had strangled Sir Edmondsbury Godfrey; and the most judicious and tolerant statesman, while smiling at the delusions which imposed on the populace, was led, by a very different road, to the same conclusion.

* Johnstone, Jan. 18, 1658; Halifax's Anatomy of an Equivalent.

The great object of William now was to unite in one body the numerous sections of the community which regarded him as their common head. In this work he had several able and trusty coadjutors, among whom two were preeminently useful, Burnet and Dykvelt. The services of Burnet indeed it was necessary to employ with some caution. The kindness with which he had been welcomed at the Hague had excited the rage of James. Mary received from her father two letters filled with invectives against the insolent and seditious divine whom she protected. But these accusations had so little effect on her that she sent back answers dictated by Burnet himself. At length, in January 1687, the King had recourse to stronger measures. Skelton, who had represented the English government in the United Provinces, was removed to Paris, and was succeeded by Albeville, the weakest and basest of all the members of the Jesuitical cabal. Money was Albeville's one object; and he took it from all who offered it. He was paid at once by France and by Holland. Nay, he stooped below even the miserable dignity of corruption, and accepted bribes so small that they seemed better suited to a porter or a lacquey than to an Envoy who had been honoured with an English baronetcy and a foreign marquisate. On one occasion he pocketed very complacently a gratuity of fifty pistoles as the price of a service which he had rendered to the States General. This man had it in charge to demand that Burnet should no longer be countenanced at the Hague. William, who was not inclined to part with a valuable friend, answered at first with his usual coldness; "I am not aware, sir, that, since the Doctor has been here, he has done or said anything of which His Majesty can justly complain." But James was peremptory: the time for an open rupture had not arrived; and it was necessary to give way. During more than eighteen months Burnet never came into the presence of either the Prince or the Princess: but he resided near them: he was fully informed of all that was passing: his advice was constantly asked: his pen was employed on all important occasions; and many of the sharpest and most effective tracts which about that time appeared in London were justly attributed to him.

The rage of James flamed high. He had always been more than sufficiently prone to the angry passions. But none of his enemies, not even those who had conspired against

CHAP. VII.

his life, not even those who had attempted by perjury to load him with the guilt of treason and assassination, had ever been regarded by him with such animosity as he now felt for Burnet. His Majesty railed daily at the Doctor in unkingly language, and meditated plans of unlawful revenge. Even blood would not slake that frantic hatred. The insolent divine must be tortured before he was permitted to die. Fortunately he was by birth a Scot; and in Scotland, before he was gibbeted in the Grassmarket, his legs might be dislocated in the boot. Proceedings were accordingly instituted against him at Edinburgh: but he had been naturalised in Holland: he had married a woman of fortune who was a native of that province; and it was certain that his adopted country would not deliver him up. It was therefore determined to kidnap him. Ruffians were hired with great sums of money to perform this perilous and infamous service. An order for three thousand pounds on this account was actually drawn up for signature in the office of the Secretary of State. Lewis was apprised of the design, and took a warm interest in it. He would lend, he said, his best assistance to convey the villain to England, and would undertake that the ministers of the vengeance of James should find a secure asylum in France. Burnet was well aware of his danger: but timidity was not among his faults. He published a courageous answer to the charges which had been brought against him at Edinburgh. He knew, he said, that it was intended to execute him without a trial: but his trust was in the King of Kings, to whom innocent blood would not cry in vain, even against the mightiest princes of the earth. He gave a farewell dinner to some friends, and, after the meal, took solemn leave of them, as a man who was doomed to death, and with whom they could no longer safely converse. Nevertheless he continued to show himself in all the public places of the Hague so boldly that his friends reproached him bitterly with his foolhardiness.*

* Burnet, i. 726—731.; Answer to the Criminal Letters issued out against Dr. Burnet; Avaux Neg. July 7/17. 1687, Jan. 3/13. 1688; Lewis to Barillon, Dec. 24/Jan. 3 1687.; Johnstone of Waristoun, Feb. 21. 1688.; Lady Russell to Dr. Fitzwilliam, Oct. 5. 1687. As it has been suspected that Burnet, who certainly was not in the habit of underrating his own importance, exaggerated the danger to which he was exposed, I will give the words of Lewis and of Johnstone. "Qui que ce soit," says Lewis, "qui entreprenne de l'enlever en Hollande trouvera son seulement une retraite assurée et une entière protection dans mes états, mais aussi toute l'assistance qu'il pourra désirer pour faire conduire surement ce scélérat en Angleterre." "The business of Bamfield (Bar-

While Burnet was William's secretary for English affairs in Holland, Dykvelt had been not less usefully employed in London. Dykvelt was one of a remarkable class of public men who, having been bred to politics in the noble school of John De Witt, had, after the fall of that great minister, thought that they should best discharge their duty to the commonwealth by rallying round the Prince of Orange. Of the diplomatists in the service of the United Provinces none was, in dexterity, temper, and manners, superior to Dykvelt. In knowledge of English affairs none seems to have been his equal. A pretence was found for despatching him, early in the year 1687, to England on a special mission with credentials from the States General. But in truth his embassy was not to the government, but to the opposition; and his conduct was guided by private instructions which had been drawn by Burnet, and approved by William.*

Dykvelt reported that James was bitterly mortified by the conduct of the Prince and Princess. "My nephew's duty," said the King, "is to strengthen my hands. But he has always taken a pleasure in crossing me." Dykvelt answered that in matters of private concern His Highness had shown, and was ready to show, the greatest deference to the King's wishes; but that it was scarcely reasonable to expect the aid of a Protestant prince against the Protestant religion.† The King was silenced, but not appeased. He saw, with ill humour which he could not disguise, that Dykvelt was mustering and drilling all the various divisions of the opposition with a skill which would have been creditable to the ablest English statesman, and which was marvellous in a foreigner. The clergy were told that they would find the Prince a friend to episcopacy and to the Book of Common Prayer. The Nonconformists were encouraged to expect from him, not only toleration, but also comprehension. Even the Roman Catholics were conciliated; and some of the most respectable among them declared, to the King's face, that they were satisfied with what Dykvelt proposed, and that they would rather have a toleration, secured by statute, than an illegal and precarious ascendency.* The chiefs of all the important sections of the nation had frequent conferences in the presence of the dexterous Envoy. At these meetings the sense of the Tory party was chiefly spoken by the Earls of Danby and Nottingham. Though more than eight years had elapsed since Danby had fallen from power, his name was still great among the old Cavaliers of England; and many even of those Whigs who had formerly persecuted him were now disposed to admit that he had suffered for faults not his own, and that his zeal for the prerogative, though it had often misled him, had been tempered by two feelings which did him honour, zeal for the established religion, and zeal for the dignity and independence of his country. He was also highly esteemed at the Hague, where it was never forgotten that he was the person who, in spite of the influence of France and of the Papists, had induced Charles to bestow the hand of the Lady Mary on her cousin.

Daniel Finch, Earl of Nottingham, a nobleman whose name will frequently recur in the history of three eventful reigns, sprang from a family of unrivalled forensic eminence. One of his kinsmen had borne the seal of Charles the First, had prostituted eminent parts and learning to evil purposes, and had been pursued by the vengeance of the Commons of England with Falkland at their head. A more honourable renown had in the succeeding generation been obtained by Heneage Finch. He had immediately after the Restoration been appointed Solicitor General. He had subsequently risen to be Attorney General, Lord Keeper, Lord Chancellor, Baron Finch, and Earl of Nottingham. Through this prosperous career he had always held the prerogative as high as he honestly or decently could; but he had never been concerned in any machinations against the fundamental laws of the realm. In the midst of a corrupt court he had kept his personal integrity unsullied. He had enjoyed high fame as an orator, though his diction, formed on models anterior to the civil wars, was, towards the close of his life, pronounced stiff and pedantic by the wits of the rising generation. In Westminster Hall he is still mentioned with respect as the

* Burnet, Spt. 12 1687.

man who first educed out of the chaos anciently called by the name of equity a new system of jurisprudence, as regular and complete as that which is administered by the Judges of the Common Law.* A considerable part of the moral and intellectual character of this great magistrate had descended with the title of Nottingham to his eldest son. This son, Earl Daniel, was an honourable and virtuous man. Though enslaved by some absurd prejudices, and though liable to strange fits of caprice, he cannot be accused of having deviated from the path of right in search either of unlawful gain or of unlawful pleasure. Like his father he was a distinguished speaker, impressive but prolix, and too monotonously solemn. The person of the orator was in perfect harmony with his oratory. His attitude was rigidly erect: his complexion was so dark that he might have passed for a native of a warmer climate than ours; and his harsh features were composed to an expression resembling that of a chief mourner at a funeral. It was commonly said that he looked rather like a Spanish Grandee than like an English gentleman. The nicknames of Dismal, Don Dismallo, and Don Diego, were fastened on him by jesters, and are not yet forgotten. He had paid much attention to the science by which his family had been raised to greatness, and was, for a man born to rank and wealth, wonderfully well read in the laws of his country. He was a devoted son of the Church, and showed his respect for her in two ways not usual among those Lords who in his time boasted that they were her especial friends, by writing tracts in defence of her dogmas, and by shaping his private life according to her precepts. Like other zealous churchmen, he had, till recently, been a strenuous supporter of monarchical authority. But to the policy which had been pursued since the suppression of the Western insurrection he was bitterly hostile, and not the less so because his younger brother Heneage had been turned out of the office of Solicitor General for refusing to defend the King's dispensing power.†

With these two great Tory Earls was now united Halifax, the accomplished chief of the Trimmers. Over the mind of Nottingham indeed Halifax appears to have had at this time a great ascendency. Between Halifax and Danby there was

CHAP. VII.

Halifax.

---

* See Lord Campbell's Life of him.
† Johnstone's Correspondence; Mackay's Memoirs; Arbuthnot's John Bull; Swift's writings from 1710 to 1714, passim; Whiston's Letter to the Earl of Nottingham and the Earl's answer.

CHAP. VII.

an enmity which began in the court of Charles, and which, at a later period, disturbed the court of William, but which, like many other enmities, remained suspended during the tyranny of James. The foes frequently met in the councils held by Dykvelt, and agreed in expressing dislike of the policy of the government and reverence for the Prince of Orange. The different characters of the two statesmen appeared strongly in their dealings with the Dutch Envoy. Halifax showed an admirable talent for disquisition, but shrank from coming to any bold and irrevocable decision. Danby, far less subtle and eloquent, displayed more energy, resolution, and practical sagacity.

Devonshire.

Several eminent Whigs were in constant communication with Dykvelt; but the heads of the great houses of Cavendish and Russell could not take quite so active and prominent a part as might have been expected from their station and their opinions. The fame and fortunes of Devonshire were at that moment under a cloud. He had an unfortunate quarrel with the Court, arising, not from a public and honourable cause, but from a private brawl in which even his warmest friends could not pronounce him altogether blameless. He had gone to Whitehall to pay his duty, and had there been insulted by a man named Colepepper, one of a set of bravoes who infested the purlieus of the court, and attempted to curry favour with the government by affronting members of the opposition. The King himself expressed great indignation at the manner in which one of his most distinguished peers had been treated under the royal roof; and Devonshire was pacified by an intimation that the offender should never again be admitted into the palace. The interdict, however, was soon taken off. The Earl's resentment revived. His servants took up his cause. Hostilities such as seemed to belong to a ruder age disturbed the streets of Westminster. The time of the Privy Council was occupied by the criminations and recriminations of the adverse parties. Colepepper's wife declared that she and her husband went in danger of their lives, and that their house had been assaulted by ruffians in the Cavendish livery. Devonshire replied that he had been fired at from Colepepper's windows. This was vehemently denied. A pistol, it was owned, loaded with gunpowder, had been discharged. But this had been done in a moment of terror merely for the purpose of alarming the Guards. While this feud was at the height the Earl met Colepepper in the drawingroom at

Whitehall, and fancied that he saw triumph and defiance in the bully's countenance. Nothing unseemly passed in the royal sight; but, as soon as the enemies had left the presence chamber, Devonshire proposed that they should instantly decide their dispute with their swords. This challenge was refused. Then the high spirited peer forgot the respect which he owed to the place where he stood and to his own character, and struck Colepepper in the face with a cane. All classes agreed in condemning this act as most indiscreet and indecent; nor could Devonshire himself, when he had cooled, think of it without vexation and shame. The government, however, with its usual folly, treated him so severely that in a short time the public sympathy was all on his side. A criminal information was filed in the King's Bench. The defendant took his stand on the privileges of the peerage; but on this point a decision was promptly given against him; nor is it possible to deny that the decision, whether it were or were not according to the technical rules of English law, was in strict conformity with the great principles on which all laws ought to framed. Nothing was then left to him but to plead guilty. The tribunal had, by successive dismissions, been reduced to such complete subjection, that the government which had instituted the prosecution was allowed to prescribe the punishment. The Judges waited in a body on Jeffreys, who insisted that they should impose a fine of not less than thirty thousand pounds. Thirty thousand pounds, when compared with the revenues of the English grandees of that age, may be considered as equivalent to a hundred and fifty thousand pounds in the nineteenth century. In the presence of the Chancellor not a word of disapprobation was uttered: but, when the Judges had retired, Sir John Powell, in whom all the little honesty of the bench was concentrated, muttered that the proposed penalty was enormous, and that one tenth part would be amply sufficient. His brethren did not agree with him; nor did he, on this occasion, show the courage by which, on a memorable day some months later, he signally retrieved his fame. The Earl was accordingly condemned to a fine of thirty thousand pounds, and to imprisonment till payment should be made. Such a sum could not then be raised at a day's notice even by the greatest of the nobility. The sentence of imprisonment, however, was more easily pronounced than executed. Devonshire had retired to Chatsworth, where he was employed in turning the old Gothic

CHAP. VII.

mansion of his family into an edifice worthy of Palladio. The Peak was in those days almost as rude a district as Connemara now is, and the Sheriff found, or pretended, that it was difficult to arrest the lord of so wild a region in the midst of a devoted household and tenantry. Some days were thus gained; but at last both the Earl and the Sheriff were lodged in prison. Meanwhile a crowd of intercessors exerted their influence. The story ran that the Countess Dowager of Devonshire had obtained admittance to the royal closet, that she had reminded James how her brother in law, the gallant Charles Cavendish, had fallen at Gainsborough fighting for the crown, and that she had produced notes, written by Charles the First and Charles the Second, in acknowledgment of great sums lent by her Lord during the civil troubles. Those loans had never been repaid, and, with the interest, amounted, it was said, to more even than the immense fine which the Court of King's Bench had imposed. There was another consideration which seems to have had more weight with the King than the memory of former services. It might be necessary to call a Parliament. Whenever that event took place it was believed that Devonshire would bring a writ of error. The point on which he meant to appeal from the judgment of the King's Bench related to the privileges of peerage. The tribunal before which the appeal must come was the House of Peers. On such an occasion the Court could not be certain of the support even of the most courtly nobles. There was little doubt that the sentence would be annulled, and that, by grasping at too much, the government would lose all. James was therefore disposed to a compromise. Devonshire was informed that, if he would give a bond for the whole fine, and thus preclude himself from the advantage which he might derive from a writ of error, he should be set at liberty. Whether the bond should be enforced or not would depend on his subsequent conduct. If he would support the dispensing power nothing would be exacted from him. If he was bent on popularity he must pay thirty thousand pounds for it. He refused, during some time, to consent to these terms; but confinement was insupportable to him. He signed the bond, and was let out of prison: but, though he consented to lay this heavy burden on his estate, nothing could induce him to promise that he would abandon his principles and his party. He was still entrusted with all the secrets of the opposition: but during some months his political friends thought it best for himself and for the good cause that he should remain in the background.*

The Earl of Bedford had never recovered from the effects of the great calamity which, four years before, had almost broken his heart. From private as well as from public feelings he was adverse to the court: but he was not active in concerting measures against it. His place in the meetings of the malecontents was supplied by his nephew. This was the celebrated Edward Russell, a man of undoubted courage and capacity, but of loose principles and turbulent temper. He was a sailor, had distinguished himself in his profession, and had in the late reign held an office in the palace. But all the ties which bound him to the royal family had been sundered by the death of his cousin William. The daring, unquiet, and vindictive seaman now sate in the councils called by the Dutch Envoy as the representative of the boldest and most eager section of the opposition, of those men who, under the names of Roundheads, Exclusionists, and Whigs, had maintained with various fortune a contest of five and forty years against three successive Kings. This party, lately prostrate and almost extinct, but now again full of life and rapidly rising to ascendency, was troubled by none of the scruples which still impeded the movements of Tories and Trimmers, and was prepared to draw the sword against the tyrant on the first day on which the sword could be drawn with reasonable hope of success.

Three men are yet to be mentioned with whom Dykvelt was in confidential communication, and by whose help he hoped to secure the good will of three great professions. Bishop Compton was the agent employed to manage the clergy; Admiral Herbert undertook to exert all his influence over the navy; and an interest was established in the army by the instrumentality of Churchill.

The conduct of Compton and Herbert requires no explanation. Having, in all things secular, served the crown with zeal and fidelity, they had incurred the royal displeasure by refusing to be employed as tools for the destruction of their

---

* Kennet's funeral sermon on the Duke of Devonshire, and Memoirs of the family of Cavendish; State Trials; Privy Council Book, March 5, 168¾; Barillon, Jan. ²⁰⁄₃₀ 1687; Johnstone, Dec. ⁷⁄₁₇ 1687; Lords' Journals, May 6, 1689. "Ses amis et ses proches," says Barillon, "lui conseillent de perdre le bon parti, mais il persiste jusqu'à présent à ne se point soumettre. S'il vouloit se bien conduire et renoncer à être populaire il ne payeroit pas l'amende, mais s'il opiniâtre, il lui en coûtera trente mille livres et il demeurera prisonnier jusqu'à l'actuel payement."

own religion. Both of them had learned by experience how soon James forgot obligations, and how bitterly he remembered what it pleased him to consider as wrongs. The Bishop had by an illegal sentence been suspended from his episcopal functions. The Admiral had in one hour been reduced from opulence to penury. The situation of Churchill was widely different. He had been raised by the royal bounty from obscurity to eminence, and from poverty to wealth. Having started in life a needy ensign, he was now, in his thirty-seventh year, a Major General, a peer of Scotland, a peer of England: he commanded a troop of Life Guards: he had been appointed to several honourable and lucrative offices; and as yet there was no sign that he had lost any part of the favour to which he owed so much. He was bound to James, not only by the common obligations of allegiance, but by military honour, by personal gratitude, and, as appeared to superficial observers, by the strongest ties of interest. But Churchill himself was no superficial observer. He knew exactly what his interest really was. If his master were once at full liberty to employ Papists, not a single Protestant would be employed. For a time a few highly favoured servants of the crown might possibly be exempted from the general proscription in the hope that they would be induced to change their religion. But even these would, after a short respite, fall one by one, as Rochester had already fallen. Churchill might indeed secure himself from this danger, and might raise himself still higher in the royal favour, by conforming to the Church of Rome; and it might seem that one who was not less distinguished by avarice and baseness than by capacity and valour was not likely to be shocked at the thought of hearing a mass. But so inconsistent is human nature that there are tender spots even in seared consciences. And thus this man, who had owed his rise to his sister's dishonour, who had been kept by the most profuse, imperious, and shameless of harlots, and whose public life, to those who can look steadily through the dazzling blaze of genius and glory, will appear a prodigy of turpitude, believed implicitly in the religion which he had learned as a boy, and shuddered at the thought of formally abjuring it. A terrible alternative was before him. The earthly evil which he most dreaded was poverty. The one crime from which his heart recoiled was apostasy. And, if the designs of the court succeeded, he could not doubt that between poverty and apostasy he must soon make his choice. He therefore determined to cross those designs; and it soon appeared that there was no guilt and no disgrace which he was not ready to incur, in order to escape from the necessity of parting either with his places or with his religion.*

It was not only as a military commander, high in rank, and distinguished by skill and courage, that Churchill was able to render services to the opposition. It was, if not absolutely essential, yet most important, to the success of William's plans that his sister in law, who, in the order of succession to the English throne, stood between his wife and himself, should act in cordial union with him. All his difficulties would have been greatly augmented if Anne had declared herself favourable to the Indulgence. Which side she might take depended on the will of others. For her understanding was sluggish; and, though there was latent in her character a hereditary wilfulness and stubbornness which, many years later, great power and great provocations developed, she was as yet a willing slave to a nature far more vivacious and imperious than her own. The person by whom she was absolutely governed was the wife of Churchill, a woman who afterwards exercised a great influence on the fate of England and of Europe.

The name of this celebrated favourite was Sarah Jennings. Her elder sister, Frances, had been distinguished by beauty and levity even among the crowd of beautiful faces and light characters which adorned and disgraced Whitehall during the wild carnival of the Restoration. On one occasion Frances dressed herself like an orange girl and cried fruit about the streets.† Sober people predicted that a girl of so little discretion and delicacy would not easily find a husband. She was however twice married, and was now the wife of Tyrconnel. Sarah, less regularly beautiful, was perhaps more attractive. Her face was expressive: her form wanted no feminine charm; and the profusion of her fine hair, not yet disguised by powder according to that barbarous fashion which she lived to see introduced, was the delight of numerous admirers. Among the gallants who sued for her

Lady Churchill and the Princess Anne.

---

* The motive which determined the conduct of the Churchills is shortly and plainly set forth in the Duchess of Marlborough's Vindication. "It was," she says, "evident to all the world that, as things were carried on by King James, every body sooner or later must be ruined, who would not become a Roman Catholic. This consideration made me very well pleased at the Prince of Orange's undertaking to rescue us from such slavery."

† Grammont's Memoirs; Pepys's Diary, Feb. 21. 1664.

favour, Colonel Churchill, young, handsome, graceful, insinuating, eloquent, and brave, obtained the preference. He must have been enamoured indeed. For he had little property except the annuity which he had bought with the infamous wages bestowed on him by the Duchess of Cleveland: he was insatiable of riches: Sarah was poor; and a plain girl with a large fortune was proposed to him. His love, after a struggle, prevailed over his avarice: marriage only strengthened his passion; and to the last hour of his life, Sarah enjoyed the pleasure and distinction of being the one human being who was able to mislead that farsighted and surefooted judgment, who was fervently loved by that cold heart, and who was servilely feared by that intrepid spirit.

In a worldly sense the fidelity of Churchill's love was amply rewarded. His bride, though slenderly portioned, brought with her a dowry which, judiciously employed, made him at length a Duke of England, a Prince of the Empire, the captain general of a great coalition, the arbiter between mighty princes, and, what he valued more, the wealthiest subject in Europe. She had been brought up from childhood with the Princess Anne; and a close friendship had arisen between the girls. In character they resembled each other very little. Anne was slow and taciturn. To those whom she loved she was meek. The form which her anger assumed was sullenness. She had a strong sense of religion, and was attached even with bigotry to the rites and government of the Church of England. Sarah was lively and voluble, domineered over those whom she regarded with most kindness, and, when she was offended, vented her rage in tears and tempestuous reproaches. To sanctity she made no pretence, and, indeed, narrowly escaped the imputation of irreligion. She was not yet what she became when one class of vices had been fully developed in her by prosperity, and another by adversity, when her brain had been turned by success and flattery, when her heart had been ulcerated by disasters and mortifications. She lived to be that most odious and miserable of human beings, an ancient crone at war with her whole kind, at war with her own children and grandchildren, great indeed and rich, but valuing greatness and riches chiefly because they enabled her to brave public opinion, and to indulge without restraint her hatred to the living and the dead. In the reign of James she was regarded as nothing worse than a fine highspirited young woman, who could now and then be cross and arbitrary, but whose flaws of temper might well be pardoned in consideration of her charms.

It is a common observation that differences of taste, understanding, and disposition, are no impediments to friendship, and that the closest intimacies often exist between minds each of which supplies what is wanting to the other. Lady Churchill was loved and even worshipped by Anne. The Princess could not live apart from the object of her romantic fondness. She married, and was a faithful and even an affectionate wife. But Prince George, a dull man whose chief pleasures were derived from his dinner and his bottle, acquired over her no influence comparable to that exercised by her female friend, and soon gave himself up with stupid patience to the dominion of the vehement and commanding spirit by which his wife was governed. Children were born to the royal pair; and Anne was by no means without the feelings of a mother. But the tenderness which she felt for her offspring was languid when compared with her devotion to the companion of her early years. At length the Princess became impatient of the restraint which etiquette imposed on her. She could not bear to hear the words Madam and Royal Highness from the lips of one who was more to her than a sister. Such words were indeed necessary in the gallery or the drawingroom; but they were disused in the closet. Anne was Mrs. Morley: Lady Churchill was Mrs. Freeman; and under these childish names was carried on during twenty years a correspondence on which at last the fate of administrations and dynasties depended. But as yet Anne had no political power and little patronage. Her friend attended her as first Lady of the Bedchamber, with a salary of only four hundred pounds a year. There is reason, however, to believe that, even at this time, Churchill was able to gratify his ruling passion by means of his wife's influence. The Princess, though her income was large and her tastes simple, contracted debts which her father, not without some murmurs, discharged; and it was rumoured that her embarrassments had been caused by her prodigal bounty to her favourite.*

At length the time had arrived when this singular friend-

---

* It would be endless to recount all the books from which I have formed my estimate of the duchess's character. Her own letters, her own Vindication, and the replies which it called forth, have been my chief materials.

ship was to exercise a great influence on public affairs. What part Anne would take in the contest which distracted England was matter of deep anxiety. Filial duty was on one side; and the interests of the religion to which she was sincerely attached, were on the other. A less inert nature might well have remained long in suspense when drawn in opposite directions by motives so strong and so respectable. But the influence of the Churchills decided the question; and their patroness became an important member of that extensive league of which the Prince of Orange was the head.

Dykvelt returns to the Hague

In June 1687 Dykvelt returned to the Hague. He presented to the States General a royal epistle filled with eulogies of his conduct during his residence in London. These eulogies however were merely formal. James, in private communications written with his own hand, bitterly complained that the Envoy had lived in close intimacy with the most factious men in the realm, and had encouraged them in all their evil purposes. Dykvelt carried with him also a packet of letters from the most eminent of those with whom he had conferred during his stay in England. The writers generally expressed unbounded reverence and affection for William, and referred him to the bearer for fuller information as to their views. Halifax discussed the state and prospects of the country with his usual subtlety and vivacity, but took care not to pledge himself to any perilous line of conduct. Danby wrote in a bolder and more determined tone, and could not refrain from slily sneering at the fears and scruples of his accomplished rival. But the most remarkable letter was from Churchill. It was written with that natural eloquence which, illiterate as he was, he never wanted on great occasions, and with that air of magnanimity which, perfidious as he was, he could with singular dexterity assume. The Princess Anne, he said, had commanded him to assure her illustrious relatives at the Hague that she was fully resolved by God's help rather to lose her life than to be guilty of apostasy. As for himself, his places and the royal favour were as nothing to him in comparison with his religion. He concluded by declaring in lofty language that, though he could not pretend to have lived the life of a saint, he should be found ready, on occasion, to die the death of a martyr.*

with letters from many eminent Englishmen.

---

* The formal epistle which Dykvelt carried back to the States is in the Archives at the Hague. The other letters mentioned in this paragraph are given by Dalrymple; Appendix to Book V.

Dykvelt's mission had succeeded so well that a pretence was soon found for sending another agent to continue the work which had been so auspiciously commenced. The new Envoy, afterwards the founder of a noble English house which became extinct in our own time, was an illegitimate cousin german of William; and bore a title taken from the lordship of Zulestein. Zulestein's relationship to the House of Orange gave him importance in the public eye. His bearing was that of a gallant soldier. He was indeed in diplomatic talents and knowledge far inferior to Dykvelt; but even this inferiority had its advantages. A military man, who had never appeared to trouble himself about political affairs, could, without exciting any suspicion, hold with the English aristocracy an intercourse which, if he had been a noted master of statecraft, would have been jealously watched. Zulestein, after a short absence, returned to his country charged with letters and verbal messages not less important than those which had been entrusted to his predecessor. A regular correspondence was from this time established between the Prince and the opposition. Agents of various ranks passed and repassed between the Thames and the Hague. Among these a Scotchman, of some parts and great activity, named Johnstone, was the most useful. He was cousin to Burnet, and son of an eminent covenanter who had, soon after the Restoration, been put to death for treason, and who was honoured by his party as a martyr.

The estrangement between the King of England and the Prince of Orange became daily more complete. A serious dispute had arisen concerning the six British regiments which were in the pay of the United Provinces. The King wished to put these regiments under the command of Roman Catholic officers. The Prince resolutely opposed this design. The King had recourse to his favourite commonplaces about toleration. The Prince replied that he only followed His Majesty's example. It was notorious that loyal and able men had been turned out of office in England merely for being Protestants. It was then surely competent to the Stadtholder and the States General to withhold high public trusts from Papists. This answer provoked James to such a degree that, in his rage, he lost sight of veracity and common sense. It was false, he vehemently said, that he had ever turned out any body on religious grounds. And if he had,

CHAP. VII.

Zulestein's mission.

Growing enmity between James and William.

what was that to the Prince or to the States? Were they his masters? Were they to sit in judgment on the conduct of foreign sovereigns? From that time he became desirous to recall his subjects who were in the Dutch service. By bringing them over to England he should, he conceived, at once strengthen himself, and weaken his worst enemies. But there were financial difficulties which it was impossible for him to overlook. The number of troops already in his pay was as great as his revenue, though large beyond all precedent, and though parsimoniously administered, would support. If the battalions now in Holland were added to the existing establishment, the Treasury would be bankrupt. Perhaps Lewis might be induced to take them into his service. They would in that case be removed from a country where they were exposed to the corrupting influence of a republican government and a Calvinistic worship, and would be placed in a country where none ventured to dispute the mandates of the sovereign or the doctrines of the true Church. The soldiers would soon unlearn every political and religious heresy. Their native prince might always, at short notice, command their help, and would, on any emergency, be able to rely on their fidelity.

A negotiation on this subject was opened between Whitehall and Versailles. Lewis had as many soldiers as he wanted; and, had it been otherwise, he would not have been disposed to take Englishmen into his service; for the pay of England, low as it must seem to our generation, was much higher than the pay of France. At the same time, it was a great object to deprive William of so fine a brigade. After some weeks of correspondence, Barillon was authorised to promise that, if James would recall the British troops from Holland, Lewis would bear the charge of supporting two thousand of them in England. This offer was accepted by James with warm expressions of gratitude. Having made these arrangements, he requested the States General to send back the six regiments. The States General, completely governed by William, answered that such a demand, in such circumstances, was not authorised by the existing treaties, and positively refused to comply. It is remarkable that Amsterdam, which had voted for keeping these troops in Holland when James needed their help against the Western insurgents, now contended vehemently that his request ought to be granted. On both occasions, the sole object of those who ruled that great city was to cross the Prince of Orange.*

The Dutch arms, however, were scarcely so formidable to James as the Dutch presses. English books and pamphlets against his government were daily printed at the Hague; nor could any vigilance prevent copies from being smuggled, by tens of thousands, into the counties bordering on the German Ocean. Among these publications, one was distinguished by its importance, and by the immense effect which it produced. The opinion which the Prince and Princess of Orange held respecting the Indulgence was well known to all who were conversant with public affairs. But, as no official announcement of that opinion had appeared, many persons who had not access to good private sources of information were deceived or perplexed by the confidence with which the partisans of the Court asserted that their Highnesses approved of the King's late acts. To contradict those assertions publicly would have been a simple and obvious course, if the sole object of William had been to strengthen his interest in England. But he considered England chiefly as an instrument necessary to the execution of his great European design. Towards that design he hoped to obtain the cooperation of both branches of the House of Austria, of the Italian princes, and even of the Sovereign Pontiff. There was reason to fear that any declaration which was satisfactory to British Protestants would excite alarm and disgust at Madrid, Vienna, Turin, and Rome. For this reason the Prince long abstained from formally expressing his sentiments. At length it was represented to him that his continued silence had excited much uneasiness and distrust among his wellwishers, and that it was time to speak out. He therefore determined to explain himself.

A Scotch Whig, named James Stewart, had fled some years before to Holland, in order to avoid the boot and the gallows, and had become intimate with the Grand Pensionary Fagel, who enjoyed a large share of the Stadtholder's confidence and favour. By Stewart had been drawn up the violent and acrimonious manifesto of Argyle. When the Indulgence appeared, Stewart conceived that he had an opportunity of obtaining,

---

* Sanderland to William, Aug. 24. 1686; William to Sunderland, Sept. 9/19. 1686; Barillon, May 5/15. May 26/June 5. Oct. 3/13. 10/20. 1687: Lewis to Barillon, Oct. 1/11. 1687; Memorial of Albeville, Dec. 16. 1687: James to William, Jan. 17., Feb. 16., March 2. 13. 1688; Avaux Neg., March 11. 12. 16. 23. 1688.

not only pardon, but reward. He offered his services to the government of which he had been the enemy; they were accepted; and he addressed to Fagel a letter, purporting to have been written by the direction of James. In that letter the Pensionary was exhorted to use all his influence with the Prince and Princess, for the purpose of inducing them to support their father's policy. After some delay Fagel transmitted a reply, deeply meditated, and drawn up with exquisite art. No person who studies that remarkable document can fail to perceive that, though it is framed in a manner well calculated to reassure and delight English Protestants, it contains not a word which could give offence, even at the Vatican. It was announced that William and Mary would, with pleasure, assist in abolishing every law which made any Englishman liable to punishment for his religious opinions. But between punishments and disabilities a distinction was taken. To admit Roman Catholics to office would, in the judgment of their Highnesses, be neither for the general interest of England nor even for the interest of the Roman Catholics themselves. This manifesto was translated into several languages, and circulated widely on the Continent. Of the English version, carefully prepared by Burnet, near fifty thousand copies were introduced into the eastern shires, and rapidly distributed over the whole kingdom. No state paper was ever more completely successful. The Protestants of our island applauded the manly firmness with which William declared that he could not consent to entrust Papists with any share in the government. The Roman Catholic princes, on the other hand, were pleased by the mild and temperate style in which his resolution was expressed, and by the hope which he held out that, under his administration, no member of their Church would be molested on account of religion.

It is probable that the Pope himself was among those who read this celebrated letter with pleasure. He had some months before dismissed Castelmaine in a manner which showed little regard for the feelings of Castelmaine's master. Innocent thoroughly disliked the whole domestic and foreign policy of the English government. He saw that the unjust and impolitic measures of the Jesuitical cabal were far more likely to make the penal laws perpetual than to bring about an abolition of the test. His quarrel with the court of Versailles was every day becoming more and more serious; nor could be, either in his character of temporal prince or in his character of Sovereign Pontiff, feel cordial friendship for a vassal of that court. Castelmaine was ill qualified to remove these disgusts. He was indeed well acquainted with Rome, and was, for a layman, deeply read in theological controversy.* But he had none of the address which his post required; and, even had he been a diplomatist of the greatest ability, there was a circumstance which would have disqualified him for the particular mission on which he had been sent. He was known all over Europe as the husband of the most shameless of women; and he was known in no other way. It was impossible to speak to him or of him without remembering in what manner the very title by which he was called had been acquired. This circumstance would have mattered little if he had been accredited to some dissolute court, such as that in which the Marchioness of Montespan had lately been dominant. But there was an obvious impropriety in sending him on an embassy rather of a spiritual than of a secular nature to a pontiff of primitive austerity. The Protestants all over Europe sneered; and Innocent, already unfavourably disposed to the English government, considered the compliment which had been paid him, at so much risk and at so heavy a cost, as little better than an affront. The salary of the Ambassador was fixed at a hundred pounds a week. Castelmaine complained that this was too little. Thrice the sum, he said, would hardly suffice. For at Rome the ministers of all the great Continental powers exerted themselves to surpass one another in splendour, under the eyes of a people whom the habit of seeing magnificent buildings, decorations, and ceremonies had made fastidious. He always declared that he had been a loser by his mission. He was accompanied by several young gentlemen of the best Roman Catholic families in England, Ratcliffes, Arundells and Tichbornes. At Rome he was lodged in the palace of the house of Pamfili on the south of the stately Place of Navona. He was early admitted to a private interview with Innocent: but the public audience was long delayed. Indeed Castelmaine's preparations for that great occasion were so sumptuous that, though commenced at Easter 1686, they were not complete till the following November; and in November the Pope had, or pretended to have, an attack of gout which caused another postponement. In January 1687, at length, the solemn in-

CHAP.
VII.

* Adda, Nov. ⅕. 1685.

troduction and homage were performed with unusual pomp. The state coaches, which had been built at Rome for the pageant, were so superb that they were thought worthy to be transmitted to posterity in fine engravings and to be celebrated by poets in several languages.* The front of the Ambassador's palace was decorated on this great day with absurd allegorical paintings of gigantic size. There was Saint George with his foot on the neck of Titus Oates, and Hercules with his club crushing College, the Protestant joiner, who in vain attempted to defend himself with his flail. After this public appearance Castelmaine invited all the persons of note then assembled at Rome to a banquet in that gay and splendid gallery which is adorned with paintings of subjects from the Æneid by Peter of Cortona. The whole city crowded to the show; and it was with difficulty that a company of Swiss guards could keep order among the spectators. The nobles of the Pontifical state in return gave costly entertainments to the Ambassador; and poets and wits were employed to lavish on him and on his master insipid and hyperbolical adulation such as flourishes most when genius and taste are in the deepest decay. Foremost among the flatterers was a crowned head. More than thirty years had elapsed since Christina, the daughter of the great Gustavus, had voluntarily descended from the Swedish throne. After long wanderings, in the course of which she had committed many follies and crimes, she had finally taken up her abode at Rome, where she busied herself with astrological calculations and with the intrigues of the conclave, and amused herself with pictures, gems, manuscripts, and medals. She now composed some Italian stanzas in honour of the English prince, who sprung, like herself, from a race of Kings heretofore regarded as the champions of the Reformation, had, like herself, been reconciled to the ancient Church. A splendid assembly met in her palace. Her verses, set to music, were sung with universal applause; and one of her literary dependents pronounced an oration on the same subject in a style so florid that it seems to have offended the taste of the

---

* The Professor of Greek in the College De Propaganda Fide expressed his admiration in some detestable hexameters and pentameters, of which the following specimen may suffice:—

English hearers. The Jesuits, hostile to the Pope, devoted to the interests of France, and disposed to pay every honour to James, received the English embassy with the utmost pomp in that princely house where the remains of Ignatius Loyola lie enshrined in lazulite and gold. Sculpture, painting, poetry, and eloquence were employed to compliment the strangers: but all these arts had sunk into deep degeneracy. There was a great display of turgid and impure Latinity unworthy of so erudite an order; and some of the inscriptions which adorned the walls had a fault more serious than even a bad style. It was said in one place that James had sent his brother as his messenger to heaven, and in another that James had furnished the wings with which his brother had soared to a higher region. There was a still more unfortunate distich, which at the time attracted little notice, but which, a few months later, was remembered and malignantly interpreted. "O King," said the poet, "cease to sigh for a son. Though nature may refuse your wish, the stars will find a way to grant it."

In the midst of these festivities Castelmaine had to suffer cruel mortifications and humiliations. The Pope treated him with extreme coldness and reserve. As often as the Ambassador pressed for an answer to the request which he had been instructed to make in favour of Petre, Innocent was taken with a violent fit of coughing, which put an end to the conversation. The fame of these singular audiences spread over Rome. Pasquin was not silent. All the curious and tattling population of the idlest of cities, the Jesuits and the prelates of the French faction only excepted, laughed at Castelmaine's discomfiture. His temper, naturally unamiable, was soon exasperated to violence; and he circulated a memorial reflecting on the Pope. He had now put himself in the wrong. The sagacious Italian had got the advantage, and took care to keep it. He positively declared that the rule which excluded Jesuits from ecclesiastical preferment should not be relaxed in favour of Father Petre. Castelmaine, much provoked, threatened to leave Rome. Innocent replied, with a mock impertinence which was the more provoking because it could scarcely be distinguished from simplicity, that His Excellency might go if he liked. "But if we must lose him," added the venerable Pontiff, "I hope that he will take care of his health on the road. English people do not know how dangerous it is in this country to travel in the heat of the day. The best way is to start before dawn, and to take some rest at noon." With this salutary advice, and with a string of beads, the unfortunate Ambassador was dismissed. In a few months appeared, both in the Italian and in the English tongue, a pompous history of the mission, magnificently printed in folio, and illustrated with plates. The frontispiece, to the great scandal of all Protestants, represented Castelmaine, in the robes of a Peer, with his coronet in his hand, kissing the toe of Innocent.*

* Correspondence of James and Innocent, in the British Museum; Burnet, i. 703—705.; Welwood's Memoirs; Commons' Journals, Oct. 28. 1689; An Account of his Excellency Roger Earl of Castelmaine's Embassy, by Michael Wright, chief steward of His Excellency's house at Rome, 1688.

CHAPTER VIII.

The marked discourtesy of the Pope might well have irritated the meekest of princes. But the only effect which it produced on James was to make him more lavish of caresses and compliments. While Castelmaine, his whole soul festering with angry passions, was on the road back to England, the Nuncio was loaded with honours which his own judgment would have led him to reject. He had, by a fiction often used in the Church of Rome, been lately raised to the episcopal dignity without having the charge of any see. He was called Archbishop of Amasia, a city of Pontus, the birthplace of Strabo and Mithridates. James insisted that the ceremony of consecration should be performed in the chapel of Saint James's Palace. The Vicar Apostolic Leyburn and two Irish prelates officiated. The doors were thrown open to the public; and it was remarked that some of those Puritans who had recently turned courtiers were among the spectators. In the evening Adda, wearing the robes of his new office, joined the circle in the Queen's apartments. James fell on his knees in the presence of the whole court and implored a blessing. In spite of the restraint imposed by etiquette, the astonishment and disgust of the bystanders could not be concealed.* It was long indeed since an English sovereign had knelt to mortal man; and those who saw the strange sight could not but think of that day of shame when John did homage for his crown between the hands of Pandolph.

In a short time a still more ostentatious pageant was performed in honour of the Holy See. It was determined that the Nuncio should go to court in solemn procession. Some persons on whose obedience the King had counted showed, on this occasion, for the first time, signs of a mutinous spirit. Among these the most conspicuous was the second temporal peer of the realm, Charles Seymour, commonly called the proud Duke of Somerset. He was in truth a man in whom

CHAP. VIII.

Consecration of the Nuncio at St. James's Palace.

His public reception.

The Duke of Somerset.

* Barillon, May 3/13. 1687.

the pride of birth and rank amounted almost to a disease. The fortune which he had inherited was not adequate to the high place which he held among the English aristocracy: but he had become possessed of the greatest estate in England by his marriage with the daughter and heiress of the last Percy who wore the ancient coronet of Northumberland. Somerset was only in his twenty-fifth year, and was very little known to the public. He was a Lord of the King's Bedchamber, and colonel of one of the regiments which had been raised at the time of the Western insurrection. He had not scrupled to carry the sword of state into the royal chapel on days of festival: but he now resolutely refused to swell the pomp of the Nuncio. Some members of his family implored him not to draw on himself the royal displeasure: but their entreaties produced no effect. The King himself expostulated. "I thought, my Lord," said he, "that I was doing you a great honour in appointing you to escort the minister of the first of all crowned heads." "Sir," said the Duke, "I am advised that I cannot obey Your Majesty without breaking the law." "I will make you fear me as well as the law," answered the King, insolently. "Do you not know that I am above the law?" "Your Majesty may be above the law," replied Somerset, "but I am not; and, while I obey the law, I fear nothing." The King turned away in high displeasure; and Somerset was instantly dismissed from his posts in the household and in the army.*

On one point, however, James showed some prudence. He did not venture to parade the Papal Envoy in state before the vast population of the capital. The ceremony was performed, on the third of July 1687, at Windsor. Great multitudes flocked to the little town. The visitors were so numerous that there was neither food nor lodging for them; and many persons of quality sate the whole day in their carriages waiting for the exhibition. At length, late in the afternoon, the Knight Marshal's men appeared on horseback. Then came a long train of running footmen; and then, in a royal coach, was seen Adda, robed in purple, with a brilliant cross on his breast. He was followed by the equipages of the principal courtiers and ministers of state. In his train the crowd recognised with disgust the arms and liveries of

* Memoirs of the Duke of Somerset; the Second, ii. 116, 117, 118.; Lord Van Cittern, July 5. 1687; Eachard's Lonsdale's Memoirs. History of the Revolution; Life of James

Crowe, Bishop of Durham, and of Cartwright, Bishop of Chester.*

On the following day appeared in the Gazette a proclamation dissolving that Parliament which of all the fifteen Parliaments held by the Stuarts had been the most obsequious.†

Meanwhile new difficulties had arisen in Westminster Hall. Only a few months had elapsed since some Judges had been turned out and others put in for the purpose of obtaining a decision favourable to the crown in the case of Sir Edward Hales; and already fresh changes were necessary.

The King had scarcely formed that army on which he chiefly depended for the accomplishing of his designs when he found that he could not himself control it. When war was actually raging in the kingdom, a mutineer or a deserter might be tried by a military tribunal, and executed by the Provost Marshal. But there was now profound peace. The common law of England, having sprung up in an age when all men bore arms occasionally and none constantly, recognised no distinction, in time of peace, between a soldier and any other subject; nor was there any Act resembling that by which the authority necessary for the government of regular troops is now annually confided to the Sovereign. Some old statutes indeed made desertion felony in certain specified cases. But those statutes were applicable only to soldiers serving the King in actual war, and could not without the grossest disingenuousness be so strained as to include the case of a man who, in a time of tranquillity, should become tired of the camp at Hounslow, and should go back to his native village. The government appears to have had no hold on such a man, except the hold which master bakers and master tailors have on their journeymen. He and his officers were, in the eye of the law, on a level. If he swore at them he might be fined for an oath. If he struck them he might be prosecuted for assault and battery. In truth the regular army was under less restraint than the militia. For the militia was a body established by an Act of Parliament; and it had been provided by that Act that slight punishments might be summarily inflicted for breaches of discipline.

It does not appear that, during the reign of Charles the Second, the practical inconvenience arising from this state of

CHAP. VIII.

Dissolution of the Parliament.

Military offences illegally punished.

* London Gazette, July 7, 1687; Tracts. Van Citters, July 7/17. Account of the ceremony reprinted among the Somers † London Gazette, July 4, 1687.

the law had been much felt. The explanation may perhaps be that, till the last year of his reign, the force which he maintained in England consisted chiefly of household troops, whose pay was so high that dismission from the service would have been felt by most of them as a great calamity. The stipend of a private in the Life Guards was a provision for the younger son of a gentleman. Even the Foot Guards were paid about as high as manufacturers in a prosperous season, and were therefore in a situation which the great body of the labouring population might regard with envy. The return of the garrison of Tangier and the raising of the new regiments had made a great change. There were now in England many thousands of soldiers, each of whom received only eightpence a day. The dread of dismission was not sufficient to keep them to their duty; and corporal punishment their officers could not legally inflict. James had therefore one plain choice before him, to let his army dissolve itself, or to induce the Judges to pronounce that the law was what every barrister in the Temple knew that it was not.

It was peculiarly important to secure the cooperation of two courts, the court of King's Bench, which was the first criminal tribunal in the realm, and the court of gaol delivery which sate at the Old Bailey, and which had jurisdiction over offences committed in the capital. In both these courts there were great difficulties. Herbert, Chief Justice of the King's Bench, servile as he had hitherto been, would go no further. Resistance still more sturdy was to be expected from Sir John Holt, who, as Recorder of the City of London, occupied the bench at the Old Bailey. Holt was an eminently learned and clearheaded lawyer: he was an upright and courageous man; and, though he had never been factious, his political opinions had a tinge of Whiggism. All obstacles, however, disappeared before the royal will. Holt was turned out of the recordership: Herbert and another Judge were removed from the King's Bench; and the vacant places were filled by persons in whom the government could confide. It was indeed necessary to go very low down in the legal profession before men could be found willing to render such services as were now required. The new Chief Justice, Sir Robert Wright, was ignorant to a proverb; yet ignorance was not his worst fault. His vices had ruined him. He had resorted to infamous ways of raising money, and had, on one occasion, made a false affidavit in order to obtain possession of five hundred pounds. Poor, dissolute, and shameless, he had become one of the parasites of Jeffreys, who promoted him and insulted him. Such was the man who was now selected by James to be Lord Chief Justice of England. One Richard Allibone, who was even more ignorant of the law than Wright, and who, as a Roman Catholic, was incapable of holding office, was appointed a puisne Judge of the King's Bench. Sir Bartholomew Shower, equally notorious as a servile Tory and a tedious orator, became Recorder of London. When these changes had been made, several deserters were brought to trial. They were convicted in the face of the letter and of the spirit of the law. Some received sentence of death at the bar of the King's Bench, and some at the Old Bailey. They were hanged in sight of the regiments to which they had belonged; and care was taken that the executions should be announced in the London Gazette, which very seldom noticed such events.*

It may well be believed, that the law, so grossly insulted by courts which derived from it all their authority, and which were in the habit of looking to it as their guide, would be little respected by a tribunal which had originated in tyrannical caprice. The new High Commission had, during the first months of its existence, merely inhibited clergymen from exercising spiritual functions. The rights of property had remained untouched. But, early in the year 1687, it was determined to strike at freehold interests, and to impress on every Anglican priest and prelate the conviction that, if he refused to lend his aid for the purpose of destroying the Church of which he was a minister, he would in an hour be reduced to beggary.

It would have been prudent to try the first experiment on some obscure individual. But the government was under an infatuation such as, in a more simple age, would have been called judicial. War was therefore at once declared against the two most venerable corporations of the realm, the Universities of Oxford and Cambridge.

The power of those bodies has during many ages been great; but it was at the height during the latter part of the

* See the statutes 18 Henry 6. c. 19.; 2 & 3 El. 6. c. 2.; Eachard's History of the Revolution; Kennet, iii. 465.; North's Life of Guildford, 247.; London Gazette, April 18., May 23. 1687; Vindication of the R. of R. (Earl of Rochester).

seventeenth century. None of the neighbouring countries could boast of such splendid and opulent seats of learning. The schools of Edinburgh and Glasgow, of Leyden and Utrecht, of Louvain and Leipsic, of Padua and Bologna, seemed mean to scholars who had been educated in the magnificent foundations of Wykeham and Wolsey, of Henry the Sixth and Henry the Eighth. Literature and science were, in the academical system of England, surrounded with pomp, armed with magistracy, and closely allied with all the most august institutions of the state. To be the Chancellor of an University was a distinction eagerly sought by the magnates of the realm. To represent an University in Parliament was a favourite object of the ambition of statesmen. Nobles and even princes were proud to receive from an University the privilege of wearing the doctoral scarlet. The curious were attracted to the Universities by ancient buildings rich with the tracery of the middle ages, by modern buildings which exhibited the highest skill of Jones and Wren, by noble halls and chapels, by museums, by botanical gardens, and by the only great public libraries which the kingdom then contained. The state which Oxford especially displayed on solemn occasions rivalled that of sovereign princes. When her Chancellor, the venerable Duke of Ormond, sate in his embroidered mantle on his throne under the painted ceiling of the Sheldonian theatre, surrounded by hundreds of graduates robed according to their rank, while the noblest youths of England were solemnly presented to him as candidates for academical honours, he made an appearance scarcely less regal than that which his master made in the Banqueting House of Whitehall. At the Universities had been formed the minds of almost all the eminent clergymen, lawyers, physicians, wits, poets, and orators of the land, and of a large proportion of the nobility and of the opulent gentry. It is also to be observed that the connection between the scholar and the school did not terminate with his residence. He often continued to be through life a member of the academical body, and to vote as such at all important elections. He therefore regarded his old haunts by the Cam and the Isis with even more than the affection which educated men ordinarily feel for the place of their education. There was no corner of England in which both Universities had not grateful and zealous sons. Any attack on the honour or interests of either Cambridge or Oxford was certain to excite the resentment of a powerful, active, and intelligent class, scattered over every county from Northumberland to Cornwall.

The resident graduates, as a body, were perhaps not superior positively to the resident graduates of our time; but they occupied a far higher position as compared with the rest of the community. For Cambridge and Oxford were then the only two provincial towns in the kingdom in which could be found a large number of men whose understandings had been highly cultivated. Even the capital felt great respect for the authority of the Universities, not only on questions of divinity, of natural philosophy, and of classical antiquity, but also on points which capitals generally claim the right of deciding in the last resort. From Will's coffee house, and from the pit of the theatre royal in Drury Lane, an appeal lay to the two great national seats of taste and learning. Plays which had been enthusiastically applauded in London were not thought out of danger till they had undergone the more severe judgment of audiences familiar with Sophocles and Terence.*

The great moral and intellectual influence of the English Universities had been strenuously exerted on the side of the crown. The head quarters of Charles the First had been at Oxford; and the silver tankards and salvers of all the colleges had been melted down to supply his military chest. Cambridge was not less loyally disposed. She had sent a large part of her plate to the royal camp; and the rest would have followed had not the town been seized by the troops of the Parliament. Both Universities had been treated with extreme severity by the victorious Puritans. Both had hailed the Restoration with delight. Both had steadily opposed the Exclusion Bill. Both had expressed the deepest horror at the Rye House plot. Cambridge had not only deposed her Chancellor Monmouth, but had marked her abhorrence of his treason in a manner unworthy of a seat of learning, by committing to the flames the canvass on which his pleasing face and figure had been portrayed by the utmost skill of Kneller.†
Oxford, which lay nearer to the Western insurgents, had given still stronger proofs of loyalty. The students, under

* Dryden's Prologues and Cibber's Memoirs contain abundant proofs of the estimation in which the taste of the Oxonians was held by the most admired poets and actors.
† See the poem called Advice to the Painter upon the Defeat of the Rebels in the West. See also another poem, a most detestable one, on the same subject, by Stepney, who was then studying at Trinity College.

the sanction of their preceptors, had taken arms by hundreds in defence of hereditary right. Such were the bodies which James now determined to insult and plunder in direct defiance of the laws and of his plighted faith.

Several Acts of Parliament, as clear as any that were to be found in the statute book, had provided that no person should be admitted to any degree in either University without taking the oath of supremacy, and another oath of similar character called the oath of obedience. Nevertheless, in February 1687, a royal letter was sent to Cambridge directing that a Benedictine monk, named Alban Francis, should be admitted a Master of Arts.

The academical functionaries, divided between reverence for the King and reverence for the law, were in great distress. Messengers were despatched in all haste to the Duke of Albemarle, who had succeeded Monmouth as Chancellor of the University. He was requested to represent the matter properly to the King. Meanwhile the Registrar and Bedells waited on Francis, and informed him that, if he would take the oaths according to law, he should instantly be admitted. He refused to be sworn, remonstrated with the officers of the University on their disregard of the royal mandate, and, finding them resolute, took horse, and hastened to relate his grievances at Whitehall.

The heads of the colleges now assembled in council. The best legal opinions were taken, and were decidedly in favour of the course which had been pursued. But a second letter from Sunderland, in high and menacing terms, was already on the road. Albemarle informed the University, with many expressions of concern, that he had done his best, but that he had been coldly and ungraciously received by the King. The academical body, alarmed by the royal displeasure, and conscientiously desirous to meet the royal wishes, but determined not to violate the clear law of the land, submitted the humblest and most respectful explanations, but to no purpose. In a short time came down a summons citing the Vicechancellor and the Senate to appear before the new High Commission at Westminster on the twenty-first of April. The Vicechancellor was to attend in person: the Senate, which consists of all the Doctors and Masters of the University, was to send deputies.

When the appointed day arrived, a great concourse filled the Council chamber. Jeffreys sate at the head of the board. Rochester, since the white staff had been taken from him,

was no longer a member. In his stead appeared the Lord
Chamberlain, John Sheffield, Earl of Mulgrave. The fate of
this nobleman has, in one respect, resembled the fate of his
colleague Sprat. Mulgrave wrote verses which scarcely ever
rose above absolute mediocrity; but as he was a man of high
note in the political and fashionable world, these verses found
admirers. Time dissolved the charm, but, unfortunately for
him, not until his lines had acquired a prescriptive right to
a place in all collections of the works of English poets. To
this day accordingly his insipid essays in rhyme and his
paltry songs to Amoretta and Gloriana are reprinted in company
with Comus and Alexander's Feast. The consequence
is that our generation knows Mulgrave chiefly as a poetaster,
and despises him as such. In truth however he was, by the
acknowledgment of those who neither loved nor esteemed
him, a man distinguished by fine parts, and in parliamentary
eloquence inferior to scarcely any orator of his time. His
moral character was entitled to no respect. He was a libertine
without that openness of heart and hand which sometimes
makes libertinism amiable, and a haughty aristocrat
without that elevation of sentiment which sometimes makes
aristocratical haughtiness respectable. The satirists of the
age nicknamed him Lord Allpride, and pronounced it strange
that a man who had so exalted a sense of his dignity should
be so hard and niggardly in all pecuniary dealings. He had
given deep offence to the royal family by venturing to entertain
the hope that he might win the heart and hand of
the Princess Anne. Disappointed in this attempt, he had
exerted himself to regain by meanness the favour which he
had forfeited by presumption. His epitaph, written by himself,
still informs all who pass through Westminster Abbey
that he lived and died a sceptic in religion; and we learn
from his memoirs, written by himself, that one of his
favourite subjects of mirth was the Romish superstition. Yet
he began, as soon as James was on the throne, to express
a strong inclination towards Popery, and at length in private
affected to be a convert. This abject hypocrisy had been rewarded
by a place in the Ecclesiastical Commission.*

Before that formidable tribunal now appeared the Vice-

---

* Mackay's character of Sheffield, with Swift's note; The Satire on the Deponents, 1688; Life of John, Duke of Buckinghamshire, 1729; Barillon, Aug. 30, 1687. I have a manuscript lampoon on Mulgrave, dated 1690. It is not destitute of spirit. The most remarkable lines are these:—

"Peters (Petre) to=day and Burnet to=morrow,
Knaves of all sides and religions he'll serve."

chancellor of the University of Cambridge, Doctor John Pechell. He was a man of no great ability or vigour; but he was accompanied by eight distinguished academicians, elected by the Senate. One of these was Isaac Newton, Fellow of Trinity College, and Professor of mathematics. His genius was then in the fullest vigour. The great work, which entitles him to the highest place among the geometricians and natural philosophers of all ages and of all nations, had been some time printing under the sanction of the Royal Society, and was almost ready for publication. He was the steady friend of civil liberty and of the Protestant religion; but his habits by no means fitted him for the conflicts of active life. He therefore stood modestly silent among the delegates, and left to men more versed in practical business the task of pleading the cause of his beloved University.

Never was there a clearer case. The law was express. The practice had been almost invariably in conformity with the law. It might perhaps have happened that, on a day of great solemnity, when many honorary degrees were conferred, a person who had not taken the oaths might have passed in the crowd. But such an irregularity, the effect of mere haste and inadvertence, could not be cited as a precedent. Foreign ambassadors of various religions, and in particular one Mussulman, had been admitted without the oaths. But it might well be doubted whether such cases fell within the reason and spirit of the Acts of Parliament. It was not even pretended that any person to whom the oaths had been tendered and who had refused them had ever taken a degree; and this was the situation in which Francis stood. The delegates offered to prove that, in the late reign, several royal mandates had been treated as nullities because the persons recommended had not chosen to qualify according to law, and that, on such occasions, the government had always acquiesced in the propriety of the course taken by the University. But Jeffreys would hear nothing. He soon found out that the Vicechancellor was weak, ignorant, and timid, and therefore gave a loose to all that insolence which had long been the terror of the Old Bailey. The unfortunate Doctor, unaccustomed to such a presence and to such treatment, was soon harassed and scared into helpless agitation. When other academicians who were more capable of defending their cause attempted to speak they were rudely silenced. "You are not Vicechancellor. When you are, you may talk. Till then it will become you to hold your peace." The defendants were thrust out of the court without a hearing. In a short time they were called in again, and informed that the Commissioners had determined to deprive Pechell of the Vicechancellorship, and to suspend him from all the emoluments to which he was entitled as Master of a college, emoluments which were strictly of the nature of freehold property. "As for you," said Jeffreys to the delegates, "most of you are divines. I will therefore send you home with a text of scripture, 'Go your way and sin no more, lest a worse thing happen to you.'"*

These proceedings might seem sufficiently unjust and violent. But the King had already begun to treat Oxford with such rigour that the rigour shown towards Cambridge might, by comparison, be called lenity. Already University College had been turned by Obadiah Walker into a Roman Catholic seminary. Already Christ Church was governed by a Roman Catholic Dean. Mass was already said daily in both those colleges. The tranquil and majestic city, so long the stronghold of monarchical principles, was agitated by passions which it had never before known. The undergraduates, with the connivance of those who were in authority over them, hooted the members of Walker's congregation, and chanted satirical ditties under his windows. Some fragments of the serenades which then disturbed the High Street have been preserved. The burden of one ballad was this:

"Old Obadiah
Sings Ave Maria."

When the actors came down to Oxford, the public feeling was expressed still more strongly. Howard's Committee was performed. This play, written soon after the Restoration, exhibited the Puritans in an odious and contemptible light, and had therefore been, during a quarter of a century, a favourite with Oxonian audiences. It was now a greater favourite than ever; for, by a lucky coincidence, one of the most conspicuous characters was an old hypocrite named Obadiah. The audience shouted with delight when, in the last scene, Obadiah was dragged in with a halter round his neck; and the acclamations redoubled when one of the players, departing from the written text of the comedy, proclaimed that Obadiah should be hanged because he had changed his

* See the proceedings against the University of Cambridge in the collection of State Trials.

religion. The King was much provoked by this insult. So mutinous indeed was the temper of the University that one of the newly raised regiments, the same which is now called the Second Dragoon Guards, was quartered at Oxford for the purpose of preventing an outbreak.*

These events ought to have convinced James that he had entered on a course which must lead him to his ruin. To the clamours of London he had been long accustomed. They had been raised against him, sometimes unjustly, and sometimes vainly. He had repeatedly braved them, and might brave them still. But that Oxford, the seat of loyalty, the head quarters of the Cavalier army, the place where his father and brother had held their court when they thought themselves insecure in their stormy capital, the place where the writings of the great republican teachers had recently been committed to the flames, should now be in a ferment of discontent, that those high-spirited youths who a few months before had eagerly volunteered to march against the Western insurgents should now be with difficulty kept down by sword and carbine, these were signs full of evil omen to the House of Stuart. The warning, however, was lost on the dull, stubborn, selfwilled tyrant. He was resolved to transfer to his own Church all the wealthiest and most splendid foundations of England. It was to no purpose that the best and wisest of his Roman Catholic counsellors remonstrated. They represented to him that he had it in his power to render a great service to the cause of his religion without violating the rights of property. A grant of two thousand pounds a year from his privy purse would support a Jesuit college at Oxford. Such a sum he might easily spare. Such a college, provided with able, learned, and zealous teachers, would be a formidable rival to the old academical institutions, which exhibited but too many symptoms of the languor almost inseparable from opulence and security. King James's College would soon be, by the confession even of Protestants, the first place of education in the island, as respected both science and moral discipline. This would be the most effectual and the least invidious method by which the Church of England could be humbled and the Church of Rome exalted.

The Earl of Ailesbury, one of the most devoted servants of

* Wood's Athenæ Oxonienses; Apology for the Life of Colley Cibber; Van Cittere, March 5/15, 1688.

the royal family, declared that, though a Protestant, and by no means rich, he would himself contribute a thousand pounds towards this design, rather than that his master should violate the rights of property, and break faith with the Established Church.* The scheme, however, found no favour in the sight of the King. It was indeed ill suited, in more ways than one, to his ungentle nature. For to bend and break the spirits of men gave him pleasure; and to part with his money gave him pain. What he had not the generosity to do at his own expense he determined to do at the expense of others. When once he was engaged, pride and obstinacy prevented him from receding; and he was at length led, step by step, to acts of Turkish tyranny, to acts which impressed the nation with a conviction that the estate of a Protestant English freeholder under a Roman Catholic King must be as insecure as that of a Greek under Moslem domination.

Magdalene College at Oxford, founded in the fifteenth century by William of Waynflete, Bishop of Winchester and Lord High Chancellor, was one of the most remarkable of our academical institutions. A graceful tower, on the summit of which a Latin hymn was annually chanted by choristers at the dawn of May day, caught far off the eye of the traveller who came from London. As he approached, he found that this tower rose from an embattled pile, low and irregular, yet singularly venerable, which, embowered in verdure, overhung the sluggish waters of the Cherwell. He passed through a gateway beneath a noble oriel†, and found himself in a spacious cloister adorned with emblems of virtues and vices, rudely carved in grey stone by the masons of the fifteenth century. The table of the society was plentifully spread in a stately refectory hung with paintings and rich with fantastic carving. The service of the Church was performed morning and evening in a chapel which had suffered much violence from the Reformers, and much from the Puritans, but which was, under every disadvantage, a building of eminent beauty, and which has, in our own time, been restored with rare taste and skill. The spacious gardens along the river side were remarkable for the size of the trees, among which towered conspicuous one of the vegetable wonders of the island, a gigantic oak, older by a century, men said, than the oldest college in the University.

* Burnet, i. 697.; Letter of Lord Ailesbury printed in the European Magazine for April 1795. † This gateway is now closed.

CHAP.
VIII.

The statutes of the society ordained that the Kings of England and Princes of Wales should be lodged at Magdalene. Edward the Fourth had inhabited the building while it was still unfinished. Richard the Third had held his court there, had heard disputations in the hall, had feasted there royally, and had mended the cheer of his hosts by a present of fat bucks from his forests. Two heirs apparent of the crown who had been prematurely snatched away, Arthur, the elder brother of Henry the Eighth, and Henry, the elder brother of Charles the First, had been members of the college. Another prince of the blood, the last and best of the Roman Catholic Archbishops of Canterbury, the gentle Reginald Pole, had studied there. In the time of the civil war Magdalene had been true to the cause of the Crown. There Rupert had fixed his quarters; and, before some of his most daring enterprises, his trumpets had been heard sounding to horse through those quiet cloisters. Most of the Fellows were divines, and could aid King Charles only by their prayers and their pecuniary contributions. But one member of the body, a Doctor of Civil Law, raised a troop of undergraduates, and fell fighting bravely at their head against the soldiers of Essex. When hostilities had terminated, and the Roundheads were masters of England, six sevenths of the members of the foundation refused to make any submission to usurped authority. They were consequently ejected from their dwellings and deprived of their revenues. After the Restoration the survivors returned to their pleasant abode. They had now been succeeded by a new generation which inherited their opinions and their spirit. During the Western rebellion such Magdalene men as were not disqualified by their age or profession for the use of arms had eagerly volunteered to fight for the Crown. It would be difficult to name any corporation in the kingdom which had higher claims to the gratitude of the House of Stuart.*

The society consisted of a President, of forty Fellows, of thirty scholars called Demies, and of a train of chaplains, clerks, and choristers. At the time of the general visitation in the reign of Henry the Eighth the revenues were far larger than those of any similar institution in the realm, larger by nearly one half than those of the magnificent foundation of Henry the Sixth at Cambridge, and considerably more than

* Wood's Athenæ Oxonienses; Walker's Sufferings of the Clergy.

twice as large as those which William of Wykeham had settled on his college at Oxford. In the days of James the Second the riches of Magdalene were immense, and were exaggerated by report. The college was popularly said to be wealthier than the wealthiest abbeys of the Continent. When the leases fell in,—so ran the vulgar rumour,—the rents would be raised to the prodigious sum of forty thousand pounds a year.*

The Fellows were, by the statutes which their founder had drawn up, empowered to select their own President from among persons who were, or had been, Fellows either of their society or of New College. This power had generally been exercised with freedom. But in some instances royal letters had been received recommending to the choice of the corporation qualified persons who were in favour at court; and on such occasions it had been the practice to show respect to the wishes of the sovereign.

In March 1687, the President of the college died. One of the Fellows, Doctor Thomas Smith, popularly nicknamed Rabbi Smith, a distinguished traveller, book collector, antiquary, and orientalist, who had been chaplain to the embassy at Constantinople, and had been employed to collate the Alexandrian manuscript, aspired to the vacant post. He conceived that he had some claims on the favour of the government as a man of learning and as a zealous Tory. His loyalty was in truth as fervent and as steadfast as was to be found in the whole Church of England. He had long been intimately acquainted with Parker, Bishop of Oxford, and hoped to obtain by the interest of that prelate a royal letter to the college. Parker promised to do his best, but soon reported that he had found difficulties. "The King," he said, "will recommend no person who is not a friend to His Majesty's religion. What can you do to pleasure him as to that matter?" Smith answered that, if he became President, he would exert himself to promote learning, true Christianity, and loyalty. "That will not do," said the Bishop. "If so," said Smith manfully, "let who will be President; I can promise nothing more."

The election had been fixed for the thirteenth of April; and the Fellows had been summoned to attend. It was

---

* Burnet, I. 697.; Tanner's Notitia Monastica. At the visitation in the twenty-sixth year of Henry the Eighth it appeared that the annual revenue of King's College was 751*l*.; of New College, 487*l*.; of Magdalene, 1076*l*.

rumoured that a royal letter would come down recommending one Anthony Farmer to the vacant place. This man's life had been a series of shameful acts. He had been a member of the University of Cambridge, and had escaped expulsion only by a timely retreat. He had then joined the Dissenters. Then he had gone to Oxford, had entered himself at Magdalene, and had soon become notorious there for every kind of vice. He generally reeled into his college at night speechless with liquor. He was celebrated for having headed a disgraceful riot at Abingdon. He had been a constant frequenter of noted haunts of libertines. At length he had turned pandar, had exceeded even the ordinary vileness of his vile calling, and had received money from dissolute young gentlemen commoners for services such as it is not good that history should record. This wretch, however, had pretended to turn Papist. His apostasy atoned for all his vices; and, though still a youth, he was selected to rule a grave and religious society in which the scandal given by his depravity was still fresh.

As a Roman Catholic he was disqualified for academical office by the general law of the land. Never having been a Fellow of Magdalene College or of New College, he was disqualified for the vacant Presidency by a special ordinance of William of Waynflete. William of Waynflete had also enjoined those who partook of his bounty to have a particular regard to moral character in choosing their head; and, even if he had left no such injunction, a body chiefly composed of divines could not with decency entrust such a man as Farmer with the government of a place of education.

The Fellows respectfully represented to the King the difficulty in which they should be placed, if, as was rumoured, Farmer should be recommended to them, and begged that, if it were His Majesty's pleasure to interfere in the election, some person for whom they could legally and conscientiously vote might be proposed. Of this dutiful request no notice was taken. The royal letter arrived. It was brought down by one of the Fellows who had lately turned Papist, Robert Charnock, a man of parts and spirit, but of a violent and restless temper, which impelled him a few years later to an atrocious crime and to a terrible fate. On the thirteenth of April the society met in the chapel. Some hope was still entertained that the King might be moved by the remonstrance which had been addressed to him. The assembly therefore adjourned till the fifteenth, which was the last day on which, by the constitution of the college, the election could take place.

Election of the President.

The fifteenth of April came. Again the Fellows repaired to their chapel. No answer had arrived from Whitehall. Two or three of the Seniors, among whom was Smith, were inclined to postpone the election once more rather than take a step which might give offence to the King. But the language of the statutes was clear. Those statutes the members of the foundation had sworn to observe. The general opinion was that there ought to be no further delay. There was a hot debate. The electors were too much excited to take their seats; and the whole choir was in a tumult. Those who were for proceeding appealed to their oaths and to the rules laid down by the founder whose bread they had eaten. The King, they truly said, had no right to force on them even a qualified candidate. Some expressions unpleasing to Tory ears were dropped in the course of the dispute; and Smith was provoked into exclaiming that the spirit of Ferguson had possessed his brethren. It was at length resolved by a great majority that it was necessary to proceed immediately to the election. Charnock left the chapel. The other Fellows, having first received the sacrament, proceeded to give their voices. The choice fell on John Hough, a man of eminent virtue and prudence, who, having borne persecution with fortitude and prosperity with meekness, having risen to high honours and having modestly declined honours higher still, died in extreme old age, yet in full vigour of mind, more than fifty-six years after this eventful day.

The society hastened to acquaint the King with the circumstances which had made it necessary to elect a President without further delay, and requested the Duke of Ormond, as patron of the whole University, and the Bishop of Winchester, as visitor of Magdalene College, to undertake the office of intercessors: but the King was far too angry and too dull to listen to explanations.

The Fellows of Magdalene cited before the High Commission.

Early in June the Fellows were cited to appear before the High Commission at Whitehall. Five of them, deputed by the rest, obeyed the summons. Jeffreys treated them after his usual fashion. When one of them, a grave Doctor named Fairfax, hinted some doubt as to the validity of the Commission, the Chancellor began to roar like a wild beast.

CHAP. VIII.

"Who is this man? What commission has he to be impudent here? Seize him. Put him into a dark room. What does he do without a keeper? He is under my care as a lunatic. I wonder that nobody has applied to me for the custody of him." But when this storm had spent its force, and the depositions concerning the moral character of the King's nominee had been read, none of the Commissioners had the front to pronounce that such a man could properly be made the head of a great college. Obadiah Walker and the other Oxonian Papists who were in attendance to support their proselyte were utterly confounded. The Commission pronounced Hough's election void, and suspended Fairfax from his fellowship: but about Farmer no more was said; and, in the month of August, arrived a royal letter recommending Parker, Bishop of Oxford, to the Fellows.

Parker recommended as President.

Parker was not an avowed Papist. Still there was an objection to him which, even if the presidency had been vacant, would have been decisive: for he had never been a Fellow of either New College or Magdalene. But the presidency was not vacant: Hough had been duly elected; and all the members of the college were bound by oath to support him in his office. They therefore, with many expressions of loyalty and concern, excused themselves from complying with the King's mandate.

The Charterhouse.

While Oxford was thus opposing a firm resistance to tyranny, a stand not less resolute was made in another quarter. James had, some time before, commanded the trustees of the Charterhouse, men of the first rank and consideration in the kingdom, to admit a Roman Catholic named Popham into the hospital which was under their care. The Master of the house, Thomas Burnet, a clergyman of distinguished genius, learning, and virtue, had the courage to represent to them, though the ferocious Jeffreys sate at the board, that what was required of them was contrary both to the will of the founder and to an Act of Parliament. "What is that to the purpose?" said a courtier who was one of the governors. "It is very much to the purpose, I think," answered a voice, feeble with age and sorrow, yet not to be heard without respect by any assembly, the voice of the venerable Ormond. "An Act of Parliament," continued the patriarch of the Cavalier party, "is, in my judgment, no light thing." The question was put whether Popham should be admitted; and it was determined to reject him. The Chancellor, who could not well ease himself by cursing and swearing at Ormond, flung away in a rage, and was followed by some of the minority. The consequence was, that there was not a quorum left, and that no formal reply could be made to the royal mandate.

The next meeting took place only two days after the High Commission had pronounced sentence of deprivation against Hough, and of suspension against Fairfax. A second mandate under the Great Seal was laid before the trustees: but the tyrannical manner in which Mugdalene College had been treated had roused instead of subduing their spirit. They drew up a letter to Sunderland in which they requested him to inform the King that they could not, in this matter, obey His Majesty without breaking the law and betraying their trust.

There can be little doubt that, had ordinary signatures been appended to this document, the King would have taken some violent course. But even he was daunted by the opposition of Ormond, Halifax, Danby, and Nottingham, the chiefs of all the sections of that great party to which he owed his crown. He therefore contented himself with directing Jeffreys to consider what course ought to be taken. It was announced at one time that a proceeding would be instituted in the King's Bench, at another that the Ecclesiastical Commission would take up the case: but these threats gradually died away.*

The summer was now far advanced; and the King set out on a progress, the longest and the most splendid that had been known during many years. From Windsor he went on the sixteenth of August to Portsmouth, walked round the fortifications, touched some scrofulous people, and then proceeded in one of his yachts to Southampton. From Southampton he travelled to Bath, where he remained a few days, and where he left the Queen. When he departed, he was attended by the High Sheriff of Somersetshire and by a large body of gentlemen to the frontier of the county, where the High Sheriff of Gloucestershire, with a not less splendid retinue, was in attendance. The Duke of Beaufort soon met the royal coaches, and conducted them to Badminton, where a banquet worthy of the fame which his splendid housekeeping had won for him was prepared. In the afternoon the cavalcade proceeded to Gloucester. It was greeted two miles

* A Relation of the Proceedings at the Charterhouse, 1689.

from the city by the Bishop and clergy. At the South Gate the Mayor waited with the keys. The bells rang and the conduits flowed with wine as the King passed through the streets to the close which encircles the venerable Cathedral. He lay that night at the deanery, and on the following morning set out for Worcester. From Worcester he went to Ludlow, Shrewsbury, and Chester, and was everywhere received with outward signs of joy and respect, which he was weak enough to consider as proofs that the discontent excited by his measures had subsided, and that an easy victory was before him. Barillon, more sagacious, informed Lewis that the King of England was under a delusion, that the progress had done no real good, and that those very gentlemen of Worcestershire and Shropshire who had thought it their duty to receive their Sovereign and their guest with every mark of honour would be found as refractory as ever when the question of the test should come on.*

On the road the royal train was joined by two courtiers who in temper and opinions differed widely from each other. Penn was at Chester on a pastoral, or, to speak more correctly, on a political tour. The chief object of his expedition was to induce the Dissenters, throughout England, to support the government. His popularity and authority among his brethren had greatly declined since he had become a tool of the King and of the Jesuits.† He was, however, most graciously received by James, and, on the Sunday, was permitted to harangue in the tennis court, while Cartwright preached in the Cathedral, and while the King heard mass at an altar which had been decked in the Shire Hall. It is said, indeed, that His Majesty deigned to look into the tennis court and to listen with decency to his friend's melodious eloquence.‡

The furious Tyrconnel had crossed the sea from Dublin to give an account of his administration. All the most respectable English Roman Catholics looked coldly on him as an

---

* See the London Gazette, from August 18. to September 1. 1687; Barillon, September 1/11.

† "Penn, chef des Quakers, qu'on mit être dans les intérêts du Roi d'Angleterre, est si fort décrié parmi ceux de son parti qu'ils n'ont plus aucune confiance en lui." — Bonrepaux to Seignelay, Sept. 11. 1687. The evidence of Gerard Croese is to the same effect. "Etiam Quakeri Pennum non amplius, ut ante, its amabant ac magnifaciebant, quidam aversabantur ac fugiebant." — Historia Quakeriana, lib. ii. 1695. As to Penn's tour, Van Citters wrote on Oct. 4/14. 1687, "Dat den bekenden Aerts-Quaker Pen door het Lant op reyse was, om die van syne gesintheyt, en sodere soo veel doenlyck, tot des Conings partie en Sinnelyckheyt te winnen."

‡ Cartwright's Diary, Aug. 30. 1687; Clarkson's Life of William Penn.

enemy of their race and a scandal to their religion. But he was cordially welcomed by his master, and dismissed with assurances of undiminished confidence and steady support. James expressed his delight at learning that in a short time the whole government of Ireland would be in Roman Catholic hands. The English colonists had already been stripped of all political power. Nothing remained but to strip them of their property; and this last outrage was deferred only till the cooperation of an Irish Parliament should have been secured.*

From Cheshire the King turned southward, and, in the full belief that the Fellows of Magdalene College, however mutinous they might be, would not dare to disobey a command uttered by his own lips, directed his course towards Oxford. By the way he made some little excursions to places which peculiarly interested him, as a King, a brother, and a son. He visited the hospitable roof of Boscobel, and the remains of the oak so conspicuous in the history of his house. He rode over the field of Edgehill, where the Cavaliers first crossed swords with the soldiers of the Parliament. On the third of September he dined in great state at the palace of Woodstock, an ancient and renowned mansion, of which not a stone is now to be seen, but of which the site is still marked on the turf of Blenheim Park by two sycamores which grow near the stately bridge. In the evening he reached Oxford. He was received there with the wonted honours. The students in their academical garb were ranged to welcome him on the right hand and on the left, from the entrance of the city to the great gate of Christ Church. He lodged at the deanery, where, among other accommodations, he found a chapel fitted up for the celebration of the mass.†
On the day after his arrival, the Fellows of Magdalene College were ordered to attend him. When they appeared before him, he treated them with an insolence such as had never been shown to their predecessors by the Puritan visitors. "You have not dealt with me like gentlemen," he

---

* London Gazette, Sept. 5.; Sheridan MS.; Barillon, Sept. 4/14 1687. "Le Roi son maitre," says Barillon, "a témoigné une grande satisfaction des mesures qu'il a prises, et a autorisé ce qu'il a fait en faveur des Catholiques. Il les établit dans les emplois et les charges, en sorte que l'autorité se trouvera bientôt entre leurs mains. Il reste encore beaucoup de choses à faire en ce pays ici pour retirer les biens injustement ôtés aux Catholiques. Mais cela ne peut s'exécuter qu'avec le tems et dans l'assemblée d'un parlement en Irlande."

† London Gazette of Sept. 5. and Sept. 8. 1687.

exclaimed. "You have been unmannerly as well as undutiful." They fell on their knees and tendered a petition. He would not look at it. "Is this your Church of England loyalty? I could not have believed that so many clergymen of the Church of England would have been concerned in such a business. Go home. Get you gone. I am King. I will be obeyed. Go to your chapel this instant; and admit the Bishop of Oxford. Let those who refuse look to it. They shall feel the whole weight of my hand. They shall know what it is to incur the displeasure of their Sovereign." The Fellows, still kneeling before him, again offered him their petition. He angrily flung it down. "Get you gone, I tell you. I will receive nothing from you till you have admitted the Bishop."

They retired and instantly assembled in their chapel. The question was propounded whether they would comply with His Majesty's command. Smith was absent. Charnock alone answered in the affirmative. The other Fellows who were at the meeting declared that in all things lawful they were ready to obey the King, but that they would not violate their statutes and their oaths.

The King, greatly incensed and mortified by his defeat, quitted Oxford and rejoined the Queen at Bath. His obstinacy and violence had brought him into an embarrassing position. He had trusted too much to the effect of his frowns and angry tones, and had rashly staked, not merely the credit of his administration, but his personal dignity, on the issue of the contest. Could he yield to subjects whom he had menaced with raised voice and furious gestures? Yet could he venture to eject in one day a crowd of respectable clergymen from their homes, because they had discharged what the whole nation regarded as a sacred duty? Perhaps there might be an escape from this dilemma. Perhaps the college might still be terrified, caressed, or bribed into submission. The agency of Penn was employed. He had too much good feeling to approve of the violent and unjust proceedings of the government, and even ventured to express part of what he thought. James was, as usual, obstinate in the wrong. The courtly Quaker, therefore, did his best to seduce the college from the path of right. He first tried intimidation. Ruin, he said, impended over the society. The King was highly incensed. The case might be a hard one. Most people thought it so. But every child knew that His Majesty loved to have his own way and could not bear to be thwarted. Penn, therefore, exhorted the Fellows not to rely on the goodness of their cause, but to submit, or at least to temporise.* Such counsel came strangely from one who had himself been expelled from the University for raising a riot about the surplice, who had run the risk of being disinherited rather than take off his hat to the princes of the blood, and who had been more than once sent to prison for haranguing in conventicles. He did not succeed in frightening the Magdalene men. In answer to his alarming hints he was reminded that in the last generation thirty-four out of the forty Fellows had cheerfully left their beloved cloisters and gardens, their hall and their chapel, and had gone forth not knowing where they should find a meal or a bed rather than violate the oath of allegiance. The King now wished them to violate another oath. He should find that the old spirit was not extinct.

* See Penn's Letter to Bailey, one of the Fellows of the College, in the Impartial Relation printed at Oxford in 1688. It has lately been asserted that Penn most certainly did not write this letter. Now, the evidence which proves the letter to be his is irresistible. Bailey, to whom the letter was addressed, ascribed it to Penn, and sent as answer to Penn. In a very short time both the letter and the answer appeared in print. Many thousands of copies were circulated. Penn was pointed out to the whole world as the author of the letter; and it is not pretended that he met this public accusation with a public contradiction. Everybody therefore believed, and was perfectly warranted in believing, that he was the author. The letter was repeatedly quoted as his, during his own lifetime, not merely in fugitive pamphlets, such as the History of the Ecclesiastical Commission, published in 1711, but in grave and elaborate books which were meant to descend to posterity. Boyer, in his History of William the Third, printed immediately after that King's death, and reprinted in 1703, pronounced the letter to be Penn's, and added some severe reflections on the writer. Kennet, in the bulky History of England published in 1706, a history which had a large sale and produced a great sensation, adopted the very words of Boyer. When these works appeared, Penn was not only alive, but in the full enjoyment of his faculties. He cannot have been ignorant of the charge brought against him by writers of so much note; and it was not his practice to hold his peace when unjust charges were brought against him even by obscure scribblers. In 1695, a pamphlet on the Exclusion Bill was falsely imputed to him in an anonymous libel. Contemptible as was the quarter from which the calumny proceeded, he hastened to vindicate himself. His denial, distinct, solemn, and indignant, speedily came forth in print. Is it possible to doubt that he would, if he could, have confounded Boyer and Kennet by a similar denial? He however silently suffered them to tell the whole nation, during many years, that this letter was written by "William Penn the head of the Quakers, or, as some then thought, an ambitious, crafty Jesuit, who under a phanatical outside, promoted King James's designs." He died without attempting to clear himself. In the year of his death appeared Eachard's huge volume, containing the History of England from the Restoration to the Revolution; and Eachard, though often differing with Boyer and Kennet, agreed with them in unhesitatingly ascribing the letter to Penn.

Such is the evidence on one side. I am not aware that any evidence deserving a serious answer has been produced on the other. (1687.)

Then Penn tried a gentler tone. He had an interview with Hough and with some of the Fellows, and, after many professions of sympathy and friendship, began to hint at a compromise. The King could not bear to be crossed. The college must give way. Parker must be admitted. But he was in very bad health. All his preferments would soon be vacant. "Doctor Hough," said Penn, " may then be Bishop of Oxford. How should you like that, gentlemen?"* Penn had passed his life in declaiming against a hireling ministry. He held that he was bound to refuse the payment of tithes, and this even when he had bought land chargeable with tithes and had been allowed the value of the tithes in the purchase money. According to his own principles, he would have committed a great sin if he had interfered for the purpose of obtaining a benefice on the most honourable terms for the most pious divine. Yet to such a degree had his manners been corrupted by evil communications, and his understanding obscured by inordinate zeal for a single object, that he did not scruple to become a broker in simony of a peculiarly discreditable kind, and to use a bishopric as a bait to tempt a divine to perjury. Hough replied with civil contempt that he wanted nothing from the Crown but common justice. "We stand," he said, "on our statutes and our oaths: but even setting aside our statutes and oaths, we feel that we have our religion to defend. The Papists

* Here again I have been accused of calumniating Penn; and some show of a case has been made out by suppression amounting to falsification. It is asserted that Penn did not "begin to hint at a compromise;" and in proof of this assertion, a few words, quoted from the letter in which Hough gives an account of the interview, are printed in italics. These words are, "I thank God, he did not offer any proposal by way of accommodation." These words, taken by themselves, undoubtedly seem to prove that Penn did not begin to hint at a compromise. But their effect is very different indeed when they are read in connection with words which immediately follow, without the intervention of a full stop, but which have been carefully suppressed. The whole sentence runs thus: "I thank God, he did not offer any proposal by way of accommodation; only once, upon the mention of the Bishop of Oxford's indisposition, he said, smiling, 'If the Bishop of Oxford die, Dr. Hough may be made Bishop. What think you of that, gentlemen?'" Can anything be clearer than that the latter part of the sentence limits the general assertion contained in the former part? Everybody knows that *only* is perpetually used as synonymous with *except that*. Instances will readily occur to all who are well acquainted with the English Bible, a book from the authority of which there is no appeal when the question is about the force of an English word. We read in the Book of Genesis, to go no further, that *every* living thing was destroyed; and Noah *only* remained, and they that were with him in the ark: and that Joseph bought *all* the land of Egypt for Pharaoh; *only* the land of the priests bought he not. The defenders of Penn reason exactly like a commentator who should construe these passages to mean that Noah was drowned in the flood, and that Joseph bought the land of the priests for Pharaoh. (1857).

have robbed us of University College. They have robbed us of Christ Church. The fight is now for Magdalene. They will soon have all the rest."

Penn was foolish enough to answer that he really believed that the Papists would now be content. "University," he said, "is a pleasant college. Christ Church is a noble place. Magdalene is a fine building. The situation is convenient. The walks by the river are delightful. If the Roman Catholics are reasonable they will be satisfied with these." This absurd avowal would alone have made it impossible for Hough and his brethren to yield.* The negotiation was broken off; and the King hastened to make the disobedient know, as he had threatened, what it was to incur his displeasure.

A special commission was directed to Cartwright, Bishop of Chester, to Wright, Chief Justice of the King's Bench, and to Sir Thomas Jenner, a Baron of the Exchequer, appointing them to exercise visitatorial jurisdiction over the college. On the twentieth of October they arrived at Oxford, escorted by three troops of cavalry with drawn swords. On the following morning the Commissioners took their seats in the hall of Magdalene. Cartwright pronounced a loyal oration, which, a few years before, would have called forth the acclamations of an Oxonian audience, but which was now heard with sullen indignation. A long dispute followed. The president defended his rights with skill, temper, and resolution. He professed great respect for the royal authority: but he steadily maintained that he had by the laws of England a freehold interest in the house and revenues annexed to the Presidency. Of that interest he could not be deprived by an arbitrary mandate of the Sovereign. "Will you submit," said the Bishop, "to our visitation?" "I submit to it," said Hough with great dexterity, "so far as it is consistent with the laws, and no further." "Will you deliver up the key of your lodg-

---

* I will give one other specimen of the arts which are thought legitimate where the fame of Penn is concerned. To vindicate the language which he held on this occasion, if we suppose him to have meant what he said, is plainly impossible. We are therefore told that he was in a merry mood; that his benevolent heart was so much exhilarated by the sight of several pious and learned men who were about to be reduced to beggary for observing their oaths and adhering to their religion, that he could not help joking; and that it would be most unjust to treat his charming facetiousness as a crime. In order to make out this defence,—a poor defence even if made out,—the following words are quoted, as part of Hough's letter, "He had a mind to droll upon us." This is given as a positive assertion made by Hough. The context is carefully suppressed. My readers will, I believe, be surprised when they learn that Hough's words really are these: "When I heard him talk at this rate, I concluded he was either off his guard, or had a mind to droll upon us."

ings?" said Cartwright. Hough remained silent. The question was repeated; and Hough returned a mild but resolute refusal. The Commissioners pronounced him an intruder, and charged the fellows to assist at the admission of the Bishop of Oxford. Charnock eagerly promised obedience: Smith returned an evasive answer: but the great body of the members of the college firmly declared that they still regarded Hough as their rightful head.

Protest of Hough.

And now Hough himself craved permission to address a few words to the Commissioners. They consented with much civility, perhaps expecting from the calmness and suavity of his manner that he would make some concession. "My Lords," said he, "you have this day deprived me of my freehold: I hereby protest against all your proceedings as illegal, unjust, and null; and I appeal from you to our Sovereign Lord the King in his courts of justice." A loud murmur of applause arose from the gownsmen who filled the hall. The Commissioners were furious. Search was made for the offenders, but in vain. Then the rage of the whole board was turned against Hough. "Do not think to huff us, sir," cried Jenner, punning on the President's name. "I will uphold His Majesty's authority," said Wright, "while I have breath in my body. All this comes of your popular protest. You have broken the peace. You shall answer it in the King's Bench. I bind you over in one thousand pounds to appear there next term. I will see whether the civil power cannot manage you. If that is not enough, you shall have the military too." In truth Oxford was in a state which made the Commissioners not a little uneasy. The soldiers were ordered to have their carbines loaded. It was said that an express was sent to London for the purpose of hastening the arrival of more troops.

Parker.

No disturbance however took place. The Bishop of Oxford was quietly installed by proxy: but only two members of Magdalene College attended the ceremony. Many signs showed that the spirit of resistance had spread to the common people. The porter of the college threw down his keys. The butler refused to scratch Hough's name out of the buttery book, and was instantly dismissed. No blacksmith could be found in the whole city who would force the lock of the President's lodgings. It was necessary for the Commissioners to employ their own servants, who broke open the door with iron bars. The sermons which on the following Sunday were preached in the University Church were full of reflections such as stung Cartwright to the quick, though such as he could not discreetly resent.

And here, if James had not been infatuated, the matter might have stopped. The Fellows in general were not inclined to carry their resistance further. They were of opinion that, by refusing to assist in the admission of the intruder, they had sufficiently proved their respect for their statutes and oaths, and that, since he was now in actual possession, they might justifiably submit to him as their head, till he should be removed by sentence of a competent court. Only one Fellow, Doctor Fairfax, refused to yield even to this extent. The Commissioners would gladly have compromised the dispute on these terms; and during a few hours there was a truce which many thought likely to end in an amicable arrangement: but soon all was again in confusion. The Fellows found that the popular voice loudly accused them of pusillanimity. The townsmen already talked ironically of a Magdalene conscience, and exclaimed that the brave Hough and the honest Fairfax had been betrayed and abandoned. Still more annoying were the sneers of Obadiah Walker and his brother renegades. This then, said those apostates, was the end of all the big words in which the society had declared itself resolved to stand by its lawful President and by its Protestant faith. While the Fellows, bitterly annoyed by the public censure, were regretting the modified submission which they had consented to make, they learned that this submission was by no means satisfactory to the King. It was not enough, he said, that they offered to obey the Bishop of Oxford as President in fact. They must distinctly admit the Commission and all that had been done under it to be legal: they must acknowledge that they had acted undutifully: they must declare themselves penitent; they must promise to behave better in future, must implore His Majesty's pardon, and must lay themselves at his feet. Two Fellows, of whom the King had no complaint to make, Charnock and Smith, were excused from the obligation of making these degrading apologies.

Even James never committed a grosser error. The Fellows, already angry with themselves for having conceded so much, and galled by the censure of the world, eagerly caught at the opportunity which was now offered them of regaining the public esteem. With one voice they declared that they would never ask pardon for being in the right, or admit that the

CHAP. VIII.

Ejection of the Fellows.

visitation of their college and the deprivation of their President had been legal.

Then the King, as he had threatened, laid on them the whole weight of his hand. They were by one sweeping edict condemned to expulsion. Yet this punishment was not deemed sufficient. It was known that many noblemen and gentlemen who possessed church patronage would be disposed to provide for men who had suffered so much for the laws of England and for the Protestant religion. The High Commission therefore pronounced the ejected Fellows incapable of ever holding any ecclesiastical preferment. Such of them as were not yet in holy orders were pronounced incapable of receiving the clerical character. James might enjoy the thought that he had reduced many of them from a situation in which they were surrounded by comforts, and had before them the fairest professional prospects, to hopeless indigence.

But all these severities produced an effect directly the opposite of that which he had anticipated. The spirit of Englishmen, that sturdy spirit which no King of the House of Stuart could ever be taught by experience to understand, swelled up high and strong against injustice. Oxford, the quiet seat of learning and loyalty, was in a state resembling that of the City of London on the morning after the attempt of Charles the First to seize the five members. The Vicechancellor had been asked to dine with the Commissioners on the day of the expulsion. He refused. "My taste," he said, "differs from that of Colonel Kirke. I cannot eat my meals with appetite under a gallows." The scholars refused to pull off their caps to the new rulers of Magdalene College. Smith was nicknamed Doctor Roguery, and was publicly insulted in a coffeehouse. When Charnock summoned the Demies to perform their academical exercises before him, they answered that they were deprived of their lawful governors and would submit to no usurped authority. They assembled apart both for study and for divine service. Attempts were made to corrupt them by offers of the lucrative fellowships which had just been declared vacant; but one undergraduate after another manfully answered that his conscience would not suffer him to profit by injustice. One lad who was induced to take a fellowship was turned out of the hall by the rest. Youths were invited from other colleges, but with small success. The richest foundation in the kingdom seemed to have lost all attractions for needy students. Meanwhile, in Lon-

don and all over the country, money was collected for the
support of the ejected Fellows. The Princess of Orange, to
the great joy of all Protestants, subscribed two hundred
pounds. Still, however, the King held on his course. The
expulsion of the Fellows was soon followed by the expulsion
of a crowd of Demies. All this time the new President was
fast sinking under bodily and mental disease. He had made
a last feeble effort to serve the government by publishing, at
the very time when the college was in a state of open rebellion against his authority, a defence of the Declaration of
Indulgence, or rather a defence of the doctrine of transubstantiation. This piece called forth many answers, and particularly one from Burnet, written with extraordinary vigour
and acrimony. A few weeks after the expulsion of the Demies, Parker died in the house of which he had violently
taken possession. Men said that his heart was broken by
remorse and shame. He lies in the beautiful antechapel of
the college; but no monument marks his grave.

Then the King's plan was carried into full effect. The
college was turned into a Popish seminary. Bonaventure
Giffard, the Roman Catholic Bishop of Madura, was appointed
President. The Roman Catholic service was performed in
the chapel. In one day twelve Roman Catholics were admitted Fellows. Some servile Protestants applied for fellowships, but met with refusals. Smith, an enthusiast in loyalty,
but still a sincere member of the Anglican Church, could not
bear to see the altered aspect of the house. He absented
himself: he was ordered to return into residence: he disobeyed: he was expelled; and the work of spoliation was
complete.*

The nature of the academical system of England is such
that no event which seriously affects the interests and honour
of either University can fail to excite a strong feeling throughout the country. Every successive blow, therefore, which
fell on Magdalene College, was felt to the extremities of the
kingdom. In the coffeehouses of London, in the Inns of Court,
in the closes of all the Cathedral towns, in parsonages and
manorhouses scattered over the remotest shires, pity for the

---

* Proceedings against Magdalene Col-
lege, in Oxon., for not electing Anthony
Farmer president of the said College, in
the Collection of State Trials; Luttrell's
Diary, June 15, 17, Oct. 21, Dec. 10,
1687; Smith's Narrative; Letter of Dr.
Richard Rawlinson, dated Oct. 31. 1687;
Reresby's Memoirs; Burnet, i. 696..;
Cartwright's Diary; Van Citters, Nov. 11/21
Nov. 15/25 1687.

CHAP.
VIII.

Resentment of the clergy.

sufferers and indignation against the government went on growing. The protest of Hough was everywhere applauded; the forcing of his door was everywhere mentioned with abhorrence; and at length the sentence of deprivation fulminated against the Fellows dissolved those ties, once so close and dear, which had bound the Church of England to the House of Stuart. Bitter resentment and cruel apprehension took the place of love and confidence. There was no prebendary, no rector, no vicar, whose mind was not haunted by the thought that, however quiet his temper, however obscure his situation, he might, in a few months, be driven from his dwelling by an arbitrary edict to beg in a ragged cassock with his wife and children, while his freehold, secured to him by laws of immemorial antiquity and by the royal word, was occupied by some apostate. This then was the reward of that heroic loyalty never once found wanting through the vicissitudes of fifty tempestuous years. It was for this that the clergy had endured spoliation and persecution in the cause of Charles the First. It was for this that they had supported Charles the Second in his hard contest with the Whig opposition. It was for this that they had stood in the front of the battle against those who sought to despoil James of his birthright. To their fidelity alone their oppressor owed the power which he was now employing to their ruin. They had long been in the habit of recounting in acrimonious language all that they had suffered at the hand of the Puritan in the day of his power. Yet for the Puritan there was some excuse. He was an avowed enemy: he had wrongs to avenge; and even he, while remodelling the ecclesiastical constitution of the country, and ejecting all who would not subscribe his Covenant, had not been altogether without compassion. He had at least granted to those whose benefices he seized a pittance sufficient to support life. But the hatred felt by the King towards that Church which had saved him from exile and placed him on a throne was not to be so easily satiated. Nothing but the utter ruin of his victims would content him. It was not enough that they were expelled from their homes and stripped of their revenues. They found every walk of life towards which men of their habits could look for a subsistence closed against them with malignant care, and nothing left to them but the precarious and degrading resource of alms.

The Anglican clergy, therefore, and that portion of the

laity which was strongly attached to Protestant episcopacy, now regarded the King with those feelings which injustice aggravated by ingratitude naturally excites. Yet had the Churchman still many scruples of conscience and honour to surmount before he could bring himself to oppose the government by force. He had been taught that passive obedience was enjoined without restriction or exception by the divine law. He had professed this opinion ostentatiously. He had treated with contempt the suggestion that an extreme case might possibly arise which would justify a people in drawing the sword against regal tyranny. Both principle and shame therefore restrained him from imitating the example of the rebellious Roundheads, while any hope of a peaceful and legal deliverance remained; and such a hope might reasonably be cherished as long as the Princess of Orange stood next in succession to the crown. If he would but endure with patience this trial of his faith, the laws of nature would soon do for him what he could not, without sin and dishonour, do for himself. The wrongs of the Church would be redressed: her property and dignity would be fenced by new guarantees; and those wicked courtiers who had, in the day of her adversity, injured and insulted her, would be signally punished.

The event to which the Church of England looked forward as an honourable and peaceful termination of her troubles was one of which even the most reckless members of the Jesuitical cabal could not think without painful apprehensions. If their master should die, leaving them no better security against the penal laws than a Declaration which the general voice of the nation pronounced to be a nullity, if a Parliament, animated by the same spirit which had prevailed in the Parliaments of Charles the Second, should assemble round the throne of a Protestant sovereign, was it not probable that a terrible retribution would be exacted, that the old laws against Popery would be rigidly enforced, and that new laws still more severe would be added to the statute book? The evil counsellors had long been tormented by these gloomy apprehensions, and some of them had contemplated strange and desperate remedies. James had scarcely mounted the throne when it began to be whispered about Whitehall that, if the Lady Anne would turn Roman Catholic, it might not be impossible, with the help of Lewis, to transfer to her the birthright of her elder sister. At the French embassy this scheme was warmly approved, and

Bonrepaux gave it as his opinion that the assent of James would be easily obtained.* Soon, however, it became manifest that Anne was unalterably attached to the Established Church. All thought of making her Queen was therefore relinquished. Nevertheless, a small knot of fanatics still continued to cherish a wild hope that they might be able to change the order of succession. The plan formed by these men was set forth in a minute of which a rude French translation has been preserved. It was to be hoped, they said, that the King might be able to establish the true faith without resorting to extremities; but in the worst event, he might leave his crown at the disposal of Lewis. It was better for Englishmen to be the vassals of France than the slaves of the Devil.† This extraordinary document was handed about from Jesuit to Jesuit, and from courtier to courtier, till some eminent Roman Catholics, in whom bigotry had not extinguished patriotism, furnished the Dutch ambassador with a copy. He put the paper into the hands of James. James, greatly agitated, pronounced it a vile forgery contrived by some pamphleteer in Holland. The Dutch minister resolutely answered that he could prove the contrary by the testimony of several distinguished members of His Majesty's own Church, nay, that there would be no difficulty in pointing out the writer, who, after all, had written only what many priests and many busy politicians said every day in the galleries of the palace. The King did not think it expedient to ask who the writer was, but, abandoning the charge of forgery, protested, with great vehemence and solemnity, that no thought of disinheriting his eldest daughter had ever crossed his mind. "Nobody," he said, "ever dared to hint such a thing to me. I never would listen to it. God does not command us to propagate the true religion by injustice, and this would be the foulest, the most unnatural injustice."‡ Notwithstanding all these professions, Barillon, a few days later, reported to his court

---

* "Quand on conçoit le dedans de cette cour aussi intimement que je la connois, on peut croire que sa Majesté Britannique donnera volontiers dans ces sortes de projets."—Bonrepaux to Seignelay, March ¹⁵/₅. 1686.

† "Que, quand pour établir la religion Catholique et pour la conserver icy, il (James) devroit se rendre en quelque façon dépendant de la France, et mettre la décision de la succession à la couronne entre les mains de ce monarque là, qu'il seroit obligé de le faire, parcequ'il vaudroit mieux pour ses sujets qu'ils devinssent vassaux du Roy de France, Haut Catholique, que de demeurer comme esclaves du Diable." This paper is in the archives of both France and Holland.

‡ Van Citters, Aug. ⁶/₁₆. ¹⁹/₂₉. 1686; Barillon, Aug. ⁹/₁₉.

that James had begun to listen to suggestions respecting a change in the order of succession, that the question was doubtless a delicate one, but that there was reason to hope that, with time and management, a way might be found to settle the crown on some Roman Catholic, to the exclusion of the two Princesses.* During many months this subject continued to be discussed by the fiercest and most extravagant Papists about the court, and candidates for the regal office were actually named.†

It is not probable however that James ever meant to take a course so insane. He must have known that England would never bear for a single day the yoke of an usurper who was also a Papist, and that any attempt to set aside the Lady Mary would have been withstood to the death, both by all those who had supported the Exclusion Bill, and by all those who had opposed it. There is, however, no doubt that the King was an accomplice in a plot less absurd, but not less unjustifiable, against the rights of his children. Tyrconnel had, with his master's approbation, made arrangements for separating Ireland from the empire, and for placing her under the protection of Lewis, as soon as the crown should devolve on a Protestant sovereign. Bonrepaux had been consulted, had imparted the design to his court, and had been instructed to assure Tyrconnel that France would lend effectual aid to the accomplishment of this great project.‡ These transactions, which, though perhaps not in all parts accurately known at the Hague, were strongly suspected there, must not be left out of the account if we would pass a just judgment on the course taken a few months later by the Princess of Orange. Those who pronounce her guilty of a breach of filial duty must admit that her fault was at

CHAP. VIII.

Scheme of James and Tyrconnel for preventing the Princess of Orange from succeeding to the kingdom of Ireland.

---

* Barillon, Sept. 14. 1686. "La matière est une matière fort délicate à traiter. Je sais pourtant qu'on en parle au Roy d'Angleterre, et qu'on ne désespère pas avec le temps de trouver des moyens pour faire passer la couronne sur la tête d'un héritier Catholique."

† Bonrepaux, July 14. 1687.

‡ Bonrepaux to Seignelay, Aug. 25. 1687. I will quote a few words from this most remarkable despatch: "Je scay bien certainement que l'intention du Roy d'Angleterre est de faire perdre ce royaume (Ireland) à son successeur, et de le fortifier en sorte que tous ses sujets Catholiques y puissent avoir un asile assuré. Son projet est de mettre les choses en cet estat dans le cours de cinq années." In the Secret Consults of the Romish party in Ireland, printed in 1690, there is a passage which shows that this negotiation had not been kept strictly secret. "Though the King kept it private from most of his council, yet certain it is that he had promised the French King the disposal of that government and kingdom when things had attained to that growth as to be fit to bear it."

least greatly extenuated by her wrongs. If, to serve the cause of her religion, she broke through the most sacred ties of consanguinity, she only followed her father's example. She did not assist to depose him until he had conspired to disinherit her.

Scarcely had Bonrepaux been informed that Lewis had resolved to assist the enterprise of Tyrconnel when all thoughts of that enterprise were abandoned. James had caught the first glimpse of a hope which delighted and elated him. The Queen was with child.

Before the end of October 1687 the great news began to be whispered. It was observed that Her Majesty had absented herself from some public ceremonies on the plea of indisposition. It was said that many relics, supposed to possess extraordinary virtue, had been hung about her. Soon the story made its way from the palace to the coffeehouses of the capital, and spread fast over the country. By a very small minority the rumour was welcomed with joy. The great body of the nation listened with mingled derision and fear. There was indeed nothing very extraordinary in what had happened. The King had but just completed his fifty-fourth year. The Queen was in the summer of life. She had already borne four children who had died young; and long afterwards she was delivered of another child whom nobody had any interest in treating as suppositious, and who was therefore never said to be so. As, however, five years had elapsed since her last pregnancy, the people, under the influence of that delusion which leads men to believe what they wish, had ceased to entertain any apprehension that she would give an heir to the throne. On the other hand, nothing seemed more natural and probable than that the Jesuits should have contrived a pious fraud. It was certain that they must consider the accession of the Princess of Orange as one of the greatest calamities which could befal their Church. It was equally certain that they would not be very scrupulous about doing whatever might be necessary to save their Church from a great calamity. In books written by eminent members of the Society, and licensed by its rulers, it was distinctly laid down that means even more shocking to all notions of justice and humanity than the introduction of a spurious heir into a family might lawfully be employed for ends less important than the conversion of a heretical kingdom. It had got abroad that some of the King's advisers, and even the King himself, had meditated schemes for defrauding the Lady Mary, either wholly or in part, of her rightful inheritance. A suspicion, not indeed well founded, but by no means so absurd as is commonly supposed, took possession of the public mind. The folly of some Roman Catholics confirmed the vulgar prejudice. They spoke of the auspicious event as strange, as miraculous, as an exertion of the same Divine power which had made Sarah proud and happy in Isaac, and had given Samuel to the prayers of Hannah. Mary's mother, the Duchess of Modena, had lately died. A short time before her death, she had, it was said, implored the Virgin of Loretto, with fervent vows and rich offerings, to bestow a son on James. The King himself had, in the preceding August, turned aside from his progress to visit the Holy Well, and had there besought Saint Winifred to obtain for him that boon without which his great designs for the propagation of the true faith could be but imperfectly executed. The imprudent zealots who dwelt on these tales foretold with confidence that the unborn infant would be a boy, and offered to back their opinion by laying twenty guineas to one. Heaven, they affirmed, would not have interfered, but for a great end. One fanatic announced that the Queen would give birth to twins, of whom the elder would be King of England, and the younger Pope of Rome. Mary could not conceal the delight with which she heard this prophecy, and her ladies found that they could not gratify her more than by talking of it. The Roman Catholics would have acted more wisely if they had spoken of the pregnancy as of a natural event, and if they had borne with moderation their unexpected good fortune. Their insolent triumph excited the popular indignation. Their predictions strengthened the popular suspicions. From the Prince and Princess of Denmark down to porters and laundresses nobody alluded to the promised birth without a sneer. The wits of London described the new miracle in rhymes which, it may well be supposed, were not the most delicate. The rough country squires roared with laughter if they met with any person simple enough to believe that the Queen was really likely to be again a mother. A royal proclamation appeared, commanding the clergy to read a form of prayer and thanksgiving which had been prepared for this joyful occasion by Crewe and Sprat. The clergy obeyed: but it was observed

CHAP. VIII.

that the congregations made no responses and showed no signs of reverence. Soon in all the coffeehouses was handed about a brutal lampoon on the courtly prelates whose pens the King had employed. Mother East had also her full share of abuse. Into that homely monosyllable our ancestors had degraded the name of the great house of Este which reigned at Modena.*

The new hope which elated the King's spirits was mingled with many fears. Something more than the birth of a Prince of Wales was necessary to the success of the plans formed by the Jesuitical party. It was not very likely that James would live till his son should be of age to exercise the royal functions. The law had made no provision for the case of a minority. The reigning sovereign was not competent to make provision for such a case by will. The legislature only could supply the defect. If James should die before the defect had been supplied, leaving a successor of tender years, the supreme power would undoubtedly devolve on Protestants. Those Tories who held most firmly the doctrine that nothing could justify them in resisting their liege lord would have no scruple about drawing their swords against a Popish woman who should dare to usurp the guardianship of the realm and of the infant sovereign. The result of a contest could scarcely be matter of doubt. The Prince of Orange, or his wife, would be Regent. The young King would be placed in the hands of heretical instructors, whose arts might speedily efface from his mind the impressions which might have been made on it in the nursery. He might prove another Edward the Sixth; and the blessing granted to the intercession of the Virgin Mother and of Saint Winifred might be turned into a curse.† This was a danger against which nothing but an Act of Parliament could be a security, and how was such an Act to be obtained? Everything seemed to indicate that, if the Houses were convoked, they would come up to Westminster animated by the spirit of 1640. The event of the country elections could

Feeling of the constituent bodies, and of the Press.

---

* Van Citters, ⁷⁄₁₇, ⁹⁄₁₉ 1687; the Princess Anne to the Princess of Orange, March 14. and 20. 168⅞; Barillon, Dec. ⁴⁄₁₄. 1687; Revolution Politics; the song "Two Toms and a Nat;" Johnstone, April 4. 1688; Secret Consults of the Romish Party in Ireland, 1690.

† The King's uneasiness on this subject is strongly described by Ronquillo,

Dec. 17. 1687. "Un Principe de Valres y un Duque de York y otro di Luchaousterna (Lancaster, I suppose,) so bastan á reducir la grete; porque el Rey tiene 54 años, y vendrá á morir, dejando los hijos pequeños, y que entonces el reyno se apoderará dellos, y los nombrará tutor, y los educará en la religion protestante, contra la disposicion que dejare el Rey, y la autoridad de la Reyna."

hardly be doubted. The whole body of freeholders, high and low, clerical and lay, was strongly excited against the government. In the great majority of those towns where the right of voting depended on the payment of local taxes, or on the occupation of a tenement, no courtly candidate could dare to show his face. A very large part of the House of Commons was returned by members of municipal corporations. These corporations had recently been remodelled for the purpose of destroying the influence of the Whigs and Dissenters. More than a hundred constituent bodies had been deprived of their charters by tribunals devoted to the crown, or had been induced to avert compulsory disfranchisement by voluntary surrender. Every Mayor, every Alderman, every Town Clerk, from Berwick to Helstone, was a Tory and a Churchman: but Tories and Churchmen were now no longer devoted to the sovereign. The new municipalities were more unmanageable than the old municipalities had ever been, and would undoubtedly return representatives whose first act would be to impeach all the Popish Privy Councillors, and all the members of the High Commission.

In the Lords the prospect was scarcely less gloomy than in the Commons. Among the temporal peers it was certain that there would be an immense majority against the King's measures; and on that episcopal bench, which seven years before had unanimously supported him against those who had attempted to deprive him of his birthright, he could now look for support only to four or five sycophants despised by their profession and by their country.*

To all men not utterly blinded by passion these difficulties appeared insuperable. The most unscrupulous slaves of power showed signs of uneasiness. Dryden muttered that the King would only make matters worse by trying to mend them, and sighed for the golden days of the careless and goodnatured Charles.† Even Jeffreys wavered. As long as he was poor,

---

* Three lists framed at this time are extant; one in the French archives, the other two in the archives of the Portland family. In these lists every peer is entered under one of three heads, For the Repeal of the Test, Against the Repeal, and Doubtful. According to one list the numbers were, 31 for, 86 against, and 20 doubtful; according to another, 33 for, 87 against, and 19 doubtful; according to the third, 35 for, 92 against, and 10 doubtful. Copies of the three lists are among the Mackintosh MSS.

† There is in the British Museum a letter of Dryden to Etherege, dated Feb. 1686. I do not remember to have seen it in print. "Oh," says Dryden, "that our monarch would encourage noble idleness by his own example, as he of blessed memory did before him. For my mind misgives me that he will not much advance his affairs by stirring."

he was perfectly ready to face obloquy and public hatred for lucre. But he had now, by corruption and extortion, accumulated great riches; and he was more anxious to secure them than to increase them. His slackness drew on him a sharp reprimand from the royal lips. In dread of being deprived of the Great Seal, he promised whatever was required of him: but Barillon, in reporting this circumstance to Lewis, remarked that the King of England could place little reliance on any man who had anything to lose.*

James determines to pack a Parliament.

Nevertheless James determined to persevere. The sanction of a Parliament was necessary to his system. The sanction of a free and lawful Parliament it was evidently impossible to obtain: but it might not be altogether impossible to bring together by corruption, by intimidation, by violent exertions of prerogative, by fraudulent distortions of law, an assembly which might call itself a Parliament, and might be willing to register any edict of the Sovereign. Returning officers must be appointed who would avail themselves of the slightest pretence to declare the King's friends duly elected. Every placeman, from the highest to the lowest, must be made to understand that, if he wished to retain his office, he must, at this conjuncture, support the throne by his vote and interest. The High Commission meanwhile would keep its eye on the clergy. The boroughs, which had just been remodelled to serve one turn, might be remodelled again to serve another. By such means the King hoped to obtain a majority in the House of Commons. The Upper House would then be at his mercy. He had undoubtedly by law the power of creating peers without limit; and this power he was fully determined to use. He did not wish, and indeed no sovereign can wish, to make the highest honour which is in the gift of the crown worthless. He cherished the hope that, by calling up some heirs apparent to the assembly in which they must ultimately sit, and by conferring English titles on some Scotch and Irish Lords, he might be able to secure a majority without ennobling new men in such numbers as to bring ridicule on the coronet and the ermine. But there was no extremity to which he was not prepared to go in case of necessity. When in a large company an opinion was expressed that the peers would prove intractable, "Oh, silly," cried Sunderland, turn-

* Barillon, Aug. 5/15. 1687.

ing to Churchill; your troop of guards shall be called up to the House of Lords."*

Having determined to pack a Parliament, James set himself energetically and methodically to the work. A proclamation appeared in the Gazette, announcing that the King had determined to revise the Commissions of Peace and of Lieutenancy, and to retain in public employment only such gentlemen as should be disposed to support his policy.† A committee of seven Privy Councillors sate at Whitehall, for the purpose of regulating,—such was the phrase,—the municipal corporations. In this committee Jeffreys alone represented the Protestant interest. Powis alone represented the moderate Roman Catholics. All the other members belonged to the Jesuitical faction. Among them was Petre, who had just been sworn of the Council. Till he took his seat at the board, his elevation had been kept a profound secret from everybody but Sunderland. The public indignation at this new violation of the law was clamorously expressed; and it was remarked that the Roman Catholics were even louder in censure than the Protestants. The vain and ambitious Jesuit was now charged with the business of destroying and reconstructing half the constituent bodies in the kingdom. Under the Committee of Privy Councillors a subcommittee consisting of bustling agents less eminent in rank was entrusted with the management of details. Local subcommittees of regulators all over the country corresponded with the central board at Westminster.‡

The persons on whom James chiefly relied for assistance in his new and arduous enterprise were the Lords Lieutenants. Every Lord Lieutenant received written orders directing him to go down immediately into his county. There he was to summon before him all his deputies, and all the Justices of the Peace, and to put to them a series of interrogatories framed for the purpose of ascertaining how they would act at a general election. He was to take down the answers in writing, and to transmit them to the government. He was to furnish a list of such Roman Catholics, and such Protestant Dissenters, as might be best qualified for the bench and for commands in the militia. He was also to examine

---

* Told by Lord Bradford who was present, to Dartmouth; note on Barnet, I. 755.
† London Gazette, Dec. 12. 1687.
‡ Roercraan to Seignelay, November 11.; Van Citters, November 11.; Lords' Journals, December 20. 1689.

into the state of all the boroughs in his county, and to make such reports as might be necessary to guide the operations of the board of regulators. It was intimated to him that he must himself perform these duties, and that he could not be permitted to delegate them to any other person.*

Many Lords Lieutenants dismissed.

The first effect produced by these orders would have at once sobered a prince less infatuated than James. Half the Lords Lieutenants of England peremptorily refused to stoop to the odious service which was required of them. They were immediately dismissed. All those who incurred this glorious disgrace were peers of high consideration; and all had hitherto been regarded as firm supporters of monarchy. Some names in the list deserve especial notice.

The Earl of Oxford.

The noblest subject in England, and indeed, as Englishmen loved to say, the noblest subject in Europe, was Aubrey de Vere, twentieth and last of the old Earls of Oxford. He derived his title, through an uninterrupted male descent, from a time when the families of Howard and Seymour were still obscure, when the Nevilles and Percies enjoyed only a provincial celebrity, and when even the great name of Plantagenet had not yet been heard in England. One chief of the house of De Vere had held high command at Hastings; another had marched, with Godfrey and Tancred, over heaps of slaughtered Moslem, to the sepulchre of Christ. The first Earl of Oxford had been minister of Henry Beauclerc. The third Earl had been conspicuous among the Lords who extorted the Great Charter from John. The seventh Earl had fought bravely at Cressy and Poictiers. The thirteenth Earl had, through many vicissitudes of fortune, been the chief of the party of the Red Rose, and had led the van on the decisive day of Bosworth. The seventeenth Earl had shone at the court of Elizabeth, and had won for himself an honourable place among the early masters of English poetry. The nineteenth Earl had fallen in arms for the Protestant religion and for the liberties of Europe under the walls of Maestricht. His son Aubrey, in whom closed the longest and most illustrious line of nobles that England has seen, a man of loose morals, but of inoffensive temper and of courtly manners, was Lord Lieutenant of Essex, and Colonel of the Blues. His nature was not factious; and his interest inclined him to avoid a rupture with the Court; for his estate was encumbered, and his military command lucrative. He was sum-

* Van Citters, Dec. 2/7, 1687.

moned to the royal closet; and an explicit declaration of his intentions was demanded from him. "Sir," answered Oxford, "I will stand by Your Majesty against all enemies to the last drop of my blood. But this is matter of conscience, and I cannot comply." He was instantly deprived of his lieutenancy and of his regiment.*

Inferior in antiquity and splendour to the house of De Vere, but to the house of De Vere alone, was the house of Talbot. Ever since the reign of Edward the Third, the Talbots had sate among the peers of the realm. The earldom of Shrewsbury had been bestowed, in the fifteenth century, on John Talbot, the antagonist of the Maid of Orleans. He had been long remembered by his countrymen with tenderness and reverence as one of the most illustrious of those warriors who had striven to erect a great English empire on the Continent of Europe. The stubborn courage which he had shown in the midst of disasters had made him an object of interest greater than more fortunate captains had inspired; and his death had furnished a singularly touching scene to our early stage. His posterity had, during two centuries, flourished in great honour. The head of the family at the time of the Restoration was Francis, the eleventh Earl, a Roman Catholic. His death had been attended by circumstances such as, even in those licentious times which immediately followed the downfall of the Puritan tyranny, had moved men to horror and pity. The Duke of Buckingham in the course of his vagrant amours was for a moment attracted by the Countess of Shrewsbury. She was easily won. Her Lord challenged the gallant and fell. Some said that the abandoned woman witnessed the combat in man's attire, and others that she clasped her victorious lover to her bosom while his shirt was still dripping with the blood of her husband. The honours of the murdered man descended to his infant son Charles. As the orphan grew up to man's estate, it was generally acknowledged that of the young nobility of England none had been so richly gifted by nature. His person was pleasing, his temper singularly sweet, his parts such as, if he had been born in a humble rank, might well have raised him to civil greatness. All these advantages

CHAP. VIII.

The Earl of Shrewsbury.

* Halstead's Succinct Genealogy of the Family of Vere, 1685; Collins's Historical Collections. See in the Lords' Journals, and in Jones's Reports, the proceedings respecting the earldom of Oxford, in March and April 1625. The exordium of the speech of Lord Chief Justice Crewe is among the finest specimens of the ancient English eloquence. Van Citters, Feb. 4/14. 1686.

he had so improved that, before he was of age, he was allowed to be one of the finest gentlemen and finest scholars of his time. His learning is proved by notes which are still extant in his handwriting on books in almost every department of literature. He spoke French like a gentleman of Lewis's bedchamber, and Italian like a citizen of Florence. It was impossible that a youth of such parts should not be anxious to understand the grounds on which his family had refused to conform to the religion of the state. He studied the disputed points closely, submitted his doubts to priests of his own faith, laid their answers before Tillotson, weighed the arguments on both sides long and attentively, and, after an investigation which occupied two years, declared himself a Protestant. The Church of England welcomed the illustrious convert with delight. His popularity was great, and became greater when it was known that royal solicitations and promises had been vainly employed to seduce him back to the superstition which he had abjured. The character of the young Earl did not however develope itself in a manner quite satisfactory to those who had borne the chief part in his conversion. His morals by no means escaped the contagion of fashionable libertinism. In truth the shock which had overturned his early prejudices had at the same time unfixed all his opinions, and left him to the unchecked guidance of his feelings. But, though his principles were unsteady, his impulses were so generous, his temper so bland, his manners so gracious and easy, that it was impossible not to love him. He was early called the King of Hearts, and never, through a long, eventful, and chequered life, lost his right to that name.*

Shrewsbury was Lord Lieutenant of Staffordshire and Colonel of one of the regiments of horse which had been raised in consequence of the Western insurrection. He now refused to act under the board of regulators, and was deprived of both his commissions.

The Earl of Dorset.

None of the English nobles enjoyed a larger measure of public favour than Charles Sackville Earl of Dorset. He was indeed a remarkable man. In his youth he had been one of the most notorious libertines of the wild time which followed

* Coxe's Shrewsbury Correspondence; Mackay's Memoirs; Life of Charles Duke of Shrewsbury, 1718; Dorset, i. 752.; Birch's Life of Tillotson, where the reader will find a letter from Tillotson to Shrewsbury, which seems to me a model of serious, friendly, and gentlemanlike reproof.

the Restoration. He had been the terror of the City watch, had passed many nights in the round house, and had at least once occupied a cell in Newgate. His passion for Betty Morrice, and for Nell Gwynn, who called him her Charles the First, had given no small amusement and scandal to the town.* Yet, in the midst of follies and vices, his courageous spirit, his fine understanding, and his natural goodness of heart, had been conspicuous. Men said that the excesses in which he indulged were common between him and the whole race of gay young Cavaliers, but that his sympathy with human suffering, and the generosity with which he made reparation to those whom his freaks had injured, were all his own. His associates were astonished by the distinction which the public made between him and them. "He may do what he chooses," said Wilmot; "he is never in the wrong." The judgment of the world became still more favourable to Dorset when he had been sobered by time and marriage. His graceful manners, his brilliant conversation, his soft heart, his open hand, were universally praised. No day passed, it was said, in which some distressed family had not reason to bless his name. And yet, with all his goodnature, such was the keenness of his wit that scoffers whose sarcasm all the town feared stood in craven fear of the sarcasm of Dorset. All political parties esteemed and caressed him: but politics were not much to his taste. Had he been driven by necessity to exert himself, he would probably have risen to the highest posts in the state: but he was born to rank so high and wealth so ample that many of the motives which impel men to engage in public affairs were wanting to him. He took just so much part in parliamentary and diplomatic business as sufficed to show that he wanted nothing but inclination to rival Danby and Sunderland, and turned away to pursuits which pleased him better. Like many other men who, with great natural abilities, are constitutionally and habitually indolent, he became an intellectual voluptuary, and a master of all those pleasing branches of knowledge which can be acquired without severe application. He was allowed to be the best judge of painting, of sculpture, of architecture, of acting, that the court could show. On questions of polite

* The King was only Nell's Charles III. Whether Dorset or Major Charles Hart had the honour of being her Charles I. is a point open to dispute. But the evidence in favour of Dorset's claim seems to me to preponderate. See the suppressed passage of Burnet, i. 263., and Pepys's Diary, Oct. 26. 1667.

learning his decisions were regarded at all the coffeehouses as without appeal. More than one clever play which had failed on the first representation was supported by his single authority against the whole clamour of the pit, and came forth successful from the second trial. The delicacy of his taste in French composition was extolled by Saint Evremond and La Fontaine. Such a patron of letters England had never seen. His bounty was bestowed with equal judgment and liberality, and was confined to no sect or faction. Men of genius, estranged from each other by literary jealousy or by difference of political opinion, joined in acknowledging his impartial kindness. Dryden owned that he had been saved from ruin by Dorset's princely generosity. Yet Montague and Prior, who had keenly satirised Dryden, were introduced by Dorset into public life; and the best comedy of Dryden's mortal enemy, Shadwell, was written at Dorset's country seat. The munificent Earl might, if such had been his wish, have been the rival of those of whom he was content to be the benefactor. For the verses which he occasionally composed, unstudied as they are, exhibit the traces of a genius which, assiduously cultivated, would have produced something great. In the small volume of his works may be found songs which have the easy vigour of Suckling, and little satires which sparkle with wit as splendid as that of Butler.*

Dorset was Lord Lieutenant of Sussex; and to Sussex the board of regulators looked with great anxiety: for in no other county, Cornwall and Wiltshire excepted, were there so many small boroughs. He was ordered to repair to his post. No person who knew him expected that he would obey. He gave such an answer as became him, and was informed that his services were no longer needed. The interest which his many noble and amiable qualities inspired was heightened when it was known that he had received by the post an anonymous billet telling him that, if he did not promptly comply with

* Pepys's Diary; Prior's Dedication of his Poems to the Duke of Dorset; Johnson's Life of Dorset; Dryden's Essay on Satire and Dedication of the Essay on Dramatic Poesy. The affection of Dorset for his wife and his strict fidelity to her are mentioned with great contempt by that prodigate coxcomb Sir George Etherege in his letters from Ratisbon, December 1/11, 1687, and January 17/27, 1688.

See also Shadwell's Dedication of the Squire of Alsatia; Burnet, i. 264.; Mackay's Characters. Some parts of Dorset's character are well touched in his epitaph, written by Pope:
" Yet soft his nature, though severe his lay;"
and again :
" Blest courtier, who could King and country please,
Yet sacred keep his friendships and his ease."

the King's wishes, all his wit and popularity should not save him from assassination. A similar warning was sent to Shrewsbury. Threatening letters were then much more rare than they afterwards became. It is therefore not strange that the people, excited as they were, should have been disposed to believe that the best and noblest Englishmen were really marked out for Popish daggers.* Just when these letters were the talk of all London, the mutilated corpse of a noted Puritan was found in the streets. It was soon discovered that the murderer had acted from no religious or political motive. But the first suspicions of the populace fell on the Papists. The mangled remains were carried in procession to the house of the Jesuits in the Savoy; and during a few hours the fear and rage of the populace were scarcely less violent than on the day when Godfrey was borne to the grave.†

The other dismissions must be more concisely related. The Duke of Somerset, whose regiment had been taken from him some months before, was now turned out of the lord lieutenancy of the East Riding of Yorkshire. The North Riding was taken from Viscount Fauconberg, Shropshire from Viscount Newport, and Lancashire from the Earl of Derby, grandson of that gallant Cavalier who had faced death so bravely, both on the field of battle and on the scaffold, for the House of Stuart. The Earl of Pembroke, who had recently served the Crown with fidelity and spirit against Monmouth, was displaced in Wiltshire, the Earl of Rutland in Leicestershire, the Earl of Bridgewater in Buckinghamshire, the Earl of Thanet in Cumberland, the Earl of Northampton in Warwickshire, the Earl of Abingdon in Oxfordshire, and the Earl of Scarsdale in Derbyshire. Scarsdale was also deprived of a regiment of cavalry, and of an office in the household of the Princess of Denmark. She made a struggle to retain his services, and yielded only to a peremptory command of her father. The Earl of Gainsborough was ejected, not only from the lieutenancy of Hampshire, but also from the government of Portsmouth and the rangership of the New Forest, two places for which he had, only a few months before, given five thousand pounds.‡

The King could not find Lords of great note, or indeed

* Barillon, Jan. 3/13. 1688; Van Citters, Jan. 3/13.
† Adda, Feb. 7/17. 1688.
‡ Barillon, Dec. 5/15. 12/22. 1687; Van Citters, Dec. 2/12. 9/19. Dec. 5/15.

Protestant Lords of any sort, who would accept the vacant offices. It was necessary to assign two shires to Jeffreys, a new man whose landed property was small, and two to Preston who was not even an English peer. The other counties which had been left without governors were entrusted, with scarcely an exception, to known Roman Catholics, or to courtiers who had secretly promised the King to declare themselves Roman Catholics as soon as they could do so with prudence.

At length the new machinery was put in action; and soon from every corner of the realm arrived the news of complete and hopeless failure. The catechism by which the Lords Lieutenants had been directed to test the sentiments of the country gentlemen consisted of three questions. Every magistrate and Deputy Lieutenant was to be asked, first, whether, if he should be chosen to serve in Parliament, he would vote for a bill framed on the principles of the Declaration of Indulgence; secondly, whether, as an elector, he would support candidates who would engage to vote for such a bill; and, thirdly, whether, in his private capacity, he would aid the King's benevolent designs by living in friendship with people of all religious persuasions.*

As soon as the questions got abroad, a form of answer, drawn up with admirable skill, was circulated all over the kingdom, and was generally adopted. It was to the following effect: "As a member of the House of Commons, should I have the honour of a seat there, I shall think it my duty carefully to weigh such reasons as may be adduced in debate for and against a Bill of Indulgence, and then to vote according to my conscientious conviction. As an elector, I shall give my support to candidates whose notions of the duty of a representative agree with my own. As a private man, it is my wish to live in peace and charity with every body." This answer, far more provoking than a direct refusal, because slightly tinged with a sober and decorous irony which could not well be resented, was all that the emissaries of the Court could extract from most of the country gentlemen. Arguments, promises, threats, were tried in vain. The Duke of Norfolk, though a Protestant, and though dissatisfied with the proceedings of the government, had consented to become its agent in two counties. He went first to Surrey, where he

* Van Citters, Dec. 7, 1687.; Lonsdale's Memoirs.

soon found that nothing could be done.* He then repaired to Norfolk, and returned to inform the King that, of seventy gentlemen who bore office in that great province, only six had held out hopes that they should support the policy of the Court.† The Duke of Beaufort, whose authority extended over four English shires and over the whole principality of Wales, came up to Whitehall with an account not less discouraging.‡ Rochester was Lord Lieutenant of Hertfordshire. All his little stock of virtue had been expended in his struggle against the strong temptation to sell his religion for lucre. He was still bound to the Court by a pension of four thousand pounds a year; and in return for this pension he was willing to perform any service, however illegal or degrading, provided only that he were not required to go through the forms of a reconciliation with Rome. He had readily undertaken to manage his county; and he exerted himself, as usual, with indiscreet heat and violence. But his anger was thrown away on the sturdy squires to whom he addressed himself. They told him with one voice that they would send up no man to Parliament who would vote for taking away the safeguards of the Protestant religion.§ The same answer was given to the Chancellor in Buckinghamshire.|| The gentry of Shropshire, assembled at Ludlow, unanimously refused to fetter themselves by the pledge which the King demanded of them.¶ The Earl of Yarmouth reported from Wiltshire that, of sixty magistrates and Deputy Lieutenants with whom he had conferred, only seven had given favourable answers, and that even those seven could not be trusted.** The renegade Peterborough made no progress in Northamptonshire.†† His brother renegade Dover was equally unsuccessful in Cambridgeshire.‡‡ Preston brought cold news from Cumberland and Westmoreland. Dorsetshire and Huntingdonshire were animated by the same spirit. The Earl of Bath, after a long canvass, returned from the West with gloomy tidings. He had been authorised to make the most tempting offers to the inhabitants of that region. In particular he had promised that, if proper respect

CHAP. VIII.

* Van Citters, $\frac{Nov.}{Dec.}\frac{11}{1}$ 1687.
† Ibid. $\frac{Dec. 17}{27}$ 1687.
‡ Ibid.
§ Rochester's offensive warmth on this occasion is twice noticed by Johnstone, November 25. and December 9. 1687. His failure is mentioned by Van Citters, December $\frac{9}{19}$.
|| Van Citters, Dec. $\frac{9}{19}$. 1687.
¶ Ibid. Dec. $\frac{13}{23}$ 1687.
** Ibid. $\frac{Nov. 25}{Dec. 5}$ 1687.
†† Ibid. $\frac{Dec. 2}{12}$ 1687.
‡‡ Ibid. Nov. $\frac{14}{24}$ 1687.

were shown to the royal wishes, the trade in tin should be freed from the oppressive restrictions under which it lay. But this lure, which at another time would have proved irresistible, was now slighted. All the Justices and Deputy Lieutenants of Devonshire and Cornwall, without a single dissenting voice, declared that they would put life and property in jeopardy for the King, but that the Protestant religion was dearer to them than either life or property. "And, sir," said Bath, "if Your Majesty should dismiss all these gentlemen, their successors would give exactly the same answer."* If there was any district in which the government might have hoped for success, that district was Lancashire. Considerable doubts had been felt as to the result of what was passing there. In no part of the realm had so many opulent and honourable families adhered to the old religion. The heads of many of those families had already, by virtue of the dispensing power, been made Justices of the Peace and entrusted with commands in the militia. Yet from Lancashire the new Lord Lieutenant, himself a Roman Catholic, reported that two thirds of his deputies and of the magistrates were opposed to the Court.† But the proceedings in Hampshire wounded the King's pride still more deeply. Arabella Churchill had, more than twenty years before, borne him a son, widely renowned, at a later period, as one of the most skilful captains of Europe. The youth, named James Fitzjames, had as yet given no promise of the eminence which he afterwards attained: but his manners were so gentle and inoffensive that he had no enemy except Mary of Modena, who had long hated the child of the concubine with the bitter hatred of a childless wife. A small part of the Jesuitical faction had, before the pregnancy of the Queen was announced, seriously thought of setting him up as a competitor of the Princess of Orange.‡ When it is remembered how signally Monmouth, though believed by the populace to be legitimate, and though the champion of the national religion, had failed in a similar competition, it must seem extraordinary that any man should have been so much blinded by fanaticism as to think of placing on the throne one who was universally known to be a Popish bastard. It does not appear that this absurd design was ever counte-

---

* Van Citters, April 1⁰. 1688.
† The anxiety about Lancashire is mentioned by Van Citters, in a despatch dated Nov. 1⁰. 1687; the result in a despatch dated four days later.
‡ Bonrepaux, July 1⁰. 1687.

nanced by the King. The boy, however, was acknowledged; and whatever distinctions a subject, not of the royal blood, could hope to attain were bestowed on him. He had been created Duke of Berwick; and he was now loaded with honourable and lucrative employments, taken from those noblemen who had refused to comply with the royal commands. He succeeded the Earl of Oxford as Colonel of the Blues, and the Earl of Gainsborough as Lord Lieutenant of Hampshire, Ranger of the New Forest, and Governor of Portsmouth. On the frontier of Hampshire Berwick expected to have been met, according to custom, by a long cavalcade of baronets, knights, and squires: but not a single person of note appeared to welcome him. He sent out letters commanding the attendance of the gentry: but only five or six paid the smallest attention to his summons. The rest did not wait to be dismissed. They declared that they would take no part in the civil or military government of their county while the King was represented there by a Papist, and voluntarily laid down their commissions.*

Sunderland, who had been named Lord Lieutenant of Warwickshire in the room of the Earl of Northampton, found some excuse for not going down to face the indignation and contempt of the gentry of that shire; and his plea was the more readily admitted because the King had, by that time, begun to feel that the spirit of the rustic gentry was not to be bent.†

It is to be observed that those who displayed this spirit were not the old enemies of the House of Stuart. The Commissions of Peace and Lieutenancy had long been carefully purged of all republican names. The persons from whom the Court had in vain attempted to extract any promise of support were, with scarcely an exception, Tories. The elder among them could still show scars given by the swords of Roundheads, and receipts for plate sent to Charles the First in his distress. The younger had adhered firmly to James against Shaftesbury and Monmouth. Such were the men who were now turned out of office in a mass by the very prince to whom they had given such signal proofs of fidelity. Dismission however only made them more resolute. It had become a sacred point of honour among them to stand stoutly by one another in this crisis. There could be no doubt that, if the suffrage of the freeholders

* Van Citters. Feb. 4/14. 1688.   † Ibid. April 1/11. 1688.

were fairly taken, not a single knight of the shire favourable to the policy of the government would be returned. Men therefore asked one another, with no small anxiety, whether the suffrages were likely to be fairly taken. The list of the Sheriffs for the new year was impatiently expected. It appeared while the Lord Lieutenants were still engaged in their canvass, and was received with a general cry of alarm and indignation. Most of the functionaries who were to preside at the county elections were either Roman Catholics or Protestant Dissenters who had expressed their approbation of the Indulgence.* For a time the most gloomy apprehensions prevailed: but soon they began to subside. There was good reason to believe that there was a point beyond which the King could not reckon on the support even of those Sheriffs who were members of his own Church. Between the Roman Catholic courtier and the Roman Catholic country gentleman there was very little sympathy. That cabal which domineered at Whitehall consisted partly of fanatics, who were ready to break through all rules of morality and to throw the world into confusion for the purpose of propagating their religion, and partly of hypocrites who, for lucre, had apostatised from the faith in which they had been brought up, and who now overacted the zeal characteristic of neophytes. Both the fanatical and the hypocritical courtiers were generally destitute of all English feeling. In some of them devotion to their Church had extinguished every national sentiment. Some were Irishmen, whose patriotism consisted in mortal hatred of the Saxon conquerors of Ireland. Some, again, were traitors, who received regular hire from a foreign power. Some had passed a great part of their lives abroad, and either were mere cosmopolites, or felt a positive distaste for the manners and institutions of the the country which was now subjected to their rule. Between such men and the lord of a Cheshire or Staffordshire manor who adhered to the old Church there was scarcely anything in common. He was neither a fanatic nor a hypocrite. He was a Roman Catholic because his father and grandfather had been so; and he held his hereditary faith, as men generally hold a hereditary faith, sincerely, but with little enthusiasm. In all other points he was a mere English squire, and, if he differed from the neighbouring squires, differed from them by being somewhat more simple and clownish

* London Gazette, Dec. 5. 1687; Van Citters, Dec. 5/15.

than they. The disabilities under which he lay had prevented his mind from expanding to the standard, moderate as that standard was, which the minds of Protestant country gentlemen then ordinarily attained. Excluded, when a boy, from Eton and Westminster, when a youth, from Oxford and Cambridge, when a man, from Parliament and from the bench of justice, he generally vegetated as quietly as the elms of the avenue which led to his ancestral grange. His cornfields, his dairy, and his cider press, his greyhounds, his fishing rod, and his gun, his ale and his tobacco, occupied almost all his thoughts. With his neighbours, in spite of his religion, he was generally on good terms. They knew him to be unambitious and inoffensive. He was almost always of a good old family. He was always a Cavalier. His peculiar notions were not obtruded, and caused no annoyance. He did not, like a Puritan, torment himself and others with scruples about everything that was pleasant. On the contrary, he was as keen a sportsman, and as jolly a boon companion, as any man who had taken the oath of supremacy and the declaration against transubstantiation. He met his brother squires at the cover, was in with them at the death, and, when the sport was over, took them home with him to a venison pasty and to October four years in bottle. The oppressions which he had undergone had not been such as to impel him to any desperate resolution. Even when his Church was barbarously persecuted, his life and property were in little danger. The most impudent false witnesses could hardly venture to shock the common sense of mankind by accusing him of being a conspirator. The Papists whom Oates selected for attack were peers, prelates, Jesuits, Benedictines, a busy political agent, a lawyer in high practice. The Roman Catholic country gentleman, protected by his obscurity, by his peaceable demeanour, and by the good will of those among whom he lived, carted his hay or filled his bag with game unmolested, while Coleman and Langhorne, Whitbread and Pickering, Archbishop Plunkett and Lord Stafford, died by the halter or the axe. An attempt was indeed made by a knot of villains to bring home a charge of treason to Sir Thomas Gascoigne, an aged Roman Catholic baronet of Yorkshire: but twelve gentlemen of the West Riding, who knew his way of life, could not be convinced that their honest old acquaintance had hired cutthroats to murder the King, and, in spite of charges which did very

CHAP. VIII.

little honour to the bench, found a verdict of Not Guilty. Sometimes, indeed, the head of an old and respectable provincial family might reflect with bitterness that he was excluded, on account of his religion, from places of honour and authority which men of humbler descent and less ample estate were thought competent to fill: but he was little disposed to risk land and life in a struggle against overwhelming odds; and his honest English spirit would have shrunk with horror from means such as were contemplated by the Petres and Tyrconnels. Indeed he would have been as ready as any of his Protestant neighbours to gird on his sword, and to put pistols in his holsters, for the defence of his native land against an invasion of French or Irish Papists. Such was the general character of the men to whom James now looked as to his most trustworthy instruments for the conduct of county elections. He soon found that they were not inclined to throw away the esteem of their neighbours, and to endanger their heads and their estates, by rendering him an infamous and criminal service. Several of them refused to be Sheriffs. Of those who accepted the shrievalty many declared that they would discharge their duty as fairly as if they were members of the Established Church, and would return no candidate who had not a real majority.*

Feeling of the Dissenters.

If the King could place little confidence even in his Roman Catholic Sheriffs, still less could he rely on the Puritans. Since the publication of the Declaration several months had elapsed, months crowded with important events, months of unintermitted controversy. Discussion had opened the eyes of many Dissenters; but the acts of the government, and especially the severity with which Magdalene College had been treated, had done more than even the pen of Halifax to alarm and to unite all classes of Protestants. Most of those sectaries who had been induced to express gratitude for the Indulgence were now ashamed of their error, and were desirous of making atonement by casting in their lot with the great body of their countrymen.

CHAP. VIII.

In consequence of this change in the feeling of the Nonconformists, the government found almost as great difficulty in the towns as in the counties. When the regulators began their work, they had taken it for granted that every Dissenter who had availed himself of the Indulgence would be favourable to the King's policy. They were therefore confident that they should be able to fill all the municipal offices in the kingdom with staunch friends. In the new charters a power had been reserved to the crown of dismissing magistrates at pleasure. This power was now exercised without limit. It was by no means equally clear that James had the power of appointing magistrates: but, whether it belonged to him or not, he determined to assume it. Everywhere, from the Tweed to the Land's End, Tory functionaries were ejected; and the vacant places were filled with Presbyterians, Independents, and Baptists. In the new charter of the City of London the crown had reserved the power of displacing the Masters, Wardens, and Assistants of all the companies. Accordingly more than eight hundred citizens of the first consideration, all of them members of that party which had opposed the Exclusion Bill, were turned out of office by a single edict. In a short time appeared a supplement to this long list.* But scarcely had the new officebearers been sworn in when it was discovered that they were as unmanageable as their predecessors. At Newcastle on Tyne the regulators appointed a Roman Catholic Mayor and Puritan Aldermen. No doubt was entertained that the municipal body, thus remodelled, would vote an address promising to support the King's measures. The address, however, was negatived. The Mayor went up to London in a fury, and told the King that the Dissenters were all knaves and rebels, and that in the whole corporation the government could not reckon on more than four votes.† At Reading

Regulation of corporations.

* Privy Council Book, Sept. 25. 1687; Feb. 21. 1688].
in Brand's History of Newcastle; Johnstone, Feb. 21. 1687.
† Records of the Corporation, quoted

twenty-four Tory Aldermen were dismissed. Twenty-four new Aldermen were appointed. Twenty-three of these immediately declared against the Indulgence, and were dismissed in their turn.* In the course of a few days the borough of Yarmouth was governed by three different sets of magistrates, all equally hostile to the Court.† These are mere examples of what was passing all over the kingdom. The Dutch Ambassador informed the States that in many towns the public functionaries had, within one month, been changed twice, and even thrice, and yet changed in vain.‡ From the records of the Privy Council it appears that the number of regulations, as they were called, exceeded two hundred.§ The regulators indeed found that, in not a few places, the change had been for the worse. The discontented Tories, even while murmuring against the King's policy, had constantly expressed respect for his person and his office, and had disclaimed all thought of resistance. Very different was the language of some of the new members of corporations. It was said that old soldiers of the Commonwealth, who, to their own astonishment and that of the public, had been made Aldermen, gave the agents of the Court very distinctly to understand that blood should flow before Popery and arbitrary power were established in England.‖

The regulators found that little or nothing had been gained by what had as yet been done. There was one way, and one way only, in which they could hope to effect their object. The charters of the boroughs must be resumed; and other charters must be granted confining the elective franchise to very small constituent bodies appointed by the sovereign.¶

But how was this plan to be carried into effect? In a few of the new charters, indeed, a right of revocation had been reserved to the crown: but the rest James could get into his hands only by voluntary surrender on the part of corporations, or by judgment of a court of law. Few corporations were now disposed to surrender their charters voluntarily; and such judgments as would suit the purposes of the government were hardly to be expected even from such a slave as Wright. The writs of Quo Warranto which had been brought a few years before for the purpose of crushing the Whig party had been

* Johnstone, Feb. 21. 168].
† Van Citters, Feb. 14. 1688.
‡ Ibid. May 4. 1688.
§ In the margin of the Privy Council Book may be observed the words "Second Regulation," and "Third Regulation," when a corporation had been remodelled more than once.
‖ Johnstone, May 25. 1688.
¶ Ibid. Feb. 21. 1688.

condemned by every impartial man. Yet those writs had at least the semblance of justice; for they were brought against ancient municipal bodies, and there were few ancient municipal bodies in which some abuse, sufficient to afford a pretext for a penal proceeding, had not grown up in the course of ages. But the corporations now to be attacked were still in the innocence of infancy. The oldest among them had not completed its fifth year. It was impossible that many of them should have committed offences meriting disfranchisement. The Judges themselves were uneasy. They represented that what they were required to do was in direct opposition to the plainest principles of law and justice: but all remonstrance was vain. The boroughs were commanded to surrender their charters. Few complied; and the course which the King took with those few did not encourage others to trust him. In several towns the right of voting was taken away from the commonalty, and given to a very small number of persons, who were required to bind themselves by oath to support the candidates recommended by the government. At Tewkesbury, for example, the franchise was confined to thirteen persons. Yet even this number was too large. Hatred and fear had spread so widely through the community that it was scarcely possible to bring together in any town, by any process of packing, thirteen men on whom the Court could absolutely depend. It was rumoured that the majority of the new constituent body of Tewkesbury was animated by the same sentiment which was general throughout the nation, and would, when the decisive day should arrive, send true Protestants to Parliament. The regulators in great wrath threatened to reduce the number of electors to three.* Meanwhile the great majority of the boroughs firmly refused to give up their privileges. Barnstaple, Winchester, and Buckingham, distinguished themselves by the boldness of their opposition. At Oxford the motion that the city should resign its franchises to the King was negatived by eighty votes to two.† The Temple and Westminster Hall were in a ferment with the sudden rush of business from all corners of the kingdom. Every lawyer in high practice was overwhelmed with the briefs from corporations. Ordinary litigants complained that their business was neglected.‡ It was evident that a considerable time must elapse before judgment could be given in so great a number of important cases. Tyranny could ill

* Johnstone, Feb. 21. 1686. ‡ Van Citters, May 4/14. 1688.
† Van Citters, March 5/15. 1688.

brook this delay. Nothing was omitted which could terrify the refractory boroughs into submission. At Buckingham some of the municipal officers had spoken of Jeffreys in language which was not laudatory. They were prosecuted, and were given to understand that no mercy should be shown to them unless they would ransom themselves by surrendering their charter.* At Winchester still more violent measures were adopted. A large body of troops was marched into the town for the sole purpose of burdening and harassing the inhabitants.† The town continued resolute; and the public voice loudly accused the King of imitating the worst crimes of his brother of France. The dragonades, it was said, had begun. There was indeed reason for alarm. It had occurred to James that he could not more effectually break the spirit of an obstinate town than by quartering soldiers on the inhabitants. He must have known that this practice had sixty years before excited formidable discontents, and had been solemnly pronounced illegal by the Petition of Right, a statute scarcely less venerated by Englishmen than the Great Charter. But he hoped to obtain from the courts of law a declaration that even the Petition of Right could not control the prerogative. He actually consulted the Chief Justice of the King's Bench on this subject‡: but the result of the consultation remained secret; and in a very few weeks the aspect of affairs became such that a fear stronger than the fear of the royal displeasure began to impose some restraint even on the most servile magistrates.

Inquisition in all the public departments

While the Lords Lieutenants were questioning the Justices of the Peace, while the regulators were remodelling the boroughs, all the public departments were subjected to a strict inquisition. The palace was first purified. Every battered old Cavalier, who, in return for blood and lands lost in the royal cause, had obtained some small place under the Keeper of the Wardrobe or the Master of the Harriers, was called upon to choose between the King and the Church. The Commissioners of Customs and Excise were ordered to attend His Majesty at the Treasury. There he demanded from them a promise to support his policy, and directed them to require a similar promise from all their subordinates.§ One Custom-house officer notified his submission to the royal will in a way

* Van Citters, May 7/17, 1688.
† Ibid. May 4/14, 1688.
‡ Ibid. May 25/June 4, 1688.

§ Van Citters, April 3/13, 1688; Treasury Letter Book, March 14, 1688; Ronquillo, April 16/26.

which excited both merriment and compassion. "I have," he said, "fourteen reasons for obeying His Majesty's commands, a wife and thirteen young children."* Such reasons were indeed cogent; yet there were not a few instances in which, even against such reasons, religious and patriotic feelings prevailed.

There is ground to believe that the government at this time seriously meditated a blow which would have reduced many thousands of families to beggary, and would have disturbed the whole social system of every part of the country. No wine, beer, or coffee could be sold without a license. It was rumoured that every person holding such a license would shortly be required to enter into the same engagements which had been imposed on public functionaries, or to relinquish his trade.† It seems certain that, if such a step had been taken, the houses of entertainment and of public resort all over the kingdom would have been at once shut up by hundreds. What effect such an interference with the comfort of all ranks would have produced must be left to conjecture. The resentment excited by grievances is not always proportioned to their dignity; and it is by no means improbable that the resumption of licenses might have done what the resumption of charters had failed to do. Men of fashion would have missed the chocolate house in Saint James's Street, and men of business the coffee pot, round which they were accustomed to smoke and talk politics, in Change Alley. Half the clubs would have been wandering in search of shelter. The traveller at nightfall would have found the inn where he had expected to sup and lodge deserted. The clown would have regretted the hedge alehouse, where he had been accustomed to take his pot on the bench before the door in summer, and at the chimney corner in winter. The nation might, perhaps, on such provocation, have risen in general rebellion without waiting for the help of foreign allies.

It was not to be expected that a prince who required all the humblest servants of the government to support his policy on pain of dismission would continue to employ an Attorney General whose aversion to that policy was no secret. Sawyer had been suffered to retain his situation more than a year and a half after he had declared against the dispensing power. This extraordinary indulgence he owed to the extreme difficulty which the government found in supplying his place. It

CHAP. VIII.

Dismission of Sawyer.

* Van Citters, May 13. 1688.   † Ibid. May 13. 1688.

CHAP. VIII.

was necessary for the protection of the pecuniary interests of the crown, that at least one of the two chief law officers should be a man of ability and knowledge; and it was by no means easy to induce any barrister of ability and knowledge to put himself in peril by committing every day acts which the next Parliament would probably treat as high crimes and misdemeanours. It had been impossible to procure a better Solicitor General than Powis, a man who indeed stuck at nothing, but who was incompetent to perform the ordinary duties of his post. In these circumstances it was thought desirable that there should be a division of labour. An Attorney, the value of whose professional talents was much diminished by his conscientious scruples, was coupled with a Solicitor whose want of scruples made some amends for his want of talents. When the government wished to enforce the law, recourse was had to Sawyer. When the government wished to break the law, recourse was had to Powis. This arrangement lasted till the King was able to obtain the services of an advocate at once baser than Powis and abler than Sawyer.

Williams Solicitor General.

No barrister living had opposed the Court with more virulence than William Williams. He had distinguished himself in the late reign as a Whig and an Exclusionist. When faction was at the height, he had been chosen Speaker of the House of Commons. After the prorogation of the Oxford Parliament he had commonly been counsel for the most noisy demagogues who had been accused of sedition. He was allowed to possess both parts and learning. His chief faults were supposed to be rashness and party spirit. It was not yet suspected that he had faults compared with which rashness and party spirit might well pass for virtues. The government sought occasion against him, and easily found it. He had published, by order of the House of Commons, a narrative which Dangerfield had written. This narrative, if published by a private man, would undoubtedly have been a seditious libel. A criminal information was filed in the King's Bench against Williams: he pleaded the privileges of Parliament in vain: he was convicted and sentenced to a fine of ten thousand pounds. A large part of this sum he actually paid: for the rest he gave a bond. The Earl of Peterborough, who had been injuriously mentioned in Dangerfield's narrative, was encouraged, by the success of the criminal information, to bring a civil action, and to demand large damages.

Williams was driven to extremity. At this juncture a way of escape presented itself. It was indeed a way which, to a man of strong principles or high spirit, would have been more dreadful than beggary, imprisonment, or death. He might sell himself to that government of which he had been the enemy and the victim. He might offer to go on the forlorn hope in every assault on those liberties and on that religion for which he had professed an inordinate zeal. He might expiate his Whiggism by performing services from which bigoted Tories, stained with the blood of Russell and Sidney, shrank in horror. The bargain was struck. The debt still due to the crown was remitted. Peterborough was induced, by royal mediation, to compromise his action. Sawyer was dismissed. Powis became Attorney General. Williams was made Solicitor, received the honour of knighthood, and was soon a favourite. Though in rank he was only the second law officer of the crown, his abilities, knowledge, and energy were such that he completely threw his superior into the shade.*

Williams had not been long in office when he was required to bear a chief part in the most memorable state trial recorded in the British annals.

On the twenty-seventh of April 1688, the King put forth a second Declaration of Indulgence. In this paper he recited at length the Declaration of the preceding April. His past life, he said, ought to have convinced his people that he was not a person who could easily be induced to depart from any resolution which he had formed. But, as designing men had attempted to persuade the world that he might be prevailed on to give way in this matter, he thought it necessary to proclaim that his purpose was immutably fixed, that he was resolved to employ those only who were prepared to concur in his design, and that he had, in pursuance of that resolution, dismissed many of his disobedient servants from civil and military employments. He announced that he meant to hold a Parliament in November at the latest; and he exhorted his subjects to choose representatives who would assist him in the great work which he had undertaken.†

CHAP. VIII.

The clergy ordered to read it.

This Declaration at first produced little sensation. It contained nothing new; and men wondered that the King should think it worth while to publish a solemn manifesto merely for the purpose of telling them that he had not changed his mind.* Perhaps James was nettled by the indifference with which the announcement of his fixed resolution was received by the public, and thought that his dignity and authority would suffer unless he without delay did something novel and striking. On the fourth of May, accordingly, he made an Order in Council that his Declaration of the preceding week should be read, on two successive Sundays, at the time of divine service, by the officiating ministers of all the churches and chapels of the kingdom. In London and in the suburbs the reading was to take place on the twentieth and twenty-seventh of May, in other parts of England on the third and tenth of June. The Bishops were directed to distribute copies of the Declaration through their respective dioceses.†

When it is considered that the clergy of the Established Church, with scarcely an exception, regarded the Indulgence as a violation of the laws of the realm, as a breach of the plighted faith of the King, and as a fatal blow levelled at the interest and dignity of their own profession, it will scarcely admit of doubt that the Order in Council was intended to be felt by them as a cruel affront. It was popularly believed that Petre had avowed this intention in a coarse metaphor borrowed from the rhetoric of the East. He would, he said, make them eat dirt, the vilest and most loathsome of all dirt. But, tyrannical and malignant as the mandate was, would the Anglican priesthood refuse to obey? The King's temper was arbitrary and severe. The proceedings of the Ecclesiastical Commission were as summary as those of a court martial. Whoever ventured to resist might in a week be ejected from his parsonage, deprived of his whole income, pronounced incapable of holding any other spiritual preferment, and left to beg from door to door. If, indeed, the whole body offered an united opposition to the royal will, it was probable that even James would scarcely venture to punish ten thousand delinquents at once. But there was not time to form an extensive combination. The Order in Council was gazetted on the seventh of May. On the twentieth the Declaration was to be read in all the pulpits of

* Van Citters, May 14. 1688.   † London Gazette, May 7. 1688.

London and the neighbourhood. By no exertion was it possible in that age to ascertain within a fortnight the intentions of one tenth part of the parochial ministers who were scattered over the kingdom. It was not easy to collect in so short a time the sense even of the episcopal order. It might also well be apprehended that, if the clergy refused to read the Declaration, the Protestant Dissenters would misinterpret the refusal, would despair of obtaining any toleration from the members of the Church of England, and would throw their whole weight into the scale of the Court.

CHAP. VIII.

The clergy therefore hesitated; and this hesitation may well be excused: for some eminent laymen, who possessed a large share of the public confidence, were disposed to recommend submission. They thought that a general opposition could hardly be expected, and that a partial opposition would be ruinous to individuals, and of little advantage to the Church and to the nation. Such was the opinion given at this time by Halifax and Nottingham. The day drew near; and still there was no concert and no formed resolution.*

They hesitate.

At this conjuncture the Protestant Dissenters of London won for themselves a title to the lasting gratitude of their country. They had hitherto been reckoned by the government as part of its strength. A few of their most active and noisy preachers, corrupted by the favours of the Court, had got up addresses in favour of the King's policy. Others, estranged by the recollection of many cruel wrongs both from the Church of England and from the House of Stuart, had seen with resentful pleasure the tyrannical prince and the tyrannical hierarchy separated by a bitter enmity, and bidding against each other for the help of sects lately persecuted and despised. But this feeling, however natural, had been indulged long enough. The time had come when it was necessary to make a choice; and the Nonconformists of the City, with a noble spirit, arrayed themselves side by side with the members of the Church in defence of the fundamental laws of the realm. Baxter, Bates, and Howe distinguished themselves by their efforts to bring about this coalition: but the generous enthusiasm which pervaded the whole Puritan body made the task easy. The zeal of the flocks outran that of the pastors. Those Presbyterian and Independent teachers who showed an inclination to take part with the King against the ecclesiastical establishment received distinct notice that,

Patriotism of the Protestant Nonconformists of London.

* Johnstone, May 27. 1688.

CHAP. VIII.

unless they changed their conduct, their congregations would neither hear them nor pay them. Alsop, who had flattered himself that he should be able to bring over a great body of his disciples to the royal side, found himself on a sudden an object of contempt and abhorrence to those who had lately revered him as their spiritual guide, sank into a deep melancholy, and hid himself from the public eye. Deputations waited on several of the London clergy imploring them not to judge of the dissenting body from the servile adulation which had lately filled the London Gazette, and exhorting them, placed as they were in the van of this great fight, to play the men for the liberties of England and for the faith delivered to the Saints. These assurances were received with joy and gratitude. Yet there was still much anxiety and much difference of opinion among those who had to decide whether, on Sunday the twentieth, they would or would not obey the King's command. The London clergy, then universally acknowledged to be the flower of their profession, held a meeting. Fifteen Doctors of Divinity were present. Tillotson, Dean of Canterbury, the most celebrated preacher of the age, came thither from a sick bed. Sherlock, Master of the Temple, Patrick, Dean of Peterborough and Rector of Saint Paul's, Covent Garden, and Stillingfleet, Archdeacon of London and Dean of Saint Paul's Cathedral, attended. The general feeling of the assembly seemed to be that it was, on the whole, advisable to obey the Order in Council. The dispute began to wax warm, and might have produced fatal consequences, if it had not been brought to a close by the firmness and wisdom of Doctor Edward Fowler, Vicar of Saint Giles's, Cripplegate, one of a small but remarkable class of divines who united that love of civil liberty which belonged to the school of Calvin with the theology of the school of Arminius.[*] Standing up, Fowler spoke thus: "I must be plain. The question is so simple that argument can throw no new light on it, and can only beget heat. Let every man say Yes or No. But I cannot consent to be bound by the vote of the majority. I shall be sorry to cause a breach of unity. But this Declaration I cannot in conscience read."

Consultation of the London clergy.

[*] That very remarkable man, the late Alexander Knox, whose eloquent conversation and elaborate letters had a great influence on the minds of his contemporaries, learned, I suspect, much of his theological system from Fowler's writings. Fowler's book on the Design of Christianity was assailed by John Bunyan with a ferocity which nothing can justify but which the birth and breeding of the honest Tinker in some degree excuse.

Tillotson, Patrick, Sherlock, and Stillingfleet declared that they were of the same mind. The majority yielded to the authority of a minority so respectable. A resolution by which all present pledged themselves to one another not to read the Declaration was then drawn up. Patrick was the first who set his hand to it; Fowler was the second. The paper was sent round the City, and was speedily subscribed by eighty-five incumbents.*

Meanwhile several of the Bishops were anxiously deliberating as to the course which they should take. On the twelfth of May a grave and learned company was assembled round the table of the Primate at Lambeth. Compton, Bishop of London, Turner, Bishop of Ely, White, Bishop of Peterborough, and Tenison, Rector of Saint Martin's Parish, were among the guests. The Earl of Clarendon, a zealous and uncompromising friend of the Church, had been invited. Cartwright, Bishop of Chester, intruded himself on the meeting, probably as a spy. While he remained, no confidential communication could take place: but, after his departure, the great question of which all minds were full was propounded and discussed. The general opinion was that the Declaration ought not to be read. Letters were forthwith written to several of the most respectable prelates of the province of Canterbury, entreating them to come up without delay to London, and to strengthen the hands of their metropolitan at this conjuncture.† As there was little doubt that these letters would be opened if they passed through the office in Lombard Street, they were sent by horsemen to the nearest country post towns on the different roads. The Bishop of Winchester, whose loyalty had been so signally proved at Sedgemoor, though suffering from indisposition, resolved to set out in obedience to the summons, but found himself unable to bear the motion of a coach. The letter addressed to William Lloyd, Bishop of Norwich, was, in spite of all precautions, detained by a postmaster; and that prelate, inferior to none of his brethren in courage and in zeal for the common cause of his order, did not reach London in time.‡ His namesake, William Lloyd, Bishop of Saint Asaph, a pious, honest, and learned

* Johnstone, May 23. 1688. There is a satirical poem on this meeting entitled the Clerical Cabal.
† Clarendon's Diary, May 22. 1688.
‡ Extracts from Tanner MSR. in Howell's State Trials; Life of Prideaux; Clarendon's Diary, May 16. 1688.

man, but of slender judgment, and half crazed by his persevering endeavours to extract from the Book of Daniel and from the Revelations some information about the Pope and the King of France, hastened to the capital and arrived on the sixteenth.* On the following day came the excellent Ken, Bishop of Bath and Wells, Lake, Bishop of Chichester, and Sir John Trelawney, Bishop of Bristol, a baronet of an old and honourable Cornish family.

Consultation at Lambeth Palace.

On the eighteenth a meeting of prelates and of other eminent divines was held at Lambeth. Tillotson, Tenison, Stillingfleet, Patrick, and Sherlock were present. Prayers were solemnly read before the consultation began. After long deliberation, a petition embodying the general sense was written by the Archbishop with his own hand. It was not drawn up with much felicity of style. Indeed, the cumbrous and inelegant structure of the sentences brought on Sancroft some raillery, which he bore with less patience than he showed under much heavier trials. But in substance nothing could be more skilfully framed than this memorable document. All disloyalty, all intolerance, was earnestly disclaimed. The King was assured that the Church still was, as she had ever been, faithful to the throne. He was assured also that the Bishops would, in proper place and time, as Lords of Parliament and members of the Upper House of Convocation, show that they by no means wanted tenderness for the conscientious scruples of Dissenters. But Parliament had, both in the late and in the present reign, pronounced that the sovereign was not constitutionally competent to dispense with statutes in matters ecclesiastical. The Declaration was therefore illegal; and the petitioners could not, in prudence, honour, or conscience, be parties to the solemn publishing of an illegal Declaration in the house of God, and during the time of divine service.

This paper was signed by the Archbishop and by six of his suffragans, Lloyd of Saint Asaph, Turner of Ely, Lake of Chichester, Ken of Bath and Wells, White of Peterborough, and Trelawney of Bristol. The Bishop of London, being under suspension, did not sign.

Petition of the seven Bishops presented to the King.

It was now late on Friday evening; and on Sunday morning the Declaration was to be read in the churches of London. It was necessary to put the paper into the King's

* Clarendon's Diary, May 16 and 17. 1688.

hands without delay. The six Bishops crossed the river to Whitehall. The Archbishop, who had long been forbidden the Court, did not accompany them. Lloyd, leaving his five brethren at the House of Lord Dartmouth in the vicinity of the palace, went to Sunderland, and begged that minister to read the petition, and to ascertain when the King would be willing to receive it. Sunderland, afraid of compromising himself, refused to look at the paper, but went immediately to the royal closet. James directed that the Bishops should be admitted. He had heard from his tool Cartwright that they were disposed to obey the royal mandate, but that they wished for some little modifications in form, and that they meant to present a humble request to that effect. His Majesty was therefore in very good humour. When they knelt before him, he graciously told them to rise, took the paper from Lloyd, and said, "This is my Lord of Canterbury's hand." "Yes, sir, his own hand," was the answer. James read the petition: he folded it up; and his countenance grew dark. "This," he said, "is a great surprise to me. I did not expect this from your Church, especially from some of you. This is a standard of rebellion." The Bishops broke out into passionate professions of loyalty: but the King, as usual, repeated the same words over and over. "I tell you, this is a standard of rebellion." "Rebellion!" cried Trelawney, falling on his knees. "For God's sake, sir, do not say so hard a thing of us. No Trelawney can be a rebel. Remember that my family has fought for the crown. Remember how I served Your Majesty when Monmouth was in the West." "We put down the last rebellion," said Lake: "we shall not raise another." "We rebel!" exclaimed Turner; "we are ready to die at your Majesty's feet." "Sir," said Ken, in a more manly tone, "I hope that you will grant to us that liberty of conscience which you grant to all mankind." Still James went on. "This is rebellion. This is a standard of rebellion. Did ever a good Churchman question the dispensing power before? Have not some of you preached for it and written for it? It is a standard of rebellion. I will have my Declaration published." "We have two duties to perform," answered Ken, "our duty to God, and our duty to Your Majesty. We honour you: but we fear God." "Have I deserved this?" said the King, more and more angry: "I who have been such a friend to your Church? I did not expect this from some of you. I will be obeyed. My Declaration

CHAP. VIII.

shall be published. You are trumpeters of sedition. What do you do here? Go to your dioceses; and see that I am obeyed. I will keep this paper. I will not part with it. I will remember you that have signed it." "God's will be done," said Ken. "God has given me the dispensing power," said the King, "and I will maintain it. I tell you that there are still seven thousand of your Church who have not bowed the knee to Baal." The Bishops respectfully retired.* That very evening the document which they had put into the hands of the King appeared word for word in print, was laid on the tables of all the coffeehouses, and was cried about the streets. Everywhere the people rose from their beds, and came up to stop the hawkers. It was said that the printer cleared a thousand pounds in a few hours by this penny broadside. This is probably an exaggeration; but it is an exaggeration which proves that the sale was enormous. How the petition got abroad is still a mystery. Sancroft declared that he had taken every precaution against publication, and that he knew of no copy except that which he had himself written, and which James had taken out of Lloyd's hand. The veracity of the Archbishop is beyond all suspicion. But it is by no means improbable that some of the divines who assisted in framing the petition may have remembered so short a composition accurately, and may have sent it to the press. The prevailing opinion, however, was that some person about the King had been indiscreet or treacherous.† Scarcely less sensation was produced by a short letter which was written with great power of argument and language, printed secretly, and largely circulated on the same day by the post and by the common carriers. A copy was sent to every clergyman in the kingdom. The writer did not attempt to disguise the danger which those who disobeyed the royal mandate would incur: but he set forth in a lively manner the still greater danger of submission. "If we read the Declaration," said he, "we fall to rise no more. We fall unpitied and despised. We fall amidst the curses of a nation whom our compliance will have ruined." Some thought that this paper came from Holland. Others attributed it to Sherlock. But Prideaux, Dean of Norwich, who was a principal agent in distributing it, believed it to be the work of Halifax.

* Sancroft's Narrative, printed from the Tanner MSS.; Van Citters, May 17, 1688.
† Burnet, i. 741.; Revolution Politics; Higgins's Short View.

The conduct of the prelates was rapturously extolled by the general voice: but some murmurs were heard. It was said that such grave men, if they thought themselves bound in conscience to remonstrate with the King, ought to have remonstrated earlier. Was it fair to leave him in the dark till within thirty-six hours of the time fixed for the reading of the Declaration? Even if he wished to revoke the Order in Council, it was too late to do so. The inference seemed to be that the petition was intended, not to move the royal mind, but merely to inflame the discontents of the people.* These complaints were utterly groundless. The King had laid on the Bishops a command new, surprising, and embarrassing. It was their duty to communicate with each other, and to ascertain as far as possible the sense of the profession of which they were the heads before they took any step. They were dispersed over the whole kingdom. Some of them were distant from others a full week's journey. James allowed them only a fortnight to inform themselves, to meet, to deliberate, and to decide; and he surely had no right to think himself aggrieved because that fortnight was drawing to a close before he learned their decision. Nor is it true that they did not leave him time to revoke his order if he had been wise enough to do so. He might have called together his Council on Saturday morning, and before night it might have been known throughout London and the suburbs that he had yielded to the entreaties of the fathers of the Church. The Saturday, however, passed over without any sign of relenting on the part of the government; and the Sunday arrived, a day long remembered.

CHAP. VIII.

In the City and Liberties of London were about a hundred parish churches. In only four of these was the Order in Council obeyed. At Saint Gregory's the Declaration was read by a divine of the name of Martin. As soon as he uttered the first words, the whole congregation rose and withdrew. At Saint Matthew's, in Friday Street, a wretch named Timothy Hall, who had disgraced his gown by acting as broker for the Duchess of Portsmouth in the sale of pardons, and who now had hopes of obtaining the vacant bishopric of Oxford, was in like manner left alone in his church. At Serjeant's Inn, in Chancery Lane, the clerk pretended that he had forgotten to bring a copy; and the Chief Justice of the King's Bench, who had attended in order to

The London Clergy disobey the royal order.

* Life of James the Second, ii. 155.

see that the royal mandate was obeyed, was forced to content himself with this excuse. Samuel Wesley, the father of John and Charles Wesley, a curate in London, took for his text that day the noble answer of the three Jews to the Chaldean tyrant, "Be it known unto thee, O King, that we will not serve thy gods, nor worship the golden image which thou hast set up." Even in the chapel of Saint James's Palace the officiating minister had the courage to disobey the order. The Westminster boys long remembered what took place that day in the Abbey. Sprat, Bishop of Rochester, officiated there as Dean. As soon as he began to read the Declaration, murmurs and the noise of people crowding out of the choir drowned his voice. He trembled so violently that men saw the paper shake in his hand. Long before he had finished, the place was deserted by all but those whose situation made it necessary for them to remain.*

Never had the Church been so dear to the nation as on the afternoon of that day. The spirit of dissent seemed to be extinct. Baxter from his pulpit pronounced an eulogium on the Bishops and parochial clergy. The Dutch minister, a few hours later, wrote to inform the States General that the Anglican priesthood had risen in the estimation of the public to an incredible degree. The universal cry of the Nonconformists, he said, was that they would rather continue to lie under the penal statutes than separate their cause from that of the prelates.†

Another week of anxiety and agitation passed away. Sunday came again. Again the churches of the capital were thronged by hundreds of thousands. The Declaration was read nowhere except at the very few places where it had been read the week before. The minister who had officiated at the chapel in Saint James's Palace had been turned out of his situation: a more obsequious divine appeared with the paper in his hand: but his agitation was so great that he could not articulate. In truth the feeling of the whole nation had now become such as none but the very best and noblest, or the very worst and basest, of mankind could without much discomposure encounter.‡

Even the King stood aghast for a moment at the violence of the tempest which he had raised. What step was he next to take? He must either advance or recede: and it was impossible to advance without peril, or to recede without humiliation. At one moment he determined to put forth a second order enjoining the clergy in high and angry terms to publish his Declaration, and menacing every one who should be refractory with instant suspension. This order was drawn up and sent to the press, then recalled, then a second time sent to the press, then recalled a second time.* A different plan was suggested by some of those who were for rigorous measures. The prelates who had signed the petition might be cited before the Ecclesiastical Commission and deprived of their sees. But to this course strong objections were urged in Council. It had been announced that the Houses would be convoked before the end of the year. The Lords would assuredly treat the sentence of deprivation as a nullity, would insist that Sancroft and his fellow petitioners should be summoned to Parliament, and would refuse to acknowledge a new Archbishop of Canterbury or a new Bishop of Bath and Wells. Thus the session, which at best was likely to be sufficiently stormy, would commence with a deadly quarrel between the crown and the peers. If therefore it were thought necessary to punish the Bishops, the punishment ought to be inflicted according to the known course of English law. Sunderland had from the beginning objected, as far as he dared, to the Order in Council. He now suggested a course which, though not free from inconveniences, was the most prudent and the most dignified that a series of errors had left open to the government. The King might with grace and majesty announce to the world that he was deeply hurt by the undutiful conduct of the Church of England; but that he could not forget all the services rendered by that Church, in trying times, to his father, to his brother, and to himself; that, as a friend to the liberty of conscience, he was unwilling to deal severely with men whom conscience, ill informed indeed, and unreasonably scrupulous, might have prevented from obeying his commands; and that he would therefore leave the offenders to that punishment which their own reflections would inflict whenever they should calmly compare their recent acts with the loyal doctrines of which they had so loudly boasted. Not only Powis and Bellasyse, who had always been for moderate counsels, but even Dover and Arundell, leaned towards this

* Van Citters, May 7/17, 1688.

proposition. Jeffreys, on the other hand, maintained that the government would be disgraced if such transgressors as the seven Bishops were suffered to escape with a mere reprimand. He did not, however, wish them to be cited before the Ecclesiastical Commission, in which he sate as chief or rather as sole Judge. For the load of public hatred under which he already lay was too much even for his shameless forehead and obdurate heart; and he shrank from the responsibility which he would have incurred by pronouncing an illegal sentence on the rulers of the Church and the favourites of the nation. He therefore recommended a criminal information. It was accordingly resolved that the Archbishop and the six other petitioners should be brought before the Court of King's Bench on a charge of seditious libel. That they would be convicted it was scarcely possible to doubt. The Judges and their officers were tools of the Court. Since the old charter of the City of London had been forfeited, scarcely one prisoner whom the government was bent on bringing to punishment had been absolved by a jury. The refractory prelates would probably be condemned to ruinous fines and to long imprisonment, and would be glad to ransom themselves by serving, both in and out of Parliament, the designs of the Sovereign.*

On the twenty-seventh of May it was notified to the Bishops that on the eighth of June they must appear before the King in Council. Why so long an interval was allowed we are not informed. Perhaps James hoped that some of the offenders, terrified by his displeasure, might submit before the day fixed for the reading of the Declaration in their dioceses, and might, in order to make their peace with him, persuade their clergy to obey his order. If such was his hope it was signally disappointed. Sunday the third of June came; and all parts of England followed the example of the capital. Already the Bishops of Norwich, Gloucester, Salisbury, Winchester, and Exeter had signed copies of the petition in token of their approbation. The Bishop of Worcester had refused to distribute the Declaration among his clergy. The Bishop of Hereford had distributed it: but it was generally understood that he was overwhelmed by remorse and shame for having done so. Not one parish priest

---

* Barillon, May 24. May 31. June 4. June 10. 1688: Van Citters, July 3.; Adda, May 25. May 25. May 30. June 4. June 8.; Life of James the Second, ii. 152.

in fifty complied with the Order in Council. In the great diocese of Chester, including the county of Lancaster, only three clergymen could be prevailed on by Cartwright to obey the King. In the diocese of Norwich are many hundreds of parishes. In only four of these was the Declaration read. The courtly Bishop of Rochester could not overcome the scruples of the minister of the ordinary of Chatham, who depended on the government for bread. There is still extant a pathetic letter which this honest priest sent to the Secretary of the Admiralty. "I cannot," he wrote, "reasonably expect Your Honour's protection. God's will be done. I must choose suffering rather than sin."*

CHAP. VIII

On the evening of the eighth of June the seven prelates, furnished by the ablest lawyers in England with full advice, repaired to the palace, and were called into the Council chamber. Their petition was lying on the table. The Chancellor took the paper up, showed it to the Archbishop, and said, "Is this the paper which your Grace wrote, and which the six Bishops present delivered to His Majesty?" Sancroft looked at the paper, turned to the King, and spoke thus: "Sir, I stand here a culprit. I never was so before. Once I little thought that I ever should be so. Least of all could I think that I should be charged with any offence against my King: but, since I am so unhappy as to be in this situation, Your Majesty will not be offended if I avail myself of my lawful right to decline saying anything which may criminate me." "This is mere chicanery," said the King. "I hope that Your Grace will not do so ill a thing as to deny your own hand." "Sir," said Lloyd, whose studies had been much among the casuists, "all divines agree that a person situated as we are may refuse to answer such a question." The King, as slow of understanding as quick of temper, could not comprehend what the prelates meant. He persisted, and was evidently becoming very angry. "Sir," said the Archbishop, "I am not bound to accuse myself. Nevertheless, if Your Majesty positively commands me to answer, I will do so in the confidence that a just and generous prince will not suffer what I say in obedience to his orders to be brought in evidence against me." "You must not capitulate with your Sovereign," said the Chancellor. "No," said the King; "I will

They are examined by the Privy Council.

* Burnet, I. 740.; Life of Prideaux; Van Citters, June 11. 11. 1688; Tanner MSS.; Life and Correspondence of Pepys.

not give any such command. If you choose to deny your own hands, I have nothing more to say to you."

The Bishops were repeatedly sent out into the antechamber, and repeatedly called back into the Council room. At length James positively commanded them to answer the question. He did not expressly engage that their confession should not be used against them. But they, not unnaturally, supposed that, after what had passed, such an engagement was implied in his command. Sancroft acknowledged his handwriting; and his brethren followed his example. They were then interrogated about the meaning of some words in the petition, and about the letter which had been circulated with so much effect all over the kingdom: but their language was so guarded that nothing was gained by the examination. The Chancellor then told them that a criminal information would be exhibited against them in the Court of King's Bench, and called upon them to enter into recognisances. They refused. They were peers of Parliament, they said. They were advised by the best lawyers in Westminster Hall that no peer could be required to enter into a recognisance in a case of libel; and they should not think themselves justified in relinquishing the privilege of their order. The King was so absurd as to think himself personally affronted because they chose, on a legal question, to be guided by legal advice. "You believe every body," he said, "rather than me." He was indeed mortified and alarmed. For he had gone so far that, if they persisted, he had no choice left but to send them to prison; and, though he by no means foresaw all the consequences of such a step, he foresaw probably enough to disturb him. They were resolute. A warrant was therefore made out directing the Lieutenant of the Tower to keep them in safe custody, and a barge was manned to convey them down the river.*

It was known all over London that the Bishops were before the Council. The public anxiety was intense. A great multitude filled the courts of Whitehall and all the neighbouring streets. Many people were in the habit of refreshing themselves at the close of a summer day with the cool air of the Thames. But on this evening the whole river was alive with wherries. When the Seven came forth under a guard, the emotions of the people broke through all restraint. Thousands fell on their knees and prayed aloud for the men

* Sancroft's Narrative, printed from the Tanner MSS.

who had, with the Christian courage of Ridley and Latimer, confronted a tyrant inflamed by all the bigotry of Mary. Many dashed into the stream, and, up to their waists in ooze and water, cried to the holy fathers to bless them. All down the river, from Whitehall to London Bridge, the royal barge passed between lines of boats, from which arose a shout of "God bless Your Lordships." The King, in great alarm, gave orders that the garrison of the Tower should be doubled, that the Guards should be held ready for action, and that two companies should be detached from every regiment in the kingdom, and sent up instantly to London. But the force on which he relied as the means of coercing the people shared all the feelings of the people. The very sentinels who were posted at the Traitors' Gate reverently asked for a blessing from the martyrs whom they were to guard. Sir Edward Hales was Lieutenant of the Tower. He was little inclined to treat his prisoners with kindness. For he was an apostate from that Church for which they suffered; and he held several lucrative posts by virtue of that dispensing power against which they had protested. He learned with indignation that his soldiers were drinking the health of the Bishops. He ordered his officers to see that it was done no more. But the officers came back with a report that the thing could not be prevented, and that no other health was drunk in the garrison. Nor was it only by carousing that the troops showed their reverence for the fathers of the Church. There was such a show of devotion throughout the Tower that pious men thanked God for bringing good out of evil, and for making the persecution of His faithful servants the means of saving many souls. All day the coaches and liveries of the first nobles of England were seen round the prison gates. Thousands of humbler spectators constantly covered Tower Hill.* But among the marks of public respect and sympathy which the prelates received there was one which more than all the rest enraged and alarmed the King. He learned that a deputation of ten Nonconformist ministers had visited the Tower. He sent for four of these persons, and himself upbraided them. They courageously answered that they thought it their duty to

CHAP. VIII.

* Burnet, i. 741.; Van Citters, June his wife, dated June 14., and printed 8. 16. 1688; Luttrell's Diary, June 8.; from the Tanner MSS.; Reresby's Memoirs. Evelyn's Diary; Letter of Dr. Nelson to

CHAP. VIII.

Birth of the Pretender.

forget past quarrels, and to stand by the men who stood by the Protestant religion.*

Scarcely had the gates of the Tower been closed on the prisoners when an event took place which increased the public excitement. It had been announced that the Queen did not expect to be confined till July. But, on the day after the Bishops had appeared before the Council, it was observed that the King seemed to be anxious about her state. In the evening, however, she sate playing cards at Whitehall till near midnight. Then she was carried in a sedan to Saint James's Palace, where apartments had been very hastily fitted up for her reception. Soon messengers were running about in all directions to summon physicians and priests, Lords of the Council, and Ladies of the Bedchamber. In a few hours many public functionaries and women of rank were assembled in the Queen's room. There, on the morning of Sunday, the tenth of June, a day long kept sacred by the too faithful adherents of a bad cause, was born the most unfortunate of princes, destined to seventy-seven years of exile and wandering, of vain projects, of honours more galling than insults, and of hopes such as make the heart sick.

He is generally believed to be suppositious.

The calamities of the poor child had begun before his birth. The nation over which, according to the ordinary course of succession, he would have reigned, was fully persuaded that his mother was not really pregnant. By whatever evidence the fact of his birth had been proved, a considerable number of people would probably have persisted in maintaining that the Jesuits had practised some skilful sleight of hand; and the evidence, partly from accident, partly from gross mismanagement, was really open to some objections. Many persons of both sexes were in the royal bedchamber when the child first saw the light; but none of them enjoyed any large measure of public confidence. Of the Privy Councillors present, half were Roman Catholics; and those who called themselves Protestants were generally regarded as traitors to their country and their God. Many of the women in attendance were French, Italian, and Portuguese. Of the English ladies some were Papists, and some were the wives of Papists. Some persons who were peculiarly entitled to be present, and whose testimony would have satisfied all minds accessible to reason, were absent;

* Reresby's Memoirs.

and for their absence the King was held responsible. The Princess Anne was, of all the inhabitants of the island, the most deeply interested in the event. Her sex and her experience qualified her to act as the guardian of her sister's birthright and her own. She had conceived strong suspicions, which were daily confirmed by circumstances trifling or imaginary. She fancied that the Queen carefully shunned her scrutiny, and ascribed to guilt a reserve which was perhaps the effect of delicacy.* In this temper Anne had determined to be present and vigilant when the critical day should arrive. But she had not thought it necessary to be at her post a month before that day, and had, in compliance, it was said, with her father's advice, gone to drink the Bath waters. Sancroft, whose great place made it his duty to attend, and on whose probity the nation placed entire reliance, had a few hours before been sent to the Tower by James. The Hydes were the proper protectors of the rights of the two Princesses. The Dutch Ambassador might be regarded as the representative of William, who, as first prince of the blood and consort of the King's eldest daughter, had a deep interest in what was passing. James never thought of summoning any member, male or female, of the family of Hyde; nor was the Dutch Ambassador invited to be present.

Posterity has fully acquitted the King of the fraud which his people imputed to him. But it is impossible to acquit him of folly and perverseness such as explain and excuse the error of his contemporaries. He was perfectly aware of the suspicions which were abroad.† He ought to have known that those suspicions would not be dispelled by the evidence of members of the Church of Rome, or of persons who, though they might call themselves members of the Church of England, had shown themselves ready to sacrifice the interests of the Church of England in order to obtain his favour. That he was taken by surprise is true. But he had twelve hours to make his arrangements. He found no difficulty in crowding St. James's Palace with bigots and sycophants on whose word the nation placed no reliance. It would have been quite as easy to procure the attendance of some eminent persons whose attachment to the Princesses and to the established religion was unquestionable.

* Correspondence between Anne and Mary, in Dalrymple; Clarendon's Diary, Oct. 31, 1688.
† This is clear from Clarendon's Diary, Oct. 21, 1688.

CHAP. VIII.

At a later period, when he had paid dearly for his foolhardy contempt of public opinion, it was the fashion at Saint Germain's to excuse him by throwing the blame on others. Some Jacobites charged Anne with having purposely kept out of the way. Nay, they were not ashamed to say that Sancroft had provoked the King to send him to the Tower, in order that the evidence which was to confound the calumnies of the malecontents might be defective.* The absurdity of these imputations is palpable. Could Anne or Sancroft possibly have foreseen that the Queen's calculations would turn out to be erroneous by a whole month? Had those calculations been correct, Anne would have been back from Bath, and Sancroft would have been out of the Tower, in ample time for the birth. At all events, the maternal uncles of the King's daughters were neither at a distance nor in a prison. The same messenger who summoned the whole bevy of renegades, Dover, Peterborough, Murray, Sunderland, and Mulgrave, could just as easily have summoned Clarendon. If they were Privy Councillors, so was he. His house was in Jermyn Street, not two hundred yards from the chamber of the Queen. Yet he was left to learn at St. James's Church, from the agitation and whispers of the congregation, that his niece had ceased to be heiress presumptive of the crown.† Was it a disqualification that he was the near kinsman of the Princesses of Orange and Denmark? Or was it a disqualification that he was unalterably attached to the Church of England?

The cry of the whole nation was that an imposture had been practised. Papists had, during some months, been predicting, from the pulpit and through the press, in prose and verse, in English and Latin, that a Prince of Wales would be given to the prayers of the Church; and they had now accomplished their own prophecy. Every witness who could not be corrupted or deceived had been studiously excluded. Anne had been tricked into visiting Bath. The Primate had, on the very day preceding that which had been fixed for the villany, been sent to prison in defiance of the rules of law and of the privileges of peerage. Not a single man or woman who had the smallest interest in detecting the fraud had been suffered to be present. The Queen had been removed suddenly and at the dead of night to Saint

* Life of James the Second, ii. 159, 160.
† Clarendon's Diary, June 10. 1688.

James's Palace, because that building, less commodious for honest purposes than Whitehall, had some rooms and passages well suited for the purpose of the Jesuits. There, amidst a circle of zealots who thought nothing a crime that tended to promote the interests of their Church, and of courtiers who thought nothing a crime that tended to enrich and aggrandise themselves, a new born child had been introduced, by means of a warming pan, into the royal bed, and then handed round in triumph, as heir of three kingdoms. Heated by such suspicions, suspicions unjust, it is true, but not altogether unnatural, men thronged more eagerly than ever to pay their homage to the saintly victims of the tyrant, who, having long foully injured his people, had now filled up the measure of his iniquities by more foully injuring his children.*

The Prince of Orange, not himself suspecting any trick, and not aware of the state of public feeling in England, ordered prayers to be said under his own roof for his little brother in law, and sent Zulestein to London with a formal message of congratulation. Zulestein, to his amazement, found all the people whom he met opened mouthed about the infamous fraud just committed by the Jesuits, and saw every hour some fresh pasquinade on the pregnancy and the delivery. He soon wrote to the Hague that not one person in ten believed the child to have been born of the Queen.†

The demeanour of the seven prelates meanwhile strengthened the interest which their situation excited. On the evening of the Black Friday, as it was called, on which they were committed, they reached their prison just at the hour of divine service. They instantly hastened to the chapel. It chanced that in the second lesson were these words: "In all things approving ourselves as the ministers of God, in much patience, in afflictions, in distresses, in stripes, in imprisonments." All zealous Churchmen were delighted by this coincidence, and remembered how much comfort a similar coincidence had given, near forty years before, to Charles the First at the time of his death.

---

* Johnstone gives in a very few words an excellent summary of the case against the King. "The generality of people conclude all is a trick; because they say the reckoning is changed. The Princess sent away, none of the Clarendon family nor the Dutch Ambassador sent for the suddenness of the thing, the sermons, the confidence of the priests, the hurry." June 13. 1688.

† Rosquillo, July 23/Aug 2. Rosquillo adds, that what Zulestein said of the state of public opinion was strictly true.

CHAP.
VIII.

On the evening of the next day, Saturday the ninth, a letter came from Sunderland enjoining the chaplain of the Tower to read the Declaration during divine service on the following morning. As the time fixed by the Order in Council for the reading in London had long expired, this proceeding of the government could be considered only as a personal insult of the meanest and most childish kind to the venerable prisoners. The chaplain refused to comply: he was dismissed from his situation; and the chapel was shut up.*

The Bishops brought before the King's Bench and bailed.

The Bishops edified all who approached them by the firmness and cheerfulness with which they endured confinement, by the modesty and meekness with which they received the applauses and blessings of the whole nation, and by the loyal attachment which they professed for the persecutor who sought their destruction. They remained only a week in custody. On Friday, the fifteenth of June, the first day of term, they were brought before the King's Bench. An immense throng awaited their coming. From the landing-place to the Court of Requests they passed through a lane of spectators who blessed and applauded them. "Friends," said the prisoners as they passed, "honour the King; and remember us in your prayers." These humble and pious expressions moved the hearers even to tears. When at length the procession had made its way through the crowd into the presence of the Judges, the Attorney General exhibited the information which he had been commanded to prepare, and moved that the defendants might be ordered to plead. The counsel on the other side objected that the Bishops had been unlawfully committed, and were therefore not regularly before the Court. The question whether a peer could be required to enter into recognisances on a charge of libel was argued at great length, and decided by a majority of the Judges in favour of the crown. The prisoners then pleaded Not Guilty. That day fortnight, the twenty-ninth of June, was fixed for their trial. In the meantime they were allowed to be at large on their own recognisances. The crown lawyers acted prudently in not requiring sureties. For Halifax had arranged that twenty-one temporal peers of the highest consideration should be ready to put in bail, three for each defendant; and such a manifestation of the feeling of the nobility would have been no slight blow to the

* Van Citters, June 11/11, 1688; Luttrell's Diary, June 18.

government. It was also known that one of the most opulent Dissenters of the City had begged that he might have the honour of giving security for Ken.

The Bishops were now permitted to depart to their own homes. The common people, who did not understand the nature of the legal proceedings which had taken place in the King's Bench, and who saw that their favourites had been brought to Westminster Hall in custody and were suffered to go away in freedom, imagined that the good cause was prospering. Loud acclamations were raised. The steeples of the churches sent forth joyous peals. Sprat was amazed to hear the bells of his own Abbey ringing merrily. He promptly silenced them; but his interference caused much angry muttering. The Bishops found it difficult to escape from the importunate crowd of their wellwishers. Lloyd was detained in Palace Yard by admirers who struggled to touch his hands and to kiss the skirt of his robe, till Clarendon, with some difficulty, rescued him and conveyed him home by a bypath. Cartwright, it is said, was so unwise as to mingle with the crowd. A person who saw his episcopal habit asked and received his blessing. A bystander cried out, "Do you know who blessed you?" "Surely," said he who had just been honoured by the benediction, " it was one of the Seven." "No," said the other, "it is the Popish Bishop of Chester." "Popish dog," cried the enraged Protestant: "take your blessing back again."

Such was the concourse, and such the agitation, that the Dutch Ambassador was surprised to see the day close without an insurrection. The King had been anxious and irritable. In order that he might be ready to suppress any disturbance, he had passed the morning in reviewing several battalions of infantry in Hyde Park. It is, however, by no means certain that his troops would have stood by him if he had needed their services. When Sancroft reached Lambeth, in the afternoon, he found the footguards, who were quartered in that suburb, assembled before the gate of his palace. They formed in two lines on his right and left, and asked his benediction as he went through them. He with difficulty prevented them from lighting a bonfire in honour of his return to his dwelling. There were, however, many bonfires that evening in the City. Two Roman Catholics, who were so indiscreet as to beat some boys for joining in these rejoicings,

CHAP. VIII.

were seized by the mob, stripped naked, and ignominiously branded.*

Sir Edward Hales now came to demand fees from those who had lately been his prisoners. They refused to pay anything for a detention which they regarded as illegal to an officer whose commission was, on their principles, a nullity. The Lieutenant hinted very intelligibly that, if they came into his hands again, they should be put into heavy irons and should lie on bare stones. "We are under our King's displeasure," was the answer; "and most deeply do we feel it: but a fellow subject who threatens us does but lose his breath." It is easy to imagine with what indignation the people, excited as they were, must have learned that a renegade from the Protestant faith, who held a command in defiance of the fundamental laws of England, had dared to menace divines of venerable age and dignity with all the barbarities of Lollard's Tower.†

Agitation of the public mind.

Before the day of trial the agitation had spread to the furthest corners of the island. From Scotland the Bishops received letters assuring them of the sympathy of the Presbyterians of that country, so long and so bitterly hostile to prelacy.‡ The people of Cornwall, a fierce, bold, and athletic race, among whom there was a stronger provincial feeling than in any other part of the realm, were greatly moved by the danger of Trelawney, whom they reverenced less as a ruler of the Church than as the head of an honourable house, and the heir through twenty descents of ancestors who had been of great note before the Normans had set foot on English ground. All over the country the peasants chanted a ballad of which the burden is still remembered:

"And shall Trelawney die, and shall Trelawney die?
Then thirty thousand Cornish boys will know the reason why."

The miners from their caverns reechoed the song with a variation:

"Then twenty thousand under ground will know the reason why."§

The rustics in many parts of the country loudly expressed a strange hope which had never ceased to live in their hearts.

* For the events of this day see the State Trials; Clarendon's Diary; Luttrell's Diary; Van Citters, June 14; Johnstone, June 15.; Revolution Politics.
† Johnstone, June 18. 1688; Evelyn's Diary, June 29.
‡ Tanner MSS.
§ This fact was communicated to me in the most obliging manner by the Reverend R. S. Hawker of Morwenstow in Cornwall.

Their Protestant Duke, their beloved Monmouth, would suddenly appear, would lead them to victory, and would tread down the King and the Jesuits under his feet.*

The ministers were appalled. Even Jeffreys would gladly have retraced his steps. He charged Clarendon with friendly messages to the Bishops, and threw on others the blame of the prosecution which he had himself recommended. Sunderland again ventured to recommend concession. The late auspicious birth, he said, had given the King an excellent opportunity of withdrawing from a position full of danger and inconvenience without incurring the reproach of timidity or of caprice. On such happy occasions it had been usual for sovereigns to make the hearts of subjects glad by acts of clemency; and nothing could be more advantageous to the Prince of Wales than that he should, while still in his cradle, be the peacemaker between his father and the agitated nation. But the King's resolution was fixed. "I will go on," he said. "I have been only too indulgent. Indulgence ruined my father."† The artful minister found that his advice had been formerly taken only because it had been shaped to suit the royal temper, and that, from the moment at which he began to counsel well, he began to counsel in vain. He had shown some signs of slackness in the proceeding against Magdalene College. He had recently attempted to convince the King that Tyrconnel's scheme of confiscating the property of the English colonists in Ireland was full of danger, and had, with the help of Powis and Bellasyse, so far succeeded that the execution of the design had been postponed for another year. But this timidity and scrupulosity had excited disgust and suspicion in the royal mind.‡ The day of retribution had arrived. Sunderland was in the same situation in which his rival Rochester had been some months before. Each of the two statesmen in turn experienced the misery of clutching with an agonising grasp, power which was perceptibly slipping away. Each in turn saw his suggestions scornfully rejected. Both endured the pain of reading displeasure and distrust in the countenance and demeanour of their master; yet both were by their country held responsible for those crimes and errors from which they

Uneasiness of Sunderland.

* Johnstone, June 18. 1688.
† Adda. ¹⁵⁻⁷⁵/₃₀ 1688.
‡ Sunderland's own narrative is, of course, not to be implicitly trusted. But he vouches Godolphin as a witness of what took place respecting the Irish Act of Settlement.

had vainly endeavoured to dissuade him. While he suspected them of trying to win popularity at the expense of his authority and dignity, the public voice loudly accused them of trying to win his favour at the expense of their own honour and of the general weal. Yet, in spite of mortifications and humiliations, they both clung to office with the gripe of drowning men. Both attempted to propitiate the King by affecting a willingness to be reconciled to his Church. But there was a point at which Rochester was determined to stop. He went to the verge of apostasy; but there he recoiled: and the world, in consideration of the firmness with which he refused to take the final step, granted him a liberal amnesty for all former compliances. Sunderland, less scrupulous and less sensible of shame, resolved to atone for his late moderation, and to recover the royal confidence, by an act which, to a mind impressed with the importance of religious truth, must have appeared to be one of the most flagitious of crimes, and which even men of the world regard as the last excess of baseness. About a week before the day fixed for the great trial, it was publicly announced that he was a Papist. The King talked with delight of this triumph of divine grace. Courtiers and envoys kept their countenances as well as they could while the renegade protested that he had been long convinced of the impossibility of finding salvation out of the communion of Rome, and that his conscience would not let him rest till he had renounced the heresies in which he had been brought up. The news spread fast. At all the coffeehouses it was told how the prime minister of England, his feet bare, and a taper in his hand, had repaired to the royal chapel and knocked humbly for admittance; how a priestly voice from within had demanded who was there; how Sunderland had made answer that a poor sinner who had long wandered from the true Church entreated her to receive and to absolve him; how the doors were opened; and how the neophyte partook of the holy mysteries.*

This scandalous apostasy could not but heighten the interest with which the nation looked forward to the day when the fate of the seven brave confessors of the English Church was to be decided. To pack a jury was now the great object of the King. The crown lawyers were ordered to make strict enquiry as to the sentiments of the persons who were regis-

tered in the freeholders' book. Sir Samuel Astry, Clerk of
the Crown, whose duty it was, in cases of this description, to
select the names, was summoned to the palace, and had an
interview with James in the presence of the Chancellor.* Sir
Samuel seems to have done his best. For, among the forty-
eight persons whom he nominated, were said to be several
servants of the King, and several Roman Catholics.† But as
the counsel for the Bishops had a right to strike off twelve,
these persons were removed. The crown lawyers also struck
off twelve. The list was thus reduced to twenty-four. The
first twelve who answered to their names were to try the issue.

On the twenty-ninth of June, Westminster Hall, Old and
New Palace Yard, and all the neighbouring streets to a great
distance were thronged with people. Such an auditory had
never before and has never since been assembled in the Court
of King's Bench. Thirty-five temporal peers of the realm
were counted in the crowd.‡

All the four Judges of the Court were on the bench.
Wright, who presided, had been raised to his high place over
the heads of many abler and more learned men solely on
account of his unscrupulous servility. Allibone was a Papist,
and owed his situation to that dispensing power, the legality
of which was now in question. Holloway had hitherto been
a serviceable tool of the government. Even Powell, whose
character for honesty stood high, had borne a part in some
proceedings which it is impossible to defend. He had, in the
great case of Sir Edward Hales, with some hesitation, it is
true, and after some delay, concurred with the majority of the
bench, and had thus brought on his character a stain which
his honourable conduct on this day completely effaced.

The counsel were by no means fairly matched. The
government had required from its law officers services so
odious and disgraceful that all the ablest jurists and advocates of the Tory party had, one after another, refused to
comply, and had been dismissed from their employments.
Sir Thomas Powis, the Attorney General, was scarcely of the
third rank in his profession. Sir William Williams, the
Solicitor General, had great abilities and dauntless courage:
but he wanted discretion; he loved wrangling; he had no
command over his temper; and he was hated and despised by
all political parties. The most conspicuous assistants of the

* Clarendon's Diary. June 31. 1688. ‡ Johnstone, July 2. 1688.
† Van Citters, June 29/July 9 1688.

Attorney and Solicitor were Serjeant Trinder, a Roman Catholic, and Sir Bartholomew Shower, Recorder of London, who had some legal learning, but whose fulsome apologies and endless repetitions were the jest of Westminster Hall. The government had wished to secure the services of Maynard: but he had plainly declared that he could not in conscience do what was asked of him.*

On the other side were arrayed almost all the eminent forensic talents of the age. Sawyer and Finch, who, at the time of the accession of James, had been Attorney and Solicitor General, and who, during the persecution of the Whigs in the late reign, had served the crown with but too much vehemence and success, were of counsel for the defendants. With them were joined two persons who, since age had diminished the activity of Maynard, were reputed the two best lawyers that could be found in the Inns of Court; Pemberton, who had, in the time of Charles the Second, been Chief Justice of the King's Bench, who had been removed from his high place on account of his humanity and moderation, and who had resumed his practice at the bar; and Pollexfen, who had long been at the head of the Western circuit, and who, though he had incurred much unpopularity by holding briefs for the crown at the Bloody Assizes, and particularly by appearing against Alice Lisle, was known to be at heart a Whig, if not a republican. Sir Creswell Levinz was also there, a man of great knowledge and experience, but of singularly timid nature. He had been removed from the bench some years before, because he was afraid to serve the purposes of the government. He was now afraid to appear as the advocate of the Bishops, and had at first refused to receive their retainer: but it had been intimated to him by the whole body of attorneys who employed him that, if he declined this brief, he should never have another.†

Sir George Treby, an able and zealous Whig, who had been Recorder of London under the old charter, was on the same side. Sir John Holt, a still more eminent Whig lawyer, was not retained for the defence, in consequence, it should seem, of some prejudice conceived against him by Sancroft, but was privately consulted on the case by the Bishop of London.‡

---

* Johnstone, July 2. 1688.
† Ibid. July 2. 1688. The editor of Levinz's Reports expresses great wonder that, after the Revolution, Levinz was not replaced on the bench. The facts related by Johnstone may perhaps explain the seeming injustice.
‡ I draw this inference from a letter of Compton to Sancroft, dated the 12th of June.

The junior counsel for the Bishops was a young barrister named John Somers. He had no advantages of birth or fortune; nor had he yet had any opportunity of distinguishing himself before the eyes of the public: but his genius, his industry, his great and various accomplishments, were well known to a small circle of friends; and, in spite of his Whig opinions, his pertinent and lucid mode of arguing and the constant propriety of his demeanour had already secured to him the ear of the Court of King's Bench. The importance of obtaining his services had been strongly represented to the Bishops by Johnstone; and Pollexfen, it is said, had declared that no man in Westminster Hall was so well qualified to treat a historical and constitutional question as Somers.

The jury was sworn. It consisted of persons of highly respectable station. The foreman was Sir Roger Langley, a baronet of old and honourable family. With him were joined a knight and ten esquires, several of whom are known to have been men of large possessions. There were some Nonconformists in the number: for the Bishops had wisely resolved not to show any distrust of the Protestant Dissenters. One name excited considerable alarm, that of Michael Arnold. He was brewer to the palace; and it was apprehended that the government counted on his voice. The story goes that he complained bitterly of the position in which he found himself. "Whatever I do," he said, "I am sure to be half ruined. If I say Not Guilty, I shall brew no more for the King; and if I say Guilty, I shall brew no more for anybody else."*

The trial then commenced, a trial which, even when coolly perused after the lapse of more than a century and a half, has all the interest of a drama. The advocates contended on both sides with far more than professional keenness and vehemence; the audience listened with as much anxiety as if the fate of every one of them was to be decided by the verdict; and the turns of fortune were so sudden and amazing that the multitude repeatedly passed in a single minute from anxiety to exultation, and back again from exultation to still deeper anxiety.

The information charged the Bishops with having written or published, in the county of Middlesex, a false, malicious, and seditious libel. The Attorney and Solicitor first tried to prove the writing. For this purpose several persons were

* Revolution Politics.

called to speak to the hands of the Bishops. But the witnesses were so unwilling that hardly a single plain answer could be extracted from any of them. Pemberton, Pollexfen, and Levinz contended that there was no evidence to go to the jury. Two of the Judges, Holloway and Powell, declared themselves of the same opinion; and the hopes of the spectators rose high. All at once the crown lawyers announced their intention to take another line. Powis, with shame and reluctance which he could not dissemble, put into the witness box Blathwayt, a Clerk of the Privy Council, who had been present when the King interrogated the Bishops. Blathwayt swore that he had heard them own their signatures. His testimony was decisive. "Why," said Judge Holloway to the Attorney, "when you had such evidence, did you not produce it at first, without all this waste of time?" It soon appeared why the counsel for the crown had been unwilling, without absolute necessity, to resort to this mode of proof. Pemberton stopped Blathwayt, subjected him to a searching cross examination, and insisted upon having all that had passed between the King and the defendants fully related. "That is a pretty thing indeed," cried Williams. "Do you think," said Powis, "that you are at liberty to ask our witnesses any impertinent question that comes into your heads?" The advocates of the Bishops were not men to be so put down. "He is sworn," said Pollexfen, "to tell the truth and the whole truth; and an answer we must and will have." The witness shuffled, equivocated, pretended to misunderstand the questions, implored the protection of the Court. But he was in hands from which it was not easy to escape. At length the Attorney again interposed. "If," he said, "you persist in asking such a question, tell us, at least, what use you mean to make of it." Pemberton, who, through the whole trial, did his duty manfully and ably, replied without hesitation: "My Lords, I will answer Mr. Attorney. I will deal plainly with the Court. If the Bishops owned this paper under a promise from His Majesty that their confession should not be used against them, I hope that no unfair advantage will be taken of them." "You put on His Majesty what I dare hardly name," said Williams. "Since you will be so pressing, I demand, for the King, that the question may be recorded." "What do you mean, Mr. Solicitor?" said Sawyer, interposing. "I know what I mean," said the apostate: "I desire that the question may be recorded in court."

"Record what you will. I am not afraid of you, Mr. Solicitor," said Pemberton. Then came a loud and fierce altercation, which Wright could with difficulty quiet. In other circumstances, he would probably have ordered the question to be recorded, and Pemberton to be committed. But on this great day the unjust judge was overawed. He often cast aside glance towards the thick rows of Earls and Barons by whom he was watched, and before whom, in the next Parliament, he might stand at the bar. He looked, a bystander said, as if all the peers present had halters in their pockets.* At length Bluthwayt was forced to give a full account of what had passed. It appeared that the King had entered into no express covenant with the Bishops. But it appeared also that the Bishops might not unreasonably think that there was an implied engagement. Indeed, from the unwillingness of the crown lawyers to put the Clerk of the Council into the witness box, and from the vehemence with which they objected to Pemberton's cross examination, it is plain that they were themselves of this opinion.

However, the handwriting was now proved. But a new and serious objection was raised. It was not sufficient to prove that the Bishops had written the alleged libel. It was necessary to prove also that they had written it in the county of Middlesex. And not only was it out of the power of the Attorney and Solicitor to prove this; but it was in the power of the defendants to prove the contrary. For it so happened that Sancroft had never once left the palace at Lambeth from the time when the Order in Council appeared till after the petition was in the King's hands. The whole case for the prosecution had therefore completely broken down; and the audience, with great glee, expected a speedy acquittal.

The crown lawyers then changed their ground again, abandoned altogether the charge of writing a libel, and undertook to prove that the Bishops had published a libel in the county of Middlesex. The difficulties were great. The delivery of the petition to the King was undoubtedly, in the eye of the law, a publication. But how was this delivery to be proved? No person had been present at the audience in the royal closet except the King and the defendants. The King could not well be sworn. It was therefore only by the admissions of the defendants that the fact of publication could be estab-

* This is the expression of an eyewitness. It is in a newsletter in the Mackintosh Collection.

lished. Blathwayt was again examined, but in vain. He
well remembered, he said, that the Bishops owned their
hands; but he did not remember that they owned the paper
which lay on the table of the Privy Council to be the same
paper which they had delivered to the King, or that they
were even interrogated on that point. Several other official
men who had been in attendance on the Council were called,
and among them Samuel Pepys, Secretary of the Admiralty,
but none of them could remember that anything was said
about the delivery. It was to no purpose that Williams put
leading questions till the counsel on the other side declared
that such twisting, such wiredrawing, was never seen in a
court of justice, and till Wright himself was forced to admit
that the Solicitor's mode of examination was contrary to all
rule. As witness after witness answered in the negative,
roars of laughter and shouts of triumph, which the Judges
did not even attempt to silence, shook the hall.

It seemed that at length this hard fight had been won.
The case for the crown was closed. Had the counsel for the
Bishops remained silent, an acquittal was certain; for nothing which the most corrupt and shameless Judge could venture to call legal evidence of publication had been given. The
Chief Justice was beginning to charge the jury, and would
undoubtedly have directed them to acquit the defendants;
but Finch, too anxious to be perfectly discreet, interfered, and
begged to be heard. "If you will be heard," said Wright,
"you shall be heard; but you do not understand your own
interests." The other counsel for the defence made Finch
sit down, and begged the Chief Justice to proceed. He was
about to do so, when a messenger came to the Solicitor
General with news that Lord Sunderland could prove the
publication, and would come down to the court immediately.
Wright maliciously told the counsel for the defence that they
had only themselves to thank for the turn which things
had taken. The countenances of the great multitude fell.
Finch was, during some hours, the most unpopular man
in the country. Why could he not sit still as his betters,
Sawyer, Pemberton, and Pollexfen, had done? His love of
meddling, his ambition to make a fine speech, had ruined
everything.

Meanwhile the Lord President was brought in a sedan
chair through the hall. Not a hat moved as he passed; and
many voices cried out "Popish dog." He came into court

pale and trembling, with eyes fixed on the ground, and grave his evidence in a faltering voice. He swore that the Bishops had informed him of their intention to present a petition to the King, and that they had been admitted into the royal closet for that purpose. This circumstance, coupled with the circumstance that, after they left the closet, there was in the King's hands a petition signed by them, was such proof as might reasonably satisfy a jury of the fact of the publication.

Publication in Middlesex was then proved. But was the paper thus published a false, malicious, and seditious libel? Hitherto the matter in dispute had been whether a fact which every body well knew to be true could be proved according to technical rules of evidence; but now the contest became one of deeper interest. It was necessary to enquire into the limits of prerogative and liberty, into the right of the King to dispense with statutes, into the right of the subject to petition for the redress of grievances. During three hours the counsel for the petitioners argued with great force in defence of the fundamental principles of the constitution, and proved from the Journals of the House of Commons that the Bishops had affirmed no more than the truth when they represented to the King that the dispensing power which he claimed had been repeatedly declared illegal by Parliament. Somers rose last. He spoke little more than five minutes: but every word was full of weighty matter; and when he sate down his reputation as an orator and a constitutional lawyer was established. He went through the expressions which were used in the information to describe the offence imputed to the Bishops, and showed that every word, whether adjective or substantive, was altogether inappropriate. The offence imputed was a false, a malicious, a seditious libel. False the paper was not; for every fact which it set forth had been shown from the journals of Parliament to be true. Malicious the paper was not; for the defendants had not sought an occasion of strife, but had been placed by the government in such a situation that they must either oppose themselves to the royal will, or violate the most sacred obligations of conscience and honour. Seditious the paper was not; for it had not been scattered by the writers among the rabble, but delivered privately into the hands of the King alone; and a libel it was not, but a decent petition such as, by the laws of England, nay by the laws of imperial Rome, by the laws of all civilised states, a subject who thinks himself aggrieved may with propriety present to the sovereign.

The Attorney replied shortly and feebly. The Solicitor spoke at great length and with great acrimony, and was often interrupted by the clamours and hisses of the audience. He went so far as to lay it down that no subject or body of subjects, except the Houses of Parliament, had a right to petition the King. The galleries were furious; and the Chief Justice himself stood aghast at the effrontery of this venal turncoat.

At length Wright proceeded to sum up the evidence. His language showed that the awe in which he stood of the government was tempered by the awe with which the audience, so numerous, so splendid, and so strongly excited, had impressed him. He said that he would give no opinion on the question of the dispensing power; that it was not necessary for him to do so; that he could not agree with much of the Solicitor's speech; that it was the right of the subject to petition; but that the particular petition before the Court was improperly worded, and was, in the contemplation of law, a libel. Allibone was of the same mind, but, in giving his opinion, showed such gross ignorance of law and history as brought on him the contempt of all who heard him. Holloway evaded the question of the dispensing power, but said that the petition seemed to him to be such as subjects who think themselves aggrieved are entitled to present, and therefore no libel. Powell took a bolder course. He avowed that, in his judgment, the Declaration of Indulgence was a nullity, and that the dispensing power, as lately exercised, was utterly inconsistent with all law. If these encroachments of prerogative were allowed, there was an end of Parliaments. The whole legislative authority would be in the King. "That issue, gentlemen," he said, "I leave to God and to your consciences."*

It was dark before the jury retired to consider of their verdict. The night was a night of intense anxiety. Some letters are extant which were despatched during that period of suspense, and which have therefore an interest of a peculiar kind. "It is very late," wrote the Papal Nuncio, "and the decision is not yet known. The judges and the culprits have gone to their own homes. The jury remain together. Tomorrow we shall learn the event of this great struggle."

* See the proceedings in the Collection of State Trials. I have taken some touches from Johnstone, and some from Van Citters.

The solicitor for the Bishops sate up all night with a body of
servants on the stairs leading to the room where the jury was
consulting. It was absolutely necessary to watch the officers
who watched the doors; for those officers were supposed to be
in the interest of the crown, and might, if not carefully observed, have furnished a courtly juryman with food, which
would have enabled him to starve out the other eleven. Strict
guard was therefore kept. Not even a candle to light a pipe
was permitted to enter. Some basins of water for washing
were suffered to pass at about four in the morning. The jurymen, raging with thirst, soon lapped up the whole. Great
numbers of people walked the neighbouring streets till dawn.
Every hour a messenger came from Whitehall to know what
was passing. Voices, high in altercation, were repeatedly
heard within the room: but nothing certain was known.*

At first nine were for acquitting and three for convicting.
Two of the minority soon gave way: but Arnold was obstinate.
Thomas Austin, a country gentleman of great estate, who
had paid close attention to the evidence and speeches, and
had taken full notes, wished to argue the question. Arnold
declined. He was not used, he doggedly said, to reasoning
and debating. His conscience was not satisfied; and he
should not acquit the Bishops. "If you come to that," said
Austin, "look at me. I am the largest and strongest of the
twelve; and before I find such a petition as this a libel, here
I will stay till I am no bigger than a tobacco pipe." It was
six in the morning before Arnold yielded. It was soon known
that the jury were agreed: but what the verdict would be
was still a secret.†

At ten the Court again met. The crowd was greater than
ever. The jury appeared in the box; and there was a breathless stillness.

Sir Samuel Astry spoke. "Do you find the defendants,
or any of them, guilty of the misdemeanour whereof they are
impeached, or not guilty?" Sir Roger Langley answered,
"Not Guilty." As the words were uttered, Halifax sprung
up and waved his hat. At that signal, benches and galleries
raised a shout. In a moment ten thousand persons, who
crowded the great hall, replied with a still louder shout,
which made the old oaken roof crack; and in another mo-

---

* Johnstone, July 2. 1688; Letter MSS.; Revolution Politics
from Mr. Ince to the Archbishop, dated † Johnstone, July 2. 1688.
at six o'clock in the morning; Tanner

ment the innumerable throng without set up a third huzza, which was heard at Temple Bar. The boats which covered the Thames gave an answering cheer. A peal of gunpowder was heard on the water, and another, and another; and so in a few moments, the glad tidings went flying past the Savoy and the Friars to London Bridge, and to the forest of masts below. As the news spread, streets and squares, marketplaces and coffeehouses, broke forth into acclamations. Yet were the acclamations less strange than the weeping. For the feelings of men had been wound up to such a point that at length the stern English nature, so little used to outward signs of emotion, gave way, and thousands sobbed aloud for very joy. Meanwhile, from the outskirts of the multitude, horsemen were spurring off to bear along all the great roads intelligence of the victory of our Church and nation. Yet not even that astounding explosion could awe the bitter and intrepid spirit of the Solicitor. Striving to make himself heard above the din, he called on the Judges to commit those who had violated, by clamour, the dignity of a court of justice. One of the rejoicing populace was seized. But the tribunal felt that it would be absurd to punish a single individual for an offence common to hundreds of thousands, and dismissed him with a gentle reprimand.*

It was vain to think of passing at that moment to any other business. Indeed the roar of the multitude was such that, during half an hour, scarcely a word could be heard in the court. Williams got to his coach amidst a tempest of hisses and curses. Cartwright, whose curiosity was ungovernable, had been guilty of the folly and indecency of coming to Westminster in order to hear the decision. He was recognised by his sacerdotal garb and by his corpulent figure, and was hooted through the hall. "Take care," said one, "of the wolf in sheep's clothing." "Make room," cried another, "for the man with the Pope in his belly." †

The acquitted prelates took refuge in the nearest chapel

from the crowd which implored their blessing. Many churches
were open on that morning throughout the capital; and many
pious persons repaired thither. The bells of all the parishes
of the City and liberties were ringing. The jury meanwhile
could scarcely make their way out of the hall. They were
forced to shake hands with hundreds. "God bless you!"
cried the people; "God prosper your families! you have done
like honest goodnatured gentlemen ı you have saved us all
to-day." As the noblemen who had attended to support the
good cause drove off, they flung from their carriage windows
handfuls of money, and bade the crowd drink to the health of
the King, the Bishops, and the jury.*

The Attorney went with the tidings to Sunderland, who
happened to be conversing with the Nuncio. "Never," said
Powis, "within man's memory, have there been such shouts
and such tears of joy as today."† The King had that morning visited the camp on Hounslow Heath. Sunderland instantly sent a courier thither with the news. James was in
Lord Feversham's tent when the express arrived. He was
greatly disturbed, and exclaimed in French, "So much the
worse for them." He soon set out for London. While he
was present, respect prevented the soldiers from giving a
loose to their feelings; but he had scarcely quitted the camp
when he heard a great shouting behind him. He was surprised, and asked what that uproar meant. "Nothing," was
the answer: "the soldiers are glad that the Bishops are acquitted." "Do you call that nothing?" said James. And
then he repeated, "So much the worse for them."‡

He might well be out of temper. His defeat had been
complete and most humiliating. Had the prelates escaped on
account of some technical defect in the case for the crown,
had they escaped because they had not written the petition in

CHAP. VIII.

Middlesex, or because it was impossible to prove, according to the strict rules of law, that they had delivered to the King the paper for which they were called in question, the prerogative would have suffered no shock. Happily for the country, the fact of publication had been fully established. The counsel for the defence had therefore been forced to attack the dispensing power. They had attacked it with great learning, eloquence, and boldness. The advocates of the government had been by universal acknowledgment overmatched in the contest. Not a single Judge had ventured to declare that the Declaration of Indulgence was legal. One Judge had in the strongest terms pronounced it illegal. The language of the whole town was that the dispensing power had received a fatal blow. Finch, who had the day before been universally reviled, was now universally applauded. He had been unwilling, it was said, to let the case be decided in a way which would have left the great constitutional question still doubtful. He had felt that a verdict which should acquit his clients, without condemning the Declaration of Indulgence, would be but half a victory. It is certain that Finch deserved neither the reproaches which had been cast on him while the event was doubtful, nor the praises which he received when it had proved happy. It was absurd to blame him because, during the short delay which he occasioned, the crown lawyers unexpectedly discovered new evidence. It was equally absurd to suppose that he deliberately exposed his clients to risk, in order to establish a general principle; and still more absurd was it to praise him for what would have been a gross violation of professional duty.

That joyful day was followed by a not less joyful evening. The Bishops, and some of their most respectable friends, in vain exerted themselves to prevent tumultuous demonstrations of public feeling. Never within the memory of the oldest, not even on that night on which it was known through London that the army of Scotland had declared for a free Parliament, had the streets been in such a glare with bonfires. Round every bonfire crowds were drinking good health to the Bishops and confusion to the Papists. The windows were lighted with rows of candles. Each row consisted of seven; and the taper in the centre, which was taller than the rest, represented the Primate. The noise of rockets, squibs, and firearms, was incessant. One huge pile of faggots blazed right in front of the great gate of Whitehall. Others were lighted before the doors of Roman Catholic peers. Lord Arundell of Wardour wisely quieted the mob with a little money; but at Salisbury House in the Strand, an attempt at resistance was made. Lord Salisbury's servants sallied out and fired: but they killed only the unfortunate beadle of the parish, who had come thither to put out the fire; and they were soon routed and driven back into the house. None of the spectacles of that night interested the common people so much as one with which they had, a few years before, been familiar, and which they now, after a long interval, enjoyed once more, the burning of the Pope. This once familiar pageant is known to our generation only by descriptions and engravings. A figure, by no means resembling those rude representations of Guy Faux which are still paraded on the fifth of November, but made of wax with some skill, and adorned at no small expense with robes and a tiara, was mounted on a chair resembling that in which the Bishops of Rome are still, on some great festivals, borne through St. Peter's Church to the high altar. His Holiness was generally accompanied by a train of Cardinals and Jesuits. At his ear stood a buffoon disguised as a devil with horns and tail. No rich and zealous Protestant grudged his guinea on such an occasion, and, if rumour could be trusted, the cost of the procession was sometimes not less than a thousand pounds. After the Pope had been borne some time in state over the heads of the multitude, he was committed to the flames with loud acclamations. In the time of the popularity of Oates and Shaftesbury, this show was exhibited annually in Fleet Street before the windows of the Whig Club on the anniversary of the birth of Queen Elizabeth. Such was the celebrity of these grotesque rites, that Barillon once risked his life in order to peep at them from a hiding place.* But from the day when the Rye House plot was discovered, till the day of the acquittal of the Bishops, the ceremony had been disused. Now, however, several Popes made their appearance in different parts of London. The Nuncio was much shocked; and the King was more hurt by this insult to his Church than by all the other affronts which he had received. The magistrates, however, could do nothing. The Sunday had dawned, and

* See a very curious narrative published, among other papers, in 1710, by Hanley, then Duke of Leeds. There is an amusing account of the ceremony of burning a Pope in North's Examen, 570. See also the note on the Epilogue to the Tragedy of Œdipus in Scott's edition of Dryden.

CHAP. VIII.

the bells of the parish churches were ringing for early prayers, before the fires began to languish and the crowd to disperse. A proclamation was speedily put forth against the rioters. Many of them, mostly young apprentices, were apprehended; but the bills were thrown out at the Middlesex sessions. The Justices, many of whom were Roman Catholics, expostulated with the grand jury and sent them three or four times back, but to no purpose.*

Peculiar state of public feeling at this time.

Meanwhile the glad tidings were flying to every part of the kingdom, and were everywhere received with rapture. Gloucester, Bedford, and Lichfield were among the places which were distinguished by peculiar zeal: but Bristol and Norwich, which stood nearest to London in population and wealth, approached nearest to London in enthusiasm on this joyful occasion.

The prosecution of the Bishops is an event which stands by itself in our history. It was the first and the last occasion on which two feelings of tremendous potency, two feelings which have generally been opposed to each other, and either of which, when strongly excited, has sufficed to convulse the state, were united in perfect harmony. Those feelings were love of the Church and love of freedom. During many generations every violent outbreak of High Church feeling, with one exception, has been unfavourable to civil liberty; every violent outbreak of zeal for liberty, with one exception, has been unfavourable to the authority and influence of the prelacy and the priesthood. In 1688 the cause of the hierarchy was for a moment that of the popular party. More than nine thousand clergymen, with the Primate and his most respectable suffragans at their head, offered themselves to endure bonds and the spoiling of their goods for the great fundamental principle of our free constitution. The effect was a coalition which included the most zealous Cavaliers, the most zealous Republicans, and all the intermediate sections of the community. The spirit which had supported Hampden in the preceding generation, the spirit which, in the succeeding generation, supported Sacheverell, combined to support the Archbishop who was Hampden and Sacheverell in one. Those classes of society which are most deeply interested in the preservation of order, which in

* Reresby's Memoirs; Van Citters, of July 4.; Oldmixon, 739.; Ellis Correspondence.
July 4/14, 1688; Adda, July 2/12; Barillon,
July 12/22; Luttrell's Diary; Newsletter

troubled times are generally most ready to strengthen the hands of government, and which have a natural antipathy to agitators, followed, without scruple, the guidance of a venerable man, the first peer of the Parliament, the first minister of the Church, a Tory in politics, a saint in manners, whom tyranny had in his own despite turned into a demagogue. Many, on the other hand, who had always abhorred episcopacy, as a relic of Popery, and as an instrument of arbitrary power, now asked on bended knees the blessing of a prelate who was ready to wear fetters and to lay his aged limbs on bare stones rather than betray the interests of the Protestant religion and set the prerogative above the laws. With love of the Church and with love of freedom was mingled, at this great crisis, a third feeling which is among the most honourable peculiarities of our national character. An individual oppressed by power, even when destitute of all claim to public respect and gratitude, generally finds strong sympathy among us. Thus, in the time of our grandfathers, society was thrown into confusion by the persecution of Wilkes. We have ourselves seen the nation roused to madness by the wrongs of Queen Caroline. It is probable, therefore, that, even if no great political or religious interest had been staked on the event of the proceeding against the Bishops, England would not have seen, without strong emotions of pity and anger, old men of stainless virtue pursued by the vengeance of a harsh and inexorable prince who owed to their fidelity the crown which he wore.

Actuated by these sentiments our ancestors arrayed themselves against the government in one huge and compact mass. All ranks, all parties, all Protestant sects, made up that vast phalanx. In the van were the Lords Spiritual and Temporal. Then came the landed gentry and the clergy, both the Universities, all the Inns of Court, merchants, shopkeepers, farmers, the porters who plied in the streets of the great towns, the peasants who ploughed the fields. The league against the King included the very foremost men who manned his ships, the very sentinels who guarded his palace. The names of Whig and Tory were for a moment forgotten. The old Exclusionist took the old Abhorrer by the hand. Episcopalians, Presbyterians, Independents, Baptists, forgot their long feud, and remembered only their common Protestantism and their common danger. Divines bred in the school of Laud talked loudly, not only of toleration, but of comprehension. The Archbishop soon after his acquittal put forth a pastoral letter which is one of the most remarkable compositions of that age. He had, from his youth up, been at war with the Nonconformists, and had repeatedly assailed them with unjust and unchristian asperity. His principal work was a hideous caricature of the Calvinistic theology.* He had drawn up for the thirtieth of January and for the twenty-ninth of May forms of prayer which reflected on the Puritans in language so strong that the government had thought fit to soften it down. But now his heart was melted and opened. He solemnly enjoined the Bishops and clergy to have a very tender regard to their brethren the Protestant Dissenters, to visit them often, to entertain them hospitably, to discourse with them civilly, to persuade them, if it might be, to conform to the Church, but, if that were found impossible, to join them heartily and affectionately in exertions for the blessed cause of the Reformation.†

Many pious persons in subsequent years remembered that time with bitter regret. They described it as a short glimpse of a golden age between two iron ages. Such lamentation, though natural, was not reasonable. The coalition of 1688 was produced, and could be produced, only by tyranny which approached to insanity, and by danger which threatened at once all the great institutions of the country. If there has never since been similar union, the reason is that there has never since been similar misgovernment. It must be remembered that, though concord is in itself better than discord, discord may indicate a better state of things than is indicated by concord. Calamity and peril often force men to combine. Prosperity and security often encourage them to separate.

* The Fur Prædestinatus.

† This document will be found in the first of the twelve collections of papers relating to the affairs of England, printed at the end of 1688 and the beginning of 1689. It was put forth on the 26th of July, not quite a month after the trial. Lloyd of Saint Asaph about the same time told Henry Wharton that the Bishops purposed to adopt an entirely new policy towards the Protestant Dissenters; "Omni modo curaturos ut ecclesiæ sordibus et corruptelis penitus exuerentur; ut sectariis reformatis reditus in ecclesiæ sinum exoptati occasio ac ratio concederetur, si qui soberii et pii essent; ut pertinacibus interim jugum leverentur, extinctis penitus legibus mulctatoriis."— Excerpta ex Vita H. Wharton

CHAPTER IX.

The acquittal of the Bishops was not the only event which makes the thirtieth of June 1688 a great epoch in history. On that day, while the bells of a hundred churches were ringing, while multitudes were busied, from Hyde Park to Mile End, in piling faggots and dressing Popes for the rejoicings of the night, was despatched from London to the Hague an instrument scarcely less important to the liberties of England than the Great Charter.

The prosecution of the Bishops, and the birth of the Prince of Wales, had produced a great revolution in the feelings of many Tories. At the very moment at which their Church was suffering the last excess of injury and insult, they were compelled to renounce the hope of peaceful deliverance. Hitherto they had flattered themselves that the trial to which their loyalty was subjected would, though severe, be temporary, and that their wrongs would shortly be redressed without any violation of the ordinary rule of succession. A very different prospect was now before them. As far as they could look forward they saw only misgovernment, such as that of the last three years, extending through ages. The cradle of the heir apparent of the crown was surrounded by Jesuits. Deadly hatred of that Church of which he would one day be the head would be studiously instilled into his infant mind, would be the guiding principle of his life, and would be bequeathed by him to his posterity. This vista of calamities had no end. It stretched beyond the life of the youngest man living, beyond the eighteenth century. None could say how many generations of Protestant Englishmen might have to bear oppression, such as, even when it had been believed to be short, had been found almost insupportable. Was there then no remedy? One remedy there was, quick, sharp, and decisive, a remedy which the Whigs had been but too ready to employ, but which had always been regarded by the Tories as, in all cases, unlawful.

Change in the opinion of the Tories concerning the lawfulness of resistance.

The greatest Anglican doctors of that age had maintained that no breach of law or contract, no excess of cruelty, rapacity, or licentiousness, on the part of a rightful king, could justify his people in withstanding him by force. Some of them had delighted to exhibit the doctrine of nonresistance in a form so exaggerated as to shock common sense and humanity. They frequently and emphatically remarked that Nero was at the head of the Roman government when Saint Paul inculcated the duty of obeying magistrates. The inference which they drew was that, if an English king should, without any law but his own pleasure, persecute his subjects for not worshipping idols, should fling them to the lions in the Tower, should wrap them up in pitched cloth and set them on fire to light up Saint James's Park, and should go on with these massacres till whole towns and shires were left without one inhabitant, the survivors would still be bound meekly to submit, and to be torn in pieces or roasted alive without a struggle. The arguments in favour of this proposition were futile indeed: but the place of sound argument was amply supplied by the omnipotent sophistry of interest and of passion. Many writers have expressed wonder that the highspirited Cavaliers of England should have been zealous for the most slavish theory that has ever been known among men. The truth is that this theory at first presented itself to the Cavalier as the very opposite of slavish. Its tendency was to make him not a slave but a freeman and a master. It exalted him by exalting one whom he regarded as his protector, as his friend, as the head of his beloved party and of his more beloved Church. When Republicans were dominant the Royalist had endured wrongs and insults which the restoration of the legitimate government had enabled him to retaliate. Rebellion was therefore associated in his imagination with subjection and degradation, and monarchical authority with liberty and ascendency. It had never crossed his imagination that a time might come when a King, a Stuart, would persecute the most loyal of the clergy and gentry with more than the animosity of the Rump or the Protector. That time had however arrived. It was now to be seen how the patience which Churchmen professed to have learned from the writings of Paul would stand the test of a persecution by no means so severe as that of Nero. The event was such as everybody who knew anything of human nature would have predicted. Oppression speedily did what philosophy and eloquence would have failed to do. The system of Filmer might have survived the attacks of Locke: but it never recovered from the death blow given by James.

That logic, which, while it was used to prove that Presbyterians and Independents ought to bear imprisonment and confiscation with meekness, had been pronounced unanswerable, seemed to be of very little force when the question was whether Anglican Bishops should be imprisoned, and the revenues of Anglican colleges confiscated. It had been often repeated, from the pulpits of all the Cathedrals of the land, that the apostolical injunction to obey the civil magistrate was absolute and universal, and that it was impious presumption in man to limit a precept which had been promulgated without any limitation in the word of God. Now, however, divines, whose sagacity had been sharpened by the imminent danger in which they stood of being turned out of their livings and prebends to make room for Papists, discovered flaws in the reasoning which had formerly seemed so convincing. The ethical parts of Scripture were not to be construed like Acts of Parliament, or like the casuistical treatises of the schoolmen. What Christian really turned the left cheek to the ruffian who had smitten the right? What Christian really gave his cloak to the thieves who had taken his coat away? Both in the Old and in the New Testament general rules were perpetually laid down unaccompanied by the exceptions. Thus there was a general command not to kill, unaccompanied by any reservation in favour of the warrior who kills in defence of his king and country. There was a general command not to swear, unaccompanied by any reservation in favour of the witness who swears to speak the truth before a judge. Yet the lawfulness of defensive war, and of judicial oaths, was disputed only by a few obscure sectaries, and was positively affirmed in the articles of the Church of England. All the arguments which showed that the Quaker, who refused to bear arms, or to kiss the Gospels, was unreasonable and perverse, might be turned against those who denied to subjects the right of resisting extreme tyranny by force. If it was contended that the texts which prohibited homicide, and the texts which prohibited swearing, though generally expressed, must be construed in subordination to the great commandment by which every man is enjoined to promote the welfare of his neighbours, and would, when so construed, be found not to apply to cases in which homicide or swearing might be absolutely necessary to protect the dearest interests of society, it was not easy to deny that the texts which prohibited resistance ought to be construed in the same manner. If the ancient people of God had been directed sometimes to destroy human life, and sometimes to bind themselves by oaths, they had also been directed sometimes to resist wicked princes. If early fathers of the Church had occasionally used language which seemed to imply that they disapproved of all resistance, they had also occasionally used language which seemed to imply that they disapproved of all war and of all oaths. In truth the doctrine of passive obedience, as taught at Oxford in the reign of Charles the Second, can be deduced from the Bible only by a mode of interpretation which would irresistibly lead us to the conclusions of Barclay and Penn.

It was not merely by arguments drawn from the letter of Scripture that the Anglican theologians had, during the years which immediately followed the Restoration, laboured to prove their favourite tenet. They had attempted to show that, even if revelation had been silent, reason would have taught wise men the folly and wickedness of all resistance to established government. It was universally admitted that such resistance was, except in extreme cases, unjustifiable. And who would undertake to draw the line between extreme cases and ordinary cases? Was there any government in the world under which there were not to be found some discontented and factious men who would say, and perhaps think, that their grievances constituted an extreme case? If, indeed, it were possible to lay down a clear and accurate rule which might forbid men to rebel against Trajan, and yet leave them at liberty to rebel against Caligula, such a rule might be highly beneficial. But no such rule had ever been, or ever would be, framed. To say that rebellion was lawful under some circumstances, without accurately defining those circumstances, was to say that every man might rebel whenever he thought fit; and a society in which every man rebelled whenever he thought fit would be more miserable than a society governed by the most cruel and licentious despot. It was therefore necessary to maintain the great principle of nonresistance in all its integrity. Particular cases might doubtless be put in which resistance would benefit a community: but it was, on the whole, better that the people should patiently endure a bad government than that they should relieve themselves by violating a law on which the security of all government depended.

Such reasoning easily convinced a dominant and prosperous party, but could ill bear the scrutiny of minds strongly excited by royal injustice and ingratitude. It is true that to trace the exact boundary between rightful and wrongful resistance is impossible: but this impossibility arises from the nature of right and wrong, and is found in every part of ethical science. A good action is not distinguished from a bad action by marks so plain as those which distinguish a hexagon from a square. There is a frontier where virtue and vice fade into each other. Who has ever been able to define the exact boundary between courage and rashness, between prudence and cowardice, between frugality and avarice, between liberality and prodigality? Who has ever been able to say how far mercy to offenders ought to be carried, and where it ceases to deserve the name of mercy and becomes a pernicious weakness? What casuist, what lawgiver, has ever been able nicely to mark the limits of the right of selfdefence? All our jurists hold that a certain quantity of risk to life or limb justifies a man in shooting or stabbing an assailant: but they have long given up in despair the attempt to describe, in precise words, that quantity of risk. They only say that it must be, not a slight risk, but a risk such as would cause serious apprehension to a man of firm mind; and who will undertake to say what is the precise amount of apprehension which deserves to be called serious, or what is the precise texture of mind which deserves to be called firm? It is doubtless to be lamented that the nature of words and the nature of things do not admit of more accurate legislation: nor can it be denied that wrong will often be done when men are judges in their own cause, and proceed instantly to execute their own judgment. Yet who would, on that account, interdict all selfdefence? The right which a people has to resist a bad government bears a close analogy to the right which an individual, in the absence of legal protection, has to slay an assailant. In both cases the evil must be grave. In both cases all regular and peaceable modes of defence must be exhausted before the aggrieved party resorts to extremities. In both cases an awful responsibility is incurred. In both cases the burden of the proof lies on him who has ventured on so desperate an expedient: and, if he fails to vindicate himself, he is justly liable to the

CHAP. IX.

severest penalties. But in neither case can we absolutely deny the existence of the right. A man beset by assassins is not bound to let himself be tortured and butchered without using his weapons, because nobody has ever been able precisely to define the amount of danger which justifies homicide. Nor is a society bound to endure passively all that tyranny can inflict, because nobody has ever been able precisely to define the amount of misgovernment which justifies rebellion.

But could the resistance of Englishmen to such a prince as James be properly called rebellion? The thoroughpaced disciples of Filmer, indeed, maintained that there was no difference whatever between the polity of our country and that of Turkey, and that, if the King did not confiscate the contents of all the tills in Lombard Street, and send mutes with bowstrings to Sancroft and Halifax, this was only because His Majesty was too gracious to use the whole power which he derived from heaven. But the great body of Tories, though, in the heat of conflict, they might occasionally use language which seemed to indicate that they approved of these extravagant doctrines, heartily abhorred despotism. The English government was, in their view, a limited monarchy. Yet how can a monarchy be said to be limited, if force is never to be employed, even in the last resort, for the purpose of maintaining the limitations? In Muscovy, where the sovereign was, by the constitution of the state, absolute, it might perhaps be, with some colour of truth, contended that, whatever excesses he might commit, he was still entitled to demand, on Christian principles, the obedience of his subjects. But here prince and people were alike bound by the laws. It was therefore James who incurred the woe denounced against those who insult the powers that be. It was James who was resisting the ordinance of God, who was mutinying against that legitimate authority to which he ought to have been subject, not only for wrath, but also for conscience sake, and who was, in the true sense of the words of Jesus, withholding from Cæsar the things which were Cæsar's.

Moved by such considerations as these, the ablest and most enlightened Tories began to admit that they had overstrained the doctrine of passive obedience. The difference between these men and the Whigs as to the reciprocal obligations of kings and subjects was now no longer a difference of principle. There still remained, it is true, many historical controversies between the party which had always maintained the lawfulness of resistance and the new converts. The memory of the blessed Martyr was still as much revered as ever by those old Cavaliers who were ready to take arms against his degenerate son. They still spoke with abhorrence of the Long Parliament, of the Rye House plot, and of the Western insurrection. But, whatever they might think about the past, the view which they took of the present was altogether Whiggish; for they now held that extreme oppression might justify resistance, and they held that the oppression which the nation suffered was extreme.*

It must not, however, be supposed that all the Tories renounced, even at that conjuncture, a tenet which they had from childhood been taught to regard as an essential part of Christianity, which they had professed during many years with ostentatious vehemence, and which they had attempted to propagate by persecution. Many were kept steady to their old creed by conscience, and many by shame. But the greater part, even of those who still continued to pronounce all resistance to the sovereign unlawful, were disposed, in the event of a civil conflict, to remain neutral. No provocation should drive them to rebel: but, if rebellion broke forth, it did not appear that they were bound to fight for James the Second as they would have fought for Charles the First. The Christians of Rome had been forbidden by Saint Paul to resist the government of Nero: but there was no reason to believe that the Apostle, if he had been alive when the Legions and the Senate rose up against that wicked Emperor, would have commanded the brethren to fly to arms in support of tyranny. The duty of the persecuted Church was clear: she must suffer patiently, and commit her cause to God. But, if God, whose providence perpetually educes good out of evil, should be pleased, as oftentimes He had been pleased, to redress her wrongs by the instrumentality of men whose angry passions her lessons had not been able to tame, she might gratefully accept from Him a deliverance which her principles did not permit her to achieve for herself. Most of those Tories, therefore, who still sincerely disclaimed

* This change in the opinion of a section of the Tory party is well illustrated by a little tract published at the beginning of 1689, and entitled "A Dialogue between Two Friends, wherein the Church of England is vindicated in joining with the Prince of Orange."

all thought of attacking the government, were yet by no means inclined to defend it, and perhaps, while glorying in their own scruples, secretly rejoiced that everybody was not so scrupulous as themselves.

The Whigs saw that their time was come. Whether they should draw the sword against the government had, during six or seven years, been, in their view, merely a question of prudence; and prudence itself now urged them to take a bold course.

Russell proposes to the Prince of Orange a descent on England.

In May, before the birth of the Prince of Wales, and while it was still uncertain whether the Declaration would or would not be read in the churches, Edward Russell had repaired to the Hague. He had strongly represented to the Prince of Orange the state of the public mind, and had advised His Highness to appear in England at the head of a strong body of troops, and to call the people to arms.

William had seen, at a glance, the whole importance of the crisis. "Now or never," he exclaimed in Latin to Van Dykvelt.* To Russell he held more guarded language, admitted that the distempers of the State were such as required an extraordinary remedy, but spoke with earnestness of the chance of failure, and of the calamities which failure might bring on Britain and on Europe. He knew well that many who talked in high language about sacrificing their lives and fortunes for their country would hesitate when the prospect of another Bloody Circuit was brought close to them. He wanted therefore to have, not vague professions of good will, but distinct invitations and promises of support subscribed by powerful and eminent men. Russell remarked that it would be dangerous to entrust the design to a great number of persons. William assented, and said that a few signatures would be sufficient, if they were the signatures of statesmen who represented great interests.†

With this answer Russell returned to London, where he found the excitement greatly increased and daily increasing. The imprisonment of the Bishops and the delivery of the Queen made his task easier than he could have anticipated. He lost no time in collecting the voices of the chiefs of the opposition. His principal coadjutor in this work was Henry Sidney, brother of Algernon. It is remarkable that both Edward Russell and Henry Sidney had been in the household

Henry Sidney.

---

* "Aut nunc, aut nunquam."—Witsen MS. quoted by Wagenaar, book lx.
† Burnet, i. 763.

of James, that both had, partly on public and partly on private grounds, become his enemies, and that both had to avenge the blood of near kinsmen who had, in the same year, fallen victims to his implacable severity. Here the resemblance ends. Russell, with considerable abilities, was proud, acrimonious, restless, and violent. Sidney, with a sweet temper and winning manners, seemed to be deficient in capacity and knowledge, and to be sunk in voluptuousness and indolence. His face and form were eminently handsome. In his youth he had been the terror of husbands; and even now, at near fifty, he was the favourite of women and the envy of younger men. He had formerly resided at the Hague in a public character, and had then succeeded in obtaining a large share of William's confidence. Many wondered at this: for it seemed that between the most austere of statesmen and the most dissolute of idlers there could be nothing in common. Swift, many years later, could not be convinced that one whom he had known only as an illiterate and frivolous old rake could really have played a great part in a great revolution. Yet a less acute observer than Swift might have been aware that there is a certain tact, resembling an instinct, which is often wanting to great orators and philosophers, and which is often found in persons who, if judged by their conversation or by their writings, would be pronounced simpletons. Indeed, when a man possesses this tact, it is in some sense an advantage to him that he is destitute of those more showy talents which would make him an object of admiration, of envy, and of fear. Sidney was a remarkable instance of this truth. Incapable, ignorant, and dissipated as he seemed to be, he understood, or rather felt, with whom it was necessary to be reserved, and with whom he might safely venture to be communicative. The consequence was, that he did what Mordaunt, with all his vivacity and invention, or Burnet, with all his multifarious knowledge and fluent elocution, never could have done.*

With the old Whigs there could be no difficulty. In their opinion there had been scarcely a moment, during many years, at which the public wrongs would not have justified resistance. Devonshire, who might be regarded as their chief, had private as well as public wrongs to revenge. He

Devonshire.

* Sidney's Diary and Correspondence, edited by Mr. Blencowe; Mackay's Memoirs with Swift's note; Burnet, I. 762.

went into the scheme with his whole heart, and answered for his party.*

Russell opened the design to Shrewsbury. Sidney sounded Halifax. Shrewsbury took his part with a courage and decision which, at a later period, seemed to be wanting to his character. He at once agreed to set his estate, his honours, and his life, on the stake. But Halifax received the first hint of the project in a way which showed that it would be useless, and perhaps hazardous, to be explicit. He was indeed not the man for such an enterprise. His intellect was inexhaustibly fertile of distinctions and objections, his temper calm and unadventurous. He was ready to oppose the Court to the utmost in the House of Lords and by means of anonymous writings: but he was little disposed to exchange his lordly repose for the insecure and agitated life of a conspirator, to be in the power of accomplices, to live in constant dread of warrants and King's messengers, nay, perhaps, to end his days on a scaffold, or to live on alms in some back street of the Hague. He therefore let fall some words which plainly indicated that he did not wish to be privy to the intentions of his more daring and impetuous friends. Sidney understood him and said no more.†

The next application was made to Danby, and had far better success. Indeed, for his bold and active spirit the danger and the excitement, which were insupportable to the more delicately organised mind of Halifax, had a strong fascination. The different characters of the two statesmen were legible in their faces. The brow, the eye, and the mouth of Halifax indicated a powerful intellect and an exquisite sense of the ludicrous; but the expression was that of a sceptic, of a voluptuary, of a man not likely to venture his all on a single hazard, or to be a martyr in any cause. To those who are acquainted with his countenance it will not seem wonderful that the writer in whom he most delighted was Montaigne.‡ Danby was a skeleton; and his meagre and wrinkled, though handsome and noble, face strongly expressed both the keenness of his parts, and the restlessness of his ambition. Already he had once risen

* Burnet, i. 764.; Letter in cipher to William, dated June 18, 1688, in Dalrymple.
† Ibid.
‡ As to Montaigne, see Halifax's Letter to Cotton. I am not sure that the head of Halifax in Westminster Abbey does not give a more lively notion of him than any painting or engraving that I have seen.

from obscurity to the height of power. He had then fallen headlong from his elevation. His life had been in danger. He had passed years in a prison. He was now free: but this did not content him; he wished to be again great. Attached as he was to the Anglican Church, hostile as he was to the French ascendency, he could not hope to be great in a court swarming with Jesuits and obsequious to the House of Bourbon. But, if he bore a chief part in a revolution which should confound all the schemes of the Papists, which should put an end to the long vassalage of England, and which should transfer the regal power to an illustrious pair whom he had united, he might emerge from his eclipse with new splendour. The Whigs, whose animosity had nine years before driven him from office, would, on his auspicious reappearance, join their acclamations to the acclamations of his old friends the Cavaliers. Already there had been a complete reconciliation between him and one of the most distinguished of those who had formerly been managers of his impeachment, the Earl of Devonshire. The two noblemen had met at a village in the Peak, and had exchanged assurances of good will. Devonshire had frankly owned that the Whigs had been guilty of a great injustice, and had declared that they were now convinced of their error. Danby, on his side, had also recantations to make. He had once held, or pretended to hold, the doctrine of passive obedience in the largest sense. Under his administration, and with his sanction, a law had been proposed which, if it had been passed, would have excluded from Parliament and office all who refused to declare on oath that they thought resistance in every case unlawful. But his vigorous understanding, now thoroughly awakened by anxiety for the public interests and for his own, was no longer to be duped, if indeed it ever had been duped, by such childish fallacies. He at once gave in his own adhesion to the conspiracy. He then exerted himself to obtain the concurrence of Compton, the suspended Bishop of London, and succeeded without difficulty. No prelate had been so insolently and unjustly treated by the government as Compton; nor had any prelate so much to expect from a revolution: for he had directed the education of the Princess of Orange, and was supposed to possess a large share of her confidence. He had, like his brethren, strongly maintained, as long as he

CHAP. IX.

Bishop Compton.

was not oppressed, that it was a crime to resist oppression; but, since he had stood before the High Commission, a new light had broken in upon his mind.*

Nottingham. Both Danby and Compton were desirous to secure the assistance of Nottingham. The whole plan was opened to him; and he approved of it. But in a few days he began to be unquiet. His mind was not sufficiently powerful to emancipate itself from the prejudices of education. He went about from divine to divine proposing in general terms hypothetical cases of tyranny, and inquiring whether in such cases resistance would be lawful. The answers which he obtained increased his distress. He at length told his accomplices that he could go no further with them. If they thought him capable of betraying them, they might stab him; and he should hardly blame them; for, by drawing back after going so far, he had given them a kind of right over his life. They had, however, he assured them, nothing to fear from him: he would keep their secret: he could not help wishing them success; but his conscience would not suffer him to take an active part in a rebellion. They heard his confession with suspicion and disdain. Sidney, whose notions of a conscientious scruple were extremely vague, informed the Prince that Nottingham had taken fright. It is due to Nottingham, however, to say that the general tenor of his life justifies us in believing his conduct on this occasion to have been perfectly honest, though most unwise and irresolute.†

Lumley. The agents of the Prince had more complete success with Lord Lumley, who knew himself to be, in spite of the eminent service which he had performed at the time of the Western insurrection, abhorred at Whitehall, not only as a heretic but as a renegade, and who was therefore more eager than most of those who had been born Protestants to take arms in defence of Protestantism.‡

Invitation to William despatched. During June the meetings of those who were in the secret were frequent. At length, on the last day of the month, the day on which the Bishops were pronounced not guilty, the decisive step was taken. A formal invitation, transcribed by Sidney, but drawn up by some person better skilled than Sidney in the art of composition, was despatched

---

* See Danby's Introduction to the papers which he published in 1710; Burnet, i. 764.
† Burnet, i. 764.; Sidney to the Prince of Orange, June 30. 1688, in Dalrymple.
‡ Burnet, i. 753.; Lumley to William, May 31. 1688, in Dalrymple.

to the Hague. In this paper William was assured that
nineteen twentieths of the English people were desirous of a
change, and would willingly join to effect it, if only they
could obtain the help of such a force from abroad as might
secure those who should rise in arms from the danger of
being dispersed and slaughtered before they could form
themselves into anything like military order. If His Highness would appear in the island at the head of some troops,
tens of thousands would hasten to his standard. He would
soon find himself at the head of a force greatly superior to
the whole regular army of England. Nor could that army
be implicitly depended on by the government. The officers
were discontented; and the common soldiers shared that
aversion to Popery which was general in the class from
which they were taken. In the navy Protestant feeling was
still stronger. It was important to take some decisive step
while things were in this state. The enterprise would be far
more arduous if it were deferred till the King, by remodelling
boroughs and regiments, had procured a Parliament and an
army on which he could rely. The conspirators, therefore,
implored the Prince to come among them with as little delay
as possible. They pledged their honour that they would
join him; and they undertook to secure the cooperation of as
large a number of persons as could safely be trusted with
so momentous and perilous a secret. On one point they
thought it their duty to remonstrate with His Highness.
He had not taken advantage of the opinion which the
great body of the English people had formed touching the
late birth. He had, on the contrary, sent congratulations
to Whitehall, and had thus seemed to acknowledge that the
child who was called Prince of Wales was rightful heir of
the throne. This was a grave error, and had damped the
zeal of many. Not one person in a thousand doubted that
the boy was supposititious; and the Prince would be wanting to his own interests if the suspicious circumstances which
had attended the Queen's confinement were not put prominently forward among his reasons for taking arms.*

This paper was signed in cipher by the seven chiefs of the
conspiracy, Shrewsbury, Devonshire, Danby, Lumley, Compton, Russell, and Sidney. Herbert undertook to be their
messenger. His errand was one of no ordinary peril. He
assumed the garb of a common sailor, and in this disguise

* See the invitation at length in Dalrymple.

reached the Dutch coast in safety, on the Friday after the trial of the Bishops. He instantly hastened to the Prince. Bentinck and Van Dykvelt were summoned, and several days were passed in deliberation. The first result of this deliberation was that the prayer for the Prince of Wales ceased to be read in the Princess's chapel.*

Conduct of Mary.

From his wife William had no opposition to apprehend. Her understanding had been completely subjugated by his; and, what is more extraordinary, he had won her entire affection. He was to her in the place of the parents whom she had lost by death and by estrangement, of the children who had been denied to her prayers, and of the country from which she was banished. His empire over her heart was divided only with her God. To her father she had probably never been attached: she had quitted him young: many years had elapsed since she had seen him; and no part of his conduct to her, since her marriage, had indicated tenderness on his part, or had been calculated to call forth tenderness on hers. He had done all in his power to disturb her domestic happiness, and had established a system of spying, eavesdropping, and talebearing under her roof. He had a far greater revenue than any of his predecessors had ever possessed, and allowed to her younger sister thirty or forty thousand pounds a year†: but the heiress presumptive of his throne had never received from him the smallest pecuniary assistance, and was scarcely able to make that appearance which became her high rank among European princesses. She had ventured to intercede with him on behalf of her old friend and preceptor Compton, who, for refusing to commit an act of flagitious injustice, had been suspended from his episcopal functions: but she had been ungraciously repulsed.‡ From the day on which it had become clear that she and her husband were determined not to be parties to the subversion of the English constitution, one chief object of the politics of James had been to injure them both. He had recalled the British regiments from Holland. He had conspired with Tyrconnel and with France against Mary's rights, and had made arrangements for depriving her of one at least of the three crowns to which, at his death, she would have been entitled. It was believed by the great body of his

* Sidney's Letter to William, June 30. 1688; Avaux Neg. July 19. 11.
† Bonrepaus, July 19. 1687.
‡ Birch's Extracts, in the British Museum.

people, and by many persons high in rank and distinguished by abilities, that he had introduced a supposititious Prince of Wales into the royal family, in order to deprive her of a magnificent inheritance; and there is no reason to doubt that she partook of the prevailing suspicion. That she should love such a father was impossible. Her religious principles, indeed, were so strict that she would probably have tried to perform what she considered as her duty, even to a father whom she did not love. On the present occasion, however, she judged that the claim of James to her obedience ought to yield to a claim more sacred. And indeed all divines and publicists agree in this, that, when the daughter of a prince of one country is married to a prince of another country, she is bound to forget her own people and her father's house, and, in the event of a rupture between her husband and her parents, to side with her husband. This is the undoubted rule even when the husband is in the wrong; and to Mary the enterprise which William meditated appeared not only just, but holy.

But, though she carefully abstained from doing or saying anything that could add to his difficulties, those difficulties were serious indeed. They were in truth but imperfectly understood even by some of those who invited him over, and have been but imperfectly described by some of those who have written the history of his expedition.

The obstacles which he might expect to encounter on English ground, though the least formidable of the obstacles which stood in the way of his design, were yet serious. He felt that it would be madness in him to imitate the example of Monmouth, to cross the sea with a few British adventurers, and to trust to a general rising of the population. It was necessary, and it was pronounced necessary by all those who invited him over, that he should carry an army with him. Yet who could answer for the effect which the appearance of such an army might produce? The government was indeed justly odious. But would the English people, altogether unaccustomed to the interference of Continental powers in English disputes, be inclined to look with favour on a deliverer who was surrounded by foreign soldiers? If any part of the royal forces resolutely withstood the invaders, would not that part soon have on its side the patriotic sympathy of millions? A defeat would be fatal to the whole undertaking. A bloody victory gained in the heart of the island by the mercenaries of the States General over the Coldstream Guards and the Buffs would be almost as great a calamity as a defeat. Such a victory would be the most cruel wound ever inflicted on the national pride of one of the proudest of nations. The crown so won would never be worn in peace or security. The hatred with which the High Commission and the Jesuits were regarded would give place to the more intense hatred which would be inspired by the alien conquerors; and many, who had hitherto contemplated the power of France with dread and loathing, would say that, if a foreign yoke must be borne, there was less ignominy in submitting to France than in submitting to Holland.

These considerations might well have made William uneasy, even if all the military means of the United Provinces had been at his absolute disposal. But in truth it seemed very doubtful whether he would be able to obtain the assistance of a single battalion. Of all the difficulties with which he had to struggle, the greatest, though little noticed by English historians, arose from the constitution of the Batavian republic. No great society has ever existed during a long course of years under a polity so inconvenient. The States General could not make war or peace, could not conclude any alliance or levy any tax, without the consent of the States of every province. The States of a province could not give such consent without the consent of every municipality which had a share in the representation. Every municipality was, in some sense, a sovereign state, and, as such, claimed the right of communicating directly with foreign ambassadors, and of concerting with them the means of defeating schemes on which other municipalities were intent. In some town councils the party, which had, during several generations, regarded the influence of the Stadtholders with jealousy, had great power. At the head of this party were the magistrates of the noble city of Amsterdam, which was then at the height of prosperity. They had, ever since the peace of Nimeguen, kept up a friendly correspondence with Lewis through the instrumentality of his able and active envoy the Count of Avaux. Propositions brought forward by the Stadtholder as indispensable to the security of the commonwealth, sanctioned by all the provinces except Holland, and sanctioned by seventeen of the eighteen town councils of Holland, had repeatedly been negatived by the single voice of Amsterdam. The only constitutional remedy in such cases was that deputies from the cities which were agreed should pay a visit to the city which dissented, for the purpose of expostulation. The number of deputies was unlimited; they might continue to expostulate as long as they thought fit; and meanwhile all their expenses were defrayed by the obstinate community which refused to yield to their arguments. This absurd mode of coercion had once been tried with success on the little town of Gorkum, but was not likely to produce much effect on the mighty and opulent Amsterdam, renowned throughout the world for its haven bristling with innumerable masts, its canals bordered by stately mansions, its gorgeous hall of state, walled, roofed, and floored with polished marble, its warehouses filled with the most costly productions of Ceylon and Surinam, and its exchange resounding with the endless hubbub of all the languages spoken by civilised men.*

The disputes between the majority which supported the Stadtholder and the minority headed by the magistrates of Amsterdam had repeatedly run so high that bloodshed had seemed to be inevitable. On one occasion the Prince had attempted to bring the refractory deputies to punishment as traitors. On another occasion the gates of Amsterdam had been barred against him, and troops had been raised to defend the privileges of the municipal council. That the rulers of this great city would ever consent to an expedition offensive in the highest degree to Lewis whom they courted, and likely to aggrandise the House of Orange which they abhorred, was not likely. Yet, without their consent, such an expedition could not legally be undertaken. To quell their opposition by main force was a course from which, in different circumstances, the resolute and daring Stadtholder would not have shrunk. But at that moment it was most important that he should carefully avoid every act which could be represented as tyrannical. He could not venture to violate the fundamental laws of Holland at the very moment at which he was drawing the sword against his father in law for violating the fundamental laws of England. The violent subversion of one free constitution would have been a strange prelude to the violent restoration of another.†

There was yet another difficulty which has been too little noticed by English writers, but which was never for a moment

---

* Avaux Neg. 1683.
† As to the relation in which the Stadtholder and the city of Amsterdam stood towards each other, see Avaux, passim.

absent from William's mind. In the expedition which he meditated he could succeed only by appealing to the Protestant feeling of England, and by stimulating that feeling till it became, for a time, the dominant and almost the exclusive sentiment of the nation. This would indeed have been a very simple course, had the end of all his politics been to effect a revolution in our island and to reign there. But he had in view an ulterior end which could be obtained only by the help of princes sincerely attached to the Church of Rome. He was desirous to unite the Empire, the Catholic King, and the Holy See, with England and Holland, in a league against the French ascendency. It was therefore necessary that, while striking the greatest blow ever struck in defence of Protestantism, he should yet contrive not to lose the goodwill of governments which regarded Protestantism as a deadly heresy.

Such were the complicated difficulties of this great undertaking. Continental statesmen saw a part of those difficulties, British statesmen another part. One capacious and powerful mind alone took them all in at one view, and determined to surmount them all. It was no easy thing to subvert the English Government by means of a foreign army without galling the national pride of Englishmen. It was no easy thing to obtain from that Batavian faction which regarded France with partiality, and the House of Orange with aversion, a decision in favour of an expedition which would confound all the schemes of France, and raise the House of Orange to the height of greatness. It was no easy thing to lead enthusiastic Protestants on a crusade against Popery with the good wishes of almost all Popish governments and of the Pope himself. Yet all these things William effected. All his objects, even those which appeared most incompatible with each other, he attained completely and at once. The whole history of ancient and of modern times records no other such triumph of statesmanship.

The task would indeed have been too arduous even for such a statesman as the Prince of Orange, had not his chief adversaries been at this time smitten with an infatuation such as by many men not prone to superstition was ascribed to the special judgment of God. Not only was the King of England, as he had ever been, stupid and perverse: but even the counsel of the politic King of France was turned into foolishness. Whatever wisdom and energy could do William did.

Those obstacles which no wisdom or energy could have overcome his enemies themselves studiously removed.

On the great day on which the Bishops were acquitted, and on which the invitation was despatched to the Hague, James returned from Hounslow to Westminster in a gloomy and unquiet mood. He made an effort that afternoon to appear cheerful*; but the bonfires, the rockets, and above all the waxen Popes who were blazing in every quarter of London, were not likely to soothe him. Those who saw him on the morrow could easily read in his face and demeanour the violent emotions which disturbed his mind.† During some days he appeared so unwilling to talk about the trial that even Barillon could not venture to introduce the subject.‡

Soon it began to be clear that defeat and mortification had only hardened the King's heart. Almost the first words which he uttered when he learned that the objects of his revenge had escaped him, were, "So much the worse for them." In a few days these words, which he, according to his fashion, repeated many times, were fully explained. He blamed himself, not for having prosecuted the Bishops, but for having prosecuted them before a tribunal where questions of fact were decided by juries, and where established principles of law could not be utterly disregarded even by the most servile Judges. This error he determined to repair. Not only the seven prelates who had signed the petition, but the whole Anglican clergy, should have reason to curse the day on which they had triumphed over their Sovereign. Within a fortnight after the trial an order was made, enjoining all Chancellors of dioceses and all Archdeacons to make a strict inquisition throughout their respective jurisdictions, and to report to the High Commission, within five weeks, the names of all such rectors, vicars, and curates, as had omitted to read the Declaration.§ The King anticipated with delight the terror with which the offenders would learn that they were to be cited before a court which would give them no quarter.‖ The number of culprits was little, if at all, short of ten thousand: and, after what had passed at Magdalene College, every one of them might reasonably expect to be interdicted from all his spiritual functions, ejected from his benefice, declared incapable of holding any other preferment, and

---

* Adda, July 9/19 1688.
† Harvey's Memoirs.
‖ Barillon, July 9/19 1688.
§ London Gazette of July 16. 1688. The order bears date July 12.
¶ Barillon's own phrase, July 9/19 1688.

CHAP. IX.

Dismissions and promotions.

charged with the costs of the proceedings which had reduced him to beggary.

Such was the persecution with which James, smarting from his great defeat in Westminster Hall, resolved to harass the clergy. Meanwhile he tried to show the lawyers, by a prompt and large distribution of rewards and punishments, that strenuous and unblushing servility, even when least successful, was a sure title to his favour, and that whoever, after years of obsequiousness, ventured to deviate but for one moment into courage and honesty was guilty of an unpardonable offence. The violence and audacity which the apostate Williams had exhibited throughout the trial of the Bishops had made him hateful to the whole nation.* He was recompensed with a baronetcy. Holloway and Powell had raised their character by declaring that, in their judgment, the petition was no libel. They were dismissed from their situations.† The fate of Wright seems to have been, during some time, in suspense. He had indeed summed up against the Bishops: but he had suffered their counsel to question the dispensing power. He had pronounced the petition a libel: but he had carefully abstained from pronouncing the Declaration legal; and, through the whole proceeding, his tone had been that of a man who remembered that a day of reckoning might come. He had indeed strong claims to indulgence: for it was hardly to be expected that any human impudence would hold out without flagging through such a task, in the presence of such a bar and of such an auditory. The members of the Jesuitical cabal, however, blamed his want of spirit: the Chancellor pronounced him a beast; and it was generally believed that a new Chief Justice would be appointed.‡ But no change was made. It would indeed have been no easy matter to supply Wright's place. The many lawyers who were far superior to him in parts and learning were, with scarcely an exception, hostile to the designs of the government: and the very few lawyers who surpassed him in turpitude and effrontery were, with scarcely an exception, to be found only in the lowest ranks of the profession, and would have been incompetent to conduct the ordinary business of the Court of King's Bench. Williams,

* In one of the numerous ballads of that time are the following lines:

"Rush our Britons are fooled,
Who the laws overruled,
And our parliament each will be plagued
nobodied."

The two Britons are Jeffreys and Williams, who were both natives of Wales.
† London Gazette, July 9. 1688.
‡ Ellis Correspondence, July 10. 1688; Clarendon's Diary, Aug. 3. 1688

it is true, united all the qualities which James required in a magistrate. But the services of Williams were needed at the bar; and had he been removed thence, the crown would have been left without the help of any advocate even of the third rate.

Nothing had amazed or mortified the King more than the enthusiasm which the Dissenters had shown in the cause of the Bishops. Penn, who, though he had himself sacrificed wealth and honours to his conscientious scruples, seems to have imagined that nobody but himself had a conscience, imputed the discontent of the Puritans to envy and dissatisfied ambition. They had not had their share of the benefits promised by the Declaration of Indulgence: none of them had been admitted to any high and honourable post; and therefore it was not strange that they were jealous of the Roman Catholics. Accordingly, within a week after the great verdict had been pronounced in Westminster Hall, Silas Titus, a noted Presbyterian, a vehement Exclusionist, and a manager of Stafford's impeachment, was invited to occupy a seat in the Privy Council. He was one of the persons on whom the opposition had most confidently reckoned. But the honour now offered to him, and the hope of obtaining a large sum due to him from the crown, overcame his virtue, and, to the great disgust of all classes of Protestants, he was sworn in.*

The vindictive designs of the King against the Church were not accomplished. Almost all the Archdeacons and diocesan Chancellors refused to furnish the information which was required. The day on which it had been intended that the whole body of the priesthood should be summoned to answer for the crime of disobedience arrived. The High Commission met. It appeared that scarcely one ecclesiastical officer had sent up a return. At the same time a paper of grave import was delivered to the board. It came from Sprat, Bishop of Rochester. During two years, supported by the hope of an Archbishopric, he had been content to bear the reproach of persecuting that Church which he was bound by every obligation of conscience and honour to defend. But his hope had been disappointed. He saw that, unless he abjured his religion, he had no chance of sitting on the metropolitan throne of York. He was too goodnatured

*London Gazette, July 9. 1688; 12.; Johnstone, Dec. 4/14. 1687. Feb. 3/13. Adda, July 11/21.; Evelyn's Diary, July 16/18.

CHAP. IX.

to find any pleasure in tyranny, and too discerning not to see the signs of the coming retribution. He therefore determined to resign his odious functions; and he communicated his determination to his colleagues in a letter written, like all his prose compositions, with great propriety and dignity of style. It was impossible, he said, that he could any longer continue to be a member of the Commission. He had himself, in obedience to the royal command, read the Declaration: but he could not presume to condemn thousands of pious and loyal divines who had taken a different view of their duty; and since it was resolved to punish them for acting according to their conscience, he must declare that he would rather suffer with them than be accessory to their sufferings.

The Commissioners read and stood aghast. The very faults of their colleague, the known laxity of his principles, the known meanness of his spirit, made his defection peculiarly alarming. A government must be indeed in danger, when men like Sprat address it in the language of Hampden. The tribunal, lately so insolent, became on a sudden strangely tame. The ecclesiastical functionaries who had defied its authority were not even reprimanded. It was not thought safe to hint any suspicion that their disobedience had been intentional. They were merely enjoined to have their reports ready in four months. The Commission then broke up in confusion. It had received a death blow.*

Discontent of the clergy.

While the High Commission shrank from a conflict with the Church, the Church, conscious of its strength, and animated by a new enthusiasm, invited, by a series of defiances, the attack of the High Commission. Soon after the acquittal of the Bishops, the venerable Ormond, the most illustrious of the Cavaliers of the great civil war, sank under his infirmities. The intelligence of his death was conveyed with speed to Oxford. Instantly the University, of which he had long been Chancellor, met to name a successor. One party was for the eloquent and accomplished Halifax, another for the grave and orthodox Nottingham. Some mentioned the Earl of Abingdon, who resided near them, and had recently been turned out of the lieutenancy of the county for refusing to join with the King against the established religion. But the majority, consisting of a hundred and eighty graduates, voted for the young Duke of Ormond,

Transactions at Oxford.

* Sprat's Letters to the Earl of Dorset; London Gazette, Aug. 23. 1688.

grandson of their late head, and son of the gallant Ossory. The speed with which they came to this resolution was caused by their apprehension that, if there were a delay even of a day, the King would attempt to force on them some chief who would betray their rights. The apprehension was reasonable: for, only two hours after they had separated, came a mandate from Whitehall requiring them to choose Jeffreys. Happily the election of young Ormond was already complete and irrevocable.* A few weeks later the infamous Timothy Hall, who had distinguished himself among the clergy of London by reading the Declaration, was rewarded with the Bishopric of Oxford, which had been vacant since the death of the not less infamous Parker. Hall came down to his see: but the Canons of his Cathedral refused to attend his installation: the University refused to create him a Doctor: not a single one of the academic youth applied to him for holy orders: no cap was touched to him; and, in his palace, he found himself alone.†

Soon afterwards a living which was in the gift of Magdalene College, Oxford, became vacant. Hough and his ejected brethren assembled and presented a clerk; and the Bishop of Gloucester, in whose diocese the living lay, instituted their presentee without hesitation.‡

The gentry were not less refractory than the clergy. The assizes of that summer wore all over the country an aspect never before known. The Judges, before they set out on their circuits, had been summoned into the King's presence, and had been directed by him to impress on the grand jurors and magistrates, throughout the kingdom, the duty of electing such members of Parliament as would support his policy. They obeyed his commands, harangued vehemently against the clergy, reviled the seven Bishops, called the memorable petition a factious libel, criticised with great asperity Sancroft's style, which was indeed open to criticism, and pronounced that His Grace ought to be whipped by Doctor Busby for writing bad English. But the only effect of these indecent declamations was to increase the public discontent. All the marks of respect which had usually been shown to

CHAP. IX.

Discontents of the gentry.

---

* London Gazette, July 26, 1688; Adda, July 27; Newsletter in the Mackintosh Collection, July 25.; Ellis Correspondence, July 28. 31.; Wood's Fasti Oxonienses.

† Wood's Athenæ Oxonienses; Luttrell's Diary, Aug. 23. 1688.

‡ Ronquillo, Sept. 17. 1688; Luttrell's Diary, Sept. 6.

the judicial office and to the royal commission were withdrawn. The old custom was that men of good birth and estate should ride in the train of the Sheriff when he escorted the Judges to the county town; but such a procession could now with difficulty be formed in any part of the kingdom. The successors of Powell and Holloway, in particular, were treated with marked indignity. The Oxford circuit had been alloted to them: and they had expected to be greeted in every shire by a cavalcade of the loyal gentry. But as they approached Wallingford, where they were to open their commission for Berkshire, the Sheriff alone came forth to meet them. As they approached Oxford, the eminently loyal capital of an eminently loyal province, they were again welcomed by the Sheriff alone.*

The army was scarcely less disaffected than the clergy or the gentry. The garrison of the Tower had drunk the health of the imprisoned Bishops. The footguards stationed at Lambeth had, with every mark of reverence, welcomed the Primate back to his palace. Nowhere had the news of the acquittal been received with more clamorous delight than at Hounslow Heath. In truth, the great force which the King had assembled for the purpose of overawing his mutinous capital had become more mutinous than the capital itself, and was more dreaded by the Court than by the citizens. Early in August, therefore, the camp was broken up, and the troops were sent to quarters in different parts of the country.†

James flattered himself that it would be easier to deal with separate battalions than with many thousands of men collected in one mass. The first experiment was tried on Lord Lichfield's regiment of infantry, now called the Twelfth of the Line. That regiment was probably selected because it had been raised at the time of the Western insurrection, in Staffordshire, a province where the Roman Catholics were more numerous and powerful than in almost any other part of England. The men were drawn up in the King's presence. Their Major informed them that His Majesty wished them to subscribe an engagement, binding them to assist in carrying into effect his intentions concerning the test, and that all who did not choose to comply must quit the service on the spot. To the King's great astonishment, whole ranks instantly laid

* Ellis Correspondence, August 4, 7. Conference of November 6, 1688, 1688; Bishop Sprat's relation of the   † Luttrell's Diary, August 8, 1688.

down their pikes and muskets. Only two officers and a few privates, all Roman Catholics, obeyed his command. He remained silent for a short time. Then he bade the men take up their arms. "Another time," he said, with a gloomy look, "I shall not do you the honour to consult you."*

It was plain that, if he determined to persist in his designs, he must remodel his army. Yet materials for that purpose he could not find in our island. The members of his Church, even in the districts where they were most numerous, were a small minority of the people. Hatred of Popery had spread through all classes of his Protestant subjects, and had become the ruling passion even of ploughmen and artisans. But there was another part of his dominions where a very different spirit animated the great body of the population. There was no limit to the number of Roman Catholic soldiers whom the good pay and quarters of England would attract across St. George's Channel. Tyrconnel had been, during some time, employed in forming out of the peasantry of his country a military force on which his master might depend. Already Papists, of Celtic blood and speech, composed almost the whole army of Ireland. Barillon earnestly and repeatedly advised James to bring over that army for the purpose of coercing the English.†

James wavered. He wished to be surrounded by troops on whom he could rely: but he dreaded the explosion of national feeling which the appearance of a great Irish force on English ground must produce. At last, as usually happens when a weak man tries to avoid opposite inconveniences, he took a course which united them all. He brought over Irishmen, not indeed enough to hold down the single city of London, or the single county of York, but more than enough to excite the alarm and rage of the whole kingdom, from Northumberland to Cornwall. Battalion after battalion, raised and trained by Tyrconnel, landed on the western coast and moved towards the capital; and Irish recruits were imported in considerable numbers, to fill up vacancies in the English regiments.‡

Of the many errors which James committed, none was

---

* This is told us by three writers who could well remember that time, Kennet, Eachard, and Oldmixon. See also the Caveat against the Whigs.

† Barillon, Aug. 20, 1685; September 3, 2, 3.

‡ Luttrell's Diary, Aug. 27, 1688.

more fatal than this. Already he had alienated the hearts of his people by violating their laws, confiscating their estates, and persecuting their religion. Of those who had once been most zealous for monarchy, he had already made many rebels in heart. Yet he might still, with some chance of success, have appealed to the patriotic spirit of his subjects against an invader. For they were a race insular in temper as well as in geographical position. Their national antipathies were, indeed, in that age, unreasonably and unamiably strong. Never had the English been accustomed to the control or interference of any stranger. The appearance of a foreign army on their soil might impel them to rally even round a King whom they had no reason to love. William might, perhaps, have been unable to overcome this difficulty; but James removed it. Not even the arrival of a brigade of Lewis's musketeers would have excited such resentment and shame as our ancestors felt when they saw armed columns of Papists, just arrived from Dublin, moving in military pomp along the high roads. No man of English blood then regarded the aboriginal Irish as his countrymen. They did not belong to our branch of the great human family. They were distinguished from us by more than one moral and intellectual peculiarity, which the difference of situation and of education, great as that difference was, did not seem altogether to explain. They had an aspect of their own, a mother tongue of their own. When they talked English their pronunciation was ludicrous; and their phraseology was grotesque, as is always the phraseology of those who think in one language and express their thoughts in another. They were therefore foreigners; and of all foreigners they were the most hated and despised; the most hated, for they had, during five centuries, always been our enemies; the most despised, for they were our vanquished, enslaved, and despoiled enemies. The Englishman felt proud when he compared his own fields with the desolate bogs whence the Rapparees issued forth to rob and murder, and his own dwelling with the hovels where the peasants and the hogs of the Shannon wallowed in filth together. He was a member of a society, far inferior, indeed, in wealth and civilisation, to the society in which we live, but still one of the wealthiest and most highly civilised societies that the world had then seen: the Irish were almost as rude as the savages of Labrador. He was a freeman: the Irish were the hereditary serfs of his race. He worshipped God after a pure and rational fashion: the Irish were sunk in idolatry and superstition. He knew that great numbers of Irish had repeatedly fled before a small English force, and that the whole Irish population had been held down by a small English colony; and he very complacently inferred that he was naturally a being of a higher order than the Irishman: for it is thus that a dominant race always explains its ascendency and excuses its tyranny. That in vivacity, humour, and eloquence, the Irish stand high among the nations of the world is now universally acknowledged. That, when well disciplined, they are excellent soldiers has been proved on a hundred fields of battle. Yet it is certain that, in the seventeenth century, they were generally despised in our island as both a stupid and a cowardly people. And these were the men who were to hold England down by main force while her civil and ecclesiastical constitution was destroyed. The blood of the whole nation boiled at the thought. To be conquered by Frenchmen or by Spaniards would have seemed comparatively a tolerable fate. With Frenchmen and Spaniards we had been accustomed to treat on equal terms. We had sometimes envied their prosperity, sometimes dreaded their power, sometimes congratulated ourselves on their friendship. In spite of our unsocial pride, we admitted that they were great nations, and that they could boast of men eminent in the arts of war and peace. But to be subjugated by an inferior caste was a degradation beyond all other degradation. The English felt as the white inhabitants of Charleston and New Orleans would feel if those towns were occupied by negro garrisons. The real facts would have been sufficient to excite uneasiness and indignation; but the real facts were lost amidst a crowd of wild rumours which flew without ceasing from coffeehouse to coffeehouse and from alebench to alebench, and became more wonderful and terrible at every stage of the progress. The number of the Irish troops who had landed on our shores might justly excite serious apprehensions as to the King's ulterior designs: but it was magnified tenfold by the public apprehensions. It may well be supposed that the rude kerne of Connaught, placed, with arms in his hands, among a foreign people whom he hated, and by whom he was hated in turn, was guilty of some excesses. These excesses were exaggerated by report; and, in addition to the outrages which the stranger had really committed, all the offences of his English comrades were set down to his account. From every corner of the kingdom a cry arose against the foreign barbarians who forced themselves into private houses, seized horses and waggons, extorted money, and insulted women. These men, it was said, were the sons of those who, forty-seven years before, had massacred Protestants by tens of thousands. The history of the rebellion of 1641, a history which, even when soberly related, might well move pity and horror, and which had been frightfully distorted by national and religious antipathies, was now the favourite topic of conversation. Hideous stories of houses burned with all the inmates, of women and young children butchered, of near relations compelled by torture to be the murderers of each other, of corpses outraged and mutilated, were told and heard with full belief and intense interest. Then it was added that the dastardly savages, who had by surprise committed all these cruelties on an unsuspecting and defenceless colony, had, as soon as Oliver came among them on his great mission of vengeance, flung down their arms in panic terror, and sunk, without trying the chances of a single pitched field, into that slavery which was their fit portion. Many signs indicated that another great spoliation and slaughter of the Saxon settlers was meditated by the Lord Lieutenant. Already thousands of Protestant colonists, flying from the injustice and insolence of Tyrconnel, had raised the indignation of the mother country by describing all that they had suffered, and all that they had, with too much reason, feared. How much the public mind had been excited by the complaints of these fugitives had recently been shown in a manner not to be mistaken. Tyrconnel had transmitted for the royal approbation the heads of a bill repealing the law by which half the soil of Ireland was held, and he had sent to Westminster, as his agents, two of his Roman Catholic countrymen who had lately been raised to high judicial office; Nugent, Chief Justice of the Irish Court of King's Bench, a personification of all the vices and weaknesses which the English then imagined to be characteristic of the Popish Celt, and Rice, a Baron of the Irish Exchequer, who, in abilities and attainments, was perhaps the foremost man of his race and religion. The object of the mission was well known; and the two judges could not venture to show themselves in the streets. If ever they were recognised, the rabble shouted, "Room for the Irish Ambassadors;" and their coach was escorted with mock solemnity by a train of ushers and harbingers bearing sticks with potatoes stuck on the points.*

So strong and general, indeed, was at that time the aversion of the English to the Irish, that the most distinguished Roman Catholics partook of it. Powis and Bellasyse expressed, in coarse and acrimonious language, even at the Council board, their antipathy to the aliens.† Among English Protestants that antipathy was far stronger; and perhaps it was strongest in the army. Neither officers nor soldiers were disposed to bear patiently the preference shown by their master to a foreign and a subject race. The Duke of Berwick, who was Colonel of the Eighth Regiment of the Line, then quartered at Portsmouth, gave orders that thirty men just arrived from Ireland should be enlisted. The English soldiers declared that they would not serve with these intruders. John Beaumont, the Lieutenant Colonel, in his own name and in the name of five of the Captains, protested to the Duke's face against this insult to the English army and nation. "We raised the regiment," he said, "at our own charges to defend His Majesty's crown in a time of danger. We had then no difficulty in procuring hundreds of English recruits. We can easily keep every company up to its full complement without admitting Irishmen. We therefore do not think it consistent with our honour to have these strangers forced on us; and we beg that we may either be permitted to command men of our own nation or to lay down our commissions." Berwick sent to Windsor for directions. The King, greatly exasperated, instantly despatched a troop of horse to Portsmouth with orders to bring the six refractory officers before him. A council of war sate on them. They refused to make any submission; and they were sentenced to be cashiered, the highest punishment which a court martial was then competent to inflict. The whole nation applauded the disgraced officers; and the prevailing sentiment was stimulated by an unfounded rumour that, while under arrest, they had been treated with cruelty.‡

* King's State of the Protestants of Ireland; Secret Consults of the Romish Party in Ireland.
† Secret Consults of the Romish Party in Ireland.
‡ History of the Desertion, 1689; compare the first and second editions; Barillon, Sept. 5, 1688; Van Citters of the same date; Life of James the Second, ii. 165. The compiler of the last mentioned work says that Churchill moved the court to sentence the six offi-

Public feeling did not then manifest itself by those signs with which we are familiar, by large meetings, and by vehement harangues. Nevertheless it found a vent. Thomas Wharton, who, in the last Parliament, had represented Buckinghamshire, and who had long been conspicuous both as a libertine and as a Whig, had written a satirical ballad on the administration of Tyrconnel. In this little poem an Irishman congratulates a brother Irishman, in a barbarous jargon, on the approaching triumph of Popery and of the Milesian race. The Protestant heir will be excluded. The Protestant officers will be broken. The Great Charter and the prators who appealed to it will be hanged in one rope. The good Talbot will shower commissions on his countrymen, and will cut the throats of the English. These verses, which were in no respect above the ordinary standard of street poetry, had for burden some gibberish which was said to have been used as a watchword by the insurgents of Ulster in 1641. The verses and the tune caught the fancy of the nation. From one end of England to the other all classes were constantly singing this idle rhyme. It was especially the delight of the English army. More than seventy years after the Revolution, Sterne delineated, with exquisite skill, a veteran who had fought at the Boyne and at Namur. One of the characteristics of the good old soldier is his trick of whistling Lillibullero.*

Wharton afterwards boasted that he had sung a King out of three kingdoms. But in truth the success of Lillibullero was the effect, and not the cause, of that excited state of public feeling which produced the Revolution.

While James was thus raising against himself all those national feelings which, but for his own folly, might have saved his throne, Lewis was in another way exerting himself not less effectually to facilitate the enterprise which William meditated.

The party in Holland which was favourable to France was

---

vers to death. This story does not appear to have been taken from the King's papers. I therefore regard it as one of the thousand fictions invented at Saint Germains for the purpose of blackening a character which was black enough without such daubing. That Churchill may have affected great indignation on this occasion, in order to hide the treason which he meditated is highly probable. But it is impossible to believe that a man of his sense would have urged the members of a council of war to inflict a punishment which was notoriously beyond their competence.

* The song of Lillibullero is among the State Poems. In Percy's Relics the first part will be found, but not the second part, which was added after William's landing. In the Examiner, and in several pamphlets of 1712, Wharton is mentioned as the author.

a minority, but a minority strong enough, according to the constitution of the Batavian Federation, to prevent the Stadtholder from striking any great blow. To keep that minority steady was an object to which, if the Court of Versailles had been wise, every other object would at that juncture have been postponed. Lewis however had, during some time, laboured, as if of set purpose, to estrange his Dutch friends; and he at length, though not without difficulty, succeeded in forcing them to become his enemies at the precise moment at which their help would have been invaluable to him.

CHAP. IX.

Politics of the United Provinces.

There were two subjects on which the people of the United Provinces were peculiarly sensitive, religion and trade; and both their religion and their trade the French King had assailed. The persecution of the Huguenots, and the revocation of the edict of Nantes, had everywhere moved the grief and indignation of Protestants. But in Holland these feelings were stronger than in any other country; for many persons of Dutch birth, confiding in the repeated and solemn declarations of Lewis that the toleration granted by his grandfather should be maintained, had, for commercial purposes, settled in France, and a large proportion of the settlers had been naturalised there. Every post now brought to Holland the tidings that these persons were treated with extreme rigour on account of their religion. Dragoons, it was reported, were quartered on one. Another had been held naked before a fire till he was half roasted. All were forbidden, under the severest penalties, to celebrate the rites of their religion, or to quit the country into which they had, under false pretences been decoyed. The partisans of the House of Orange exclaimed against the cruelty and perfidy of the tyrant. The opposition was abashed and dispirited. Even the town council of Amsterdam, though strongly attached to the French interest and to the Arminian theology, and though little inclined to find fault with Lewis or to sympathise with the Calvinists whom he persecuted, could not venture to oppose itself to the general sentiment; for in that great city there was scarcely one wealthy merchant who had not some kinsman or friend among the sufferers. Petitions numerously and respectably signed were presented to the Burgomasters, imploring them to make strong representations to Avaux. There were even suppliants who made their way into the Stadthouse, flung themselves on their knees, described with tears and sobs the lamentable condition of those whom they

Errors of the French king.

most loved, and besought the intercession of the magistrates. The pulpits resounded with invectives and lamentations. The press poured forth heartrending narratives and stirring exhortations. Avaux saw the whole danger. He reported to his court that even the well intentioned,—for so he always called the enemies of the House of Orange,—either partook of the public feeling or were overawed by it; and he suggested the policy of making some concession to their wishes. The answers which he received from Versailles were cold and acrimonious. Some Dutch families, indeed, which had not been naturalised in France, were permitted to return to their country. But to those natives of Holland who had obtained letters of naturalisation Lewis refused all indulgence. No power on earth, he said, should interfere between him and his subjects. These people had chosen to become his subjects; and how he treated them was a matter with which no neighbouring state had anything to do. The magistrates of Amsterdam naturally resented the scornful ingratitude of the potentate whom they had strenuously and unscrupulously served against the general sense of their own countrymen. Soon followed another provocation which they felt even more keenly. Lewis began to make war on their trade. He first put forth an edict prohibiting the importation of herrings into his dominions. Avaux hastened to inform his court that this step had excited great alarm and indignation, that sixty thousand persons in the United Provinces subsisted by the herring fishery, and that some strong measure of retaliation would probably be adopted by the States. The answer which he received was that the King was determined, not only to persist, but also to increase the duties on many of those articles in which Holland carried on a lucrative commerce with France. The consequence of these errors, errors committed in defiance of repeated warnings, and, as it should seem, in the mere wantonness of selfwill, was that now, when the voice of a single powerful member of the Batavian federation might have averted an event fatal to all the politics of Lewis, no such voice was raised. The Envoy, with all his skill, vainly endeavoured to rally the party by the help of which he had, during several years, held the Stadtholder in check. The arrogance and obstinacy of the master counteracted all the efforts of the servant. At length Avaux was compelled to send to Versailles the alarming tidings that no reliance could be placed on Amsterdam, so

long devoted to the French cause, that some of the well CHAP.
intentioned were alarmed for their religion, that others were IX.
alarmed for their trade, and that the few whose inclinations
were unchanged could not venture to utter what they thought.
The fervid eloquence of preachers who declaimed against the
horrors of the French persecution, and the lamentations of
bankrupts who ascribed their ruin to the French decrees, had
wrought up the people to such a temper, that no citizen could
declare himself favourable to France without imminent risk
of being flung into the nearest canal. Men remembered that,
only fifteen years before, the most illustrious chief of the
party adverse to the House of Orange had been torn to pieces
by an infuriated mob in the very precinct of the palace of
the States General. A similar fate might not improbably
befall those who should, at this crisis, be accused of serving
the purposes of France against their native land, and against
the reformed religion.*

While Lewis was thus forcing his friends in Holland to His
become, or to pretend to become, his enemies, he was labour- quarrel
ing with not less success to remove all the scruples which Pope con-
might have prevented the Roman Catholic princes of the cerning
continent from countenancing William's designs. A new franchises.
quarrel had arisen between the Court of Versailles and the
Vatican, a quarrel in which the injustice and insolence of the
French King were perhaps more offensively displayed than in
any other transaction of his reign.

It had long been the rule at Rome that no officer of justice
or finance could enter the dwelling inhabited by the minister
who represented a Catholic state. In process of time not
only the dwelling, but a large precinct round it, was held inviolable. It was a point of honour with every Ambassador
to extend as widely as possible the limits of the region which
was under his protection. At length half the city consisted
of privileged districts, within which the Papal government
had no more power than within the Louvre or the Escurial.
Every asylum was thronged with contraband traders, fraudulent bankrupts, thieves and assassins. In every asylum were

* See the Negotiations of the Count Oct. 5., Dec. 20.; 1686, Jan. 3., Nov. 22.;
of Avaux. It would be almost impos- 1687, Oct. 2., Nov. 6., Nov. 19.; 1688,
sible for me to cite all the passages July 29., Aug. 20. Lord Lonsdale, in his
which have furnished me with materials Memoirs, justly remarks that, but for
for this part of my narrative. The most the mismanagement of Lewis, the city of
important will be found under the fol- Amsterdam would have prevented the
lowing dates: 1685, Sept. 20., Sept. 21., Revolution.

collected magazines of stolen or smuggled goods. From every asylum ruffians sallied forth nightly to plunder and stab. In no town of Christendom, consequently, was law so impotent and wickedness so audacious as in the ancient capital of religion and civilisation. On this subject Innocent felt as became a priest and a prince. He declared that he would receive no Ambassador who insisted on a right so destructive of order and morality. There was at first much murmuring; but his resolution was so evidently just that all governments but one speedily acquiesced. The Emperor, highest in rank among Christian monarchs, the Spanish Court, distinguished among all courts by sensitiveness and pertinacity on points of etiquette, renounced the odious privilege. Lewis alone was impracticable. What other sovereigns might choose to do, he said, was nothing to him. He therefore sent a mission to Rome, escorted by a great force of cavalry and infantry. The Ambassador marched to his palace as a general marches in triumph through a conquered town. The house was strongly guarded. Round the limits of the protected district sentinels paced the rounds day and night, as on the walls of a fortress. The Pope was unmoved. "They trust, he cried, "in chariots and in horses; but we will remember the name of the Lord our God." He betook himself to his spiritual weapons, and laid the region garrisoned by the French under an interdict.*

This dispute was at the height when another dispute arose, in which the Germanic body was as deeply concerned as the Pope.

The Archbishopric of Cologne.

Cologne and the surrounding district were governed by an Archbishop, who was an elector of the empire. The right of choosing this great prelate belonged, under certain limitations, to the Chapter of the Cathedral. The Archbishop was also Bishop of Liege, of Munster, and of Hildesheim. His dominions were extensive, and included several strong fortresses, which in the event of a campaign on the Rhine would be of the highest importance. In time of war he could bring twenty thousand men into the field. Lewis had spared no effort to gain so valuable an ally, and had succeeded so well that Cologne had been almost separated from Germany, and had become an outwork of France. Many ecclesiastics devoted to the Court of Versailles had been brought into the Chapter, and Cardinal Furstemberg, a mere creature of that court, had been appointed Coadjutor.

* Professor Von Ranke, Die Römischen Papste, book viii.; Burnet, I. 749.

In the summer of the year 1688 the archbishopric became vacant. Furstemberg was the candidate of the House of Bourbon. The enemies of that house proposed the young Prince Clement of Bavaria. Furstemberg was already a Bishop, and therefore could not be moved to another diocese except by a special dispensation from the Pope, or by a postulation, in which it was necessary that two thirds of the Chapter of Cologne should join. The Pope would grant no dispensation to a creature of France. The Emperor induced more than a third part of the Chapter to vote for the Bavarian prince. Meanwhile, in the Chapters of Liege, Munster, and Hildesheim, the majority was adverse to France. Lewis saw, with indignation and alarm, that an extensive province which he had begun to regard as a fief of his crown was about to become, not merely independent of him, but hostile to him. In a paper written with great acrimony he complained of the injustice with which France was on all occasions treated by that See which ought to extend a parental protection to every part of Christendom. Many signs indicated his fixed resolution to support the pretensions of his candidate by arms against the Pope and the Pope's confederates.*

Thus Lewis, by two opposite errors, raised against himself at once the resentment of both the religious parties between which Western Europe was divided. Having alienated one great section of Christendom by persecuting the Huguenots, he alienated another by insulting the Holy See. These faults he committed at a conjuncture at which no fault could be committed with impunity, and under the eye of an opponent second in vigilance, sagacity, and energy, to no statesman whose memory history has preserved. William saw with stern delight his adversaries toiling to clear away obstacle after obstacle from his path. While they raised against themselves the enmity of all sects, he laboured to conciliate all. The great design which he meditated he with exquisite skill presented to different governments in different lights; and it must be added that, though those lights were different, none of them was false. He called on the princes of Northern Germany to rally round him in defence of the common cause of all reformed Churches. He set before the two heads of the House of Austria the danger with which they were

* Burnet, i. 755.; Lewis's paper bears date Aug. 7. 1688. It will be found in the Recueil des Traités, vol. iv. no. 219.

threatened by French ambition, and the necessity of rescuing England from vassalage and of uniting her to the European confederacy.* He disclaimed, and with truth, all bigotry. The real enemy, he said, of the British Roman Catholics was that shortsighted and headstrong monarch who, when he might easily have obtained for them a legal toleration, had trampled on law, liberty, property, in order to raise them to an odious and precarious ascendency. If the misgovernment of James were suffered to continue, it must produce, at no remote time, a popular outbreak, which might be followed by a barbarous persecution of the Papists. The Prince declared that to avert the horrors of such a persecution was one of his chief objects. If he succeeded in his design, he would use the power which he must then possess, as head of the Protestant interest, to protect the members of the Church of Rome. Perhaps the passions excited by the tyranny of James might make it impossible to efface the penal laws from the statute book: but those laws should be mitigated by a lenient administration. No class would really gain more by the proposed expedition than those peaceable and unambitious Roman Catholics who merely wished to follow their callings and to worship their Maker without molestation. The only losers would be the Tyrconnels, the Dovers, the Albevilles, and other political adventurers who, in return for flattery and evil counsel, had obtained from their credulous master governments, regiments, and embassies.

His military and naval preparations.

While William exerted himself to enlist on his side the sympathies both of Protestants and of Roman Catholics, he exerted himself with not less vigour and prudence to provide the military means which his undertaking required. He could not make a descent on England without the sanction of the United Provinces. If he asked for that sanction before his design was ripe for execution, his intentions might possibly be thwarted by the faction hostile to his house, and would certainly be divulged to the whole world. He therefore determined to make his preparations with all speed, and, when they were complete, to seize some favourable moment for re-

* For the consummate dexterity with which he exhibited two different views of his policy to two different parties he was afterwards bitterly reviled by the Court of Saint Germain's. "Licet Foederatis publicum ille perdo haud alicui aperte propinat nisi ut Galliei imperii exuberans amputetur potestas, veruntamen sibi et suis ex haereticis facere complicibus, ut pro comperto habemus, longe alind promisit, tempo at, excuso vel exerrato Francorum regno, ubi Catholicarum partium summum jam robur situm est, haereticis ipsorum pravitas per orbem Christianum universum prævaleat."— Letter of James to the Pope, written in 1689.

questing the consent of the federation. It was observed by the agents of France that he was more busy than they had ever known him. Not a day passed on which he was not seen spurring from his villa to the Hague. He was perpetually closeted with his most distinguished adherents. Twenty-four ships of war were fitted out for sea in addition to the ordinary force which the commonwealth maintained. There was, as it chanced, an excellent pretence for making this addition to the marine: for some Algerine corsairs had recently dared to show themselves in the German Ocean. A camp was formed near Nimeguen. Many thousands of troops were assembled there. In order to strengthen this army the garrisons were withdrawn from the strongholds in Dutch Brabant. Even the renowned fortress of Bergopzoom was left almost defenceless. Field pieces, bombs, and tumbrels from all the magazines of the United Provinces were collected at the head quarters. All the bakers of Rotterdam toiled day and night to make biscuit. All the gunmakers of Utrecht were found too few to execute the orders for pistols and muskets. All the saddlers of Amsterdam were hard at work on harness and holsters. Six thousand sailors were added to the naval establishment. Seven thousand new soldiers were raised. They could not, indeed, be formally enlisted without the sanction of the federation: but they were well drilled, and kept in such a state of discipline that they might without difficulty be distributed into regiments within twenty-four hours after that sanction should be obtained. These preparations required ready money: but William had, by strict economy, laid up against a great emergency a treasure amounting to about two hundred and fifty thousand pounds sterling. What more was wanting was supplied by the zeal of his partisans. Great quantities of gold, not less, it was said, than a hundred thousand guineas, came to him from England. The Huguenots, who had carried with them into exile large quantities of the precious metals, were eager to lend him all that they possessed; for they fondly hoped that, if he succeeded, they should be restored to the country of their birth; and they feared that, if he failed, they should scarcely be safe even in the country of their adoption.*

Through the latter part of July and the whole of August the preparations went on rapidly, yet too slowly for the vehe-

* Avaux Neg. August 5. 8. 11. 14. 18. 19. 22. 26. 1688.

CHAP. IX.

He receives numerous assurances of support from England.

ment spirit of William. Meanwhile the intercourse between England and Holland was active. The ordinary modes of conveying intelligence and passengers were no longer thought safe. A light bark of marvellous speed constantly ran backward and forward between Schevening and the eastern coast of our island.* By this vessel William received a succession of letters from persons of high note in the Church, the state, and the army. Two of the seven prelates who had signed the memorable petition, Lloyd, Bishop of Saint Asaph, and Trelawney, Bishop of Bristol, had, during their residence in the Tower, reconsidered the doctrine of nonresistance, and were ready to welcome an armed deliverer. A brother of the Bishop of Bristol, Colonel Charles Trelawney, who commanded one of the Tangier regiments, now known as the Fourth of the Line, signified his readiness to draw his sword for the Protestant religion. Similar assurances arrived from the savage Kirke. Churchill, in a letter written with a certain elevation of language, which was the sure mark that he was going to commit a baseness, declared that he was determined to perform his duty to heaven and to his country, and that he put his honour absolutely into the hands of the Prince of Orange. William doubtless read these words with one of those bitter and cynical smiles which gave his face its least pleasing expression. It was not his business to take care of the honour of other men; nor had the most rigid casuists pronounced it unlawful in a general to invite, to use, and to reward the services of deserters whom he could not but despise.†

Churchill's letter was brought by Sidney, whose situation in England had become hazardous, and who, having taken many precautions to hide his track, had passed over to Holland about the middle of August.‡ About the same time Shrewsbury and Edward Russell crossed the German Ocean in a boat which they had hired with great secrecy, and appeared at the Hague. Shrewsbury brought with him twelve thousand pounds, which he had raised by a mortgage on his estates, and which he lodged in the Bank of Amsterdam.§ Devonshire, Danby, and Lumley remained in England, where they undertook to rise in arms as soon as the Prince should set foot on the island.

* Avaux Neg. September 6/16. 1688.
† Burnet, i. 765.; Churchill's letter bears date Aug. 4. 1688.
‡ William to Bentinck, Aug. 11/21. 1688.
§ Memoirs of the Duke of Shrewsbury, 1718.

There is reason to believe that, at this conjuncture, William first received assurances of support from a very different quarter. Part of the history of Sunderland's intrigues is covered with an obscurity which it is not probable that any enquirer will ever succeed in penetrating: but, though it is impossible to discover the whole truth, it is easy to detect some palpable fictions. The Jacobites, for obvious reasons, affirmed that the revolution of 1688 was the result of a plot concerted long before. Sunderland they represented as the chief conspirator. He had, they averred, in pursuance of his great design, incited his too confiding master to dispense with statutes, to create an illegal tribunal, to confiscate freehold property, and to send the fathers of the Established Church to a prison. This romance rests on no evidence, and, though it has been repeated down to our time, seems hardly to deserve confutation. No fact is more certain than that Sunderland opposed some of the most imprudent steps which James took, and in particular the prosecution of the Bishops, which really brought on the decisive crisis. But, even if this fact were not established, there would still remain one argument sufficient to decide the controversy. What conceivable motive had Sunderland to wish for a revolution? Under the existing system he was at the height of dignity and prosperity. As President of the Council he took precedence of the whole temporal peerage. As Principal Secretary of State he was the most active and powerful member of the cabinet. He might look forward to a dukedom. He had obtained the garter lately worn by the brilliant and versatile Buckingham, who, having squandered away a princely fortune and a vigorous intellect, had sunk into the grave deserted, contemned, and brokenhearted.* Money, which Sunderland valued more than honours, poured in upon him in such abundance that, with ordinary management, he might hope to become, in a few years, one of the wealthiest subjects in Europe. The direct emolument of his posts, though considerable, was a very small part of what he received. From France alone he drew a regular stipend of near six thousand pounds a year, besides large occasional gratuities. He had bargained with Tyrconnel for five thousand a year, or fifty thousand pounds down, from Ireland. What sums he made by selling places, titles, and pardons can only be conjectured, but must have been enormous. James seemed to take a plea-

* London Gazette, April 25. 28. 1687.

sure in loading with wealth one whom he regarded as his own convert. All fines, all forfeitures, went to Sunderland. On every grant toll was paid to him. If any suitor ventured to ask any favour directly from the King, the answer was, "Have you spoken to my Lord President?" One bold man ventured to say that the Lord President got all the money of the court. "Well," replied His Majesty; "he deserves it all."* We shall scarcely overrate the amount of the minister's gains, if we put them at thirty thousand pounds a year: and it must be remembered that fortunes of thirty thousand pounds a year were in his time rarer than fortunes of a hundred thousand pounds a year now are. It is probable that there was then not one peer of the realm whose private income equalled Sunderland's official income.

What chance was there that, in a new order of things, a man so deeply implicated in illegal and unpopular acts, a member of the High Commission, a renegade whom the multitude, in places of general resort, pursued with the cry of Popish dog, would be greater and richer? What chance that he would even be able to escape condign punishment?

He had undoubtedly been long in the habit of looking forward to the time when William and Mary might be, in the ordinary course of nature and law, at the head of the English government, and had probably attempted to make for himself an interest in their favour, by promises and services which, if discovered, would not have raised his credit at Whitehall. But it may with confidence be affirmed that he had no wish to see them raised to power by a revolution, and that he did not at all foresee such a revolution when, towards the close of June 1688, he solemnly joined the communion of the Church of Rome.

Scarcely however had he, by that inexpiable crime, made himself an object of hatred and contempt to the whole nation, when he learned that the civil and ecclesiastical polity of England would shortly be vindicated by foreign and domestic arms. From that moment all his plans seem to have undergone a change. Fear bowed down his whole soul, and was so written in his face that all who saw him could read.† It

* Secret Consults of the Romish Party in Ireland. This account is strongly confirmed by what Ronsrpaux wrote to Seignelay, Sept. 1?. 1687. "Il (Sunderland) assure beaucoup d'argent, le roi son maître lui donnant la plus grande partie de celui qui provient des confiscations on des accommodemens que ceux qui out encoru des peines font pour obtenir leur grace."

† Adda says that Sunderland's terror was visible. Oct. 16. Nov. 5. 1688.

could hardly be doubted that, if there were a revolution, the evil counsellors who surrounded the throne would be called to a strict account: and among those counsellors he stood in the foremost rank. The loss of his places, his salaries, his pensions, was the least that he had to dread. His patrimonial mansion and woods at Althorpe might be confiscated. He might lie many years in a prison. He might end his days in a foreign land a pensioner on the bounty of France. Even this was not the worst. Visions of an innumerable crowd covering Tower Hill and shouting with savage joy at the sight of the apostate, of a scaffold hung with black, of Burnet reading the prayer for the departing, and of Ketch leaning on the axe with which Russell and Monmouth had been mangled in so butcherly a fashion, began to haunt the unhappy statesman. There was yet one way in which he might escape, a way more terrible to a noble spirit than a prison or a scaffold. He might still, by a well timed and useful treason, earn his pardon from the foes of the government. It was in his power to render to them at this conjuncture services beyond all price: for he had the royal ear: he had great influence over the Jesuitical cabal; and he was blindly trusted by the French Ambassador. A channel of communication was not wanting, a channel worthy of the purpose which it was to serve. The Countess of Sunderland was an artful woman, who, under a show of devotion which imposed on some grave men, carried on, with great activity, both amorous and political intrigues.* The handsome and dissolute Henry Sidney had long been her favourite lover. Her husband was well pleased to see her thus connected with the court of the Hague. Whenever he wished to transmit a secret message to Holland, he spoke to his wife: she wrote to Sidney; and Sidney communicated her letter to William. One of her communications was intercepted and carried to James. She vehemently protested that it was a forgery. Her husband, with characteristic ingenuity, defended himself by representing that it was quite impossible for any man to be so base as to do what he was in the habit of doing. "Even if this is Lady Sunderland's hand," he said, "that is no affair of mine. Your Majesty knows my domestic misfortunes. The footing on which my wife and Mr. Sidney are is but too public. Who can believe that I would make a confidant of the man who has injured

---

* Compare Evelyn's account of her wrote about her to the Hague, and with with what the Princess of Denmark her own letters to Henry Sidney.

my honour in the tenderest point, of the man whom, of all others, I ought most to hate?"* This defence was thought satisfactory; and secret intelligence was still transmitted from the wittol to the adulteress, from the adulteress to the gallant, and from the gallant to the enemies of James.

It is highly probable that the first decisive assurances of Sunderland's support were conveyed orally by Sidney to William about the middle of August. It is certain that, from that time till the expedition was ready to sail, a most significant correspondence was kept up between the Countess and her lover. A few of her letters, partly written in cipher, are still extant. They contain professions of goodwill and promises of service mingled with earnest entreaties for protection. The writer intimates that her husband will do all that his friends at the Hague can wish: she supposes that it will be necessary for him to go into temporary exile: but she hopes that his banishment will not be perpetual, and that his patrimonial estate will be spared; and she earnestly begs to be informed in what place it will be best for him to take refuge till the first fury of the storm is over.†

Anxiety of William.

The help of Sunderland was most welcome. For, as the time of striking the great blow drew near, the anxiety of William became intense. From common eyes his feelings were concealed by the icy tranquillity of his demeanour: but his whole heart was open to Bentinck. The preparations were not quite complete. The design was already suspected, and could not be long concealed. The King of France or the city of Amsterdam might still frustrate the whole plan. If Lewis were to send a great force into Brabant, if the faction which hated the Stadtholder were to raise its head, all was over. "My sufferings, my disquiet," the Prince wrote, "are dreadful. I hardly see my way. Never in my life did I so much feel the need of God's guidance."‡ Bentinck's wife was at this time dangerously ill; and both the friends were painfully anxious about her. "God support you," William wrote, "and enable you to bear your part in a work on which, as far as human beings can see, the welfare of his Church depends."§

* Bonrepaux to Seignelay, July 1¹/₁. 1688.
† See her letters in the Sidney Diary and Correspondence lately published. Mr. Fox, in his copy of Barillon's despatches, marked the 30th of August N.S. 1688, as the date from which it was quite certain that Sunderland was playing false.
‡ Aug. 1¹/₁. 1688.
§ September ₁/₁₁. 1688.

It was indeed impossible that a design so vast as that which had been formed against the King of England should remain during many weeks a secret. No art could prevent intelligent men from perceiving that William was making great military and naval preparations, and from suspecting the object with which those preparations were made. Early in August hints that some great event was approaching were whispered up and down London. The weak and corrupt Albeville was then on a visit to England, and was, or affected to be, certain that the Dutch government entertained no design unfriendly to James. But, during the absence of Albeville from his post, Avaux performed, with eminent skill, the duties both of French and English Ambassador to the States, and supplied Barillon as well as Lewis with ample intelligence. Avaux was satisfied that a descent on England was in contemplation, and succeeded in convincing his master of the truth. Every courier who arrived at Westminster, either from the Hague or from Versailles, brought earnest warnings.* But James was under a delusion which appears to have been artfully encouraged by Sunderland. The Prince of Orange, said the cunning minister, would never dare to engage in an expedition beyond sea, leaving Holland defenceless. The States, remembering what they had suffered and what they had been in danger of suffering during the great agony of 1672, would never incur the risk of again seeing an invading army encamped on the plain between Utrecht and Amsterdam. There was doubtless much discontent in England; but the interval was immense between discontent and rebellion. Men of rank and fortune were not disposed lightly to hazard their honours, their estates, and their lives. How many eminent Whigs had held high language when Monmouth was in the Netherlands? And yet, when he set up his standard, what eminent Whig had joined it? It was easy to understand why Lewis affected to give credit to these idle rumours. He doubtless hoped to frighten the King of England into taking the French side in the dispute about Cologne. By such reasoning James was easily lulled into stupid security.† The alarm and indignation of Lewis increased daily. The style of his letters became sharp and

---

* Avaux, July 11/21, Aug 3/13. August 14/24. Adda, Aug 3/13; Life of James, II. 177. 1688; Lewis to Barillon, August 4/14. Orig. Mem.
† Barillon, Aug. 9/19, Aug 6/16, 1688;

vehement.* He could not understand, he wrote, this lethargy on the eve of a terrible crisis. Was the King bewitched? Were his ministers blind? Was it possible that nobody at Whitehall was aware of what was passing in England and on the Continent? Such foolhardy security could scarcely be the effect of mere improvidence. There must be foul play. James was evidently in bad hands. Barillon was earnestly cautioned not to repose implicit confidence in the English ministers: but he was cautioned in vain. On him, as on James, Sunderland had cast a spell which no exhortation could break.

Lewis bestirred himself vigorously. Bonrepaux, who was far superior to Barillon in shrewdness, and who had always disliked and distrusted Sunderland, was despatched to London with an offer of naval assistance. Avaux was at the same time ordered to declare to the States General that France had taken James under her protection. A large body of troops was held in readiness to march towards the Dutch frontier. This bold attempt to save the infatuated tyrant in his own despite was made with the full concurrence of Skelton, who was now Envoy from England to the Court of Versailles.

Avaux, in conformity with his instructions, demanded an audience of the States. It was readily granted. The assembly was unusually large. The general belief was that some overture respecting commerce was about to be made; and the President brought a written answer framed on that supposition. As soon as Avaux began to disclose his errand, signs of uneasiness were discernible. Those who were believed to enjoy the confidence of the Prince of Orange cast down their eyes. The agitation became great when the Envoy announced that his master was strictly bound by the ties of friendship and alliance to His Britannic Majesty, and that any attack on England would be considered as a declaration of war against France. The President, completely taken by surprise, stammered out a few evasive phrases; and the conference terminated. It was at the same time notified to the States that Lewis had taken under his protection Cardinal Furstemberg and the Chapter of Cologne.†

The Deputies were in great agitation. Some recommended caution and delay. Others breathed nothing but war. Fagel spoke vehemently of the French insolence, and implored his brethren not to be daunted by threats. The proper answer to such a communication, he said, was to levy more soldiers, and to equip more ships. A courier was instantly despatched to recall William from Minden, where he was holding a consultation of high moment with the Elector of Brandenburg.

But there was no cause for alarm. James was bent on ruining himself; and every attempt to stop him only made him rush more eagerly to his doom. When his throne was secure, when his people were submissive, when the most obsequious of Parliaments was eager to anticipate all his reasonable wishes, when foreign kingdoms and commonwealths paid emulous court to him, when it depended only on himself whether he would be the arbiter of Christendom, he had stooped to be the slave and the hireling of France. And now when, by a series of crimes and follies, he had succeeded in alienating his neighbours, his subjects, his soldiers, his sailors, his children, and had left himself no refuge but the protection of France, he was taken with a fit of pride, and determined to assert his independence. That help which, when he did not want it, he had accepted with ignominious tears, he now, when it was indispensable to him, threw contemptuously away. Having been abject when he might, with propriety, have been punctilious in maintaining his dignity, he became ungratefully haughty at a moment when haughtiness must bring on him at once derision and ruin. He resented the friendly intervention which might have saved him. Was ever King so used? Was he a child, or an idiot, that others must think for him? Was he a petty prince, a Cardinal Furstemberg, who must fall if not upheld by a powerful patron? Was he to be degraded in the estimation of all Europe, by an ostentatious patronage which he had never asked? Skelton was recalled to answer for his conduct, and, as soon as he arrived, was committed prisoner to the Tower. Van Citters was well received at Whitehall, and had a long audience. He could, with more truth than diplomatists on such occasions think at all necessary, disclaim, on the part of the States General, any hostile project. For the States General had, as yet, no official knowledge of the design of William; nor was it by any means impossible that they might, even now, refuse to sanction that design. James declared that he gave not the least credit to the rumours of a Dutch invasion, and that the conduct of the French government had surprised and annoyed him. Middleton was

CHAP. IX.

James frustrates them

directed to assure all the foreign ministers that there existed no such alliance between France and England as the Court of Versailles had, for its own ends, pretended. To the Nuncio the King said that the designs of Lewis were palpable and should be frustrated. This officious protection was at once an insult and a snare. "My good brother," said James, "has excellent qualities; but flattery and vanity have turned his head."* Adda, who was much more anxious about Cologne than about England, encouraged this strange delusion. Albeville, who had now returned to his post, was commanded to give friendly assurances to the States General, and to add some high language, which might have been becoming in the mouth of Elizabeth or Oliver. "My master," he said, "is raised, alike by his power and by his spirit, above the position which France affects to assign to him. There is some difference between a King of England and an Archbishop of Cologne." The reception of Bonrepaux at Whitehall was cold. The naval succours which he offered were not absolutely declined: but he was forced to return without having settled anything; and the Envoys, both of the United Provinces and of the House of Austria, were informed that his mission had been disagreeable to the King and had produced no result. After the Revolution Sunderland boasted, and probably with truth, that he had induced his master to reject the proffered assistance of France.†

The perverse folly of James naturally excited the indignation of his powerful neighbour. Lewis complained that, in return for the greatest service which he could render to the English government, that government had given him the lie in the face of all Christendom. He justly remarked that what Avaux had said, touching the alliance between France and Great Britain, was true according to the spirit, though perhaps not according to the letter. There was not indeed a treaty digested into articles, signed, sealed, and ratified: but assurances equivalent in the estimation of honourable men to such a treaty had, during some years, been frequently exchanged between the two Courts. Lewis added that, high as

* "Che l' adulazione e la vanità gli avevano tornato il capo."—Adda, Aug. 31/Sept. 10 1688.

† Van Citters, Sept. 11/21 1688; Avaux, Sept. 14/24; Barillon, Sept. 13/23 L; Wagenaar, book lx.; Sunderland's Apology. It has been often asserted that James declined the help of a French army. The truth is that no such army was offered. Indeed, the French troops would have served James much more effectually by menacing the frontiers of Holland than by crossing the Channel.

was his own place in Europe, he should never be so absurdly jealous of his dignity as to see an insult in any act prompted by friendship. But James was in a very different situation, and would soon learn the value of that aid which he had so ungraciously rejected.*

Yet, notwithstanding the stupidity and ingratitude of James, it would have been wise in Lewis to persist in the resolution which had been notified to the States General. Avaux, whose sagacity and judgment made him an antagonist worthy of William, was decidedly of this opinion. The first object of the French government,—so the skilful Envoy reasoned,—ought to be to prevent the intended descent on England. The way to prevent that descent was to invade the Spanish Netherlands, and to menace the Batavian frontier. The Prince of Orange, indeed, was so bent on his darling enterprise that he would persist, even if the white flag were flying on the walls of Brussels. He had actually said that, if the Spaniards could only manage to keep Ostend, Mons, and Namur till the next spring, he would then return from England with a force which would soon recover all that had been lost. But, though such was the Prince's opinion, it was not the opinion of the States. They would not readily consent to send their Captain General and the flower of their army across the German Ocean, while a formidable enemy threatened their own territory.†

Lewis admitted the force of these reasonings: but he had already resolved on a different line of action. Perhaps he had been provoked by the discourtesy and wrongheadedness of the English government, and indulged his temper at the expense of his interest. Perhaps he was misled by the counsels of his minister of war, Louvois, whose influence was great, and who regarded Avaux with no friendly feeling. It was determined to strike in a quarter remote from Holland a great and unexpected blow. Lewis suddenly withdrew his troops from Flanders, and poured them into Germany. One army, placed under the nominal command of the Dauphin, but really directed by the Duke of Duras and by Vauban, the father of the science of fortification, invested Philipsburg. Another, led by the Marquess of Boufflers, seized Worms, Mentz, and Treves. A third, commanded by the Marquess of Humieres, entered Bonn. All down the Rhine, from Baden

* Lewis to Barillon, Sept. 17. 1688.   † Avaux, Sept. V., Oct. 4. 1688.

to Cologne, the French arms were victorious. The news of the fall of Philipsburg reached Versailles on All Saints day, while the Court was listening to a sermon in the chapel. The King made a sign to the preacher to stop, announced the good news to the congregation, and, kneeling down, returned thanks to God for this great success. The audience wept for joy.[a] The tidings were eagerly welcomed by the sanguine and susceptible people of France. Poets celebrated the triumphs of their magnificent patron. Orators extolled from the pulpit the wisdom and magnanimity of the oldest son of the Church. The Te Deum was sung with unwonted pomp; and the solemn notes of the organ were mingled with the clash of the cymbal and the blast of the trumpet. But there was little cause for rejoicing. The great statesman who was at the head of the European coalition smiled inwardly at the misdirected energy of his foe. Lewis had indeed, by his promptitude, gained some advantages on the side of Germany: but those advantages would avail little if England, inactive and inglorious under four successive kings, should suddenly resume her old rank in Europe. A few weeks would suffice for the enterprise on which the fate of the world depended; and for a few weeks the United Provinces were in security.

William obtains the sanction of the States General to his expedition.

William now urged on his preparations with indefatigable activity, and with less secrecy than he had hitherto thought necessary. Assurances of support came pouring in daily from foreign courts. Opposition had become extinct at the Hague. It was in vain that Avaux, even at this last moment, exerted all his skill to reanimate the faction which had contended against three generations of the House of Orange. The chiefs of that faction, indeed, still regarded the Stadtholder with no friendly feeling. They had reason to fear that, if he prospered in England, he would become absolute master of Holland. Nevertheless the errors of the court of Versailles, and the dexterity with which he had availed himself of those errors, made it impossible to continue the struggle against him. He saw that the time had come for demanding the sanction of the States. Amsterdam was the head quarters of the party hostile to his line, his office, and his person; and even from Amsterdam he had at this moment nothing to apprehend. Some of the chief function-

---

[a] Madame de Sévigné, Nov. 14 1688.

aries of that city had been repeatedly closeted with him, with Van Dykvelt, and with Bentinck, and had been induced to promise that they would promote, or at least that they would not oppose, the great design: some were exasperated by the commercial edicts of Lewis: some were in deep distress for kinsmen and friends who were harassed by the French dragoons: some shrank from the responsibility of causing a schism which might be fatal to the Batavian federation; and some were afraid of the common people, who, stimulated by the exhortations of zealous preachers, were ready to execute summary justice on any traitor who should, at this crisis, be false to the Protestant cause. The majority, therefore, of that town council which had long been devoted to France pronounced in favour of William's undertaking. Thenceforth all fear of opposition in any part of the United Provinces was at an end; and the full sanction of the federation to his enterprise was, in secret sittings, formally given.*

The Prince had already fixed upon a general well qualified to be second in command. This was indeed no light matter. A random shot or the dagger of an assassin might in a moment leave the expedition without a head. It was necessary that a successor should be ready to fill the vacant place. Yet it was impossible to make choice of any Englishman without giving offence either to the Whigs or to the Tories; nor had any Englishman then living shown that he possessed the military skill necessary for the conduct of a campaign. On the other hand it was not easy to assign preeminence to a foreigner without wounding the national sensibility of the haughty islanders. One man there was, and only one in Europe, to whom no objection could be found, Frederic, Count of Schomberg, a German, sprung from a noble house of the Palatinate. He was generally esteemed the greatest living master of the art of war. His rectitude and piety, tried by strong temptations and never found wanting, commanded general respect and confidence. Though a Protestant, he had been, during many years, in the service of Lewis, and had, in spite of the ill offices of the Jesuits, extorted from his employer, by a series of great actions, the staff of a Marshal of France. When persecution began to rage, the brave veteran steadfastly refused to purchase the

Schomberg.

---

* Witsen MS. quoted by Wagenaar; the States General, dated Oct. 1⁄7, will Lord Lonsdale's Memoirs; Avaux, Oct. be found in the Recueil des Traités, vol. 1⁄4. 1688. The formal declaration of iv. No. 252.

royal favour by apostasy, resigned, without one murmur, all his honours and commands, quitted his adopted country for ever, and took refuge at the court of Berlin. He had long passed his seventieth year: but both his mind and his body were still in full vigour. He had been in England, and was much loved and honoured there. He had indeed a recommendation of which very few foreigners could then boast; for he spoke our language not only intelligibly, but with grace and purity. He was, with the consent of the Elector of Brandenburg, and with the warm approbation of the chiefs of all the English parties, appointed William's lieutenant.*

British adventurers at the Hague.

And now the Hague was crowded with British adventurers of all the various factions which the tyranny of James had united in a strange coalition, old royalists who had shed their blood for the throne, old agitators of the army of the Parliament, Tories who had been persecuted in the days of the Exclusion Bill, Whigs who had fled to the Continent for their share in the Rye House plot.

Conspicuous in this great assemblage were Charles Gerard, Earl of Macclesfield, an ancient Cavalier who had fought for Charles the First and had shared the exile of Charles the Second; Archibald Campbell, who was the eldest son of the unfortunate Argyle, but had inherited nothing except an illustrious name and the inalienable affection of a numerous clan; Charles Paulet, Earl of Wiltshire, heir apparent of the Marquisate of Winchester; and Peregrine Osborne, Lord Dumblane, heir apparent of the Earldom of Danby. Mordaunt, exulting in the prospect of adventures irresistibly attractive to his fiery nature, was among the foremost volunteers. Fletcher of Saltoun had learned, while guarding the frontier of Christendom against the infidels, that there was once more a hope of deliverance for his country, and had hastened to offer the help of his sword. Sir Patrick Hume, who had, since his flight from Scotland, lived humbly at Utrecht, now emerged from his obscurity: but, fortunately, his eloquence could, on this occasion, do little mischief; for the Prince of Orange was by no means disposed to be the lieutenant of a debating society such as that which had ruined the enterprise of Argyle. The subtle and restless Wildman, who had some time before found England an unsafe residence, and had escaped to Germany, repaired from his retreat to the

---

* Abrégé de la Vie de Frédéric Duc de Schomberg, 1690; Sidney to William, June 30, 1688; Burnet, i. 677.

Prince's Court. There too was Carstairs, a Presbyterian minister from Scotland, who in craft and courage had no superior among the politicians of his age. He had been entrusted some years before by Fagel with important secrets, and had resolutely kept them in spite of the most horrible torments which could be inflicted by boot and thumbscrew. His rare fortitude had earned for him as large a share of the Prince's confidence and esteem as was granted to any man except Bentinck.* Ferguson could not remain quiet when a revolution was preparing. He secured for himself a passage in the fleet, and made himself busy among his fellow emigrants: but he found himself generally distrusted and despised. He had been a great man in the knot of ignorant and hotheaded outlaws who had urged the feeble Monmouth to destruction: but there was no place for a lowminded agitator, half maniac and half knave, among the grave statesmen and generals who partook the cares of the resolute and sagacious William.

The difference between the expedition of 1685 and the expedition of 1688 was sufficiently marked by the difference between the manifestoes which the leaders of those expeditions published. For Monmouth Ferguson had scribbled an absurd and brutal libel about the burning of London, the strangling of Godfrey, the butchering of Essex, and the poisoning of Charles. The Declaration of William was drawn up by the Grand Pensionary Fagel, who was highly renowned as a publicist. Though weighty and learned, it was, in its original form, much too prolix: but it was abridged and translated into English by Burnet, who well understood the art of popular composition. It began by a solemn preamble, setting forth that, in every community, the strict observance of law was necessary alike to the happiness of nations and to the security of governments. The Prince of Orange had therefore seen with deep concern that the fundamental laws of a kingdom, with which he was by blood and by marriage closely connected, had, by the advice of evil counsellors, been grossly and systematically violated. The power of dispensing with Acts of Parliament had been strained to such a point that the whole legislative authority had been transferred to the crown. Decisions at variance with the spirit of the constitution had been obtained from the tribunals by turning out Judge after Judge, till the bench had been filled with men ready to obey

William's Declaration.

* Burnet, i. 591.; Mackay's Memoirs.

implicitly the directions of the government. Notwithstanding the King's repeated assurances that he would maintain the established religion, persons notoriously hostile to that religion had been promoted, not only to civil offices, but also to ecclesiastical benefices. The government of the Church had, in defiance of express statutes, been entrusted to a new court of High Commission; and in that court an avowed Papist had a seat. Good subjects, for refusing to violate their duty and their oaths, had been ejected from their property, in contempt of the Great Charter of the liberties of England. Meanwhile persons who could not legally set foot on the island had been placed at the head of seminaries for the corruption of youth. Lieutenants, Deputy Lieutenants, Justices of the Peace, had been dismissed in multitudes for refusing to support a pernicious and unconstitutional policy. The franchises of almost every borough in the realm had been invaded. The courts of justice were in such a state that their decisions, even in civil matters, had ceased to inspire confidence, and that their servility in criminal cases had brought on the kingdom the stain of innocent blood. All these abuses, loathed by the English nation, were to be defended, it seemed, by an army of Irish Papists. Nor was this all. The most arbitrary princes had never accounted it an offence in a subject modestly and peaceably to represent his grievances and to ask for relief. But supplication was now treated as a high misdemeanour in England. For no crime but that of offering to the Sovereign a petition drawn up in the most respectful terms, the fathers of the Church had been imprisoned and prosecuted; and every Judge who had given his voice in their favour had instantly been turned out. The calling of a free and lawful Parliament might indeed be an effectual remedy for all these evils; but such a Parliament, unless the whole spirit of the administration was changed, the nation could not hope to see. It was evidently the intention of the Court to bring together, by means of regulated corporations and of Popish returning officers, a body which would be a House of Commons in name alone. Lastly, there were circumstances which raised a grave suspicion that the child who was called Prince of Wales was not really born of the Queen. For these reasons the Prince, mindful of his near relation to the royal house, and grateful for the affection which the English people had ever shown to his beloved wife and to himself, had resolved, in compliance with the request of many Lords

Spiritual and Temporal, and of many other persons of all ranks, to go over at the head of a force sufficient to repel violence. He abjured all thought of conquest. He protested that, while his troops remained in the island, they should be kept under the strictest restraints of discipline, and that, as soon as the nation had been delivered from tyranny, they should be sent back. His single object was to have a free and legal Parliament assembled: and to the decision of such a Parliament he solemnly pledged himself to leave all questions both public and private.

As soon as copies of this Declaration were handed about the Hague, signs of dissension began to appear among the English. Wildman, indefatigable in mischief, prevailed on some of his countrymen, and, among others, on the headstrong and volatile Mordaunt, to declare that they would not take up arms on such grounds. The paper had been drawn up merely to please the Cavaliers and the parsons. The injuries of the Church and the trial of the Bishops had been put too prominently forward; and nothing had been said of the tyrannical manner in which the Tories, before their rupture with the Court, had treated the Whigs. Wildman then brought forward a counterproject, prepared by himself, which, if it had been adopted, would have disgusted all the Anglican clergy and four fifths of the landed aristocracy. The leading Whigs strongly opposed him. Russell in particular declared that, if such an insane course were taken, there would be an end of the coalition from which alone the nation could expect deliverance. The dispute was at length settled by the authority of William, who, with his usual good sense, determined that the manifesto should stand nearly as Fagel and Burnet had framed it.*

While these things were passing in Holland, James had at length become sensible of his danger. Intelligence which could not be disregarded came pouring in from various quarters. At length a despatch from Albeville removed all doubts. It is said that, when the King had read it, the blood left his cheeks, and he remained some time speechless.† He might, indeed, well be appalled. The first easterly wind would bring a hostile armament to the shores of his realm. All Europe, one single power alone excepted, was impatiently waiting for the news of his downfall. The help of that single

* Burnet, i. 775, 780.
† Eachard's History of the Revolution, ii. 2.

CHAP.
IX.

power he had madly rejected. Nay, he had requited with insult the friendly intervention which might have saved him. The French armies which, but for his own folly, might have been employed in overawing the States General, were besieging Philipsburg or garrisoning Mentz. In a few days he might have to fight, on English ground, for his crown and for the birthright of his infant son. His means were indeed in appearance great. The navy was in a much more efficient state than at the time of his accession; and the improvement is partly to be attributed to his own exertions. He had appointed no Lord High Admiral or Board of Admiralty, but had kept the chief direction of maritime affairs in his own hands, and had been strenuously assisted by Pepys. It is a proverb that the eye of a master is more to be trusted than that of a deputy; and, in an age of corruption and peculation, a department, on which a sovereign, even of very slender capacity, bestows close personal attention, is likely to be comparatively free from abuses. It would have been easy to find an abler minister of marine than James: but it would not have been easy to find, among the public men of that age, any minister of marine, except James, who would not have embezzled stores, taken bribes from contractors, and charged the crown with the cost of repairs which had never been made.

His naval

The King was, in truth, almost the only person who could be trusted not to rob the King. There had therefore been, during the last three years, much less waste and pilfering in the dockyards than formerly. Ships had been built which were fit to go to sea. An excellent order had been issued increasing the allowances of Captains, and at the same time strictly forbidding them to carry merchandise from port to port without the royal permission. The effect of these reforms was already perceptible; and James found no difficulty in fitting out, at short notice, a considerable fleet. Thirty ships of the line, all third rates and fourth rates, were collected in the Thames, under the command of Lord Dartmouth. The loyalty of Dartmouth was not suspected; and he was thought to have as much professional skill and knowledge as any of the patrician sailors who, in that age, rose to the highest naval commands without a regular naval training, and who were at once flag officers on the sea and colonels of infantry on shore.*

* Pepys's Memoirs relating to the Royal Navy, 1690; Life of James the

The regular army had, during some years, been the largest that any king of England had ever commanded, and was now rapidly augmented. New companies were incorporated with the existing regiments. Commissions for the raising of fresh regiments were issued. Four thousand men were added to the English establishment. Three thousand were sent for with all speed from Ireland. As many more were ordered to march southward from Scotland. James estimated the force with which he should be able to meet the invaders at near forty thousand troops, exclusive of the militia.*

The navy and army were therefore far more than sufficient to repel a Dutch invasion. But could the navy, could the army, be trusted? Would not the trainbands flock by thousands to the standard of the deliverer? The party which had, a few years before, drawn the sword for Monmouth would undoubtedly be eager to welcome the Prince of Orange. And what had become of the party which had, during seven and forty years, been the bulwark of monarchy? Where were now those gallant gentlemen who had ever been ready to shed their blood for the crown? Outraged and insulted, driven from the bench of justice, and deprived of all military command, they saw the peril of their ungrateful sovereign with undisguised delight. Where were those priests and prelates who had, from ten thousand pulpits, proclaimed the duty of obeying the anointed delegate of God? Some of them had been imprisoned: some had been plundered: all had been placed under the iron rule of the High Commission, and were in hourly fear lest some new freak of tyranny should deprive them of their freeholds and leave them without a morsel of bread. That Churchmen would even now so completely forget the doctrine which had been their peculiar boast as to join in active resistance seemed incredible. But could their oppressor expect to find among them the spirit which, in the preceding generation, had triumphed over the armies of Essex and Waller, and had yielded only after a desperate struggle to the genius and vigour of Cromwell? The tyrant was overcome by fear. He ceased to repeat that concession had always ruined princes, and sullenly owned that he must stoop to court the Tories once more.† There is reason to believe that Halifax was, at this time, invited to return to

* Life of James the Second, ii. 166. Orig. Mem.; Adda, [illegible]; Van Citters, [illegible].

† Adda, [illegible] 1688. This despatch describes strongly James's dread of an universal defection of his subjects.

office, and that he was not unwilling to do so. The part of mediator between the throne and the nation was, of all parts, that for which he was best qualified, and of which he was most ambitious. How the negotiation with him was broken off is not known: but it is not improbable that the question of the dispensing power was the insurmountable difficulty. His hostility to the dispensing power had caused his disgrace three years before: nothing that had since happened had been of a nature to change his views; and James was fully determined to make no concession on that point.* As to other matters His Majesty was less pertinacious. He put forth a proclamation in which he solemnly promised to protect the Church of England and to maintain the Act of Uniformity. He declared himself willing to make great sacrifices for the sake of concord. He would no longer insist that Roman Catholics should be admitted into the House of Commons; and he trusted that his people would justly appreciate such a proof of his disposition to meet their wishes. Three days later he notified his intention to replace all the magistrates and Deputy Lieutenants who had been dismissed for refusing to support his policy. On the day after the appearance of this notification Compton's suspension was taken off.†

He gives audience to the Bishops.

At the same time the King gave an audience to all the Bishops who were then in London. They had requested admittance to his presence for the purpose of tendering their counsel in this emergency. The Primate was spokesman. He respectfully asked that the administration might be put into the hands of persons duly qualified, that all acts done under pretence of the dispensing power might be revoked, that the Ecclesiastical Commission might be annulled, that the wrongs of Magdalene College might be redressed, and that the old franchises of the municipal corporations might be restored. He hinted very intelligibly that there was one most desirable event which would completely secure the throne and quiet the distracted realm. If His Majesty would reconsider the points in dispute between the Churches of Rome and England, perhaps, by the divine blessing on the arguments which the Bishops wished to lay before him, he might be convinced that it was his duty to return to the religion of

* All the scanty light which we have respecting this negotiation is derived from Reresby. His informant was a lady whom he does not name, and who certainly was not to be implicitly trusted.
† London Gazette, Sept. 24. 27., Oct 1. 1688.

his father and of his grandfather. Thus far, Sancroft said, he had spoken the sense of his brethren. There remained a subject on which he had not taken counsel with them, but to which he thought it his duty to advert. He was indeed the only man of his profession who could advert to that subject without being suspected of an interested motive. The metropolitan see of York had been three years vacant. The Archbishop implored the King to fill it speedily with a pious and learned divine, and added that such a divine might without difficulty be found among those who then stood in the royal presence. The King commanded himself sufficiently to return thanks for this unpalatable counsel, and promised to consider what had been said.* Of the dispensing power he would not yield one tittle. No unqualified person was removed from any civil or military office. But some of Sancroft's suggestions were adopted. Within forty-eight hours the Court of High Commission was abolished.† It was determined that the charter of the City of London, which had been forfeited six years before, should be restored; and the Chancellor was sent in state to carry back the venerable parchment to Guildhall.‡ A week later the public was informed that the Bishop of Winchester, who was by virtue of his office Visitor of Magdalene College, had it in charge from the King to correct whatever was amiss in that society. It was not without a long struggle and a bitter pang that James stooped to this last humiliation. Indeed he did not yield till the Vicar Apostolic Leyburn, who seems to have behaved on all occasions like a wise and honest man, declared that in his judgment the ejected President and Fellows had been wronged, and that on religious as well as on political grounds, restitution ought to be made to them.§ In a few days appeared a proclamation restoring the forfeited franchises of all the municipal corporations.||

James flattered himself that concessions so great, made in

---

* Tanner MSS.; Burnet, i. 764. Burnet has, I think, confounded this audience with an audience which took place a few weeks later.

† London Gazette, Oct. 8. 1688.

‡ Ibid.

§ London Gazette, Oct. 15. 1688; Adda, Oct. 14. The Nuncio, though generally an enemy to violent courses, seems to have opposed the restoration of Hough, probably from regard for the interests of Giffard and the other Roman Catholics who were quartered in Magdalene College. Leyburn declared himself "del sentimento che fosse stato uno spoglio, e che il possesso in cui si trovano ora li Cattolici fosse violento ed illegale, onde non era privar quelli di un dritto acquisto, ma rendere agli altri quello che era stato levato con violenza."

|| London Gazette, Oct. 18. 1688.

CHAP. IX.

His concessions ill received.

the short space of a month, would bring back to him the hearts of his people. Nor can it be doubted that such concessions, if they had been made before there was reason to expect an invasion from Holland, would have done much to conciliate the Tories. But gratitude is not to be expected by rulers who give to fear what they have refused to justice. During three years the King had been proof to all argument and to all entreaty. Every minister who had dared to raise his voice in favour of the civil and ecclesiastical constitution of the realm had been disgraced. A Parliament eminently loyal had ventured to protest gently and respectfully against a violation of the fundamental laws of England, and had been sternly reprimanded, prorogued, and dissolved. Judge after Judge had been stripped of the ermine for declining to give decisions opposed to the whole common and statute law. The most respectable Cavaliers had been excluded from all share in the government of their counties for refusing to betray the public liberties. Scores of clergymen had been deprived of their livelihood for observing their oaths. Prelates, to whose steadfast fidelity the King owed the crown which he wore, had on their knees besought him not to command them to violate the laws of God and of the land. Their modest petition had been treated as a seditious libel. They had been browbeaten, threatened, imprisoned, prosecuted, and had narrowly escaped utter ruin. Then at length the nation, finding that right was borne down by might, and that even supplication was regarded as a crime, began to think of trying the chances of war. The oppressor learned that an armed deliverer was at hand and would be eagerly welcomed by Whigs and Tories, Dissenters and Churchmen. All was immediately changed. That government which had requited constant and zealous service with spoliation and persecution, that government which to weighty reasons and pathetic entreaties had replied only by injuries and insults, became in a moment strangely gracious. Every Gazette now announced the removal of some grievance. It was then evident that on the equity, the humanity, the plighted word of the King, no reliance could be placed, and that he would govern well only so long as he was under the strong dread of resistance. His subjects were therefore by no means disposed to restore to him a confidence which he had justly forfeited, or to relax the pressure which had wrung from him the only good acts of his whole reign. The general impatience for the arrival of the Dutch became every day stronger. The gales which at this time blew obstinately from the west, and which at once prevented the Prince's armament from sailing and brought fresh Irish regiments from Dublin to Chester, were bitterly cursed and reviled by the common people. The weather, it was said, was Popish.* Crowds stood in Cheapside gazing intently at the weathercock on the graceful steeple of Bow Church, and praying for a Protestant wind.†

The general feeling was strengthened by an event which, though merely accidental, was not unnaturally ascribed to the perfidy of the King. The Bishop of Winchester announced that, in obedience to the royal commands, he designed to restore the ejected members of Magdalene College. He fixed the twenty-first of October for this ceremony, and on the twentieth went down to Oxford. The whole University was in expectation. The expelled Fellows had arrived from all parts of the kingdom, eager to take possession of their beloved home. Three hundred gentlemen on horseback escorted the Visitor to his lodgings. As he passed the bells rang, and the High Street was crowded with shouting spectators. He retired to rest. The next morning a joyous crowd assembled at the gates of Magdalene: but the Bishop did not make his appearance; and soon it was known that he had been roused from his bed by a royal messenger, and had been directed to repair immediately to Whitehall. This strange disappointment caused much wonder and anxiety; but in a few hours came news which, to minds disposed, not without reason, to think the worst, seemed completely to explain the King's change of purpose. The Dutch armament had put out to sea, and had been driven back by a storm. The disaster was exaggerated by rumour. Many ships, it was said, had been lost. Thousands of horses had perished. All thought of a design on England must be relinquished, at least for the present year. Here was a lesson for the nation. While James expected immediate invasion and rebellion, he had given orders that reparation should be made to those whom he had unlawfully despoiled. As soon as he found himself safe, those orders had been revoked. This imputation,

* "Vento Papista," says Adda, Oct. 14/Nov. 2. 1688.
† The expression Protestant wind seems to have been first applied to the wind which kept Tyrconnel, during some time, from taking possession of the government of Ireland. See the first part of Lillibullero.

though at that time generally believed, and though, since that time, repeated by writers who ought to have been well informed, was without foundation. It is certain that the mishap of the Dutch fleet could not, by any mode of communication, have been known at Westminster till some hours after the Bishop of Winchester had received the summons which called him away from Oxford. The King, however, had little right to complain of the suspicions of his people. If they sometimes, without severely examining evidence, ascribed to his dishonest policy what was really the effect of accident or inadvertence, the fault was his own. That men who are in the habit of breaking faith should be distrusted when they mean to keep it is part of their just and natural punishment.*

It is remarkable that James, on this occasion, incurred one unmerited imputation solely in consequence of his eagerness to clear himself from another imputation equally unmerited. The Bishop of Winchester had been hastily summoned from Oxford to attend an extraordinary meeting of the Privy Council, or rather an assembly of Notables, which had been convoked at Whitehall. With the Privy Councillors were joined, in this solemn sitting, all the Peers Spiritual and Temporal who chanced to be in or near the capital, the Judges, the crown lawyers, the Lord Mayor and the Aldermen of the City of London. A hint had been given to Petre that he would do well to absent himself. In truth few of the Peers would have chosen to sit with him. Near the head of the board a chair of state was placed for the Queen Dowager. The Princess Anne had been requested to attend, but had excused herself on the plea of delicate health.

Proofs of the birth of the Prince of Wales submitted to the Privy Council.

James informed this great assembly that he thought it necessary to produce proofs of the birth of his son. The arts of bad men had poisoned the public mind to such an extent that very many believed the Prince of Wales to be a suppositious child. But Providence had graciously ordered things so that scarcely any prince had ever come into the world in the presence of so many witnesses. Those witnesses then appeared and gave their evidence. After all the depositions had been taken, James with great solemnity declared that the imputation thrown on him was utterly false, and that he would rather die a thousand deaths than wrong any of his children.

* All the evidence on this point is collected in Howell's edition of the State Trials.

All who were present appeared to be satisfied. The evidence was instantly published, and was allowed by judicious and impartial persons to be decisive.* But the judicious are always a minority; and scarcely anybody was then impartial. The whole nation was convinced that all sincere Papists thought it a duty to perjure themselves whenever they could, by perjury, serve the interests of their Church. Men who, having been bred Protestants, had for the sake of lucre pretended to be converted to Popery, were, if possible, less trustworthy than sincere Papists. The depositions of all who belonged to these two classes were therefore regarded as mere nullities. Thus the weight of the testimony on which James had relied was greatly reduced. What remained was malignantly scrutinised. To every one of the few Protestant witnesses who had said anything material some exception was taken. One was notoriously a greedy sycophant. Another had not indeed yet apostatised, but was nearly related to an apostate. The people asked, as they had asked from the first, why, if all was right, the King, knowing, as he knew, that many doubted the reality of his wife's pregnancy, had not taken care that the birth should be more satisfactorily proved. Was there nothing suspicious in the false reckoning, in the sudden change of abode, in the absence of the Princess Anne and of the Archbishop of Canterbury? Why was no prelate of the Established Church in attendance? Why was not the Dutch Ambassador summoned? Why, above all, were not the Hydes, loyal servants of the crown, faithful sons of the Church, and natural guardians of the interest of their nieces, suffered to mingle with the crowd of Papists which was assembled in and near the royal bedchamber? Why, in short, was there, in the long list of assistants, not a single name which commanded public confidence and respect? The true answer to these questions was that the King's understanding was weak, that his temper was despotic, and that he had willingly seized an opportunity of manifesting his contempt for the opinion of his subjects. But the multitude, not contented with this explanation, attributed to deep laid villany what was really the effect of folly and perverseness. Nor was this opinion confined to the multitude. The Lady Anne, at her toilette, on the morning after the Council, spoke of the investigation

* The evidence will be found with much illustrative matter in Howell's edition of the State Trials.

with such scorn as emboldened the very tirewomen who were dressing her to put in their jests. Some of the Lords who had heard the examination, and had appeared to be satisfied, were really unconvinced. Lloyd, Bishop of St. Asaph, whose piety and learning commanded general respect, continued to the end of his life to believe that a fraud had been practised.

Disgrace of Sunderland.

The depositions taken before the Council had not been many hours in the hands of the public when it was noised abroad that Sunderland had been dismissed from all his places. The news of his disgrace seems to have taken the politicians of the coffeehouses by surprise, but did not astonish those who had observed what was passing in the palace. Treason had not been brought home to him by legal, or even by tangible, evidence: but there was a strong suspicion among those who watched him closely that, through some channel or other, he was in communication with the enemies of that government in which he occupied so high a place. He, with unabashed forehead, imprecated on his own head all evil here and hereafter if he was guilty. His only fault, he protested, was that he had served the crown too well. Had he not given hostages to the royal cause? Had he not broken down every bridge by which he could, in case of a disaster, effect his retreat? Had he not gone all lengths in favour of the dispensing power, sate in the High Commission, signed the warrant for the committment of the Bishops, appeared as a witness against them, at the hazard of his life, amidst the hisses and curses of the thousands who filled Westminster Hall? Had he not given the last proof of fidelity by renouncing his religion, and publicly joining a Church which the nation detested? What had he to hope from a change? What had he not to dread? These arguments, though plausible, and though set off by the most insinuating address, could not remove the impression which whispers and reports arriving at once from a hundred different quarters had produced. The King became daily colder and colder. Sunderland attempted to support himself by the Queen's help, obtained an audience of Her Majesty, and was actually in her apartment when Middleton entered, and, by the King's orders, demanded the seals. That evening the fallen minister was for the last time closeted with the Prince whom he had flattered and betrayed. The interview was a strange one. Sunderland acted calumniated virtue to perfection. He regretted not, he said, the Secretaryship of

State or the Presidency of the Council, if only he retained his Sovereign's esteem. "Do not, sir, do not make me the most unhappy gentleman in your dominions, by refusing to declare that you acquit me of disloyalty." The King hardly knew what to believe. There was no positive proof of guilt; and the energy and pathos with which Sunderland lied might have imposed on a keener understanding than that with which he had to deal. At the French embassy his professions still found credit. There he declared that he should remain a few days in London, and show himself at court. He would then retire to his country seat at Althorpe, and try to repair his dilapidated fortunes by economy. If a revolution should take place he must fly to France. His ill requited loyalty had left him no other place of refuge.*

The seals which had been taken from Sunderland were delivered to Preston. The same Gazette which announced this change contained the official intelligence of the disaster which had befallen the Dutch fleet.† That disaster was serious, though far less serious than the King and his few adherents, misled by their wishes, were disposed to believe.

On the sixteenth of October, according to the English reckoning, was held a solemn sitting of the States of Holland. The Prince came to bid them farewell. He thanked them for the kindness with which they had watched over him when he was left an orphan child, for the confidence which they had reposed in him during his administration, and for the assistance which they had granted to him at this momentous crisis. He entreated them to believe that he had always meant and endeavoured to promote the interest of his country. He was now quitting them, perhaps never to return. If he should fall in defence of the reformed religion and of the independence of Europe, he commended his beloved wife to their care. The Grand Pensionary answered in a faltering voice; and in all that grave senate there was none who could refrain from shedding tears. But the iron stoicism of William never gave way; and he stood among his weeping friends calm and austere as if he had been about to leave them only for a short visit to his hunting grounds at Loo.‡

The deputies of the principal towns accompanied him to

CHAP. IX.

William takes leave of the States of Holland

---

* Barillon, Oct. 4/14, 11/21 Oct. 22/ Nov. 1, 1688; Adda, Oct. 23/ Nov. 2.
† London Gazette, Oct. 29, 1688.
‡ Register of the Proceedings of the States of Holland and West Friesland; Burnet, i. 782.

his yacht. Even the representatives of Amsterdam, so long the chief seat of opposition to his administration, joined in paying him this compliment. Public prayers were offered for him on that day in all the churches of the Hague.

In the evening he arrived at Helvoetsluys and went on board of a frigate called the Brill. His flag was immediately hoisted. It displayed the arms of Nassau quartered with those of England. The motto, embroidered in letters three feet long, was happily chosen. The House of Orange had long used the elliptical device, "I will maintain." The ellipsis was now filled up with words of high import, "The liberties of England and the Protestant religion."

The Prince had not been many hours on board when the wind became fair. On the nineteenth the armament put out to sea, and traversed, before a strong breeze, about half the distance between the Dutch and English coasts. Then the wind changed, blew hard from the west, and swelled into a violent tempest. The ships, scattered and in great distress, regained the shore of Holland as they best might. The Brill reached Helvoetsluys on the twenty-first. The Prince's fellow passengers had observed with admiration that neither peril nor mortification had for one moment disturbed his composure. He now, though suffering from sea sickness, refused to go on shore: for he conceived that, by remaining on board, he should in the most effectual manner notify to Europe that the late misfortune had only delayed for a very short time the execution of his purpose. In two or three days the fleet reassembled. One vessel only had been cast away. Not a single soldier or sailor was missing. Some horses had perished: but this loss the Prince with great expedition repaired; and, before the London Gazette had spread the news of his mishap, he was again ready to sail.*

His Declaration preceded him only by a few hours. On the first of November it began to be mentioned in mysterious whispers by the politicians of London, was passed secretly from man to man, and was slipped into the boxes of the post office. One of the agents was arrested, and the packets of which he was in charge were carried to Whitehall. The King read, and was greatly troubled. His first impulse was to hide the paper from all human eyes. He threw into the

* London Gazette, October 29, 1688; Burnet, i. 782.; Bentinck to his wife, October 11. Oct. 72. Oct. 94. Oct. 17. 1688.

fire every copy which had been brought to him, except one; and that one he would scarcely trust out of his own hands.*

The paragraph in the manifesto which disturbed him most was that in which it was said that some of the Peers, Spiritual and Temporal, had invited the Prince of Orange to invade England. Halifax, Clarendon, and Nottingham were then in London. They were immediately summoned to the palace and interrogated. Halifax, though conscious of innocence, refused at first to make any answer. "Your Majesty asks me," said he, "whether I have committed high treason. If I am suspected, let me be brought before my peers. And how can Your Majesty place any dependence on the answer of a culprit whose life is at stake? Even if I had invited His Highness over, I should without scruple plead Not Guilty." The King declared that he did not at all consider Halifax as a culprit, and that he had asked the question as one gentleman asks another who has been calumniated whether there be the least foundation for the calumny. "In that case," said Halifax, "I have no objection to aver, as a gentleman speaking to a gentleman, on my honour, which is as sacred as my oath, that I have not invited the Prince of Orange over."† Clarendon and Nottingham said the same. The King was still more anxious to ascertain the temper of the Prelates. If they were hostile to him, his throne was indeed in danger. But it could not be. There was something monstrous in the supposition that any Bishop of the Church of England could rebel against his Sovereign. Compton was called into the royal closet, and was asked whether he believed that there was the slightest ground for the Prince's assertion. The Bishop was in a strait; for he was himself one of the seven who had signed the invitation; and his conscience, not a very enlightened conscience, would not suffer him, it seems, to utter a direct falsehood. "Sir," he said, "I am quite confident that there is not one of my brethren who is not as guiltless as myself in this matter." The equivocation was ingenious; but whether the difference between the sin of such an equivocation and the sin of a lie be worth any expense of ingenuity may perhaps be doubted. The King was satisfied. "I fully acquit you all," he said. "But I

* Van Citters, Nov. 4/14. 1688; Adda, "respuestas," says Ronquillo, "con ciertas, Nov. 4/14. aunque mas las escabrian en la corte."
† Ronquillo, Nov. 14/24. 1688. = Estas

think it necessary that you should publicly contradict the slanderous charge brought against you in the Prince's Declaration." The Bishop very naturally begged that he might be allowed to read the paper which he was required to contradict: but the King would not suffer him to look at it.

On the following day appeared a proclamation threatening with the severest punishment all who should circulate, or who should even dare to read William's manifesto.* The Primate and the few Spiritual Peers who happened to be then in London had orders to wait upon the King. Preston was in attendance with the Prince's Declaration in his hand. "My Lords," said James, "listen to this passage. It concerns you." Preston then read the sentence in which the Spiritual Peers were mentioned. The King proceeded: "I do not believe one word of this: I am satisfied of your innocence: but I think it fit to let you know of what you are accused."

The Primate, with many dutiful expressions, protested that the King did him no more than justice. "I was born in Your Majesty's allegiance. I have repeatedly confirmed that allegiance by my oath. I can have but one King at one time. I have not invited the Prince over; and I do not believe that a single one of my brethren has done so." "I am sure I have not," said Crewe of Durham. "Nor I," said Cartwright of Chester. Crewe and Cartwright might well be believed; for both had sate in the Ecclesiastical Commission. When Compton's turn came, he parried the question with an adroitness which a Jesuit might have envied. "I gave Your Majesty my answer yesterday."

James repeated again and again that he fully acquitted them all. Nevertheless it would, in his judgment, be for his service and for their own honour that they should publicly vindicate themselves. He therefore required them to draw up a paper setting forth their abhorrence of the Prince's design. They remained silent: their silence was supposed to imply consent; and they were suffered to withdraw.†

Meanwhile the fleet of William was on the German Ocean. It was on the evening of Thursday the first of November that he put to sea the second time. The wind blew fresh from the east. The armament, during twelve hours, held a course

* London Gazette, Nov. 5, 1688. The Proclamation is dated November 2.
† Tanner MSS.

towards the northwest. The light vessels sent out by the
English Admiral for the purpose of obtaining intelligence
brought back news which confirmed the prevailing opinion
that the enemy would try to land in Yorkshire. All at once,
on a signal from the Prince's ship, the whole fleet tacked,
and made sail for the British Channel. The same breeze
which favoured the voyage of the invaders, prevented Dartmouth from coming out of the Thames. His ships were
forced to strike yards and topmasts; and two of his frigates,
which had gained the open sea, were shattered by the violence
of the weather and driven back into the river.*

The Dutch fleet ran fast before the gale, and reached the
Straits at about ten in the morning of Saturday, the third
of November. William himself, in the Brill, led the way.
More than six hundred vessels, with canvas spread to a
favourable wind, followed in his train. The transports were
in the centre. The men of war, more than fifty in number,
formed an outer rampart. Herbert, with the title of Lieutenant Admiral General, commanded the whole fleet. His
post was in the rear, and many English sailors, inflamed
against Popery, and attracted by high pay, served under him.
It was not without great difficulty that the Prince had prevailed on some Dutch officers of high reputation to submit to
the authority of a stranger. But the arrangement was eminently judicious. There was, in the King's fleet, much discontent and an ardent zeal for the Protestant faith. But
within the memory of old mariners the Dutch and English
navies had thrice, with heroic spirit and various fortune, contended for the empire of the sea. Our sailors had not forgotten the broom with which Tromp had threatened to sweep
the Channel, or the fire which De Ruyter had lighted in the
dockyards of the Medway. Had the rival nations been once
more brought face to face on the element of which both claimed
the sovereignty, all other thoughts might have given place to
mutual animosity. A bloody and obstinate battle might have
been fought. Defeat would have been fatal to William's
enterprise. Even victory would have deranged all his deeply
meditated schemes of policy. He therefore wisely determined that the pursuers, if they overtook him, should be
hailed in their own mother tongue, and adjured, by an admiral

* Burnet, I. 787.; Rapin; Whittle's the Desertion, 1688; Dartmouth to
Exact Diary; Expedition of the Prince James, Nov. 5. 1688, in Dalrymple.
of Orange to England, 1688; History of

CHAP. IX.

He passes the Straits.

under whom they had served, and whom they esteemed, not to fight against old messmates for Popish tyranny. Such an appeal might possibly avert a conflict. If a conflict took place, one English commander wouldbe opposed to another; nor would the pride of the islanders be wounded by learning that Dartmouth had been compelled to strike to Herbert.*

Happily William's precautions were not necessary. Soon after midday he passed the Straits. His fleet spread to within a league of Dover on the north and of Calais on the south. The men of war on the extreme right and left saluted both fortresses at once. The troops appeared under arms on the decks. The flourish of trumpets, the clash of cymbals, and the rolling of drums were distinctly heard at once on the English and French shores. An innumerable company of gazers blackened the white beach of Kent. Another mighty multitude covered the coast of Picardy. Rapin de Thoyras, who, driven by persecution from his country, had taken service in the Dutch army, and now went with the Prince to England, described the spectacle, many years later, as the most magnificent and affecting that was ever seen by human eyes. At sunset the armament was off Beachy Head. Then the lights were kindled. The sea was in a blaze for many miles. But the eyes of all the steersmen were directed throughout the night to three huge lanterns which flamed on the stern of the Brill.†

Meanwhile a courier had been riding post from Dover Castle to Whitehall with news that the Dutch had passed the Straits and were steering westward. It was necessary to make an immediate change in all the military arrangements. Messengers were despatched in every direction. Officers were roused from their beds at dead of night. At three on the Sunday morning there was a great muster by torchlight in Hyde Park. The King had sent several regiments northward in the expectation that William would land in Yorkshire. Expresses were despatched to recall them. All the

* Avaux, July 14/24, Aug. 13/23, 1688. On this subject, Mr. De Jonge, who is connected by affinity with the descendants of the Dutch Admiral Evertsen, has kindly communicated to me some interesting information derived from family papers. In a letter to Bentinck, dated Sept. 4/14, 1688, William insists strongly on the importance of avoiding an action, and begs Bentinck to represent this to Herbert. "Ce n'est pas le tems de faire voir sa bravoure, ni de sa battre si l'on le peut éviter. Je luy l'ai déjà dit: mais il sera nécessaire que vous le répétiez, et que vous le luy fassiez bien comprendre."

† Rapin's History; Whittle's Exact Diary. I have seen a contemporary Dutch chart of the order in which the fleet sailed.

forces except those which were necessary to keep the peace of the capital were ordered to move to the West. Salisbury was appointed as the place of rendezvous; but, as it was thought possible that Portsmouth might be the first point of attack, three battalions of guards and a strong body of cavalry set out for that fortress. In a few hours it was known that Portsmouth was safe; and these troops then received orders to change their route and to hasten to Salisbury.*

When Sunday the fourth of November dawned, the cliffs of the Isle of Wight were full in view of the Dutch armament. That day was the anniversary both of William's birth and of his marriage. Sail was slackened during part of the morning; and divine service was performed on board of the ships. In the afternoon and through the night the fleet held on its course. Torbay was the place where the Prince intended to land. But the morning of Monday the fifth of November was hazy. The pilot of the Brill could not discern the sea marks, and carried the fleet too far to the west. The danger was great. To return in the face of the wind was impossible. Plymouth was the next port. But at Plymouth a garrison had been posted under the command of the Earl of Bath. The landing might be opposed: and a check might produce serious consequences. There could be little doubt, moreover, that by this time the royal fleet had got out of the Thames and was hastening full sail down the Channel. Russell saw the whole extent of the peril, and exclaimed to Burnet, "You may go to prayers, Doctor. All is over." At that moment the wind changed: a soft breeze sprang up from the south; the mist dispersed; the sun shone forth; and, under the mild light of an autumnal noon, the fleet turned back, passed round the lofty cape of Berry Head, and rode safe in the harbour of Torbay.†

Since William looked on that harbour its aspect has greatly changed. The amphitheatre which surrounds the spacious basin, now exhibits everywhere the signs of prosperity and civilisation. At the northeastern extremity has sprung up a great watering place, to which strangers are attracted from the most remote parts of our island by the Italian softness of the air: for in that climate the myrtle flourishes unsheltered, and even the winter is milder than the Northumbrian April.

He lands at Torbay.

* Adda, Nov. 5. 1688; Newsletter in the Mackintosh Collection; Van Citters, Nov. 5.
† Burnet, I. 788.; Extracts from the Legge Papers in the Mackintosh Collection.

The inhabitants are about ten thousand in number. The newly built churches and chapels, the baths and libraries, the hotels and public gardens, the infirmary and the museum, the white streets, rising terrace above terrace, the gay villas peeping from the midst of shrubberies and flower beds, present a spectacle widely different from any that in the seventeenth century England could show. At the opposite end of the bay lies, sheltered by Berry Head, the stirring market town of Brixham, the wealthiest seat of our fishing trade. A pier and a haven were formed there at the beginning of the present century, but have been found insufficient for the increasing traffic. The population is about six thousand souls. The shipping amounts to more than two hundred sail. The tonnage exceeds many times the tonnage of the port of Liverpool under the kings of the House of Stuart. But Torbay, when the Dutch fleet cast anchor there, was known only as a haven where ships sometimes took refuge from the tempests of the Atlantic. Its quiet shores were undisturbed by the bustle either of commerce or of pleasure; and the huts of ploughmen and fishermen were thinly scattered over what is now the site of crowded marts and of luxurious pavilions.

The peasantry of the coast of Devonshire remembered the name of Monmouth with affection, and held Popery in detestation. They therefore crowded down to the seaside with provisions and offers of service. The disembarkation instantly commenced. Sixty boats conveyed the troops to the coast. Mackay was sent on shore first with the British regiments. The Prince soon followed. He landed where the quay of Brixham now stands. The whole aspect of the place has been altered. Where we now see a port crowded with shipping, and a market place swarming with buyers and sellers, the waves then broke on a desolate beach; but a fragment of the rock on which the deliverer stepped from his boat has been carefully preserved, and is set up as an object of public veneration in the centre of that busy wharf.

As soon as the Prince had planted his foot on dry ground he called for horses. Two beasts, such as the small yeomen of that time were in the habit of riding, were procured from the neighbouring village. William and Schomberg mounted and proceeded to examine the country.

As soon as Burnet was on shore he hastened to the Prince. An amusing dialogue took place between them. Burnet poured forth his congratulations with genuine delight, and then eagerly asked what were His Highness's plans. Military men are seldom disposed to take counsel with gownsmen on military matters; and William regarded the interference of unprofessional advisers, in questions relating to war with even more than the disgust ordinarily felt by soldiers on such occasions. But he was at that moment in an excellent humour, and, instead of signifying his displeasure by a short and cutting reprimand, graciously extended his hand, and answered his chaplain's question by another question: "Well Doctor, what do you think of predestination now?" The reproof was so delicate that Burnet, whose perceptions were not very fine, did not perceive it. He answered with great fervour that he should never forget the signal manner in which Providence had favoured their undertaking.*

During the first day the troops who had gone on shore had many discomforts to endure. The earth was soaked with rain. The baggage was still on board of the ships. Officers of high rank were compelled to sleep in wet clothes on the wet ground; the Prince himself had no better quarters than a hut afforded. His banner was displayed on the thatched roof; and some bedding brought from the Brill was spread for him on the floor.† There was some difficulty about landing the horses; and it seemed probable that this operation would occupy several days. But on the following morning the prospect cleared. The wind was gentle. The water in the bay was as even as glass. Some fishermen pointed out a place where the ships could be brought within sixty feet of the beach. This was done; and in three hours many hundreds of horses swam safely to shore.

The disembarkation had hardly been effected when the wind rose again, and swelled into a fierce gale from the west. The enemy coming in pursuit down the Channel had been stopped by the same change of weather which enabled William to land. During two days the King's fleet lay on an unruffled sea in sight of Beachy Head. At length Dartmouth was able to proceed. He passed the Isle of Wight, and one of his ships came in sight of the Dutch topmasts in Torbay. Just at this moment he was encountered by the tempest, and compelled to take shelter in the harbour of

---

* I think that nobody who compares Burnet's account of this conversation with Dartmouth's can doubt that I have correctly represented what passed.

† I have seen a contemporary Dutch print of the disembarkation. Some men are bringing the Prince's bedding into the hut on which his flag is flying.

Portsmouth.* At that time James, who was not incompetent to form a judgment on a question of seamanship, declared himself perfectly satisfied that his admiral had done all that man could do, and had yielded only to the irresistible hostility of the winds and waves. At a later period the unfortunate prince began, with little reason, to suspect Dartmouth of treachery, or at least of slackness.†

The weather had indeed served the Protestant cause so well that some men of more piety than judgment fully believed the ordinary laws of nature to have been suspended for the preservation of the liberty and religion of England. Exactly a hundred years before, they said, the Armada, invincible by man, had been scattered by the wrath of God. Civil freedom and divine truth were again in jeopardy, and again the obedient elements had fought for the good cause. The wind had blown strong from the east while the Prince wished to sail down the Channel, had turned to the south when he wished to enter Torbay, had sunk to a calm during the disembarkation, and as soon as the disembarkation was completed, had risen to a storm, and had met the pursuers in the face. Nor did men omit to remark that, by an extraordinary coincidence, the Prince had reached our shores on a day on which the Church of England commemorated, by prayer and thanksgiving, the wonderful escape of the Royal House and of the three estates from the blackest plot ever devised by Papists. Carstairs, whose suggestions were sure to meet with attention from the Prince, recommended that, as soon as the landing had been effected, public thanks should be offered to God for the protection so conspicuously accorded to the great enterprise. This advice was taken, and with excellent effect. The troops, taught to regard themselves as favourites of heaven, were inspired with new courage; and the English people formed the most favourable opinion of a general and an army so attentive to the duties of religion.

On Tuesday, the sixth of November, William's army began to march up the country. Some regiments advanced as far as Newton Abbot. A stone, set up in the midst of that little town, still marks the spot where the Prince's Declaration

---

* Burnet, i. 789.; Legge Papers.
† On Nov. 9. 1688, James wrote to Dartmouth thus: "Nobody could work otherwise than you did. I am sure all knowing seamen must be of the same mind." But see the Life of James, ii. 207. Orig. Mem.

was solemnly read to the people. The movements of the troops were slow: for the rain fell in torrents, and the roads of England were then in a state which seemed frightful to persons accustomed to the excellent communications of Holland. William took up his quarters, during two days, at Ford, a seat of the ancient and illustrious family of Courtenay, in the neighbourhood of Newton Abbot. He was magnificently lodged and feasted there; but it is remarkable that the owner of the house, though a strong Whig, did not choose to be the first to put life and fortune in peril, and cautiously abstained from doing anything which, if the King should prevail, could be treated as a crime.

Exeter, in the meantime, was greatly agitated. Lamplugh, the bishop, as soon as he heard that the Dutch were at Torbay, set off in terror for London. The Dean fled from the deanery. The magistrates were for the King, the body of the inhabitants for the Prince. Everything was in confusion when, on the morning of Thursday, the eighth of November, a body of troops, under the command of Mordaunt, appeared before the city. With Mordaunt came Burnet, to whom William had entrusted the duty of protecting the clergy of the Cathedral from injury and insult.* The Mayor and Aldermen had ordered the gates to be closed, but yielded on the first summons. The deanery was prepared for the reception of the Prince. On the following day, Friday the ninth, he arrived. The magistrates had been pressed to receive him in state at the entrance of the city, but had steadfastly refused. The pomp of that day, however, could well spare them. Such a sight had never been seen in Devonshire. Many of the citizens went forth half a day's journey to meet the champion of their religion. All the neighbouring villages poured forth their inhabitants. A great crowd, consisting chiefly of young peasants, brandishing their cudgels, had assembled on the top of Haldon Hill, whence the army, marching from Chudleigh, first descried the rich valley of the Exe, and the two massive towers rising from the cloud of smoke which overhung the capital of the West. The road, all down the long descent, and through the plain to the banks of the river, was lined, mile after mile, with spectators. From the West Gate to the Cathedral Close, the pressing and shouting on each side was such as reminded Londoners of the crowds on the

* Burnet, I. 790.

Lord Mayor's day. The houses were gaily decorated. Doors, windows, balconies, and roofs were thronged with gazers. An eye accustomed to the pomp of war would have found much to criticise in the spectacle. For several toilsome marches in the rain, through roads where one who travelled on foot sank at every step up to the ankles in clay, had not improved the appearance either of the men or of their accoutrements. But the people of Devonshire, altogether unused to the splendour of well ordered camps, were overwhelmed with delight and awe. Descriptions of the martial pageant were circulated all over the kingdom. They contained much that was well fitted to gratify the vulgar appetite for the marvellous. For the Dutch army, composed of men who had been born in various climates, and had served under various standards, presented an aspect at once grotesque, gorgeous, and terrible to islanders who had, in general, a very indistinct notion of foreign countries. First rode Macclesfield at the head of two hundred gentlemen, mostly of English blood, glittering in helmets and cuirasses, and mounted on Flemish war horses. Each was attended by a negro, brought from the sugar plantations on the coast of Guiana. The citizens of Exeter, who had never seen so many specimens of the African race, gazed with wonder on those black faces set off by embroidered turbans and white feathers. Then, with drawn broadswords, came a squadron of Swedish horsemen in black armour and fur cloaks. They were regarded with a strange interest; for it was rumoured that they were natives of a land where the ocean was frozen and where the night lasted through half the year, and that they had themselves slain the huge bears whose skins they wore. Next, surrounded by a goodly company of gentlemen and pages, was borne aloft the Prince's banner. On its broad folds the crowd which covered the roofs and filled the windows read with delight that memorable inscription, "The Protestant religion and the liberties of England." But the acclamations redoubled when, attended by forty running footmen, the Prince himself appeared, armed on back and breast, wearing a white plume and mounted on a white charger. With how martial an air he curbed his horse, how thoughtful and commanding was the expression of his ample forehead and falcon eye, may still be seen on the canvas of Kneller. Once those grave features relaxed into a smile. It was when an ancient woman, perhaps one of the zealous Puritans who, through twenty-eight years of persecution, had waited with firm faith for the consolation of Israel, perhaps the mother of some rebel who had perished in the carnage of Sedgemoor, or in the more fearful carnage of the Bloody Circuit, broke from the crowd, rushed through the drawn swords and curvetting horses, touched the hand of the deliverer, and cried out that now she was happy. Near to the Prince was one who divided with him the gaze of the multitude. That, men said, was the great Count Schomberg, the first soldier in Europe, since Turenne and Condé were gone, the man whose genius and valour had saved the Portuguese monarchy on the field of Montes Claros, the man who had earned a still higher glory by resigning the truncheon of a Marshal of France for the sake of the true religion. It was not forgotten that the two heroes who, indissolubly united by their common Protestantism, were entering Exeter together, had twelve years before been opposed to each other under the walls of Maestricht, and that the energy of the young Prince had not then been found a match for the cool science of the veteran who now rode in friendship by his side. Then came a long column of the whiskered infantry of Switzerland, distinguished in all the Continental wars of two centuries by preeminent valour and discipline, but never till that week seen on English ground. And then marched a succession of bands, designated, as was the fashion of that age, after their leaders, Bentinck, Solmes, and Ginkell, Talmash and Mackay. With peculiar pleasure Englishmen might look on one gallant regiment which still bore the name of the honoured and lamented Ossory. The effect of the spectacle was heightened by the recollection of more than one renowned event in which the warriors now pouring through the West Gate had borne a share. For they had seen service very different from that of the Devonshire militia, or of the camp at Hounslow. Some of them had repelled the fiery onset of the French on the field of Seneff; and others had crossed swords with the infidels in the cause of Christendom on that great day when the siege of Vienna was raised. The very senses of the multitude were fooled by imagination. Newsletters conveyed to every part of the kingdom fabulous accounts of the size and strength of the invaders. It was affirmed that they were, with scarcely an exception, above six feet high, and that they wielded such huge pikes, swords, and muskets, as had never before been seen in England. Nor did the wonder of the population diminish when the artillery arrived, twenty-one heavy pieces of brass cannon, which were with difficulty tugged along by sixteen cart horses to each. Much curiosity was excited by a strange structure mounted on wheels. It proved to be a movable smithy, furnished with all tools and materials necessary for repairing arms and carriages. But nothing caused so much astonishment as the bridge of boats, which was laid with great speed on the Exe for the conveyance of waggons, and afterwards as speedily taken to pieces and carried away. It was made, if report said true, after a pattern contrived by the Christians who were warring against the Great Turk on the Danube. The foreigners inspired as much good will as admiration. Their politic leader took care to distribute the quarters in such a manner as to cause the smallest possible inconvenience to the inhabitants of Exeter and of the neighbouring villages. The most rigid discipline was maintained. Not only were pillage and outrage effectually prevented, but the troops were required to demean themselves with civility towards all classes. Those who had formed their notions of an army from the conduct of Kirke and his Lambs were amazed to see soldiers who never swore at a landlady or took an egg without paying for it. In return for this moderation the people furnished the troops with provisions in great abundance and at reasonable prices.*

Much depended on the course which, at this great crisis, the clergy of the Church of England might take; and the members of the Chapter of Exeter were the first who were called upon to declare their sentiments. Burnet informed the Canons, now left without a head by the flight of the Dean, that they could not be permitted to use the prayer for the Prince of Wales, and that a solemn service must be performed in honour of the safe arrival of the Prince. The

Canons did not choose to appear in their stalls; but some of the choristers and prebendaries attended. William repaired in military state to the Cathedral. As he passed under the gorgeous screen, that renowned organ, scarcely surpassed by any of those which are the boast of his native Holland, gave out a peal of triumph. He mounted the Bishop's seat, a stately throne rich with the carving of the fifteenth century. Burnet stood below; and a crowd of warriors and nobles appeared on the right hand and on the left. The singers, robed in white, sang the Te Deum. When the chaunt was over, Burnet read the Prince's Declaration: but, as soon as the first words were uttered, prebendaries and singers crowded in all haste out of the choir. At the close Burnet cried in a loud voice, "God save the Prince of Orange!" and many fervent voices answered, "Amen."*

On Sunday, the eleventh of November, Burnet preached before the Prince in the Cathedral, and dilated on the signal mercy vouchsafed by God to the English Church and nation. At the same time a singular event happened in a humbler place of worship. Ferguson resolved to preach at the Presbyterian meeting house. The minister and elders would not consent: but the turbulent and halfwitted knave, fancying that the times of Fleetwood and Harrison were come again, forced the door, went through the congregation sword in hand, mounted the pulpit, and there poured forth a fiery invective against the King. The time for such follies had gone by: and this exhibition excited nothing but derision and disgust.†

While these things were passing in Devonshire the ferment was great in London. The Prince's Declaration, in spite of all precautions, was now in every man's hands. On the sixth of November James, still uncertain on what part of the coast the invaders had landed, summoned the Primate and three other Bishops, Compton of London, White of Peterborough, and Sprat of Rochester, to a conference in the closet. The King listened graciously while the prelates made warm professions of loyalty, and assured them that he did not suspect them. "But where," said he, "is the paper that you were to bring me?" "Sir," answered Sancroft, "we have brought no paper. We are not solicitous to clear our fame to the

* Expedition of the Prince of Orange; Oldmixon, 755.; Whittle's Diary; Echard, iii. 911.; London Gazette, Nov. 15.
† London Gazette, Nov. 15. 1688; Expedition of the Prince of Orange.

world. It is no new thing to us to be reviled and falsely accused. Our consciences acquit us: Your Majesty acquits us; and we are satisfied." "Yes," said the King; "but a declaration from you is necessary to my service." He then produced a copy of the Prince's manifesto. "See," he said, "how you are mentioned here." "Sir," answered one of the Bishops, "not one person in five hundred believes this manifesto to be genuine." "No!" cried the King fiercely: "then those five hundred would bring the Prince of Orange to cut my throat." "God forbid," exclaimed the prelates in concert. But the King's understanding, never very clear, was now quite bewildered. One of his peculiarities was that, whenever his opinion was not adopted, he fancied that his veracity was questioned. "This paper not genuine!" he exclaimed, turning over the leaves with his hands. "Am I not worthy to be believed? Is my word not to be taken?" "At all events, sir," said one of the Bishops, "this is not an ecclesiastical matter. It lies within the sphere of the civil power. God has entrusted Your Majesty with the sword: and it is not for us to invade your functions." Then the Archbishop, with that gentle and temperate malice which inflicts the deepest wounds, declared that he must be excused from setting his hand to any political document. "I and my brethren, sir," he said, "have already smarted severely for meddling with affairs of state; and we shall be very cautious how we do so again. We once subscribed a petition of the most harmless kind: we presented it in the most respectful manner; and we found that we had committed a high offence. We were saved from ruin only by the merciful protection of God. And, sir, the ground then taken by Your Majesty's Attorney and Solicitor was that, out of Parliament, we were private men, and that it was criminal presumption in private men to meddle with politics. They attacked us so fiercely that for my part I gave myself over for lost." "I thank you for that, my Lord of Canterbury," said the King: "I should have hoped that you would not have thought yourself lost by falling into my hands." Such a speech might have become the mouth of a merciful sovereign, but it came with a bad grace from a prince who had burned a woman alive for harbouring one of his flying enemies, from a prince round whose knees his own nephew had clung in vain agonies of supplication. The Archbishop was not to be so silenced. He resumed his story, and recounted the insults which the creatures of the Court had offered to the Church of England, among which some ridicule thrown on his own style occupied a conspicuous place. The King had nothing to say but that there was no use in repeating old grievances, and that he had hoped that these things had been quite forgotten. He, who never forgot the smallest injury that he had suffered, could not understand how others should remember for a few weeks the most deadly injuries that he had inflicted.

At length the conversation came back to the point from which it had wandered. The King insisted on having from the Bishops a paper declaring their abhorrence of the Prince's enterprise. They, with many professions of the most submissive loyalty, pertinaciously refused. The Prince, they said, asserted that he had been invited by temporal as well as by spiritual peers. The imputation was common. Why should not the purgation be common also? "I see how it is," said the King. "Some of the temporal peers have been with you, and have persuaded you to cross me in this matter." The Bishops solemnly averred that it was not so. But it would, they said, seem strange that, on a question involving grave political and military considerations, the temporal peers should be entirely passed over, and the prelates alone should be required to take a prominent part. "But this," said James, "is my method. I am your King. It is for me to judge what is best. I will go my own way; and I call on you to assist me." The Bishops assured him that they would assist him in their proper department, as Christian ministers with their prayers, and as peers of the realm with their advice in his Parliament. James, who wanted neither the prayers of heretics nor the advice of Parliaments, was bitterly disappointed. After a long altercation, "I have done," he said; "I will urge you no further. Since you will not help me, I must trust to myself and to my own arms."*

The Bishops had hardly left the royal presence, when a courier arrived with the news that on the preceding day the Prince of Orange had landed in Devonshire. During the following week London was violently agitated. On Sunday, the eleventh of November, a rumour was circulated that knives, gridirons, and caldrons, intended for the torturing of heretics, were concealed in the monastery which had been established under the King's protection at Clerkenwell. Great multi-

* Life of James, ii. 210. Orig. Mem.; Sprat's Narrative; Vas Citters, Nov. 4/14 1688.

tudes assembled round the building, and were about to demolish it, when a military force arrived. The crowd was dispersed, and several of the rioters were slain. An inquest sate on the bodies, and came to a decision which strongly indicated the temper of the public mind. The jury found that certain loyal and well disposed persons, who had gone to put down the meetings of traitors and public enemies at a mass house, had been wilfully murdered by the soldiers; and this strange verdict was signed by all the jurors. The ecclesiastics at Clerkenwell, naturally alarmed by these symptoms of popular feeling, were desirous to place their property in safety. They succeeded in removing most of their furniture before any report of their intentions got abroad. But at length the suspicions of the rabble were excited. The last two carts were stopped in Holborn, and all that they contained was publicly burned in the middle of the street. So great was the alarm among the Catholics that all their places of worship were closed, except those which belonged to the royal family and to foreign Ambassadors.*

On the whole, however, things as yet looked not unfavourably for James. The invaders had been more than a week on English ground. Yet no man of note had joined them. No rebellion had broken out in the north or the east. No servant of the crown appeared to have betrayed his trust. The royal army was assembling fast at Salisbury, and, though inferior in discipline to that of William, was superior in numbers.

Men of rank begin to repair to the Prince.

The Prince was undoubtedly surprised and mortified by the slackness of those who had invited him to England. By the common people of Devonshire, indeed, he had been received with every sign of good will: but no nobleman, no gentleman of high consideration, had yet repaired to his quarters. The explanation of this singular fact is probably to be found in the circumstance that he had landed in a part of the island where he had not been expected. His friends in the north had made their arrangements for a rising, on the supposition that he would be among them with an army. His friends in the west had made no arrangements at all, and were naturally disconcerted at finding themselves suddenly called upon take the lead in a movement so important and perilous. They had also fresh in their recollection, and

* Luttrell's Diary; Newsletter in the Mackintosh Collection; Adda. Nov. 11. 1688.

indeed full in their sight, the disastrous consequences of rebellion, gibbets, heads, mangled quarters, families still in deep mourning for brave sufferers who had loved their country well but not wisely. After a warning so terrible and so recent, some hesitation was natural. It was equally natural, however, that William, who, trusting to promises from England, had put to hazard, not only his own fame and fortunes, but also the prosperity and independence of his native land, should feel deeply mortified. He was, indeed, so indignant, that he talked of falling back to Torbay, reembarking his troops, returning to Holland, and leaving those who had betrayed him to the fate which they deserved. At length, on Monday, the twelfth of November, a gentleman named Burrington, who resided in the neighbourhood of Crediton, joined the Prince's standard, and his example was followed by several of his neighbours.

Men of higher consequence had already set out from different parts of the country for Exeter. The first of these was John Lord Lovelace, distinguished by his taste, by his magnificence, and by the audacious and intemperate vehemence of his Whiggism. He had been five or six times arrested for political offences. The last crime laid to his charge was, that he had contemptuously denied the validity of a warrant, signed by a Roman Catholic Justice of the Peace. He had been brought before the Privy Council and strictly examined, but to little purpose. He resolutely refused to criminate himself; and the evidence against him was insufficient. He was dismissed; but, before he retired, James exclaimed in great heat, "My Lord, this is not the first trick that you have played me." "Sir," answered Lovelace with undaunted spirit, "I never played any trick to Your Majesty, or to any other person. Whoever has accused me to Your Majesty of playing tricks is a liar."* Lovelace had subsequently been admitted into the confidence of those who planned the Revolution. His mansion, built by his ancestors out of the spoils of Spanish galleons from the Indies, rose on the ruins of a house of Our Lady in that beautiful valley through which the Thames, not yet defiled by the precincts of a great capital, nor rising and falling with the flow and ebb of the sea, rolls under woods of beech round the gentle hills of Berkshire. Beneath the stately saloon, adorned by Italian pencils, was a subterraneous vault, in which the bones of ancient monks

* Johnstone, Feb. 27. 1688; Van Citters of the same date.

had sometimes been found. In this dark chamber some zealous and daring opponents of the government had held many midnight conferences during that anxious time when England was impatiently expecting the Protestant wind.* The season for action had now arrived. Lovelace, with seventy followers, well armed and mounted, quitted his dwelling, and directed his course westward. He reached Gloucestershire without difficulty. But Beaufort, who governed that county, was exerting all his great authority and influence in support of the crown. The militia had been called out. A strong party had been posted at Cirencester. When Lovelace arrived there he was informed that he could not be suffered to pass. It was necessary for him either to relinquish his undertaking or to fight his way through. He resolved to force a passage; and his friends and tenants stood gallantly by him. A sharp conflict took place. The militia lost an officer and six or seven men; but at length the followers of Lovelace were overpowered: he was made a prisoner, and sent to Gloucester Castle.†

Colchester. Others were more fortunate. On the day on which the skirmish took place at Cirencester, Richard Savage, Lord Colchester, son and heir of the Earl Rivers, and father, by a lawless amour, of that unhappy poet whose misdeeds and misfortunes form one of the darkest portions of literary history, came with between sixty and seventy horse to Exeter. With him arrived the bold and turbulent Thomas Wharton. A few hours later came Edward Russell, son of the Earl of Bedford, and brother of the virtuous nobleman whose blood had been shed on the scaffold. Another arrival still more important was speedily announced. Colchester, Wharton, and Russell belonged to that party which had been constantly opposed to the Court. James Bertie, Earl of Abingdon, had, on the contrary, been regarded as a supporter of arbitrary government. He had been true to James in the days of the Exclusion Bill. He had, as Lord Lieutenant of Oxfordshire, acted with vigour and severity against the adherents of Monmouth, and had lighted bonfires to celebrate the defeat of Argyle. But dread of Popery had driven him into opposition and rebellion. He was the first peer of the realm who made his appearance at the quarters of the Prince of Orange.‡

* Lysons, Magna Britannia, Berkshire. Luttrell's Diary.
† London Gazette, Nov. 15. 1688; ‡ Burnet, i. 790.; Life of William, 1702.

But the King had less to fear from those who openly arrayed themselves against his authority, than from the dark conspiracy which had spread its ramifications through his army and his family. Of that conspiracy Churchill, unrivalled in sagacity and address, endowed by nature with a certain cool intrepidity which never failed him either in fighting or lying, high in military rank, and high in the favour of the Princess Anne, must be regarded as the soul. It was not yet time for him to strike the decisive blow. But even thus early he inflicted, by the instrumentality of a subordinate agent, a wound, serious if not deadly, on the royal cause.

Edward Viscount Cornbury, eldest son of the Earl of Clarendon, was a young man of slender abilities, loose principles, and violent temper. He had been early taught to consider his relationship to the Princess Anne as the groundwork of his fortunes, and had been exhorted to pay her assiduous court. It had never occurred to his father that the hereditary loyalty of the Hydes could run any risk of contamination in the household of the King's favourite daughter: but in that household the Churchills held absolute sway; and Cornbury became their tool. He commanded one of the regiments of dragoons which had been sent westward. Such dispositions had been made that, on the fourteenth of November, he was, during a few hours, the senior officer at Salisbury, and all the troops assembled there were subject to his authority. It seems extraordinary that, at such a crisis, the army on which everything depended should have been left, even for a moment, under the command of a young Colonel, who had neither abilities nor experience. There can be little doubt that so strange an arrangement was the result of deep design, and as little doubt to what head and to what heart the design is to be imputed.

Suddenly three of the regiments of cavalry which had assembled at Salisbury were ordered to march westward. Cornbury put himself at their head, and conducted them first to Blandford and thence to Dorchester. From Dorchester, after a halt of an hour or two, they set out for Axminster. Some of the officers began to be uneasy, and demanded an explanation of these strange movements. Cornbury replied that he had instructions to make a night attack on some troops which the Prince of Orange had posted at Honiton. But suspicion was awake. Searching questions were put, and were evasively answered. At last Cornbury was pressed to produce his orders. He perceived, not only that it would be impossible for him to carry over all the three regiments, as he had hoped, but that he was himself in a situation of considerable peril. He accordingly stole away with a few followers to the Dutch quarters. Most of his troops returned to Salisbury: but some who had been detached from the main body, and who had no suspicion of the designs of their commander, proceeded to Honiton. There they found themselves in the midst of a large force which was fully prepared to receive them. Resistance was impossible. Their leader pressed them to take service under William. A gratuity of a month's pay was offered to them, and was by most of them accepted.*

The news of these events reached London on the fifteenth. James had been on the morning of that day in high good humour. Bishop Lamplugh had just presented himself at court on his arrival from Exeter, and had been most graciously received. "My Lord," said the King, "you are a genuine old Cavalier." The archbishopric of York, which had now been vacant more than two years and a half, was immediately bestowed on Lamplugh as the reward of loyalty. That afternoon, just as the King was sitting down to dinner, arrived an express with the tidings of Cornbury's defection. James turned away from his untasted meal, swallowed a crust of bread and a glass of wine, and retired to his closet. He afterwards learned that, as he was rising from table, several of the Lords in whom he reposed the greatest confidence were shaking hands and congratulating each other in the adjoining gallery. When the news was carried to the Queen's apartments she and her ladies broke out into tears and loud cries of sorrow.†

The blow was indeed a heavy one. It was true that the direct loss to the crown and the direct gain to the invaders hardly amounted to two hundred men and as many horses. But where could the King henceforth expect to find those sentiments in which consists the strength of states and of armies? Cornbury was the heir of a house conspicuous for its attachment to monarchy. His father Clarendon, his uncle Rochester, were men whose loyalty was supposed to be proof to all temptation. What must be the strength of that feeling against which the most deeply rooted hereditary prejudices

* Life of James, ii. 216. Orig. Mem.; Burnet, i. 790.; Clarendon's Diary, Nov. 15. 1688; London Gazette, Nov. 17.
† Life of James, ii. 215.; Clarendon's Diary, Nov. 15, 1688; Van Citters, Nov. 16/26.

were of no avail, of that feeling which could reconcile a young officer of high birth to desertion, aggravated by breach of trust and by gross falsehood? That Cornbury was not a man of brilliant parts or enterprising temper made the event more alarming. It was impossible to doubt that he had in some quarter a powerful and artful prompter. Who that prompter was soon became evident. In the meantime no man in the royal camp could feel assured that he was not surrounded by traitors. Political rank, military rank, the honour of a nobleman, the honour of a soldier, the strongest professions, the purest Cavalier blood, could no longer afford security. Every man might reasonably doubt whether every order which he received from his superior was not meant to serve the purposes of the enemy. That prompt obedience without which an army is merely a rabble was necessarily at an end. What discipline could there be among soldiers who had just been saved from a snare by refusing to follow their commanding officer on a secret expedition, and by insisting on a sight of his orders?

Cornbury was soon kept in countenance by a crowd of deserters superior to him in rank and capacity: but during a few days he stood alone in his shame, and was bitterly reviled by many who afterwards imitated his example and envied his dishonourable precedence. Among these was his own father. The first outbreak of Clarendon's rage and sorrow was highly pathetic. "Oh God!" he ejaculated, "that a son of mine should be a rebel!" A fortnight later he made up his mind to be a rebel himself. Yet it would be unjust to pronounce him a mere hypocrite. In revolutions men live fast: the experience of years is crowded into hours: old habits of thought and action are violently broken; and novelties which at first sight inspire dread and disgust, become in a few days familiar, endurable, attractive. Many men of far purer virtue and higher spirit than Clarendon were prepared, before that memorable year ended, to do what they would have pronounced wicked and infamous when it began.

The unhappy father composed himself as well as he could, and sent to ask a private audience of the King. It was granted. James said, with more than his usual graciousness, that he from his heart pitied Cornbury's relations, and should not hold them at all accountable for the crime of their unworthy kinsman. Clarendon went home, scarcely daring to look his friends in the face. Soon, however, he learned with surprise that the act, which had, as he at first thought, for ever dishonoured his family, was applauded by some persons of high station. His niece, the Princess of Denmark, asked him why he shut himself up. He answered that he had been overwhelmed with confusion by his son's villany. Anne seemed not at all to understand this feeling. "People," she said, "are very uneasy about Popery. I believe that many of the army will do the same."*

And now the King, greatly disturbed, called together the principal officers who were still in London. Churchill, who was about this time promoted to the rank of Lieutenant General, made his appearance with that bland serenity which neither peril nor infamy could ever disturb. The meeting was attended by Henry Fitzroy, Duke of Grafton, whose audacity and activity made him conspicuous among the natural children of Charles the Second. Grafton was colonel of the first regiment of Foot Guards. He seems to have been at this time completely under Churchill's influence, and was prepared to desert the royal standard as soon as the favourable moment should arrive. Two other traitors were in the circle, Kirke and Trelawney, who commanded those two fierce and lawless bands then known as the Tangier regiments. Both of them had, like the other Protestant officers of the army, long seen with extreme displeasure the partiality which the King had shown to members of his own Church; and Trelawney remembered with bitter resentment the persecution of his brother the Bishop of Bristol. James addressed the assembly in language worthy of a better man and of a better cause. It might be, he said, that some of the officers had conscientious scruples about fighting for him. If so, he was willing to receive back their commissions. But he adjured them as gentlemen and soldiers not to imitate the shameful example of Cornbury. All seemed moved; and none more than Churchill. He was the first to vow with well feigned enthusiasm that he would shed the last drop of his blood in the service of his gracious master: Grafton was loud and forward in similar protestations; and the example was followed by Kirke and Trelawney.†

Petition of the Lords for a Parliament.

Deceived by these professions, the King prepared to set out for Salisbury. Before his departure he was informed that a considerable number of peers, temporal and spiritual, desired

* Clarendon's Diary, Nov. 13, 16, 17, 20. 1688.
† Life of James, ii. 219. Orig. Mem.

to be admitted to an audience. They came, with Sancroft at their head, to present a petition, praying that a free and legal Parliament might be called, and that a negotiation might be opened with the Prince of Orange.

The history of this petition is curious. The thought seems to have occurred at once to two great chiefs of parties who had long been rivals and enemies, Rochester and Halifax. They both, independently of one another, consulted the Bishops. The Bishops warmly approved the suggestion. It was then proposed that a general meeting of peers should be called to deliberate on the form of an address to the King. It was term time; and in term time men of rank and fashion then lounged every day in Westminster Hall as they now lounge in the clubs of Pall Mall and Saint James's Street. Nothing could be easier than for the Lords who assembled there to step aside into some adjoining room and to hold a consultation. But unexpected difficulties arose. Halifax became first cold and then adverse. It was his nature to discover objections to everything; and on this occasion his sagacity was quickened by rivalry. The scheme, which he had approved while he regarded it as his own, began to displease him as soon as he found that it was also the scheme of Rochester, by whom he had been long thwarted and at length supplanted, and whom he disliked as much as it was in his easy nature to dislike anybody. Nottingham was at that time much under the influence of Halifax. They both declared that they would not join in the address if Rochester signed it. Clarendon expostulated in vain. "I mean no disrespect," said Halifax, "to my Lord Rochester: but he has been a member of the Ecclesiastical Commission: the proceedings of that court must soon be the subject of a very serious enquiry; and it is not fit that one who has sate there should take any part in our petition." Nottingham, with strong expressions of personal esteem for Rochester, avowed the same opinion. The authority of the two dissentient Lords prevented several other noblemen from subscribing the address; but the Hydes and the Bishops persisted. Nineteen signatures were procured; and the petitioners waited in a body on the King.*

He received their address ungraciously. He assured them, indeed, that he passionately desired the meeting of a free Parliament; and he promised them, on the faith of a King,

* Clarendon's Diary, from Nov. 8. to Nov. 17. 1688.

that he would call one as soon as the Prince of Orange should have left the island. "But how," said he, "can a Parliament be free when an enemy is in the kingdom, and can return near a hundred votes?" To the prelates he spoke with peculiar acrimony. "I could not," he said, "prevail on you the other day to declare against this invasion: but you are ready enough to declare against me. Then you would not meddle with politics. You have no scruple about meddling now. You have excited this rebellious temper among your flocks; and now you foment it. You would be better employed in teaching them how to obey than in teaching me how to govern." He was much incensed against his nephew Grafton, whose signature stood next to that of Sancroft, and said to the young man, with great asperity, "You know nothing about religion: you care nothing about it; and yet, forsooth, you must pretend to have a conscience." "It is true, sir," answered Grafton, with impudent frankness, "that I have very little conscience: but I belong to a party which has a great deal."*

Bitter as was the King's language to the petitioners, it was far less bitter than that which he held after they had withdrawn. He had done, he said, far too much already in the hope of satisfying an undutiful and ungrateful people. He had always hated the thought of concession: but he had suffered himself to be talked over: and now he, like his father before him, had found that concession only made subjects more encroaching. He would yield nothing more, not an atom; and, after his fashion, he vehemently repeated many times, "Not an atom." Not only would he make no overtures to the invaders, but he would receive none. If the Dutch sent flags of truce, the first messenger should be dismissed without an answer; the second should be hanged.†

The King goes to Salisbury.

In such a mood James set out for Salisbury. His last act before his departure was to appoint a Council of five Lords to represent him in London during his absence. Of the five, two were Papists, and by law incapable of office. Joined with them was Jeffreys, a Protestant indeed, but more detested by the nation than any Papist. To the other two members of this board, Preston and Godolphin, no serious

* Life of James, ii. 212. Orig. Mem.; Clarendon's Diary, Nov. 17. 1688; Van Citters, Nov. 13.; Barnet, i. 791.; Some Reflections upon the most Humble Petition to the King's most Excellent Majesty, 1688; Modest Vindication of the Petition; First Collection of Papers relating to English Affairs, 1688.

† Adda, Nov. 16. 1688.

objection could be made. On the day on which the King left CHAP. IX.
London the Prince of Wales was sent to Portsmouth. That
fortress was strongly garrisoned, and was under the government of Berwick. The fleet commanded by Dartmouth lay
close at hand: and it was supposed that, if things went ill,
the royal infant would, without difficulty, be conveyed from
Portsmouth to France.*

On the nineteenth James reached Salisbury, and took up
his quarters in the episcopal palace. Evil news was now
fast pouring in upon him from all sides. The western counties had at length risen. As soon as the news of Cornbury's
desertion was known, many wealthy landowners took heart
and hastened to Exeter. Among them was Sir William
Portman of Bryanstone, one of the greatest men in Dorsetshire, and Sir Francis Warre of Hestercombe, whose interest
was great in Somersetshire.† But the most important of the
new comers was Seymour, who had recently inherited a baronetcy which added nothing to his dignity, and who, in birth, Seymour.
in political influence, and in parliamentary abilities, was beyond comparison the foremost among the Tory gentlemen of
England. At his first audience he is said to have exhibited
his characteristic pride in a way which surprised and amused
the Prince. "I think, Sir Edward," said William, meaning
to be very civil, "that you are of the family of the Duke of
Somerset." "Pardon me, sir," said Sir Edward, who never
forgot that he was the head of the elder branch of the Seymours: "the Duke of Somerset is of my family."‡

The quarters of William now began to present the appearance of a court. More than sixty men of rank and fortune William
were lodged at Exeter; and the daily display of rich liveries, at Exeter.
and of coaches drawn by six horses, in the Cathedral Close,
gave to that quiet precinct something of the splendour
and gaiety of Whitehall. The common people were eager
to take arms; and it would have been easy to form many
battalions of infantry. But Schomberg, who thought little of
soldiers fresh from the plough, maintained that, if the expedition could not succeed without such help, it would not
succeed at all; and William, who had as much professional

---

* Life of James, ii. 220, 221.
† Eachard's History of the Revolution.
‡ Seymour's reply to William is related by many writers. It much resembles a story which is told of the Manriques family. They, it is said, took for their device the words, "Nos no descendemos de los Reyes; sino los Reyes descienden de nos."—Carpesiana.

VOL. II. T

feeling as Schomberg, concurred in this opinion. Commissions therefore for raising new regiments were very sparingly given; and none but picked recruits were enlisted.

It was now thought desirable that the Prince should give a public reception to the whole body of noblemen and gentlemen who had assembled at Exeter. He addressed them in a short but dignified and well considered speech. He was not, he said, acquainted with the faces of all whom he saw. But he had a list of their names, and knew how high they stood in the estimation of their country. He gently chid their tardiness, but expressed a confident hope that it was not yet too late to save the kingdom. "Therefore," he said, "gentlemen, friends, and fellow Protestants, we bid you and all your followers most heartily welcome to our court and camp."*

Seymour, a keen politician, long accustomed to the tactics of faction, saw in a moment that the party which had begun to rally round the Prince stood in need of organisation. It was as yet, he said, a mere rope of sand: no common object had been publicly and formally avowed: nobody was pledged to anything. As soon as the assembly at the deanery broke up, he sent for Burnet, and suggested that an association should be formed, and that all the English adherents of the Prince should put their hands to an instrument binding them to be true to their leader and to each other. Burnet carried the suggestion to the Prince and to Shrewsbury, by both of whom it was approved. A meeting was held in the Cathedral. A short paper drawn up by Burnet was produced, approved, and eagerly signed. The subscribers engaged to pursue in concert the objects set forth in the Prince's Declaration; to stand by him and by each other; to take signal vengeance on all who should make any attempt on his person; and, even if such an attempt should unhappily succeed, to persist in their undertaking till the liberties and the religion of the nation should be effectually secured.†

About the same time a messenger arrived at Exeter from the Earl of Bath, who commanded at Plymouth. Bath declared that he placed himself, his troops, and the fortress which he governed at the Prince's disposal. The invaders therefore had now not a single enemy in their rear.‡

---

* Fourth Collection of Papers, 1688; Letter from Exon; Burnet, i. 792.
† Burnet, i. 792.; History of the Desertion; Second Collection of Papers, 1688.
‡ Letter of Bath to the Prince of Orange, Nov. 18. 1688; Dalrymple.

While the West was thus rising to confront the King, the North was all in a flame behind him. On the sixteenth Delamere took arms in Cheshire. He convoked his tenants, called upon them to stand by him, promised that, if they fell in the cause, their leases should be renewed to their children, and exhorted every one who had a good horse either to take the field or to provide a substitute.* He appeared at Manchester with fifty men armed and mounted, and his force had trebled before he reached Boaden Downs.

The neighbouring counties were violently agitated. It had been arranged that Danby should seize York, and that Devonshire should appear at Nottingham. At Nottingham no resistance was anticipated. But at York there was a small garrison under the command of Sir John Reresby. Danby acted with rare dexterity. A meeting of the gentry and freeholders of Yorkshire had been summoned for the twenty-second of November to address the King on the state of affairs. All the Deputy Lieutenants of the three Ridings, several noblemen, and a multitude of opulent esquires and substantial yeomen had been attracted to the provincial capital. Four troops of militia had been drawn out under arms to preserve the public peace. The Common Hall was crowded with freeholders, and the discussion had begun, when a cry was suddenly raised that the Papists were up, and were slaying the Protestants. The Papists of York were much more likely to be employed in seeking for hiding places than in attacking enemies who outnumbered them in the proportion of a hundred to one. But at that time no story of Popish atrocity could be so wild and marvellous as not to find ready belief. The meeting separated in dismay. The whole city was in confusion. At this moment Danby at the head of about a hundred horsemen rode up to the militia, and raised the cry "No Popery! A free Parliament! The Protestant religion!" The militia echoed the shout. The garrison was instantly surprised and disarmed. The governor was placed under arrest. The gates were closed. Sentinels were posted everywhere. The populace was suffered to pull down a Roman Catholic chapel; but no other harm appears to have been done. On the following morning the Guildhall was crowded with the first gentlemen of the shire, and with the principal magistrates of the city. The Lord Mayor was placed in the chair. Danby proposed a Declaration setting forth

* First Collection of Papers, 1688; London Gazette, November 22.

the reasons which had induced the friends of the constitution and of the Protestant religion to rise in arms. This Declaration was eagerly adopted, and received in a few hours the signatures of six peers, of five baronets, of six knights, and of many gentlemen of high consideration.*

Devonshire meantime, at the head of a great body of friends and dependents, quitted the palace which he was rearing at Chatsworth, and appeared in arms at Derby. There he formally delivered to the municipal authorities a paper setting forth the reasons which had moved him to this enterprise. He then proceeded to Nottingham, which soon became the head quarters of the Northern insurrection. Here a proclamation was put forth couched in bold and severe terms. The name of rebellion, it was said, was a bugbear which could frighten no reasonable men. Was it rebellion to defend those laws and that religion which every King of England bound himself by oath to maintain? How that oath had lately been observed was a question on which, it was to be hoped, a free Parliament would soon pronounce. In the meantime, the insurgents declared that they held it to be not rebellion, but legitimate self defence, to resist a tyrant who knew no law but his own will. The Northern rising became every day more formidable. Four powerful and wealthy Earls, Manchester, Stamford, Rutland, and Chesterfield, repaired to Nottingham, and were joined there by Lord Cholmondeley and by Lord Grey de Ruthyn.†

All this time the hostile armies in the south were approaching each other. The Prince of Orange, when he learned that the King had arrived at Salisbury, thought it time to leave Exeter. He placed that city and the surrounding country under the government of Sir Edward Seymour, and set out on Wednesday the twenty-first of November, escorted by many of the most considerable gentlemen of the Western counties, for Axminster, where he remained several days.

The King was eager to fight; and it was obviously his interest to do so. Every hour took away something from his own strength, and added something to the strength of his enemies. It was most important, too, that his troops should be blooded. A great battle, however it might terminate, could not but injure the Prince's popularity. All this William

* Reresby's Memoirs; Life of James, ii. 231. Orig. Mem.
† Cibber's Apology; History of the Desertion; Luttrell's Diary; Second Collection of Papers, 1689.

perfectly understood, and determined to avoid an action as long as possible. It is said that, when Schomberg was told that the enemy were advancing and were determined to fight, he answered, with the composure of a tactician confident in his skill, "That will be just as we may choose." It was, however, impossible to prevent all skirmishing between the advanced guards of the armies. William was desirous that in such skirmishing nothing might happen which could wound the pride or rouse the vindictive feelings of the nation which he meant to deliver. He therefore, with admirable prudence, placed his British regiments in the situations where there was most risk of collision. The outposts of the royal army were Irish. The consequence was that, in the little combats of this short campaign, the invaders had on their side the hearty sympathy of all Englishmen.

The first of these encounters took place at Wincanton. Mackay's regiment, composed of British soldiers, lay near a body of the King's Irish troops, commanded by their countryman, the gallant Sarsfield. Mackay sent out a small party under a lieutenant named Campbell, to procure horses for the baggage. Campbell found what he wanted at Wincanton, and was just leaving that town on his return, when a strong detachment of Sarsfield's troops approached. The Irish were four to one; but Campbell resolved to fight it out to the last. With a handful of resolute men he took his stand in the road. The rest of his soldiers lined the hedges which overhung the highway on the right and on the left. The enemy came up. "Stand," cried Campbell; "for whom are you?" "I am for King James," answered the leader of the other party. "And I for the Prince of Orange," cried Campbell. "We will prince you," answered the Irishman with a curse. "Fire!" exclaimed Campbell; and a sharp fire was instantly poured in from both the hedges. The King's troops received three well aimed volleys before they could make any return. At length they succeeded in carrying one of the hedges; and would have overpowered the little band which was opposed to them, had not the country people, who mortally hated the Irish, given a false alarm that more of the Prince's troops were coming up. Sarsfield recalled his men and fell back; and Campbell proceeded on his march unmolested with the baggage horses. This affair, creditable undoubtedly to the valour and discipline of the Prince's army, was magnified by report into a victory won against great odds by British Pro-

CHAP. IX.

Skirmish at Wincanton.

testants over Popish barbarians who had been brought from Connaught to oppress our island.*

A few hours after this skirmish an event took place which put an end to all risk of a more serious struggle between the armies. Churchill and some of his principal accomplices were assembled at Salisbury. Two of the conspirators, Kirke and Trelawney, had proceeded to Warminster, where their regiments were posted. All was ripe for the execution of the long meditated treason.

Churchill advised the King to visit Warminster, and to inspect the troops stationed there. James assented; and his coach was at the door of the episcopal palace when his nose began to bleed violently. He was forced to postpone his expedition and to put himself under medical treatment. Three days elapsed before the hemorrhage was entirely subdued; and during those three days alarming rumours reached his ears.

It was impossible that a conspiracy so widely spread as that of which Churchill was the head could be kept altogether secret. There was no evidence which could be laid before a jury or a court martial; but strange whispers wandered about the camp. Feversham, who held the chief command, reported that there was a bad spirit in the army. It was hinted to the King that some who were near his person were not his friends, and that it would be a wise precaution to send Churchill and Grafton under a guard to Portsmouth. James rejected this counsel. A propensity to suspicion was not among his vices. Indeed the confidence which he reposed in professions of fidelity and attachment was such as might rather have been expected from a goodhearted and inexperienced stripling than from a politician who was far advanced in life, who had seen much of the world, who had suffered much from villanous arts, and whose own character was by no means a favourable specimen of human nature. It would be difficult to mention any other man who, having himself so little scruple about breaking faith with his neighbours, was so slow to believe that his neighbours could break faith with him. Nevertheless the reports which he had received of the state of his army disturbed him greatly. He was now no longer impatient for a battle. He even began to think of retreating. On the evening of Saturday, the twenty-fourth of November, he called a council of war. The meeting was attended by those officers against whom he had been most

* Whittle's Diary; History of the Desertion; Luttrell's Diary.

earnestly cautioned. Feversham expressed an opinion that it was desirable to fall back. Churchill argued on the other side. The consultation lasted till midnight. At length the King declared that he had decided for a retreat. Churchill saw or imagined that he was distrusted, and, though gifted with a rare self command, could not conceal his uneasiness. Before the day broke he fled to the Prince's quarters, accompanied by Grafton.*

Churchill left behind him a letter of explanation. It was written with that decorum which he never failed to preserve in the midst of guilt and dishonour. He acknowledged that he owed everything to the royal favour. Interest, he said, and gratitude impelled him in the same direction. Under no other government could he hope to be so great and prosperous as he had been: but all such considerations must yield to a paramount duty. He was a Protestant; and he could not conscientiously draw his sword against the Protestant cause. As to the rest he would ever be ready to hazard life and fortune in defence of the sacred person and of the lawful rights of his gracious master.†

Next morning all was confusion in the royal camp. The King's friends were in dismay. His enemies could not conceal their exultation. The consternation of James was increased by news which arrived on the same day from Warminster. Kirke, who commanded at that post, had refused to obey orders which he had received from Salisbury. There could no longer be any doubt that he too was in league with the Prince of Orange. It was rumoured that he had actually gone over with all his troops to the enemy; and the rumour, though false, was, during some hours, fully believed.‡ A new light flashed on the mind of the unhappy King. He thought that he understood why he had been pressed, a few days before, to visit Warminster. There he would have found himself helpless, at the mercy of the conspirators, and in the vicinity of the hostile outposts. Those who might have attempted to defend him would have been easily overpowered. He would have been carried a prisoner to the head quarters of the invading army. Perhaps some still blacker treason might have been committed; for men who have once engaged

* Life of James, ii. 222. Orig. Mem.; Barillon, Nov. 11/21 1688; Sheridan MS.
† First Collection of Papers, 1688.
‡ Letter from Middleton to Preston, dated Salisbury, Nov. 25. "Villany upon villany," says Middleton, "the last still greater than the former." Life of James, ii. 224, 225. Orig. Mem.

CHAP.
IX.

Desertion of Churchill and Grafton.

in a wicked and perilous enterprise are no longer their own masters, and are often impelled, by a fatality which is part of their just punishment, to crimes such as they would at first have shuddered to contemplate. Surely it was not without the special intervention of some guardian Saint that a King devoted to the Catholic Church had, at the very moment when he was blindly hastening to captivity, perhaps to death, been suddenly arrested by what he had then thought a disastrous malady.

Retreat of the royal army from Salisbury.

All these things confirmed James in the resolution which he had taken on the preceding evening. Orders were given for an immediate retreat. Salisbury was in an uproar. The camp broke up with the confusion of a flight. No man knew whom to trust or whom to obey. The material strength of the army was little diminished: but its moral strength had been destroyed. Many whom shame would have restrained from leading the way to the Prince's quarters were eager to imitate an example which they never would have set; and many, who would have stood by the King while he appeared to be resolutely advancing against the invaders, felt no inclination to follow a receding standard.*

James went that day as far as Andover. He was attended by his son in law, Prince George, and by the Duke of Ormond. Both were among the conspirators, and would probably have accompanied Churchill, had he not, in consequence of what had passed at the council of war, thought it expedient to take his departure suddenly. The impenetrable stupidity of Prince George served his turn on this occasion better than cunning would have done. It was his habit, when any news was told him, to exclaim in French, "Est-il-possible?" "Is it possible?" This catchword was now of great use to him. "Est-il-possible?" he cried, when he had been made to understand that Churchill and Grafton were missing. And when the ill tidings came from Warminster, he again ejaculated, "Est-il-possible?"

Desertion of Prince George and Ormond.

Prince George and Ormond were invited to sup with the King at Andover. The meal must have been a sad one. The King was overwhelmed by his misfortunes. His son in law was the dullest of companions. "I have tried Prince George sober," said Charles the Second; "and I have tried him drunk; and, drunk or sober, there is nothing in him."†

* History of the Desertion; Luttrell's Diary.
† Dartmouth's note on Burnet, l. 643.

JAMES THE SECOND. 281

Ormond, who was through life taciturn and bashful, was not likely to be in high spirits at such a moment. At length the repast terminated. The King retired to rest. Horses were in waiting for the Prince and Ormond, who, as soon as they left the table, mounted and rode off. They were accompanied by the Earl of Drumlanrig, eldest son of the Duke of Queensberry. The defection of this young nobleman was no insignificant event. For Queensberry was the head of the Protestant Episcopalians of Scotland, a class compared with whom the bitterest English Tories might be called Whiggish; and Drumlanrig himself was Lieutenant Colonel of Dundee's regiment, a band more detested by the Whigs than even Kirke's lambs. This fresh calamity was announced to the King on the following morning. He was less disturbed by the news than might have been expected. The shock which he had undergone twenty-four hours before had prepared him for almost any disaster; and it was impossible to be seriously angry with Prince George, who was hardly an accountable being, for having yielded to the arts of such a tempter as Churchill. "What!" said James, "Is Est-il-possible gone too? After all, a good trooper would have been a greater loss."* In truth the King's whole anger seems, at this time, to have been concentrated, and not without cause, on one object. He set off for London, breathing vengeance against Churchill, and learned, on arriving, a new crime of the archdeceiver. The Princess Anne had been some hours missing.

CHAP. IX.

Anne, who had no will but that of the Churchills, had been induced by them to notify under her own hand to William, a week before, her approbation of his enterprise. She assured him that she was entirely in the hands of her friends, and that she would remain in the palace, or take refuge in the City, as they might determine.† On Sunday, the twenty-fifth of November, she, and those who thought for her, were under the necessity of coming to a sudden resolution. That afternoon a courier from Salisbury brought tidings that Churchill had disappeared, that he had been accompanied by Grafton, that Kirke had proved false, and that the royal forces were in full retreat. There was, as usually happened when great news, good or bad, arrived in town, an immense crowd that evening

Flight of the Princess Anne.

* Clarendon's Diary, Nov. 26.; Life of James, ii. 224.; Prince George's letter to the King has often been printed.
† The letter, dated Nov. 18, will be found in Dalrymple.

in the galleries of Whitehall. Curiosity and anxiety sate on every face. The Queen broke forth into natural expressions of indignation against the chief traitor, and did not altogether spare his too partial mistress. The sentinels were doubled round that part of the palace which Anne occupied. The Princess was in dismay. In a few hours her father would be at Westminster. It was not likely that he would treat her personally with severity; but that he would permit her any longer to enjoy the society of her friend was not to be hoped. It could hardly be doubted that Sarah would be placed under arrest, and would be subjected to a strict examination by shrewd and rigorous inquisitors. Her papers would be seized. Perhaps evidence affecting her life might be discovered. If so, the worst might well be dreaded. The vengeance of the implacable King knew no distinction of sex. For offences much smaller than those which might probably be brought home to Lady Churchill he had sent women to the scaffold and the stake. Strong affection braced the feeble mind of the Princess. There was no tie which she would not break, no risk which she would not run, for the object of her idolatrous affection. "I will jump out of the window," she cried, "rather than be found here by my father." The favourite undertook to manage an escape. She communicated in all haste with some of the chiefs of the conspiracy. In a few hours everything was arranged. That evening Anne retired to her chamber as usual. At dead of night she rose, and, accompanied by her friend Sarah and two other female attendants, stole down the back stairs in a dressing gown and slippers. The fugitives gained the open street unchallenged. A hackney coach was in waiting for them there. Two men guarded the humble vehicle. One of them was Compton, Bishop of London, the Princess's old tutor: the other was the magnificent and accomplished Dorset, whom the extremity of the public danger had roused from his luxurious repose. The coach drove instantly to Aldersgate Street, where the town residence of the Bishops of London then stood, within the shadow of their Cathedral. There the Princess passed the night. On the following morning she set out for Epping Forest. In that wild tract Dorset possessed a venerable mansion, which has long since been destroyed. In his hospitable dwelling, the favourite resort, during many years, of wits and poets, the fugitives made a short stay. They could not safely attempt to reach William's quarters; for the road thither lay through a country occupied by the royal forces. It was therefore determined that Anne should take refuge with the northern insurgents. Compton wholly laid aside, for the time, his sacerdotal character. Danger and conflict had rekindled in him all the military ardour which he had felt twenty-eight years before, when he rode in the Life Guards. He preceded the Princess's carriage in a buff coat and jackboots, with a sword at his side and pistols in his holsters. Long before she reached Nottingham she was surrounded by a body guard of gentlemen who volunteered to escort her. They invited the Bishop to act as their colonel; and he consented with an alacrity which gave great scandal to rigid Churchmen, and did not much raise his character even in the opinion of Whigs.*

When, on the morning of the twenty-sixth, Anne's apartment was found empty, the consternation was great in Whitehall. While the Ladies of her Bedchamber ran up and down the courts of the palace, screaming and wringing their hands, while Lord Craven, who commanded the Foot Guards, was questioning the sentinels in the gallery, while the Chancellor was sealing up the papers of the Churchills, the Princess's nurse broke into the royal apartments crying out that the dear lady had been murdered by the Papists. The news flew to Westminster Hall. There the story was that Her Highness had been hurried away by force to a place of confinement. When it could no longer be denied that her flight had been voluntary, numerous fictions were invented to account for it. She had been grossly insulted: she had been threatened; nay, though she was in that situation in which woman is entitled to peculiar tenderness, she had been beaten by her cruel stepmother. The populace, which years of misrule had made suspicious and irritable, was so much excited by these calumnies that the Queen was scarcely safe. Many Roman Catholics, and some Protestant Tories whose loyalty was proof to all trials, repaired to the palace that they might be in readiness to defend her in the event of an outbreak. In the midst of this distress and terror arrived the news of Prince George's flight. The courier who brought these evil tidings was fast followed by the King himself. The evening

---

* Clarendon's Diary, Nov. 25, 26. 1688; Van Citters, Dec. 14; Ellis Correspondence, Dec. 10.; Duchess of Marlborough's Vindication; Burnet, i. 793.; Compton to the Prince of Orange, Dec. 2. 1688, in Dalrymple. The Bishop's military costume is mentioned in innumerable pamphlets and lampoons.

was closing in when James arrived, and was informed that his daughter had disappeared. After all that he had suffered, this affliction forced a cry of misery from his lips. "God help me!" he said; "my own children have forsaken me."*

That evening he sate in Council with his principal ministers till a late hour. It was determined that he should summon all the Lords Spiritual and Temporal who were then in London to attend him on the following day, and that he should solemnly ask their advice. Accordingly, on the afternoon of Tuesday the twenty-seventh, the Lords met in the dining room of the palace. The assembly consisted of nine prelates and between thirty and forty noblemen, all Protestants. The two Secretaries of State, Middleton and Preston, though not peers of England, were in attendance. The King himself presided. The traces of severe bodily and mental suffering were discernible in his countenance and deportment. He opened the proceedings by referring to the petition which had been put into his hands just before he set out for Salisbury. The prayer of that petition was that he would convoke a free Parliament. Situated as he then was, he had not, he said, thought it right to comply. But, during his absence from London, great changes had taken place. He had also observed that his people everywhere seemed anxious that the Houses should meet. He had therefore commanded the attendance of his faithful Peers, in order to ask their counsel.

For a time there was silence. Then Oxford, whose pedigree, unrivalled in antiquity and splendour, gave him a kind of primacy in the meeting, said that, in his opinion, those Lords who had signed the petition to which His Majesty had referred ought now to explain their views.

These words called up Rochester. He defended the petition, and declared that he still saw no hope for the throne or the country but in a Parliament. He would not, he said, venture to affirm that, in so disastrous an extremity, even that remedy would be efficacious; but he had no other remedy to propose. He added that it might be advisable to open a negotiation with the Prince of Orange. Jeffreys and Godolphin followed; and both declared that they agreed with Rochester.

Then Clarendon rose, and, to the astonishment of all, who remembered his loud professions of loyalty, and the agony of shame and sorrow into which he had been thrown, only a few

* Dartmouth's note on Burnet, I. 792.; II. 226. Orig. Mem.; Clarendon's Diary, Van Citters, Nov. 16. 1688; Life of James, Nov. 26.; Revolution Politics.

days before, by the news of his son's defection, broke forth into a vehement invective against tyranny and Popery. "Even now," he said, "His Majesty is raising in London a regiment into which no Protestant is admitted." "That is not true," cried James, in great agitation from the head of the board. Clarendon persisted, and left this offensive topic only to pass to a topic still more offensive. He accused the unfortunate King of pusillanimity. Why retreat from Salisbury? Why not try the event of a battle? Could people be blamed for submitting to the invader when they saw their sovereign run away at the head of his army? James felt these insults keenly, and remembered them long. Indeed even Whigs thought the language of Clarendon indecent and ungenerous. Halifax spoke in a very different tone. During several years of peril he had defended with admirable ability the civil and ecclesiastical constitution of his country against the prerogative. But his serene intellect, singularly unsusceptible of enthusiasm, and singularly averse to extremes, began to lean towards the cause of royalty at the very moment at which those noisy Royalists who had lately execrated the Trimmers as little better than rebels were everywhere rising in rebellion. It was his ambition to be, at this conjuncture, the peacemaker between the throne and the nation. His talents and character fitted him for that office; and, if he failed, the failure is to be ascribed to causes against which no human skill could contend, and chiefly to the folly, faithlessness, and obstinacy of the Prince whom he tried to save.

Halifax now gave utterance to much unpalatable truth, but with a delicacy which brought on him the reproach of flattery from spirits too abject to understand that what would justly be called flattery when offered to the powerful is a debt of humanity to the fallen. With many expressions of sympathy and deference, he declared it to be his opinion that the King must make up his mind to great sacrifices. It was not enough to convoke a Parliament or to open a negotiation with the Prince of Orange. Some at least of the grievances of which the nation complained should be instantly redressed without waiting till redress was demanded by the Houses or by the captain of the hostile army. Nottingham, in language equally respectful, declared that he agreed with Halifax. The chief concessions which these Lords pressed the King to make were three. He ought, they said, forthwith to dismiss all Roman Catholics from office, to separate himself wholly from France,

CHAP. IX.

and to grant an unlimited amnesty to those who were in arms against him. The last of these propositions, it should seem, admitted of no dispute. For, though some of those who were banded together against the King had acted towards him in a manner which might not unreasonably excite his bitter resentment, it was more likely that he would soon be at their mercy than that they would ever be at his. It would have been childish to open a negotiation with William, and yet to denounce vengeance against men whom William could not without infamy abandon. But the clouded understanding and implacable temper of James held out long against the arguments of those who laboured to convince him that it would be wise to pardon offences which he could not punish. "I cannot do it," he exclaimed: "I must make examples; Churchill above all; Churchill whom I raised so high. He and he alone has done all this. He has corrupted my army. He has corrupted my child. He would have put me into the hands of the Prince of Orange, but for God's special providence. My Lords, you are strangely anxious for the safety of traitors. None of you troubles himself about my safety." In answer to this burst of impotent anger, those who had recommended the amnesty represented with profound respect, but with firmness, that a prince attacked by powerful enemies can be safe only by conquering or by conciliating. "If Your Majesty, after all that has happened, has still any hope of safety in arms, we have done: but if not, you can be safe only by regaining the affections of your people." After a long and animated debate the King broke up the meeting. "My Lords," he said, "you have used great freedom: but I do not take it ill of you. I have made up my mind on one point. I shall call a Parliament. The other suggestions which have been offered are of grave importance; and you will not be surprised that I take a night to reflect on them before I decide."*

* Life of James, II. 236. Orig. Mem.; Burnet, i. 791.; Luttrell's Diary; Clarendon's Diary, November 27. 1688; Van Citters, and . Van Citters evidently had his intelligence from one of the Lords who were present. As the matter is important, I will give two short passages from his despatches. The King said, "Dat het by na voor hem onmogelyck was te pardonneren persoonen wie so hoog in syn regaarde schuldig stonden, vooral aen uyttrawende jegens den Lord Churchill, wien hy hadde groot gemaekt, en nogtans meyrade de eenigste oorsake van alle dese desertie en van de retraite van hare Coninglycke Hoogheden te wesen." One of the lords, probably Halifax or Nottingham, "sert hadde gearguert op de securiteyt van de lords die nu met syn Hoogheyt gereageerrt staan. Soo hoor ick," says Van Citters, "dat syn Ma-

JAMES THE SECOND.   287

At first James seemed disposed to make excellent use of   CHAP.
the time which he had taken for consideration. The Chan-   IX.
cellor was directed to issue writs convoking a Parliament for   He
the thirteenth of January. Halifax was sent for to the   appoints
closet, had a long audience, and spoke with much more   sioners to
freedom than he had thought it decorous to use in the   treat with
presence of a large assembly. He was informed that he   William.
had been appointed a Commissioner to treat with the Prince
of Orange. With him were joined Nottingham and Godolphin. The King declared that he was prepared to make
great sacrifices for the sake of peace. Halifax answered
that great sacrifices would doubtless be required. "Your
Majesty," he said, "must not expect that those who have the
power in their hands will consent to any terms which would
leave the laws at the mercy of the prerogative." With this
distinct explanation of his views, he accepted the Commission which the King wished him to undertake.* The concessions which a few hours before had been so obstinately
refused were now made in the most liberal manner. A proclamation was put forth by which the King not only granted
a free pardon to all who were in rebellion against him, but
declared them eligible to be members of the approaching
Parliament. It was not even required as a condition of
eligibility that they should lay down their arms. The same
Gazette which announced that the Houses were about to
meet contained a notification that Sir Edward Hales, who,
as a Papist, as a renegade, as the foremost champion of
the dispensing power, and as the harsh gaoler of the Bishops,
was one of the most unpopular men in the realm, had ceased
to be Lieutenant of the Tower, and had been succeeded by his
late prisoner, Bevil Skelton, who, though he held no high
place in the esteem of his countrymen, was at least not disqualified by law for public trust.†

But these concessions were meant only to blind the Lords   The
and the nation to the King's real designs. He had secretly   negotiation
                                                             a feint.

jesteyt onder anderen soude gesegt hebben : ' Men spreekt al voor de securiteyt
vanr andere, en niet voor de myne.' Waar op een der Pairs resolut dan met groot
respect soude geantwoordt hebben dat, soo syne Majesteyt's wapenen in staat
waren om hem te connen maintenneren, dat dan sulk syne securiteyte houde
wesen; soo niet, en soo de difficulteyt dan nog te surmonteren was, dat het dan
soude geschieden door de meeste condescendance, en hoe meer die was, en hy
gaorgen om aan de natie contentement te geven, dat syne securiteyt ook des te
grooter soude wesen."

* Letter of the Bishop of Saint Amph to the Prince of Orange. Dec. 17. 1688.
† London Gazette, Nov. 29., Dec. 3, 1688; Clarendon's Diary, Nov. 29, 30.

determined that, even in this extremity, he would yield nothing. On the very day on which he issued the proclamation of amnesty, he fully explained his intentions to Barillon. "This negotiation," said James, "is a mere feint. I must send Commissioners to my nephew, that I may gain time to ship off my wife and the Prince of Wales. You know the temper of my troops. None but the Irish will stand by me; and the Irish are not in sufficient force to resist the enemy. A Parliament would impose on me conditions which I could not endure. I should be forced to undo all that I have done for the Catholics, and to break with the King of France. As soon, therefore, as the Queen and my child are safe, I will leave England, and take refuge in Ireland, in Scotland, or with your master."*

Already James had made preparations for carrying this scheme into effect. Dover had been sent to Portsmouth with instructions to take charge of the Prince of Wales; and Dartmouth, who commanded the fleet there, had been ordered to obey Dover's directions in all things concerning the royal infant, and to have a yacht manned by trusty sailors in readiness to sail for France at a moment's notice.† The King now sent positive orders that the child should instantly be conveyed to the nearest Continental port.‡ Next to the Prince of Wales the chief object of anxiety was the Great Seal. To that symbol of kingly authority our jurists have always ascribed a peculiar and almost mysterious importance. It is held that, if the Keeper of the Seal should affix it, without taking the royal pleasure, to a patent of peerage or to a pardon, though he may be guilty of a high offence, the instrument cannot be questioned by any court of law, and can be annulled only by an Act of Parliament. James seems to have been afraid that his enemies might get this organ of his will into their hands, and might thus give a legal validity to acts which might affect him injuriously. Nor will his apprehensions be thought unreasonable when it is remembered that, exactly a hundred years later, the Great Seal of a King was used, with the assent of the Lords and the Commons, and with the approbation of many great statesmen and lawyers, for the purpose of transferring his prerogatives to his son. Lest the talisman which possessed such formidable powers should be abused, James determined that it should

* Barillon, December 4/14. 1688.   The letters are in Dalrymple.
† James to Dartmouth, Nov. 25. 1688.   ‡ James to Dartmouth, Dec. 1. 1688.

be kept within a few yards of his own closet. Jeffreys was therefore ordered to quit the costly mansion which he had lately built in Duke Street, and to take up his residence in a small apartment at Whitehall.*

The King had made all his preparations for flight, when an unexpected impediment compelled him to postpone the execution of his design. His agents at Portsmouth began to entertain scruples. Even Dover, though a member of the Jesuitical cabal, showed signs of hesitation. Dartmouth was still less disposed to comply with the royal wishes. He was zealous for the crown, and had done all that he could do, with a disaffected fleet, and in the face of an adverse wind, to prevent the Dutch from landing in England: but he was also zealous for the Established Church, and was by no means friendly to the policy of that government of which he was the defender. The mutinous temper of the officers and men under his command had caused him much anxiety; and he had been greatly relieved by the news that a free Parliament had been convoked, and that Commissioners had been named to treat with the Prince of Orange. The joy was clamorous throughout the fleet. An address, warmly thanking the King for these gracious concessions to public feeling, was drawn up on board of the flag ship. The Admiral signed first. Thirty-eight Captains wrote their names under his. This paper on its way to Whitehall crossed the messenger who brought to Portsmouth the order that the Prince of Wales should instantly be conveyed to France. Dartmouth learned, with bitter grief and resentment, that the free Parliament, the general amnesty, the negotiation, were all parts of a great fraud on the nation, and that in this fraud he was expected to be an accomplice. His conduct on this occasion was the most honourable part of a not very honourable life. In a sensible and spirited letter he declared that he had already carried his obedience to the furthest point to which a Protestant and an Englishman could go. To put the heir apparent of the British crown into the hands of Lewis would be nothing less than treason against the monarchy. The nation, already too much alienated from the Sovereign, would be roused to madness. The Prince of Wales would either not return at all, or would return attended by a French army.

* Luttrell's Diary.

CHAP. IX.

If His Royal Highness remained in the island, the worst that could be apprehended was that he would be brought up a member of the national Church; and that he might be so brought up ought to be the prayer of every loyal subject. Dartmouth concluded by declaring that he would risk his life in defence of the throne, but that he would be no party to the transporting of the Prince into France.*

This letter deranged all the projects of James. He learned too that he could not on this occasion expect from his Admiral even passive obedience. For Dartmouth had gone so far as to station several sloops at the mouth of the harbour of Portsmouth with orders to suffer no vessel to pass out unexamined. A change of plan was necessary. The child must be brought back to London, and sent thence to France. An interval of some days must elapse before this could be done. During that interval the public mind must be amused by the hope of a Parliament and the semblance of a negotiation. Writs were sent out for the elections. Trumpeters went backward and forward between the capital and the Dutch head quarters. At length passes for the King's Commissioners arrived; and the three Lords set out on their embassy.

Agitation of London.

They left the capital in a state of fearful distraction. The passions which, during three troubled years, had been gradually gathering force, now, emancipated from the restraint of fear, and stimulated by victory and sympathy, showed themselves without disguise, even in the precincts of the royal dwelling. The grand jury of Middlesex found a bill against the Earl of Salisbury for turning Papist.† The Lord Mayor ordered the houses of the Roman Catholics of the city to be searched for arms. The mob broke into the house of one respectable merchant who held the unpopular faith, in order to ascertain whether he had not run a mine from his cellars under the neighbouring parish church, for the purpose of blowing up parson and congregation.‡ The hawkers bawled about the streets a hue and cry after Father Petre, who had withdrawn himself, and not before it was time,

* Second Collection of Papers, 1688; Dartmouth's Letter, dated December 3, 1688, will be found in Dalrymple; Life of James, ii. 253. Orig. Mem. James accuses Dartmouth of having got up an address from the fleet demanding a Parliament. This is a mere calumny. The address is one of thanks to the King for having called a Parliament, and was framed before Dartmouth had the least suspicion that His Majesty was deceiving the nation.

† Luttrell's Diary.

‡ Adda. Dec. $\frac{8}{18}$. 1688.

from his apartments in Whitehall.* Wharton's celebrated song, with many additional verses, was chaunted more loudly than ever in all the streets of the capital. The very sentinels who guarded the palace hummed, as they paced their rounds,

> "The English confusion to Popery drink,
> Lillibullero bullen a la."

The secret presses of London worked without ceasing. Many papers daily came into circulation by means which the magistracy could not discover, or would not check. One of these has been preserved from oblivion by the skilful audacity with which it was written, and by the immense effect which it produced. It purported to be a supplemental declaration under the hand and seal of the Prince of Orange: but it was written in a style very different from that of his genuine manifesto. Vengeance alien from the usages of Christian and civilised nations was denounced against all Papists who should dare to espouse the royal cause. They should be treated, not as soldiers or gentlemen, but as freebooters. The ferocity and licentiousness of the invading army, which had hitherto been restrained with a strong hand, should be let loose on them. Good Protestants, and especially those who inhabited the capital, were adjured, as they valued all that was dear to them, and commanded, on peril of the Prince's highest displeasure, to seize, disarm, and imprison their Roman Catholic neighbours. This document, it is said, was found by a Whig bookseller one morning under his shop door. He made haste to print it. Many copies were dispersed by the post, and passed rapidly from hand to hand. Discerning readers had no difficulty in pronouncing it a forgery devised by some unquiet and unprincipled adventurer, such as, in troubled times, are always busied in the foulest and darkest offices of faction. But the multitude was completely duped. Indeed to such a height had national and religious feeling been excited against the Irish Papists that most of those who believed the spurious proclamation to be genuine were inclined to applaud it as a seasonable exhibition of vigour. When it was known that no such document had really proceeded from William, men asked anxiously what impostor had so daringly and so successfully personated His

CHAP.
IX.

Forged proclamation.

* The Nuncio says, "Se lo avesse fatto prima di ora, per il Rè ne sarebbe stato meglio."

Highness. Some suspected Ferguson, others Johnson. At length, after the lapse of twenty-seven years, Hugh Speke avowed the forgery, and demanded from the House of Brunswick a reward for so eminent a service rendered to the Protestant religion. He asserted, in the tone of a man who conceives himself to have done something eminently virtuous and honourable, that, when the Dutch invasion had thrown Whitehall into consternation, he had offered his services to the Court, had pretended to be estranged from the Whigs, and had promised to act as a spy upon them; that he had thus obtained admittance to the royal closet, had vowed fidelity, had been promised large pecuniary rewards, and had procured blank passes which enabled him to travel backwards and forwards across the hostile lines. All these things he protested that he had done solely in order that he might, unsuspected, aim a deadly blow at the government, and produce a violent outbreak of popular feeling against the Roman Catholics. The forged proclamation he claimed as one of his contrivances: but whether his claim were well founded may be doubted. He delayed to make it so long that we may reasonably suspect him of having waited for the death of those who could confute him; and he produced no evidence but his own.*

While these things happened in London, every post from every part of the country brought tidings of some new insurrection. Lumley had seized Newcastle. The inhabitants had welcomed him with transport. The statue of the King, which stood on a lofty pedestal of marble, had been pulled down and hurled into the Tyne. The third of December was long remembered at Hull as the Towntaking Day. That place had a garrison commanded by Lord Langdale, a Roman Catholic. The Protestant officers concerted with the magistracy a plan of revolt; Langdale and his adherents were arrested; and soldiers and citizens united in declaring for the Protestant religion and a free Parliament.†

The Eastern counties were up. The Duke of Norfolk, attended by three hundred gentlemen armed and mounted, appeared in the stately marketplace of Norwich. The Mayor and Aldermen met him there, and engaged to stand by him

---

* See the Secret History of the Revolution, by Hugh Speke, 1715. In the London Library is a copy of this rare work with a manuscript note which seems to be in Speke's own hand.
† Brand's History of Newcastle; Tickell's History of Hull.

against Popery and arbitrary power.* Lord Herbert of Cherbury and Sir Edward Harley took up arms in Worcestershire.† Bristol, the second city of the realm, opened its gates to Shrewsbury. Trelawney, the Bishop, who had entirely unlearned in the Tower the doctrine of nonresistance, was the first to welcome the Prince's troops. Such was the temper of the inhabitants that it was thought unnecessary to leave any garrison among them.‡ The people of Gloucester rose and delivered Lovelace from confinement. An irregular army soon gathered round him. Some of his horsemen had only halters for bridles. Many of his infantry had only clubs for weapons. But this force, such as it was, marched unopposed through counties once devoted to the House of Stuart, and at length entered Oxford in triumph. The magistrates came in state to welcome the insurgents. The University itself, exasperated by recent injuries, was little disposed to pass censures on rebellion. Already some of the Heads of Houses had despatched one of their number to assure the Prince of Orange that they were cordially with him, and that they would gladly coin their plate for his service. The Whig chief, therefore, rode through the capital of Toryism amidst general acclamation. Before him the drums beat Lillibullero. Behind him came a long stream of horse and foot. The whole High Street was gay with orange ribands. For already the orange riband had the double signification which, after the lapse of one hundred and sixty years, it still retains. Already it was the emblem to the Protestant Englishman of civil and religious freedom, to the Roman Catholic Celt of subjugation and persecution.§

While foes were thus rising up all round the King, friends were fast shrinking from his side. The idea of resistance had become familiar to every mind. Many, who had been struck with horror when they heard of the first defections, now blamed themselves for having been so slow to discern the signs of the times. There was no longer any difficulty or danger in repairing to William. The King, in calling on

---

* An account of what passed at Norwich may still be seen in several collections on the original broadside. See also the Fourth Collection of Papers, 1688.

† Life of James, ii. 233.; MS. Memoir of the Harley family in the Mackintosh Collection.

‡ Van Citters, Dec. 4/14 1688; Letter of the Bishop of Bristol to the Prince of Orange, Dec. 5. 1688, in Dalrymple.

§ Van Citters, Nov. 27/Dec. 7 1688; Clarendon's Diary, Dec. 11.; Song on Lord Lovelace's Entry into Oxford, 1688; Burnet, i. 792.

the nation to elect representatives, had, by implication, authorised all men to repair to the places where they had votes or interest; and many of those places were already occupied by invaders or insurgents. Clarendon eagerly caught at this opportunity of deserting the falling cause. He knew that his speech in the Council of Peers had given deadly offence; and he was mortified by finding that he was not to be one of the royal Commissioners. He had estates in Wiltshire; and he determined that his son, the son of whom he had lately spoken with grief and horror, should be a candidate for that county. Under pretence of looking after the election, Clarendon set out for the West. He was speedily followed by the Earl of Oxford, and by others who had hitherto disclaimed all connection with the Prince's enterprise.*

By this time the invaders, steadily though slowly advancing, were within seventy miles of London. Though midwinter was approaching, the weather was fine: the way was pleasant; and the turf of Salisbury Plain seemed luxuriously smooth to men who had been toiling through the miry ruts of the Devonshire and Somersetshire highways. The route of the army lay close by Stonehenge; and regiment after regiment halted to examine that mysterious ruin, celebrated all over the Continent as the greatest wonder of our island. William entered Salisbury with the same military pomp which he had displayed at Exeter, and was lodged there in the palace which the King had occupied a few days before.†

Clarendon joins the Prince at Salisbury.

The Prince's train was now swelled by the Earls of Clarendon and Oxford, and by other men of high rank, who had, till within a few days, been considered as zealous Royalists. Van Citters also made his appearance at the Dutch head quarters. He had been during some weeks almost a prisoner in his house near Whitehall, under the constant observation of relays of spies. Yet, in spite of those spies, or perhaps by their help, he had succeeded in obtaining full and accurate intelligence of all that passed in the palace; and now, full fraught with valuable information about men and things, he came to assist the deliberations of William.‡

Dissension in the Prince's camp.

Thus far the Prince's enterprise had prospered beyond the anticipations of the most sanguine. And now, according to the general law which governs human affairs, prosperity

---

* Clarendon's Diary, Dec. 3, 4, 5. History of the Revolution. 1688. ‡ Van Citters, Nov. 30/Dec. 4, 1688.
† Whittle's Exact Diary; Echard's.

began to produce disunion. The English assembled at Salisbury were divided into two parties. One party consisted of Whigs who had always regarded the doctrines of passive obedience and of indefeasible hereditary right as slavish superstitions. Many of them had passed years in exile. All had been long shut out from participation in the favours of the crown. They now exulted in the near prospect of greatness and of vengeance. Burning with resentment, flushed with victory and hope, they would hear of no compromise. Nothing less than the deposition of their enemy would content them; nor can it be disputed that herein they were perfectly consistent. They had exerted themselves, nine years earlier, to exclude him from the throne, because they thought it likely that he would be a bad King. It could therefore scarcely be expected that they would willingly leave him on the throne, now that he had turned out a far worse King than any reasonable man could have anticipated.

On the other hand, not a few of William's followers were zealous Tories, who had, till very recently, held the doctrine of nonresistance in the most absolute form, but whose faith in that doctrine had, for a moment, given way to the strong passions excited by the ingratitude of the King and by the peril of the Church. No situation could be more painful or perplexing than that of the old Cavalier who found himself in arms against the throne. The scruples which had not prevented him from repairing to the Dutch camp began to torment him cruelly as soon as he was there. His mind misgave him that he had committed a crime. At all events he had exposed himself to reproach, by acting in diametrical opposition to the professions of his whole life. He felt insurmountable disgust for his new allies. They were people whom, ever since he could remember, he had been reviling and persecuting, Presbyterians, Independents, Anabaptists, old soldiers of Cromwell, brisk boys of Shaftesbury, accomplices in the Rye House plot, captains of the Western insurrection. He naturally wished to find out some salvo which might soothe his conscience, which might vindicate his consistency, and which might put a distinction between him and the crew of schismatical rebels whom he had always despised and abhorred, but with whom he was now in danger of being confounded. He therefore disclaimed with vehemence all thought of taking the crown from that anointed head which the ordinance of heaven and the fundamental laws of the realm had made sacred. His dearest wish was to see a reconciliation effected on terms which would not lower the royal dignity. He was no traitor. He was not, in truth, resisting the kingly authority. He was in arms only because he was convinced that the best service which could be rendered to the throne was to rescue His Majesty, by a little gentle coercion, from the hands of wicked counsellors.

The evils which the mutual animosity of these factions tended to produce were, to a great extent, averted by the ascendency and by the wisdom of the Prince. Surrounded by eager disputants, officious advisers, abject flatterers, vigilant spies, malicious talebearers, he remained serene and inscrutable. He preserved silence while silence was possible. When he was forced to speak, the earnest and peremptory tone in which he uttered his well weighed opinions soon silenced everybody else. Whatever some of his too zealous adherents might say, he uttered not a word indicating any design on the English crown. He was doubtless well aware that between him and that crown were still interposed obstacles which no prudence might be able to surmount, and which a single false step would make insurmountable. His only chance of obtaining the splendid prize was not to seize it rudely, but to wait till, without any appearance of exertion or stratagem on his part, his secret wish should be accomplished by the force of circumstances, by the blunders of his opponents, and by the free choice of the Estates of the Realm. Those who ventured to interrogate him learned nothing, and yet could not accuse him of shuffling. He quietly referred them to his Declaration, and assured them that his views had undergone no change since that instrument had been drawn up. So skilfully did he manage his followers that their discord seems rather to have strengthened than to have weakened his hands: but it broke forth with violence when his control was withdrawn, interrupted the harmony of convivial meetings, and did not respect even the sanctity of the house of God. Clarendon, who tried to hide from others and from himself, by an ostentatious display of loyal sentiments, the plain fact that he was a rebel, was shocked to hear some of his new associates laughing over their wine at the royal amnesty which had just been graciously offered to them. They wanted no pardon, they said. They would make the King ask pardon before they had done with him. Still more alarming and disgusting to every good Tory was an incident

which happened at Salisbury Cathedral. As soon as the
officiating minister began to read the collect for the King,
Burnet, among whose many good qualities selfcommand and
a fine sense of the becoming cannot be reckoned, rose from
his knees, sate down in his stall, and uttered some contemptuous noises which disturbed the devotions of the congregation.*

CHAP. IX.

In a short time the factions which divided the Prince's
camp had an opportunity of measuring their strength. The
royal Commissioners were on their way to him. Several
days had elapsed since they had been appointed; and it was
thought strange that, in a case of such urgency, there should
be such delay. But in truth neither James nor William
was desirous that negotiations should speedily commence;
for James wished only to gain time sufficient for sending his wife and son into France; and the position of
William became every day more commanding. At length
the Prince caused it to be notified to the Commissioners
that he would meet them at Hungerford. He probably
selected this place because, lying at an equal distance from
Salisbury and from Oxford, it was well situated for a rendezvous of his most important adherents. At Salisbury were
those noblemen and gentlemen who had accompanied him
from Holland or had joined him in the West; and at Oxford
were many chiefs of the Northern insurrection.

Late on Thursday, the sixth of December, he reached
Hungerford. The little town was soon crowded with men of
rank and note who came thither from opposite quarters.
The Prince was escorted by a strong body of troops. The
northern Lords brought with them hundreds of irregular
cavalry, whose accoutrements and horsemanship moved the
mirth of men accustomed to the splendid aspect and exact
movements of regular armies.†

The Prince reaches Hungerford.

While the Prince lay at Hungerford a sharp encounter
took place between two hundred and fifty of his troops and
six hundred Irish who were posted at Reading. The superior
discipline of the invaders was signally proved on this occasion. Though greatly outnumbered, they, at one onset, drove
the King's forces in confusion through the streets of the
town into the marketplace. There the Irish attempted to
rally; but, being vigorously attacked in front, and fired upon

Skirmish at Read-
ing.

* Clarendon's Diary, Dec. 6, 7. 1688. † Ibid. Dec. 7. 1688.

at the same time by the inhabitants from the windows of the neighbouring houses, they soon lost heart, and fled with the loss of their colours and of fifty men. Of the conquerors only five fell. The satisfaction which this news gave to the Lords and gentlemen who had joined William was unmixed. There was nothing in what had happened to gall their national feelings. The Dutch had not beaten the English, but had assisted an English town to free itself from the insupportable dominion of the Irish.*

On the morning of Saturday, the eighth of December, the King's Commissioners reached Hungerford. The Prince's body guard was drawn up to receive them with military respect. Bentinck welcomed them, and proposed to conduct them immediately to his master. They expressed a hope that the Prince would favour them with a private audience; but they were informed that he had resolved to hear them and answer them in public. They were ushered into his bedchamber, where they found him surrounded by a crowd of noblemen and gentlemen. Halifax, whose rank, age, and abilities entitled him to precedence, was spokesman. The proposition which the Commissioners had been instructed to make was that the points in dispute should be referred to the Parliament, for which the writs were already sealing, and that in the meantime the Prince's army would not come within thirty or forty miles of London. Halifax, having explained that this was the basis on which he and his colleagues were prepared to treat, put into William's hand a letter from the King, and retired. William opened the letter and seemed unusually moved. It was the first letter which he had received from his father in law since they had become avowed enemies. Once they had been on good terms and had written to each other familiarly; nor had they, even when they had begun to regard each other with suspicion and aversion, banished from their correspondence those forms of kindness which persons nearly related by blood and marriage commonly use. The letter which the Commissioners had brought was drawn up by a secretary in diplomatic form and in the French language. "I have had many letters from the King," said William, "but they were all in English, and in his own hand." He spoke with a sensibility which he was little in the habit of displaying.

* History of the Desertion; Van Citters, Dec. $\frac{8}{18}$. 1688; Exact Diary; Oldmixon, 760.

Perhaps he thought at that moment how much reproach his enterprise, just, beneficent, and necessary as it was, must bring on him and on the wife who was devoted to him. Perhaps he repined at the hard fate which had placed him in such a situation that he could fulfil his public duties only by breaking through domestic ties, and envied the happier condition of those who are not responsible for the welfare of nations and Churches. But such thoughts, if they rose in his mind, were firmly suppressed. He requested the Lords and gentlemen whom he had convoked on this occasion to consult together, unrestrained by his presence, as to the answer which ought to be returned. To himself, however, he reserved the power of deciding in the last resort, after hearing their opinion. He then left them, and retired to Littlecote Hall, a manor house situated about two miles off, and renowned down to our own times, not more on account of its venerable architecture and furniture than on account of a horrible and mysterious crime which was perpetrated there in the days of the Tudors.*

Before he left Hungerford, he was told that Halifax had expressed a great desire to see Burnet. In this desire there was nothing strange; for Halifax and Burnet had long been on terms of friendship. No two men, indeed, could resemble each other less. Burnet was utterly destitute of delicacy and tact. Halifax's taste was fastidious, and his sense of the ludicrous morbidly quick. Burnet viewed every act and every character through a medium distorted and coloured by party spirit. The tendency of Halifax's mind was always to see the faults of his allies more strongly than the faults of his opponents. Burnet was, with all his infirmities, and through all the vicissitudes of a life passed in circumstances not very favourable to piety, a sincerely pious man. The sceptical and sarcastic Halifax lay under the imputation of infidelity. Halifax therefore often incurred Burnet's indignant censure; and Burnet was often the butt of Halifax's keen and polished pleasantry. Yet they were drawn to each other by a mutual attraction, liked each other's conversation, appreciated each other's abilities, interchanged opinions freely, and interchanged also good offices in perilous times. It was not, however, merely from personal regard that Halifax now wished to see his old acquaintance. The Commissioners must have been anxious to know what was the

* See a very interesting note on the fifth canto of Sir Walter Scott's Rokeby.

Prince's real aim. He had refused to see them in private; and little could be learned from what he might say in a formal and public interview. Almost all those who were admitted to his confidence were men taciturn and impenetrable as himself. Burnet was the only exception. He was notoriously garrulous and indiscreet. Yet circumstances had made it necessary to trust him; and he would doubtless, under the dexterous management of Halifax, have poured out secrets as fast as words. William knew this well, and, when he was informed that Halifax was asking for the Doctor, could not refrain from exclaiming, "If they get together there will be fine tattling." Burnet was forbidden to see the Commissioners in private: but he was assured in very courteous terms that his fidelity was regarded by the Prince as above all suspicion; and, that there might be no ground for complaint, the prohibition was made general.

That afternoon the noblemen and gentlemen whose advice William had asked met in the great room of the principal inn at Hungerford. Oxford was placed in the chair; and the King's overtures were taken into consideration. It soon appeared that the assembly was divided into two parties, a party anxious to come to terms with the King, and a party bent on his destruction. The latter party had the numerical superiority: but it was observed that Shrewsbury, who of all the English nobles was supposed to enjoy the largest share of William's confidence, though a Whig, sided on this occasion with the Tories. After much altercation the question was put. The majority was for rejecting the proposition which the royal Commissioners had been instructed to make. The resolution of the assembly was reported to the Prince at Littlecote. On no occasion during the whole course of his eventful life did he show more prudence and selfcommand. He could not wish the negotiation to succeed. But he was far too wise a man not to know that, if unreasonable demands made by him should cause it to fail, public feeling would no longer be on his side. He therefore overruled the opinion of his too eager followers, and declared his determination to treat on the basis proposed by the King. Many of the Lords and gentlemen assembled at Hungerford remonstrated: a whole day was spent in bickering: but William's purpose was immovable. He declared himself willing to refer all the questions in dispute to the Parliament which had just been summoned, and not to advance within forty miles of London.

On his side he made some demands which even those who were least disposed to commend him allowed to be moderate. He insisted that the existing statutes should be obeyed till they should be altered by competent authority, and that all persons who held offices without a legal qualification should be forthwith dismissed. The deliberations of the Parliament, he justly conceived, could not be free if it was to sit surrounded by Irish regiments while he and his army lay at a distance of several marches. He therefore thought it reasonable that, since his troops were not to advance within forty miles of London on the west, the King's troops should fall back as far to the east. There would thus be, round the spot where the Houses were to meet, a wide circle of neutral ground. Within that circle, indeed, there were two fastnesses of great importance to the people of the capital, the Tower, which commanded their dwellings, and Tilbury Fort, which commanded their maritime trade. It was impossible to leave these places ungarrisoned. William therefore proposed that they should be temporarily entrusted to the care of the City of London. It might possibly be convenient that, when the Parliament assembled, the King should repair to Westminster with a body guard. The Prince announced that, in that case, he should claim the right of repairing thither with an equal number of soldiers. It seemed to him just that, while military operations were suspended, both the armies should be considered as alike engaged in the service of the English nation, and should be alike maintained out of the English revenue. Lastly, he required some guarantee that the King would not take advantage of the armistice for the purpose of introducing a French force into England. The point where there was most danger was Portsmouth. The Prince did not insist that this important fortress should be delivered up to him, but proposed that it should, during the truce, be under the government of an officer in whom both himself and James could confide.

The propositions of William were framed with a punctilious fairness, such as might have been expected rather from a disinterested umpire pronouncing an award than from a victorious prince dictating to a helpless enemy. No fault could be found with them by the partisans of the King. But among the Whigs there was much murmuring. They wanted no reconciliation with their old master. They thought themselves absolved from all allegiance to him.

CHAP.
IX.

They were not disposed to recognise the authority of a Parliament convoked by his writ. They were averse to an armistice; and they could not conceive why, if there was to be an armistice, it should be an armistice on equal terms. By all the laws of war the stronger party had a right to take advantage of his strength; and what was there in the character of James to justify any extraordinary indulgence? Those who reasoned thus little knew from how elevated a point of view, and with how discerning an eye, the leader whom they censured contemplated the whole situation of England and Europe. They were eager to ruin James, and would therefore either have refused to treat with him on any conditions, or have imposed on him conditions insupportably hard. To the success of William's vast and profound scheme of policy it was necessary that James should ruin himself by rejecting conditions ostentatiously liberal. The event proved the wisdom of the course which the majority of the Englishmen at Hungerford were inclined to condemn.

On Sunday, the ninth of December, the Prince's demands were put in writing, and delivered to Halifax. The Commissioners dined at Littlecote. A splendid assemblage had been invited to meet them. The old hall, hung with coats of mail which had seen the wars of the Roses, and with portraits of gallants who had adorned the court of Philip and Mary, was now crowded with Peers and Generals. In such a throng a short question and answer might be exchanged without attracting notice. Halifax seized this opportunity, the first which had presented itself, of extracting all that Burnet knew or thought. "What is it that you want?" said the dexterous diplomatist: "do you wish to get the King into your power?" "Not at all," said Burnet: "we would not do the least harm to his person." "And if he were to go away?" said Halifax. "There is nothing," said Burnet, "so much to be wished." There can be no doubt that Burnet expressed the general sentiment of the Whigs in the Prince's camp. They were all desirous that James should fly from the country; but only a few of the wisest among them understood how important it was that his flight should be ascribed by the nation to his own folly and perverseness, and not to harsh usage and well grounded apprehension. It seems probable that, even in the extremity to which he was now reduced, all his enemies united would have been unable to effect his complete overthrow had he not been his own worst enemy: but while his Commissioners were labouring to save him, he was labouring as earnestly to make all their efforts useless.*

His plans were at length ripe for execution. The pretended negotiation had answered its purpose. On the same day on which the three Lords reached Hungerford the Prince of Wales arrived at Westminster. It had been intended that he should come over London Bridge; and some Irish troops were sent to Southwark to meet him. But they were received by a great multitude with such hooting and execration that they thought it advisable to retire with all speed. The poor child crossed the Thames at Kingston, and was brought into Whitehall so privately that many believed him to be still at Portsmouth.†

CHAP. IX.

The Queen and the Prince of Wales sent to France.

To send him and the Queen out of the country without delay was now the first object of James. But who could be trusted to manage the escape? Dartmouth was accounted the most loyal of Protestant Tories; and Dartmouth had refused. Dover was a creature of the Jesuits; and even Dover had hesitated. It was not very easy to find an Englishman of rank and honour who would undertake to place the heir apparent of the English crown in the hands of the King of France. In these circumstances James bethought him of a French nobleman who then resided in London, Antonine Count of Lauzun. Of this man it has been said that his life was stranger than the dreams of other people. At an early age he had been the intimate associate of Lewis, and had been encouraged to expect the highest employments under the French crown. Then his fortunes had undergone an eclipse. Lewis had driven from him the friend of his youth with bitter reproaches, and had, it was said, scarcely refrained from adding blows. The fallen favourite had been sent prisoner to a fortress; but he had emerged from his confinement, had again enjoyed the smiles of his master, and had gained the heart of one of the greatest ladies in Europe, Anna Maria, daughter of Gaston Duke of Orleans, granddaughter of King Henry the Fourth, and heiress of the immense domains of the house of Montpensier. The lovers

Lauzun.

---

* My account of what passed at Hungerford is taken from Clarendon's Diary, December 8, 9, 1688; Burnet, i. 794.; the Paper delivered to the Prince by the Commissioners, and the Prince's Answer; Sir Patrick Hume's Diary; Van Citters, December 7/17.

† Life of James II. 237. Burnet, strange to say, had not heard, or had forgotten, that the prince was brought back to London: i. 796.

were bent on marriage. The royal consent was obtained. During a few hours Lauzun was regarded by the court as an adopted member of the house of Bourbon. The portion which the princess brought with her might well have been an object of competition to sovereigns; three great dukedoms, an independent principality with its own mint and with its own tribunals, and an income greatly exceeding the whole revenue of the kingdom of Scotland. But this splendid prospect had been overcast. The match had been broken off. The aspiring suitor had been, during many years, shut up in a remote castle. At length Lewis relented. Lauzun was forbidden to appear in the royal presence, but was allowed to enjoy liberty at a distance from the court. He visited England, and was well received at the palace of James and in the fashionable circles of London; for in that age the gentlemen of France were regarded throughout Europe as models of grace; and many Chevaliers and Viscounts who had never been admitted to the interior circle at Versailles, found themselves objects of general curiosity and admiration at Whitehall. Lauzun was in every respect the man for the present emergency. He had courage and a sense of honour, had been accustomed to eccentric adventures, and, with the keen observation and ironical pleasantry of a finished man of the world, had a strong propensity to knight errantry. All his national feelings and all his personal interests impelled him to undertake the adventure from which the most devoted subjects of the English crown seemed to shrink. As the guardian, at a perilous crisis, of the Queen of Great Britain and of the Prince of Wales, he might return with honour to his native land: he might once more be admitted to see Lewis dress and dine, and might, after so many vicissitudes, recommence, in the decline of life, the strangely fascinating chase of royal favour.

Animated by such feelings, Lauzun eagerly accepted the high trust which was offered to him. The arrangements for the flight were promptly made: a vessel was ordered to be in readiness at Gravesend: but to reach Gravesend was not easy. The city was in a state of extreme agitation. The slightest cause sufficed to bring a crowd together. No foreigner could appear in the streets without risk of being stopped, questioned, and carried before a magistrate as a Jesuit in disguise. It was, therefore, necessary to take the road on the south of the Thames. No precaution which could quiet suspicion was omitted. The King and Queen retired to rest as usual. When the palace had been some time profoundly quiet, James rose and called a servant who was in attendance. "You will find," said the King, "a man at the door of the antechamber: bring him hither." The servant obeyed, and Lauzun was ushered into the royal bedchamber. "I confide to you," said James, "my Queen and my son; everything must be risked to carry them into France." Lauzun, with a truly chivalrous spirit, returned thanks for the dangerous honour which had been conferred on him, and begged permission to avail himself of the assistance of his friend Saint Victor, a gentleman of Provence, whose courage and faith had been often tried. The services of so valuable an assistant were readily accepted. Lauzun gave his hand to Mary. Saint Victor wrapped up in his warm cloak the ill fated heir of so many Kings. The party stole down the back stairs, and embarked in an open skiff. It was a miserable voyage. The night was bleak: the rain fell: the wind roared: the water was rough: at length the boat reached Lambeth; and the fugitives landed near an inn, where a coach and horses were in waiting. Some time elapsed before the horses could be harnessed. Mary, afraid that her face might be known, would not enter the house. She remained with her child, cowering for shelter from the storm under the tower of Lambeth Church, and distracted by terror whenever the ostler approached her with his lantern. Two of her women attended her, one who gave suck to the Prince, and one whose office was to rock his cradle; but they could be of little use to their mistress; for both were foreigners who could hardly speak the English language, and who shuddered at the rigour of the English climate. The only consolatory circumstance was that the little boy was well, and uttered not a single cry. At length the coach was ready. Saint Victor followed it on horseback. The fugitives reached Gravesend safely, and embarked in the yacht which waited for them. They found there Lord Powis and his wife. Three Irish officers were also on board. These men had been sent thither in order that they might assist Lauzun in any desperate emergency; for it was thought not impossible that the captain of the ship might prove false; and it was fully determined that, on the first suspicion of treachery, he should be stabbed to the heart. There was, however, no necessity for violence. The yacht proceeded down the river with a fair wind; and

CHAP. IX.

Saint Victor, having seen her under sail, spurred back with the good news to Whitehall.*

On the morning of Monday, the tenth of December, the King learned that his wife and son had begun their voyage with a fair prospect of reaching their destination. About the same time a courier arrived at the palace with despatches from Hungerford. Had James been a little more discerning, or a little less obstinate, those despatches would have induced him to reconsider all his plans. The Commissioners wrote hopefully. The conditions proposed by the conqueror were strangely liberal. The King himself could not refrain from exclaiming that they were more favourable than he could have expected. He might indeed not unreasonably suspect that they had been framed with no friendly design: but this mattered nothing; for, whether they were offered in the hope that, by closing with them, he would lay the ground for a happy reconciliation, or, as is more likely, in the hope that, by rejecting them, he would exhibit himself to the whole nation as utterly unreasonable and incorrigible, his course was equally clear. In either case his policy was to accept them promptly and to observe them faithfully.

The King's preparations for flight.

But it soon appeared that William had perfectly understood the character with which he had to deal, and, in offering those terms which the Whigs at Hungerford had censured as too indulgent, had risked nothing. The solemn farce by which the public had been amused since the retreat of the royal army from Salisbury was prolonged during a few hours. All the Lords who were still in the capital were invited to the palace that they might be informed of the progress of the negotiation which had been opened by their advice. Another meeting of Peers was appointed for the following day. The Lord Mayor and the Sheriffs of London were summoned to attend the King. He exhorted them to perform their duties vigorously, and owned that he had thought it expedient to send his wife and child out of the country, but assured them that he would himself remain at his post. While he uttered this unkingly and unmanly falsehood, his fixed purpose was to depart before daybreak. Already he had entrusted his most valuable movables to the care of several foreign Am-

* Life of James, ii. 246.; Père d'Orléans, Révolutions d'Angleterre, xi.; Madame de Sévigné, Dec. 11. 1688; Dangeau, Mémoires, Dec. 11. As to Lauzun, see the Memoirs of Mademoiselle and of the Duke of Saint Simon, and the Characters of Labruyère.

bassadors. His most important papers had been deposited with the Tuscan minister. But before the flight there was still something to be done. The tyrant pleased himself with the thought that he might avenge himself on a people who had been impatient of his despotism by inflicting on them at parting all the evils of anarchy. He ordered the Great Seal and the writs for the new Parliament to be brought to his apartment. The writs he threw into the fire. Some which had been already sent out he annulled by an instrument drawn up in legal form. To Feversham he wrote a letter which could be understood only as a command to disband the army. Still, however, he concealed, even from his chief ministers, his intention of absconding. Just before he retired he directed Jeffreys to be in the closet early on the morrow, and, while stepping into bed, whispered to Mulgrave that the news from Hungerford was highly satisfactory. Everybody withdrew except the Duke of Northumberland. This young man, a natural son of Charles the Second by the Duchess of Cleveland, commanded a troop of Life Guards, and was a Lord of the Bedchamber. It seems to have been then the custom of the court that, in the Queen's absence, a Lord of the Bedchamber should sleep on a pallet in the King's room; and it was Northumberland's turn to perform this duty.

At three in the morning of Tuesday the eleventh of December, James rose, took the Great Seal in his hand, laid his commands on Northumberland not to open the door of the bedchamber till the usual hour, and disappeared through a secret passage, the same passage probably through which Huddleston had been brought to the bedside of the late King. Sir Edward Hales was in attendance with a hackney coach. James was conveyed to Millbank, where he crossed the Thames in a small wherry. As he passed Lambeth he flung the Great Seal into the midst of the stream, where, after many months, it was accidentally caught by a fishing net and dragged up.

At Vauxhall he landed. A carriage and horses had been stationed there for him; and he immediately took the road towards Sheerness, where a hoy belonging to the Custom House had been ordered to await his arrival.*

CHAP. IX.

His flight.

---

* History of the Desertion; Life of Account of the Revolution; Burnet, James, ii. 251. Orig. Mem.; Mulgrave's i. 79b.

CHAPTER X.

The flight of James known.

NORTHUMBERLAND strictly obeyed the injunction which had been laid on him, and did not open the door of the royal apartment till it was broad day. The antechamber was filled with courtiers who came to make their morning bow and with Lords who had been summoned to Council. The news of James's flight passed in an instant from the galleries to the streets; and the whole capital was in commotion.

Great agitation.

It was a terrible moment. The King was gone. The Prince had not arrived. No Regency had been appointed. The Great Seal, essential to the administration of ordinary justice, had disappeared. It was soon known that Feversham had, on the receipt of the royal order, instantly disbanded his forces. What respect for law or property was likely to be found among soldiers, armed and congregated, emancipated from the restraints of discipline, and destitute of the necessaries of life? On the other hand, the populace of London had, during some weeks, shown a strong disposition to turbulence and rapine. The urgency of the crisis united for a short time all who had any interest in the peace of society. Rochester had till that day adhered firmly to the royal cause. He now saw that there was only one way of averting general confusion. "Muster your troop of Guards," he said to Northumberland; "and declare for the Prince of Orange." The advice was promptly followed. The principal officers of the army who were then in London held a meeting at Whitehall, and resolved that they would submit to William's authority, and would, till his pleasure should be known, keep their men together, and assist the civil power to preserve order.*

The Lords meet at Guildhall.

Who was to supply, at that awful crisis, the place of the King? In the days of the Plantagenets, if a suspension of the regal functions took place, the Lords Spiritual and Temporal generally assumed the supreme executive power. It was

* History of the Desertion; Mulgrave's Account of the Revolution; Echard's History of the Revolution.

by the Lords that provision was made for the government of the kingdom during the minority of Henry the Third and during the absence of Edward the First. Both when Henry the Sixth succeeded to the crown in his infancy, and when many years later he sank into imbecility, the Lords took upon themselves to administer the government in his stead till the legislature had appointed a Protector. Whether our old Barons and Prelates, in acting for a King who could not act for himself, exercised a strictly legal right, or committed an irregularity which only extreme necessity could excuse, is a question which has been much debated. But the morning of the eleventh of December 1688 was not a time for controversy. It was necessary to the public safety that there should be a provisional government; and the eyes of men naturally turned to the magnates of the realm. Most of the Peers who were in the capital repaired to Guildhall, and were received there with all honour by the magistracy of the City. The extremity of the danger drew Sancroft forth from his palace. He took the chair; and, under his presidency, the new Archbishop of York, five Bishops, and twenty-two temporal Lords determined to draw up, subscribe, and publish a Declaration. By this instrument they declared that they were firmly attached to the religion and constitution of their country, and that they had cherished the hope of seeing grievances redressed and tranquillity restored by the Parliament which the King had lately summoned, but that this hope had been extinguished by his flight. They had therefore determined to join with the Prince of Orange, in order that the freedom of the nation might be vindicated, that the rights of the Church might be secured, that a just liberty of conscience might be given to Dissenters, and that the Protestant interest throughout the world might be strengthened. Till His Highness should arrive, they were prepared to take on themselves the responsibility of giving such directions as might be necessary for the preservation of order. A deputation was instantly sent to lay this Declaration before the Prince, and to inform him that he was impatiently expected in London.*

The Lords then proceeded to deliberate on the course which it was necessary to take for the prevention of tumult. They sent for the two Secretaries of State. Middleton refused to submit to what he regarded as an illegitimate authority; but Preston, astounded by his master's flight, and not knowing

* London Gazette, Dec. 13. 1688.

what to expect, or whither to turn, obeyed the summons. A message was sent to Skelton, who was Lieutenant of the Tower, requesting his attendance at Guildhall. He came, and was told that his services were no longer wanted, and that he must instantly deliver up his keys. He was succeeded by Lord Lucas. At the same time the Peers ordered a letter to be written to Dartmouth, enjoining him to refrain from all hostile operations against the Dutch fleet, and to displace all the Popish officers who held commands under him.*

The part taken in these proceedings by Sancroft, and by some other persons who had, up to that day, been strictly faithful to the principle of passive obedience, deserves especial notice. To usurp the command of the military and naval forces of the state, to remove the officers whom the King had set over his castles and his ships, and to prohibit his Admiral from giving battle in defence of the royal cause, was surely nothing less than rebellion. Yet several honest and able Tories of the school of Filmer persuaded themselves that they could do all these things without incurring the guilt of resisting their Sovereign. The distinction which they took was, at least, ingenious. Government, they said, is the ordinance of God. Hereditary monarchical government is eminently the ordinance of God. While the King commands what is lawful we must obey him actively. When he commands what is unlawful we must obey him passively. In no extremity are we justified in withstanding him by force. But if he chooses to resign his office, his rights over us are at an end. While he governs us, though he may govern us ill, we are bound to submit; but, if he refuses to govern us at all, we are not bound to remain for ever without a government. Anarchy is not the ordinance of God; nor will he impute it to us as a sin that, when a prince, whom, in spite of extreme provocations, we have never ceased to honour and obey, has departed we know not whither, leaving no vicegerent, we take the only course which can prevent the entire dissolution of society. Had our Sovereign remained among us, we were ready, little as he deserved our love, to die at his feet. Had he, when he quitted us, appointed a regency to govern us with vicarious authority during his absence, to that regency alone should we have looked for direction. But he has dis-

* Life of James, II. 259; Mulgrave's Account of the Revolution; Legge Papers in the Mackintosh Collection.

appeared, having made no provision for the preservation of order or the administration of justice. With him, and with his Great Seal, has vanished the whole machinery by which a murderer can be punished, by which the right to an estate can be decided, by which the effects of a bankrupt can be distributed. His last act has been to free thousands of armed men from the restraints of military discipline, and to place them in such a situation that they must plunder or starve. Yet a few hours, and every man's hand will be against his neighbour. Life, property, female honour, will be at the mercy of every lawless spirit. We are at this moment actually in that state of nature about which theorists have written so much; and in that state we have been placed, not by our fault, but by the voluntary defection of him who ought to have been our protector. His defection may be justly called voluntary: for neither his life nor his liberty was in danger. His enemies had just consented to treat with him on a basis proposed by himself, and had offered immediately to suspend all hostile operations, on conditions which he could not deny to be liberal. In such circumstances it is that he has abandoned his trust. We retract nothing. We are in nothing inconsistent. We still assert our old doctrines without qualification. We still hold that it is in all cases sinful to resist the magistrate: but we say that there is no longer any magistrate to resist. He who was the magistrate, after long abusing his powers, has at last abdicated them. The abuse did not give us a right to depose him: but the abdication gives us a right to consider how we may best supply his place.

It was on these grounds that the Prince's party was now swollen by many adherents who had previously stood aloof from it. Never, within the memory of man, had there been so near an approach to entire concord among all intelligent Englishmen as at this conjuncture; and never had concord been more needed. All those evil passions which it is the office of government to restrain, and which the best governments restrain but imperfectly, were on a sudden emancipated from control; avarice, licentiousness, revenge, the hatred of sect to sect, the hatred of nation to nation. On such occasions it will ever be found that the human vermin, which, neglected by ministers of state, and ministers of religion, barbarous in the midst of civilisation, heathen in the midst of Christianity, burrows, among all physical and all moral pollution, in the cellars and garrets of great cities, will at once rise into a terrible importance. So it was now in London. When the night, the longest night, as it chanced, of the year approached, forth came from every den of vice, from the bear garden at Hockley, and from the labyrinth of tippling houses and brothels in the Friars, thousands of housebreakers and highwaymen, cutpurses and ringdroppers. With these were mingled thousands of idle apprentices, who wished merely for the excitement of a riot. Even men of peaceable and honest habits were impelled by religious animosity to join the lawless part of the population. For the cry of No Popery, a cry which has more than once endangered the existence of London, was the signal for outrage and rapine. First the rabble fell on the Roman Catholic places of worship. The buildings were demolished. Benches, pulpits, confessionals, breviaries were heaped up and set on fire. A great mountain of books and furniture blazed on the site of the convent at Clerkenwell. Another pile was kindled before the ruins of the Franciscan house in Lincoln's Inn Fields. The chapel in Lime Street, the chapel in Ducklersbury, were pulled down. The pictures, images, and crucifixes were carried along the streets in triumph, amidst lighted tapers torn from the altars. The procession bristled thick with swords and staves, and on the point of every sword and of every staff was an orange. The King's printing house, whence had issued, during the preceding three years, innumerable tracts in defence of Papal supremacy, image worship, and monastic vows, was—to use a coarse metaphor which then, for the first time, came into fashion—completely gutted. The vast stock of paper, much of which was still unpolluted by types, furnished an immense bonfire. From monasteries, temples, and public offices, the fury of the multitude turned to private dwellings. Several houses were pillaged and destroyed; but the smallness of the booty disappointed the plunderers; and soon a rumour was spread that the most valuable effects of the Papists had been placed under the care of the foreign Ambassadors. To the savage and ignorant populace the law of nations and the risk of bringing on their country the just vengeance of all Europe were as nothing. The houses of the Ambassadors were besieged. A great crowd assembled before Barillon's door in St. James's Square. He, however, fared better than might have been expected. For, though the government which he represented was held in abhorrence, his liberal housekeeping and exact payments had made him personally popular. Moreover he had taken the precaution of asking for a guard of soldiers; and, as several men of rank, who lived near him had done the same, a considerable force was collected in the square. The rioters, therefore, when they were assured that no arms or priests were concealed under his roof, left him unmolested. The Venetian Envoy was protected by a detachment of troops: but the mansions occupied by the ministers of the Elector Palatine and of the Grand Duke of Tuscany were destroyed. One precious box the Tuscan minister was able to save from the marauders. It contained nine volumes of memoirs, written in the hand of James himself. These volumes reached France in safety, and, after the lapse of more than a century, perished there in the havoc of a revolution far more terrible than that from which they had escaped. But some fragments still remain, and, though grievously mutilated, and imbedded in masses of childish fiction, well deserve to be attentively studied.*

The rich plate of the Chapel Royal had been deposited at Wild House, near Lincoln's Inn Fields, the residence of the Spanish ambassador Ronquillo. Ronquillo, conscious that he and his court had not deserved ill of the English nation, had thought it unnecessary to ask for soldiers: but the mob was not in a mood to make nice distinctions. The name of Spain had long been associated in the public mind with the Inquisition and the Armada, with the cruelties of Mary and the

---

* I take this opportunity of giving an explanation which well informed persons may think superfluous. Several critics have complained that I treat the Saint Germain's Life of James the Second sometimes as a work of the highest authority, and sometimes as a mere romance. They seem to imagine that the book is all from the same hand, and ought either to be uniformly quoted with respect or uniformly thrown aside with contempt. The truth is that part of the Life is of the very highest authority, and that the rest is the work of an ignorant and silly compiler, and is of no more value than any common Jacobite pamphlet. Those passages which were copied from the Memoirs written by James, and those passages which were carefully revised by his son, are among the most useful materials for history. They contain the testimony of witnesses, who were undoubtedly under a strong bias, and for whose bias large allowance ought to be made, but who had the best opportunities of learning the truth. The interstices between these precious portions of the narrative are sometimes filled with trash. Whoever will take the trouble to examine the references in my notes will see that I have constantly borne in mind the distinction which I have now pointed out. Surely I may cite, as of high authority, an account of the last moments of Charles the Second, which was written by his brother, or an account of the plottings of Penn, of Dartmouth, and of Churchill, which was corrected by the hand of the Pretender, and yet may, with perfect consistency, reject the fables of a nameless scribbler who makes Argyle, with all his cavalry, swim across the Clyde at a place where the Clyde is more than four miles wide. (1857.)

314   HISTORY OF ENGLAND.

CHAP. X. plots against Elizabeth. Ronquillo had also made himself
many enemies among the common people by availing himself
of his privilege to avoid the necessity of paying his debts.
His house was therefore sacked without mercy; and a noble
library, which he had collected, perished in the flames. His
only comfort was that the host in his chapel was rescued from
the same fate.*

The morning of the twelfth of December rose on a ghastly
sight. The capital in many places presented the aspect of a
city taken by storm. The Lords met at Whitehall, and exerted themselves to restore tranquillity. The trainbands were
ordered under arms. A body of cavalry was kept in readiness
to disperse tumultuous assemblages. Such atonement as was
at that moment possible was made for the gross insults which
had been offered to foreign governments. A reward was
promised for the discovery of the property taken from Wild
House; and Ronquillo, who had not a bed or an ounce of
plate left, was splendidly lodged in the deserted palace of the
Kings of England. A sumptuous table was kept for him;
and the yeomen of the guard were ordered to wait in his antechamber with the same observance which they were in the
habit of paying to the Sovereign. These marks of respect
soothed even the punctilious pride of the Spanish court, and
averted all danger of a rupture.†

Arrest of Jeffreys. In spite, however, of the well meant efforts of the provisional government, the agitation grew hourly more formidable.
It was heightened by an event which, even at this distance of
time, can hardly be related without a feeling of vindictive
pleasure. A scrivener who lived at Wapping, and whose
trade was to furnish the seafaring men there with money at
high interest, had some time before lent a sum on bottomry.
The debtor applied to equity for relief against his own bond;
and the case came before Jeffreys. The counsel for the bor-

* London Gazette, Dec. 13. 1688; Barillon, Dec. 13/23.; Van Citters, same date; Luttrell's Diary; Life of James, ii. 256. Orig. Mem.; Ellis Correspondence, Dec. 13; Consultation of the Spanish Council of State, Jan. 19. 1689. It appears that Ronquillo complained bitterly to his government of his losers; "Sirviendole solo de consuelo al haber tenido prevencion de poder consumir El Santissimo."

† London Gazette, Dec. 13. 1688; Luttrell's Diary; Mulgrave's Account of

the Revolution; Consultation of the Spanish Council of State, Jan. 19. 1689. Something was said about reprisals; but the Spanish council treated the suggestion with contempt. "Habiendo sido este hecho por un furor de pueblo, sin consentimiento del gobierno, y antes contra su voluntad, como lo ha mostrado la satisfaccion que le han dado y lo han prometido, parece que no hay juicio humano que puede aconsejar que se pase á semejante remedio."

rower, having little else to say, said that the lender was a Trimmer. The Chancellor instantly fired. "A Trimmer! where is he? Let me see him. I have heard of that kind of monster. What is it made like?" The unfortunate creditor was forced to stand forth. The Chancellor glared fiercely on him, stormed at him, and sent him away half dead with fright. "While I live," the poor man said, as he tottered out of the court, "I shall never forget that terrible countenance." And now the day of retribution had arrived. The Trimmer was walking through Wapping, when he saw a well known face looking out of the window of an alehouse. He could not be deceived. The eyebrows, indeed, had been shaved away. The dress was that of a common sailor from Newcastle, and was black with coal dust: but there was no mistaking the savage eye and mouth of Jeffreys. The alarm was given. In a moment the house was surrounded by hundreds of people shaking bludgeons and bellowing curses. The fugitive's life was saved by a company of the trainbands; and he was carried before the Lord Mayor. The Mayor was a simple man who had passed his whole life in obscurity, and was bewildered by finding himself an important actor in a mighty revolution. The events of the last twenty-four hours, and the perilous state of the city which was under his charge, had disordered his mind and his body. When the great man, at whose frown, a few days before, the whole kingdom had trembled, was dragged into the justice room begrimed with ashes, half dead with fright, and followed by a raging multitude, the agitation of the unfortunate Mayor rose to the height. He fell into fits, and was carried to his bed, whence he never rose. Meanwhile the throng without was constantly becoming more numerous and more savage. Jeffreys begged to be sent to prison. An order to that effect was procured from the Lords who were sitting at Whitehall; and he was conveyed in a carriage to the Tower. Two regiments of militia were drawn out to escort him, and found the duty a difficult one. It was repeatedly necessary for them to form, as if for the purpose of repelling a charge of cavalry, and to present a forest of pikes to the mob. The thousands who were disappointed of their revenge pursued the coach, with howls of rage, to the gate of the Tower, brandishing cudgels, and holding up halters full in the prisoner's view. The wretched man meantime was in convulsions of terror. He wrung his hands: he looked wildly out, sometimes at one window, sometimes at the other, and

CHAP. X.

was heard even above the tumult, crying "Keep them off, gentlemen! For God's sake keep them off!" At length, having suffered far more than the bitterness of death, he was safely lodged in the fortress where some of his most illustrious victims had passed their last days, and where his own life was destined to close in unspeakable ignominy and horror.*

All this time an active search was making after Roman Catholic priests. Many were arrested. Two Bishops, Ellis and Leyburn, were sent to Newgate. The Nuncio, who had little reason to expect that either his spiritual or his political character would be respected by the multitude, made his escape, disguised as a lacquey, in the train of the minister of the Duke of Savoy.†

The Irish Night.

Another day of agitation and alarm closed, and was followed by a night the strangest and most terrible that England had ever seen. Early in the evening an attack was made by the rabble on a stately house which had been built a few months before for Lord Powis, which, in the reign of George the Second, was the residence of the Duke of Newcastle, and which is still conspicuous at the northwestern angle of Lincoln's Inn Fields. Some troops were sent thither: the mob was dispersed, tranquillity seemed to be restored, and the citizens were retiring quietly to their beds. Just at this time arose a whisper which swelled fast into a fearful clamour, passed in an hour from Piccadilly to Whitechapel, and spread into every street and alley of the capital. It was said that the Irish whom Feversham had let loose were marching on London and massacring every man, woman, and child on the road. At one in the morning the drums of the militia beat to arms. Everywhere terrified women were weeping and wringing their hands, while their fathers and husbands were equipping themselves for fight. Before two the capital wore a face of stern preparedness which might well have daunted a real enemy, if such an enemy had been approaching. Candles were blazing at all the windows. The public places were as bright as at noonday. All the great avenues were barricaded. More than twenty thousand pikes and muskets lined the streets. The late daybreak of the winter solstice found the whole City still in arms. During many years the Londoners retained a vivid recollection of what they

* North's Life of Guildford, 220.; Jeffreys' Elegy; Luttrell's Diary; Oldmixon, 762. Oldmixon was in the crowd, and was, I doubt not, one of the most furious there. He tells the story well. Ellis Correspondence; Burnet, I. 797. and Onslow's note.
† Adda, Dec. 4/14; Van Cittars, Dec. 14/24

called the Irish Night. When it was known that there had
been no danger, attempts were made to discover the origin of
the rumour which had produced so much agitation. It appeared that some persons who had the look and dress of clowns
just arrived from the country had first spread the report in
the suburbs a little before midnight: but whence these men
came, and by whom they were employed, remained a mystery.
And soon news arrived from many quarters which bewildered
the public mind still more. The panic had not been confined
to London. The cry that disbanded Irish soldiers were coming
to murder the Protestants had, with malignant ingenuity, been
raised at once in many places widely distant from each other.
Great numbers of letters, skilfully framed for the purpose of
frightening ignorant people, had been sent by stage coaches,
by waggons, and by the post, to various parts of England.
All these letters came to hand almost at the same time. In
a hundred towns at once the populace was possessed with the
belief that armed barbarians were at hand, bent on perpetrating crimes as foul as those which had disgraced the rebellion
of Ulster. No Protestant would find mercy. Children would
be compelled by torture to murder their parents. Babes
would be stuck on pikes, or flung into the blazing ruins of
what had lately been happy dwellings. Great multitudes assembled with weapons: the people in some places began to
pull down bridges, and to throw up barricades: but soon the
excitement went down. In many districts those who had been
so foully imposed upon learned with delight, alloyed by shame,
that there was not a single Popish soldier within a week's
march. There were places, indeed, where some struggling
bands of Irish made their appearance and demanded food;
but it can scarcely be imputed to them as a crime that they
did not choose to die of hunger; and there is no evidence that
they committed any wanton outrage. In truth they were
much less numerous than was commonly supposed; and their
spirit was cowed by finding themselves left on a sudden, without leaders or provisions, in the midst of a mighty population
which felt towards them as men feel towards a drove of wolves.
Of all the subjects of James none had more reason to execrate
him than these unfortunate members of his church and defenders of his throne.*

* Van Citters, Dec. 14. 1688; Luttrell's Diary; Ellis Correspondence; Oldmixon, 751.; Speke's Secret History of the Revolution; Life of James, II., 257.; Fachard's History of the Revolution; History of the Desertion.

It is honourable to the English character that, notwithstanding the aversion with which the Roman Catholic religion and the Irish race were then regarded, notwithstanding the anarchy which was the effect of the flight of James, notwithstanding the artful machinations which were employed to scare the multitude into cruelty, no atrocious crime was perpetrated at this conjuncture. Much property, indeed, was destroyed and carried away. The houses of many Roman Catholic gentlemen were attacked. Parks were ravaged. Deer were slain and stolen. Some venerable specimens of the domestic architecture of the middles ages bear to this day the marks of the popular violence. The roads were in many places made impassable by a self-appointed police, which stopped every traveller till he proved that he was not a Papist. The Thames was infested by a set of pirates who, under pretence of searching for arms or delinquents, rummaged every boat that passed. Obnoxious persons were insulted and hustled. Many persons who were not obnoxious were glad to ransom their persons and effects by bestowing some guineas on the zealous Protestants who had, without any legal authority, assumed the office of inquisitors. But in all this confusion, which lasted several days and extended over many counties, not a single Roman Catholic lost his life. The mob showed no inclination to blood, except in the case of Jeffreys; and the hatred which that bad man inspired had more affinity with humanity than with cruelty.*

Many years later Hugh Speke affirmed that the Irish Night was his work, that he had prompted the rustics who raised London, and that he was the author of the letters which had spread dismay through the country. His assertion is not intrinsically improbable: but it rests on no evidence except his own word. He was a man quite capable of committing such a villany, and quite capable also of falsely boasting that he had committed it.†

At London William was impatiently expected: for it was not doubted that his vigour and ability would speedily restore order and security. There was however some delay for which the Prince cannot justly be blamed. His original intention had been to proceed from Hungerford to Oxford, where he was assured of an honourable and affectionate

* Life of James ii. 248.   † Secret History of the Revolution.

reception: but the arrival of the deputation from Guildhall induced him to change his intention and to hasten directly towards the capital. On the way he learned that Feversham, in pursuance of the King's orders, had dismissed the royal army, and that thousands of soldiers, freed from restraint and destitute of necessaries, were scattered over the counties through which the road to London lay. It was therefore impossible for William to proceed slenderly attended without great danger, not only to his own person, about which he was not much in the habit of being solicitous, but also to the great interests which were under his care. It was necessary that he should regulate his own movements by the movements of his troops; and troops could then move but slowly along the highways of England in midwinter. He was, on this occasion, a little moved from his ordinary composure. "I am not to be thus dealt with," he exclaimed with bitterness; "and that my Lord Feversham shall find." Prompt and judicious measures were taken to remedy the evils which James had caused. Churchill and Grafton were entrusted with the task of reassembling the dispersed army and bringing it into order. The English soldiers were invited to resume their military character. The Irish were commanded to deliver up their arms on pain of being treated as banditti, but were assured that, if they would submit quietly, they should be supplied with necessaries.*

The Prince's orders were carried into effect with scarcely any opposition, except from the Irish soldiers who had been in garrison at Tilbury. One of these men snapped a pistol at Grafton. It missed fire, and the assassin was instantly shot dead by an Englishman. About two hundred of the unfortunate strangers made a gallant attempt to return to their own country. They seized a richly laden East Indiaman which had just arrived in the Thames, and tried to procure pilots by force at Gravesend. No pilot, however, was to be found; and they were under the necessity of trusting to their own skill in navigation. They soon ran their ship aground, and, after some bloodshed, were compelled to lay down their arms.†

William had now been five weeks on English ground; and during the whole of that time his good fortune had been

* Clarendon's Diary, December 13. † Van Citters, Dec. 14. 1688; Luttrell's Diary.
1688; Van Citters, December 14; Eachard's History of the Revolution.

uninterrupted. His own prudence and firmness had been conspicuously displayed, and yet had done less for him than the folly and pusillanimity of others. And now, at the moment when it seemed that his plans were about to be crowned with entire success, they were disconcerted by one of those strange incidents which so often confound the most exquisite devices of human policy.

The King detained near Sheerness.

On the morning of the thirteenth of December the people of London, not yet fully recovered from the agitation of the Irish Night, were surprised by a rumour that the King had been detained, and was still in the island. The report gathered strength during the day, and was fully confirmed before the evening.

James had travelled with relays of coach horses along the southern shore of the Thames, and on the morning of the twelfth had reached Emley Ferry near the island of Sheppey. There lay the hoy in which he was to sail. He went on board: but the wind blew fresh; and the master would not venture to put to sea without more ballast. A tide was thus lost. Midnight was approaching before the vessel began to float. By that time the news that the King had disappeared, that the country was without a government, and that London was in confusion, had travelled fast down the Thames, and wherever it spread had produced outrage and misrule. The rude fishermen of the Kentish coast eyed the hoy with suspicion and with cupidity. It was whispered that some persons in the garb of gentlemen had gone on board of her in great haste. Perhaps they were Jesuits: perhaps they were rich. Fifty or sixty boatmen, animated at once by hatred of Popery and by love of plunder, boarded the hoy just as she was about to make sail. The passengers were told that they must go on shore and be examined by a magistrate. The King's appearance excited suspicion. "It is Father Petre," cried one ruffian; "I know him by his lean jaws." "Search the hatchet faced old Jesuit," became the general cry. He was rudely pulled and pushed about. His money and watch were taken from him. He had about him his coronation ring, and some other trinkets of great value: but these escaped the search of the robbers, who indeed were so ignorant of jewellery that they took his diamond buckles for bits of glass.

At length the prisoners were put on shore and carried to an inn. A crowd had assembled there to see them; and

James, though disguised by a wig of different shape and colour from that which he usually wore, was at once recognised. For a moment the rabble seemed to be overawed: but the exhortations of their chiefs revived their courage; and the sight of Hales, whom they well knew and bitterly hated, inflamed their fury. His park was in the neighbourhood; and at that very moment a band of rioters was employed in pillaging his house and shooting his deer. The multitude assured the King that they would not hurt him: but they refused to let him depart. It chanced that the Earl of Winchelsea, a Protestant, but a zealous royalist, head of the Finch family, and a kinsman of Nottingham, was then at Canterbury. As soon as he learned what had happened he hastened to the coast, accompanied by some Kentish gentlemen. By their intervention the King was removed to a more convenient lodging: but he was still a prisoner. The mob kept constant watch round the house to which he had been carried; and some of the ringleaders lay at the door of his bedroom. His demeanour meantime was that of a man, all the nerves of whose mind had been broken by the load of misfortunes. Sometimes he spoke so haughtily that the rustics who had charge of him were provoked into making insolent replies. Then he betook himself to supplication. " Let me go," he cried; " get me a boat. The Prince of Orange is hunting for my life. If you do not let me fly now, it will be too late. My blood will be on your heads. He that is not with me is against me." On this last text he preached a sermon half an hour long. He harangued on a strange variety of subjects, on the disobedience of the fellows of Magdalene College, on the miracles wrought by Saint Winifred's well, on the disloyalty of the black coats, and on the virtues of a piece of the true cross which he had unfortunately lost. " What have I done?" he demanded of the Kentish squires who attended him. " Tell me the truth. What error have I committed?" Those to whom he put these questions were too humane to return the answer which must have risen to their lips, and listened to his wild talk in pitying silence.*

When the news that he had been stopped, insulted, roughly handled, and plundered, and that he was still a

* Life of James, ii. 251. Orig. Mem.; of Rapin. This curious letter is in the Letter printed in Tindal's Continuation Harl MSS. 6852.

prisoner in the hands of rude churls, reached the capital, many passions were roused. Rigid Churchmen, who had, a few hours before, begun to think that they were freed from their allegiance to him, now felt misgivings. He had not quitted his kingdom. He had not consummated his abdication. If he should resume his regal office, could they, on their principles, refuse to pay him obedience? Enlightened statesmen foresaw with concern that all the disputes which his flight had for a moment set at rest would be revived and exasperated by his return. Some of the common people, though still smarting from recent wrongs, were touched with compassion for a great prince outraged by ruffians, and were willing to entertain a hope, more honourable to their good nature than to their discernment, that he might even now repent of the errors which had brought on him so terrible a punishment.

From the moment when it was known that the King was still in England, Sancroft, who had hitherto acted as chief of the Provisional Government, absented himself from the sittings of the Peers. Halifax, who had just returned from the Dutch head quarters, was placed in the chair. His sentiments had undergone a great change in a few hours. Both public and private feelings now impelled him to join the Whigs. Those who candidly examine the evidence which has come down to us will be of opinion that he accepted the office of royal Commissioner in the sincere hope of effecting an accommodation between the King and the Prince on fair terms. The negotiation had commenced prosperously: the Prince had offered terms which the King could not but acknowledge to be fair; the eloquent and ingenious Trimmer might flatter himself that he should be able to mediate between infuriated factions, to dictate a compromise between extreme opinions, to secure the liberties and religion of his country, without exposing her to the risks inseparable from a change of dynasty and a disputed succession. While he was pleasing himself with thoughts so agreeable to his temper, he learned that he had been deceived, and had been used as an instrument for deceiving the nation. His mission to Hungerford had been a fool's errand. The King had never meant to abide by the terms which he had instructed his Commissioners to propose. He had charged them to declare that he was willing to submit all the questions in dispute to the Parliament which he had summoned; and, while they were delivering his message, he had burned the writs, made away with the seal, let loose the army, suspended the administration of justice, dissolved the government, and fled from the capital. Halifax saw that an amicable arrangement was no longer possible. He also felt, it may be suspected, the vexation natural to a man widely renowned for wisdom, who finds that he has been duped by an understanding immeasurably inferior to his own, and the vexation natural to a great master of ridicule, who finds himself placed in a ridiculous situation. His judgment and his resentment alike induced him to relinquish the schemes of reconciliation on which he had hitherto been intent, and to place himself at the head of those who were bent on raising William to the throne.*

A journal of what passed in the Council of Lords while Halifax presided is still extant in his own handwriting.† No precaution, which seemed necessary for the prevention of outrage and robbery, was omitted. The Peers took on themselves the responsibility of giving orders that, if the rabble rose again, the soldiers should fire with bullets. Jeffreys was brought to Whitehall and interrogated as to what had become of the Great Seal and the writs. At his own earnest request he was remanded to the Tower, as the only place where his life could be safe; and he retired thanking and blessing those who had given him the protection of a prison. A Whig nobleman moved that Oates should be set at liberty: but this motion was overruled.‡

The business of the day was nearly over, and Halifax was about to rise, when he was informed that a messenger from Sheerness was in attendance. No occurrence could be more perplexing or annoying. To do anything, to do nothing, was to incur a grave responsibility. Halifax, wishing probably to obtain time for communication with the Prince, would have adjourned the meeting: but Mulgrave begged the Lords to keep their seats, and introduced the messenger. The man told his story with many tears, and produced a letter written

---

* Reresby was told, by a lady whom he does not name, that the King had no intention of withdrawing till he received a letter from Halifax, who was then at Hungerford. The letter, she said, informed His Majesty that, if he staid, his life would be in danger. This was certainly a fiction. The King, before the Commissioners left London, had told Barillon that their embassy was a mere feint, and had expressed a full resolution to leave the country. It is clear from Reresby's own narrative that Halifax thought himself shamefully used.

† Harl. MS. 255.

‡ Halifax MS.; Van Citters, Dec. 14. 1688.

CHAP. X.

The Lords order him to be set at liberty.

in the King's hand, and addressed to no particular person, but imploring the aid of all good Englishmen.*

Such an appeal it was hardly possible to disregard. The Lords ordered Feversham to hasten with a troop of the Life Guards to the place where the King was detained, and to set His Majesty at liberty.

Already Middleton and a few other adherents of the royal cause had set out to assist and comfort their unhappy master. They found him strictly confined, and were not suffered to enter his presence till they had delivered up their swords. The concourse of people about him was by this time immense. Some Whig gentlemen of the neighbourhood had brought a large body of militia to guard him. They had imagined most erroneously that by detaining him they were ingratiating themselves with his enemies, and were greatly disturbed when they learned that the treatment which the King had undergone was disapproved by the Provisional Government in London, and that a body of cavalry was on the road to release him. Feversham soon arrived. He had left his troop at Sittingbourne : but there was no occasion to use force. The King was suffered to depart without opposition, and was removed by his friends to Rochester, where he took some rest, which he greatly needed. He was in a pitiable state. Not only was his understanding, which had never been very clear, altogether bewildered : but the personal courage which, when a young man, he had shown in several battles, both by sea and by land, had forsaken him. The rough corporal usage which he had now, for the first time, undergone, seems to have discomposed him more than any other event of his chequered life. The desertion of his army, of his favourites, of his family, affected him less than the indignities which he had suffered when his boy was boarded. The remembrance of those indignities continued long to rankle in his heart, and showed itself, after the lapse of more than three years, in a way which moved all Europe to contemptuous mirth.

Yet, had he possessed an ordinary measure of good sense, he would have seen that those who had detained him had unintentionally done him a great service. The events which had taken place during his absence from his capital ought to have convinced him that, if he had succeeded in escaping, he never would have returned. In his own despite he had been saved from ruin. He had another chance, a last chance.

* Mulgrave's Account of the Revolution.

Great as his offences had been, to dethrone him, while he remained in his kingdom and offered to assent to such conditions as a free Parliament might impose, would have been almost impossible.

During a short time he seemed disposed to remain. He sent Feversham from Rochester with a letter to William. The substance of the letter was that His Majesty was on his way back to Whitehall, that he wished to have a personal conference with the Prince, and that Saint James's Palace should be fitted up for His Highness.*

William was now at Windsor. He had learned with deep mortification the events which had taken place on the coast of Kent. Just before the news arrived, those who approached him had observed that his spirits were unusually high. He had, indeed, reason to rejoice. A vacant throne was before him. All parties, it seemed, would, with one voice, invite him to mount it. On a sudden his prospects were overcast. The abdication, it appeared, had not been completed. A large proportion of his own followers would have scruples about deposing a King who remained among them, who invited them to represent their grievances in a Parliamentary way, and who promised full redress. It was necessary that the Prince should examine his new position, and should determine on a new line of action. No course was open to him which was altogether free from objections, no course which would place him in a situation so advantageous as that which he had occupied a few hours before. Yet something might be done. The King's first attempt to escape had failed. What was now most to be desired was that he should make a second attempt with better success. He must be at once frightened and enticed. The liberality with which he had been treated in the negotiation at Hungerford, and which he had requited by a breach of faith, would now be out of season. No terms of accommodation must be proposed to him. If he should propose terms he must be coldly answered. No violence must be used towards him, or even threatened. Yet it might not be impossible, without either using or threatening violence, to make so weak a man uneasy about his personal safety. He would soon be eager to fly. All facilities for flight must then be placed within his reach; and care must be taken that he should not again be stopped by any officious blunderer.

Such was William's plan; and the ability and determina-

* Life of James, ii. 261. Orig. Mem.

tion with which he carried it into effect present a strange contrast to the folly and cowardice with which he had to deal. He soon had an excellent opportunity of commencing his system of intimidation. Feversham arrived at Windsor with James's letter. The messenger had not been very judiciously selected. It was he who had disbanded the royal army. To him primarily were to be imputed the confusion and terror of the Irish Night. His conduct was loudly blamed by the public. William had been provoked into muttering a few words of menace; and a few words of menace from William's lips generally meant something. Feversham was asked for his safe conduct. He had none. By coming without one into the midst of a hostile camp, he had, according to the laws of war, made himself liable to be treated with the utmost severity. William refused to see him, and ordered him to be put under arrest.* Zulestein was instantly despatched to inform James that the Prince declined the proposed conference, and desired that His Majesty would remain at Rochester.

But it was too late. James was already in London. He had hesitated about the journey, and had, at one time, determined to make another attempt to reach the Continent. But at length he yielded to the urgency of friends who were wiser than himself, and set out for Whitehall. He arrived there on the afternoon of Sunday the sixteenth of December. He had been apprehensive that the common people, who, during his absence, had given so many proofs of their aversion to Popery, would offer him some affront. But the very violence of the recent outbreak had produced a remission. The storm had spent itself. Good humour and pity had succeeded to fury. In no quarter was any disposition shown to insult the King. Some cheers were raised as his coach passed through the City. The bells of some churches were rung; and a few bonfires were lighted in honour of his return.† His feeble

---

* Clarendon's Diary, Dec. 16. 1688; Burnet, i. 800.

† Life of James, ii. 262. Orig. Mem; Burnet, i. 799. In the History of the Desertion (1689) it is affirmed that the shouts on this occasion were uttered merely by some idle boys, and that the great body of the people looked on in silence. Oldmixon, who was in the crowd, says the same; and Ralph, whose prejudices were very different from Oldmixon's, tells us that the information which he had received from a respectable eyewitness was to the same effect. The truth probably is that the signs of joy were in themselves slight, but seemed extraordinary because a violent explosion of public indignation had been expected. Hamilton mentions that there had been acclamations and some bonfires, but adds, "Le peuple dans le fond est pour le Prince d'Orange." December 17. 1688.

mind, which had just before been sunk in despondency, was extravagantly elated by these unexpected signs of popular goodwill and compassion. He entered his dwelling in high spirits. It speedily resumed its old aspect. Roman Catholic priests, who had, during the preceding week, been glad to hide themselves from the rage of the multitude in vaults and cocklofts, now came forth from their lurking places, and demanded possession of their old apartments in the palace. Grace was said at the royal table by a Jesuit. The Irish brogue, then the most hateful of all sounds to English ears, was heard everywhere in the courts and galleries. The King himself had resumed all his old haughtiness. He held a Council, his last council, and, even in that extremity, summoned to the board persons not legally qualified to sit there. He expressed high displeasure at the conduct of those Lords who, during his absence, had dared to take the administration on themselves. It was their duty, he conceived, to let society be dissolved, to let the houses of Ambassadors be pulled down, to let London be set on fire, rather than assume the functions which he had thought fit to abandon. Among those whom he thus censured were some nobles and prelates who, in spite of all his errors, had been constantly true to him, and who, even after this provocation, never could be induced by hope or fear to transfer their allegiance from him to any other sovereign.*

But his courage was soon cast down. Scarcely had he entered his palace when Zulestein was announced. William's cold and stern message was delivered. The King still pressed for a personal conference with his nephew. "I would not have left Rochester," he said, "if I had known that he wished me not to do so: but, since I am here, I hope that he will come to Saint James's." "I must plainly tell Your Majesty," said Zulestein, "that His Highness will not come to London while there are any troops here which are not under his orders." The King, confounded by this answer, remained silent. Zulestein retired; and soon a gentleman entered the bedchamber with the news that Feversham had been put under arrest.† James was greatly disturbed. Yet the recollection of the applause with which he had been greeted still buoyed up his spirits. A wild hope rose in his mind. He fancied that London, so long the stronghold of Protestantism

* London Gazette, Dec. 18, 1688; 702.; Evelyn's Diary, Dec. 13, 17, 1688. Mulgrave's Account of the Revolution; † History of James, ii. 263. Orig. History of the Desertion; Burnet, i. Mem.

CHAP. X.

and Whiggism, was ready to take arms in his defence. He sent to ask the Common Council whether, if he took up his residence in the City, they would engage to defend him against the Prince. But the Common Council had not forgotten the seizure of the charter and the judicial murder of Cornish, and refused to give the pledge which was demanded. Then the King's heart again sank within him. Where, he asked, was he to look for protection? He might as well have Dutch troops about him as his own Life Guards. As to the citizens, he now understood what their huzzas and bonfires were worth. Nothing remained but flight; and yet, he said, he knew that there was nothing which his enemies so much desired as that he would fly.*

Consultation at Windsor.

While he was in this state of trepidation, his fate was the subject of grave deliberation at Windsor. The court of William was now crowded to overflowing with eminent men of all parties. Most of the chiefs of the Northern insurrection had joined him. Several of the Lords, who had, during the anarchy of the preceding week, taken upon themselves to act as a Provisional Government, had, as soon as the King returned, quitted London for the Dutch head quarters. One of these was Halifax. William had welcomed him with great satisfaction, but had not been able to suppress a sarcastic smile at seeing the ingenious and accomplished politician, who had aspired to be the umpire in that great contention, forced to abandon the middle course and to take a side. Among those who, at this conjuncture, repaired to Windsor were some men who had purchased the favour of James by ignominious services, and who were now impatient to atone, by betraying their master, for the crime of having betrayed their country. Such a man was Titus, who had sate at the Council board in defiance of law, and who had laboured to unite the Puritans with the Jesuits in a league against the constitution. Such a man was Williams, who had been converted by interest from a demagogue into a champion of prerogative, and who was now ready for a second apostasy. These men the Prince, with just contempt, suffered to wait at the door of his apartment in vain expectation of an audience.†

On Monday, the seventeenth of December, all the Peers who were at Windsor were summoned to a solemn consul-

* Barillon, Dec. 17. 1688; Life of James, ii. 271.
† Mulgrave's Account of the Revolution; Clarendon's Diary, Dec. 16. 1688.

lation at the Castle. The subject proposed for deliberation was what should be done with the King. William did not think it advisable to be present during the discussion. He retired; and Halifax was called to the chair. On one point the Lords were agreed. The King could not be suffered to remain where he was. That one prince should fortify himself in Whitehall and the other in Saint James's, that there should be two hostile garrisons within an area of a hundred acres, was universally felt to be inexpedient. Such an arrangement could scarcely fail to produce suspicions, insults, and bickerings which might end in blood. The assembled Lords, therefore, thought it advisable that James should be sent out of London. Ham, which had been built and decorated by Lauderdale, on the banks of the Thames, out of the plunder of Scotland and the bribes of France, and which was regarded as the most luxurious of villas, was proposed as a convenient retreat. When the Lords had come to this conclusion, they requested the Prince to join them. Their opinion was then communicated to him by Halifax. William listened and approved. A short message to the King was drawn up. "Whom," said William, "shall we send with it?" "Ought it not," said Halifax, "to be conveyed by one of Your Highness's officers?" "Nay, my Lord," answered the Prince; "by your favour, it is sent by the advice of your Lordships, and some of you ought to carry it." Then, without pausing to give time for remonstrance, he appointed Halifax, Shrewsbury, and Delamere to be the messengers.*

The resolution of the Lords appeared to be unanimous. But there were in the assembly those who by no means approved of the decision in which they affected to concur, and who wished to see the King treated with a severity which they did not venture openly to recommend. It is a remarkable fact that the chief of this party was a peer who had been a vehement Tory, and who afterwards died a Nonjuror, Clarendon. The rapidity with which, at this crisis, he went backward and forward from extreme to extreme, might seem incredible to people living in quiet times, but will not surprise those who have had an opportunity of watching the course of revolutions. He knew that the asperity, with which he had, in the royal presence, censured the whole

* Burnet, i. 800.; Clarendon's Diary, Dec. 17. 1688; Van Citters, Dec. 18. 1688.

system of government, had given mortal offence to his old master. On the other hand he might, as the uncle of the Princesses, hope to be great and rich in the new world which was about to commence. The English colony in Ireland regarded him as a friend and patron; and he felt that on the confidence and attachment of that great interest much of his importance depended. To such considerations as these the principles, which he had, during his whole life, ostentatiously professed, now gave way. He repaired to the Prince's closet, and represented the danger of leaving the King at liberty. The Protestants of Ireland were in extreme peril. There was only one way to secure their estates and their lives; and that was to keep His Majesty close prisoner. It might not be prudent to shut him up in an English castle. But he might be sent across the sea and confined in the fortress of Breda till the affairs of the British Islands were settled. If the Prince were in possession of such a hostage, Tyrconnel would probably lay down the sword of state; and the English ascendency would be restored in Ireland without a blow. If, on the other hand, James should escape to France and make his appearance at Dublin, accompanied by a foreign army, the consequences must be disastrous. William owned that there was great weight in these reasons: but it could not be. He knew his wife's temper, and he knew that she never would consent to such a step. Indeed it would not be for his own honour to treat his vanquished kinsman so ungraciously. Nor was it quite clear that generosity might not be the best policy. Who could say what effect such severity as Clarendon recommended might produce on the public mind of England? Was it impossible that the loyal enthusiasm, which the King's misconduct had extinguished, might revive as soon as it was known that he was within the walls of a foreign fortress? On these grounds William determined not to subject his father in law to personal restraint; and there can be little doubt that the determination was wise.*

James, while his fate was under discussion, remained at Whitehall, fascinated, as it seemed, by the greatness and nearness of the danger, and unequal to the exertion of either struggling or flying. In the evening news came that the Dutch had occupied Chelsea and Kensington. The King,

* Burnet, i. 800.; Conduct of the Duchess of Marlborough; Mulgrave's Account of the Revolution. Clarendon says nothing of this under the proper date; but see his Diary, August 19, 1689.

however, prepared to go to rest as usual. The Coldstream Guards were on duty at the palace. They were commanded by William Earl of Craven, an aged man, who, more than fifty years before, had been distinguished in war and love, who had led the forlorn hope at Creutznach with such courage that he had been patted on the shoulder by the great Gustavus, and who was believed to have won from a thousand rivals the heart of the unfortunate Queen of Bohemia. Craven was now in his eightieth year; but time had not tamed his spirit.*

It was past ten o'clock when he was informed that three battalions of the Prince's foot, mingled with some troops of horse, were pouring down the long avenue of Saint James's Park, with matches lighted, and in full readiness for action. Count Solmes, who commanded the foreigners, said that his orders were to take military possession of the posts round Whitehall, and exhorted Craven to retire peaceably. Craven swore that he would rather be cut in pieces: but when the King, who was undressing himself, learned what was passing, he forbade the stout old soldier to attempt a resistance which must have been ineffectual. By eleven the Coldstream Guards had withdrawn; and Dutch sentinels were pacing the rounds on every side of the palace. Some of the King's attendants asked whether he would venture to lie down surrounded by enemies. He answered that they could hardly use him worse than his own subjects had done, and, with the apathy of a man stupefied by disasters, went to bed and to sleep.†

Scarcely was the palace again quiet when it was again roused. A little after midnight the three Lords arrived from Windsor. Middleton was called up to receive them. They informed him that they were charged with an errand which did not admit of delay. The King was awakened from his first slumber; and they were ushered into his bedchamber. They delivered into his hand the letter with which they had been entrusted, and informed him that the Prince would be at Westminster in a few hours, and that His Majesty would do well to set out for Ham before ten in the morning. James made some difficulties. He did not like Ham. It was a pleasant place in the summer, but cold and comfortless

---

* Harte's Life of Gustavus Adolphus.
† Life of James, ii. 261, mostly from Orig. Mem.; Mulgrave's Account of the Revolution; Rapin de Thoyras. It must be remembered that in these events Rapin was himself an actor.

at Christmas, and was moreover unfurnished. Halifax answered that furniture should be instantly sent in. The three messengers retired, but were speedily followed by Middleton, who told them that the King would greatly prefer Rochester to Ham. They answered that they had not authority to accede to His Majesty's wish, but that they would instantly send off an express to the Prince, who was to lodge that night at Sion House. A courier started immediately, and returned before daybreak with William's consent. That consent, indeed, was most gladly given: for there could be no doubt that Rochester had been named because it afforded facilities for flight; and that James might fly was the first wish of his nephew.*

James sets out for Rochester.

On the morning of the eighteenth of December, a rainy and stormy morning, the royal barge was early at Whitehall stairs: and round it were eight or ten boats filled with Dutch soldiers. Several noblemen and gentlemen attended the King to the waterside. It is said, and may well be believed, that many tears were shed. For even the most zealous friend of liberty could scarcely have seen, unmoved, the sad and ignominious close of a dynasty which might have been so great. Shrewsbury did all in his power to soothe the fallen Sovereign. Even the bitter and vehement Delamere was softened. But it was observed that Halifax, who was generally distinguished by his tenderness to the vanquished, was, on this occasion, less compassionate than his two colleagues. The mock embassy to Hungerford was doubtless still rankling in his mind.†

While the King's barge was slowly working its way on rough waves down the river, brigade after brigade of the Prince's troops marched into London from the west. It had been wisely determined that the duty of the capital should be chiefly done by the British soldiers in the service of the States General. The three English regiments were quartered in and round the Tower, the three Scotch regiments in Southwark.‡

Arrival of William at St. James's.

In defiance of the weather a great multitude assembled between Albemarle House and Saint James's Palace to greet the Prince. Every hat, every cane, was adorned with an

* Life of James, II. 205. Orig. Mem.; Mulgrave's Account of the Revolution; Burnet, i. 801.; Van Citters, Dec. 18/28.
† Van Citters, Dec. 18/28. 1688; Evelyn's Diary, same date; Life of James, ii. 266, 267. Orig. Mem.
‡ Van Citters, December 18/28. 1688.

orange riband. The bells were ringing all over London. Candles for an illumination were disposed in the windows. Faggots for bonfires were heaped up in the streets. William, however, who had no taste for crowds and shouting, took the road through the Park. Before nightfall he arrived at Saint James's in a light carriage, accompanied by Schomberg. In a short time all the rooms and staircases in the palace were thronged by those who came to pay their court. Such was the press, that men of the highest rank were unable to elbow their way into the presence chamber.* While Westminster was in this state of excitement, the Common Council was preparing at Guildhall an address of thanks and congratulation. The Lord Mayor was unable to preside. He had never held up his head since the Chancellor had been dragged into the justice room in the garb of a collier. But the Aldermen and the other officers of the corporation were in their places. On the following day the magistrates of the City went in state to pay their duty to their deliverer. Their gratitude was eloquently expressed by their Recorder, Sir George Treby. Some princes of the House of Nassau, he said, had been the chief officers of a great republic. Others had worn the imperial crown. But the peculiar title of that illustrious line to the public veneration was this, that God had set it apart and consecrated it to the high office of defending truth and freedom against tyrants from generation to generation. On the same day all the prelates who were in town, Sancroft excepted, waited on the Prince in a body. Then came the clergy of London, the foremost men of their profession in knowledge, eloquence, and influence, with their Bishop at their head. With them were mingled some eminent dissenting ministers, whom Compton, much to his honour, treated with marked courtesy. A few months earlier, or a few months later, such courtesy would have been considered by many Churchmen as treason to the Church. Even then it was but too plain to a discerning eye that the armistice to which the Protestant sects had been forced would not long outlast the danger from which it had sprung. About a hundred Nonconformist divines, resident in the capital, presented a separate address. They were introduced by Devonshire, and were received with every mark of respect and kindness. The lawyers paid their homage, headed by Maynard, who, at

---

* Luttrell's Diary; Evelyn's Diary; Clarendon's Diary, Dec. 18. 1668; Revolution Politics.

CHAP. X.

ninety years of age, was as alert and clearheaded as when he stood up in Westminster Hall to accuse Strafford. "Mr. Serjeant," said the Prince, "you must have survived all the lawyers of your standing." "Yes, sir," said the old man, "and, but for Your Highness, I should have survived the laws too."*

But, though the addresses were numerous and full of eulogy, though the acclamations were loud, though the illuminations were splendid, though Saint James's Palace was too small for the crowd of courtiers, though the theatres were every night, from the pit to the ceiling, one blaze of orange ribands, William felt that the difficulties of his enterprise were but beginning. He had pulled a government down. The far harder task of reconstruction was now to be performed. From the moment of his landing till he reached London, he had exercised the authority which, by the laws of war, acknowledged throughout the civilised world, belongs to the commander of an army in the field. It was now necessary that he should exchange the character of a general for that of a magistrate; and this was no easy task. A single false step might be fatal; and it was impossible to take any step without offending prejudices and rousing angry passions.

He is advised to assume the crown by right of conquest.

Some of the Prince's advisers pressed him to assume the crown at once as his own by right of conquest, and then, as King, to send out, under his Great Seal, writs calling a Parliament. This course was strongly recommended by some eminent lawyers. It was, they said, the shortest way to what could otherwise be attained only through innumerable difficulties and disputes. It was in strict conformity with the auspicious precedent set after the battle of Bosworth by Henry the Seventh. It would also quiet the scruples which many respectable people felt as to the lawfulness of transferring allegiance from one ruler to another. Neither the law of England nor the Church of England recognised any right in subjects to depose a sovereign. But no jurist, no divine, had ever denied that a nation, overcome in war, might, without sin, submit to the decision of the God of battles. Thus, after the Chaldean conquest, the most pious and patriotic Jews did not think that they violated their duty to their native King by serving with loyalty the new master

* Fourth Collection of Papers relating to the present juncture of affairs in England, 1689; Burnet, i. 802, 803.; Calamy's Life and Times of Baxter, chapter xiv.

whom Providence had set over them. The three confessors, who were marvellously preserved in the furnace, held high office in the province of Babylon. Daniel was minister successively of the Assyrian who subjugated Judea, and of the Persian who subjugated Assyria. Nay, Jesus himself, who was, according to the flesh, a prince of the house of David, had, by commanding his countrymen to pay tribute to Cæsar, pronounced that foreign conquest annuls hereditary right and is a legitimate title to dominion. It was therefore probable that great numbers of Tories, though they could not, with a clear conscience, choose a king for themselves, would accept, without hesitation, a king given to them by the event of war.*

On the other side, however, there were reasons which greatly preponderated. The Prince could not claim the crown as won by his sword without a gross violation of faith. In his Manifesto he had declared that he had no design of conquering England; that those who imputed to him such a design foully calumniated, not only himself, but the patriotic noblemen and gentlemen who had invited him over; that the force which he brought with him was evidently inadequate to an enterprise so arduous; and that it was his full resolution to refer all the public grievances, and all his own pretensions, to a free Parliament. For no earthly object could it be right or wise that he should forfeit his word so solemnly pledged in the face of all Europe. Nor was it certain that, by calling himself a conqueror, he would have removed the scruples which made rigid Churchmen unwilling to acknowledge him as king. For, call himself what he might, all the world knew that he was not really a conqueror. It was notoriously a mere fiction to say that this great kingdom, with a mighty fleet on the sea, with a regular army of forty thousand men, and with a militia of a hundred and fifty thousand men, had been, without one siege or battle, reduced to the state of a province by fifteen thousand invaders. Such a fiction was not likely to quiet consciences really sensitive: but it could scarcely fail to gall the national pride, already sore and irritable. The English soldiers were in a temper which required the most delicate management. They were conscious that, in the late campaign, their part had not been brilliant. Captains and privates were alike impatient to prove that they had not given way before an inferior force from want of

* Burnet, I. 803.

courage. Some Dutch officers had been indiscreet enough to boast, at a tavern over their wine, that they had driven the King's army before them. This insult had raised among the English troops a ferment which, but for the Prince's prompt interference, would probably have ended in a terrible slaughter.* What, in such circumstances, was likely to be the effect of a proclamation announcing that the commander of the foreigners considered the whole island as lawful prize of war?

It was also to be remembered that, by putting forth such a proclamation, the Prince would at once abrogate all the rights of which he had declared himself the champion. For the authority of a foreign conqueror is not circumscribed by the customs and statutes of the conquered nation, but is, by its own nature, despotic. Either, therefore, it was not competent to William to declare himself King, or it was competent to him to declare the Great Charter and the Petition of Right nullities, to abolish trial by jury, and to raise taxes without the consent of Parliament. He might, indeed, reestablish the ancient constitution of the realm. But, if he did so, he did so in the exercise of an arbitrary discretion. English liberty would thenceforth be held by a base tenure. It would be, not as heretofore, an immemorial inheritance, but a recent gift which the generous master who had bestowed it might, if such had been his pleasure, have withheld.

He calls together the Lords and the members of the Parliaments of Charles II.

William therefore righteously and prudently determined to observe the promises contained in his Declaration, and to leave to the legislature the office of settling the government. So carefully did he avoid whatever looked like usurpation that he would not, without some semblance of parliamentary authority, take upon himself even to convoke the Estates of the Realm, or to direct the executive administration during the elections. Authority strictly parliamentary there was none in the state: but it was possible to bring together, in a few hours, an assembly which would be regarded by the nation with a large portion of the respect due to a Parliament. One Chamber might be formed of the numerous Lords Spiritual and Temporal who were then in London, and another of old members of the House of Commons and of the magistrates of the City. The scheme was ingenious, and was promptly executed. The Peers were summoned to Saint

* Gazette de France, Jan. 24/Feb. 3, 1689.

James's on the twenty-first of December. About seventy attended. The Prince requested them to consider the state of the country, and to lay before him the result of their deliberations. Shortly after appeared a notice inviting all gentlemen who had sate in the House of Commons during the reign of Charles the Second to attend His Highness on the morning of the twenty-sixth. The Aldermen of London were also summoned, and the Common Council was requested to send a deputation.*

It has often been asked, in a reproachful tone, why the invitation was not extended to the members of the Parliament which had been dissolved in the preceding year. The answer is obvious. One of the chief grievances of which the nation complained was the manner in which that Parliament had been elected. The majority of the burgesses had been returned by constituent bodies remodelled in a manner which was generally regarded as illegal, and which the Prince had, in his Declaration, condemned. James himself had, just before his downfall, consented to restore the old municipal franchises. It would surely have been the height of inconsistency in William, after taking up arms for the purpose of vindicating the invaded charters of corporations, to recognise persons chosen in defiance of those charters as the legitimate representatives of the towns of England.

On Saturday the twenty-second the Lords met in their own house. That day was employed in settling the order of proceeding. A clerk was appointed; and, as no confidence could be placed in any of the twelve Judges, some serjeants and barristers of great note were requested to attend, for the purpose of giving advice on legal points. It was resolved that on the Monday the state of the kingdom should be taken into consideration.†

The interval between the sitting of Saturday and the sitting of Monday was anxious and eventful. A strong party among the Peers still cherished the hope that the constitution and religion of England might be secured without the deposition of the King. This party resolved to move a solemn address to him, imploring him to consent to such terms as might remove the discontents and apprehensions which his past conduct had excited. Sancroft, who, since the return of

---

* History of the Desertion; Clarendon's Diary, Dec. 21, 1688; Burnet, i. 803, and Onslow's note.
† Clarendon's Diary, Dec. 21, 1688. Van Citters, same date.

James from Kent to Whitehall), had taken no part in public affairs, determined to come forth from his retreat on this occasion, and to put himself at the head of the Royalists. Several messengers were sent to Rochester with letters for the King. He was assured that his interests would be strenuously defended, if only he could, at this last moment, make up his mind to renounce designs abhorred by his people. Some respectable Roman Catholics followed him, in order to implore him, for the sake of their common faith, not to carry the vain contest further.*

The advice was good; but James was in no condition to take it. His understanding had always been dull and feeble; and, such as it was, womanish tremors and childish fancies now disabled him from using it. He was aware that his flight was the thing which his adherents most dreaded, and which his enemies most desired. Even if there had been serious personal risk in remaining, the occasion was one on which he ought to have thought it infamous to flinch: for the question was whether he and his posterity should reign on an ancestral throne, or should be vagabonds and beggars. But in his mind all other feelings had given place to a craven fear for his life. To the earnest entreaties and unanswerable arguments of the agents whom his friends had sent to Rochester, he had only one answer. His head was in danger. In vain he was assured that there was no ground for such an apprehension, that common sense, if not principle, would restrain his kinsman from incurring the guilt and shame of regicide and parricide, and that many, who never would consent to depose their Sovereign while he remained on English ground, would think themselves absolved from their allegiance by his desertion. Fright overpowered every other feeling. James determined to depart; and it was easy for him to do so. He was negligently guarded: all persons were suffered to repair to him: vessels ready to put to sea lay at no great distance, and their boats might come close to the garden of the house in which he was lodged. Had he been wise, the pains which his keepers took to facilitate his escape would have sufficed to convince him that he ought to stay where he was. In truth the snare was so ostentatiously exhibited that it could impose on nothing but folly bewildered by terror.

The arrangements were expeditiously made. On the evening

* Clarendon's Diary, Dec. 21, 22, 1688; Life of James, ii. 268, 270. Orig. Mem.

of Saturday the twenty-second the King assured some of the gentlemen who had been sent to him from London with intelligence and advice, that he would see them again in the morning. He went to bed, rose at dead of night, and, attended by Berwick, stole out at a back door, and went through the garden to the shore of the Medway. A small skiff was in waiting. Soon after the dawn of Sunday the fugitives were on board of a smack which was running down the Thames.*

That afternoon the tidings of the flight reached London. The King's adherents were confounded. The Whigs could not conceal their joy. The good news encouraged the Prince to take a bold and important step. He was informed that communications were passing between the French embassy and the party hostile to him. It was well known that at that embassy all the arts of corruption were well understood; and there could be little doubt that, at such a conjuncture, neither intrigues nor pistoles would be spared. Barillon was most desirous to remain a few days longer in London, and for that end omitted no art which could conciliate the victorious party. In the streets he quieted the populace, who looked angrily at his coach, by throwing money among them. At his table he publicly drank the health of the Prince of Orange. But William was not to be so cajoled. He had not, indeed, taken on himself to exercise regal authority: but he was a general: and, as such, he was not bound to tolerate, within the territory of which he had taken military occupation, the presence of one whom he regarded as a spy. Before that day closed Barillon was informed that he must leave England within twenty-four hours. He begged hard for a short delay: but minutes were precious; the order was repeated in more peremptory terms; and he unwillingly set off for Dover. That no mark of contempt and defiance might be omitted, he was escorted to the coast by one of his Protestant countrymen whom persecution had driven into exile. So bitter was the resentment excited by the French ambition and arrogance that even those Englishmen who were not generally disposed to take a favourable view of William's conduct loudly applauded him for retorting with so much spirit the insolence with which Lewis had, during many years, treated every court in Europe.†

---

* Clarendon, Dec. 23. 1688; Life of James, ii. 271. 273. 276. Orig. Mem. † Van Citters, Jan. 4/14. 1689; Witsen MS. quoted by Wagenaar, book lx.

CHAP. X.

Debates and resolutions of the Lords.

On Monday the Lords met again. Halifax was chosen to preside. The Primate was absent, the Royalists sad and gloomy, the Whigs eager and in high spirits. It was known that James had left a letter behind him. Some of his friends moved that it might be produced, in the faint hope that it might contain propositions which might furnish a basis for a happy settlement. On this motion the previous question was put and carried. Godolphin, who was known not to be unfriendly to his old master, uttered a few words which were decisive. "I have seen the paper," he said; "and I grieve to say that there is nothing in it which will give your Lordships any satisfaction." In truth it contained no expression of regret for past errors: it held out no hope that those errors would in future be avoided; and it threw the blame of all that had happened on the malice of William and on the blindness of a nation deluded by the specious names of religion and property. None ventured to propose that a negotiation should be opened with a prince whom the most rigid discipline of adversity seemed only to have made more obstinate in wrong. Something was said about inquiring into the birth of the Prince of Wales; but the Whig peers treated the suggestion with disdain. "I did not expect, my Lords," exclaimed Philip, Lord Wharton, an old Roundhead, who had commanded a regiment against Charles the First at Edgehill, "I did not expect to hear anybody at this time of day mention the child who was called Prince of Wales; and I hope that we have now heard the last of him." After long discussion it was resolved that two addresses should be presented to William. One address requested him to take on himself provisionally the administration of the government; the other recommended that he should, by circular letters subscribed with his own hand, invite all the constituent bodies of the kingdom to send up representatives to Westminster. At the same time the Peers took upon themselves to issue an order banishing all Papists, except a few privileged persons, from London and the vicinity.*

The Lords presented their addresses to the Prince on the following day, without waiting for the issue of the deliberations of the commoners whom he had called together. It seems, indeed, that the hereditary nobles were disposed at this

* Halifax's notes; Lansdowne MS. 255.; Clarendon's Diary, December 24. 1688; London Gazette, December 31.

moment to be punctilious in asserting their dignity, and were unwilling to recognise a coordinate authority in an assembly unknown to the law. They conceived that they were a real House of Lords. The other Chamber they despised as only a mock House of Commons. William, however, wisely excused himself from coming to any decision till he had ascertained the sense of the gentlemen who had formerly been honoured with the confidence of the counties and towns of England.*

CHAP.
X.

The commoners who had been summoned met in Saint Stephen's Chapel, and formed a numerous assembly. They placed in the chair Henry Powle, who had represented Cirencester in several Parliaments, and had been eminent among the supporters of the Exclusion Bill.

Debates and resolutions of the commoners summoned by the Prince.

Addresses were proposed and adopted similar to those which the Lords had already presented. No difference of opinion appeared on any serious question; and some feeble attempts which were made to raise a debate on points of form were put down by the general contempt. Sir Robert Sawyer declared that he could not conceive how it was possible for the Prince to administer the government without some distinguishing title, such as Regent or Protector. Old Maynard, who as a lawyer, had no equal, and who was also a politician versed in the tactics of revolutions, was at no pains to conceal his disdain for so puerile an objection, taken at a moment when union and promptitude were of the highest importance. "We shall sit here very long," he said, "if we sit till Sir Robert can conceive how such a thing is possible;" and the assembly thought the answer as good as the cavil deserved."†

The resolutions of the meeting were communicated to the Prince. He forthwith announced his determination to comply with the joint request of the two Chambers which he had called together, to issue letters summoning a Convention of the Estates of the Realm, and, till the Convention should meet, to take on himself the executive administration.‡

A Convention called.

He had undertaken no light task. The whole machine of government was disordered. The Justices of the Peace had abandoned their functions. The officers of the revenue had ceased to collect the taxes. The army which Feversham had

Exertions of the Prince to restore order.

* Van Citters, Dec. 28/Jan. 7 1688.
† The objector was designated in contemporary books and pamphlets only by his initials; and these were sometimes misinterpreted. Echard attributes the cavil to Sir Robert Southwell. But I have little doubt that Oldmixon is right in putting it into the mouth of Sawyer.
‡ History of the Desertion; Life of William, 1703; Van Citters, Dec. 28/Jan. 7 1688.

disbanded was still in confusion, and ready to break out into mutiny. The fleet was in a scarcely less alarming state. Large arrears of pay were due to the civil and military servants of the crown; and only forty thousand pounds remained in the Exchequer. The Prince addressed himself with vigour to the work of restoring order. He published a proclamation by which all magistrates were continued in office, and another containing orders for the collection of the revenue.* The new modelling of the army went rapidly on. Many of the noblemen and gentlemen who had been removed from the command of the English regiments were reappointed. A way was found of employing the thousands of Irish soldiers whom James had brought into England. They could not safely be suffered to remain in a country where they were objects of religious and national animosity. They could not safely be sent home to reinforce the army of Tyrconnel. It was therefore determined that they should be conveyed to the Continent, where they might, under the banners of the House of Austria, render indirect but effectual service to the cause of the English constitution and of the Protestant religion. Dartmouth was removed from his command; and the navy was conciliated by assurances that every sailor should speedily receive his due. The City of London undertook to extricate the Prince from his financial difficulties. The Common Council, by an unanimous vote, engaged to find him two hundred thousand pounds. It was thought a great proof, both of the wealth and of the public spirit of the merchants of the capital, that, in forty-eight hours, the whole sum was raised on no security but the Prince's word. A few weeks before, James had been unable to procure a much smaller loan, though he had offered to pay higher interest, and to pledge valuable property.†

His tolerant policy.

In a very few days the confusion, which the invasion, the insurrection, the flight of James, and the suspension of all regular government had produced, was at an end, and the kingdom wore again its accustomed aspect. There was a general sense of security. Even the classes which were most obnoxious to public hatred, and which had most reason to apprehend persecution, were protected by the politic clemency

---

* London Gazette, Jan. 3. 7. 168⁹⁄₉.
† London Gazette, January 10. 17. 168⁹⁄₉; Luttrell's Diary; Legge Papers; Van Citters, January ⁷⁄₁₇. ¹⁰⁄₂₀. ¹¹⁄₂₁. 1689;

Ronquillo, January ¹⁴⁄₂₄. ²¹⁄₃₁.; Consultation of the Spanish Council of State, Mar. 24.

of the conqueror. Persons deeply implicated in the illegal transactions of the late reign not only walked the streets in safety, but offered themselves as candidates for seats in the Convention. Mulgrave was received not ungraciously at Saint James's. Feversham was released from arrest, and was permitted to resume the only office for which he was qualified, that of keeping the bank at the Queen Dowager's basset table. But no body of men had so much reason to feel grateful to William as the Roman Catholics. It would not have been safe to rescind formally the severe resolutions which the Peers had passed against the professors of a religion generally abhorred by the nation: but, by the prudence and humanity of the Prince, those resolutions were practically annulled. On his line of march from Torbay to London, he had given orders that no outrage should be committed on the persons or dwellings of Papists. He now renewed those orders, and directed Burnet to see that they were strictly obeyed. A better choice could not have been made; for Burnet was a man of such generosity and good nature, that his heart always warmed towards the unhappy; and at the same time his known hatred of Popery was a sufficient guarantee to the most zealous Protestants that the interests of their religion would be safe in his hands. He listened kindly to the complaints of the Roman Catholics, procured passports for those who wished to go beyond sea, and went himself to Newgate to visit the prelates who were imprisoned there. He ordered them to be removed to a more commodious apartment and supplied with every indulgence. He solemnly assured them that not a hair of their heads should be touched, and that, as soon as the Prince could venture to act as he wished, they should be set at liberty. The Spanish minister reported to his government, and, through his government, to the Pope, that no Catholic need feel any scruple of conscience on account of the late revolution in England, that for the danger to which the members of the true Church were exposed James alone was responsible, and that William alone had saved them from a sanguinary persecution.*

* Burnet, I. 802.; Ronquillo, Jan. 4/14, Feb. 4/14, 1689. The originals of these despatches were entrusted to me by the kindness of the late Lady Holland and of the present Lord Holland. From the latter despatch I will quote a very few words: "La toma de S. M. Britanica á acquir imprudentes consejos perdió á los Catolicos aquella quietud en que los dexó Carlos segundo. V. E. asegure á su Santidad que mas seguro del Principe para los Catolicos que pudiera ser del Rey."

There was, therefore, little alloy to the satisfaction with which the princes of the House of Austria and the Sovereign Pontiff learned that the long vassalage of England was at an end. When it was known at Madrid that William was in the full career of success, a single voice in the Spanish Council of State faintly expressed regret that an event which, in a political point of view, was most auspicious, should be prejudicial to the interests of the true Church.* But the tolerant policy of the Prince soon quieted all scruples, and his elevation was seen with scarcely less satisfaction by the bigoted Grandees of Castile than by the English Whigs.

With very different feelings had the news of this great revolution been received in France. The politics of a long, eventful, and glorious reign had been confounded in a day. England was again the England of Elizabeth and of Cromwell; and all the relations of all the states of Christendom were completely changed by the sudden introduction of this new power into the system. The Parisians could talk of nothing but what was passing in London. National and religious feeling impelled them to take the part of James. They knew nothing of the English constitution. They abominated the English Church. Our revolution appeared to them, not as the triumph of public liberty over despotism, but as a frightful domestic tragedy in which a venerable and pious Servius was hurled from his throne by a Tarquin, and crushed under the chariot wheels of a Tullia. They cried shame on the traitorous captains, execrated the unnatural daughters, and regarded William with a mortal loathing, tempered, however, by the respect which valour, capacity, and success seldom fail to inspire.† The Queen, exposed to the night wind and rain, with the infant heir of three crowns clasped to her breast, the King stopped, robbed, and outraged by ruffians, were objects of pity and of romantic interest to all France. But Lewis saw with peculiar emotion the calamities of the House of Stuart. All the selfish and all the generous

---

* On December 11, 1688, the Admiral of Castile gave his opinion thus: "Esta materia es de calidad que no puede dexar de padecer nuestra sagrada religion ó el servicio de V. M.; porque, si el Principe de Orange tiene buenos successos, nos aseguraremos de Franceses, pero peligrará la religion." The Council was much pleased on February 14, by a letter of the Prince, in which he promised "que los Catolicos que se portarren con prudencia no sean molestados, y guera libertad de conciencia, pues ser contra su dictamen el forzar ni castigar por esta razon á nadie."

† In the chapter of La Bruyère, entitled "Sur les Jugemens," is a passage which deserves to be read, as showing in what light our revolution appeared to a Frenchman of distinguished abilities.

parts of his nature were moved alike. After many years of prosperity he had at length met with a great check. He had reckoned on the support or neutrality of England. He had now nothing to expect from her but energetic and pertinacious hostility. A few weeks earlier he might not unreasonably have hoped to subjugate Flanders and to give law to Germany. At present he might think himself fortunate if he should be able to defend his own frontiers against a confederacy such as Europe had not seen during many ages. From this position, so new, so embarrassing, so alarming, nothing but a counter revolution or a civil war in the British Islands could extricate him. He was therefore impelled by ambition and by fear to espouse the cause of the fallen dynasty. And it is but just to say that motives nobler than ambition or fear had a large share in determining his course. His heart was naturally compassionate; and this was an occasion which could not fail to call forth all his compassion. His situation had prevented his good feelings from fully developing themselves. Sympathy is rarely strong where there is a great inequality of condition; and he was raised so high above the mass of his fellow creatures that their distresses excited in him only a languid pity, such as that with which we regard the sufferings of the inferior animals, of a famished redbreast, or of an overdriven posthorse. The devastation of the Palatinate and the persecution of the Huguenots had therefore given him no uneasiness which pride and bigotry could not effectually soothe. But all the tenderness of which he was capable was called forth by the misery of a great King who had a few weeks ago been served on the knee by Lords, and who was now a destitute exile. With that tenderness was mingled, in the soul of Lewis, a not ignoble vanity. He would exhibit to the world a pattern of munificence and courtesy. He would show mankind what ought to be the bearing of a perfect gentleman in the highest station and on the greatest occasion; and, in truth, his conduct was marked by a chivalrous generosity and urbanity, such as had not embellished the annals of Europe since the Black Prince had stood behind the chair of King John at the supper on the field of Poitiers.

As soon as the news that the Queen of England was on the French coast had been brought to Versailles, a palace was prepared for her reception. Carriages and troops of guards were despatched to await her orders. Workmen

Reception of the Queen of England in France.

were employed to mend the Calais road that her journey might be easy. Lauzun was not only assured that his past offences were forgiven for her sake, but was honoured with a friendly letter in the handwriting of Lewis. Mary was on the road towards the French court when news came that her husband had, after a rough voyage, landed safe at the little village of Ambleteuse. Persons of high rank were instantly despatched from Versailles to greet and escort him. Meanwhile Lewis, attended by his family and his nobility, went forth in state to receive the exiled Queen. Before his gorgeous coach went the Swiss halberdiers. On each side of it and behind it rode the body guards with cymbals clashing and trumpets pealing. After the King, in a hundred carriages each drawn by six horses, came the most splendid aristocracy of Europe, all feathers, ribands, jewels, and embroidery. Before the procession had gone far it was announced that Mary was approaching. Lewis alighted and advanced on foot to meet her. She broke forth into passionate expressions of gratitude. "Madam," said her host, "it is but a melancholy service that I am rendering you today. I hope that I may be able hereafter to render you services greater and more pleasing." He embraced the little Prince of Wales, and made the Queen seat herself in the royal state coach on the right hand. The cavalcade then turned towards Saint Germains.

At Saint Germains, on the verge of a forest swarming with beasts of chase, and on the brow of a hill which looks down on the windings of the Seine, Francis the First had built a castle, and Henry the Fourth had constructed a noble terrace. Of the residences of the French kings none stood in a more salubrious air or commanded a fairer prospect. The huge size and venerable age of the trees, the beauty of the gardens, the abundance of the springs, were widely famed. Lewis the Fourteenth had been born there, had, when a young man, held his court there, had added several stately pavilions to the mansion of Francis, and had completed the terrace of Henry. Soon, however, the magnificent King conceived an inexplicable disgust for his birthplace. He quitted Saint Germains for Versailles, and expended sums almost fabulous in the vain attempt to create a paradise on a spot singularly sterile and unwholesome, all sand or mud, without wood, without water, and without game. Saint Germains had now been selected to be

the abode of the royal family of England. Sumptuous
furniture had been hastily sent in. The nursery of the
Prince of Wales had been carefully furnished with everything that an infant could require. One of the attendants
presented to the Queen the key of a superb casket which
stood in her apartment. She opened the casket, and found
in it six thousand pistoles.

On the following day James arrived at Saint Germains.
Lewis was already there to welcome him. The unfortunate
exile bowed so low that it seemed as if he was about to embrace the knees of his protector. Lewis raised him, and
embraced him with brotherly tenderness. The two Kings
then entered the Queen's room. "Here is a gentleman,"
said Lewis to Mary, "whom you will be glad to see." Then,
after entreating his guests to visit him next day at Versailles,
and to let him have the pleasure of showing them his buildings, pictures, and plantations, he took the unceremonious
leave of an old friend.

In a few hours the royal pair were informed that, as long
as they would do the King of France the favour to accept of
his hospitality, forty-five thousand pounds sterling a year
would be paid them from his treasury. Ten thousand pounds
sterling were sent for outfit.

The liberality of Lewis, however, was much less rare and
admirable than the exquisite delicacy with which he laboured
to soothe the feelings of his guests and to lighten the almost
intolerable weight of the obligations which he laid upon
them. He who had hitherto, on all questions of precedence,
been sensitive, litigious, insolent, who had been more than
once ready to plunge Europe into war rather than concede
the most frivolous point of etiquette, was now punctilious indeed, but punctilious for his unfortunate friends against himself. He gave orders that Mary should receive all the marks
of respect that had ever been paid to his own deceased wife.
A question was raised whether the Princes of the House of
Bourbon were entitled to be indulged with chairs in the presence of the Queen. Such trifles were serious matters at the
old court of France. There were precedents on both sides:
but Lewis decided the point against his own blood. Some
ladies of illustrious rank omitted the ceremony of kissing the
hem of Mary's robe. Lewis remarked the omission, and
noticed it in such a voice and with such a look that the
whole peerage was ever after ready to kiss her shoe. When

Esther, just written by Racine, was acted at Saint Cyr, Mary had the seat of honour. James was at her right hand. Lewis modestly placed himself on the left. Nay, he was well pleased that, in his own palace, an outcast living on his bounty should assume the title of King of France, should, as King of France, quarter the lilies with the English lions, and should, as King of France, dress in violet on days of court mourning.

The demeanour of the French nobility on public occasions was absolutely regulated by their sovereign: but it was beyond even his power to prevent them from thinking freely, and from expressing what they thought, in private circles, with the keen and delicate wit characteristic of their nation and of their order. Their opinion of Mary was favourable. They found her person agreeable and her deportment dignified: they respected her courage and her maternal affection; and they pitied her ill fortune. But James they regarded with extreme contempt. They were disgusted by his insensibility, by the cool way in which he talked to everybody of his ruin, and by the childish pleasure which he took in the pomp and luxury of Versailles. This strange apathy they attributed, not to philosophy or religion, but to stupidity and meanness of spirit, and remarked that nobody who had had the honour to hear His Britannic Majesty tell his own story could wonder that he was at Saint Germains and his son in law at Saint James's.*

State of feeling in the United Provinces.

In the United Provinces the excitement produced by the tidings from England was even greater than in France. This was the moment at which the Batavian federation reached the highest point of power and glory. From the day on which the expedition sailed, the anxiety of the whole Dutch nation had been intense. Never had there been such crowds in the churches. Never had the enthusiasm of the preachers been so ardent. The inhabitants of the Hague could not be restrained from insulting Albeville. His house was so closely beset by the populace, day and night, that scarcely any person ventured to visit him; and he was afraid that his chapel would be burned to the ground.† As mail after mail arrived with news of the Prince's progress, the

---

* My account of the reception of James and his wife in France is taken chiefly from the letters of Madame de Sévigné and the Memoirs of Dangeau.
† Albeville to Preston, Nov. 23, Dec. 2, 1688, in Mackintosh Collection.

spirits of his countrymen rose higher and higher; and when at length it was known that he had, on the invitation of the Lords and of an assembly of eminent commoners, taken on himself the executive administration, a general cry of pride and joy rose from all the Dutch factions. An extraordinary mission was, with great speed, despatched to congratulate him. Dykvelt, whose adroitness and intimate knowledge of English politics made his assistance, at such a conjuncture, peculiarly valuable, was one of the Ambassadors; and with him was joined Nicholas Witsen, a Burgomaster of Amsterdam, who seems to have been selected for the purpose of proving to all Europe that the long feud between the House of Orange and the chief city of Holland was at an end. On the eighth of January Dykvelt and Witsen made their appearance at Westminster. William talked to them with a frankness and an effusion of heart which seldom appeared in his conversations with Englishmen. His first words were, "Well, and what do our friends at home say now?" In truth, the only applause by which his stoical nature seems to have been strongly moved was the applause of his dear native country. Of his immense popularity in England he spoke with cold disdain, and predicted, too truly, the reaction which followed. "Here," said he, "the cry is all Hosannah today, and will, perhaps, be Crucify tomorrow."*

On the following day the first members of the Convention were chosen. The City of London led the way, and elected, without any contest, four great merchants who were zealous Whigs. The King and his adherents had hoped that many returning officers would treat the Prince's letter as a nullity; but the hope was disappointed. The elections went on rapidly and smoothly. There were scarcely any contests. For the nation had, during more than a year, been kept in constant expectation of a Parliament. Writs, indeed, had been issued and recalled. Some constituent bodies had, under those writs, actually proceeded to the choice of representatives. There was scarcely a county in which the gentry and

CHAP. X.

Election of members to serve in the Convention.

* "Tis hier as Hosanna: maar 't sal veelligt, haast Kruist hem, Kruist hem, syn."— Witsen, MS. In Wagenaar, book lxi. It is an odd coincidence that, a very few years before, Richard Duke, a Tory poet, once well known, but now scarcely remembered, except by Johnson's biographical sketch, had used exactly the same illustration about James: "Was not of old the Jewish rabble's cry, Hosannah first, and after crucify?" The Review. Despatch of the Dutch Ambassadors Extraordinary, Jan. 8/18. 1689; Van Citters, same date.

yeomanry had not, many months before, fixed upon candidates, good Protestants, whom no exertions must be spared to carry, in defiance of the King and of the Lord Lieutenant; and these candidates were now generally returned without opposition.

The Prince gave strict orders that no person in the public service should, on this occasion, practise those arts which had brought so much obloquy on the late government. He especially directed that no soldiers should be suffered to appear in any town where an election was going on.* His admirers were able to boast, and his enemies seem not to have been able to deny, that the sense of the constituent bodies was fairly taken. It is true that he risked little. The party which was attached to him was triumphant, enthusiastic, full of life and energy. The party from which alone he could expect serious opposition was disunited and disheartened, out of humour with itself, and still more out of humour with its natural chief. A great majority, therefore, of the shires and boroughs returned Whig members.

Affairs of Scotland.

It was not over England alone that William's guardianship now extended. Scotland had risen on her tyrants. All the regular soldiers by whom she had long been held down had been summoned by James to his help against the Dutch invaders, with the exception of a very small force, which, under the command of the Duke of Gordon, a great Roman Catholic Lord, garrisoned the Castle of Edinburgh. Every mail which had gone northward during the eventful month of November had carried news which stirred the passions of the oppressed Scots. While the event of the military operations was still doubtful, there were disturbances at Edinburgh; and those disturbances became more formidable after James had retreated from Salisbury. Great crowds assembled at first by night, and then by broad daylight. Popes were publicly burned: loud shouts were raised for a free Parliament; placards were stuck up setting prices on the heads of the ministers of the crown. Among those ministers Perth, as filling the great place of Chancellor, as standing high in the royal favour, as an apostate from the reformed faith, and as the man who had first introduced the thumbscrew into the jurisprudence of his country, was the most detested. His nerves were weak: his spirit was abject; and the only courage which he possessed was that evil courage which

* London Gazette, Jan. 7. 168⁸⁄₉.

braves infamy, and which looks steadily on the torments of others. His post, at such a time, was at the head of the Council board; but his heart failed him, and he determined to take refuge at his country seat from the danger which, as he judged by the looks and the cries of the fierce and resolute populace of Edinburgh, was not remote. A strong guard escorted him safe to Castle Drummond; but scarcely had he departed when the city rose up. A few troops tried to suppress the insurrection, but were overpowered. The palace of Holyrood, which had been turned into a Roman Catholic seminary and printing house, was stormed and sacked. Huge heaps of Popish books, beads, crucifixes, and pictures were burned in the High Street. In the midst of the agitation came down the tidings of the King's flight. The members of the government gave up all thought of contending with the popular fury, and changed sides with a promptitude then common among Scottish politicians. The Privy Council by one proclamation ordered that all Papists should be disarmed, and by another invited Protestants to muster for the defence of pure religion. The nation had not waited for the call. Town and country were already up in arms for the Prince of Orange. Nithisdale and Clydesdale were the only regions in which there was the least chance that the Roman Catholics would make head; and both Nithisdale and Clydesdale were soon occupied by bands of armed Presbyterians. Among the insurgents were some fierce and moody men who had formerly disowned Argyle, and who were now equally eager to disown William. His Highness, they said, was plainly a malignant. There was not a word about the Covenant in his Declaration. The Dutch were a people with whom no true servant of the Lord would unite. They consorted with Lutherans; and a Lutheran was as much a child of perdition as a Jesuit. The general voice of the kingdom, however, effectually drowned the growl of this hateful faction.*

The commotion soon reached the neighbourhood of Castle Drummond. Perth found that he was no longer safe among his own servants and tenants. He gave himself up to an agony as bitter as that into which his merciless tyranny had often thrown better men. He wildly tried to find consolation in the rites of his new Church. He importuned his priests for comfort, prayed, confessed, and communicated; but his

* The Sixth Collection of Papers, 151.; Faithful Contendings Displayed; 1680; Wodrow, III. xii. 4. App. 150. Burnet, I. 801.

faith was weak; and he owned that, in spite of all his devotions, the strong terrors of death were upon him. At this time he learned that he had a chance of escaping on board of a ship which lay off Brentisland. He disguised himself as well as he could, and, after a long and difficult journey by unfrequented paths over the Ochil mountains, which were then deep in snow, he succeeded in embarking; but, in spite of all his precautions, he had been recognised, and the alarm had been given. As soon as it was known that the cruel renegade was on the waters, and that he had gold with him, pursuers, inflamed at once by hatred and by avarice, were on his track. A skiff, commanded by an old buccaneer, overtook the flying vessel and boarded her. Perth was dragged out of the hold on deck in woman's clothes, stripped, hustled, and plundered. Bayonets were held to his breast. Begging for life with unmanly cries, he was hurried to the shore, and flung into the common gaol of Kirkaldy. Thence, by order of the Council over which he had lately presided, and which was filled with men who had been partakers in his guilt, he was removed to Stirling Castle. It was on a Sunday, during the time of public worship, that he was conveyed under a guard to his place of confinement: but even rigid Puritans forgot the sanctity of the day. The churches poured forth their congregations as the torturer passed by, and the noise of threats, execrations, and screams of hatred accompanied him to the gate of his prison.*

Several eminent Scotsmen were in London when the Prince arrived there; and many others now hastened thither to pay their court to him. On the seventh of January he requested them to attend him at Whitehall. The assemblage was large and respectable. The Duke of Hamilton and his eldest son, the Earl of Arran, the chiefs of a house of almost regal dignity, appeared at the head of the procession. They were accompanied by thirty Lords and about eighty gentlemen of note. William desired them to consult together, and to let him know in what way he could best promote the welfare of their country. He then withdrew, and left them to deliberate unrestrained by his presence. They repaired to the Council chamber, and put Hamilton into the chair. Though there seems to have been little difference of opinion, their debates lasted three days, a fact which is sufficiently explained by the

* Perth to Lady Errol, Dec. 29. 1688; to Melfort, Dec. 21. 1688; Sixth Collection of Papers, 1689.

circumstance that Sir Patrick Hume was one of the debaters. Arran ventured to recommend a negotiation with the King. But this motion was ill received by the mover's father and by the whole assembly, and did not even find a seconder. At length resolutions were carried closely resembling the resolutions which the English Lords and Commoners had presented to the Prince a few days before. He was requested to call together a Convention of the Estates of Scotland, to fix the fourteenth of March for the day of meeting, and, till that day, to take on himself the civil and military administration. To this request he acceded: and thenceforth the government of the whole island was in his hands.*

The decisive moment approached; and the agitation of the public mind rose to the height. Knots of politicians were whispering and consulting in every part of London. The coffeehouses were in a ferment. The presses were hard at work. Of the pamphlets which appeared at that time enough may still be collected to form several volumes; and from those pamphlets it is not difficult to gather a correct notion of the state of parties.

There was a very small faction which wished to recall James without stipulations. There was also a very small faction which wished to set up a commonwealth, and to entrust the administration to a council of state under the presidency of the Prince of Orange. But these extreme opinions were generally held in abhorrence. Nineteen twentieths of the nation consisted of persons in whom love of hereditary monarchy and love of constitutional freedom were combined, though in different proportions, and who were equally opposed to the total abolition of the kingly office and to the unconditional restoration of the King.

But, in the wide interval which separated the bigots who still clung to the doctrines of Filmer from the enthusiasts who still dreamed the dreams of Harrington, there was room for many shades of opinion. If we neglect minute subdivisions, we shall find that the great majority of the nation and of the Convention was divided into four bodies. Three of these bodies consisted of Tories. The Whig party formed the fourth.

The amity of the Whigs and Tories had not survived the peril which had produced it. On several occasions, during the Prince's march from the West, dissension had appeared

* Burnet, i. 805.; Sixth Collection of Papers, 1689.

among his followers. While the event of his enterprise was doubtful, that dissension had, by his skilful management, been easily quieted. But, from the day on which he entered Saint James's palace in triumph, such management could no longer be practised. His victory, by relieving the nation from the strong dread of Popish tyranny, had deprived him of half his influence. Old antipathies, which had slept when Bishops were in the Tower, when Jesuits were at the Council board, when loyal clergymen were deprived of their bread by scores, when loyal gentlemen were put out of the commission of the peace by hundreds, were again strong and active. The Royalist shuddered at the thought that he was allied with all that from his youth up he had most hated, with old parliamentary Captains who had stormed his country house, with old parliamentary Commissioners who had sequestrated his estate, with men who had plotted the Rye House butchery and headed the Western rebellion. That beloved Church, too, for whose sake he had, after a painful struggle, broken through his allegiance to the throne, was she really in safety? Or had he rescued her from one enemy only that she might be exposed to another? The Popish priests, indeed, were in exile, in hiding, or in prison. No Jesuit or Benedictine who valued his life now dared to show himself in the habit of his order. But the Presbyterian and Independent teachers went in long procession to salute the chief of the government, and were as graciously received as the true successors of the Apostles. Some schismatics avowed the hope that every fence which excluded them from ecclesiastical preferment would soon be levelled; that the Articles would be softened down; that the Liturgy would be garbled; that Christmas would cease to be a feast; that Good Friday would cease to be a fast; that canons on whom no Bishop had ever laid his hand would, without the sacred vestment of white linen, distribute, in the choirs of Cathedrals, the eucharistic bread and wine to communicants lolling on benches. The Prince, indeed, was not a fanatical Presbyterian; but he was at best a Latitudinarian. He had no scruple about communicating in the Anglican form; but he cared not in what form other people communicated. His wife, it was to be feared, had imbibed too much of his spirit. Her conscience was under the direction of Burnet. She heard preachers of different Protestant sects. She had recently said that she saw no essential difference between the Church of England and the other reformed Churches.* It was necessary, therefore, that the Cavaliers should, at this conjuncture, follow the example set by their fathers in 1641, should draw off from Roundheads and sectaries, and should, in spite of all the faults of the hereditary monarch, uphold the cause of hereditary monarchy.

The body which was animated by these sentiments was large and respectable. It included about one half of the House of Lords, about one third of the House of Commons, a majority of the country gentlemen, and at least nine tenths of the clergy; but it was torn by dissensions, and beset on every side by difficulties.

One section of this great party, a section which was especially strong among divines, and of which Sherlock was the chief organ, wished that a negotiation should be opened with James, and that he should be invited to return to Whitehall on such conditions as might fully secure the civil and ecclesiastical constitution of the realm.† It is evident that this plan, though strenuously supported by the clergy, was altogether inconsistent with the doctrines which the clergy had been teaching during many years. It was, in truth, an attempt to make a middle way where there was no room for a middle way, to effect a compromise between two things which do not admit of compromise, resistance and nonresistance. The Tories had formerly taken their stand on the principle of nonresistance. But that ground most of them had now abandoned, and were not disposed again to occupy. The Cavaliers of England had, as a class, been so deeply concerned, directly or indirectly, in the late rising against the King, that they could not, for very shame, talk at that moment about the sacred duty of obeying Nero; nor, indeed, were they disposed to recall the prince under whose misgovernment they had suffered so much, without exacting from him terms which might make it impossible for him again to abuse his power. They were, therefore, in a false position. Their old theory, sound or unsound, was at least complete and coherent. If that theory were sound, the King ought to be immediately invited back, and permitted, if such were his pleasure, to put Seymour and Danby, the Bishop of London and the Bishop of Bristol, to death for high treason, to reestablish the Ecclesiastical Commission, to fill the Church

Sherlock's plan

---

* Allerville, Nov. 4. 1688. a Member of the Convention, and the
† See the pamphlet entitled Letter to   answer, 1689; Burnet, i. 809.

CHAP. X.

with Popish dignitaries, and to place the army under the command of Popish officers. But if, as the Tories themselves now seemed to confess, that theory was unsound, why treat with the King? If it was admitted that he might lawfully be excluded till he gave satisfactory guarantees for the security of the constitution in Church and State, it was not easy to deny that he might lawfully be excluded for ever. For what satisfactory guarantee could he give? How was it possible to draw up an Act of Parliament in language clearer than the language of the Acts of Parliament which required that the Dean of Christchurch should be a Protestant? How was it possible to put any promise into words stronger than those in which James had repeatedly declared that he would strictly respect the legal rights of the Anglican clergy? If law or honour could have bound him, he would never have been forced to fly from his kingdom. If neither law nor honour could bind him, could he safely be permitted to return?

It is probable, however, that in spite of these arguments, a motion for opening a negotiation with James would have been made in the Convention, and would have been supported by a great body of Tories, had he not been, on this as on every other occasion, his own worst enemy. Every post which arrived from Saint Germains brought intelligence which damped the ardour of his adherents. He did not think it worth his while to feign regret for his past errors, or to promise amendment. He put forth a manifesto, telling his people that it had been his constant care to govern them with justice and moderation, and that they had been cheated into ruin by imaginary grievances.* The effect of his folly and obstinacy was that those who were most desirous to see him restored to his throne on fair conditions felt that, by proposing at that moment to treat with him, they should injure the cause which they wished to serve. They therefore determined to coalesce with another body of Tories of whom Sancroft was the chief. Sancroft fancied that he had found out a device by which provision might be made for the government of the country without recalling James, and yet without despoiling him of his crown. This device was a Regency. The most uncompromising of those divines who had inculcated the doctrine of passive obedience had never maintained that such obedience was due to a babe or to a madman. It was universally acknowledged that, when the rightful sovereign was intellectually incapable of

Sancroft's plan.

* Letter to the Lords of the Council, Jan. 4/14. 1688/9; Clarendon's Diary, Jan. 6/16.

performing his office, a deputy might be appointed to act in his stead, and that any person who should resist the deputy, and should plead as an excuse for doing so the command of a prince who was in the cradle, or who was raving, would justly incur the penalties of rebellion. Stupidity, perverseness, and superstition,—such was the reasoning of the Primate,—had made James as unfit to rule his dominions as any child in swaddling clothes, or as any maniac who was grinning and chattering in the straw of Bedlam. That course must therefore be taken which had been taken when Henry the Sixth was an infant, and again when he became lethargic. James could not be King in effect: but he must still continue to be King in semblance. Writs must still run in his name. His image and superscription must still appear on the coin and on the Great Seal. Acts of Parliament must still be called from the years of his reign. But the administration must be taken from him and confided to a Regent named by the Estates of the Realm. In this way, Sancroft gravely maintained, the people would remain true to their allegiance; the oaths of fealty which they had sworn to their King would be strictly observed; and the most orthodox Churchmen might, without any scruple of conscience, take office under the Regent.*

The opinion of Sancroft had great weight with the whole Tory party, and especially with the clergy. A week before the day for which the Convention had been summoned, a grave party assembled at Lambeth Palace, heard prayers in the chapel, dined with the Primate, and then consulted on the

---

* It seems incredible that any man should really have been imposed upon by such nonsense. I therefore think it right to quote Sancroft's words, which are still extant in his own handwriting:—

"The political capacity or authority of the King, and his name in the government, are perfect and cannot fail; but his person being human and mortal, and not otherwise privileged than the rest of mankind, is subject to all the defects and failings of it. He may therefore be incapable of directing the government and dispensing the public treasure, &c. either by absence, by infancy, lunacy, deliracy, or apathy, whether by nature or casual infirmity, or lastly, by some invincible prejudices of mind, contracted and fixed by education and habit, with unalterable resolutions superinduced, in matters wholly inconsistent and incompatible with the laws, religion, peace,

and true policy of the kingdom. In all these cases (I say) there must be some one or more persons appointed to supply such defect, and vicariously to him, and by his power and authority, to direct public affairs. And this done, I say further, that all proceedings, authorities, commissions, grants, &c. issued so formerly, are legal and valid to all intents, and the people's allegiance is the same still, their oaths and obligations no way thwarted. . . . . So long as the government moves by the King's authority, and in his name, all those sacred ties and settled forms of proceedings are kept, and no man's conscience burthened with anything he needs scruple to undertake."—Tanner MSS.; Doyly's Life of Sancroft. It was not altogether without reason that the creatures of James made themselves merry with the good Archbishop's English.

state of public affairs. Four suffragans of the Archbishop, who had shared his perils and his glory in the preceding summer, were present. The Earls of Clarendon and Ailesbury represented the Tory laity. The unanimous sense of the meeting appeared to be that those who had taken the oath of allegiance to James might justifiably withdraw their obedience from him, but could not with a safe conscience call any other by the name of King.*

Danby's plan.

Thus two sections of the Tory party, a section which looked forward to an accommodation with James, and a section which was opposed to any such accommodation, agreed in supporting the plan of Regency. But a third section, which, though not very numerous, had great weight and influence, recommended a very different plan. The leaders of this small band were Danby and the Bishop of London in the House of Lords, and Sir Robert Sawyer in the House of Commons. They conceived that they had found out a way of effecting a complete revolution under strictly legal forms. It was contrary to all principle, they said, that the King should be deposed by his subjects; nor was it necessary to depose him. He had himself, by his flight, abdicated his power and dignity. A demise had actually taken place. All constitutional lawyers held that the throne of England could not be one moment vacant. The next heir had therefore succeeded. Who, then, was the next heir? As to the infant who had been carried into France, his entrance into the world had been attended by many suspicious circumstances. It was due to the other members of the royal family and to the nation that all doubts should be cleared up. An investigation had been solemnly demanded, in the name of the Princess of Orange, by her husband, and would have been instituted if the parties who were accused of fraud had not taken a course which, in any ordinary case, would have been considered as a decisive proof of guilt. They had not chosen to await the issue of a solemn parliamentary proceeding: they had stolen away into a foreign country: they had carried with them the child: they had carried with them all those French and Italian women of the bedchamber who, if there had been foul play, must have been privy to it, and who ought therefore to have been subjected to a rigorous cross examination. To admit the boy's claim without enquiry was impossible; and those who called themselves his parents had made enquiry impossible. Judg-

* Evelyn, Jan. 15. 168⅘.

ment must therefore go against him by default. If he was wronged, he was wronged, not by the nation, but by those whose strange conduct at the time of his birth had justified the nation in demanding investigation, and who had then avoided investigation by flight. He might, therefore, with perfect equity, be considered as a pretender. And thus the crown had legally devolved on the Princess of Orange. She was actually Queen Regnant. The Houses had nothing to do but to proclaim her. She might, if such were her pleasure, make her husband her first minister, and might even, with the consent of Parliament, bestow on him the title of King.

The persons who preferred this scheme to any other were few; and it was certain to be opposed, both by all who still bore any good will to James, and by all the adherents of William. Yet Danby, confident in his own knowledge of parliamentary tactics, and well aware how much, when great parties are nearly balanced, a small flying squadron can effect, was not without hopes of being able to keep the event of the contest in suspense till both Whigs and Tories, despairing of complete victory, and afraid of the consequences of delay, should suffer him to act as umpire. Nor is it impossible that he might have succeeded if his efforts had been seconded, nay if they had not been counteracted, by her whom he wished to raise to the height of human greatness. Quicksighted as he was and versed in affairs, he was altogether ignorant of the character of Mary, and of the feeling with which she regarded her husband; nor was her old preceptor, Compton, better informed. William's manners were dry and cold: his constitution was infirm, and his temper by no means bland: he was not a man who would commonly be thought likely to inspire a fine young woman of twenty-six with a violent passion. It was known that he had not always been strictly constant to his wife; and talebearers had reported that she did not live happily with him. The most acute politicians therefore never suspected that, with all his faults, he had obtained such an empire over her heart as princes the most renowned for their success in gallantry, Francis the First and Henry the Fourth, Lewis the Fourteenth and Charles the Second, had never obtained over the heart of any woman, and that the three kingdoms of her forefathers were valuable in her estimation chiefly because, by bestowing them on him, she could prove to him the intensity and disinterestedness of her affection. Danby, in profound ignorance of her sentiments, assured her

CHAP. X.

The Whig plan.

that he would defend her rights, and that, if she would support him, he hoped to place her alone on the throne.*

The course of the Whigs, meanwhile, was simple and consistent. Their doctrine was that the foundation of our government was a contract expressed on one side by the oath of allegiance, and on the other by the coronation oath, and that the duties imposed by this contract were mutual. They held that a sovereign who grossly abused his power might lawfully be withstood and dethroned by his people. That James had grossly abused his power was not disputed: and the whole Whig party was ready to pronounce that he had forfeited it. Whether the Prince of Wales was supposititious, was a point not worth discussing. There were now far stronger reasons than any which could be drawn from the circumstances of his birth for excluding him from the throne. A child, brought to the royal couch in a warming pan, might possibly prove a good King of England. But there could be no such hope for a child educated by a father who was the most stupid and obstinate of tyrants, in a foreign country, the seat of despotism and superstition; in a country where the last traces of liberty had disappeared; where the States General had ceased to meet; where parliaments had long registered without one remonstrance the most oppressive edicts of the sovereign; where valour, genius, learning, seemed to exist only for the purpose of aggrandising a single man; where adulation was the main business of the press, the pulpit, and the stage; and where one chief subject of adulation was the barbarous persecution of the Reformed Church. Was the boy likely to learn, under such tuition and in such a situation, respect for the institutions of his native land? Could it be doubted that he would be brought up to be the slave of the Jesuits and the Bourbons, and that he would be, if possible, more bitterly prejudiced than any preceding Stuart against the laws of England?

Nor did the Whigs think that, situated as the country then was, a departure from the ordinary rule of succession was in itself an evil. They were of opinion that, till that rule had been broken, the doctrines of indefeasible hereditary right and passive obedience would be pleasing to the Court, would be inculcated by the clergy, and would retain a strong hold on the public mind. The notion would still prevail that

* Clarendon's Diary, December 24. offered in behalf of the Princess of 1688; Burnet, i. 819.; Proposals humbly Orange, January 28. 1689.

the kingly office is the ordinance of God in a sense different from that in which all government is His ordinance. It was plain that, till this superstition was extinct, the constitution could never be secure. For a really limited monarchy cannot long exist in a society which regards monarchy as something divine, and the limitations as mere human inventions. Royalty, in order that it might exist in perfect harmony with our liberties, must be unable to show any higher or more venerable title than that by which we hold our liberties. The King must be henceforth regarded as a magistrate, a great magistrate indeed and highly to be honoured, but subject, like all other magistrates, to the law, and deriving his power from heaven in no other sense than that in which the Lords and the Commons may be said to derive their power from heaven. The best way of effecting this salutary change would be to interrupt the course of descent. Under sovereigns who would consider it as little short of high treason to preach nonresistance and the patriarchal theory of government, under sovereigns whose authority, springing from resolutions of the two Houses, could never rise higher than its source, there would be little risk of oppression such as had compelled two generations of Englishmen to rise in arms against two generations of Stuarts. On these grounds the Whigs were prepared to declare the throne vacant, to fill it by election, and to impose on the prince of their choice such conditions as might secure the country against misgovernment.

The time for the decision of these great questions had now arrived. At break of day on the twenty-second of January, the House of Commons was crowded with knights and burgesses. On the benches appeared many faces which had been well known in that place during the reign of Charles the Second, but had not been seen there under his successor. Most of those Tory squires, and of those needy retainers of the Court, who had been returned in multitudes to the Parliament of 1685, had given place to the men of the old country party, the men who had driven the Cabal from power, who had carried the Habeas Corpus Act, and who had sent up the Exclusion Bill to the Lords. Among them was Powle, deeply read in the history and law of Parliament, and distinguished by the species of eloquence which is required when grave questions are to be solemnly brought under the notice of senates, and Sir Thomas Littleton, versed in European politics, and gifted with a vehement and piercing logic which

Meeting of the Convention. Leading members of the House of Commons.

had often, when, after a long sitting, the candles had been lighted, roused the languishing House, and decided the event of the debate. There, too, was William Sacheverell, an orator whose great parliamentary abilities were, many years later, a favourite theme of old men who lived to see the conflicts of Walpole and Pulteney.* With these eminent persons was joined Sir Robert Clayton, the wealthiest merchant of London, whose palace in the Old Jewry surpassed in splendour the aristocratical mansions of Lincoln's Inn Fields and Covent Garden, whose villa among the Surrey hills was described as a garden of Eden, whose banquets vied with those of kings, and whose judicious munificence, still attested by numerous public monuments, had obtained for him in the annals of the City a place second only to that of Gresham. In the Parliament which met at Oxford in 1681, Clayton had, as member for the capital, and at the request of his constituents, moved for leave to bring in the Bill of Exclusion, and had been seconded by Lord Russell. In 1685 the City, deprived of its franchises and governed by the creatures of the Court, had returned four Tory representatives. But the old charter had now been restored; and Clayton had been again chosen by acclamation.† Nor must John Birch be passed over. He had begun life as a carter, but had, in the civil wars, left his team, had turned soldier, had risen to the rank of Colonel in the army of the Commonwealth, had, in high fiscal offices, shown great talents for business, had sate many years in Parliament, and, though retaining to the last the rough manners and plebeian dialect of his youth, had, by strong sense and mother wit, gained the ear of the Commons, and was regarded as a formidable opponent by the most accomplished debaters of his time.‡ These were the most conspicuous among the veterans who now, after a long seclusion, returned to public life. But they were all speedily thrown into the shade by two younger Whigs, who, on this great day, took their seats for the first time, who soon rose to the highest honours of the state, who weathered together the fiercest storms of faction, and who having been long and widely renowned as statesmen, as orators, and as munificent patrons of genius and learning, died, within a few

* Burnet, i. 359.; and the notes of Speaker Onslow.
† Evelyn's Diary, September 24. 1672, October 12. 1679, July 13. 1700; Strype's Survey of London.
‡ Burnet, i. 388.; and Speaker Onslow's note.

months of each other, soon after the accession of the House of Brunswick. These were Charles Montague and John Somers.

One other name must be mentioned, a name then known only to a small circle of philosophers, but now pronounced beyond the Ganges and the Mississippi with reverence exceeding that which is paid to the memory of the greatest warriors and rulers. Among the crowd of silent members appeared the majestic forehead and pensive face of Isaac Newton. The renowned University on which his genius had already begun to impress a peculiar character, still plainly discernible after the lapse of more than a hundred and sixty years, had sent him to the Convention; and he sate there, in his modest greatness, the unobtrusive but unflinching friend of civil and religious freedom.

The first act of the Commons was to choose a Speaker; and the choice which they made indicated in a manner not to be mistaken their opinion touching the great questions which they were about to decide. Down to the very eve of the meeting, it had been understood that Seymour would be placed in the chair. He had formerly sate there during several years. He had great and various titles to consideration; descent, fortune, knowledge, experience, eloquence. He had long been at the head of a powerful band of members from the Western counties. Though a Tory, he had in the last Parliament headed, with conspicuous ability and courage, the opposition to Popery and arbitrary power. He had been among the first gentlemen who had repaired to the Dutch head quarters at Exeter, and had been the author of that Association by which the Prince's adherents had bound themselves to stand or fall together. But, a few hours before the Houses met, a rumour was spread that Seymour was against declaring the throne vacant. As soon, therefore, as the benches had filled, the Earl of Wiltshire, who represented Hampshire, stood up, and proposed that Powle should be Speaker. Sir Vere Fane, member for Kent, seconded the motion. A plausible objection might have been raised; for it was known that a petition was about to be presented against Powle's return; but the general cry of the House called him to the chair; and the Tories thought it prudent to acquiesce.* The mace was then laid on the table; the

CHAP. X.

Choice of a Speaker.

* Van Citters, 1689; Grey's Debates.

list of members was called over; and the names of the defaulters were noted.

Meanwhile the Peers, about a hundred in number, had met, had chosen Halifax to be their Speaker, and had appointed several eminent lawyers to perform the functions which, in regular Parliaments, belong to the Judges. There was, in the course of that day, frequent communication between the Houses. They joined in requesting that the Prince would continue to administer the government till he should hear further from them, in expressing to him their gratitude for the deliverance which he, under God, had wrought for the nation, and in directing that the thirty-first of January should be observed as a day of thanksgiving for that deliverance.*

Thus far no difference of opinion had appeared: but both sides were preparing for the conflict. The Tories were strong in the Upper House, and weak in the Lower; and they knew that, at such a conjuncture, the House which should be the first to come to a resolution would have a great advantage over the other. There was not the least chance that the Commons would send up to the Lords a vote in favour of the plan of Regency: but, if such a vote were sent down from the Lords to the Commons, it was not absolutely impossible that many even of the Whig representatives of the people might be disposed to acquiesce rather than take the grave responsibility of causing discord and delay at a crisis which required union and expedition. The Commons had determined that, on Monday the twenty-eighth of January, they would take into consideration the state of the nation. The Tory Lords therefore proposed, on Friday the twenty-fifth, to enter instantly on the great business for which they had been called together. But their motives were clearly discerned and their tactics frustrated by Halifax, who, ever since his return from Hungerford, had seen that the settlement of the government could be effected on Whig principles only, and who had therefore, for the time, allied himself closely with the Whigs. Devonshire moved that Tuesday the twenty-ninth should be the day. "By that time," he said with more truth than discretion, "we may have some lights from below which may be useful for our guidance." His motion was carried; but his language was severely

* Lords' and Commons' Journals, Jan. 23, 1688; Van Citter's dispatch and Clarendon's Diary of the same date.

censured by some of his brother peers as derogatory to their order.*

On the twenty-eighth the Commons resolved themselves into a Committee of the whole House. A member who had, more than thirty years before, been one of Cromwell's Lords, Richard Hampden, son of the illustrious leader of the Roundheads, and father of the unhappy man who had, by large bribes and degrading submissions, narrowly escaped with life from the vengeance of James, was placed in the chair, and the great debate began.

It was soon evident that an overwhelming majority considered James as no longer King. Gilbert Dolben, son of a late Archbishop of York, was the first who declared himself to be of that opinion. He was supported by many members, particularly by the bold and vehement Wharton, by Sawyer, whose steady opposition to the dispensing power had, in some measure, atoned for old offences, by Maynard, whose voice, though so feeble with age that it could not be heard on distant benches, still commanded the respect of all parties, and by Somers, whose luminous eloquence and varied stores of knowledge were on that day exhibited, for the first time, within the walls of Parliament. The unblushing forehead and voluble tongue of Sir William Williams were found on the same side. Already he had been deeply concerned in the excesses both of the worst of oppositions and of the worst of governments. He had persecuted innocent Papists and innocent Protestants. He had been the patron of Oates and the tool of Petre. His name was associated with seditious violence which was remembered with regret and shame by all respectable Whigs, and with freaks of despotism abhorred by all respectable Tories. How men live under such infamy it is not easy to understand: but even such infamy was not enough for Williams. He was not ashamed to attack the fallen master to whom he had hired himself out for work which no honest man in the Inns of Court would undertake, and from whom he had, within six months, accepted a baronetcy as the reward of servility.

Only three members ventured to oppose themselves to what was evidently the general sense of the assembly. Sir Christopher Musgrave, a Tory gentleman of great weight and ability, hinted some doubts. Heneage Finch let fall some expressions which were understood to mean that he

* Lords' Journals, Jan. 25. 1688; Clarendon's Diary, Jan. 28. 28.

CHAP. X.

Debate on the state of the nation.

wished a negotiation to be opened with the King. This suggestion was so ill received that he made haste to explain it away. He protested that he had been misapprehended. He was convinced that, under such a prince, there could be no security for religion, liberty, or property. To recall King James, or to treat with him, would be a fatal course; but many who would never consent that he should exercise the regal power had conscientious scruples about depriving him of the royal title. There was one expedient which would remove all difficulties, a Regency. This proposition found so little favour that Finch did not venture to demand a division. Richard Fanshaw, Viscount Fanshaw of the kingdom of Ireland, said a few words in behalf of James, and recommended an adjournment; but the recommendation was met by a general outcry. Member after member stood up to represent the importance of despatch. Every moment, it was said, was precious: the public anxiety was intense: trade was suspended. The minority sullenly submitted, and suffered the predominant party to take its own course.

What that course would be was not perfectly clear. For the majority was made up of two classes. One class consisted of eager and vehement Whigs, who, if they had been able to take their own course, would have given to the proceedings of the Convention a decidedly revolutionary character. The other class admitted that a revolution was necessary, but regarded it as a necessary evil, and wished to disguise it, as much as possible, under the show of legitimacy. The former class demanded a distinct recognition of the right of subjects to dethrone bad princes. The latter class desired to rid the country of one bad prince, without promulgating any doctrine which might be abused for the purpose of weakening the just and salutary authority of future monarchs. The former class dwelt chiefly on the King's misgovernment; the latter on his flight. The former class considered him as having forfeited his crown; the latter as having resigned it. It was not easy to draw up any form of words which would please all whose assent it was important to obtain; but at length, out of many suggestions offered from different quarters, a resolution was framed which gave general satisfaction. It was moved that King James the Second, having endeavoured to subvert the constitution of the kingdom by breaking the original contract between King and people, and, by the advice of Jesuits and other wicked persons,

Resolution declaring the throne vacant.

having violated the fundamental laws, and having withdrawn himself out of the kingdom, had abdicated the government, and that the throne had thereby become vacant.

This resolution has been many times subjected to criticism as minute and severe as was ever applied to any sentence written by man: and perhaps there never was a sentence written by man which would bear such criticism less. That a King by grossly abusing his power may forfeit it is true. That a King, who absconds without making any provision for the administration, and leaves his people in a state of anarchy, may, without any violent straining of language, be said to have abdicated his functions is also true. But no accurate writer would affirm that long continued misgovernment and desertion, added together, make up an act of abdication. It is evident too that the mention of the Jesuits and other evil advisers of James weakens, instead of strengthening, the case against him. For it is a well known maxim of English law that, when a king is misled by pernicious counsel, his counsellors, and not himself, ought to be held accountable for his errors. It is idle, however, to examine these memorable words as we should examine a chapter of Aristotle or of Hobbes. Such words are to be considered, not as words, but as deeds. If they effect that which they are intended to effect, they are rational though they may be contradictory. If they fail of attaining their end, they are absurd, though they carry demonstration with them. Logic admits of no compromise. The essence of politics is compromise. It is therefore not strange that some of the most important and most useful political instruments in the world should be among the most illogical compositions that ever were penned. The object of Somers, of Maynard, and of the other eminent men who shaped this celebrated motion was, not to leave to posterity a model of definition and partition, but to make the restoration of a tyrant impossible, and to place on the throne a sovereign under whom law and liberty might be secure. This object they attained by using language which, in a philosophical treatise, would justly be reprehended as inexact and confused. They cared little whether their major agreed with their conclusion, if the major secured two hundred votes, and the conclusion two hundred more. In fact the one beauty of the resolution is its inconsistency. There was a phrase for every subdivision of the majority. The mention of the original contract

CHAP. X.

gratified the disciples of Sidney. The word abdication conciliated politicians of a more timid school. There were doubtless many fervent Protestants who were pleased with the censure cast on the Jesuits. To the real statesman the single important clause was that which declared the throne vacant; and, if that clause could be carried, he cared little by what preamble it might be introduced. The force which was thus united made all resistance hopeless. The motion was adopted by the Committee without a division. It was ordered that the report should be instantly made. Powle returned to the chair: the mace was laid on the table: Hampden brought up the resolution: the House instantly agreed to it, and ordered him to carry it to the Lords.*

It is sent up to the Lords.

On the following morning the Lords assembled early. The benches both of the spiritual and of the temporal peers were crowded. Hampden appeared at the bar, and put the resolution of the Commons into the hands of Halifax. The Upper House then resolved itself into a Committee; and Danby took the chair.

The discussion was soon interrupted by the reappearance of Hampden with another message. The House resumed and was informed that the Commons had just voted it inconsistent with the safety and welfare of this Protestant nation to be governed by a Popish King. To this resolution, irreconcilable as it obviously was with the doctrine of indefeasible hereditary right, the Peers gave an immediate and unanimous assent. The principle which was thus affirmed has always, down to our own time, been held sacred by all Protestant statesmen, and has never been considered by any reasonable Roman Catholic as objectionable. If, indeed, our sovereigns were, like the Presidents of the United States, mere civil functionaries, it would not be easy to vindicate such a restriction. But the headship of the English Church is annexed to the English crown; and there is no intolerance in saying that a Church ought not to be subjected to a head who regards her as schismatical and heretical.†

Debate in the Lords on the plan of Regency.

After this short interlude the Lords again went into committee. The Tories insisted that their plan should be discussed before the vote of the Commons which declared the

* Commons' Journals, Jan. 28. 168⅔; Grey's Debates; Van Citters, Jan. 29. If the report in Grey's Debates be correct, Van Citters must have been misinformed as to Sawyer's speech.
† Lords' and Commons' Journals, Jan. 29. 168⅔.

throne vacant was considered. This was conceded to them; and the question was put whether a Regency, exercising kingly power during the life of James, in his name, would be the best expedient for preserving the laws and liberties of the nation?

The contest was long and animated. The chief speakers in favour of a Regency were Rochester and Nottingham. Halifax and Danby led the other side. The Primate, strange to say, did not make his appearance, though earnestly importuned by the Tory peers to place himself at their head. His absence drew on him many contumelious censures; nor have even his eulogists been able to find any explanation of it which raises his character.[*] The plan of Regency was his own. He had, a few days before, in a paper written with his own hand, pronounced that plan to be clearly the best that could be adopted. The deliberations of the Lords who supported that plan had been carried on under his roof. His situation made it his clear duty to declare publicly what he thought. Nobody can suspect him of personal cowardice or of vulgar cupidity. It was probably from a nervous fear of doing wrong that, at this great conjuncture, he did nothing: but he should have known that, situated as he was, to do nothing was to do wrong. A man who is too scrupulous to take on himself a grave responsibility at an important crisis ought to be too scrupulous to accept the place of first minister of the Church and first peer of the Parliament.

It is not strange, however, that Sancroft's mind should have been ill at ease; for he could hardly be blind to the obvious truth that the scheme which he had recommended to his friends was utterly inconsistent with all that he and his brethren had been teaching during many years. That the King had a divine and indefeasible right to the regal power, and that the regal power, even when most grossly abused, could not, without sin, be resisted, was the doctrine in which the Anglican Church had long gloried. Did this doctrine then really mean only that the King had a divine and indefeasible right to have his effigy and name cut on a seal which was to be daily employed in despite of him for the purpose of commissioning his enemies to levy war on him, and of sending his friends to the gallows for obeying him? Did the whole duty of a good subject consist in using the word King?

---

[*] Clarendon's Diary, Jan. 21. 168⁹⁄₉; Burnet, I. 810.; Doyly's Life of Sancroft.

If so, Fairfax and Cromwell at Naseby had performed all the duty of good subjects. For Charles had been designated as King even by the generals who commanded against him. Nothing in the conduct of the Long Parliament had been more severely blamed by the Church than the ingenious device of using his name against himself. Every one of her ministers had been required to sign a declaration condemning as traitorous the fiction by which the authority of the sovereign had been separated from his person.* Yet this traitorous fiction was now considered by the Primate and by many of his suffragans as the only basis on which they could, in strict conformity with Christian principles, erect a government.

The distinction which Sancroft had borrowed from the Roundheads of the preceding generation subverted from the foundation that system of politics which the Church and the Universities pretended to have learned from Saint Paul. The Holy Spirit, it had been a thousand times repeated, had commanded the Romans to be subject to Nero. The meaning of the precept now appeared to be only that the Romans were to call Nero Augustus. They were perfectly at liberty to chase him beyond the Euphrates, to leave him a pensioner on the bounty of the Parthians, to withstand him by force if he attempted to return, to punish all who aided him or corresponded with him, and to transfer the Tribunitian power and the Consular power, the Presidency of the Senate and the command of the Legions, to Galba or Vespasian.

The analogy which the Archbishop imagined that he had discovered between the case of a wrongheaded king and the case of a lunatic king will not bear a moment's examination. It was plain that James was not in that state of mind in which, if he had been a country gentleman or a merchant, any tribunal would have held him incapable of executing a contract or a will. He was of unsound mind only as all bad kings are of unsound mind; as Charles the First had been of unsound mind when he went to seize the five members; as Charles the Second had been of unsound mind when he concluded the treaty of Dover. If this sort of mental unsoundness did not justify subjects in withdrawing their obedience from princes, the plan of a Regency was evidently indefensible. If this sort of mental unsoundness did justify subjects

* See the Act of Uniformity.

in withdrawing their obedience from princes, the doctrine of nonresistance was completely given up; and all that any moderate Whig had ever contended for was fully admitted.

As to the oath of allegiance about which Sancroft and his disciples were so anxious, one thing at least is clear, that, whoever might be right, they were wrong. The Whigs held that, in the oath of allegiance, certain conditions were implied, that the King had violated these conditions, and that the oath had therefore lost its force. But, if the Whig doctrine were false, if the oath were still binding, could men of sense really believe that they escaped the guilt of perjury by voting for a Regency? Could they affirm that they bore true allegiance to James, while they were, in defiance of his protestations made before all Europe, authorising another person to receive the royal revenues, to summon and prorogue Parliaments, to create Dukes and Earls, to name Bishops and Judges, to pardon offenders, to command the forces of the state, and to conclude treaties with foreign powers? Had Pascal been able to find, in all the folios of the Jesuitical casuists, a sophism more contemptible than that which now, as it seemed, sufficed to quiet the consciences of the fathers of the Anglican Church.

Nothing could be more evident than that the plan of Regency could be defended only on Whig principles. Between the rational supporters of that plan and the majority of the House of Commons there could be no dispute as to the question of right. All that remained was a question of expediency. And would any statesman seriously contend that it was expedient to constitute a government with two heads, and to give to one of those heads regal power without regal dignity, and to the other regal dignity without regal power? It was notorious that such an arrangement, even when made necessary by the infancy or insanity of a prince, had serious disadvantages. That times of Regency were times of weakness, of trouble, and of disaster, was a truth proved by the whole history of England, of France, and of Scotland, and had almost become a proverb. Yet, in a case of infancy or of insanity, the King was at least passive. He could not actively counterwork the Regent. What was now proposed was that England should have two first magistrates, of ripe age and sound mind, waging with each other an irreconcilable war. It was absurd to talk of leaving James merely the kingly name, and depriving him of all the kingly power. For the name was a part of the power. The word King was a word of conjuration. It was associated in the minds of many Englishmen with the idea of a mysterious character derived from above, and in the minds of almost all Englishmen with the idea of legitimate and venerable authority. Surely, if the title carried with it such power, those who maintained that James ought to be deprived of all power could not deny that he ought to be deprived of the title.

And how long was the anomalous government planned by the genius of Sancroft to last? Every argument which could be urged for setting it up at all might be urged with equal force for retaining it to the end of time. If the boy who had been carried into France was really born of the Queen, he would hereafter inherit the divine and indefeasible right to be called King. The same right would very probably be transmitted from Papist to Papist through the whole of the eighteenth and nineteenth centuries. Both the Houses had unanimously resolved that England should not be governed by a Papist. It might well be, therefore, that, from generation to generation, Regents would continue to administer the government in the name of vagrant and mendicant Kings. There was no doubt that the Regents must be appointed by Parliament. The effect, therefore, of this contrivance, a contrivance intended to preserve unimpaired the sacred principle of hereditary monarchy, would be that the monarchy would become really elective.

Another unanswerable reason was urged against Sancroft's plan. There was in the statute book a law which had been passed soon after the close of the long and bloody contest between the Houses of York and Lancaster, and which had been framed for the purpose of averting calamities such as the alternate victories of those Houses had brought on the nobility and gentry of the realm. By this law it was provided that no person should, by adhering to a King in possession, incur the penalties of treason. When the regicides were brought to trial after the Restoration, some of them insisted that their case lay within the equity of this act. They had obeyed, they said, the government which was in possession, and were therefore not traitors. The Judges admitted that this would have been a good defence if the prisoners had acted under the authority of an usurper who, like Henry the Fourth and Richard the Third, bore the regal title, but declared that such a defence could not avail men who had indicted, sentenced, and executed one who, in the indictment, in the sentence, and in the death warrant, was designated as King. It followed, therefore, that whoever should support a Regent in opposition to James would run great risk of being hanged, drawn, and quartered, if ever James should recover supreme power; but that no person could, without such a violation of law as Jeffreys himself would hardly venture to commit, be punished for siding with a King who was reigning, though wrongfully, at Whitehall, against a rightful King who was in exile at Saint Germains.*

It should seem that these arguments admit of no reply; and they were doubtless urged with force by Danby, who had a wonderful power of making every subject which he treated clear to the dullest mind, and by Halifax, who, in fertility of thought and brilliancy of diction, had no rival among the orators of that age. Yet so numerous and powerful were the Tories in the Upper House that, notwithstanding the weakness of their case, the defection of their leader, and the ability of their opponents, they very nearly carried the day. A hundred Lords divided. Forty-nine voted for a Regency, fifty-one against it. In the minority were the natural children of Charles, the brothers in law of James, the Dukes of Somerset and Ormond, the Archbishop of York and eleven Bishops. No prelate voted in the majority except Compton and Trelawney.†

It was near nine in the evening before the House rose. The following day was the thirtieth of January, the anniversary of the death of Charles the First. The great body of the Anglican clergy had, during many years, thought it a sacred duty to inculcate on that day the doctrines of nonresistance and passive obedience. Their old sermons were now of little use; and many divines were even in doubt whether they could venture to read the whole Liturgy. The Lower House had declared that the throne was vacant. The Upper had not yet expressed any opinion. It was therefore not easy to decide whether the prayers for the sovereign

---

* Stat. 2 Hen. 7. c. 1.; Lord Coke's Institutes, part III. chap. I.; Trial of Cook for High treason, in the Collection of State Trials; Burnet, i. 813. and Swift's note.

† Lords' Journals, January 29, 168⅞; Clarendon's Diary; Evelyn's Diary; Van Citters; Eachard's History of the Revolution; Burnet, i. 813.; History of the Reestablishment of the Government, 1689. The numbers of the Contents and Not Contents are not given in the journals, and are differently reported by different writers. I have followed Clarendon, who took the trouble to make out lists of the majority and minority.

ought to be used. Every officiating minister took his own course. In most of the churches of the capital the petitions for James were omitted; but at Saint Margaret's, Sharp, Dean of Norwich, who had been requested to preach before the Commons, not only read to their faces the whole service as it stood in the book, but, before his sermon, implored, in his own words, a blessing on the King, and, towards the close of his discourse, declaimed against the Jesuitical doctrine that princes might lawfully be deposed by their subjects. The Speaker, that very afternoon, complained to the House of this affront. "You pass a vote one day," he said; "and on the next day it is contradicted from the pulpit in your own hearing." Sharp was strenuously defended by the Tories, and had friends even among the Whigs: for it was not forgotten that he had incurred serious danger in the evil times by the courage with which, in defiance of the royal injunction, he had preached against Popery. Sir Christopher Musgrave very ingeniously remarked that the House had not ordered the resolution which declared the throne vacant to be published. Sharp, therefore, was not only not bound to know anything of that resolution, but could not have taken notice of it without a breach of privilege for which he might have been called to the bar and reprimanded on his knees. The majority felt that it was not wise at that conjuncture to quarrel with the clergy; and the subject was suffered to drop.*

While the Commons were discussing Sharp's sermon, the Lords had again gone into a Committee on the state of the nation, and had ordered the resolution which pronounced the throne vacant to be read clause by clause.

The first expression on which a debate arose was that which recognised the original contract between king and people. It was not to be expected that the Tory peers would suffer a phrase which contained the quintessence of Whiggism to pass unchallenged. A division took place; and it was determined by fifty-three votes to forty-six that the words should stand.

The severe censure passed by the Commons on the administration of James was next considered, and was approved without one dissentient voice. Some verbal objections were made to the proposition that James had abdicated the govern-

* Grey's Debates; Evelyn's Diary; letter to Dr. John Sharp, Archbishop of York, 1691. Life of Archbishop Sharp, by his son; Apology for the New Separation, in a

ment. It was urged that he might more correctly be said to have deserted it. This amendment was adopted, it should seem, with scarcely any debate, and without a division. By this time it was late; and the Lords again adjourned.*

Up to this moment the small body of peers which was under the guidance of Danby had acted in firm union with Halifax and the Whigs. The effect of this union had been that the plan of Regency had been rejected, and the doctrine of the original contract affirmed. The proposition that James had ceased to be King had been the rallying point of the two parties which had made up the majority. But from that point their path diverged. The next question to be decided was whether the throne was vacant; and this was a question not merely verbal, but of grave practical importance. If the throne was vacant, the Estates of the Realm might place William in it. If it was not vacant, he could succeed to it only after his wife, after Anne, and after Anne's posterity.

It was, according to the followers of Danby, an established maxim that our country could not be, even for a moment, without a rightful prince. The man might die; but the magistrate was immortal. The man might abdicate; but the magistrate was irremovable. If, these politicians said, we once admit that the throne is vacant, we admit that it is elective. The sovereign whom we may place on it will be a sovereign, not after the English, but after the Polish, fashion. Even if we choose the very person who would reign by right of birth, still that person will reign not by right of birth, but in virtue of our choice, and will take as a gift what ought to be regarded as an inheritance. That salutary reverence with which the blood royal and the order of primogeniture have hitherto been regarded will be greatly diminished. Still more serious will the evil be, if we not only fill the throne by election, but fill it with a prince who has doubtless the qualities of a great and good ruler, and who has wrought a wonderful deliverance for us, but who is not first nor even second in the order of succession. If we once say that merit, however eminent, shall be a title to the crown, we disturb the very foundations of our polity, and furnish a precedent of which every ambitious warrior or statesman who may have rendered any great service to the public will be tempted to avail himself. This danger we avoid if we logically follow out the principles of the constitution to their consequences.

CHAP. X.

Schism between the Whigs and the followers of Danby.

* Lords' Journals, Jan. 30. 1685; Clarendon's Diary

CHAP. X.

There has been a demise of the crown. At the instant of the demise the next heir became our lawful sovereign. We consider the Princess of Orange as next heir; and we hold that she ought, without any delay, to be proclaimed, what she already is, our Queen.

The Whigs answered that it was idle to apply ordinary rules to a country in a state of revolution, that the great question now depending was not to be decided by the saws of pedantic Templars, and that, if it were to be so decided, such saws might be quoted on one side as well as the other. If it were a legal maxim that the throne could never be vacant, it was also a legal maxim that a living man could have no heir. James was still living. How then could the Princess of Orange be his heir? The truth was that the laws of England had made full provision for the succession when the power of a sovereign and his natural life terminated together, but had made no provision for the very rare cases in which his power terminated before the close of his natural life; and with one of those very rare cases the Convention had now to deal. That James no longer filled the throne both Houses had pronounced. Neither common law nor statute law designated any person as entitled to fill the throne between his demise and his decease. It followed that the throne was vacant, and that the Houses might invite the Prince of Orange to fill it. That he was not next in order of birth was true: but this was no disadvantage; on the contrary, it was a positive recommendation. Hereditary monarchy was a good political institution, but was by no means more sacred than other good political institutions. Unfortunately, bigoted and servile theologians had turned it into a religious mystery, almost as awful and as incomprehensible as transubstantiation itself. To keep the institution, and yet to get rid of the abject and noxious superstitions with which it had of late years been associated and which had made it a curse instead of a blessing to society, ought to be the first object of English statesmen; and that object would be best attained by slightly deviating for a time from the general rule of descent, and then returning to it.

Meeting at the Earl of Devonshire's.

Many attempts were made to prevent an open breach between the party of the Prince and the party of the Princess. A great meeting was held at the Earl of Devonshire's house, and the dispute was warm. Halifax was the chief speaker for William, Danby for Mary. Of the mind of Mary Danby knew nothing. She had been some time expected in London, but had been detained in Holland, first by masses of ice which had blocked up the rivers, and, when the thaw came, by strong westerly winds. Had she arrived earlier the dispute would probably have been at once quieted. Halifax on the other side had no authority to say anything in William's name. The Prince, true to his promise that he would leave the settlement of the government to the Convention, had maintained an impenetrable reserve, and had not suffered any word, look, or gesture, indicative either of satisfaction or of displeasure, to escape him. One of his countrymen, who had a large share of his confidence, had been invited to the meeting, and was earnestly pressed by the Peers to give them some information. He long excused himself. At last he so far yielded to their urgency as to say, "I can only guess at His Highness's mind. If you wish to know what I guess, I guess that he would not like to be his wife's gentleman usher; but I know nothing." "I know something now, however," said Danby. "I know enough, and too much." He then departed; and the assembly broke up.*

On the thirty-first of January the debate which had terminated thus in private was publicly renewed in the House of Peers. That day had been fixed for the national thanksgiving. An office had been drawn up for the occasion by several Bishops, among whom were Ken and Sprat. It is perfectly free both from the adulation and from the malignity by which such compositions were in that age too often deformed, and sustains, better perhaps than any occasional service which has been framed during two centuries, a comparison with that great model of chaste, lofty, and pathetic eloquence, the Book of Common Prayer. The Lords went in the morning to Westminster Abbey. The Commons had desired Burnet to preach before them at Saint Margaret's. He was not likely to fall into the same error which had been committed in the same place on the preceding day. His vigorous and animated discourse doubtless called forth the loud hums of his auditors. It was not only printed by command of the House, but was

* Dartmouth's note on Burnet, i. 393. Dartmouth says that it was from Fagel that the Lords extracted the hint. This was a slip of the pen very pardonable in a hasty marginal note; but Dalrymple and others ought not to have copied so palpable a blunder. Fagel died in Holland on the 5th of December 1688, when William was at Salisbury and James at Whitehall. The real person was, I suppose, Zulestein or Dykvelt.

translated into French for the edification of foreign Protestants.* The day closed with the festivities usual on such occasions. The whole town shone bright with fireworks and bonfires: the roar of guns and the pealing of bells lasted till the night was far spent: but, before the lights were extinct and the streets silent, an event had taken place which threw a damp on the public joy.

Debate in the Lords on the question whether the throne was vacant.

The Peers had repaired from the Abbey to their house, and had resumed the discussion on the state of the nation. The last words of the resolution of the Commons were taken into consideration; and it soon became clear that the majority was not disposed to assent to those words. To near fifty Lords who held that the regal title still belonged to James were now added seven or eight who held that it had already devolved on Mary. The Whigs, finding themselves outnumbered, tried to compromise the dispute. They proposed to omit the words which pronounced the throne vacant, and simply to declare the Prince and Princess King and Queen. It was manifest that such a declaration implied, though it did not expressly affirm, all that the Tories were unwilling to concede. For nobody could pretend that William had succeeded to the regal office by right of birth. To pass a resolution acknowledging him as King was therefore an act of election; and how could there be an election without a vacancy?

Majority for the negative.

The proposition of the Whig Lords was rejected by fifty-two votes to forty-seven. The question was then put whether the throne was vacant. The Contents were only forty-one: the Noncontents fifty-five. Of the minority thirty-six protested.†

Agitation in London.

During the two following days London was in an unquiet and anxious state. The Tories began to hope that they might be able again to bring forward their favourite plan of Regency with better success. Perhaps the Prince himself, when he found that he had no chance of wearing the crown, might prefer Sancroft's scheme to Danby's. It was better doubtless to be a King than to be a Regent: but it was better to be a Regent than to be a gentleman usher. On the other side the lower and fiercer class of Whigs, the old emissaries of Shaftesbury, the old associates of College, began to stir in the City. Crowds assembled in Palace Yard, and held threatening language. Lord Lovelace, who

---

* Both the service and Burnet's sermon are still to be found in our great libraries, and will repay the trouble of perusal. † Lords' Journals, Jan 31. 168⅝.

was suspected of having encouraged these assemblages, informed the Peers that he was charged with a petition requesting them instantly to declare the Prince and Princess of Orange King and Queen. He was asked by whom the petition was signed. "There are no hands to it yet," he answered; "but, when I bring it here next, there shall be hands enough." This menace alarmed and disgusted his own party. The leading Whigs were, in truth, even more anxious than the Tories that the deliberations of the Convention should be perfectly free, and that it should not be in the power of any adherent of James to allege that either House had acted under force. A petition, similar to that which had been entrusted to Lovelace, was brought into the House of Commons, but was contemptuously rejected. Maynard was foremost in protesting against the attempt of the rabble in the streets to overawe the Estates of the Realm. William sent for Lovelace, expostulated with him strongly, and ordered the magistrates to act with vigour against all unlawful assemblies.* Nothing in the history of our revolution is more deserving of admiration and of imitation than the manner in which the two parties in the Convention, at the very moment at which their disputes ran highest, joined like one man to resist the dictation of the mob of the capital.

But, though the Whigs were fully determined to maintain order and to respect the freedom of debate, they were equally determined to make no concession. On Saturday, the second of February, the Commons, without a division, resolved to adhere to their resolution as it originally stood. James, as usual, came to the help of his enemies. A letter from him to the Convention had just arrived in London. It had been transmitted to Preston by the apostate Melfort, who was now high in favour at Saint Germains. The name of Melfort was an abomination to every Churchman. That he was still a confidential minister was alone sufficient to prove that his master's folly and perverseness were incurable. No member of either House ventured to propose that a paper which came from such a quarter should be read. The contents, however, were well known to all the town. His Majesty exhorted the Lords and Commons not to despair of his clemency, and graciously

Letter of James to the Convention.

---

* Van Citters, Feb. 4. 1689; Clarendon's Diary, Feb. 2. The story is greatly exaggerated in the work entitled Revolution Politics, an eminently absurd book, yet of some value as a record of the foolish reports of the day. Grey's Debates.

assured them that he would pardon those who had betrayed him, some few excepted, whom he did not name. How was it possible to do anything for a prince who, vanquished, deserted, banished, living on alms, told those who were the arbiters of his fate that, if they would set him on his throne again, he would hang only a few of them?*

Debates. The contest between the two branches of the legislature lasted some days longer. On Monday, the fourth of February, the Peers resolved that they would insist on their amendments: but a protest to which thirty-nine names were subscribed was entered on the journals.† On the following day the *Negotiations.* Tories determined to try their strength in the Lower House. They mustered there in great force. A motion was made to agree to the amendments of the Lords. Those who were for the plan of Sancroft and those who were for the plan of Danby divided together; but they were beaten by two hundred and eighty-two votes to a hundred and fifty-one. The House then resolved to request a free conference with the Lords.‡

Letter of the Princess of Orange to Danby. At the same time strenuous efforts were making without the walls of Parliament to bring the dispute between the two branches of the legislature to a close. Burnet thought that the importance of the crisis justified him in publishing the great secret which the Princess had confided to him. He knew, he said, from her own lips, that it had long been her full determination, even if she came to the throne in the regular course of descent, to surrender her power, with the sanction of Parliament, into the hands of her husband. Danby received from her an earnest, and almost angry reprimand. She was, she wrote, the Prince's wife; she had no other wish than to be subject to him: the most cruel injury that could be done to her would be to set her up as his competitor; and *The Princess Anne acquiesces in the Whig plan.* she never could regard any person who took such a course as her true friend.§ The Tories had still one hope. Anne might insist on her own rights, and on those of her children. No effort was spared to stimulate her ambition, and to alarm her conscience. Her uncle Clarendon was especially active. A few

* The letter of James, dated Jan. 24 / Feb. 3, 1689, will be found in Kennet. It is most disingenuously garbled in his Life. See Clarendon's Diary, Feb. 2. 4.; Grey's Debates; Lords' Journals, Feb. 2. 4. 1689.

† It has been asserted by several writers, and, among others, by Ralph and by M. Mazure, that Danby signed this protest. This is a mistake. Probably some person who examined the journals before they were printed mistook Derby for Danby. Lords' Journals, Feb. 4. 1689. Evelyn, a few days before, wrote Derby, by mistake, for Danby. Diary, Jan. 29. 1689.

‡ Commons' Journal, Feb. 5. 1689.

§ Burnet, i. 819.

weeks only had elapsed since the hope of wealth and greatness had impelled him to belie the boastful professions of his whole life, to desert the royal cause, to join with the Wildmans and Fergusons, nay, to propose that the King should be sent a prisoner to a foreign land and immured in a fortress begirt by pestilential marshes. The lure which had produced this strange transformation was the Viceroyalty of Ireland. Soon, however, it appeared that the proselyte had little chance of obtaining the splendid prize on which his heart was set. He found that others were consulted on Irish affairs. His advice was never asked, and, when obtrusively and importunately offered, was coldly received. He repaired many times to Saint James's Palace, but could scarcely obtain a word or a look. One day the Prince was writing: another day he wanted fresh air and must ride in the Park: on a third he was closeted with officers on military business and could see nobody. Clarendon saw that he was not likely to gain anything by the sacrifice of his principles, and determined to take them back again. In December ambition had converted him into a rebel. In January disappointment reconverted him into a Royalist. The uneasy consciousness that he had not been a consistent Tory gave a peculiar acrimony to his Toryism.* In the House of Lords he had done all in his power to prevent a settlement. He now exerted, for the same end, all his influence over the Princess Anne. But his influence over her was small indeed when compared with that of the Churchills, who wisely called to their help two powerful allies, Tillotson, who, as a spiritual director, had, at that time, immense authority, and Lady Russell, whose noble and gentle virtues, proved by the most cruel of all trials, had gained for her the reputation of a saint. The Princess of Denmark, it was soon known, was willing that William should reign for life; and it was evident that to defend the cause of the daughters of James against themselves was a hopeless task.†

And now William thought that the time had come when he ought to explain himself. He accordingly sent for Halifax, Danby, Shrewsbury, and some other political leaders of great note, and with that air of stoical apathy under which he had, from a boy, been in the habit of concealing his

William explains his views.

---

* Clarendon's Diary, Jan. 1. 4. 8, 9, 10, 11, 12, 13, 14. 168⅔; Burnet, i. 807. Duchess of Marlborough's Vindication; Mulgrave's Account of the Revolution.
† Clarendon's Diary, Feb. 5. 168⅔;

strongest emotions, addressed to them a few deeply meditated and weighty words.

He had hitherto, he said, remained silent: he had used neither solicitation nor menace: he had not even suffered a hint of his opinions or wishes to get abroad: but a crisis had now arrived at which it was necessary for him to declare his intentions. He had no right and no wish to dictate to the Convention. All that he claimed was the privilege of declining any office which he felt that he could not hold with honour to himself and with benefit to the public.

A strong party was for a Regency. It was for the Houses to determine whether such an arrangement would be for the interest of the nation. He had a decided opinion on that point; and he thought it right to say distinctly that he would not be Regent.

Another party was for placing the Princess on the throne, and for giving to him, during her life, the title of King, and such a share in the administration as she might be pleased to allow him. He could not stoop to such a post. He esteemed the Princess as much as it was possible for man to esteem woman: but not even from her would he accept a subordinate and a precarious place in the government. He was so made that he could not submit to be tied to the apron strings even of the best of wives. He did not desire to take any part in English affairs; but, if he did consent to take a part, there was one part only which he could usefully or honourably take. If the Estates offered him the crown for life, he would accept it. If not, he should, without repining, return to his native country. He concluded by saying that he thought it reasonable that the Lady Anne and her posterity should be preferred in the succession to any children whom he might have by any other wife than the Lady Mary.[*]

The meeting broke up; and what the Prince had said was in a few hours known all over London. That he must be King was now clear. The only question was whether he should hold the regal dignity alone or conjointly with the Princess. Halifax and a few other politicians, who saw in a strong light the danger of dividing the supreme executive

---

[*] Burnet, i. 820. Burnet says that he has not related the events of this stirring time in chronological order. I have therefore been forced to arrange them by guess; but I think that I can scarcely be wrong in supposing that the letter of the Princess of Orange to Danby arrived, and that the Prince's explanation of his views was given, between Thursday the 31st of January, and Wednesday the 6th of February.

authority, thought it desirable that, during William's life, Mary should be only Queen Consort and a subject. But this arrangement, though much might doubtless be said for it in argument, shocked the general feeling even of those Englishmen who were most attached to the Prince. His wife had given an unprecedented proof of conjugal submission and affection; and the very least return that could be made to her would be to bestow on her the dignity of Queen Regnant. William Harbord, one of the most zealous of the Prince's adherents, was so much exasperated that he sprang out of the bed to which he was confined by gout, and vehemently declared that he never would have drawn a sword in His Highness's cause if he had foreseen that so shameful an arrangement would be made. No person took the matter up so eagerly as Burnet. His blood boiled at the wrong done to his kind patroness. He expostulated vehemently with Bentinck, and begged to be permitted to resign the chaplainship. "While I am His Highness's servant," said the brave and honest divine, "it would be unseemly in me to oppose any plan which may have his countenance. I therefore desire to be set free, that I may fight the Princess's battle with every faculty that God has given me." Bentinck prevailed on Burnet to defer an open declaration of hostilities till William's resolution should be distinctly known. In a few hours the scheme which had excited so much resentment was entirely given up; and all those who considered James as no longer King were agreed as to the way in which the throne must be filled. William and Mary must be King and Queen. The heads of both must appear together on the coin: writs must run in the names of both: both must enjoy all the personal dignities and immunities of royalty: but the administration, which could not be safely divided, must belong to William alone.*

And now the time arrived for the free conference between the Houses. The managers for the Lords, in their robes, took their seats along one side of the table in the Painted Chamber; but the crowd of members of the House of Commons on the other side was so great that the gentlemen who were to argue the question in vain tried to get through. It was not without much difficulty and long delay that the Serjeant at Arms was able to clear a passage.†

* Mulgrave's Account of the Revolution.
† Commons' Journals, Feb. 6. 1688.

CHAP. X.

At length the discussion began. A full report of the speeches on both sides has come down to us. There are few students of history who have not taken up that report with eager curiosity and laid it down with disappointment. The question between the Houses was argued on both sides as a question of law. The objections which the Lords made to the resolution of the Commons were verbal and technical, and were met by verbal and technical answers. Somers vindicated the use of the word abdication by quotations from Grotius and Brissonius, Spigelius and Bartolus. When he was challenged to show any authority for the proposition that England could be without a sovereign, he produced the Parliament roll of the year 1399, in which it was expressly set forth that the kingly office was vacant during the interval between the resignation of Richard the Second and the enthroning of Henry the Fourth. The Lords replied by producing the Parliament roll of the first year of Edward the Fourth, from which it appeared that the record of 1399 had been solemnly annulled. They therefore maintained that the precedent on which Somers relied was no longer valid. Treby then came to Somers's assistance, and laid on the table the Parliament roll of the first year of Henry the Seventh, which repealed the act of Edward the Fourth, and consequently restored the validity of the record of 1399. After a colloquy of several hours the disputants separated.* The Lords assembled in their own house. It was well understood that they were about to yield, and that the conference had been a mere form. The friends of Mary had found that, by setting her up as her husband's rival, they had deeply displeased her. Some of the Peers who had formerly voted for a Regency had determined to absent themselves or to support the resolution of the Lower House. Their opinion, they said, was unchanged: but any government was better than no government; and the country could not bear a prolongation of this agony of suspense. Even Nottingham, who, in the Painted Chamber, had taken the lead against the Commons, declared that, though his own conscience would not suffer him to give way, he was glad that the consciences of other men were less squeamish. Several Lords who had not yet voted in the Convention had been induced to attend; Lord Lexington, who had just hurried over from the Continent;

* See the Lords' and Commons' Journals of Feb. 6. 1688/9. and the Report of the Conference.

the Earl of Lincoln, who was half mad; the Earl of Carlisle, who limped in on crutches; and the Bishop of Durham, who had been in hiding and had intended to fly beyond sea, but had received an intimation that, if he would vote for the settling of the government, his conduct in the Ecclesiastical Commission should not be remembered against him. Danby, desirous to heal the schism which he had caused, exhorted the House, in a speech distinguished by even more than his usual ability, not to persevere in a contest which might be fatal to the state. He was strenuously supported by Halifax. The spirit of the opposite party was quelled. When the question was put whether King James had abdicated the government, only three Lords said Not Content. On the question whether the throne was vacant, a division was demanded. The Contents were sixty-two; the Not Contents forty-seven. It was immediately proposed and carried, without a division, that the Prince and Princess of Orange should be declared King and Queen of England.*

The Lords yield.

Nottingham then moved that the wording of the oaths of allegiance and supremacy should be altered in such a way that they might be conscientiously taken by persons who, like himself, disapproved of what the Convention had done, and yet fully purposed to be loyal and dutiful subjects of the new sovereigns. To his proposition no objection was made. Indeed there can be little doubt that there was an understanding on this subject between the Whig leaders and those Tory Lords whose votes had turned the scale on the last division. The new oaths were sent down to the Commons, together with the resolution that the Prince and Princess should be declared King and Queen.†

It was now known to whom the crown would be given. On what conditions it should be given, still remained to be decided. The Commons had appointed a committee to consider what steps it might be advisable to take, in order to secure law and liberty against the aggressions of future sovereigns, and the committee had made a report.‡ This report recommended, first, that those great principles of the constitution which had been violated by the dethroned King should

New laws proposed for the security of liberty.

---

* Lords' Journals, February 6, 1688; Clarendon's Diary; Burnet, i. 827. and Dartmouth's note; Van Citters, February 1⁸⁄₁₉. I have followed Clarendon as to the numbers. Some writers make the majority smaller and some larger.
† Lords' Journals, Feb. 6, 7, 1688; Clarendon's Diary.
‡ Commons' Journals, Jan. 29., Feb. 2, 1688.

be solemnly asserted, and, secondly, that many new laws should be enacted, for the purpose of curbing the prerogative and purifying the administration of justice. Most of the suggestions of the committee were excellent; but it was utterly impossible that the Houses could, in a month, or even in a year, deal properly with matters so numerous, so various, and so important. It was proposed, among other things, that the militia should be remodelled, that the power which the sovereign possessed of proroguing and dissolving Parliaments should be restricted; that the duration of Parliaments should be limited; that the royal pardon should no longer be pleadable to a parliamentary impeachment; that toleration should be granted to Protestant Dissenters; that the crime of high treason should be more precisely defined; that trials for high treason should be conducted in a manner more favourable to innocence; that the Judges should hold their places for life; that the mode of appointing Sheriffs should be altered; that juries should be nominated in such a way as might exclude partiality and corruption; that the practice of filing criminal informations in the King's Bench should be abolished; that the Court of Chancery should be reformed; that the fees of public functionaries should be regulated; and that the law of Quo Warranto should be amended. It was evident that cautious and deliberate legislation on these subjects must be the work of more than one laborious session; and it was equally evident that hasty and crude legislation on subjects so grave could not but produce new grievances, worse than those which it might remove. If the committee meant to give a list of the reforms which ought to be accomplished before the throne was filled, the list was absurdly long. If, on the other hand, the committee meant to give a list of all the reforms which the legislature would do well to make in proper season, the list was strangely imperfect. Indeed, as soon as the report had been read, member after member rose to suggest some addition. It was moved and carried that the selling of offices should be prohibited, that the Habeas Corpus Act should be made more efficient, and that the law of Mandamus should be revised. One gentleman fell on the chimneymen, another on the excisemen; and the House resolved that the malpractices of both chimneymen and excisemen should be restrained. It is a most remarkable circumstance that, while the whole political, military, judicial, and fiscal system of the kingdom was thus passed in review, not a single representative of the people proposed the repeal

of the statute which subjected the press to a censorship. It
was not yet understood, even by the most enlightened men,
that the liberty of discussion is the chief safeguard of all
other liberties.*

The House was greatly perplexed. Some orators vehemently said that too much time had already been lost, and that
the government ought to be settled without the delay of a day.
Society was unquiet; trade was languishing; the English
colony in Ireland was in imminent danger of perishing: a
foreign war was impending: the exiled King might, in a few
weeks, be at Dublin with a French army, and from Dublin
he might soon cross to Chester. Was it not insanity, at such
a crisis, to leave the throne unfilled, and, while the very
existence of Parliaments was in jeopardy, to waste time in
debating whether Parliaments should be prorogued by the
sovereign or by themselves? On the other side it was asked
whether the Convention could think that it had fulfilled its
mission by merely pulling down one prince and putting up
another. Surely now or never was the time to secure public
liberty by such fences as might effectually prevent the encroachments of prerogative.† There was doubtless great
weight in what was urged on both sides. The able chiefs of
the Whig party, among whom Somers was fast rising to
ascendency, proposed a middle course. The House had, they
said, two objects in view, which ought to be kept distinct.
One object was to secure the old polity of the realm against
illegal attacks: the other was to improve that polity by legal
reforms. The former object might be attained by solemnly
putting on record, in the resolution which called the new
sovereigns to the throne, the claim of the English nation to
its ancient franchises, so that the King might hold his crown,
and the people their privileges, by one and the same title
deed. The latter object would require a whole volume of
elaborate statutes. The former object might be attained in
a day; the latter, scarcely in five years. As to the former
object, all parties were agreed: as to the latter, there were
innumerable varieties of opinion. No member of either
House would hesitate for a moment to vote that the King
could not levy taxes without the consent of Parliament; but
it would be hardly possible to frame any new law of procedure in cases of high treason which would not give rise to

* Commons' Journals, Feb. 2. 1689.   † Grey's Debates; Burnet, i. 822.

long debate, and be condemned by some persons as unjust to
the prisoner, and by others as unjust to the crown. The
business of an extraordinary convention of the Estates of the
Realm was not to do the ordinary work of Parliaments, to
regulate the fees of masters in Chancery, and to provide
against the exactions of gaugers, but to put right the great
machine of government. When this had been done, it would
be time to inquire what improvement our institutions needed:
nor would anything be risked by delay; for no sovereign
who reigned merely by the choice of the nation, could long
refuse his assent to any improvement which the nation,
speaking through its representatives, demanded.

On these grounds the Commons wisely determined to postpone all reforms till the ancient constitution of the kingdom
should have been restored in all its parts, and forthwith to
fill the throne without imposing on William and Mary any
other obligation than that of governing according to the
existing laws of England. In order that the questions which
had been in dispute between the Stuarts and the nation
might never again be stirred, it was determined that the
instrument by which the Prince and Princess of Orange were
called to the throne, and by which the order of succession
was settled, should set forth, in the most distinct and solemn
manner, the fundamental principles of the constitution. This
instrument, known by the name of the Declaration of Right,
was prepared by a committee, of which Somers was chairman.
The fact that the lowborn young barrister was appointed to
so honourable and important a post in a Parliament filled
with able and experienced men, only ten days after he had
spoken in the House of Commons for the first time, sufficiently proves the superiority of his abilities. In a few hours
the Declaration was framed and approved by the Commons.
The Lords assented to it with some amendments of no great
importance.*

The Declaration began by recapitulating the crimes and
errors which had made a revolution necessary. James had
invaded the province of the legislature; had treated modest
petitioning as a crime; had oppressed the Church by means
of an illegal tribunal; had, without the consent of Parliament, levied taxes and maintained a standing army in time
of peace; had violated the freedom of election, and perverted

* Commons' Journals, Feb. 4. 8. 11, 12.; Lords' Journals, Feb. 9. 11, 12. 1688.

the course of justice. Proceedings which could lawfully be questioned only in Parliament had been made the subjects of prosecution in the King's Bench. Partial and corrupt juries had been returned: excessive bail had been required from prisoners: excessive fines had been imposed: barbarous and unusual punishments had been inflicted: the estates of accused persons had been granted away before conviction. He, by whose authority these things had been done, had abdicated the government. The Prince of Orange, whom God had made the glorious instrument of delivering the nation from superstition and tyranny, had invited the Estates of the Realm to meet and to take counsel together for the securing of religion, of law, and of freedom. The Lords and Commons, having deliberated, had resolved that they would first, after the example of their ancestors, assert the ancient rights and liberties of England. Therefore it was declared that the dispensing power, as lately assumed and exercised, had no legal existence; that, without grant of Parliament, no money could be exacted by the sovereign from the subject; that, without consent of Parliament, no standing army could be kept up in time of peace. The right of subjects to petition, the right of electors to choose representatives freely, the right of the legislature to freedom of debate, the right of the nation to a pure and merciful administration of justice according to the spirit of our mild laws, were solemnly affirmed. All these things the Convention claimed, as the undoubted inheritance of Englishmen. Having thus vindicated the principles of the constitution, the Lords and Commons, in the entire confidence that the deliverer would hold sacred the laws and liberties which he had saved, resolved that William and Mary, Prince and Princess of Orange, should be declared King and Queen of England for their joint and separate lives, and that, during their joint lives, the administration of the government should be in the Prince alone. After them the crown was settled on the posterity of Mary, then on Anne and her posterity, and then on the posterity of William.

CHAP. X.

By this time the wind had ceased to blow from the west. The ship in which the Princess of Orange had embarked lay off Margate on the eleventh of February, and, on the following morning, anchored at Greenwich.* She was received with many signs of joy and affection: but her demeanour shocked the Tories, and was not thought faultless even by

Arrival of Mary.

* London Gazette, Feb. 14. 168⅔; Van Citters, Feb. 1⅟.

the Whigs. A young woman, placed, by a destiny as mournful and awful as that which brooded over the fabled houses of Labdacus and Pelops, in such a situation that she could not, without violating her duty to her God, her husband, and her country, refuse to take her seat on the throne from which her father had just been hurled, should have been sad, or at least serious. Mary was not merely in high, but in extravagant, spirits. She entered Whitehall, it was asserted, with a girlish delight at being mistress of so fine a house, ran about the rooms, peeped into the closets, and examined the quilt of the state bed, without seeming to remember by whom those magnificent apartments had last been occupied. Burnet, who had, till then, thought her an angel in human form, could not, on this occasion, refrain from blaming her. He was the more astonished because, when he took leave of her at the Hague, she had, though fully convinced that she was in the path of duty, been deeply dejected. To him, as to her spiritual guide, she afterwards explained her conduct. William had written to inform her that some of those who had tried to separate her interest from his still continued their machinations: they gave it out that she thought herself wronged: and, if she wore a gloomy countenance, the report would be confirmed. He therefore entreated her to make her first appearance with an air of cheerfulness. Her heart, she said, was far indeed from cheerful; but she had done her best; and, as she was afraid of not sustaining well a part which was uncongenial to her feelings, she had overacted it. Her deportment was the subject of much spiteful prose and verse: it lowered her in the opinion of some whose esteem she valued: nor did the world know, till she was beyond the reach of praise and censure, that the conduct which had brought on her the reproach of levity and insensibility was really a signal instance of that perfect disinterestedness and selfdevotion of which man seems to be incapable, but which is sometimes found in woman.*

Tender and new pieces of the Crown.

On the morning of Wednesday, the thirteenth of February, the court of Whitehall and all the neighbouring streets were filled with gazers. The magnificent Banqueting House, the masterpiece of Inigo, embellished by masterpieces of Rubens, had been prepared for a great ceremony. The walls were lined by the yeomen of the guard. Near the northern door,

* Duchess of Marlborough's Vindication; Review of the Vindication; Burnet, i. 781. 825. and Dartmouth's note; Evelyn's Diary, Feb. 21, 1685.

on the right hand, a large number of Peers had assembled. On the left were the Commons with their Speaker, attended by the mace. The southern door opened: and the Prince and Princess of Orange, side by side, entered, and took their place under the canopy of state.

Both Houses approached bowing low. William and Mary advanced a few steps. Halifax on the right, and Powle on the left, stood forth; and Halifax spoke. The Convention, he said, had agreed to a resolution which he prayed Their Highnesses to hear. They signified their assent; and the clerk of the House of Lords read, in a loud voice, the Declaration of Right. When he had concluded, Halifax, in the name of all the Estates of the Realm, requested the Prince and Princess to accept the crown.

William, in his own name and in that of his wife, answered that the crown was, in their estimation, the more valuable because it was presented to them as a token of the confidence of the nation. "We thankfully accept," he said, "what you have offered us." Then, for himself, he assured them that the laws of England, which he had once already vindicated, should be the rules of his conduct, that it should be his study to promote the welfare of the kingdom, and that, as to the means of doing so, he should constantly recur to the advice of the Houses, and should be disposed to trust their judgment rather than his own.* These words were received with a shout of joy which was heard in the streets below, and was instantly answered by huzzas from many thousands of voices. The Lords and Commons then reverently retired from the Banqueting House and went in procession to the great gate of Whitehall, where the heralds and pursuivants were waiting in their gorgeous tabards.

All the space as far as Charing Cross was one sea of heads. The kettle drums struck up: the trumpets pealed; and Garter King at Arms, in a loud voice, proclaimed the Prince and Princess of Orange King and Queen of England, charged all Englishmen to bear, from that moment, true allegiance to the new sovereigns, and besought God, who had already wrought so signal a deliverance for our Church and nation, to bless William and Mary with a long and happy reign.†

William and Mary proclaimed.

---

* Lords' and Commons' Journals, Feb. 13. 1688; Van Citters, Feb. 1/9. Van Citters puts into William's mouth stronger expressions of respect for the authority of Parliament than appear in the journals; but it is clear from what Powle said that the report in the journals was not strictly accurate.

† London Gazette, Feb. 14. 1688; Lords' and Commons' Journals, Feb. 13.; Van Citters, Feb. 1/1.; Evelyn, Feb. 21.

Thus was consummated the English Revolution. When we compare it with those revolutions which have, during the last sixty years, overthrown so many ancient governments, we cannot but be struck by its peculiar character. Why that character was so peculiar is sufficiently obvious, and yet seems not to have been always understood either by eulogists or by censors.

The Continental revolutions of the eighteenth and nineteenth centuries took place in countries where all trace of the limited monarchy of the middle ages had long been effaced. The right of the prince to make laws and to levy money had, during many generations, been undisputed. His throne was guarded by a great regular army. His administration could not, without extreme peril, be blamed even in the mildest terms. His subjects held their personal liberty by no other tenure than his pleasure. Not a single institution was left which had, within the memory of the oldest man, afforded efficient protection to the subject against the utmost excess of tyranny. Those great councils which had once curbed the regal power had sunk into oblivion. Their composition and their privileges were known only to antiquaries. We cannot wonder, therefore, that, when men who had been thus ruled succeeded in wresting supreme power from a government which they had long in secret hated, they should have been impatient to demolish and unable to construct, that they should have been fascinated by every specious novelty, that they should have proscribed every title, ceremony, and phrase associated with the old system, and that, turning away with disgust from their own national precedents and traditions, they should have sought for principles of government in the writings of theorists, or aped, with ignorant and ungraceful affectation, the patriots of Athens and Rome. As little can we wonder that the violent action of the revolutionary spirit should have been followed by reaction equally violent, and that confusion should speedily have engendered despotism sterner than that from which it had sprung.

Had we been in the same situation; had Strafford succeeded in his favourite scheme of Thorough; had he formed an army as numerous and as well disciplined as that which, a few years later, was formed by Cromwell; had a series of judicial decisions, similar to that which was pronounced by the Exchequer Chamber in the case of shipmoney, transferred to the crown the right of taxing the people; had the Star Chamber and the High Commission continued to fine mutilate, and imprison every man who dared to raise his voice against the government; had the press been as completely enslaved here as at Vienna or at Naples; had our Kings gradually drawn to themselves the whole legislative power; had six generations of Englishmen passed away without a single session of Parliament; and had we then at length risen up in some moment of wild excitement against our masters, what an outbreak would that have been! With what a crash, heard and felt to the farthest ends of the world, would the whole vast fabric of society have fallen! How many thousands of exiles, once the most prosperous and the most refined members of this great community, would have begged their bread in Continental cities, or have sheltered their heads under huts of bark in the uncleared forests of America! How often should we have seen the pavement of London piled up in barricades, the houses dinted with bullets, the gutters foaming with blood! How many times should we have rushed wildly from extreme to extreme, sought refuge from anarchy in despotism, and been again driven by despotism into anarchy! How many years of blood and confusion would it have cost us to learn the very rudiments of political science! How many childish theories would have duped us! How many rude and ill poised constitutions should we have set up, only to see them tumble down! Happy would it have been for us if a sharp discipline of half a century had sufficed to educate us into a capacity of enjoying true freedom.

These calamities our Revolution averted. It was a revolution strictly defensive, and had prescription and legitimacy on its side. Here, and here only, a limited monarchy of the thirteenth century had come down unimpaired to the seventeenth century. Our parliamentary institutions were in full vigour. The main principles of our government were excellent. They were not, indeed, formally and exactly set forth in a single written instrument; but they were to be found scattered over our ancient and noble statutes; and, what was of far greater moment, they had been engraven on the hearts of Englishmen during four hundred years. That, without the consent of the representatives of the nation, no legislative act could be passed, no tax imposed, no regular soldiery kept up, that no man could be imprisoned, even for a day, by the arbitrary will of the sovereign, that no tool of power could plead the royal command as a justification for violating any right of the humblest subject, were held, both by Whigs and Tories, to be fundamental laws of the realm. A realm of which these were the fundamental laws stood in no need of a new constitution.

But, though a new constitution was not needed, it was plain that changes were required. The misgovernment of the Stuarts, and the troubles which that misgovernment had produced, sufficiently proved that there was somewhere a defect in our polity; and that defect it was the duty of the Convention to discover and to supply.

Some questions of great moment were still open to dispute. Our constitution had begun to exist in times when statesmen were not much accustomed to frame exact definitions. Anomalies, therefore, inconsistent with its principles and dangerous to its very existence, had sprung up almost imperceptibly, and, not having, during many years, caused any serious inconvenience, had gradually acquired the force of prescription. The remedy for these evils was to assert the rights of the people in such language as should terminate all controversy, and to declare that no precedent could justify any violation of those rights.

When this had been done it would be impossible for our rulers to misunderstand the law: but, unless something more were done, it was by no means improbable that they might violate it. Unhappily the Church had long taught the nation that hereditary monarchy, alone among our institutions, was divine and inviolable; that the right of the House of Commons to a share in the legislative power was a right merely human, but that the right of the King to the obedience of his people was from above; that the Great Charter was a statute which might be repealed by those who had made it, but that the rule which called the princes of the blood royal to the throne in order of succession was of celestial origin, and that any Act of Parliament inconsistent with that rule was a nullity. It is evident that, in a society in which such superstitions prevail, constitutional freedom must ever be insecure. A power which is regarded merely as the ordinance of man cannot be an efficient check on a power which is regarded as the ordinance of God. It is vain to hope that laws, however excellent, will permanently restrain a king who, in his own opinion, and in the opinion of a great part of his people, has an authority infinitely higher in kind than the authority which belongs to those laws. To deprive royalty of these mysterious attributes, and to establish the principle that Kings reigned by a right in no respect differing from the right by which freeholders chose knights of the shire, or from the right by which Judges granted writs of Habeas Corpus, was absolutely necessary to the security of our liberties.

Thus the Convention had two great duties to perform. The first was to clear the fundamental laws of the realm from ambiguity. The second was to eradicate from the minds, both of the governors and of the governed, the false and pernicious notion that the royal prerogative was something more sublime and holy than those fundamental laws. The former object was attained by the solemn recital and claim with which the Declaration of Right commences; the latter by the resolution which pronounced the throne vacant, and invited William and Mary to fill it.

The change seems small. Not a single flower of the crown was touched. Not a single new right was given to the people. The whole English law, substantive and adjective, was, in the judgment of all the greatest lawyers, of Holt and Treby, of Maynard and Somers, almost exactly the same after the Revolution as before it. Some controverted points had been decided according to the sense of the best jurists; and there had been a slight deviation from the ordinary course of succession. This was all; and this was enough.

As our Revolution was a vindication of ancient rights, so it was conducted with strict attention to ancient formalities. In almost every word and act may be discerned a profound reverence for the past. The Estates of the Realm deliberated in the old halls and according to the old rules. Powle was conducted to his chair between his mover and his seconder with the accustomed forms. The Serjeant with his mace brought up the messengers of the Lords to the table of the Commons; and the three obeisances were duly made. The conference was held with all the antique ceremonial. On one side of the table, in the Painted Chamber, the managers for the Lords sate covered and robed in ermine and gold. The managers for the Commons stood bareheaded on the other side. The speeches present an almost ludicrous contrast to the revolutionary oratory of every other country. Both the English parties agreed in treating with solemn respect the ancient constitutional traditions of the state. The only question was, in what sense those traditions were to be understood. The assertors of liberty said not a word about the natural equality of men and the inalienable sovereignty of the people, about Harmodius or Timoleon, Brutus the elder or Brutus the younger. When they were told that, by the English law, the crown, at the moment of a demise, must descend to the next heir, they answered that, by the English law, a living man could have no heir. When they were told that there was no precedent for declaring the throne vacant, they produced from among the records in the Tower a roll of parchment, near three hundred years old, on which, in quaint characters and barbarous Latin, it was recorded that the Estates of the Realm had declared vacant the throne of a perfidious and tyrannical Plantagenet. When at length the dispute had been accommodated, the new sovereigns were proclaimed with the old pageantry. All the fantastic pomp of heraldry was there, Clarencieux and Norroy, Portcullis and Rouge Dragon, the trumpets, the banners, the grotesque coats embroidered with lions and lilies. The title of King of France, assumed by the conqueror of Cressy, was not omitted in the royal style. To us, who have lived in the year 1848, it may seem almost an abuse of terms to call a proceeding, conducted with so much deliberation, with so much sobriety, and with such minute attention to prescriptive etiquette, by the terrible name of Revolution.

And yet this revolution, of all revolutions the least violent, has been of all revolutions the most beneficent. It finally decided the great question whether the popular element which had, ever since the age of Fitzwalter and De Montfort, been found in the English polity, should be destroyed by the monarchical element, or should be suffered to develope itself freely, and to become dominant. The strife between the two principles had been long, fierce, and doubtful. It had lasted through four reigns. It had produced seditions, impeachments, rebellions, battles, sieges, proscriptions, judicial massacres. Sometimes liberty, sometimes royalty, had seemed to be on the point of perishing. During many years one half of the energy of England had been employed in counteracting the other half. The executive power and the legislative power had so effectually impeded each other that the state had been of no account in Europe. The King at Arms, who proclaimed William and Mary before Whitehall Gate, did in truth announce that this great struggle was over; that there was entire union between the throne and the Parliament; that England, long dependent and degraded, was again a power of the first rank; that the ancient laws by which the prerogative was bounded would thenceforth be held as sacred as the prerogative itself, and would be followed out to all their consequences; that the executive administration would be conducted in conformity with the sense of the representatives of the nation; and that no reform, which the two Houses should, after mature deliberation, propose, would be obstinately withstood by the sovereign. The Declaration of Right, though it made nothing law which had not been law before, contained the germ of the law which gave religious freedom to the Dissenter, of the law which secured the independence of the judges, of the law which limited the duration of Parliaments, of the law which placed the liberty of the press under the protection of juries, of the law which prohibited the slave trade, of the law which abolished the sacramental test, of the law which relieved the Roman Catholics from civil disabilities, of the law which reformed the representative system, of every good law which has been passed during more than a century and a half, of every good law which may hereafter, in the course of ages, be found necessary to promote the public weal, and to satisfy the demands of public opinion.

The highest eulogy which can be pronounced on the revolution of 1688 is this, that it was our last revolution. Several generations have now passed away since any wise and patriotic Englishman has meditated resistance to the established government. In all honest and reflecting minds there is a conviction, daily strengthened by experience, that the means of effecting every improvement which the constitution requires may be found within the constitution itself.

Now, if ever, we ought to be able to appreciate the whole importance of the stand which was made by our forefathers against the House of Stuart.* All around us the world is convulsed by the agonies of great nations. Governments which lately seemed likely to stand during ages have been on a sudden shaken and overthrown. The proudest capitals of Western Europe have streamed with civil blood. All evil passions, the thirst of gain and the thirst of vengeance, the antipathy of class to class, the antipathy of race to race, have

* This passage was written in November 1848.

broken loose from the control of divine and human laws. Fear and anxiety have clouded the faces and depressed the hearts of millions. Trade has been suspended, and industry paralysed. The rich have become poor; and the poor have become poorer. Doctrines hostile to all sciences, to all arts, to all industry, to all domestic charities, doctrines which, if carried into effect, would, in thirty years, undo all that thirty centuries have done for mankind, and would make the fairest provinces of France and Germany as savage as Congo or Patagonia, have been avowed from the tribune and defended by the sword. Europe has been threatened with subjugation by barbarians, compared with whom the barbarians who marched under Attila and Alboin were enlightened and humane. The truest friends of the people have with deep sorrow owned that interests more precious than any political privileges were in jeopardy, and that it might be necessary to sacrifice even liberty in order to save civilisation. Meanwhile in our island the regular course of government has never been for a day interrupted. The few bad men who longed for license and plunder have not had the courage to confront for one moment the strength of a loyal nation, rallied in firm array round a parental throne. And, if it be asked what has made us to differ from others, the answer is that we never lost what others are wildly and blindly seeking to regain. It is because we had a preserving revolution in the seventeenth century that we have not had a destroying revolution in the nineteenth. It is because we had freedom in the midst of servitude that we have order in the midst of anarchy. For the authority of law, for the security of property, for the peace of our streets, for the happiness of our homes, our gratitude is due, under Him who raises and pulls down nations at his pleasure, to the Long Parliament, to the Convention, and to William of Orange.

CHAPTER XL

THE Revolution had been accomplished. The decrees of the Convention were everywhere received with submission. London, true during fifty eventful years to the cause of civil freedom and of the reformed religion, was foremost in professing loyalty to the new Sovereigns. Garter King at Arms, after making proclamation under the windows of Whitehall, rode in state along the Strand to Temple Bar. He was followed by the maces of the two Houses, by the two Speakers, Halifax and Powle, and by a long train of coaches filled with noblemen and gentlemen. The magistrates of the City threw open their gates and joined the procession. Four regiments of militia lined the way up Ludgate Hill, round Saint Paul's Cathedral, and along Cheapside. The streets, the balconies, and the very housetops were crowded with gazers. All the steeples from the Abbey to the Tower sent forth a joyous din. The proclamation was repeated, with sound of trumpet, in front of the Royal Exchange, amidst the shouts of the citizens.

In the evening every window from Whitechapel to Piccadilly was lighted up. The state rooms of the palace were thrown open, and were filled by a gorgeous company of courtiers desirous to kiss the hands of the King and Queen. The Whigs assembled there, flushed with victory and prosperity. There were among them some who might be pardoned if a vindictive feeling mingled with their joy. The most deeply injured of all who had survived the evil times was absent. Lady Russell, while her friends were crowding the galleries of Whitehall, remained in her retreat, thinking of one who, if he had been still living, would have held no undistinguished place in the ceremonies of that great day. But her daughter, who had a few months before become the wife of Lord Cavendish, was presented to the royal pair by his mother the Countess of Devonshire. A letter is still extant in which the young lady described with great vivacity the roar of the populace, the blaze in the streets, the throng in the presence

CHAP. XI.
1689.
William and Mary proclaimed in London.

chamber, the beauty of Mary, and the expression which ennobled and softened the harsh features of William. But the most interesting passage is that in which the orphan girl avowed the stern delight with which she had witnessed the tardy punishment of her father's murderer.*

Rejoicings throughout England.

The example of London was followed by the provincial towns. During three weeks the Gazettes were filled with accounts of the solemnities by which the public joy manifested itself, cavalcades of gentlemen and yeomen, processions of Sheriffs and Bailiffs in scarlet gowns, musters of zealous Protestants with orange flags and ribands, salutes, bonfires, illuminations, music, balls, dinners, gutters running with ale, and conduits spouting claret.†

Rejoicings in Holland.

Still more cordial was the rejoicing among the Dutch, when they learned that the first minister of their Commonwealth had been raised to a throne. On the very day of his accession he had written to assure the States General that the change in his situation had made no change in the affection which he bore to his native land, and that his new dignity would, he hoped, enable him to discharge his old duties more efficiently than ever. That oligarchical party, which had always been hostile to the doctrines of Calvin and to the House of Orange, muttered faintly that His Majesty ought to resign the Stadtholdership. But all such mutterings were drowned by the acclamations of a people proud of the genius and success of their great countryman. A day of thanksgiving was appointed. In all the cities of the Seven Provinces the public joy manifested itself by festivities of which the expense was chiefly defrayed by voluntary gifts. Every class assisted. The poorest labourer could help to set up an arch of triumph, or to bring sedge to a bonfire. Even the ruined Huguenots of France could contribute the aid of their ingenuity. One art which they had carried with them into banishment was the art of making fireworks; and they now, in honour of the victorious champion of their faith, lighted up the canals of Amsterdam with showers of splendid constellations.‡

* Letter from Lady Cavendish to Sylvia. Lady Cavendish, like most of the clever girls of that generation, had Scudéry's romances in her head. She is Dorinda: her correspondent, supposed to be her cousin Jane Allington, is Sylvia: William is Ormasdes, and Mary Pheninnus. London Gazette, Feb. 11. 168⅔; Luttrell's Diary.

† See the London Gazettes of February and March 168⅔, and Luttrell's Diary.

‡ Wagenaar, lxi. He quotes the proceedings of the States of the 2nd of March, 1689. London Gazette, April 11. 1689; Monthly Mercury for April, 1689.

To superficial observers it might well seem that William
was, at this time, one of the most enviable of human beings.
He was in truth one of the most anxious and unhappy. He
well knew that the difficulties of his task were only beginning.
Already that dawn which had lately been so bright was overcast;
and many signs portended a dark and stormy day.
It was observed that two important classes took little or
no part in the festivities by which, all over England, the inauguration
of the new government was celebrated. Very
seldom could either a priest or a soldier be seen in the assemblages
which gathered round the market crosses where
the King and Queen were proclaimed. The professional
pride both of the clergy and of the army had been deeply
wounded. The doctrine of nonresistance had been dear to
the Anglican divines. It was their distinguishing badge. It
was their favourite theme. If we are to judge by that portion
of their oratory which has come down to us, they had
preached about the duty of passive obedience at least as often
and as zealously as about the Trinity or the Atonement.*
Their attachment to their political creed had indeed been
severely tried, and had, during a short time, wavered. But
with the tyranny of James the bitter feeling which that
tyranny had excited among them had passed away. The parson
of a parish was naturally unwilling to join in what was
really a triumph over those principles which, during twentyeight
years, his flock had heard him proclaim on every anniversary
of the Martyrdom and on every anniversary of the
Restoration.

The soldiers, too, were discontented. They hated Popery
indeed; and they had not loved the banished King. But
they keenly felt that, in the short campaign which had decided
the fate of their country, theirs had been an inglorious
part. A regular army such as had never before marched to
battle under the royal standard of England, had retreated
precipitately before an invader, and had then, without a
struggle, submitted to him. That great force had been absolutely
of no account in the late change, had done nothing
towards keeping William out, and had done nothing towards

CHAP XL.

Discontent of the clergy and of the army.

---

* "I may be positive," says a writer who had been educated at Westminster school, "where I heard one sermon of repentance, faith, and the renewing of the Holy Ghost, I heard three of the other; and 'tis hard to say whether Jesus Christ or King Charles the First were oftener mentioned and magnified." —Bisset's Modern Fanatic, 1710.

bringing him in. The clowns, who, armed with pitchforks and mounted on carthorses, had straggled in the train of Lovelace or Delamere, had borne a greater part in the Revolution than those splendid household troops, whose plumed hats, embroidered coats, and curvetting chargers the Londoners had so often seen with admiration in Hyde Park. The mortification of the army was increased by the taunts of the foreigners, taunts which neither orders nor punishments could entirely restrain.* At several places the anger which a brave and highspirited body of men might, in such circumstances, be expected to feel, showed itself in an alarming manner. A battalion which lay at Cirencester put out the bonfires, huzzaed for King James, and drank confusion to his daughter and his nephew. The garrison of Plymouth disturbed the rejoicings of the County of Cornwall: blows were exchanged; and a man was killed in the fray.†

Reaction of public feeling.

The ill humour of the clergy and of the army could not but be noticed by the most heedless; for the clergy and the army were distinguished from other classes by obvious peculiarities of garb. "Black coats and red coats," said a vehement Whig in the House of Commons, "are the curses of the nation."‡ But the discontent was not confined to the black coats and the red coats. The enthusiasm with which men of all classes had welcomed William to London at Christmas had greatly abated before the close of February. The new King had, at the very moment at which his fame and fortune reached the highest point, predicted the coming reaction. That reaction might, indeed, have been predicted by a less sagacious observer of human affairs. For it is to be chiefly ascribed to a law as certain as the laws which regulate the succession of the seasons and the course of the trade winds. It is the nature of man to overrate present evil, and to underrate present good; to long for what he has not, and to be dissatisfied with what he has. This propensity, as it appears in individuals, has often been noticed both by laughing and by weeping philosophers. It was a favourite theme of Horace and of Pascal, of Voltaire and of Johnson. To its influence on the fate of great communities may be ascribed most of the revolutions and counterrevolutions recorded in history. A hundred generations have passed away since

---

* Paris Gazette, Feb. 26/Mar. 7, 1689; Orange Gazette, London, Jan. 10, 1689. Feb. 26. 1689; Boscawen's Speech, March 1.; Luttrell's Diary, Feb. 23-27.
† Grey's Debates, Howe's Speech. ‡ Grey's Debates, Feb. 26. 1689.

the first great national emancipation, of which an account has come down to us. We read in the most ancient of books that a people bowed to the dust under a cruel yoke, scourged to toil by hard taskmasters, not supplied with straw, yet compelled to furnish the daily tale of bricks, became sick of life, and raised such a cry of misery as pierced the heavens. The slaves were wonderfully set free: at the moment of their liberation they raised a song of gratitude and triumph: but, in a few hours, they began to regret their slavery, and to reproach the leader who had decoyed them away from the savoury fare of the house of bondage to the dreary waste which still separated them from the land flowing with milk and honey. Since that time the history of every great deliverer has been the history of Moses retold. Down to the present hour rejoicings like those on the shore of the Red Sea have ever been speedily followed by murmurings like those at the Waters of Strife.* The most just and salutary revolution must produce much suffering. The most just and salutary revolution cannot produce all the good that had been expected from it by men of uninstructed minds and sanguine tempers. Even the wisest cannot, while it is still recent, weigh quite fairly the evils which it has caused against the evils which it has removed. For the evils which it has caused are felt; and the evils which it has removed are felt no longer.

Thus it was now in England. The public was, as it always is during the cold fits which follow its hot fits, sullen, hard to please, dissatisfied with itself, dissatisfied with those who had lately been its favourites. The truce between the two great parties was at an end. Separated by the memory of all that had been done and suffered during a conflict of half a century, they had been, during a few months, united by a common danger. But the danger was over: the union was dissolved; and the old animosity broke forth again in all its strength.

James had, during the last year of his reign, been even more hated by the Tories than by the Whigs; and not without cause: for to the Whigs he was only an enemy; and to the Tories he had been a faithless and thankless friend. But the

CHAP. XL.

Temper of the Tories.

---

* This illustration is repeated to satiety in sermons and pamphlets of the time of William the Third. There is a poor imitation of Absalom and Ahitophel entitled the Murmurers. William is Moses; Corah, Dathan, and Abiram, nonjuring Bishops; Balaam, I think, Dryden; and Phinehas Shrewsbury.

old Royalist feeling, which had seemed to be extinct in the time of his lawless domination, had been partially revived by his misfortunes. Many lords and gentlemen who had, in December, taken arms for the Prince of Orange and a Free Parliament, muttered two months later, that they had been drawn in; that they had trusted too much to His Highness's Declaration; that they had given him credit for a disinterestedness which it now appeared was not in his nature. They had meant to put on King James, for his own good, some gentle force, to punish the Jesuits and renegades who had misled him, to obtain from him some guarantee for the safety of the civil and ecclesiastical institutions of the realm, but not to uncrown and banish him. For his maladministration, gross as it had been, excuses were found. Was it strange that, driven from his native land, while still a boy, by rebels who were a disgrace to the Protestant name, and forced to pass his youth in countries where the Roman Catholic religion was established, he should have been captivated by that most attractive of all superstitions? Was it strange that, persecuted and calumniated as he had been by an implacable faction, his disposition should have become sterner and more severe than it had once been thought, and that, when those who had tried to blast his honour and to rob him of his birthright were at length in his power, he should not have sufficiently tempered justice with mercy? As to the worst charge which had been brought against him, the charge of trying to cheat his daughters out of their inheritance by fathering a supposititious child, on what grounds did it rest? Merely on slight circumstances, such as might well be imputed to accident, or to that imprudence which was but too much in harmony with his character. Did ever the most stupid country justice put a boy in the stocks without requiring stronger evidence than that on which the English people had pronounced their King guilty of the basest and most odious of all frauds? Some great faults he had doubtless committed: nothing could be more just or constitutional than that for those faults his advisers and tools should be called to a severe reckoning; nor did any of those advisers and tools more richly deserve punishment than the Roundhead sectaries whose adulation had encouraged him to persist in the fatal exercise of the dispensing power. It was a fundamental principle of law that the King could do no wrong, and that, if wrong were done by his authority, his counsellors

and agents were responsible. That great rule, essential to
our polity, was now inverted. The sycophants, who were
legally punishable, enjoyed impunity: the King, who was
not legally punishable, was punished with merciless severity.
Was it possible for the Cavaliers of England, the sons of the
warriors who had fought under Rupert, not to feel bitter sorrow
and indignation when they reflected on the fate of their
rightful liege lord, the heir of a long line of princes, lately
enthroned in splendour at Whitehall, now an exile, a suppliant, a mendicant? His calamities had been greater than
even those of the Blessed Martyr from whom he sprang. The
father had been slain by avowed and deadly foes: the ruin of
the son had been the work of his own children. Surely the
punishment, even if deserved, should have been inflicted by
other hands. And was it altogether deserved? Had not the
unhappy man been rather weak and rash than wicked? Had
he not some of the qualities of an excellent prince? His
abilities were certainly not of a high order: but he was diligent: he was thrifty: he had fought bravely: he had been
his own minister for maritime affairs, and had, in that capacity acquitted himself respectably: he had, till his spiritual
guides obtained a fatal ascendency over his mind, been
regarded as a man of strict justice; and, to the last, when
he was not misled by them, he generally spoke truth and
dealt fairly. With so many virtues he might, if he had been
a Protestant, nay, if he had been a moderate Roman Catholic,
have had a prosperous and glorious reign. Perhaps it might
not be too late for him to retrieve his errors. It was difficult
to believe that he could be so dull and perverse as not to have
profited by the terrible discipline which he had recently undergone; and, if that discipline had produced the effects
which might reasonably be expected from it, England might
still enjoy, under her legitimate ruler, a larger measure of
happiness and tranquillity than she could expect from the
administration of the best and ablest usurper.

We should do great injustice to those who held this language, if we supposed that they had, as a body, ceased to
regard Popery and despotism with abhorrence. Some zealots
might indeed be found who could not bear the thought of
imposing conditions on their King, and who were ready to
recall him without the smallest assurance that the Declaration of Indulgence should not be instantly republished, that
the High Commission should not be instantly revived, that

Petre should not be again seated at the Council Board, and that the Fellows of Magdalene should not again be ejected. But the number of these men was small. On the other hand, the number of those Royalists, who, if James would have acknowledged his mistakes and promised to observe the laws, were ready to rally round him, was very large. It is a remarkable fact that two able and experienced statesmen, who had borne a chief part in the Revolution, frankly acknowledged, a few days after the Revolution had been accomplished, their apprehension that a Restoration was close at hand. "If King James were a Protestant," said Halifax to Reresby, "we could not keep him out four months." "If King James," said Danby to Reresby about the same time, "would but give the country some satisfaction about religion, which he might easily do, it would be very hard to make head against him."* Happily for England, James was, as usual, his own worst enemy. No word indicating that he took blame to himself on account of the past, or that he intended to govern constitutionally for the future, could be extracted from him. Every letter, every rumour, that found its way from Saint Germains to England made men of sense fear that, if, in his present temper, he should be restored to power, the second tyranny would be worse than the first. Thus the Tories, as a body, were forced to admit, very unwillingly, that there was, at that moment, no choice but between William and public ruin. They therefore, without altogether relinquishing the hope that he who was King by right might at some future time be disposed to listen to reason, and without feeling anything like loyalty towards him who was King in possession, discontentedly endured the new government.

Temper of the Whigs. It may be doubted whether that government was not, during the first months of its existence, in more danger from the affection of the Whigs than from the disaffection of the Tories. Enmity can hardly be more annoying than querulous, jealous, exacting fondness; and such was the fondness which the Whigs felt for the Sovereign of their choice. They were loud in his praise. They were ready to support him with purse and sword against foreign and domestic foes. But their attachment to him was of a peculiar kind. Loyalty such as had animated the gallant gentlemen who had fought for Charles the First, loyalty such as had rescued Charles the Second from the fearful dangers and difficulties caused by

* Reresby's Memoirs.

twenty years of maladministration, was not a sentiment to which the doctrines of Milton and Sidney were favourable: nor was it a sentiment which a prince, just raised to power by a rebellion, could hope to inspire. The Whig theory of government is that kings exist for the people, and not the people for kings; that the right of a king is divine in no other sense than that in which the right of a member of parliament, of a judge, of a juryman, of a mayor, of a headborough, is divine; that while the chief magistrate governs according to law, he ought to be obeyed and reverenced; that, when he violates the law, he ought to be withstood; and that, when he violates the law grossly, systematically, and pertinaciously, he ought to be deposed. On the truth of these principles depended the justice of William's title to the throne. It is obvious that the relation between subjects who held these principles, and a ruler whose accession had been the triumph of these principles, must have been altogether different from the relation which had subsisted between the Stuarts and the Cavaliers. The Whigs loved William indeed: but they loved him, not as a king, but as a party leader; and it was not difficult to foresee that their enthusiasm would cool fast if he should refuse to be the mere leader of their party, and should attempt to be king of the whole nation. What they expected from him in return for their devotion to his cause was that he should be one of themselves, a stanch and ardent Whig; that he should show favour to none but Whigs; that he should make all the old grudges of the Whigs his own; and there was but too much reason to apprehend that, if he disappointed this expectation, the only section of the community which was zealous in his cause would be estranged from him.*

Such were the difficulties by which, at the moment of his elevation, he found himself beset. Where there was a good path he had seldom failed to choose it. But now he had only a choice among paths every one of which seemed likely to lead to destruction. From one faction he could hope for no cordial support. The cordial support of the other faction he could retain only by becoming the most factious man in his kingdom, a Shaftesbury on the throne. If he persecuted the

---

* Here, and in many other places, I abstain from citing authorities, because my authorities are too numerous to cite. My notions of the temper and relative position of political and religious parties in the reign of William the Third, have been derived, not from any single work, but from thousands of forgotten tracts, sermons, and satires; in fact, from a whole literature which is mouldering in old libraries.

Tories, their sulkiness would infallibly be turned into fury. If he showed favour to the Tories, it was by no means certain that he would gain their goodwill; and it was but too probable that he might lose his hold on the hearts of the Whigs. Something however he must do: something he must risk: a Privy Council must be sworn in: all the great offices, political and judicial, must be filled. It was impossible to make an arrangement that would please everybody, and difficult to make an arrangement that would please anybody: but an arrangement must be made.

Ministerial arrangements.

What is now called a ministry he did not think of forming. Indeed what is now called a ministry was never known in England till he had been some years on the throne. Under the Plantagenets, the Tudors, and the Stuarts, there had been ministers: but there had been no ministry. The servants of the Crown were not, as now, bound in frankpledge for each other. They were not expected to be of the same opinion even on questions of the gravest importance. Often they were politically and personally hostile to each other, and made no secret of their hostility. It was not yet felt to be inconvenient or unseemly that they should accuse each other of high crimes, and demand each other's heads. No man had been more active in the impeachment of the Lord Chancellor Clarendon than Coventry, who was a Commissioner of the Treasury. No man had been more active in the impeachment of the Lord Treasurer Danby than Winnington, who was Solicitor General. Among the members of the Government there was only one point of union, their common head, the Sovereign. The nation considered him as the proper chief of the administration, and blamed him severely if he delegated his high functions to any subject. Clarendon has told us that nothing was so hateful to the Englishmen of his time as a Prime Minister. They would rather, he said, be subject to an usurper like Oliver, who was first magistrate in fact as well as in name, than to a legitimate King who referred them to a Grand Vizier. One of the chief accusations which the country party had brought against Charles the Second was that he was too indolent and too fond of pleasure to examine with care the balance sheets of public accountants and the inventories of military stores. James, when he came to the crown, had determined to appoint no Lord High Admiral or Board of Admiralty, and to keep the entire direction of maritime affairs in his own hands; and this arrangement, which would now be thought by men of all parties unconstitutional and pernicious in the highest degree, was then generally applauded even by people who were not inclined to see his conduct in a favourable light. How completely the relation in which the King stood to his Parliament and to his ministers had been altered by the Revolution was not at first understood even by the most enlightened statesmen. It was universally supposed that the government would, as in time past, be conducted by functionaries independent of each other, and that William would exercise a general superintendence over them all. It was also fully expected that a prince of William's capacity and experience would transact much important business without having recourse to any adviser.

There were therefore no complaints when it was understood that he had reserved to himself the direction of foreign affairs. This was indeed scarcely matter of choice: for, with the single exception of Sir William Temple, whom nothing would induce to quit his retreat for public life, there was no Englishman who had proved himself capable of conducting an important negotiation with foreign powers to a successful and honourable issue. Many years had elapsed since England had interfered with weight and dignity in the affairs of the great commonwealth of nations. The attention of the ablest English politicians had long been almost exclusively occupied by disputes concerning the civil and ecclesiastical constitution of their own country. The contests about the Popish Plot and the Exclusion Bill, the Habeas Corpus Act and the Test Act, had produced an abundance, indeed a glut, of those talents which raise men to eminence in societies torn by internal factions. All the Continent could not show such skilful and wary leaders of parties, such dexterous parliamentary tacticians, such ready and eloquent debaters, as were assembled at Westminster. But a very different training was necessary to form a great minister for foreign affairs; and the Revolution had on a sudden placed England in a situation in which the services of a great minister for foreign affairs were indispensable to her.

William was admirably qualified to supply that in which the most accomplished statesmen of his kingdom were deficient. He had long been preeminently distinguished as a negotiator. He was the author and the soul of the European coalition against the French ascendency. The clue, without which it was perilous to enter the vast and intricate maze of

CHAP. XI.

William his own minister for foreign affairs.

CHAP. XL.

Continental politics, was in his hands. His English counsellors, therefore, however able and active, seldom, during his reign, ventured to meddle with that part of the public business which he had taken as his peculiar province.*

The internal government of England could be carried on only by the advice and agency of English ministers. Those ministers William selected in such a manner as showed that he was determined not to proscribe any set of men who were willing to support his throne. On the day after the crown had been presented to him in the Banqueting House, the Privy Council was sworn in. Most of the Councillors were Whigs: but the names of several eminent Tories appeared in the list.† The four highest offices in the state were assigned to four noblemen, the representatives of four classes of politicians.

Danby.

In practical ability and official experience Danby had no superior among his contemporaries. To the gratitude of the new Sovereigns he had a strong claim; for it was by his dexterity that their marriage had been brought about in spite of difficulties which had seemed insuperable. The enmity which he had always borne to France was a scarcely less powerful recommendation. He had signed the invitation of the thirtieth of June, had excited and directed the Northern insurrection, and had, in the Convention, exerted all his influence and eloquence in opposition to the scheme of Regency. Yet the Whigs regarded him with unconquerable distrust and aversion. They could not forget that he had, in evil days, been the first minister of the state, the head of the Cavaliers, the champion of prerogative, the persecutor of dissenters. Even in becoming a rebel, he had not ceased to be a Tory. If he had drawn the sword against the crown, he had drawn it only in defence of the Church. If he had, in the Convention, done good by opposing the scheme of Regency, he had done harm by obstinately maintaining that the throne was not vacant, and that the Estates had no right to determine who should fill it. The Whigs were therefore of opinion that he ought to think himself amply rewarded for his recent merits by being suffered to escape the punishment of those offences for which he had been impeached ten years before. He, on the other hand, estimated his own abilities and services,

---

* The following passage in a tract of that time expresses the general opinion. " He has better knowledge of foreign affairs than we have; but in English business it is no dishonour to him to be told his relation to us, the nature of it, and what is fit for him to do."—An Honest Commoner's Speech.

† London Gazette, Feb. 14. 168⁹⁄₉.

which were doubtless considerable, at their full value, and
thought himself entitled to the great place of Lord High
Treasurer, which he had formerly held. But he was disappointed. William, on principle, thought it desirable to divide
the power and patronage of the Treasury among several Commissioners. He was the first English King who never, from
the beginning to the end of his reign, trusted the white staff
in the hands of a single subject. Danby was offered his
choice between the Presidency of the Council and a Secretaryship of State. He sullenly accepted the Presidency, and,
while the Whigs murmured at seeing him placed so high,
hardly attempted to conceal his anger at not having been
placed higher.*

Halifax, the most illustrious man of that small party which
boasted that it kept the balance even between Whigs and
Tories, took charge of the Privy Seal, and continued to be
Speaker of the House of Lords.† He had been foremost in
strictly legal opposition to the late Government, and had
spoken and written with great ability against the dispensing
power; but he had refused to know any thing about the
design of invasion: he had laboured, even when the Dutch
were in full march towards London, to effect a reconciliation;
and he had never deserted James till James had deserted the
throne. But, from the moment of that shameful flight, the
sagacious Trimmer, convinced that compromise was thenceforth impossible, had taken a decided part. He had distinguished himself preeminently in the Convention; nor was
it without a peculiar propriety that he had been appointed to
the honourable office of tendering the crown, in the name of
all the Estates of England, to the Prince and Princess of
Orange: for our Revolution, as far as it can be said to bear
the character of any single mind, assuredly bears the character
of the large yet cautious mind of Halifax. The Whigs, however, were not in a temper to accept a recent service as an
atonement for an old offence; and the offence of Halifax had
been grave indeed. He had long before been conspicuous in
their front rank during a hard fight for liberty. When they
were at length victorious, when it seemed that Whitehall
was at their mercy, when they had a near prospect of dominion
and revenge, he had changed sides; and fortune had changed
sides with him. In the great debate on the Exclusion Bill,

* London Gazette, Feb. 18, 168⅔; † London Gazette, Feb 18 168⅔;
Sir J. Reresby's Memoirs.   Lords' Journals.

his eloquence had struck the Opposition dumb, and had put new life into the inert and desponding party of the Court. It was true that, though he had left his old friends in the day of their insolent prosperity, he had returned to them in the day of their distress. But, now that their distress was over, they forgot that he had returned to them, and remembered only that he had left them.*

The vexation with which they saw Danby presiding in the Council, and Halifax bearing the Privy Seal, was not diminished by the news that Nottingham was appointed Secretary of State. Some of those zealous churchmen who had never ceased to profess the doctrine of nonresistance, who thought the Revolution unjustifiable, who had voted for a Regency, and who had to the last maintained that the English throne could never be one moment vacant, yet conceived it to be their duty to submit to the decision of the Convention. They had not, they said, rebelled against James. They had not elected William. But, now that they saw on the throne a Sovereign whom they never would have placed there, they were of opinion that no law, divine or human, bound them to carry the contest further. They thought that they found, both in the Bible and in the Statute Book, directions which could not be misunderstood. The Bible enjoins obedience to the powers that be. The Statute Book contains an Act providing that no subject shall be deemed a wrongdoer for adhering to the King in possession. On these grounds many, who had not concurred in setting up the new government, believed that they might give it their support without offence to God or man. One of the most eminent politicians of this school was Nottingham. At his instance the Convention had, before the throne was filled, made such changes in the oath of allegiance as enabled him and those who agreed with him to take that oath without scruple. "My principles," he said, "do not permit me to bear any part in making a King. But when a King has been made, my principles bind me to pay him an obedience more strict than he can expect from those who have made him." He now, to the surprise of some of those who most esteemed him, consented to sit in the council, and to accept the seals of Secretary. William doubtless hoped that this appointment would be considered by the clergy and the Tory country gentlemen as a sufficient guarantee that no evil was meditated against the Church. Even Burnet, who at a later period

* Burnet, ii. 4.

felt a strong antipathy to Nottingham, owned, in some memoirs written soon after the Revolution, that the King had judged well, and that the influence of the Tory Secretary, honestly exerted in support of the new Sovereigns, had saved England from great calamities.*

CHAP. XL

The other secretary was Shrewsbury.† No man so young had within living memory occupied so high a post in the government. He had but just completed his twenty-eighth year. Nobody, however, except the solemn formalists at the Spanish embassy, thought his youth an objection to his promotion.‡ He had already secured for himself a place in history by the conspicuous part which he had taken in the deliverance of his country. His talents, his accomplishments, his graceful manners, his bland temper, made him generally popular. By the Whigs especially he was almost adored. None suspected that, with many great and many amiable qualities, he had such faults both of head and of heart as would make the rest of a life which had opened under the fairest auspices burdensome to himself and almost useless to his country.

Shrewsbury.

The naval administration and the financial administration were confided to Boards. Herbert was First Commissioner of the Admiralty. He had in the late reign given up wealth and dignities when he had found that he could not retain them with honour and with a good conscience. He had carried the memorable invitation to the Hague. He had commanded the Dutch fleet during the voyage from Helvoetsluys to Torbay. His character for courage and professional skill stood high. That he had had his follies and vices was well known. But his recent conduct in the time of severe trial had atoned for

The Board of Admiralty.

---

* These memoirs will be found in a manuscript volume, which is part of the Harleian Collection, and is numbered 6584. They are in fact, the first outlines of a great part of Burnet's History of His Own Times. The dates at which the different portions of this most curious and interesting book were composed are marked. Almost the whole was written before the death of Mary. Burnet did not begin to prepare his History of William's Reign for the press till ten years later. By that time his opinions, both of men and of things, had undergone considerable changes. The value of the rough draught is therefore very great: for it contains some facts which he afterwards thought it advisable to suppress, and some judgments which he afterwards saw cause to alter. I must own that I generally like his first thoughts best. Whenever his History is reprinted, it ought to be carefully collated with this volume.

When I refer to the Burnet MS. Harl. 6584, I wish the reader to understand that the MS. contains something which is not to be found in the History.

As to Nottingham's appointment, see Burnet, ii. 8.; the London Gazette of March 7. 168 9/8 0 ; and Clarendon's Diary of Feb. 15.

† London Gazette, Feb. 18. 168 9/8 0 .
‡ Don Pedro de Ronquillo makes this objection.

all, and seemed to warrant the hope that his future career would be glorious. Among the commissioners who sate with him at the Admiralty were two distinguished members of the House of Commons, William Sacheverell, a veteran Whig, who had great authority in his party, and Sir John Lowther, an honest and very moderate Tory, who in fortune and parliamentary interest was among the first of the English gentry.*

The Board of Treasury.

Mordaunt, one of the most vehement of the Whigs, was placed at the head of the Treasury; why, it is difficult to say. His romantic courage, his flighty wit, his eccentric invention, his love of desperate risks and startling effects, were not qualities likely to be of much use to him in financial calculations and negotiations. Delamere, a more vehement Whig, if possible, than Mordaunt, sate second at the board, and was Chancellor of the Exchequer. Two Whig members of the House of Commons were in the Commission, Sir Henry Capel, brother of that Earl of Essex who died by his own hand in the Tower, and Richard Hampden, son of the great leader of the Long Parliament. But the Commissioner on whom the chief weight of business lay was Godolphin. This man, taciturn, clearminded, laborious, inoffensive, zealous for no government, and useful to every government, had gradually become an almost indispensable part of the machinery of the state. Though a churchman, he had prospered in a Court governed by Jesuits. Though he had voted for a Regency, he was the real head of a Treasury filled with Whigs. His abilities and knowledge, which had in the late reign supplied the deficiencies of Bellasyse and Dover, were now needed to supply the deficiencies of Mordaunt and Delamere.†

The Great Seal.

There were some difficulties in disposing of the Great Seal. The King at first wished to confide it to Nottingham, whose father had borne it during several years with high reputation.‡ Nottingham, however, declined the trust; and it was offered to Halifax, but was again declined. Both these lords doubtless felt that it was a trust which they could not discharge with honour to themselves or with advantage to the public. In old times, indeed, the Seal had been generally held by persons who were not lawyers. Even in the seventeenth

* London Gazette, March 11. 168⅞.
† Ibid.
‡ I have followed what seems to me the most probable story. But it has been doubted whether Nottingham was invited to be Chancellor, or only to be First Commissioner of the Great Seal. Compare Burnet, ii. 2, and Boyer's History of William. 1702. Narcissus Luttrell repeatedly, and even as late as the close of 1692, speaks of Nottingham as likely to be Chancellor.

century it had been confided to two eminent men who had never studied at any Inn of Court. Williams had been Lord Keeper to James the First. Shaftesbury had been Lord Chancellor to Charles the Second. But such appointments could no longer be made without serious inconvenience. Equity had been gradually shaping itself into a refined science, which no human faculties could master without long and intense application. Even Shaftesbury, vigorous as was his intellect, had painfully felt his want of technical knowledge *; and, during the fifteen years which had elapsed since Shaftesbury had resigned the Seal, technical knowledge had constantly been becoming more and more necessary to his successors. Neither Nottingham, therefore, though he had a stock of legal learning such as is rarely found in any person who has not received a legal education, nor Halifax, though in the judicial sittings of the House of Lords, the quickness of his apprehension, and the sublicty of his reasoning had often astonished the bar, ventured to accept the highest office which an English layman can fill. After some delay the Seal was confided to a commission of eminent lawyers, with Maynard at their head.†

The choice of Judges did honour to the new government. Every Privy Councillor was directed to bring a list. The lists were compared; and twelve men of conspicuous merit were selected.‡ The professional attainments and Whig principles of Pollexfen gave him pretensions to the highest place. But it was remembered that he had held briefs for the Crown, in the Western counties, at the assizes which followed the battle of Sedgemoor. It seems indeed from the reports of the trials that he did as little as he could do if he held the briefs at all, and that he left to the Judges the business of browbeating witnesses and prisoners. Nevertheless his name was inseparably associated in the public mind with the Bloody Circuit. He, therefore, could not with propriety be put at the head of the first criminal court in the realm.§ After acting during a few weeks as Attorney General, he was made Chief Justice of the Common Pleas. Sir John Holt, a young man, but distinguished by learning, integrity, and courage, became Chief Justice of the King's Bench. Sir Robert Atkyns, an eminent lawyer who had passed some years in rural retirement, but

CHAP. XI.

The Judges.

* Roger North relates an amusing story about Shaftesbury's embarrassments.
† London Gazette, March 4, 1688.
‡ Burnet, ii. 5.
§ The Protestant Mask taken off from the Jesuited Englishman, 1692.

whose reputation was still great in Westminster Hall, was appointed Chief Baron. Powell, who had been disgraced on account of his honest declaration in favour of the Bishops, again took his seat among the Judges. Treby succeeded Pollexfen as Attorney General; and Somers was made Solicitor.*

Two of the chief places in the Royal household were filled by two English noblemen eminently qualified to adorn a court. The high spirited and accomplished Devonshire was named Lord Steward. No man had done more or risked more for England during the crisis of her fate. In retrieving her liberties he had retrieved also the fortunes of his own house. His bond for thirty thousand pounds was found among the papers which James had left at Whitehall, and was cancelled by William.†

Dorset became Lord Chamberlain, and employed the influence and patronage annexed to his functions, as he had long employed his private means, in encouraging genius and in alleviating misfortune. One of the first acts which he was under the necessity of performing must have been painful to a man of so generous a nature, and of so keen a relish for whatever was excellent in arts and letters. Dryden could no longer remain Poet Laureate. The public would not have borne to see any Papist among the servants of Their Majesties; and Dryden was not only a Papist, but an apostate. He had moreover aggravated the guilt of his apostasy by calumniating and ridiculing the church which he had deserted. He had, it was facetiously said, treated her as the Pagan persecutors of old treated her children. He had dressed her up in the skin of a wild beast, and then baited her for the public amusement.‡ He was removed; but he received from the private bounty of the magnificent Chamberlain a pension equal to the salary which had been withdrawn. The deposed Laureate, however, as poor of spirit as rich in intellectual gifts, continued to complain piteously, year after year, of the losses which he had not suffered, till at length his wailings drew forth expressions of well merited contempt from brave and honest Jacobites, who had sacrificed everything to their principles without deigning to utter one word of deprecation or lamentation.†

---

* These appointments were not announced in the Gazette till the 6th of May; but some of them were made earlier.

† Kennet's Funeral Sermon on the first Duke of Devonshire, and Memoirs of the family of Cavendish, 1708.

‡ See a poem entitled, A Votive Tablet to the King and Queen.

§ See Prior's Dedication of his Poem's to Dorset's son and successor, and Dryden's Essay on Satire prefixed to the

WILLIAM AND MARY.

In the Royal household were placed some of those Dutch nobles who stood highest in the favour of the King. Bentinck had the great office of Groom of the Stole, with a salary of five thousand pounds a year. Zulestein took charge of the robes. The Master of the Horse was Auverquerque, a gallant soldier, who united the blood of Nassau to the blood of Horn, and who wore with just pride a costly sword presented to him by the States General in acknowledgment of the courage with which he had, on the bloody day of Saint Dennis, saved the life of William.

The place of Vice Chamberlain to the Queen was given to a man who had just become conspicuous in public life, and whose name will frequently recur in the history of this reign. John Howe, or, as he was more commonly called, Jack Howe, had been sent up to the Convention by the borough of Cirencester. His appearance was that of a man whose body was worn by the constant workings of a restless and acrid mind. He was tall, lean, pale, with a haggard eager look, expressive at once of flightiness and of shrewdness. He had been known, during several years, as a small poet; and some of the most savage lampoons which were handed about the coffeehouses were imputed to him. But it was in the House of Commons that both his parts and his illnature were most signally displayed. Before he had been a member three weeks, his volubility, his asperity, and his pertinacity had made him conspicuous. Quickness, energy, and audacity, united, soon raised him to the rank of a privileged man. His enemies,—and he had many enemies,—said that he consulted his personal safety even in his most petulant moods, and that he treated soldiers with a civility which he never showed to ladies or to Bishops. But no man had in larger measure that evil courage which braves and even courts disgust and hatred. No decencies restrained him: his spite was implacable: his skill in finding out the vulnerable parts of strong minds was consummate. All his great

---

Translations from Juvenal. There is a bitter sneer on Dryden's affectionate querulousness in Collier's Short View of the Stage. In Blackmore's Prince Arthur, a poem which, worthless as it is, contains some curious allusions to contemporary men and events, are the following lines:

"The poets' nation did obsequious wait
For the kind drop distilled at his gate,
Laureus among the meagre crowd appeared.

As old, revolted, unbelieving bard,
Who thronged, and shoved, and pressed,
      and would be heard.
Sahil's high roof, the Muses' palace, rung
With endless cries, and endless songs he sung,
To hire good Sahil Laureus would be first;
But Sahil's prince and Sahil's God he cursed.
Sahil without distinction threw his bread,
Despised the flatterer, but the poet fed."

I need not say that Sahil is Sackville, or that Laureus is a translation of the famous nickname Bayes.

CHAP. XI.

contemporaries felt his sting in their turns. Once it inflicted a wound which deranged even the stern composure of William, and constrained him to utter a wish that he were a private gentleman, and could invite Mr. Howe to a short interview behind Montague House. As yet, however, Howe was reckoned among the most strenuous supporters of the new government, and directed all his sarcasms and invectives against the malecontents.*

Subordinate appointments.

The subordinate places in every public office were divided between the two parties; but the Whigs had the larger share. Some persons, indeed, who did little honour to the Whig name, were largely recompensed for services which no good man would have performed. Wildman was made Postmaster General. A lucrative sinecure in the Excise was bestowed on Ferguson. The duties of the Solicitor of the Treasury were both very important and very invidious. It was the business of that officer to conduct political prosecutions, to collect the evidence, to instruct the counsel for the Crown, to see that the prisoners were not liberated on insufficient bail, to see that the juries were not composed of persons hostile to the government. In the days of Charles and James, the Solicitors of the Treasury had been, with too much reason, accused of employing all the vilest artifices of chicanery against men obnoxious to the Court. The new government ought to have made a choice which was above all suspicion. Unfortunately Mordaunt and Delamere pitched upon Aaron Smith, an acrimonious and unprincipled politician, who had been the legal adviser of Titus Oates in the days of the Popish plot, and who had been deeply implicated in the Rye House plot. Richard Hampden, a man of decided opinions, but of moderate temper, objected to this appointment. His objections however were overruled. The Jacobites, who hated Smith and had reason to hate him, affirmed that he had obtained his place by bullying the Lords of the Treasury, and particularly by threatening that, if his just claims were disregarded, he would be the death of Hampden.†

Some weeks elapsed before all the arrangements which

* Scarcely any man of that age is more frequently mentioned in pamphlets and satires than Howe. In the famous Petition of Legion, he is designated as "that impudent scandal of Parliaments." Mackay's account of him is curious. In a poem written in 1690, which I have never seen except in manuscript, are the following lines:

"First for Jack Howe with his terrible talent, Happy the female that scapes his lampoon; Armed at the belt a pierce-lively valiant, But very respectful to a Dragoon."

† Bent's True Account, North's Examen; Letter to Chief Justice Holt, 1691; Letter to Secretary Trenchard, 1694.

have been mentioned were publicly announced: and meanwhile many important events had taken place. As soon as the new Privy Councillors had been sworn in, it was necessary to submit to them a grave and pressing question. Could the Convention now assembled be turned into a Parliament? The Whigs, who had a decided majority in the Lower House, were all for the affirmative. The Tories, who knew that, within the last month, the public feeling had undergone a considerable change, and who hoped that a general election would add to their strength, were for the negative. They maintained that to the existence of a Parliament royal writs were indispensably necessary. The Convention had not been summoned by such writs; the original defect could not now be supplied: the Houses were therefore mere clubs of private men, and ought instantly to disperse.

It was answered that the royal writ was mere matter of form, and that to expose the substance of our laws and liberties to serious hazard for the sake of a form would be the most senseless superstition. Wherever the Sovereign, the Peers spiritual and temporal, and the Representatives freely chosen by the constituent bodies of the realm were met together, there was the essence of a Parliament. Such a Parliament was now in being; and what could be more absurd than to dissolve it at a conjuncture when every hour was precious, when numerous important subjects required immediate legislation, and when dangers, only to be averted by the combined efforts of King, Lords, and Commons, menaced the state? A Jacobite indeed might consistently refuse to recognise the Convention as a Parliament. For he held that it had from the beginning been an unlawful assembly, that all its resolutions were nullities, and that the Sovereigns whom it had set up were usurpers. But with what consistency could any man, who maintained that a new Parliament ought to be immediately called by writs under the great seal of William and Mary, question the authority which had placed William and Mary on the throne? Those who held that William was rightful King must necessarily hold that the body from which he derived his right was itself a rightful Great Council of the Realm. Those who, though not holding him to be rightful King, conceived that they might lawfully swear allegiance to him as King in fact, might surely, on the same principle, acknowledge the Convention as a Parliament in fact. It was plain that the Convention was the fountainhead from which the authority of all future Parliaments must be derived, and that on the validity of the votes of the Convention must depend the validity of every future statute. And how could the stream rise higher than the source? Was it not absurd to say that the Convention was supreme in the state, and yet a nullity; a legislature for the highest of all purposes, and yet no legislature for the humblest purposes; competent to declare the throne vacant, to change the succession, to fix the landmarks of the constitution, and yet not competent to pass the most trivial Act for the repairing of a pier or the building of a parish church?

These arguments would have had considerable weight, even if every precedent had been on the other side. But in truth our history afforded only one precedent which was at all in point; and that precedent was decisive in favour of the doctrine that royal writs are not indispensably necessary to the existence of a Parliament. No royal writ had summoned the Convention which recalled Charles the Second. Yet that Convention had, after his Restoration, continued to sit and to legislate, had settled the revenue, had passed an Act of amnesty, had abolished the feudal tenures. These proceedings had been sanctioned by authority of which no party in the state could speak without reverence. Hale, a jurist held in honour by every Whig, had borne a considerable share in them, and had always maintained that they were strictly legal. Clarendon, a statesman whose memory was respected by the great body of Tories, little as he was inclined to favour any doctrine derogatory to the rights of the Crown, or to the dignity of that seal of which he was keeper, had declared that, since God had, at a most critical conjuncture, given the nation a good Parliament, it would be the height of folly to look for technical flaws in the instrument by which that Parliament was called together. Would it be pretended that the Convention of 1660 had a more respectable origin than the Convention of 1689? Was not a letter written by the first Prince of the Blood, at the request of the whole peerage, and of hundreds of gentlemen who had represented counties and towns, at least as good a warrant as a vote of the Rump?

Weaker reasons than these would have satisfied the Whigs who formed the majority of the Privy Council. The King, therefore, on the fifth day after he had been proclaimed, went with royal state to the House of Lords, and took his seat on the throne. The Commons were called in; and he, with many gracious expressions, reminded his hearers of the perilous situation of the country, and exhorted them to take such steps as might prevent unnecessary delay in the transaction of public business. His speech was received by the gentlemen who crowded the bar with the deep hum by which our ancestors were wont to indicate approbation, and which was often heard in places more sacred than the Chamber of the Peers.* As soon as he had retired, a Bill declaring the Convention a Parliament was laid on the table of the Lords, and rapidly passed by them. In the Commons the debates were warm. The House resolved itself into a Committee; and so great was the excitement that, when the authority of the Speaker was withdrawn, it was hardly possible to preserve order. Sharp personalities were exchanged. The phrase, "Hear him," a phrase which had originally been used only to silence irregular noises, and to remind members of the duty of attending to the discussion, had, during some years, been gradually becoming what it now is; that is to say, a cry indicative, according to the tone, of admiration, acquiescence, indignation, or derision. On this occasion, the Whigs vociferated "Hear, hear," so tumultuously that the Tories complained of unfair usage. Seymour, the leader of the minority, declared that there could be no freedom of debate while such clamour was tolerated. Some old Whig members were provoked into reminding him that the same clamour had occasionally been heard when he presided, and had not then been repressed. Yet, eager and angry as both sides were, the speeches on both sides indicated that profound reverence for law and prescription which has long been characteristic of Englishmen, and which, though it runs sometimes into pedantry and sometimes into superstition, is not without its advantages. Even at that momentous crisis, when the nation was still in the ferment of a revolution, our public men talked long and seriously about all the circumstances of the deposition of Edward the Second, and of the deposition of Richard the Second, and anxiously enquired whether the assembly which, with Archbishop Lanfranc at its head, set aside Robert of Normandy, and put William Rufus on the throne, did or did not afterwards continue to act as the legislature of the realm. Much was said about the history of writs; much about the etymology of the word Parliament.

CHAP. XL.

* Van Citters, Feb. 1½ 1688.

It is remarkable, that the orator who took the most statesmanlike view of the subject was old Maynard. In the civil conflicts of fifty eventful years he had learned that questions affecting the highest interests of the commonwealth were not to be decided by verbal cavils and by scraps of Law French and Law Latin; and, being by universal acknowledgment the most subtle and the most learned of English jurists, he could express what he felt without the risk of being accused of ignorance and presumption. He scornfully thrust aside as frivolous and out of place all that blackletter learning, which some men, far less versed in such matters than himself, had introduced into the discussion. "We are," he said, "at this moment out of the beaten path. If therefore we are determined to move only in that path, we cannot move at all. A man in a revolution resolving to do nothing which is not strictly according to established form resembles a man who has lost himself in the wilderness, and who stands crying 'Where is the king's highway? I will walk nowhere but on the king's highway.' In a wilderness a man should take the track which will carry him home. In a revolution we must have recourse to the highest law, the safety of the state." Another veteran Roundhead, Colonel Birch, took the same side, and argued with great force and keenness from the precedent of 1660. Seymour and his supporters were beaten in the Committee, and did not venture to divide the House on the Report. The Bill passed rapidly, and received the royal assent on the tenth day after the accession of William and Mary.*

The law which turned the Convention into a Parliament contained a clause providing that no person should, after the first of March, sit or vote in either House without taking the oaths to the new King and Queen. This enactment produced great agitation throughout society. The adherents of the exiled dynasty hoped and confidently predicted that the recusants would be numerous. The minority in both Houses, it was said, would be true to the cause of hereditary monarchy. There might be here and there a traitor; but the great body of those who had voted for a Regency would be firm. Only two Bishops at most would recognise the usurpers. Seymour would retire from public life rather than abjure his principles.

* Stat. 1 W. & M. sess. i. c. 1. See the Journals of the two Houses, and Grey's Debates. The argument in favour of the bill is well stated in the Paris Gazettes of March 5, and 12, 1689.

Grafton had determined to fly to France and to throw himself at the feet of his uncle. With such rumours as these all the coffeehouses of London were filled during the latter part of February. So intense was the public anxiety that, if any man of rank was missed, two days running, at his usual haunts, it was immediately whispered that he had stolen away to Saint Germains.*

The second of March arrived; and the event quieted the fears of one party, and confounded the hopes of the other. The Primate indeed and several of his suffragans stood obstinately aloof: but three Bishops and seventy-three temporal peers took the oaths. At the next meeting of the Upper House several more prelates came in. Within a week about a hundred Lords had qualified themselves to sit. Others, who were prevented by illness from appearing, sent excuses and professions of attachment to their Majesties. Grafton refuted all the stories which had been circulated about him by coming to be sworn on the first day. Two members of the Ecclesiastical Commission, Mulgrave and Sprat, hastened to make atonement for their fault by plighting their faith to William. Beaufort, who had long been considered as the type of a royalist of the old school, submitted after a very short hesitation. Ailesbury and Dartmouth had as little scruple about taking the oath of allegiance as they afterwards had about breaking it.† The Hydes took different paths. Rochester complied with the law; but Clarendon proved refractory. Many thought it strange that the brother who had adhered to James till James absconded should be less sturdy than the brother who had been in the Dutch camp. The explanation perhaps is that Rochester would have sacrificed much more than Clarendon by refusing to take the oaths. Clarendon's income did not depend on the pleasure of the Government: but Rochester had a pension of four thousand a year, which he could not hope to retain if he refused to acknowledge the new Sovereigns. Indeed, he had so many enemies that, during some months, it seemed doubtful whether he would, on any terms, be suffered to retain the splendid reward which he had earned by persecuting the Whigs and by sitting in the High Commission. He was saved from what would have been a fatal blow to his fortunes

* Both Van Citters and Ronquillo London till the result was known. mention the anxiety which was felt in   † Lords' Journals, March 1689.

CHAP. XL.

by the intercession of Burnet, who had been deeply injured by him, and who revenged himself as became a Christian divine.*

In the Lower House four hundred members were sworn in on the second of March; and among them was Seymour. The spirit of the Jacobites was broken by his defection; and the minority, with very few exceptions, followed his example.†

Questions relating to the Revenue.

Before the day fixed for the taking of the oaths, the Commons had begun to discuss a momentous question which admitted of no delay. During the interregnum, William had, as provisional chief of the administration, collected the taxes and applied them to the public service; nor could the propriety of this course be questioned by any person who approved of the Revolution. But the Revolution was now over: the vacancy of the throne had been supplied: the Houses were sitting: the law was in full force; and it became necessary immediately to decide to what revenue the Government was entitled.

It was not denied that all the lands and hereditaments of the Crown had passed with the Crown to the new Sovereigns. It was not denied that all duties which had been granted to the Crown for a fixed term of years might be constitutionally exacted till that term should expire. But large revenues had been settled by Parliament on James for life; and whether what had been settled on James for life could, while he lived, be claimed by William and Mary, was a question about which opinions were divided.

Holt, Treby, Pollexfen, indeed all the eminent Whig lawyers, Somers excepted, held that these revenues had been granted to the late King, in his political capacity, but for his natural life, and ought therefore, as long as he continued to drag on his existence in a strange land, to be paid to William and Mary. It appears from a very concise and unconnected report of the debate that Somers dissented from this doctrine. His opinion was that, if the Act of Parliament which had imposed the duties in question was to be construed according to the spirit, the word life must be understood to mean reign, and that therefore the term for which the grant had been made had expired. This was surely the sound opinion: for it was plainly irrational to

---

* See the letters of Rochester and of Lady Ranelagh to Burnet on this occasion.
† Journals of the Commons, March 2. 168⅘. Ronquillo wrote as follows:

"Es de gran consideracion que Seimor haya tomado el juramento; porque es el arrengador y el director principal, en la cam de los Comunes, de los Anglicanos." March ⁵⁄₁₅. 168⅘.

treat the interest of James in this grant as at once a thing annexed to his person and a thing annexed to his office; to say in the same breath that the merchants of London and Bristol must pay money because he was in one sense alive, and that his successors must receive that money because he was in another sense defunct. The House was decidedly with Somers. The members generally were bent on effecting a great reform, without which it was felt that the Declaration of Right would be but an imperfect guarantee for public liberty. During the conflict which fifteen successive Parliaments had maintained against four successive Kings, the chief weapon of the Commons had been the power of the purse; nor had the representatives of the people ever been induced to surrender that weapon without having speedy cause to repent of their too credulous loyalty. In the season of tumultuous joy which followed the Restoration, a large revenue for life had been almost by acclamation granted to Charles the Second. A few months later there was scarcely a respectable Cavalier in the kingdom who did not own that the stewards of the nation would have acted more wisely if they had kept in their hands the means of checking the abuses which disgraced every department of the government. James the Second had obtained from his submissive Parliament, without a dissentient voice, an income amply sufficient to defray the ordinary expenses of the state during his life; and, before he had enjoyed that income half a year, the great majority of those who had dealt thus liberally with him blamed themselves severely for their liberality. If experience was to be trusted, a long and painful experience, there could be no effectual security against maladministration, unless the Sovereign were under the necessity of recurring frequently to his Great Council for pecuniary aid. Almost all honest and enlightened men were therefore agreed in thinking that a part at least of the supplies ought to be granted only for a short term. And what time could be fitter for the introduction of this new practice than the year 1689, the commencement of a new reign, of a new dynasty, of a new era of constitutional government? The feeling on this subject was so strong and general that the dissentient minority gave way. No formal resolution was passed: but the House proceeded to act on the supposition that the grants which had been made to James for life had been annulled by his abdication.*

* Grey's Debates, Feb. 25, 26, and 27. 1689.

It was impossible to make a new settlement of the revenue without enquiry and deliberation. The Exchequer was ordered to furnish such returns as might enable the House to form estimates of the public expenditure and income. In the meantime, liberal provision was made for the immediate exigencies of the state. An extraordinary aid, to be raised by direct monthly assessment, was voted to the King. An Act was passed indemnifying all who had, since his landing, collected by his authority the duties settled on James; and those duties which had expired were continued for some months.

Abolition of the hearth money.

Along William's whole line of march, from Torbay to London, he had been importuned by the common people to relieve them from the intolerable burden of the hearth money. In truth, that tax seems to have united all the worst evils which can be imputed to any tax. It was unequal, and unequal in the most pernicious way: for it pressed heavily on the poor, and lightly on the rich. A peasant, all whose property was not worth twenty pounds, had to pay several shillings, while the mansion of an opulent nobleman in Lincoln's Inn Fields or Saint James's Square was seldom assessed at two guineas. The collectors were empowered to examine the interior of every house in the realm, to disturb families at meals, to force the doors of bedrooms, and, if the sum demanded were not punctually paid, to sell the trencher on which the barley loaf was divided among the poor children, and the pillow from under the head of the lying-in woman. Nor could the Treasury effectually restrain the chimneyman from using his powers with harshness; for the tax was farmed; and the Government was consequently forced to connive at outrages and exactions such as have, in every age, made the name of publican a proverb for all that is most hateful.

William had been so much moved by what he had heard of these grievances that, at one of the earliest sittings of the Privy Council, he introduced the subject. He sent a message requesting the House of Commons to consider whether better regulations would effectually prevent the abuses which had excited so much discontent. He added that he would willingly consent to the entire abolition of the tax if it should appear that the tax and the abuses were inseparable.* This communication was received with loud applause. There

---

* Commons' Journals, and Grey's Debates, March 1. 168⁹⁄₉.

were indeed some financiers of the old school who muttered that tenderness for the poor was a fine thing, but that no part of the revenue of the state came in so exactly to the day as the hearth money; that the goldsmiths of the City could not always be induced to lend on the security of the next quarter's customs or excise, but that on an assignment of hearth money there was no difficulty in obtaining advances. In the House of Commons, those who thought thus did not venture to raise their voices in opposition to the general feeling. But in the Lords there was a conflict of which the event for a time seemed doubtful. At length the influence of the Court, strenuously exerted, carried an Act by which the chimney tax was declared a badge of slavery, and was, with many expressions of gratitude to the King, abolished for ever.*

The Commons granted, with little dispute, and without a division, six hundred thousand pounds for the purpose of repaying to the United Provinces the charges of the expedition which had delivered England. The facility with which this large sum was voted to a shrewd, diligent, and thrifty people, our allies, indeed, politically, but commercially our most formidable rivals, excited some murmurs out of doors, and was, during many years, a favourite subject of sarcasm with Tory pamphleteers.† The liberality of the House admits however of an easy explanation. On the very day on which the subject was under consideration, alarming news arrived at Westminster, and convinced many, who would at another time have been disposed to scrutinise severely any account sent in by the Dutch, that our country could not yet dispense with the services of the foreign troops.

France had declared war against the States General, and the States General had consequently demanded from the King of England those succours which he was bound by the treaty of Nimeguen to furnish.‡ He had ordered some battalions to march to Harwich, that they might be in readiness to cross to the Continent. The old soldiers of James were generally in a very bad temper, and this order did not produce a soothing effect. The discontent was greatest in the

Repayment of the expenses of the United Provinces.

Mutiny at Ipswich.

---

* 1 W. & M. sess. 1. c. 10.; Burnet, ii. 13.
† Commons' Journals, March 15. 1697. So late as 1713, Arbuthnot, in the fifth part of John Bull, alluded to this transaction with much pleasantry. "As to your Venire Facias," says John to Nick Frog, "I have paid you for one already." 1 Wagoner, lxl.

regiment which now ranks as the first of the line. Though borne on the English establishment, that regiment, from the time when it first fought under the great Gustavus, had been almost exclusively composed of Scotchmen; and Scotchmen have never, in any region to which their adventurous and aspiring temper has led them, failed to note and to resent every slight offered to Scotland. Officers and men muttered that a vote of a foreign assembly was nothing to them. If they could be absolved from their allegiance to King James the Seventh, it must be by the Estates at Edinburgh, and not by the Convention at Westminster. Their ill humour increased when they heard that Schomberg had been appointed their colonel. They ought perhaps to have thought it an honour to be called by the name of the greatest soldier in Europe. But, brave and skilful as he was, he was not their countryman; and their regiment, during the fifty-six years which had elapsed since it gained its first honourable distinctions in Germany, had never been commanded but by a Hepburn or a Douglas. While they were in this angry and punctilious mood, they were ordered to join the forces which were assembling at Harwich. There was much murmuring; but there was no outbreak till the regiment arrived at Ipswich. There the signal of revolt was given by two captains who were zealous for the exiled King. The market place was soon filled with pikemen and musketeers running to and fro. Gunshots were wildly fired in all directions. Those officers who attempted to restrain the rioters were overpowered and disarmed. At length the chiefs of the insurrection established some order, and marched out of Ipswich at the head of their adherents. The little army consisted of about eight hundred men. They had seized four pieces of cannon, and had taken possession of the military chest, which contained a considerable sum of money. At the distance of half a mile from the town a halt was called; a general consultation was held; and the mutineers resolved that they would hasten back to their native country, and would live and die with their rightful King. They instantly proceeded northward by forced marches.*

When the news reached London the dismay was great. It was rumoured that alarming symptoms had appeared in other regiments, and particularly that a body of fusileers

* Commons' Journals, March 15. 168⅔.

which lay at Harwich was likely to imitate the example set at Ipswich. "If these Scots," said Halifax to Reresby, "are unsupported, they are lost. But if they are acting in concert with others, the danger is serious indeed."* The truth seems to be that there was a conspiracy which had ramifications in many parts of the army, but that the conspirators were awed by the firmness of the Government and of the Parliament. A committee of the Privy Council was sitting when the tidings of the mutiny arrived in London. William Harbord, who represented the borough of Launceston, was at the board. His colleagues entreated him to go down instantly to the House of Commons, and to relate what had happened. He went, rose in his place, and told his story. The spirit of the assembly rose to the occasion. Howe was the first to call for vigorous action. "Address the King," he said, "to send his Dutch troops after these men. I know not who else can be trusted." "This is no jesting matter," said old Birch, who had been a colonel in the service of the Parliament, and had seen the most powerful and renowned House of Commons that ever sate twice purged and twice expelled by its own soldiers; "if you let this evil spread, you will have an army upon you in a few days. Address the King to send horse and foot instantly, his own men, men whom he can trust, and to put these people down at once." The men of the long robe caught the flame. "It is not the learning of my profession that is needed here," said Treby. "What is now to be done is to meet force with force, and to maintain in the field what we have done in the senate." "Write to the Sheriffs," said Colonel Mildmay, member for Essex. "Raise the militia. There are a hundred and fifty thousand of them: they are good Englishmen; they will not fail you." It was resolved that all members of the House who held commissions in the army should be dispensed from parliamentary attendance, in order that they might repair instantly to their military posts. An address was unanimously voted requesting the King to take effectual steps for the suppression of the rebellion, and to put forth a proclamation denouncing public vengeance on the rebels. One gentleman hinted that it might be well to advise His Majesty to offer a pardon to those who should peaceably submit; but the House wisely rejected the suggestion. "This

* Reresby's Memoirs.

CHAP.
XL.

is no time," it was well said, "for anything that looks like fear." The address was instantly sent up to the Lords. The Lords concurred in it. Two peers, two knights of shires, and two burgesses were sent with it to Court. William received them graciously, and informed them that he had already given the necessary orders. In fact, several regiments of horse and dragoons had been sent northwards under the command of Ginkell, one of the bravest and ablest officers of the Dutch army.*

Meanwhile the mutineers were hastening across the country which lies between Cambridge and the Wash. Their way lay through a vast and desolate fen, saturated with the moisture of thirteen counties, and overhung during the greater part of the year by a low grey mist, high above which rose, visible many miles, the magnificent tower of Ely. In that dreary region, covered by vast flights of wild fowl, a half savage population, known by the name of the Breedlings, then led an amphibious life, sometimes wading, and sometimes rowing, from one islet of firm ground to another.† The roads were among the worst in the island, and, as soon as rumour announced the approach of the rebels, were studiously made worse by the country people. Bridges were broken down. Trees were laid across the highways to obstruct the progress of the cannon. Nevertheless the Scotch veterans not only pushed forward with great speed, but succeeded in carrying their artillery with them. They entered Lincolnshire, and were not far from Sleaford, when they learned that Ginkell with an irresistible force was close on their track. Victory and escape were equally out of the question. The bravest warriors could not contend against fourfold odds. The most active infantry could not outrun horsemen. Yet the leaders, probably despairing of pardon, urged the men to try the chance of battle. In that region, a spot almost surrounded by swamps and pools was without difficulty found. Here the insurgents were drawn up; and the cannon were planted at the only point which was thought not to be sufficiently protected by natural defences. Ginkell ordered the attack to be made at a place which was out of the range of the guns; and his dragoons

* Commons' Journals, and Grey's Debates, March 15. 168⁹⁄₀; London Gazette, March 18.
† As to the state of this region in the latter part of the seventeenth and the earlier part of the eighteenth century, see Pepys's Diary, Sept. 18. 1663, and the Tour through the whole Island of Great Britain, 1724.

dashed gallantly into the water, though it was so deep that
their horses were forced to swim. Then the mutineers lost
heart. They beat a parley, surrendered at discretion, and
were brought up to London under a strong guard. Their
lives were forfeit; for they had been guilty, not merely of
mutiny, which was then not a legal crime, but of levying
war against the King. William, however, with politic
clemency, abstained from shedding the blood even of the
most culpable. A few of the ringleaders were brought to
trial at the next Bury assizes, and were convicted of high
treason; but their lives were spared. The rest were merely
ordered to return to their duty. The regiment, lately so
refractory, went submissively to the Continent, and there,
through many hard campaigns, distinguished itself by fidelity,
by discipline, and by valour.*

This event facilitated an important change in our polity, a
change which, it is true, could not have been long delayed,
but which would not have been easily accomplished except
at a moment of extreme danger. The time had at length
arrived at which it was necessary to make a legal distinction
between the soldier and the citizen. Under the Plantagenets
and the Tudors there had been no standing army. The
standing army which had existed under the last kings of the
House of Stuart had been regarded by every party in the
state with strong and not unreasonable aversion. The common
law gave the Sovereign no power to control his troops.
The Parliament, regarding them as mere tools of tyranny,
had not been disposed to give such power by statute. James
indeed had induced his corrupt and servile Judges to put on
some obsolete laws a construction which enabled him to
punish desertion capitally. But this construction was considered
by all respectable jurists as unsound, and, had it
been sound, would have been far from effecting all that was
necessary for the purpose of maintaining military discipline.
Even James did not venture to inflict death by sentence of
a court martial. The deserter was treated as an ordinary
felon, was tried at the assizes by a petty jury on a bill found
by a grand jury, and was at liberty to avail himself of any
technical flaw which might be discovered in the indictment.

CHAP.
XI.

The first
Mutiny
Bill

* London Gazette, March 25. 1689;
Van Citters to the States General, March 22/April 1;
Letters of Nottingham in the State Paper Office, dated July 23. and August 9.
1689; Historical Record of the First
Regiment of Foot, printed by authority.
See also a curious digression in the Compleat History of the Life and Military
Actions of Richard, Earl of Tyrconnel, 1689.

CHAP. XI.

The Revolution, by altering the relative position of the Sovereign and the Parliament, had altered also the relative position of the army and the nation. The King and the Commons were now at unity; and both were alike menaced by the greatest military power which had existed in Europe since the downfall of the Roman empire. In a few weeks thirty thousand veterans, accustomed to conquer, and led by able and experienced captains, might cross from the ports of Normandy and Britanny to our shores. That such a force would with little difficulty scatter three times that number of militia, no man well acquainted with war could doubt. There must then be regular soldiers; and, if there were to be regular soldiers, it must be indispensable, both to their efficiency, and to the security of every other class, that they should be kept under a strict discipline. An ill disciplined army has ever been a more costly and a more licentious militia, impotent against a foreign enemy, and formidable only to the country which it is paid to defend. A strong line of demarcation must therefore be drawn between the soldiers and the rest of the community. For the sake of public freedom, they must, in the midst of freedom, be placed under a despotic rule. They must be subject to a sharper penal code, and to a more stringent code of procedure, than are administered by the ordinary tribunals. Some acts which in the citizen are innocent must in the soldier be crimes. Some acts which in the citizen are punished with fine or imprisonment must in the soldier be punished with death. The machinery by which courts of law ascertain the guilt or innocence of an accused citizen is too slow and too intricate to be applied to an accused soldier. For, of all the maladies incident to the body politic, military insubordination is that which requires the most prompt and drastic remedies. If the evil be not stopped as soon as it appears, it is certain to spread; and it cannot spread far without danger to the very vitals of the commonwealth. For the general safety, therefore, a summary jurisdiction of terrible extent must, in camps, be entrusted to rude tribunals composed of men of the sword.

But, though it was certain that the country could not, at that moment, be secure without professional soldiers, and equally certain that professional soldiers must be worse than useless unless they were placed under a rule more arbitrary and severe than that to which other men were subject, it was not without great misgivings that a House of Commons could venture to recognise the existence and to make provision for the government of a standing army. There was scarcely a public man of note who had not often avowed his conviction that our polity and a standing army could not exist together. The Whigs had been in the constant habit of repeating that standing armies had destroyed the free institutions of the neighbouring nations. The Tories had repeated as constantly that, in our own island, a standing army had subverted the Church, oppressed the gentry, and murdered the King. No leader of either party could, without laying himself open to the charge of gross inconsistency, propose that such an army should henceforth be one of the permanent establishments of the realm. The mutiny at Ipswich, and the panic which that mutiny produced, made the first step in the right direction easy; and by that step the whole course of our subsequent legislation was determined. A short bill was brought in which began by declaring, in explicit terms, that standing armies and courts martial were unknown to the law of England. It was then enacted that, on account of the extreme perils impending at that moment over the state, no man mustered on pay in the service of the Crown should, on pain of death, or of such lighter punishment as a court martial should deem sufficient, desert his colours or mutiny against his commanding officers. This statute was to be in force only six months; and many of those who voted for it probably believed that it would, at the close of that period, be suffered to expire. The bill passed rapidly and easily. Not a single division was taken upon it in the House of Commons. A mitigating clause indeed, which illustrates somewhat curiously the manners of that age, was added by way of rider after the third reading. This clause provided that no court martial should pass sentence of death except between the hours of six in the morning and one in the afternoon. The dinner hour was then early; and it was but too probable that a gentleman who had dined would be in a state in which he could not safely be trusted with the lives of his fellow creatures. With this amendment, the first and most concise of our many Mutiny Bills was sent up to the Lords, and was, in a few hours, hurried by them through all its stages and passed by the King.*

* Stat. 1 W. & M. sess. 1. c. 5.; Commons' Journals, March 28. 1689.

Thus began, without one dissentient voice in Parliament, without one murmur in the nation, a change which had become necessary to the safety of the state, yet which every party in the state then regarded with extreme dread and aversion. Six months passed; and still the public danger continued. The power necessary to the maintenance of military discipline was a second time entrusted to the Crown for a short term. The trust again expired, and was again renewed. By slow degrees familiarity reconciled the public mind to the names, once so odious, of standing army and court martial. It was proved by experience that, in a well constituted society, professional soldiers may be terrible to a foreign enemy, and yet submissive to the civil power. What had been at first tolerated as the exception began to be considered as the rule. Not a session passed without a Mutiny Bill. During two generations, indeed, an annual clamour against the new system was raised by some factious men desirous to weaken the hands of the Government, and by some respectable men who felt an honest but injudicious reverence for every old constitutional tradition, and who were unable to understand that what at one stage in the progress of society is pernicious may at another stage be indispensable. But this clamour, as years rolled on, became fainter and fainter. The debate which recurred every spring on the Mutiny Bill came to be regarded merely as an occasion on which hopeful young orators, fresh from Christchurch, were to deliver maiden speeches, setting forth how the guards of Pisistratus seized the citadel of Athens, and how the Prætorian cohorts sold the Roman empire to Didius. At length these declamations became too ridiculous to be repeated. The most oldfashioned, the most eccentric, politician could hardly, in the reign of George the Third, contend that there ought to be no regular soldiers, or that the ordinary law, administered by the ordinary courts, would effectually maintain discipline among such soldiers. All parties being agreed as to the general principle, a long succession of Mutiny Bills passed without any discussion, except when some particular article of the military code appeared to require amendment. It is perhaps because the army became thus gradually, and almost imperceptibly, one of the institutions of England, that it has acted in such perfect harmony with all her other institutions, has never once, during a hundred and sixty years, been untrue to the throne or disobedient to the law, has never once defied the tribunals or overawed the constituent bodies. To this day, however, the Estates of the Realm continue to set up periodically, with laudable jealousy, a landmark on the frontier which was traced at the time of the Revolution. They solemnly reassert every year the doctrine laid down in the Declaration of Right; and they then grant to the Sovereign an extraordinary power to govern a certain number of soldiers according to certain rules during twelve months more.

In the same week in which the first Mutiny Bill was laid on the table of the Commons, another temporary law, made necessary by the unsettled state of the kingdom, was passed. Since the flight of James many persons who were believed to have been deeply implicated in his unlawful acts, or to be engaged in plots for his restoration, had been arrested and confined. During the vacancy of the throne, these men could derive no benefit from the Habeas Corpus Act. For the machinery by which alone that Act could be carried into execution had ceased to exist; and, through the whole of Hilary term, all the courts in Westminster Hall had remained closed. Now that the ordinary tribunals were about to resume their functions, it was apprehended that those prisoners whom it was not convenient to bring instantly to trial would demand and obtain their liberty. A bill was therefore brought in which empowered the King to detain in custody during a few weeks such persons as he should suspect of evil designs against his government. This bill passed the two Houses with little or no opposition.* But the malecontents out of doors did not fail to remark that, in the late reign, the Habeas Corpus Act had not been one day suspended. It was the fashion to call James a tyrant, and William a deliverer. Yet, before the deliverer had been a month on the throne, he had deprived Englishmen of a precious right which the tyrant had respected.† This is a kind of reproach which a government sprung from a popular revolution almost inevitably incurs. From such a government men naturally think themselves entitled to demand a more gentle and liberal administration than is expected from old and deeply rooted power. Yet such a government, having, as it always has, many active enemies, and not having the strength derived from legitimacy and prescription, can at first main-

CHAP. XI.

Suspension of the Habeas Corpus Act.

* Stat. 1 W. & M. sess. 1. c. 2.   † Ronquillo, March 4/14. 1689.

CHAP. XL.

tain itself only by a vigilance and a severity of which old and deeply rooted power stands in no need. Extraordinary and irregular vindications of public liberty are sometimes necessary: yet, however necessary, they are almost always followed by some temporary abridgments of that very liberty; and every such abridgment is a fertile and plausible theme for sarcasm and invective.

Unpopularity of William.

Unhappily sarcasm and invective directed against William were but too likely to find favourable audience. Each of the two great parties had its own reasons for being dissatisfied with him; and there were some complaints in which both parties joined. His manners gave almost universal offence. He was in truth far better qualified to save a nation than to adorn a court. In the highest parts of statesmanship, he had no equal among his contemporaries. He had formed plans not inferior in grandeur and boldness to those of Richelieu, and had carried them into effect with a tact and wariness worthy of Mazarin. Two countries, the seats of civil liberty and of the Reformed Faith, had been preserved by his wisdom and courage from extreme perils. Holland he had delivered from foreign, and England from domestic foes. Obstacles apparently insurmountable had been interposed between him and the ends on which he was intent; and those obstacles his genius had turned into stepping stones. Under his dexterous management the hereditary enemies of his house had helped him to mount a throne; and the persecutors of his religion had helped him to rescue his religion from persecution. Fleets and armies, collected to withstand him, had, without a struggle, submitted to his orders. Factions and sects, divided by mortal antipathies, had recognised him as their common head. Without carnage, without devastation, he had won a victory compared with which all the victories of Gustavus and Turenne were insignificant. In a few weeks he had changed the relative position of all the states in Europe, and had restored the equilibrium which the preponderance of one power had destroyed. Foreign nations did ample justice to his great qualities. In every Continental country where Protestant congregations met, fervent thanks were offered to God, who, from among the progeny of His servants, Maurice, the deliverer of Germany, and William, the deliverer of Holland, had raised up a third deliverer, the wisest and mightiest of all. At Vienna, at Madrid, nay, at Rome, the valiant and sagacious heretic was held in honour as the chief of the great confederacy against the House of Bourbon; and even at Versailles the hatred which he inspired was largely mingled with admiration.

Here he was less favourably judged. In truth, our ancestors saw him in the worst of all lights. By the French, the Germans, and the Italians, he was contemplated at such a distance that only what was great could be discerned, and that small blemishes were invisible. To the Dutch he was brought close: but he was himself a Dutchman. In his intercourse with them he was seen to the best advantage: he was perfectly at his ease with them; and from among them he had chosen his earliest and dearest friends. But to the English he appeared in a most unfortunate point of view. He was at once too near to them and too far from them. He lived among them, so that the smallest peculiarity of temper or manner could not escape their notice. Yet he lived apart from them, and was to the last a foreigner in speech, tastes, and habits.

One of the chief functions of our Sovereigns had long been to preside over the society of the capital. That function Charles the Second had performed with immense success. His easy bow, his good stories, his style of dancing and playing tennis, the sound of his cordial laugh, were familiar to all London. One day he was seen among the elms of Saint James's Park chatting with Dryden about poetry.* Another day his arm was on Tom Durfey's shoulder; and His Majesty was taking a second, while his companion sang "Phillida, Phillida," or "To horse, brave boys, to Newmarket, to horse."† James, with much less vivacity and good nature, was accessible, and, to people who did not cross him, civil. But of this sociableness William was entirely destitute. He seldom came forth from his closet; and, when he appeared in the public rooms, he stood among the crowd of courtiers and ladies, stern and abstracted, making no jest and smiling at none. His freezing look, his silence, the dry and concise answers which he uttered when he could keep silence no longer, disgusted noblemen and gentlemen who had been accustomed to be slapped on the back by their royal masters, called Jack or Harry, congratulated about race cups or rallied about actresses. The women missed the homage due to their sex. They observed that the King spoke in a somewhat im-

* See the account given in Spence's Anecdotes of the Origin of Dryden's Medal.
† Guardian, No. 67.

CHAP. XI.

perious tone even to the wife to whom he owed so much, and whom he sincerely loved and esteemed.* They were amused and shocked to see him, when the Princess Anne dined with him, and when the first green peas of the year were put on the table, devour the whole dish without offering a spoonful to Her Royal Highness; and they pronounced that this great soldier and politician was no better than a Low Dutch bear.†

One misfortune, which was imputed to him as a crime, was his bad English. He spoke our language, but not well. His accent was foreign; his diction was inelegant; and his vocabulary seems to have been no larger than was necessary for the transaction of business. To the difficulty which he felt in expressing himself, and to his consciousness that his pronunciation was bad, must be partly ascribed the taciturnity and the short answers which gave so much offence. Our literature he was incapable of enjoying or of understanding. He never once, during his whole reign, showed himself at the theatre.‡ The poets who wrote Pindaric verses in his praise, complained that their flights of sublimity were beyond his comprehension.§ Those who are acquainted with the panegyrical odes of that age will perhaps be of opinion that he did not lose much by his ignorance.

Popularity of Mary.

It is true that his wife did her best to supply what was wanting, and that she was excellently qualified to be the head of the Court. She was English by birth, and English also in her tastes and feelings. Her face was handsome, her port majestic, her temper sweet and lively, her manners affable and graceful. Her understanding, though very imperfectly cultivated, was quick. There was no want of

* There is abundant proof that William, though a very affectionate, was not always a polite husband. But no credit is due to the story contained in the letter which Dalrymple was foolish enough to publish as Nottingham's in 1773, and wise enough to omit in his edition of 1790. How any person who knew anything of the history of those times could be so strangely deceived, it is not easy to understand, particularly as the handwriting bears no resemblance to Nottingham's, with which Dalrymple was familiar. The letter is evidently a common newsletter, written by a scribbler, who had never seen the King and Queen except at some public place, and whose anecdotes of their private life rested on no better authority than coffeehouse gossip.

† Ronquillo; Burnet, ii. 2.; Duchess of Marlborough's Vindication. In a pastoral dialogue between Philander and Palæmon, published in 1091, the dislike with which women of fashion regarded William is mentioned. Philander says,
"Bet man methinks his reason should recall,
Nor let frail woman work his second fall."

‡ Tutchin's Observator of November 16. 1708.

§ Prior, who was treated by William with much kindness, and who was very grateful for it, informs us that the King did not understand poetical eulogy. The passage is in a highly curious manuscript, the property of Lord Lansdowne.

feminine wit and shrewdness in her conversation; and her letters were so well expressed that they deserved to be well spelt. She took much pleasure in the lighter kinds of literature, and did something towards bringing books into fashion among ladies of quality. The stainless purity of her private life and the strict attention which she paid to her religious duties were the more respectable, because she was singularly free from censoriousness, and discouraged scandal as much as vice. In dislike of backbiting indeed she and her husband cordially agreed; but they showed that dislike in different and in very characteristic ways. William preserved profound silence, and gave the talebearer a look which, as was said by a person who had once encountered it, and who took good care never to encounter it again, made your story go back down your throat.* Mary had a way of interrupting tattle about elopements, duels, and playdebts, by asking the tattlers, very quietly yet significantly, whether they had ever read her favourite sermon, Doctor Tillotson's on Evil Speaking. Her charities were munificent and judicious; and, though she made no ostentatious display of them, it was known that she retrenched from her own state in order to relieve Protestants whom persecution had driven from France and Ireland, and who were starving in the garrets of London. So amiable was her conduct, that she was generally spoken of with esteem and tenderness by the most respectable of those who disapproved of the manner in which she had been raised to the throne, and even of those who refused to acknowledge her as Queen. In the Jacobite lampoons of that time, lampoons which, in virulence and malignity, far exceed anything that our age has produced, she was not often mentioned with severity. Indeed she sometimes expressed her surprise at finding that libellers who respected nothing else respected

---

* Mémoires Originaux sur le Règne et la Cour de Frédéric I., Roi de Prusse, écrits par Christophe Comte de Dohna. Berlin, 1833. It is strange that this interesting volume should be almost unknown in England. The only copy that I have ever seen of it was kindly given to me by Sir Robert Adair. "Le Roi," Dohna says, "avoit une autre qualité très estimable, qui est celle de n'aimer point qu'on rendît de mauvais offices à personne par des railleries." The Marquis de la Forêt tried to entertain His Majesty at the expense of an English nobleman.

"Ce prince," says Dohna, "prit son air sévère, et, le regardant sans mot dire, lui fit rentrer les paroles dans le ventre. Le Marquis m'en fit ses plaintes quelques heures après. 'J'ai mal pris ma besogne,' dit-il; 'j'ai cru faire l'agréable sur le chapitre de Milord . . . mais j'ai trouvé à qui parler, et j'ai attrapé un regard de roi qui m'a fait passer l'envie de rire.'" Dohna supposed that William might be less sensitive about the character of a Frenchman, and tried the experiment. But, says he, "j'eus à peu près le même sort que M. de la Forêt."

her name. God, she said, knew where her weakness lay. She was too sensitive to abuse and calumny: He had mercifully spared her a trial which was beyond her strength; and the best return which she could make to Him was to discountenance all malicious reflections on the characters of others. Assured that she possessed her husband's entire confidence and affection, she turned the edge of his sharp speeches sometimes by soft and sometimes by playful answers, and employed all the influence which she derived from her many pleasing qualities to gain the hearts of the people for him.*

The Court removed from Whitehall to Hampton Court.

If she had long continued to assemble round her the best society of London, it is probable that her kindness and courtesy would have done much to efface the unfavourable impression made by his stern and frigid demeanour. Unhappily his physical infirmities made it impossible for him to reside at Whitehall. The air of Westminster, mingled with the fog of the river which in spring tides overflowed the courts of his palace, with the smoke of seacoal from two hundred thousand chimneys, and with the fumes of all the filth which was then suffered to accumulate in the streets, was insupportable to him; for his lungs were weak, and his sense of smell exquisitely keen. His constitutional asthma made rapid progress. His physicians pronounced it impossible that he could live to the end of the year. His face was so ghastly that he could hardly be recognised. Those who had to transact business with him were shocked to hear him gasping for breath, and coughing till the tears ran down his cheeks.† His mind, strong as it was, sympathised with his body. His judgment was indeed as clear as ever. But there was, during some months, a perceptible relaxation of that energy by which he had been distinguished. Even his Dutch friends whispered that he was not the man that he had been at the Hague.* It was absolutely necessary that he should quit London. He accordingly took up his residence in the purer air of Hampton Court. That mansion, begun by the magnificent Wolsey, was a fine specimen of the architecture which flourished in England under the first Tudors; but the apartments were not, according to the notions of the seventeenth century, well fitted for purposes of state. Our princes therefore had, since the Restoration, repaired thither seldom, and only when they wished to live for a time in retirement. As William purposed to make the deserted edifice his chief palace, it was necessary for him to build and to plant; nor was the necessity disagreeable to him. For he had, like most of his countrymen, a pleasure in decorating a country house; and next to hunting, though at a great interval, his favourite amusements were architecture and gardening. He had already created on a sandy heath in Guelders a paradise, which attracted multitudes of the curious from Holland and Westphalia. Mary had laid the first stone of the house. Bentinck had superintended the digging of the fishponds. There were cascades and grottoes, a spacious orangery, and an aviary which furnished Hondekoeter with numerous specimens of manycoloured plumage.† The King, in his splendid banishment, pined for this favourite seat, and found some consolation in creating another Loo on the banks of the Thames. Soon a wide extent of ground was laid out in formal walks and parterres. Much idle ingenuity was employed in forming that intricate labyrinth of verdure which has puzzled and amused five generations of holiday visitors from London. Limes thirty years old were transplanted from neighbouring woods to shade the alleys. Artificial fountains spouted among the flower beds. A new court, not designed with the purest taste, but stately, spacious, and commodious, rose under the direction of Wren. The wainscots were adorned with the rich and delicate carvings of Gibbons. The staircases were in a blaze with

---

* "Hasta decir los mismos Hollandeses que lo desconocian," says Ronquillo. "Il est absolument mal propre pour le rôle qu'il a à jouer à l'heure qu'il est," says Avaux. "Slothful and sickly," says Evelyn, March 29. 1689.

† See Harris's description of Loo, 1699.

the glaring frescoes of Verrio. In every corner of the mansion appeared a profusion of gewgaws, not yet familiar to English eyes. Mary had acquired at the Hague a taste for the porcelain of China, and amused herself by forming at Hampton a vast collection of hideous images, and of vases on which houses, trees, bridges, and mandarins, were depicted in outrageous defiance of all the laws of perspective. The fashion, a frivolous and inelegant fashion it must be owned, which was thus set by the amiable Queen, spread fast and wide. In a few years almost every great house in the kingdom contained a museum of these grotesque baubles. Even statesmen and generals were not ashamed to be renowned as judges of teapots and dragons; and satirists long continued to repeat that a fine lady valued her mottled green pottery quite as much as she valued her monkey, and much more than she valued her husband.*

But the new palace was embellished with works of art of a very different kind. A gallery was erected for the cartoons of Raphael. Those great pictures, then and still the finest on our side of the Alps, had been preserved by Cromwell from the fate which befel most of the other masterpieces in the collection of Charles the First, but had been suffered to lie during many years nailed up in deal boxes. Peter, raising the cripple at the Beautiful Gate, and Paul, proclaiming the Unknown God to the philosophers of Athens, were now brought forth from obscurity to be contemplated by artists with admiration and despair. The expense of the works at Hampton was a subject of bitter complaint to many Tories, who had very gently blamed the boundless profusion with which Charles the Second had built and rebuilt, furnished and refurnished, the dwelling of the Duchess of Portsmouth.† The expense, however, was not the chief cause of the discontent which William's change of residence excited. There was no longer a Court at Westminster. Whitehall, once the daily resort of the noble and the powerful, the beautiful and

* Every person who is well acquainted with Pope and Addison will remember their sarcasms on this taste. Lady Mary Wortley Montague took the other side. "Old China," she says, "is below nobody's taste, since it has been the Duke of Argyle's, whose understanding has never been doubted either by his friends or enemies."

† As to the works at Hampton Court, see Evelyn's Diary, July 16. 1689; the Tour through Great Britain, 1724; the British Apelles; Horace Walpole on Modern Gardening; Burnet, ii. 2, 3.

When Evelyn was at Hampton Court, in 1662, the cartoons were not to be seen. The triumphs of Andrea Mantegna were then supposed to be the finest pictures in the palace.

the gay, the place to which fops came to show their new peruques, men of gallantry to exchange glances with fine ladies, politicians to push their fortunes, loungers to hear the news, country gentlemen to see the royal family, was now, in the busiest season of the year, when London was full, when Parliament was sitting, left desolate. A solitary sentinel paced the grassgrown pavement before that door which had once been too narrow for the opposite streams of entering and departing courtiers. The services which the metropolis had rendered to the King were great and recent; and it was thought that he might have requited those services better than by treating it as Lewis had treated Paris. Halifax ventured to hint this, but was silenced by a few words which admitted of no reply. "Do you wish," said William peevishly, "to see me dead?"*

In a short time it was found that Hampton Court was too far from the Houses of Lords and Commons, and from the public offices, to be the ordinary abode of the Sovereign. Instead, however, of returning to Whitehall, William determined to have another dwelling, near enough to his capital for the transaction of business, but not near enough to be within that atmosphere in which he could not pass a night without risk of suffocation. At one time he thought of Holland House, the villa of the noble family of Rich; and he actually resided there some weeks.† But he at length fixed his choice on Kensington House, the suburban residence of the Earl of Nottingham. The purchase was made for eighteen thousand guineas, and was followed by more building, more planting, more expense, and more discontent.‡ At present Kensington House is considered as a part of London. It was then a rural mansion, and could not, in those days of highwaymen and scourers, of roads deep in mire and nights without lamps, be the rallying point of fashionable society.

It was well known that the King, who treated the English

The Court at Kensington.

* Burnet, ii. 2.; Reresby's Memoirs. Ronquillo wrote repeatedly to the same effect. For example, "Bien quisiera que el Rey fuese mas communicable, y se acomodase un poco mas al humor sociable de los Ingleses, y que estubieran en Londres; pero es cierto que nos achaques no se lo permiten." July 4, 1689. Avaux, about the same time, wrote thus to Croissy from Ireland: "Le Prince d'Orange est toujours à Hampton Court, et jamais à la ville: et le peuple est fort mal satisfait de cette manière bizarre et retirée."
† Several of his letters to Heinsius are dated from Holland House.
‡ Luttrell's Diary; Evelyn's Diary, Feb. 25. 1⅜⅜.

nobility and gentry so ungraciously, could, in a small circle of his own countrymen, be easy, friendly, even jovial, could pour out his feelings garrulously, could fill his glass, perhaps too often; and this was, in the view of our forefathers, an aggravation of his offences. Yet our forefathers should have had the sense and the justice to acknowledge that the patriotism, which they considered as a virtue in themselves, could not be a fault in him. It was unjust to blame him for not at once transferring to our island the love which he bore to the country of his birth. If, in essentials, he did his duty towards England, he might well be suffered to feel at heart an affectionate preference for Holland. Nor is it a reproach to him that he did not, in this season of his greatness, discard companions who had played with him in his childhood, who had stood by him firmly through all the vicissitudes of his youth and manhood, who had, in defiance of the most loathsome and deadly forms of infection, kept watch by his sick bed, who had, in the thickest of the battle, thrust themselves between him and the French swords, and whose attachment was, not to the Stadtholder or to the King, but to plain William of Nassau. It may be added that his old friends could not but rise in his estimation by comparison with his new courtiers. To the end of his life all his Dutch comrades, without exception, continued to deserve his confidence. They could be out of humour with him, it is true; and, when out of humour, they could be sullen and rude; but never did they, even when most angry and unreasonable, fail to keep his secrets and to watch over his interests with gentlemanlike and soldier-like fidelity. Among his English counsellors such fidelity was rare.* It is painful, but it is no more than just, to acknowledge that he had but too good reason for thinking meanly of our national character. That character was indeed, in essentials, what it has always been. Veracity, uprightness, and manly boldness were then, as now, qualities eminently English. But those qualities, though widely diffused among the great body of the people, were seldom to be found in the class with which William was best acquainted.

---

* De Foe makes this excuse for William:

"We blame the King that he relies too much
On strangers, Germans, Huguenots, and
Dutch,
And seldom does his great affairs of state
To English counsellors communicate.

The fact might very well be answered thus;
He has too often been betrayed by us,
He must have been a madman to rely
On English gentlemen's fidelity.
The foreigners have faithfully obeyed him,
And none but Englishmen have e'er betrayed him."

The True Born Englishman, Part II.

The standard of honour and virtue among our public men was, during his reign, at the very lowest point. His predecessors had bequeathed to him a court foul with all the vices of the Restoration, a court swarming with sycophants, who were ready, on the first turn of fortune, to abandon him as they had abandoned his uncle. Here and there, lost in that ignoble crowd, was to be found a man of true integrity and public spirit. Yet even such a man could not long live in such society without much risk that the strictness of his principles would be relaxed, and the delicacy of his sense of right and wrong impaired. It was surely unjust to blame a prince surrounded by flatterers and traitors for wishing to keep near him four or five servants whom he knew by proof to be faithful even to death.

Nor was this the only instance in which our ancestors were unjust to him. They had expected that, as soon as so distinguished a soldier and statesman was placed at the head of affairs, he would give some signal proof, they scarcely knew what, of genius and vigour. Unhappily, during the first months of his reign, almost everything went wrong. His subjects, bitterly disappointed, threw the blame on him, and began to doubt whether he merited that reputation which he had won at his first entrance into public life, and which the splendid success of his last great enterprise had raised to the highest point. Had they been in a temper to judge fairly, they would have perceived that for the maladministration of which they with good reason complained he was not responsible. He could as yet work only with the machinery which he had found; and the machinery which he had found was all rust and rottenness. From the time of the Restoration to the time of the Revolution, neglect and fraud had been almost constantly impairing the efficiency of every department of the government. Honours and public trusts, peerages, baronetcies, regiments, frigates, embassies, governments, commissionerships, leases of crown lands, contracts for clothing, for provisions, for ammunition, pardons for murder, for robbery, for arson, were sold at Whitehall scarcely less openly than asparagus at Covent Garden or herrings at Billingsgate. Brokers had been incessantly plying for custom in the purlieus of the court; and of these brokers the most successful had been, in the days of Charles, the harlots, and in the days of James, the priests. From the palace, which was the chief seat of this pestilence, the taint had diffused itself through every office, and through every rank in every office, and had everywhere produced feebleness and disorganisation. So rapid was the progress of the decay, that within eight years after the time when Oliver had been the umpire of Europe, the roar of the guns of De Ruyter was heard in the Tower of London. The vices which had brought that great humiliation on the country had ever since been rooting themselves deeper and spreading themselves wider. James had, to do him justice, corrected a few of the gross abuses which disgraced the naval administration. Yet the naval administration, in spite of his attempts to reform it, moved the contempt of men who were acquainted with the dockyards of France and Holland. The military administration was still worse. The courtiers took bribes from the colonels; the colonels cheated the soldiers: the commissaries sent in long bills for what had never been furnished: the keepers of the magazines sold the public stores and pocketed the price. But these evils, though they had sprung into existence and grown to maturity under the government of Charles and James, first made themselves severely felt under the government of William. For Charles and James were content to be the vassals and pensioners of a powerful and ambitious neighbour: they submitted to his ascendency: they shunned with pusillanimous caution whatever could give him offence: and thus, at the cost of the independence and dignity of that ancient and glorious crown which they unworthily wore, they avoided a conflict which would instantly have shown how helpless, under their misrule, their once formidable kingdom had become. Their ignominious policy it was neither in William's power nor in his nature to follow. It was only by arms that the liberty and religion of England could be protected against the mightiest enemy that had threatened our island since the Hebrides were strown with the wrecks of the Armada. The body politic, which, while it remained in repose, had presented a superficial appearance of health and vigour, was now under the necessity of straining every nerve in a wrestle for life or death, and was immediately found to be unequal to the exertion. The first efforts showed an utter relaxation of fibre, an utter want of training. Those efforts were, with scarcely an exception, failures; and every failure was popularly imputed, not to the rulers whose mismanagement had produced the infirmities of the state, but to the ruler in whose time the infirmities of the state became visible.

William might indeed, if he had been as absolute as Lewis, have used such sharp remedies as would speedily have restored to the English administration that firm tone which had been wanting since the death of Oliver. But the instantaneous reform of inveterate abuses was a task far beyond the powers of a prince strictly restrained by law, and restrained still more strictly by the difficulties of his situation.*

Some of the most serious difficulties of his situation were caused by the conduct of the ministers on whom, new as he was to the details of English affairs, he was forced to rely for information about men and things. There was indeed no want of ability among his chief counsellors: but one half of their ability was employed in counteracting the other half. Between the Lord President and the Lord Privy Seal there was an inveterate enmity.† It had begun twelve years before when Danby was Lord High Treasurer, a persecutor of nonconformists, an uncompromising defender of prerogative, and when Halifax was rising to distinction as one of the most eloquent leaders of the country party. In the reign of James, the two statesmen had found themselves in opposition together; and their common hostility to France and to Rome, to the High Commission and to the dispensing power, had produced an apparent reconciliation; but as soon as they were in office together the old antipathy revived. The hatred which the Whig party felt towards them both ought, it should seem, to have produced a close alliance between them: but in fact each of them saw with complacency the danger which threatened the other. Danby exerted himself to rally round him a strong phalanx of Tories. Under the plea of ill health, he withdrew from court, seldom came to the Council over which it was his duty to preside, passed much time in the country, and took scarcely any part in public affairs except by grumbling and sneering at all the acts of the government, and by doing jobs and getting places for his personal retainers.‡ In consequence of this defection, Halifax became prime minister, as far as any minister could, in that reign, be called prime minister. An immense load of business fell on him; and that load he was unable to sustain. In wit and eloquence, in amplitude of comprehension and subtlety of disquisition, he had no equal among the statesmen of his time. But that very fertility, that very acuteness, which gave a singular charm to his conversation, to his oratory, and to his writings, unfitted him for the work of promptly deciding practical questions. He was slow from very quickness. For he saw so many arguments for and against every possible course that he was longer in making up his mind than a dull man would have been. Instead of acquiescing in his first thoughts, he replied on himself, rejoined on himself, and surrejoined on himself. Those who heard him talk owned that he talked like an angel: but too often, when he had exhausted all that could be said, and came to act, the time for action was over.

Meanwhile the two Secretaries of State were constantly labouring to draw their master in diametrically opposite directions. Every scheme, every person, recommended by one of them was reprobated by the other. Nottingham was never weary of repeating that the old Roundhead party, the party which had taken the life of Charles the First and had plotted against the life of Charles the Second, was in principle republican, and that the Tories were the only true friends of monarchy. Shrewsbury replied that the Tories might be friends of monarchy, but that they regarded James as their monarch. Nottingham was always bringing to the closet intelligence of the wild daydreams in which a few old eaters of calf's head, the remains of the once formidable party of Bradshaw and Ireton, still indulged at taverns in the City. Shrewsbury produced ferocious lampoons which the Jacobites dropped every day in the coffeehouses. "Every Whig," said the Tory Secretary, "is an enemy of Your Majesty's prerogative." "Every Tory," said the Whig Secretary, "is an enemy of Your Majesty's title." *

At the Treasury there was a complication of jealousies and quarrels.† Both the First Commissioner, Mordaunt, and the Chancellor of the Exchequer, Delamere, were zealous Whigs: but though they held the same political creed, their tempers differed widely. Mordaunt was volatile, dissipated and generous. The wits of that time laughed at the way in which he

* Burnet, ii. 3, 4. 15. † Burnet, ii. 6.

flew about from Hampton Court to the Royal Exchange, and from the Royal Exchange back to Hampton Court. How he found time for dress, politics, lovemaking, and balladmaking was a wonder.* Delamere was gloomy and acrimonious, austere in his private morals, and punctual in his devotions, but greedy of ignoble gain. The two principal ministers of finance, therefore, became enemies, and agreed only in hating their colleague Godolphin. What business had he at Whitehall in these days of Protestant ascendency, he who had sate at the same board with Papists, he who had never scrupled to attend Mary of Modena to the idolatrous worship of the Mass? The most provoking circumstance was that Godolphin, though his name stood only third in the commission, was really first Lord. For in financial knowledge and in habits of business Mordaunt and Delamere were mere children when compared with him; and this William soon discovered.*

Similar feuds raged at the other great boards and through all the subordinate ranks of public functionaries. In every customhouse, in every arsenal, were a Shrewsbury and a Nottingham, a Delamere and a Godolphin. The Whigs complained that there was no department in which creatures of the fallen tyranny were not to be found. It was idle to allege that these men were versed in the details of business, that they were the depositaries of official traditions, and that the friends of liberty, having been, during many years, excluded from public employment, must necessarily be incompetent to take on themselves at once the whole management of affairs. Experience doubtless had its value: but surely the first of all the qualifications of a servant was fidelity; and no Tory could be a really faithful servant of the new government. If King William were wise, he would rather trust novices zealous for his interest and honour than veterans, who might indeed possess ability and knowledge, but who would use that ability and that knowledge to effect his ruin.

The Tories, on the other hand, complained that their share of power bore no proportion to their number, or to their weight in the country, and that everywhere old and useful public servants were, for the crime of being friends to monarchy and to the Church, turned out of their posts to make way

* "How does he do to distribute his hours,
  ......to the Court, and some to the City,
  Some to the Stage, and some to Love's powers,
  Same to be vain, and some to be witty?"
  The Modern Lampooners, a poem of 1690.
† Burnet, ii. 4.

for Rye House plotters and haunters of conventicles. These upstarts, adepts in the art of factious agitation, but ignorant of all that belonged to their new calling, would be just beginning to learn their business when they had undone the nation by their blunders. To be a rebel and a schismatic was surely not all that ought to be required of a man in high employment. What would become of the finances, what of the marine, if Whigs who could not understand the plainest balance sheet were to manage the revenue, and Whigs who had never walked over a dockyard to fit out the fleet?*

The truth is that the charges which the two parties brought against each other were, to a great extent, well founded, but that the blame which both threw on William was unjust. Official experience was to be found almost exclusively among the Tories, hearty attachment to the new settlement almost exclusively among the Whigs. It was not the fault of the King that the knowledge and the zeal, which, combined, make a valuable servant of the state, must at that time be had separately or not at all. If he employed men of one party, there was great risk of mistakes. If he employed men of the other party, there was great risk of treachery. If he employed men of both parties there was still some risk of mistakes; there was still some risk of treachery; and to these risks was added the certainty of dissension. He might join Whigs and Tories: but it was beyond his power to mix them. In the same office, at the same desk, they were still enemies, and agreed only in murmuring at the Prince who tried to mediate between them. It was inevitable that, in such circumstances, the administration, fiscal, military, naval, should be feeble and unsteady; that nothing should be done in quite the right way or at quite the right time; that the distractions from which scarcely any public office was exempt should produce disasters, and that every disaster should increase the distractions from which it had sprung.

Department of Foreign Affairs.

There was indeed one department of which the business was well conducted; and that was the department of Foreign Affairs. There William directed everything, and, on important occasions, neither asked the advice nor employed the agency

---

* Ronquillo calls the Whig functionaries "Gente que no tienen pratica ni experiencia." He adds, "Y de esto procede el passarse un mes y un otro, sin executarse nada." June 14. 1689. In one of the innumerable Dialogues which appeared at that time, the Tory interlocutor puts the question, "Do you think the government would be better served by strangers to business?" The Whig answers, "Better ignorant friends than understanding enemies."

of any English politician. One invaluable assistant he had, Anthony Heinsius, who, a few weeks after the Revolution had been accomplished, became Pensionary of Holland. Heinsius had entered public life as a member of that party which was jealous of the power of the House of Orange, and desirous to be on friendly terms with France. But he had been sent in 1681 on a diplomatic mission to Versailles; and a short residence there had produced a complete change in his views. On a near acquaintance, he was alarmed by the power and provoked by the insolence of that Court of which, while he contemplated it only at a distance, he had formed a favourable opinion. He found that his country was despised. He saw his religion persecuted. His official character did not save him from some personal affronts which, to the latest day of his long career, he never forgot. He went home a devoted adherent of William and a mortal enemy of Lewis.*

The office of Pensionary, always important, was peculiarly important when the Stadtholder was absent from the Hague. Had the politics of Heinsius been still what they once were, all the great designs of William might have been frustrated. But happily there was between these two eminent men a perfect friendship, which, till death dissolved it, appears never to have been interrupted for one moment by suspicion or ill humour. On all large questions of European policy they cordially agreed. They corresponded assiduously and most unreservedly. For, though William was slow to give his confidence, yet, when he gave it, he gave it entire. The correspondence is still extant, and is most honourable to both. The King's letters would alone suffice to prove that he was one of the greatest statesmen whom Europe has produced. While he lived, the Pensionary was content to be the most obedient, the most trusty, and the most discreet of servants. But, after the death of the master, the servant proved himself capable of supplying with eminent ability the master's place, and was renowned throughout Europe as one of the great Triumvirate which humbled the pride of Lewis the Fourteenth.†

* Négociations de M. Le Comte d' Avaux, 4 Mars 1685; Torcy's Memoirs.

† The original correspondence of William and Heinsius is in Dutch. A French translation of all William's letters, and an English translation of a few of Heinsius's letters, are among the Mackintosh MSS. The Baron Sirtema de Grovestins, who has had access to the originals, frequently quotes passages in his "Histoire des luttes et rivalités entre les puissances maritimes et la France." There is very little difference in substance, though much in phraseology, between his version and that which I have used.

CHAP. XI.

Religious disputes.

The foreign policy of England, directed immediately by William in close concert with Heinsius, was, at this time, eminently skilful and successful. But in every other part of the administration the evils arising from the mutual animosity of factions were but too plainly discernible. Nor was this all. To the evils arising from the mutual animosity of factions were added other evils arising from the mutual animosity of sects.

The year 1689 is a not less important epoch in the ecclesiastical than in the civil history of England. In that year was granted the first legal indulgence to Dissenters. In that year was made the last serious attempt to bring the Presbyterians within the pale of the Church of England. From that year dates a new schism, made in defiance of ancient precedents, by men who had always professed to regard schism with peculiar abhorrence, and ancient precedents with peculiar veneration. In that year began the long struggle between two great parties of conformists. Those parties indeed had, under various forms, existed within the Anglican communion ever since the Reformation; but till after the Revolution they did not appear marshalled in regular and permanent order of battle against each other, and were therefore not known by established names. Some time after the accession of William they began to be called the High Church party and the Low Church party; and, long before the end of his reign, these appellations were in common use.*

In the summer of 1688 the breaches which had long divided the great body of English Protestants had seemed to be almost closed. Disputes about Bishops and Synods, written prayers and extemporaneous prayers, white gowns and black gowns, sprinkling and dipping, kneeling and sitting, had been for a short space intermitted. The serried array which was then drawn up against Popery measured the whole of the vast interval which separated Sancroft from Bunyan. Prelates, recently conspicuous as persecutors, now declared themselves friends of religious liberty, and exhorted their clergy to live in a constant interchange of hospitality and of kind offices with the Separatists. Separatists, on the other

* Though these very convenient names are not, as far as I know, to be found in any book printed during the earlier years of William's reign, I shall use them without scruple, as others have done, in writing about the transactions of those years.

hand, who had recently considered mitres and lawn sleeves as the livery of Antichrist, were putting candles in windows and throwing faggots on bonfires in honour of the prelates.

These feelings continued to grow till they attained their greatest height on the memorable day on which the common oppressor finally quitted Whitehall, and on which an innumerable multitude, tricked out in orange ribands, welcomed the common deliverer to St. James's. When the clergy of London came, headed by Compton, to express their gratitude to him by whose instrumentality God had wrought salvation for the Church and the State, the procession was swollen by some eminent nonconformist divines. It was delightful to many good men to hear that pious and learned Presbyterian ministers had walked in the train of a Bishop, had been greeted by him with fraternal kindness, and had been announced by him in the presence chamber as his dear and respected friends, separated from him indeed by some differences of opinion on minor points, but united to him by Christian charity and by common zeal for the essentials of the reformed faith. There had never before been such a day in England; and there has never since been such a day. The tide of feeling was already on the turn; and the ebb was even more rapid than the flow had been. In a very few hours the High Churchman began to feel tenderness for the enemy whose tyranny was now no longer feared, and dislike of the allies whose services were now no longer needed. It was easy to gratify both feelings by imputing to the Dissenters the misgovernment of the exiled King. His Majesty,—such was now the language of too many Anglican divines,—would have been an excellent sovereign had he not been too confiding, too forgiving. He had put his trust in a class of men who hated his office, his family, his person, with implacable hatred. He had ruined himself in the vain attempt to conciliate them. He had relieved them, in defiance of law and of the unanimous sense of the old royalist party, from the pressure of the penal code; had allowed them to worship God publicly after their own mean and tasteless fashion; had admitted them to the bench of justice and to the Privy Council; had gratified them with fur robes, gold chains, salaries, and pensions. In return for his liberality, these people, once so uncouth in demeanour, once so savage in opposition even to legitimate authority, had become the most abject of flatterers. They had continued to applaud and encourage him when the most devoted friends of his family had retired in shame and sorrow from his palace. Who had more foully sold the religion and liberty of England than Titus? Who had been more zealous for the dispensing power than Alsop? Who had urged on the persecution of the seven Bishops more fiercely than Lobb? What chaplain impatient for a deanery had ever, even when preaching in the royal presence on the thirtieth of January or the twenty-ninth of May, uttered adulation more gross than might easily be found in those addresses by which dissenting congregations had testified their gratitude for the illegal Declaration of Indulgence? Was it strange that a prince who had never studied law books should have believed that he was only exercising his rightful prerogative, when he was thus encouraged by a faction which had always ostentatiously professed hatred of arbitrary power? Misled by such guidance he had gone further and further in the wrong path: he had at length estranged from him hearts which would once have poured forth their best blood in his defence: he had left himself no supporters except his old foes; and, when the day of peril came, he had found that the feeling of his old foes towards him was still what it had been when they had attempted to rob him of his inheritance, and when they had plotted against his life. Every man of sense had long known that the sectaries bore no love to monarchy. It had now been found that they bore as little love to freedom. To trust them with power would be an error not less fatal to the nation than to the throne. If, in order to redeem pledges somewhat rashly given, it should be thought necessary to grant them relief, every concession ought to be accompanied by limitations and precautions. Above all, no man who was an enemy to the ecclesiastical constitution of the realm ought to be permitted to bear any part in the civil government.

The Low Church party.

Between the nonconformists and the rigid conformists stood the Low Church party. That party contained, as it still contains, two very different elements, a Puritan element and a Latitudinarian element. On almost every question, however, relating either to ecclesiastical polity or to the ceremonial of public worship, the Puritan Low Churchman and the Latitudinarian Low Churchman were perfectly agreed. They saw in the existing polity and in the existing ceremonial no defect, no blemish, which could make it their duty to become dissenters. Nevertheless they held that both the polity and the ceremonial were means and not ends, and that the essential spirit of Christianity might exist without episcopal orders and without a Book of Common Prayer. They had, while James was on the throne, been mainly instrumental in forming the great Protestant coalition against Popery and tyranny; and they continued in 1689 to hold the same conciliatory language which they had held in 1688. They gently blamed the scruples of the nonconformists. It was undoubtedly a great weakness to imagine that there could be any sin in wearing a white robe, in tracing a cross, in kneeling at the rails of an altar. But the highest authority had given the plainest directions as to the manner in which such weakness was to be treated. The weak brother was not to be judged: he was not to be despised; believers who had stronger minds were commanded to soothe him by large compliances, and carefully to remove out of his path every stumblingblock which could cause him to offend. An apostle had declared that, though he had himself no misgivings about the use of animal food or of wine, he would eat herbs and drink water rather than give scandal to the feeblest of his flock. What would he have thought of ecclesiastical rulers who, for the sake of a vestment, a gesture, a posture, had not only torn the Church asunder, but had filled all the gaols of England with men of orthodox faith and saintly life? The reflections thrown by the High Churchmen on the recent conduct of the dissenting body the Low Churchmen pronounced to be grossly unjust. The wonder was, not that a few nonconformists should have accepted with thanks an indulgence which, illegal as it was, had opened the doors of their prisons and given security to their hearths, but that the nonconformists generally should have been true to the cause of a constitution from the benefits of which they had been long excluded. It was most unfair to impute to a great party the faults of a few individuals. Even among the Bishops of the Established Church James had found tools and sycophants. The conduct of Cartwright and Parker had been much more inexcusable than that of Alsop and Lobb. Yet those who held the Dissenters answerable for the errors of Alsop and Lobb would doubtless think it most unreasonable to hold the Church answerable for the far deeper guilt of Cartwright and Parker.

The Low Church clergymen were a minority, and not a large minority, of their profession: but their weight was

CHAP.
XI.

much more than proportioned to their numbers: for they mustered strong in the capital; they had great influence there; and the average of intellect and knowledge was higher among them than among their order generally. We should probably overrate their numerical strength, if we were to estimate them at a tenth part of the priesthood. Yet it will scarcely be denied that there were among them as many men of distinguished eloquence and learning as could be found in the other nine tenths. Among the laity who conformed to the established religion the parties were not unevenly balanced. Indeed the line which separated them deviated very little from the line which separated the Whigs and the Tories. In the House of Commons, which had been elected when the Whigs were triumphant, the Low Church party greatly preponderated. In the Lords there was an almost exact equipoise; and very slight circumstances sufficed to turn the scale.

William's views concerning ecclesiastical polity.

The head of the Low Church party was the King. He had been bred a Presbyterian: he was, from rational conviction, a Latitudinarian; and personal ambition, as well as higher motives, prompted him to act as mediator among Protestant sects. He was bent on effecting three great reforms in the laws touching ecclesiastical matters. His first object was to obtain for dissenters permission to celebrate their worship in freedom and security. His second object was to make such changes in the Anglican ritual and polity as, without offending those to whom that ritual and that polity were dear, might conciliate the moderate nonconformists. His third object was to throw open civil offices to Protestants without distinction of sect. All his three objects were good; but the first only was at that time attainable. He came too late for the second, and too early for the third.

Burnet, Bishop of Salisbury.

A few days after his accession, he took a step which indicated, in a manner not to be mistaken, his sentiments touching ecclesiastical polity and public worship. He found only one see unprovided with a Bishop. Seth Ward, who had during many years had charge of the diocese of Salisbury, and who had been honourably distinguished as one of the founders of the Royal Society, having long survived his faculties, died while the country was agitated by the elections for the Convention, without knowing that great events, of which not the least important had passed under his own roof, had saved his Church and his country from ruin. The choice of a successor was no light matter. That choice would inevitably be considered by the country as a prognostic of the highest import. The King too might well be perplexed by the number of divines whose erudition, eloquence, courage, and uprightness had been conspicuously displayed during the contentions of the last three years. The preference was given to Burnet. His claims were doubtless great. Yet William might have had a more tranquil reign if he had postponed for a time the well earned promotion of his chaplain, and had bestowed the first great spiritual preferment, which, after the Revolution, fell to the disposal of the Crown, on some eminent theologian, attached to the new settlement, yet not generally hated by the clergy. Unhappily the name of Burnet was odious to the great majority of the Anglican priesthood. Though, as respected doctrine, he by no means belonged to the extreme section of the Latitudinarian party, he was popularly regarded as the personification of the Latitudinarian spirit. This distinction he owed to the prominent place which he held in literature and politics, to the readiness of his tongue and of his pen, and above all to the frankness and boldness of his nature, frankness which could keep no secret, and boldness which flinched from no danger. He had formed but a low estimate of the character of his clerical brethren considered as a body; and with his usual indiscretion, he frequently suffered his opinion to escape him. They hated him in return with a hatred which has descended to their successors, and which, after the lapse of a century and a half, does not appear to languish.

As soon as the King's decision was known, the question was everywhere asked, What will the Archbishop do? Sancroft had absented himself from the Convention: he had refused to sit in the Privy Council: he had ceased to confirm, to ordain, and to institute; and he was seldom seen beyond the walls of his palace at Lambeth. He, on all occasions, professed to think himself still bound by his old oath of allegiance. Burnet he regarded as a scandal to the priesthood, a Presbyterian in a surplice. The prelate who should lay hands on that unworthy head would commit more than one great sin. He would, in a sacred place, and before a great congregation of the faithful, at once acknowledge an usurper as a King, and confer on a schismatic the character of a Bishop. During some time Sancroft positively declared that he would not obey the precept of William. Lloyd of Saint

Asaph, who was the common friend of the Archbishop and of the Bishop elect, entreated and expostulated in vain. Nottingham, who, of all the laymen connected with the new government, stood best with the clergy, tried his influence, but to no better purpose. The Jacobites said everywhere that they were sure of the good old Primate; that he had the spirit of a martyr; that he was determined to brave, in the cause of the Monarchy and of the Church, the utmost rigour of those laws with which the obsequious parliaments of the sixteenth century had fenced the Royal Supremacy. He did in truth hold out long. But at the last moment his heart failed him, and he looked round him for some mode of escape. Fortunately, as childish scruples often disturbed his conscience, childish expedients often quieted it. A more childish expedient than that to which he now resorted is not to be found in all the tomes of the casuists. He would not himself bear a part in the service. He would not publicly pray for the Prince and Princess as King and Queen. He would not call for their mandate, order it to be read, and then proceed to obey it. But he issued a commission empowering any three of his suffragans to commit, in his name, and as his delegates, the sins which he did not choose to commit in person. The reproaches of all parties soon made him ashamed of himself. He then tried to suppress the evidence of his fault by means more discreditable than the fault itself. He abstracted from among the public records of which he was the guardian the instrument by which he had authorised his brethren to act for him, and was with difficulty induced to give it up.*

Burnet however had, under the authority of this instrument, been consecrated. When he next waited on Mary, she reminded him of the conversations which they had held at the Hague about the high duties and grave responsibility of Bishops. "I hope," she said, "that you will put your notions in practice." Her hope was not disappointed. Whatever may be thought of Burnet's opinions touching civil and ecclesiastical polity, or of the temper and judgment which he showed in defending those opinions, the utmost malevolence of faction could not venture to deny that he tended his flock with a zeal, diligence, and disinterestedness worthy of the purest ages of the Church. His jurisdiction extended over Wiltshire and Berkshire. These counties he divided into dis-

* Burnet, ii. 6.; Birch's Life of Tillotson; Life of Kettlewell, part iii. section 62.

tricts which he sedulously visited. About two months of every summer he passed in preaching, catechising, and confirming daily from church to church. When he died there was no corner of his diocese in which the people had not had seven or eight opportunities of receiving his instructions and of asking his advice. The worst weather, the worst roads, did not prevent him from discharging these duties. On one occasion, when the floods were out, he exposed his life to imminent risk rather than disappoint a rural congregation which was in expectation of a discourse from the Bishop. The poverty of the inferior clergy was a constant cause of uneasiness to his kind and generous heart. He was indefatigable and at length successful in his attempts to obtain for them from the Crown that grant which is known by the name of Queen Anne's Bounty.* He was especially careful, when he travelled through his diocese, to lay no burden on them. Instead of requiring them to entertain him, he entertained them. He always fixed his head quarters at a market town, kept a table there, and, by his decent hospitality and munificent charities, tried to conciliate those who were prejudiced against his doctrines. When he bestowed a poor benefice,—and he had many such to bestow,—his practice was to add out of his own purse twenty pounds a year to the income. Ten promising young men, to each of whom he allowed thirty pounds a year, studied divinity under his own eye in the close of Salisbury. He had several children: but he did not think himself justified in hoarding for them. Their mother had brought him a good fortune. With that fortune, he always said, they must be content. He would not, for their sakes, be guilty of the crime of raising an estate out of revenues sacred to piety and charity. Such merits as these will, in the judgment of wise and candid men, appear fully to atone for every offence which can be justly imputed to him.†

When he took his seat in the House of Lords, he found that assembly busied in ecclesiastical legislation. A states-

* Swift, writing under the name of Gregory Misosarm, most malignantly and dishonestly represents Burnet as grudging this grant to the Church. Swift cannot have been ignorant that the Church was indebted for the grant chiefly to Burnet's persevering exertions.

† See the Life of Burnet, at the end of the second volume of his history, his manuscript memoirs, Harl. 6584, his memorials touching the First Fruits and Tenths, and Somers's letter to him on that subject. See also what Dr. King, Jacobite as he was, had the justice to say in his Anecdotes. A most honourable testimony to Burnet's virtues, given by another Jacobite who had attacked him fiercely, and whom he had treated generously, the learned and upright Thomas Baker, will be found in the Gentleman's Magazine for August and September, 1791.

CHAP. XI.

Nottingham's views concerning ecclesiastical polity.

man who was well known to be devoted to the Church had undertaken to plead the cause of the Dissenters. No subject in the realm occupied so important and commanding a position with reference to religious parties as Nottingham. To the influence derived from rank, from wealth, and from office, he added the higher influence which belongs to knowledge, to eloquence, and to integrity. The orthodoxy of his creed, the regularity of his devotions, and the purity of his morals gave a peculiar weight to his opinions on questions in which the interests of Christianity were concerned. Of all the ministers of the new Sovereigns, he had the largest share of the confidence of the clergy. Shrewsbury was certainly a Whig, and probably a freethinker: he had lost one religion; and it did not very clearly appear that he had found another. Halifax had been during many years accused of scepticism, deism, atheism. Danby's attachment to episcopacy and the liturgy was rather political than religious. But Nottingham was such a son as the Church was proud to own. Propositions therefore, which, if made by his colleagues, would infallibly produce a violent panic among the clergy, might, if made by him, find a favourable reception even in universities and chapter houses. The friends of religious liberty were with good reason desirous to obtain his cooperation; and, up to a certain point, he was not unwilling to cooperate with them. He was decidedly for a toleration. He was even for what was then called a comprehension: that is to say, he was desirous to make some alterations in the Anglican discipline and ritual for the purpose of removing the scruples of the moderate Presbyterians. But he was not prepared to give up the Test Act. The only fault which he found with that Act was that it was not sufficiently stringent, and that it left loopholes through which schismatics sometimes crept into civil employments. In truth it was because he was not disposed to part with the Test that he was willing to consent to some changes in the Liturgy. He conceived that, if the entrance of the Church were but a very little widened, great numbers who had hitherto lingered near the threshold would press in. Those who still remained without would then not be sufficiently numerous or powerful to extort any further concession, and would be glad to compound for a bare toleration.*

* Oldmixon would have us believe that Nottingham was not, at this time, unwilling to give up the Test Act. But Oldmixon's assertion, unsupported by evidence, is of no weight whatever; and all the evidence which he produces makes against his assertion.

The opinion of the Low Churchmen concerning the Test Act differed widely from his. But many of them thought that it was of the highest importance to have his support on the great questions of Toleration and Comprehension. From the scattered fragments of information which have come down to us, it appears that a compromise was made. It is quite certain that Nottingham undertook to bring in a Toleration Bill and a Comprehension Bill, and to use his best endeavours to carry both bills through the House of Lords. It is highly probable that, in return for this great service, some of the leading Whigs consented to let the Test Act remain for the present unaltered.

There was no difficulty in framing either the Toleration Bill or the Comprehension Bill. The situation of the dissenters had been much discussed nine or ten years before, when the kingdom was distracted by the fear of a Popish plot, and when there was among Protestants a general disposition to unite against the common enemy. The government had then been willing to make large concessions to the Whig party, on condition that the crown should be suffered to descend according to the regular course. A draught of a law authorising the public worship of the Nonconformists, and a draught of a law making some alterations in the public worship of the Established Church, had been prepared, and would probably have been passed by both Houses without difficulty, had not Shaftesbury and his coadjutors refused to listen to any terms, and, by grasping at what was beyond their reach, missed advantages which might easily have been secured. In the framing of these draughts, Nottingham, then an active member of the House of Commons, had borne a considerable part. He now brought them forth from the obscurity in which they had remained since the dissolution of the Oxford Parliament, and laid them, with some slight alterations, on the table of the Lords.*

The Toleration Bill passed both Houses with little debate. This celebrated statute, long considered as the Great Charter of religious liberty, has since been extensively modified, and is hardly known to the present generation except by name. The name, however, is still pronounced with respect by many

CHAP. XI.

The Toleration Bill.

* Burnet, ii. 4.; Van Citters to the States General, March 1/11 1689; King William's Toleration, being an explanation of that liberty of conscience which may be expected from His Majesty's Declaration, with a Bill for Comprehension and Indulgence, drawn up in order to an Act of Parliament, licensed March 25, 1689.

who will perhaps learn with surprise and disappointment the real nature of the law which they have been accustomed to hold in honour.

Several statutes which had been passed between the accession of Queen Elizabeth and the Revolution required all people under severe penalties to attend the services of the Church of England, and to abstain from attending conventicles. The Toleration Act did not repeal any of these statutes, but merely provided that they should not be construed to extend to any person who should testify his loyalty by taking the Oaths of Allegiance and Supremacy, and his Protestantism by subscribing the Declaration against Transubstantiation.

The relief thus granted was common between the dissenting laity and the dissenting clergy. But the dissenting clergy had some peculiar grievances. The Act of Uniformity had laid a mulct of a hundred pounds on every person who, not having received episcopal ordination, should presume to administer the Eucharist. The Five Mile Act had driven many pious and learned ministers from their houses and their friends, to live among rustics in obscure villages of which the name was not to be seen on the map. The Conventicle Act had imposed heavy fines on divines who should preach in any meeting of separatists; and, in direct opposition to the humane spirit of our law, the Courts were enjoined to construe this act largely and beneficially for the suppressing of dissent and for the encouraging of informers. These severe statutes were not repealed, but were, with many conditions and precautions, relaxed. It was provided that every dissenting minister should, before he exercised his function, profess under his hand his belief in the Articles of the Church of England, with a few exceptions. The propositions to which he was not required to assent were these; that the Church has power to regulate ceremonies; that the doctrines set forth in the Book of Homilies are sound; and that there is nothing superstitious or idolatrous in the ordination service. If he declared himself a Baptist, he was also excused from affirming that the baptism of infants is a laudable practice. But, unless his conscience suffered him to subscribe thirty-four of the thirty-nine Articles, and the greater part of two other Articles, he could not preach without incurring all the punishments which the Cavaliers, in the day of their power and their vengeance, had devised for the tormenting and ruining of schismatical teachers.

The situation of the Quaker differed from that of other dissenters, and differed for the worse. The Presbyterian, the Independent, and the Baptist had no scruple about the Oath of Supremacy. But the Quaker refused to take it, not because he objected to the proposition that foreign sovereigns and prelates have no jurisdiction in England, but because his conscience would not suffer him to swear to any proposition whatever. He was therefore exposed to the severity of part of that penal code which, long before Quakerism existed, had been enacted against Roman Catholics by the Parliaments of Elizabeth. Soon after the Restoration, a severe law, distinct from the general law which applied to all conventicles, had been passed against meetings of Quakers. The Toleration Act permitted the members of this harmless sect to hold their assemblies in peace, on condition of signing three documents, a declaration against Transubstantiation, a promise of fidelity to the government, and a confession of Christian belief. The objections which the Quaker had to the Athanasian phraseology had brought on him the imputation of Socinianism: and the strong language in which he sometimes asserted that he derived his knowledge of spiritual things directly from above had raised a suspicion that he thought lightly of the authority of Scripture. He was therefore required to profess his faith in the divinity of the Son and of the Holy Ghost, and in the inspiration of the Old and New Testaments.

Such were the terms on which the Protestant dissenters of England were, for the first time, permitted by law to worship God according to their own conscience. They were very properly forbidden to assemble with barred doors, but were protected against hostile intrusion by a clause which made it penal to enter a meeting house for the purpose of molesting the congregation.

As if the numerous limitations and precautions which have been mentioned were insufficient, it was emphatically declared that the legislature did not intend to grant the smallest indulgence to any Papist, or to any person who denied the doctrine of the Trinity as that doctrine is set forth in the formularies of the Church of England.

Of all the Acts that have ever been passed by Parliament, the Toleration Act is perhaps that which most strikingly illustrates the peculiar vices and the peculiar excellences of English legislation. The science of Politics bears in one respect a close analogy to the science of Mechanics. The mathematician can easily demonstrate that a certain power, applied by means of a certain lever or of a certain system of pulleys, will suffice to raise a certain weight. But his demonstration proceeds on the supposition that the machinery is such as no load will bend or break. If the engineer, who has to lift a great mass of real granite by the instrumentality of real timber and real hemp, should absolutely rely on the propositions which he finds in treatises on Dynamics, and should make no allowance for the imperfection of his materials, his whole apparatus of beams, wheels, and ropes would soon come down in ruin, and, with all his geometrical skill, he would be found a far inferior builder to those painted barbarians who, though they never heard of the parallelogram of forces, managed to pile up Stonehenge. What the engineer is to the mathematician, the active statesman is to the contemplative statesman. It is indeed most important that legislators and administrators should be versed in the philosophy of government, as it is most important that the architect, who has to fix an obelisk on its pedestal, or to hang a tubular bridge over an estuary, should be versed in the philosophy of equilibrium and motion. But, as he who has actually to build must bear in mind many things never noticed by D'Alembert and Euler, so must he who has actually to govern be perpetually guided by considerations to which no allusion can be found in the writings of Adam Smith or Jeremy Bentham. The perfect lawgiver is a just temper between the mere man of theory, who can see nothing but general principles, and the mere man of business, who can see nothing but particular circumstances. Of lawgivers in whom the speculative element has prevailed to the exclusion of the practical, the world has during the last eighty years been singularly fruitful. To their wisdom Europe and America have owed scores of abortive constitutions, scores of constitutions which have lived just long enough to make a miserable noise, and have then gone off in convulsions. But in English legislation the practical element has always predominated, and not seldom unduly predominated, over the speculative. To think nothing of symmetry and much of convenience; never to remove an anomaly merely because it is an anomaly; never to innovate except when some grievance is felt; never to innovate except so far as to get rid of the grievance; never to lay down any proposition of wider extent than the particular case for which it is necessary to provide; these are the rules which have, from the age of John to the age of Victoria, generally guided the deliberations of our two hundred and fifty Parliaments. Our national distaste for whatever is abstract in political science amounts undoubtedly to a fault. Yet it is, perhaps, a fault on the right side. That we have been far too slow to improve our laws must be admitted. But, though in other countries there may have occasionally been more rapid progress, it would not be easy to name any other country in which there has been so little retrogression.

The Toleration Act approaches very near to the idea of a great English law. To a jurist, versed in the theory of legislation, but not intimately acquainted with the temper of the sects and parties into which the nation was divided at the time of the Revolution, that Act would seem to be a mere chaos of absurdities and contradictions. It will not bear to be tried by sound general principles. Nay, it will not bear to be tried by any principle, sound or unsound. The sound principle undoubtedly is, that mere theological error ought not to be punished by the civil magistrate. This principle the Toleration Act not only does not recognise, but positively disclaims. Not a single one of the cruel laws enacted against nonconformists by the Tudors or the Stuarts is repealed. Persecution continues to be the general rule. Toleration is the exception. Nor is this all. The freedom which is given to conscience is given in the most capricious manner. A Quaker, by making a declaration of faith in general terms, obtains the full benefit of the Act without signing one of the thirty-nine Articles. An Independent minister, who is perfectly willing to make the declaration required from the Quaker, but who has doubts about six or seven of the Articles, remains still subject to the penal laws. Howe is liable to punishment if he preaches before he has solemnly declared his assent to the Anglican doctrine touching the Eucharist. Penn, who altogether rejects the Eucharist, is at perfect liberty to preach without making any declaration whatever on the subject.

These are some of the obvious faults which must strike every person who examines the Toleration Act by that standard of just reason which is the same in all countries and in all ages. But these very faults may perhaps appear to be merits, when we take into consideration the passions and prejudices of those for whom the Toleration Act was framed. This law, abounding with contradictions which every smatterer in political philosophy can detect, did what a law framed by the utmost skill of the greatest masters of political philosophy might have failed to do. That the provisions which have been recapitulated are cumbrous, puerile, inconsistent with each other, inconsistent with the true theory of religious liberty, must be acknowledged. All that can be said in their defence is this; that they removed a vast mass of evil without shocking a vast mass of prejudice; that they put an end, at once and for ever, without one division in either House of Parliament, without one riot in the streets, with scarcely one audible murmur even from the classes most deeply tainted with bigotry, to a persecution which had raged during four generations, which had broken innumerable hearts, which had made innumerable firesides desolate, which had filled the prisons with men of whom the world was not worthy, which had driven thousands of those honest, diligent, and godfearing yeomen and artisans, who are the true strength of a nation, to seek a refuge beyond the ocean among the wigwams of red Indians and the lairs of panthers. Such a defence, however weak it may appear to some shallow speculators, will probably be thought complete by statesmen.

The English, in 1689, were by no means disposed to admit the doctrine that religious error ought to be left unpunished. That doctrine was just then more unpopular than it had ever been. For it had, only a few months before, been hypocritically put forward as a pretext for persecuting the Established Church, for trampling on the fundamental laws of the realm, for confiscating freeholds, for treating as a crime the modest exercise of the right of petition. If a bill had then been drawn up granting entire freedom of conscience to all Protestants, it may be confidently affirmed that Nottingham would never have introduced such a bill; that all the bishops, Burnet included, would have voted against it; that it would have been denounced, Sunday after Sunday, from ten thousand pulpits, as an insult to God and to all Christian men, and as a license to the worst heretics and blasphemers; that it would have been condemned almost as vehemently by Bates and Baxter as by Ken and Sherlock; that it would have been burned by the mob in half the marketplaces of England; that it would never have become the law of the land, and that it would have made the very name of toleration odious during many years to the majority of the people. And yet, if such a bill had been passed, what would it have effected beyond what was effected by the Toleration Act?

It is true that the Toleration Act recognised persecution as the rule, and granted liberty of conscience only as the exception. But it is equally true that the rule remained in force only against a few hundreds of Protestant dissenters, and that the benefit of the exceptions extended to hundreds of thousands.

It is true that it was in theory absurd to make Howe sign thirty-four or thirty-five of the Anglican Articles before he could preach, and to let Penn preach without signing one of those Articles. But it is equally true that under this arrangement both Howe and Penn got as entire liberty to preach as they could have had under the most philosophical code that Beccaria or Jefferson could have framed.

The progress of the bill was easy. Only one amendment of grave importance was proposed. Some zealous churchmen in the Commons suggested that it might be desirable to grant the toleration only for a term of seven years, and thus to bind over the nonconformists to good behaviour. But this suggestion was so unfavourably received that those who made it did not venture to divide the House.[*]

The King gave his consent with hearty satisfaction: the bill became law; and the Puritan divines thronged to the Quarter Sessions of every county to swear and sign. Many of them probably professed their assent to the Articles with some tacit reservations. But the tender conscience of Baxter would not suffer him to qualify, till he had put on record an explanation of the sense in which he understood every proposition which seemed to him to admit of misconstruction. The instrument delivered by him to the Court before which he took the oaths is still extant, and contains two passages of peculiar interest. He declared that his approbation of the Athanasian Creed was confined to that part which was properly a Creed, and that he did not mean to express any assent to the damnatory clauses. He also declared that he did not, by signing the article which anathematises all who maintain that there is any other salvation than through Christ, mean to condemn those who entertain a hope that sincere and virtuous unbelievers may be admitted to partake in the benefits of Redemption. Many of the dissenting clergy of

[*] Commons' Journals, May 17. 1689.

London expressed their concurrence in these charitable sentiments.*

The history of the Comprehension Bill presents a remarkable contrast to the history of the Toleration Bill. The two bills had a common origin, and, to a great extent, a common object. They were framed at the same time, and laid aside at the same time; they sank together into oblivion, and they were, after the lapse of several years, again brought together before the world. Both were laid by the same peer on the table of the Upper House; and both were referred to the same select committee. But it soon began to appear that they would have widely different fates. The Comprehension Bill was indeed a neater specimen of legislative workmanship than the Toleration Bill, but was not, like the Toleration Bill, adapted to the wants, the feelings, and the prejudices of the existing generation. Accordingly while the Toleration Bill found support in all quarters, the Comprehension Bill was attacked from all quarters, and was at last coldly and languidly defended even by those who had introduced it. About the same time at which the Toleration Bill became law with the general concurrence of public men, the Comprehension Bill was, with a concurrence not less general, suffered to drop. The Toleration Bill still ranks among those great statutes which are epochs in our constitutional history. The Comprehension Bill is forgotten. No collector of antiquities has thought it worth preserving. A single copy, the same which Nottingham presented to the Peers, is still among our parliamentary records, but has been seen by only two or three persons now living. It is a fortunate circumstance that, in this copy, almost the whole history of the Bill can be read. In spite of cancellations and interlineations, the original words can easily be distinguished from those which were inserted in the committee or on the report.†

The first clause, as it stood when the bill was introduced, dispensed all the ministers of the Established Church from the necessity of subscribing the Thirty-nine Articles. For the Articles was substituted a Declaration which ran thus;

* Sense of the subscribed articles by the Ministers of London, 1689; Calamy's Historical Additions to Baxter's Life.
† The bill will be found among the Archives of the House of Lords. It is strange that this vast collection of important documents should have been altogether neglected, even by our most exact and diligent historians. It was opened to me by one of the most valued of my friends, Sir John Lefevre; and my researches were greatly assisted by the kindness of Mr. Thoms.

"I do approve of the doctrine and worship and government of the Church of England by law established, as containing all things necessary to salvation; and I promise, in the exercise of my ministry, to preach and practise according thereunto." Another clause granted similar indulgence to the members of the two universities.

Then it was provided that any minister who had been ordained after the Presbyterian fashion might, without reordination, acquire all the privileges of a priest of the Established Church. He must, however, be admitted to his new functions by the imposition of the hands of a bishop, who was to pronounce the following form of words; "Take thou authority to preach the word of God, and administer the sacraments, and to perform all other ministerial offices in the Church of England." The person thus admitted was to be capable of holding any rectory or vicarage in the kingdom.

Then followed clauses providing that a clergyman might, except in a few churches of peculiar dignity, wear the surplice or not as he thought fit, that the sign of the cross might be omitted in baptism, that children might be christened, if such were the wish of their parents, without godfathers or godmothers, and that persons who had a scruple about receiving the Eucharist kneeling might receive it sitting.

The concluding clause was drawn in the form of a petition. It was proposed that the two Houses should request the King and Queen to issue a commission empowering thirty divines of the Established Church to revise the liturgy, the canons, and the constitution of the ecclesiastical courts, and to recommend such alterations as might on enquiry appear to be desirable.

The bill went smoothly through the first stages. Compton, who, since Sancroft had shut himself up at Lambeth, was virtually Primate, supported Nottingham with ardour.* In the committee, however, it appeared that there was a strong body of churchmen, who were as obstinately determined not to give up a single word or form as if they had thought that prayers were no prayers if read without the surplice, that a babe could be no Christian if not marked with the cross, that

* Among the Tanner MSS. in the Bodleian Library is a very curious letter from Compton to Sancroft, about the Toleration Bill and the Comprehension Bill. "These," says Compton, "are two great works in which the being of our Church is concerned; and I hope you will send to the House for copies. For though we are under a conquest, God has given us favour in the eyes of our rulers; and we may keep our Church if we will." Sancroft seems to have returned no answer.

bread and wine could be no memorials of redemption or vehicles of grace if not received on bended knee. Why, these persons asked, was the docile and affectionate son of the Church to be disgusted by seeing the irreverent practices of a conventicle introduced into her majestic choirs? Why should his feelings, his prejudices, if prejudices they were, be less considered than the whims of schismatics? If, as Burnet and men like Burnet were never weary of repeating, indulgence was due to a weak brother, was it less due to the brother whose weakness consisted in the excess of his love for an ancient, a decent, a beautiful ritual, associated in his imagination from childhood with all that is most sublime and endearing, than to him whose morose and litigious mind was always devising frivolous objections to innocent and salutary usages? But, in truth, the scrupulosity of the Puritan was not that sort of scrupulosity which the Apostle had commanded believers to respect. It sprang, not from morbid tenderness of conscience, but from censoriousness and spiritual pride; and none who had studied the New Testament could have failed to observe that, while we are charged carefully to avoid whatever may give scandal to the feeble, we are taught by divine precept and example to make no concession to the supercilious and uncharitable Pharisee. Was everything which was not of the essence of religion to be given up as soon as it became unpleasing to a knot of zealots whose heads had been turned by conceit and the love of novelty? Painted glass, music, holidays, fast days, were not of the essence of religion. Were the windows of King's College chapel to be broken at the demand of one set of fanatics? Was the organ of Exeter to be silenced to please another? Were all the village bells to be mute because Tribulation Wholesome and Deacon Ananias thought them profane? Was Christmas no longer to be a day of rejoicing? Was Passion week no longer to be a season of humiliation? These changes, it is true, were not yet proposed. But if,—so the High Churchmen reasoned,—we once admit that what is harmless and edifying is to be given up because it offends some narrow understandings and some gloomy tempers, where are we to stop? And is it not probable that, by thus attempting to heal one schism, we may cause another? All those things which the Puritans regard as the blemishes of the Church are by a large part of the population reckoned among her attractions. May she not, in ceasing to give scandal to a few sour precisians, cease also to influence the hearts of many who now delight in her ordinances? Is it not to be apprehended that, for every proselyte whom she allures from the meeting house, ten of her old disciples may turn away from her maimed rites and dismantled temples, and that those new separatists may either form themselves into a sect far more formidable than the sect which we are now seeking to conciliate, or may, in the violence of their disgust at a cold and ignoble worship, be tempted to join in the solemn and gorgeous idolatry of Rome?

It is remarkable that those who held this language were by no means disposed to contend for the doctrinal Articles of the Church. The truth is that, from the time of James the First, that great party which has been peculiarly zealous for the Anglican polity and the Anglican ritual has always leaned strongly towards Arminianism, and has therefore never been much attached to a confession of faith framed by reformers who, on questions of metaphysical divinity, generally agreed with Calvin. One of the characteristic marks of that party is the disposition which it has always shown to appeal, on points of dogmatic theology, rather to the Liturgy, which was derived from Rome, than to the Articles and Homilies, which were derived from Geneva. The Calvinistic members of the Church, on the other hand, have always maintained that her deliberate judgment on such points is much more likely to be found in an Article or a Homily than in an ejaculation of penitence or a hymn of thanksgiving. It does not appear that, in the debates on the Comprehension Bill, a single High Churchman raised his voice against the clause which relieved the clergy from the necessity of subscribing the Articles, and of declaring the doctrine contained in the Homilies to be sound. Nay, the Declaration, which, in the original draught, was substituted for the Articles, was much softened down on the report. As the clause finally stood, the ministers of the Church were required, not to profess that they approved of her doctrine, but merely to acknowledge, what probably few Baptists, Quakers, or Unitarians would deny, that her doctrine contained all things necessary to salvation. Had the bill become law, the only people in the kingdom who would have been under the necessity of signing the Articles would have been the dissenting preachers.*

* The distaste of the High Churchmen for the Articles is the subject of a curious pamphlet published in 1689, and entitled a Dialogue between Timothy and Titus.

CHAP. XL.

The easy manner in which the zealous friends of the Church gave up her confession of faith presents a striking contrast to the spirit with which they struggled for her polity and her ritual. The clause which admitted Presbyterian ministers to hold benefices without episcopal ordination was rejected. The clause which permitted scrupulous persons to communicate sitting very narrowly escaped the same fate. In the Committee it was struck out, and, on the report, was with great difficulty restored. The majority of peers in the House was against the proposed indulgence, and the scale was but just turned by the proxies.

But by this time it began to appear that the bill which the High Churchmen were so keenly assailing was menaced by dangers from a very different quarter. The same considerations which had induced Nottingham to support a comprehension made comprehension an object of dread and aversion to a large body of dissenters. The truth is that the time for such a scheme had gone by. If, a hundred years earlier, when the division in the Protestant body was recent, Elizabeth had been so wise as to abstain from requiring the observance of a few forms which a large part of her subjects considered as Popish, she might perhaps have averted those fearful calamities which, forty years after her death, afflicted the Church. But the general tendency of schism is to widen. Had Leo the Tenth, when the exactions and impostures of the Pardoners first roused the indignation of Saxony, corrected those evil practices with a vigorous hand, it is not improbable that Luther would have died in the bosom of the Church of Rome. But the opportunity was suffered to escape; and, when, a few years later, the Vatican would gladly have purchased peace by yielding the original subject of quarrel, the original subject of quarrel was almost forgotten. The enquiring spirit which had been roused by a single abuse had discovered or imagined a thousand: controversies engendered controversies: every attempt that was made to accommodate one dispute ended by producing another; and at length the General Council, which, during the earlier stages of the distemper, had been supposed to be an infallible remedy, made the case utterly hopeless. In this respect, as in many others, the history of Puritanism in England bears a close analogy to the history of Protestantism in Europe. The Parliament of 1689 could no more put an end to nonconformity by tolerating a garb or a posture than the Doctors of Trent could have reconciled the Teutonic nations to the Papacy by regulating the sale of indulgences. In the sixteenth century Quakerism was unknown; and there was not in the whole realm a single congregation of Independents or Baptists. At the time of the Revolution, the Independents, Baptists, and Quakers were probably a majority of the dissenting body; and these sects could not be gained over on any terms which the lowest of Low Churchmen would have been willing to offer. The Independent held that a national Church, governed by any central authority whatever, Pope, Patriarch, King, Bishop, or Synod, was an unscriptural institution, and that every congregation of believers was, under Christ, a sovereign society. The Baptist was even more irreclaimable than the Independent, and the Quaker even more irreclaimable than the Baptist. Concessions, therefore, which would once have extinguished nonconformity, would not now satisfy even one half of the nonconformists; and it was the obvious interest of every nonconformist whom no concession would satisfy that none of his brethren should be satisfied. The more liberal the terms of comprehension, the greater was the alarm of every separatist who knew that he could, in no case, be comprehended. There was but slender hope that the dissenters, unbroken and acting as one man, would be able to obtain from the legislature full admission to civil privileges; and all hope of obtaining such admission must be relinquished if Nottingham should, by the help of some wellmeaning but shortsighted friends of religious liberty, be enabled to accomplish his design. If his bill passed, there would doubtless be a considerable defection from the dissenting body; and every defection must be severely felt by a class already outnumbered, depressed, and struggling against powerful enemies. Every proselyte, too must be reckoned twice over, as a loss to the party which was even now too weak, and as a gain to the party which was even now too strong. The Church was but too well able to hold her own against all the sects in the kingdom; and, if those sects were to be thinned by a large desertion, and the Church strengthened by a large reinforcement, it was plain that all chance of obtaining any relaxation of the Test Act would be at an end; and it was but too probable that the Toleration Act might not long remain unrepealed.

Even those Presbyterian ministers whose scruples the Comprehension Bill was especially intended to remove were by no means unanimous in wishing it to pass. The ablest and most

CHAP. XI.

CHAP. XI.

eloquent preachers among them had, since the Declaration of Indulgence had appeared, been very agreeably settled in the capital and in other large towns, and were now about to enjoy, under the sure guarantee of an Act of Parliament, that toleration which, under the Declaration of Indulgence, had been illicit and precarious. The situation of these men was such as the great majority of the divines of the Established Church might well envy. Few indeed of the parochial clergy were so abundantly supplied with comforts as the favourite orator of a great assembly of nonconformists in the City. The voluntary contributions of his wealthy hearers, Aldermen and Deputies, West India Merchants and Turkey merchants, Wardens of the Company of Fishmongers and Wardens of the Company of Goldsmiths, enabled him to become a landowner or a mortgagee. The best broadcloth from Blackwell Hall, and the best poultry from Leadenhall Market, were frequently left at his door. His influence over his flock was immense. Scarcely any member of a congregation of separatists entered into a partnership, married a daughter, put a son out as apprentice, or gave his vote at an election, without consulting his spiritual guide. On all political and literary questions the minister was the oracle of his own circle. It was popularly remarked, during many years, that an eminent dissenting minister had only to determine whether he would make his son an attorney or a physician; for that the attorney was sure to have clients and the physician to have patients. While a waiting woman was generally considered as a help meet for a chaplain in holy orders of the Established Church, the widows and daughters of opulent citizens were supposed to belong in a peculiar manner to nonconformist pastors. One of the great Presbyterian Rabbies, therefore, might well doubt whether, in a worldly view, he should be a gainer by a comprehension. He might indeed hold a rectory or a vicarage, when he could get one. But in the meantime he would be destitute: his meeting house would be closed; his congregation would be dispersed among the parish churches: if a benefice were bestowed on him, it would probably be a very slender compensation for the income which he had lost. Nor could he hope to have, as a minister of the Anglican Church, the authority and dignity which he had hitherto enjoyed. He would always, by a large portion of the members of that Church, be regarded as a deserter. He might, therefore, on the whole, very naturally wish to be left where he was.*

There was consequently a division in the Whig party. One section of that party was for relieving the dissenters from the Test Act, and giving up the Comprehension Bill. Another section was for pushing forward the Comprehension Bill, and postponing to a more convenient time the consideration of the Test Act. The effect of this division among the friends of religious liberty was that the High Churchmen, though a minority in the House of Commons and not a majority in the House of Lords, were able to oppose with success both the reforms which they dreaded. The Comprehension Bill was not passed; and the Test Act was not repealed.

Just at the moment when the question of the test and the question of the Comprehension became complicated together in a manner which might well perplex an enlightened and honest politician, both questions became complicated with a third question of great importance.

The ancient oaths of allegiance and supremacy contained some expressions which had always been disliked by the Whigs, and other expressions which Tories, honestly attached to the new settlement, thought inapplicable to princes who had not the hereditary right. The Convention had therefore, while the throne was still vacant, framed those oaths of allegiance and supremacy by which we still testify our loyalty to our Sovereign. By the Act which turned the Convention into a Parliament, the members of both Houses were required to take the new oaths. As to other persons in public trust, it was hard to say how the law stood. One form of words was

The bill for settling the oaths of allegiance and supremacy.

---

* Tom Brown says, in his scurrilous way, of the Presbyterian divines of that time, that their preaching "brings in money, and money buys land; and land is an amusement they all desire, in spite of their hypocritical cant. If it were not for the quarterly contributions, there would be no longer schism or separation." He asks how it can be imagined that, while "they are maintained like gentlemen by the breach, they will ever preach up healing doctrines?"—Brown's Amusements, Serious and Comical. Some curious instances of the influence exercised by the chief dissenting ministers may be found in Hawkins's Life of Johnson. In the Journal of the retired citizen (Spectator, 317.) Addison has indulged in some exquisite pleasantry on this subject. The Mr. Nisby whose opinions about the peace, the Grand Vizier, and laced coffee, are quoted with so much respect, and who is so well regaled with marrow bones, or cheek, and a bottle of Brooks and Hellier, was John Nesbit, a highly popular preacher, who, about the time of the Revolution, became pastor of a dissenting congregation in Hare Court, Aldersgate Street. In Wilson's History and Antiquities of Dissenting Churches and Meeting Houses in London, Westminster, and Southwark, will be found several instances of nonconformist preachers who, about this time, made handsome fortunes, generally, it should seem, by marriage.

enjoined by statutes, regularly passed, and not yet regularly abrogated. A different form was enjoined by the Declaration of Right, an instrument which was indeed revolutionary and irregular, but which might well be thought equal in authority to any statute. The practice was in as much confusion as the law. It was therefore felt to be necessary that the legislature should, without delay, pass an Act abolishing the old oaths, and determining when and by whom the new oaths should be taken.

The bill which settled this important question originated in the Upper House. As to most of the provisions there was little room for dispute. It was unanimously agreed that no person should, at any future time, be admitted to any office, civil, military, ecclesiastical, or academical, without taking the oaths to William and Mary. It was also unanimously agreed that every person who already held any civil or military office should be ejected from it, unless he took the oaths on or before the first of August 1689. But the strongest passions of both parties were excited by the question whether persons who already possessed ecclesiastical or academical offices should be required to swear fealty to the King and Queen on pain of deprivation. None could say what might be the effect of a law enjoining all the members of a great, a powerful, a sacred profession to make, under the most solemn sanction of religion, a declaration which might be plausibly represented as a formal recantation of all that they had been writing and preaching during many years. The Primate and some of the most eminent Bishops had already absented themselves from Parliament, and would doubtless relinquish their palaces and revenues, rather than acknowledge the new Sovereigns. The example of these great prelates might perhaps be followed by a multitude of divines of humbler rank, by hundreds of canons, prebendaries, and fellows of colleges, by thousands of parish priests. To such an event no Tory, however clear his own conviction that he might lawfully swear allegiance to the King who was in possession, could look forward without the most painful emotions of compassion for the sufferers and of anxiety for the Church.

There were some persons who went so far as to deny that the Parliament was competent to pass a law requiring a Bishop to swear on pain of deprivation. No earthly power, they said, could break the tie which bound the successor of the apostles to his diocese. What God had joined no man could sunder. Kings and senates might scrawl words on parchment or impress figures on wax; but those words and figures could no more change the course of the spiritual than the course of the physical world. As the Author of the universe had appointed a certain order, according to which it was His pleasure to send winter and summer, seedtime and harvest, so He had appointed a certain order, according to which He communicated His grace to His Catholic Church; and the latter order was, like the former, independent of the powers and principalities of the world. A legislature might alter the names of the months, might call June December, and December June; but in spite of the legislature, the snow would fall when the sun was in Capricorn, and the flowers would bloom when he was in Cancer. And so the legislature might enact that Ferguson or Muggleton should live in the palace at Lambeth, should sit on the throne of Augustin, should be called Your Grace, and should walk in processions before the Premier Duke: but, in spite of the legislature, Sancroft would, while Sancroft lived, be the only true Archbishop of Canterbury: and the person who should presume to usurp the archiepiscopal functions would be a schismatic. This doctrine was proved by reasons drawn from the budding of Aaron's rod, and from a certain plate which Saint James the Less, according to a legend of the fourth century, used to wear on his forehead. A Greek manuscript, relating to the deprivation of bishops, was discovered, about this time, in the Bodleian Library, and became the subject of a furious controversy. One party held that God had wonderfully brought this precious volume to light, for the guidance of His Church at a most critical moment. The other party wondered that any importance could be attached to the nonsense of a nameless scribbler of the thirteenth century. Much was written about the deprivations of Chrysostom and Photius, of Nicolaus Mysticus and Cosmas Atticus. But the case of Abiathar, whom Solomon put out of the sacerdotal office for treason, was discussed with peculiar eagerness. No small quantity of learning and ingenuity was expended in the attempt to prove that Abiathar, though he wore the ephod and answered by Urim, was not really High Priest, that he ministered only when his superior Zadoc was incapacitated by sickness or by some ceremonial pollution, and that therefore the act of Solomon was not a precedent which would warrant King William in deposing a real Bishop.*

* See, among many other tracts Dodwell's Cautionary Discourses, his Vindication of the Deprived Bishops, his Defence of the Vindication, and his Parae-

But such reasoning as this, though backed by copious citations from the Misna and Maimonides, was not generally satisfactory even to zealous churchmen. For it admitted of one answer, short, but perfectly intelligible to a plain man who knew nothing about Greek fathers or Levitical genealogies. There might be some doubt whether King Solomon had ejected a high priest; but there could be no doubt at all that Queen Elizabeth had ejected the Bishops of more than half the sees in England. It was notorious that fourteen prelates had, without any proceeding in any spiritual court, been deprived by Act of Parliament for refusing to acknowledge her supremacy. Had that deprivation been null? Had Bonner continued to be, to the end of his life, the only true Bishop of London? Had his successor been an usurper? Had Parker and Jewel been schismatics? Had the Convocation of 1562, that Convocation which had finally settled the doctrine of the Church of England, been itself out of the pale of the Church of Christ? Nothing could be more ludicrous than the distress of those controversialists who had to invent a plea for Elizabeth which should not be also a plea for William. Some zealots, indeed, gave up the vain attempt to distinguish between two cases which every man of common sense perceived to be undistinguishable, and frankly owned that the deprivations of 1559 could not be justified. But no person, it was said, ought to be troubled in mind on that account; for, though the Church of England might once have been schismatical, she had become Catholic when the last of the Bishops deprived by Elizabeth ceased to live.* The Tories, however, were not generally disposed to admit that the religious society to which they were fondly attached had originated in an unlawful breach of unity. They therefore took ground lower and more tenable. They argued the question as a question of humanity and of expediency. They spoke much of the debt of gratitude which the nation owed to the priesthood; of the courage and fidelity with which the order, from the primate down to the youngest deacon, had recently defended the civil and ecclesiastical constitution of the realm; of the memorable Sunday when, in all the hundred churches of the capital, scarcely one slave could be found to read the Declaration of Indulgence; of the Black Friday when, amidst the blessings and the loud weeping of a mighty population, the barge of the seven prelates passed through the watergate of the Tower. The firmness with which the clergy had lately, in defiance of menace and of seduction, done what they conscientiously believed to be right, had saved the liberty and religion of England. Was no indulgence to be granted to them if they now refused to do what they conscientiously apprehended to be wrong? And where, it was said, is the danger of treating them with tenderness? Nobody is so absurd as to propose that they shall be permitted to plot against the Government, or to stir up the multitude to insurrection. They are amenable to the law, like other men. If they are guilty of treason, let them be hanged. If they are guilty of sedition, let them be fined and imprisoned. If they omit, in their public ministrations, to pray for King William, for Queen Mary, and for the Parliament assembled under those most religious sovereigns, let the penal clauses of the Act of Uniformity be put in force. If this be not enough, let His Majesty be empowered to tender the oaths to any clergyman; and, if the oaths so tendered are refused, let deprivation follow. In this way any nonjuring bishop or rector who may be suspected, though he cannot be legally convicted, of intriguing, of writing, of talking, against the present settlement, may be at once removed from his office. But why insist on ejecting a pious and laborious minister of religion, who never lifts a finger or utters a word against the government, and who, as often as he performs morning or evening service, prays from his heart for a blessing on the rulers set over him by Providence, but who will not take an oath which seems to him to imply a right in the people to depose a sovereign? Surely we do all that is necessary if we leave men of this sort at the mercy of the very prince to whom they refuse to swear fidelity. If he is willing to bear with their scrupulosity, if he considers them, notwithstanding their prejudices, as innocent and useful members of society, who else can be entitled to complain?

The Whigs were vehement on the other side. They scrutinised, with ingenuity sharpened by hatred, the claims of the clergy to the public gratitude, and sometimes went so

CHAP. XI.

far as altogether to deny that the order had in the preceding year deserved well of the nation. It was true that bishops and priests had stood up against the tyranny of the late King: but it was equally true that, but for the obstinacy with which they had opposed the Exclusion Bill, he never would have been King, and that, but for their adulation and their doctrine of passive obedience, he would never have ventured to be guilty of such tyranny. Their chief business, during a quarter of a century, had been to teach the people to cringe and the prince to domineer. They were guilty of the blood of Russell, of Sidney, of every brave and honest Englishman who had been put to death for attempting to save the realm from Popery and despotism. Never had they breathed a whisper against arbitrary power till arbitrary power began to menace their own property and dignity. Then, no doubt, forgetting all their old commonplaces about submitting to Nero, they had made haste to save themselves. Grant,— such was the cry of these eager disputants,—grant that, in saving themselves, they saved the constitution. Are we therefore to forget that they had previously endangered it? And are we to reward them by now permitting them to destroy it? Here is a class of men closely connected with the state. A large part of the produce of the soil has been assigned to them for their maintenance. Their chiefs have seats in the legislature, wide domains, stately palaces. By this privileged body the great mass of the population is lectured every week from the chair of authority. To this privileged body has been committed the supreme direction of liberal education. Oxford and Cambridge, Westminster, Winchester, and Eton, are under priestly government. By the priesthood will to a great extent be formed the character of the nobility and gentry of the next generation. Of the higher clergy some have in their gift numerous and valuable benefices; others have the privilege of appointing judges who decide grave questions affecting the liberty, the property, the reputation of Their Majesties' subjects. And is an order thus favoured by the state to give no guarantee to the state? On what principle can it be contended that it is unnecessary to ask from an Archbishop of Canterbury or from a Bishop of Durham that promise of fidelity to the government which all allow that it is necessary to demand from every layman who serves the Crown in the humblest office? Every exciseman, every collector of the customs, who refuses to swear, is to be deprived of his bread. For these humble martyrs of passive obedience and hereditary right nobody has a word to say. Yet an ecclesiastical magnate who refuses to swear is to be suffered to retain emoluments, patronage, power, equal to those of a great minister of state. It is said that it is superfluous to impose the oaths on a clergyman, because he may be punished if he breaks the laws. Why is not the same argument urged in favour of the layman? And why, if the clergyman really means to observe the laws, does he scruple to take the oaths? The law commands him to designate William and Mary as King and Queen, to do this in the most sacred place, to do this in the administration of the most solemn of all the rites of religion. The law commands him to pray that the illustrious pair may be defended by a special providence, that they may be victorious over every enemy, and that their Parliament may by divine guidance be led to take such a course as may promote their safety, honour, and welfare. Can we believe that his conscience will suffer him to do all this, and yet will not suffer him to promise that he will be a faithful subject to them?

To the proposition that the nonjuring clergy should be left to the mercy of the King, the Whigs, with some justice, replied that no scheme could be devised more unjust to His Majesty. The matter, they said, is one of public concern, one in which every Englishman who is unwilling to be the slave of France and of Rome has a deep interest. In such a case it would be unworthy of the Estates of the Realm to shrink from the responsibility of providing for the common safety, to try to obtain for themselves the praise of tenderness and liberality, and to leave to the Sovereign the odious task of proscription. A law requiring all public functionaries, civil, military, ecclesiastical, without distinction of persons, to take the oaths is at least equal. It excludes all suspicion of partiality, of personal malignity, of secret spying and talebearing. But, if an arbitrary discretion is left to the Government, if one nonjuring priest is suffered to keep a lucrative benefice while another is turned with his wife and children into the street, every ejection will be considered as an act of cruelty, and will be imputed as a crime to the sovereign and his ministers.*

---

* As to this controversy, see Burnet, 22. 1689; Commons' Journals of April 11, 7, 8, 9.; Grey's Debates, April 19. and 20. and 22.; Lords' Journals, April 21.

Thus the Parliament had to decide, at the same moment, what quantity of relief should be granted to the consciences of nonconformists and what quantity of pressure should be applied to the consciences of the clergy of the Established Church. The King conceived a hope that it might be in his power to effect a compromise agreeable to all parties. He flattered himself that the Tories might be induced to make some concession to the dissenters, on condition that the Whigs would be lenient to the Jacobites. He determined to try what his personal intervention would effect. It chanced that, a few hours after the Lords had read the Comprehension Bill a second time and the Bill touching the Oaths a first time, he had occasion to go down to Parliament for the purpose of giving his assent to a law. From the throne he addressed both Houses, and expressed an earnest wish that they would consent to modify the existing laws in such a manner that all Protestants might be admitted to public employment.* It was well understood that he was willing, if the legislature would comply with his request, to let clergymen who were already beneficed continue to hold their benefices without swearing allegiance to him. His conduct on this occasion deserves undoubtedly the praise of disinterestedness. It is honourable to him that he attempted to purchase liberty of conscience for his subjects by giving up a safeguard of his own crown. But it must be acknowledged that he showed less wisdom than virtue. The only Englishman in his Privy Council whom he had consulted, if Burnet was correctly informed, was Richard Hampden †; and Richard Hampden, though a highly respectable man, was so far from being able to answer for the Whig party that he could not answer even for his own son John, whose temper, naturally vindictive, had been exasperated into ferocity by the stings of remorse and shame. The King soon found that there was in the hatred of the two great factions an energy which was wanting to their love. The Whigs, though they were almost unanimous in thinking that the sacramental test ought to be abolished, were by no means unanimous in thinking that moment well chosen for the abolition; and even those Whigs who were most desirous to see the nonconformists relieved without delay from civil disabilities were fully determined not to forego the opportunity of humbling and punish-

* Lords' Journals, March 16. 1689.   † Burnet, ii. 7, 8.

ing the class to whose instrumentality chiefly was to be ascribed that tremendous reflux of public feeling which had followed the dissolution of the Oxford Parliament. To put the Janes, the Souths, the Sherlocks into such a situation that they must either starve, or recant, publicly, and with the Gospel at their lips, all the ostentatious professions of many years, was a revenge too delicious to be relinquished. The Tory, on the other hand, sincerely respected and pitied those clergymen who felt scruples about the oaths. But the Test was, in his view, essential to the safety of the established religion, and must not be surrendered for the purpose of saving any man however eminent from any hardship however serious. It would be a sad day doubtless for the Church when the episcopal bench, the chapter houses of cathedrals, the halls of colleges, would miss some men renowned for piety and learning. But it would be a still sadder day for the Church when an Independent should bear the white staff or a Baptist sit on the woolsack. Each party tried to serve those for whom it was interested: but neither party would consent to grant favourable terms to its enemies. The result was that the nonconformists remained excluded from office in the State, and the nonjurors were ejected from office in the Church.

In the House of Commons, no member thought it expedient to propose the repeal of the Test Act. But leave was given to bring in a bill repealing the Corporation Act, which had been passed by the Cavalier Parliament soon after the Restoration, and which contained a clause requiring all municipal magistrates to receive the sacrament according to the forms of the Church of England. When this bill was about to be committed, it was moved by the Tories that the committee should be instructed to make no alteration in the law touching the sacrament. Those Whigs who were zealous for the Comprehension must have been placed by this motion in an embarrassing position. To vote for the instruction would have been inconsistent with their principles. To vote against it would have been to break with Nottingham. A middle course was found. The adjournment of the debate was moved and carried by a hundred and sixteen votes to a hundred and fourteen; and the subject was not revived.* In the House of

---

* Burnet says (ii. 8.) that the proposition to abolish the sacramental test was rejected by a great majority in both Houses. But his memory deceived him; for the only division on the subject in the House of Commons was that men-

Lords a motion was made for the abolition of the sacramental test, but was rejected by a large majority. Many of those who thought the motion right in principle thought it ill timed. A protest was entered; but it was signed only by a few peers of no great authority. It is a remarkable fact that two great chiefs of the Whig party, who were in general very attentive to their parliamentary duty, Devonshire and Shrewsbury, absented themselves on this occasion.*

The debate on the Test in the Upper House was speedily followed by a debate on the last clause of the Comprehension Bill. By that clause it was provided that thirty Bishops and priests should be commissioned to revise the liturgy and canons, and to suggest amendments. On this subject the Whig peers were almost all of one mind. They mustered strong and spoke warmly. Why, they asked, were none but members of the sacerdotal order to be entrusted with this duty? Were the laity no part of the Church of England? When the Commission should have made its report, laymen would have to decide on the recommendations contained in that report. Not a line of the Book of Common Prayer could be altered but by the authority of King, Lords, and Commons. The King was a layman. Five sixths of the Lords were laymen. All the members of the House of Commons were laymen. Was it not absurd to say that laymen were incompetent to examine into a matter which it was acknowledged that laymen must in the last resort determine? And could anything be more opposite to the whole spirit of Protestantism than the notion that a certain preternatural power of judging in spiritual cases was vouchsafed to a particular caste, and to that caste alone; that such men as Selden, as Hale, as Boyle, were less competent to give an opinion on a collect or a creed than the youngest and silliest chaplain who, in a remote manor house, passed his life in drinking ale and playing at shovelboard? What God had instituted no earthly power, lay or clerical, could alter; and of things instituted by human beings a layman was surely as competent as a clergyman to judge. That the Anglican liturgy and canons were of purely human institution the Parliament acknowledged by referring them to a Commission for revision and correction. How could it then be maintained that

tioned in the text. It is remarkable that Gwyn and Rowe, who were tellers for the majority, were two of the strongest Whigs in the House.

* Lords' Journals, March 21. 1689.

in such a Commission the laity, so vast a majority of the population, the laity, whose edification was the main end of all ecclesiastical regulations, and whose innocent tastes ought to be carefully consulted in the framing of the public services of religion, ought not to have a single representative? Precedent was directly opposed to this odious distinction. Repeatedly, since the light of reformation had dawned on England, Commissioners had been empowered by law to revise the canons; and on every one of those occasions some of the Commissioners had been laymen. In the present case the proposed arrangement was peculiarly objectionable. For the object of issuing the commission was the conciliating of dissenters; and it was therefore most desirable that the Commissioners should be men in whose fairness and moderation dissenters could confide. Would thirty such men be easily found in the higher ranks of the clerical profession? The duty of the legislature was to arbitrate between two contending parties, the Nonconformist divines and the Anglican divines, and it would be the grossest injustice to commit to one of those parties the office of umpire.

On these grounds the Whigs proposed an amendment to the effect that laymen should be joined with clergymen in the Commission. The contest was sharp. Burnet, who had just taken his seat among the peers, and who seems to have been bent on winning at almost any price the good will of his brethren, argued with all his constitutional warmth for the clause as it stood. The numbers on the division proved to be exactly equal. The consequence was that, according to the rules of the House, the amendment was lost.*

At length the Comprehension Bill was sent down to the Commons. There it would easily have been carried by two to one, if it had been supported by all the friends of religious liberty. But on this subject the High Churchmen could count on the support of a large body of Low Churchmen. Those members who wished well to Nottingham's plan saw that they were outnumbered, and, despairing of a victory, begun to meditate a retreat. Just at this time a suggestion was thrown out which united all suffrages. The ancient usage was that a Convocation should be summoned together with a Parliament; and it might well be argued that, if ever the advice of a Convocation could be needed, it must be when

* Lords' Journals, April 8. 1689; Burnet ii. 10.

changes in the ritual and discipline of the Church were under consideration. But, in consequence of the irregular manner in which the Estates of the Realm had been brought together during the vacancy of the throne, there was no Convocation. It was proposed that the House should advise the King to take measures for supplying this defect, and that the fate of the Comprehension Bill should not be decided till the clergy had had an opportunity of declaring their opinion through the ancient and legitimate organ.

This proposition was received with general acclamation. The Tories were well pleased to see such honour done to the priesthood. Those Whigs who were against the Comprehension Bill were well pleased to see it laid aside, certainly for a year, probably for ever. Those Whigs who were for the Comprehension Bill were well pleased to escape without a defeat. Some of them indeed were not without hopes that mild and liberal counsels might prevail in the ecclesiastical senate. An address requesting William to summon the Convocation was voted without a division: the concurrence of the Lords was asked: the Lords concurred: the address was carried up to the throne by both Houses: the King promised that he would, at a convenient season, do what his Parliament desired; and Nottingham's bill was not again mentioned.

Many writers, imperfectly acquainted with the history of that age, have inferred from these proceedings that the House of Commons was an assembly of High Churchmen: but nothing is more certain than that two thirds of the members were either Low Churchmen or not Churchmen at all. A very few days before this time an occurrence had taken place unimportant in itself, but highly significant as an indication of the temper of the majority. It had been suggested that the House ought, in conformity with ancient usage, to adjourn over the Easter holidays. The Puritans and Latitudinarians objected: there was a sharp debate: the High Churchmen did not venture to divide; and, to the great scandal of many grave persons, the Speaker took the chair at nine o'clock on Easter Monday; and there was a long and busy sitting.*

* Commons' Journals, March 28, April 1, 1689; Paris Gazette, April 23. Part of the passage in the Paris Gazette is worth quoting. "Il y eut, ce jour là (March 28.), une grande contestation dans la Chambre Basse, sur la proposition qui fut faite de remettre les séances après les fêtes de l'anque observées toujours par l'Eglise Anglicane. Les Protestans conformistes furent de cet avis; et les Presbytériens emportèrent à la pluralité des voix que les séances recommenceroient

This however was by no means the strongest proof which the Commons gave that they were far indeed from feeling extreme reverence or tenderness for the Anglican hierarchy. The bill for settling the oaths had just come down from the Lords framed in a manner favourable to the clergy. All lay functionaries were required to swear fealty to the King and Queen on pain of expulsion from office. But it was provided that every divine who already held a benefice might continue to hold it without swearing, unless the Government should see reason to call on him specially for an assurance of his loyalty. Burnet had, partly, no doubt, from the goodnature and generosity which belonged to his character, and partly from a desire to conciliate his brethren, supported this arrangement in the Upper House with great energy. But in the Lower House the feeling against the Jacobite priests was irresistibly strong. On the very day on which that House voted, without a division, the address requesting the King to summon the Convocation, a clause was proposed and carried which required every person who held any ecclesiastical or academical preferment to take the oaths by the first of August 1689, on pain of suspension. Six months to be reckoned from that day, were allowed to the nonjuror for reconsideration. If, on the first of February 1690, he still continued obstinate, he was to be finally deprived.

The bill, thus amended, was sent back to the Lords. The Lords adhered to their original resolution. Conference after conference was held. Compromise after compromise was suggested. From the imperfect reports which have come down to us it appears that every argument in favour of lenity was forcibly urged by Burnet. But the Commons were firm; time pressed: the unsettled state of the law caused inconvenience in every department of the public service; and the Peers very reluctantly gave way. They at the same time added a clause, empowering the King to bestow pecuniary allowances out of the forfeited benefices on a few nonjuring clergymen. The number of clergymen thus favoured was not to exceed twelve. The allowance was not to exceed one third of the income forfeited. Some zealous Whigs were unwilling to grant even this indulgence; but the Commons

CHAP.
XL.

le Lundy, seconds fois de Pasques." The low Churchmen are frequently designated as Presbyterians by the French and Dutch writers of that age. There were not twenty Presbyterians, properly so called, in the House of Commons. See A Smith and Cutler's plain Dialogue about Whig and Tory, 1690.

were content with the victory which they had won, and justly thought that it would be ungracious to refuse so slight a concession.*

The bill for settling the coronation oath.

These debates were interrupted, during a short time, by the solemnities and festivities of the Coronation. When the day fixed for that great ceremony drew near, the House of Commons resolved itself into a committee for the purpose of settling the form of words in which our Sovereigns were thenceforward to enter into covenant with the nation. All parties were agreed as to the propriety of requiring the King to swear that, in temporal matters, he would govern according to law, and would execute justice in mercy. But about the terms of the oath which related to the spiritual institutions of the realm there was much debate. Should the chief magistrate promise simply to maintain the Protestant religion established by law, or should he promise to maintain that religion as it should be hereafter established by law? The majority preferred the former phrase. The latter phrase was preferred by those Whigs who were for a Comprehension. But it was admitted that the two phrases really meant the same thing, and that the oath, however it might be worded, would bind the Sovereign in his executive capacity only. This was indeed evident from the very nature of the transaction. Any compact may be annulled by the free consent of the party who alone is entitled to claim the performance. It was never doubted by the most rigid casuist that a debtor, who has bound himself under the most awful imprecations to pay a debt, may lawfully withhold payment if the creditor is willing to cancel the obligation. And it is equally clear that no assurance, exacted from a King by the Estates of his kingdom, can bind him to refuse compliance with what may at a future time be the wish of those Estates.

A bill was drawn up in conformity with the resolutions of the Committee, and was rapidly passed through every stage. After the third reading, a foolish man stood up to propose a rider, declaring that the oath was not meant to restrain the Sovereign from consenting to any change in the ceremonial of the Church, provided always that episcopacy and a written form of prayer were retained. The gross absurdity of this motion was exposed by several eminent members. Such a clause, they justly remarked, would bind the King under pre-

* Accounts of what passed at the Conferences will be found in the Journals of the Houses, and deserve to be read.

tence of setting him free. The coronation oath, they said, was never intended to trammel him in his legislative capacity. Leave that oath as it is now drawn, and no prince can misunderstand it. No prince can seriously imagine that the two Houses mean to exact from him a promise that he will put a Veto on laws which they may hereafter think necessary to the wellbeing of the country. Or if any prince should so strangely misapprehend the nature of the contract between him and his subjects, any divine, any lawyer, to whose advice he may have recourse, will set his mind at ease. But if this rider should pass, it will be impossible to deny that the coronation oath is meant to prevent the King from giving his assent to bills which may be presented to him by the Lords and Commons; and the most serious inconveniences may follow. These arguments were felt to be unanswerable, and the proviso was rejected without a division.*

Every person who has read these debates must be fully convinced that the statesmen who framed the coronation oath did not mean to bind the King in his legislative capacity.† Unhappily, more than a hundred years later, a scruple, which those statesmen thought too absurd to be seriously entertained by any human being, found its way into a mind, honest, indeed, and religious, but narrow and obstinate by nature, and at once debilitated and excited by disease. Seldom, indeed, have the ambition and perfidy of tyrants produced evils greater than those which were brought on our country by that fatal conscientiousness. A conjuncture singularly auspicious, a conjuncture at which wisdom and justice might perhaps have reconciled races and sects long hostile, and might have made the British Islands one truly United Kingdom, was suffered to pass away. The opportunity, once lost, returned no more.

* Journals, March 28. 1689; Grey's Debates.
† I will quote some expressions which have been preserved in the concise reports of these debates. These expressions are quite decisive as to the sense in which the oath was understood by the legislators who framed it. Musgrave said, "There is no occasion for this proviso. It cannot be imagined that any bill from hence will ever destroy the legislative power." Finch said, "The words, 'established by law,' hinder not the King from passing any bill for the relief of Dissenters. The proviso makes the scruple, and gives the occasion for it." Sawyer said, "This is the first proviso of this nature that ever was in any bill. It seems to strike at the legislative power." Sir Robert Cotton said, "Though the proviso looks well and healing, yet it seems to imply a defect. Not able to alter laws as occasion required! This, instead of one scruple, raises more, as if you were so bound up to the ecclesiastical government that you cannot make any new laws without such a proviso." Sir Thomas Lee said, "It will, I fear, creep in that other laws cannot be made without such a proviso: therefore I would lay it aside."

CHAP. XI.

The coronation.

Two generations of public men have since laboured with imperfect success to repair the error which was then committed; nor is it improbable that some of the penalties of that error may continue to afflict a remote posterity.

The bill by which the oath was settled passed the Upper House without amendment. All the preparations were complete; and, on the eleventh of April, the coronation took place. In some things it differed from ordinary coronations. The representatives of the people attended the ceremony in a body, and were sumptuously feasted in the Exchequer Chamber. Mary, being not merely Queen Consort, but also Queen Regnant, was inaugurated in all things like a King, was girt with the sword, lifted up into the throne, and presented with the Bible, the spurs, and the orb. Of the temporal grandees of the realm, and of their wives and daughters, the muster was great and splendid. None could be surprised that the Whig aristocracy should swell the triumph of Whig principles. But the Jacobites saw, with concern, that many Lords who had voted for a Regency bore a conspicuous part in the ceremonial. The King's crown was carried by Grafton, the Queen's by Somerset. The pointed sword, emblematical of temporal justice, was borne by Pembroke. Ormond was Lord High Constable for the day, and rode up the hall on the right hand of the hereditary champion, who thrice flung down his glove on the pavement, and thrice defied to mortal combat the false traitor who should gainsay the title of William and Mary. Among the noble damsels who supported the gorgeous train of the Queen was her beautiful and gentle cousin, the Lady Henrietta Hyde, whose father, Rochester, had to the last contended against the resolution which declared the throne vacant.* The show of Bishops, indeed, was scanty. The Primate did not make his appearance, and his place was supplied by Compton. On one side of Compton, the paten was carried by Lloyd, Bishop of Saint Asaph, eminent among the seven confessors of the preceding year. On the other side, Sprat, Bishop of Rochester, lately a member of the High Commission, had charge of the chalice. Burnet, the junior prelate, preached with all his wonted ability, and more than his wonted taste and judgment. His grave and

* Lady Henrietta, whom her uncle Clarendon calls "pretty little Lady Henrietta," and "the best child in the world" (Diary, Jan. 168¾), was soon after married to the Earl of Dalkeith, eldest son of the unfortunate Duke of Monmouth.

eloquent discourse was polluted neither by flattery nor by
malignity. He is said to have been greatly applauded; and
it may well be believed that the animated peroration in which
he implored heaven to bless the royal pair with long life and
mutual love, with obedient subjects, wise counsellors, and
faithful allies, with gallant fleets and armies, with victory,
with peace, and finally with crowns more glorious and more
durable than those which then glittered on the altar of the
Abbey, drew forth the loudest hums of the Commons.*

On the whole, the ceremony went off well, and produced
something like a revival, faint, indeed, and transient, of the
enthusiasm of the preceding December. The day was, in
London, and in many other places, a day of general rejoicing.
The churches were filled in the morning: the afternoon was
spent in sport and carousing; and at night bonfires were
kindled, rockets discharged, and windows lighted up. The
Jacobites however contrived to discover or to invent abundant
matter for scurrility and sarcasm. They complained bitterly
that the way from the hall to the western door of the Abbey
had been lined by Dutch soldiers. Was it seemly that an
English king should enter into the most solemn of engagements with the English nation behind a triple hedge of
foreign swords and bayonets? Little affrays, such as, at
every great pageant, almost inevitably take place between
those who are eager to see the show and those whose business
it is to keep the communications clear, were exaggerated
with all the artifices of rhetoric. One of the alien mercenaries had backed his horse against an honest citizen who
pressed forward to catch a glimpse of the royal canopy.
Another had rudely pushed back a woman with the butt end
of his musket. On such grounds as these the strangers were
compared to those Lord Danes whose insolence, in the old
time, had provoked the Anglosaxon population to insurrection and massacre. But there was no more fertile theme for
censure than the coronation medal, which really was absurd
in design and mean in execution. A chariot appeared conspicuous on the reverse; and plain people were at a loss to
understand what this emblem had to do with William and
Mary. The disaffected wits solved the difficulty by suggest-
ing that the artist meant to allude to that chariot which a

* The sermon deserves to be read. and the Despatch of the Dutch Ambassa-
See the London Gazette of April 14. dors to the States General.
1689; Evelyn's Diary; Luttrell's Diary;

CHAP.
XL

Promotions

Roman princess, lost to all filial affection, and blindly devoted to the interests of an ambitious husband, drove over the still warm remains of her father.*

Honours were, as usual, liberally bestowed at this festive season. Three garters which happened to be at the disposal of the Crown were given to Devonshire, Ormond, and Schomberg. Prince George was created Duke of Cumberland. Several eminent men took new appellations by which they must henceforth be designated. Danby became Marquess of Caermarthen, Churchill Earl of Marlborough, and Bentinck Earl of Portland. Mordaunt was made Earl of Monmouth, not without some murmuring on the part of old Exclusionists, who still remembered with fondness their Protestant Duke, and who had hoped that his attainder would be reversed, and that his title would be borne by his descendants. It was remarked that the name of Halifax did not appear in the list of promotions. None could doubt that he might easily have obtained either a blue riband or a ducal coronet; and, though he was honourably distinguished from most of his contemporaries by his scorn of illicit gain, it was well known that he desired honorary distinctions with a greediness of which he was himself ashamed, and which was unworthy of his fine understanding. The truth is that his ambition was at this time chilled by his fears. To those whom he trusted he hinted his apprehensions that evil times were at hand. The King's life was not worth a year's purchase; the government was disjointed, the clergy and the army disaffected, the par-

* A specimen of the prose which the Jacobites wrote on this subject will be found among the Somers Tracts. The Jacobite verses were generally too loathsome to be quoted. I select some of the most decent lines from a very rare lampoon:

"The eleventh of April has come about,
To Westminster went the rabble rout,
In order to crown a bundle of clouts,
A dainty fine King indeed.

"Descended he is from the Orange tree;
But, if I can read his destiny,
He'll once more descend from another tree,
A dainty fine King is he.

"He has gotten part of the shape of a man,
But more of a monkey, deny it who can;
He has the head of a groom, but the legs of a crane,
A dainty fine King indeed."

A Frenchman named Le Noble, who had been banished from his own country for his crimes, but by the connivance of the police, lurked in Paris, and earned a precarious livelihood as a bookseller's hack, published on this occasion two pasquinades, now extremely scarce, "Le Couronnement de Guillemot et de Guillemette, avec le Sermon du grand Docteur Barnet," and "Le Festin de Guillemot." In wit, taste, and good sense, Le Noble's writings are not inferior to the English poem which I have quoted. He tells us that the Archbishop of York and the Bishop of London had a boxing match in the Abbey; that the champion rode up the Hall on an ass, which turned restive and kicked over the royal table with all the plate; and that the banquet ended in a fight between the peers armed with stools and benches, and the cooks armed with spits. This sort of pleasantry, strange to say, found readers; and the writer's portrait was pompously engraved with the motto "Laissantes rire: te tua fama manet."

liament torn by factions; civil war was already raging in one part of the empire; foreign war was impending. At such a moment a minister, whether Whig or Tory, might well be uneasy: but neither Whig nor Tory had so much to fear as the Trimmer, who might not improbably find himself the common mark at which both parties would take aim. For these reasons Halifax determined to avoid all ostentation of power and influence, to disarm envy by a studied show of moderation, and to attach to himself by civilities and benefits persons whose gratitude might be useful in the event of a counterrevolution. The next three months, he said, would be the time of trial. If the government got safe through the summer it would probably stand.*

Meanwhile questions of external policy were every day becoming more and more important. The work at which William had toiled indefatigably during many gloomy and anxious years was at length accomplished. The great coalition was formed. It was plain that a desperate conflict was at hand. The oppressor of Europe would have to defend himself against England allied with Charles the Second King of Spain, with the Emperor Leopold, and with the Germanic and Batavian federations, and was likely to have no ally except the Sultan, who was waging war against the House of Austria on the Danube.

Lewis had, towards the close of the preceding year, taken his enemies at a disadvantage, and had struck the first blow before they were prepared to parry it. But that blow, though heavy, was not aimed at the part where it might have been mortal. Had hostilities been commenced on the Batavian frontier, William and his army would probably have been detained on the Continent, and James might have continued to govern England. Happily, Lewis, under an infatuation which many pious Protestants confidently ascribed to the righteous judgment of God, had neglected the point on which the fate of the whole civilised world depended, and had made a great display of power, promptitude, and energy, in a quarter where the most splendid achievements could produce nothing more than an illumination and a Te Deum. A French army under the command of Marshal Duras had invaded the Palatinate and some of the neighbouring principalities. But this expedition, though it had been completely

* Reresby's Memoirs.

successful, and though the skill and vigour with which it had been conducted had excited general admiration, could not perceptibly affect the event of the tremendous struggle which was approaching. France would soon be attacked on every side. It would be impossible for Duras long to retain possession of the provinces which he had surprised and overrun. An atrocious thought rose in the mind of Louvois, who, in military affairs, had the chief sway at Versailles. He was a man distinguished by zeal for what he thought the public interests, by capacity, and by knowledge of all that related to the administration of war, but of a savage and obdurate nature. If the cities of the Palatinate could not be retained, they might be destroyed. If the soil of the Palatinate was not to furnish supplies to the French, it might be so wasted that it would at least furnish no supplies to the Germans. The ironhearted statesman submitted his plan, probably with much management and with some disguise, to Lewis; and Lewis, in an evil hour for his fame, assented. Duras received orders to turn one of the fairest regions of Europe into a wilderness. Fifteen years had elapsed since Turenne had ravaged part of that fine country. But the ravages committed by Turenne, though they have left a deep stain on his glory, were mere sport in comparison with the horrors of this second devastation. The French commander announced to near half a million of human beings that he granted them three days of grace, and that, within that time, they must shift for themselves. Soon the roads and fields, which then lay deep in snow, were blackened by innumerable multitudes of men, women, and children flying from their homes. Many died of cold and hunger: but enough survived to fill the streets of all the cities of Europe with lean and squalid beggars, who had once been thriving farmers and shopkeepers. Meanwhile the work of destruction began. The flames went up from every marketplace, every hamlet, every parish church, every country seat, within the devoted provinces. The fields where the corn had been sown were ploughed up. The orchards were hewn down. No promise of a harvest was left on the fertile plains near what had once been Frankenthal. Not a vine, not an almond tree, was to be seen on the slopes of the sunny hills round what had once been Heidelberg. No respect was shown to palaces, to temples, to monasteries, to infirmaries, to beautiful works of art, to monuments of the illustrious dead. The farfamed castle of the Elector Palatine was turned into a heap of ruins. The adjoining hospital was sacked. The provisions, the medicines, the pallets on which the sick lay were destroyed. The very stones of which Manheim had been built were flung into the Rhine. The magnificent Cathedral of Spires perished, and with it the marble sepulchres of eight Cæsars. The coffins were broken open. The ashes were scattered to the winds.* Treves, with its fair bridge, its Roman baths and amphitheatre, its venerable churches, convents, and colleges, was doomed to the same fate. But, before this last crime had been perpetrated, Lewis was recalled to a better mind by the execrations of all the neighbouring nations, by the silence and confusion of his flatterers, and by the expostulations of his wife. He had been more than two years secretly married to Frances de Maintenon, the governess of his natural children. It would be hard to name any woman who, with so little romance in her temper, has had so much in her life. Her early years had been passed in poverty and obscurity. Her first husband had supported himself by writing burlesque farces and poems. When she attracted the notice of her sovereign, she could no longer boast of youth or beauty: but she possessed in an extraordinary degree those more lasting charms, which men of sense, whose passions age has tamed, and whose life is a life of business and care, prize most highly in a female companion. Her character was such as has been well compared to that soft green on which the eye, wearied by warm tints and glaring lights, reposes with pleasure. A just understanding; an inexhaustible yet never redundant flow of rational, gentle, and sprightly conversation; a temper of which the serenity was never for a moment ruffled; a tact which surpassed the tact of her sex as much as the tact of her sex surpasses the tact of ours; such were the qualities which made the widow of a buffoon first the confidential friend, and then the spouse, of the proudest and most powerful of European kings. It was said that Lewis had been with difficulty prevented by the arguments and vehement entreaties of Louvois from declaring her Queen of France. It is certain that she regarded Louvois as her

CHAP. XI.

* For the history of the devastation of the Palatinate, see the Memoirs of La Fare, Dangeau, Madame de la Fayette, Villars, and Saint Simon, and the Monthly Mercuries for March and April 1689. The pamphlets and broadsides are too numerous to quote. One broadside, entitled "A true Account of the barbarous Cruelties committed by the French in the Palatinate in January and February last," is perhaps the most remarkable.

enemy. Her hatred of him, cooperating perhaps with better feelings, induced her to plead the cause of the unhappy people of the Rhine. She appealed to those sentiments of compassion which, though weakened by many corrupting influences, were not altogether extinct in her husband's mind, and to those sentiments of religion which had too often impelled him to cruelty, but which, on the present occasion, were on the side of humanity. He relented; and Treves was spared.* In truth he could hardly fail to perceive that he had committed a great error. The devastation of the Palatinate, while it had not in any sensible degree lessened the power of his enemies, had inflamed their animosity, and had furnished them with inexhaustible matter for invective. The cry of vengeance rose on every side. Whatever scruple either branch of the House of Austria might have felt about coalescing with Protestants was completely removed. It was in vain that Lewis accused the Emperor and the Catholic King of having betrayed the cause of the Church; of having allied themselves with an usurper who was the avowed champion of the great schism; of having been accessary to the foul wrong done to a lawful sovereign who was guilty of no crime but zeal for the true religion. It was in vain that James sent to Vienna and Madrid piteous letters, in which he recounted his misfortunes, and implored the assistance of his brother kings, his brethren also in the faith, against the unnatural children and the rebellious subjects who had driven him into exile. There was little difficulty in framing a plausible answer both to the reproaches of Lewis and to the supplications of James. Leopold and Charles declared that they had not, even for purposes of just selfdefence, leagued themselves with heretics, till their enemy had, for purposes of unjust aggression, leagued himself with Mahometans. Nor was this the worst. The French King, not content with assisting the Moslem against the Christians, was himself treating Christians with a barbarity which would have shocked the very Moslem. His infidel allies, to do them justice, had not perpetrated on the Danube such outrages against the edifices and the members of the Holy Catholic Church as he who called himself the eldest son of that Church was perpetrating on the Rhine. On these grounds, the princes to whom James had appealed replied by appealing, with many professions of good will and compassion, to him-

* Memoirs of Saint Simon.

self. He was surely too just to blame them for thinking that it was their first duty to defend their own people against such outrages as had turned the Palatinate into a desert, or for calling in the aid of Protestants against an enemy who had not scrupled to call in the aid of Turks.*

During the winter and the earlier part of the spring, the powers hostile to France were gathering their strength for a great effort, and were in constant communication with one another. As the season for military operations approached, the solemn appeals of injured nations to the God of battles came forth in rapid succession. The manifesto of the Germanic body appeared in February; that of the States General in March; that of the House of Brandenburg in April; and that of Spain in May.†

Here, as soon as the ceremony of the coronation was over, the House of Commons determined to take into consideration the late proceedings of the French King.‡ In the debate, that hatred of the powerful, unscrupulous, and imperious Lewis, which had, during twenty years of vassalage, been festering in the hearts of Englishmen, broke violently forth. He was called the most Christian Turk, the most Christian ravager of Christendom, the most Christian barbarian who had perpetrated on Christians outrages of which his infidel allies would have been ashamed.§ A committee, consisting chiefly of ardent Whigs, was appointed to prepare an address. John Hampden, the most ardent Whig among them, was put into the chair; and he produced a composition too long, too rhetorical, and too vituperative, to suit the lips of the Speaker or the ears of the King. Invectives against Lewis might perhaps, in the temper in which the

---

* I will quote a few lines from Leopold's letter to James: "Nunc autem quo loco res nostræ sint, ut Serenitati vestræ auxilium præstari possit a nobis, qui non Turcico tantum bello implicati, sed insuper etiam crudelissimo et iniquissimo a Gallis securis, contra datam fidem impetiti sumus, ipsimet Servaitati vestræ judicandum relinquimus. . . . Galli non tantum in nostram et totius Christianæ orbis perniciem fœdifraga arma cum juratis Sanctæ Crucis hostibus sociare fas sibi durant; sed etiam in imperio, perfidiam perfidis cumulando, urbes deditione occupatas contra datam fidem immensis tributis exhaurire, exhaustas, diripere, direptas funditus excindere ant flammis delere, palatia principum ab omni antiquitate inter sæviasima bellorum incendia intacta servata exurere, templa spoliare, dedititios in servitutem more apud barbaros usitato abducere, denique passim, imprimis vero etiam in Catholicorum ditionibus, alia horrenda, et ipsam Turcorum tyrannidem repræsentia immanitatis et sevitiæ exempla edere pro lubo habent."

† See the London Gazettes of Feb. 25., March 11., April 22., May 2., and the Monthly Mercuries. Some of the Declarations will be found in Dumont's Corps Universel Diplomatique.

‡ Commons' Journals, April 15. 16. 1689.

§ Oldmixon.

House then was, have passed without censure, if they had not been accompanied by severe reflections on the character and administration of Charles the Second, whose memory, in spite of all his faults, was affectionately cherished by the Tories. There were some very intelligible allusions to Charles's dealings with the Court at Versailles, and to the foreign woman whom that Court had sent to lie like a snake in his bosom. The House was with good reason dissatisfied. The address was recommitted, and, having been made more concise, and less declamatory and acrimonious, was approved and presented.* William's attention was called to the wrongs which France had done to him and to his kingdom; and he was assured that, whenever he should resort to arms for the redress of those wrongs, he should be heartily supported by his people. He thanked the Commons warmly. Ambition, he said, should never induce him to draw the sword: but he had no choice: France had already attacked England; and it was necessary to exercise the right of self-defence. A few days later war was proclaimed.†

Of the grounds of quarrel alleged by the Commons in their address, and by the King in his manifesto, the most serious was the interference of Lewis in the affairs of Ireland. In that country great events had, during several months, followed one another in rapid succession. Of those events it is now time to relate the history, a history dark with crime and sorrow, yet full of interest and instruction.

* Commons' Journals, April 19, 24, 26, 1689.
† The declaration is dated on the 7th of May, but was not published in the London Gazette till the 13th.

CHAPTER XII.

WILLIAM had assumed, together with the title of King of England, the title of King of Ireland. For all our jurists then regarded Ireland as a mere colony, more important indeed than Massachusetts, Virginia, or Jamaica, but, like Massachusetts, Virginia, and Jamaica, dependent on the mother country, and bound to pay allegiance to the Sovereign whom the mother country had called to the throne.*

In fact, however, the Revolution found Ireland emancipated from the dominion of the English colony. As early as the year 1686, James had determined to make that island a place of arms which might overawe Great Britain, and a place of refuge where, if any disaster happened in Great Britain, the members of his Church might find refuge. With this view he had exerted all his power for the purpose of inverting the relation between the conquerors and the aboriginal population. The execution of his design he had entrusted, in spite of the remonstrances of his English counsellors, to the Lord Deputy Tyrconnel. In the autumn of 1688, the process was complete. The highest offices in the state, in the army, and in the Courts of Justice, were, with scarcely an exception, filled by Papists. A pettifogger named Alexander Fitton, who had been detected in forgery, who had been fined for misconduct by the House of Lords at Westminster, who had been many years in prison, and who was equally deficient in legal knowledge and in the natural good sense and acuteness by which the want of legal knowledge has sometimes been supplied, was Lord Chancellor. His single merit was that he had apostatised from the Protestant religion; and this merit was thought sufficient to wash out even the stain of his Saxon extraction. He soon proved himself worthy of the confidence of his patrons. On the bench of justice he declared that

---

* The general opinion of the English on this subject is clearly expressed in a little tract entitled "Aphorisms relating to the Kingdom of Ireland," which appeared during the vacancy of the throne.

there was not one heretic in forty thousand who was not a villain. He often, after hearing a cause in which the interests of his Church were concerned, postponed his decision, for the purpose, as he avowed, of consulting his spiritual director, a Spanish priest, well read doubtless in Escobar.* Thomas Nugent, a Roman Catholic who had never distinguished himself at the bar except by his brogue and his blunders, was Chief Justice of the King's Bench.† Stephen Rice, a Roman Catholic, whose abilities and learning were not disputed even by the enemies of his nation and religion, but whose known hostility to the Act of Settlement excited the most painful apprehensions in the minds of all who held property under that Act, was Chief Baron of the Exchequer.‡ Richard Nagle, an acute and well read lawyer, who had been educated in a Jesuit college, and whose prejudices were such as might have been expected from his education, was Attorney General.§

Keating, a highly respectable Protestant, was still Chief Justice of the Common Pleas: but two Roman Catholic Judges sate with him. It ought to be added that one of those judges, Daly, was a man of sense, moderation, and integrity. The matters however which came before the Court of Common Pleas were not of great moment. Even the King's Bench was at this time almost deserted. The Court of Exchequer overflowed with business; for it was the only court at Dublin from which no writ of error lay to England, and consequently the only court in which the English could be oppressed and pillaged without hope of redress. Rice, it was said, had declared that they should have from him exactly what the law, construed with the utmost strictness, gave them, and nothing more. What, in his opinion, the law, strictly construed, gave them, they could easily infer from a saying which, before he became a Judge, was often in his mouth. "I will drive," he used to say, "a coach and six through the Act of Settlement." He now carried his threat daily into execution. The cry of all Protestants was that it mattered not what evidence they produced before him ; that, when their titles were to be set aside, the rankest forgeries, the most in-

---

* King's State of the Protestants of Ireland, II. 6. and lii. 3.

† King, lii. 3. Clarendon in a letter to Rochester (June 1. 1686), calls Nagent "a very troublesome, impertinent creature."

‡ King, III. 3.

§ King, ii. 6., iii. 3. Clarendon, in a letter to Ormond (Sept. 28. 1686), speaks highly of Nagle's knowledge and ability, but in the Diary (Jan. 31. 168?) calls him "a covetous, ambitious man."

famous witnesses, were sure to have his countenance. To his court his countrymen came in multitudes with writs of ejectment and writs of trespass. In his court the government attacked at once the charters of all the cities and boroughs in Ireland; and he easily found pretexts for pronouncing all those charters forfeited. The municipal corporations, about a hundred in number, had been instituted to be the strongholds of the reformed religion and of the English interest, and had consequently been regarded by the Irish Roman Catholics with an aversion which cannot be thought unnatural or unreasonable. Had those bodies been remodelled in a judicious and impartial manner, the irregularity of the proceedings by which so desirable a result had been attained might have been pardoned. But it soon appeared that one exclusive system had been swept away only to make room for another. The boroughs were subjected to the absolute authority of the Crown. Towns in which almost every householder was an English Protestant were placed under the government of Irish Roman Catholics. Many of the new Aldermen had never even seen the places over which they were appointed to bear rule. At the same time the Sheriffs, to whom belonged the execution of writs and the nomination of juries, were selected in almost every instance from the caste which had till very recently been excluded from all public trust. It was affirmed that some of these important functionaries had been burned in the hand for theft. Others had been servants to Protestants; and the Protestants added, with bitter scorn, that it was fortunate for the country when this was the case; for that a menial who had cleaned the plate and rubbed down the horse of an English gentleman might pass for a civilised being, when compared with many of the native aristocracy whose lives had been spent in coshering or marauding. To such Sheriffs no colonist, even if he had been so strangely fortunate as to obtain a judgment, dared to entrust an execution.*

CHAP.
XII.

Thus the civil power had, in the space of a few months, been transferred from the Saxon to the Celtic population. The transfer of the military power had been not less complete. The army, which, under the command of Ormond, had been the chief safeguard of the English ascendency, had ceased to exist. Whole regiments had been dissolved and

The military power in the hands of the Roman Catholics.

* King, II. 6. 1., III. 3. 5.; A Short View of the Methods made use of in Ireland for the Subversion and Destruction of the Protestant Religion and Interests, by a Clergyman lately escaped from thence, licensed October 17, 1689.

reconstructed. Six thousand Protestant veterans, deprived of their bread, were brooding in retirement over their wrongs, or had crossed the sea and joined the standard of William. Their place was supplied by men who had long suffered oppression, and who, finding themselves suddenly transformed from slaves into masters, were impatient to pay back, with accumulated usury, the heavy debt of injuries and insults. The new soldiers, it was said, never passed an Englishman without cursing him and calling him by some foul name. They were the terror of every Protestant innkeeper; for, from the moment when they came under his roof, they ate and drank everything: they paid for nothing; and by their rude swaggering they scared more respectable guests from his door.*

Mutual enmity between the English and Irish.

Such was the state of Ireland when the Prince of Orange landed at Torbay. From that time every packet which arrived at Dublin brought tidings, such as could not but increase the mutual fear and loathing of the hostile races. The colonist, who, after long enjoying and abusing power, had now tasted for a moment the bitterness of servitude, the native, who, having drunk to the dregs all the bitterness of servitude, had at length for a moment enjoyed and abused power, were alike sensible that a great crisis, a crisis like that of 1641, was at hand. The majority impatiently expected Phelim O'Neil to revive in Tyrconnel. The minority saw in William a second Oliver.

On which side the first blow was struck was a question which Williamites and Jacobites afterwards debated with much asperity. But no question could be more idle. History must do to both parties the justice which neither has ever done to the other, and must admit that both had fair pleas and cruel provocations. Both had been placed, by a fate for which neither was answerable, in such a situation that, human nature being what it is, they could not but regard each other with enmity. A king, who perhaps might

* King. lii. 2. I cannot find that Charles Leslie, who was zealous on the other side, has, in his answer to King, contradicted any of these facts. Indeed Leslie gives up Tyrconnel's administration. "I desire to obviate one objection which I know will be made, as if I were about wholly to vindicate all that the Lord Tyrconnel and other of King James's ministers have done in Ireland, especially before this revolution began, and which most of anything brought it on. No; I am far from it. I am sensible that their carriage in many particulars gave greater occasion to King James's enemies than all the other maladministrations which were charged upon his government."—Leslie's Answer to King, 1692.

have reconciled them, had, year after year, systematically employed his whole power for the purpose of inflaming their enmity to madness. It was now impossible to establish in Ireland a just and beneficent government, a government which should know no distinction of race or of sect, a government which, while strictly respecting the rights guaranteed by law to the new landowners, should alleviate by a judicious liberality, the misfortunes of the ancient gentry. The opportunity had passed away: compromise had become impossible: the two infuriated castes were alike convinced that it was necessary to oppress or to be oppressed, and that there could be no safety but in victory, vengeance, and dominion. They agreed only in spurning out of the way every mediator who sought to reconcile them.

During some weeks there were outrages, insults, evil reports, violent panics, the natural preludes of the terrible conflict which was at hand. A rumour spread over the whole island that, on the ninth of December, there would be a general massacre of the Englishry. Tyrconnel sent for the chief Protestants of Dublin to the Castle, and, with his usual energy of diction, invoked on himself all the vengeance of heaven, if the report was not a cursed, a blasted, a confounded lie. It was said that, in his rage at finding his oaths ineffectual, he pulled off his hat and wig, and flung them into the fire.* But lying Dick Talbot was so well known that his imprecations and gesticulations only strengthened the apprehension which they were meant to allay. Ever since the recall of Clarendon there had been a large emigration of timid and quiet people from the Irish ports to England. That emigration now went on faster than ever. It was not easy to obtain a passage on board of a well built or commodious vessel. But many persons, made bold by the excess of fear, and choosing rather to trust the winds and waves than the exasperated Irishry, ventured to encounter all the dangers of St. George's Channel and of the Welsh coast in open boats and in the depth of winter. The English who remained began, in almost every county, to draw close together. Every large country house became a fortress. Every visitor who arrived after nightfall was challenged from a loophole or from a barricaded window; and if he attempted

CHAP. XII.

Panic among the Englishry.

* A True and Impartial Account of who was an Eye-witness; licensed July the most material Passages in Ireland 22. 1689. since December 1688, by a Gentleman

CHAP. XII.

to enter without passwords and explanations, a blunderbuss was presented to him. On the dreaded night of the ninth of December, there was scarcely one Protestant mansion from the Giant's Causeway to Bantry Bay in which armed men were not watching and lights burning from the early sunset to the late sunrise.*

History of the town of Kenmare.

A minute account of what passed in one district at this time has come down to us, and well illustrates the general state of the kingdom. The south-western part of Kerry is now well known as the most beautiful tract in the British isles. The mountains, the glens, the capes stretching far into the Atlantic, the crags on which the eagles build, the rivulets brawling down rocky passes, the lakes overhung by groves in which the wild deer find covert, attract every summer crowds of wanderers sated with the business and the pleasures of great cities. The beauties of that country are indeed too often hidden in the mist and rain which the west wind brings up from a boundless ocean. But, on the rare days when the sun shines out in all his glory, the landscape has a freshness and a warmth of colouring seldom found in our latitude. The myrtle loves the soil. The arbutus thrives better than even on the sunny shore of Calabria.† The turf is of livelier hue than elsewhere: the hills glow with a richer purple: the varnish of the holly and ivy is more glossy; and berries of a brighter red peep through foliage of a brighter green. But during the greater part of the seventeenth century this paradise was as little known to the civilised world as Spitzbergen or Greenland. If ever it was mentioned, it was mentioned as a horrible desert, a chaos of bogs, thickets, and precipices, where the she wolf still littered, and where some half naked savages, who could not speak a word of English, made themselves burrows in the mud, and lived on roots and sour milk.‡

---

* A True and Impartial Account, 1689; Leslie's Answer to King, 1692.

† There have been in the neighbourhood of Killarney specimens of the arbutus thirty feet high and four feet and a half round. See the Philosophical Transactions, 727.

‡ In a very full account of the British lakes published at Nuremberg in 1690, Kerry is described as "an vielen Orten unwegsam und voller Wälder und Gebürge." Wölfe sind Infested Ireland. "Kein schädlich Thier ist da, ausser halb Wölff und Füchse." So late as the year 1710 money was levied on presentments of the Grand Jury of Kerry for the destruction of wolves in that county. See Smith's Ancient and Modern State of the County of Kerry, 1756. I do not know that I have ever met with a better book of the kind and of the size. In a poem published as late as 1719, and entitled Maccleremot, or the Irish Fortune Hunter, in six cantos, wolf-hunting and wolfspearing are represented as common sports in Munster. In Wil-

At length, in the year 1670, the benevolent and enlightened Sir William Petty determined to form an English settlement in this wild district. He possessed a large domain there, which has descended to a posterity worthy of such an ancestor. On the improvement of that domain, he expended, it was said, not less than ten thousand pounds. The little town which he founded, named from the bay of Kenmare, stood at the head of that bay, under a mountain ridge, on the summit of which travellers now stop to gaze upon the loveliest of the three lakes of Killarney. Scarcely any village, built by an enterprising band of New Englanders, far from the dwellings of their countrymen, in the midst of the hunting grounds of the Red Indians, was more completely out of the pale of civilisation than Kenmare. Between Petty's settlement and the nearest English habitation the journey by land was of two days through a wild and dangerous country. Yet the place prospered. Forty-two houses were erected. The population amounted to a hundred and eighty. The land round the town was well cultivated. The cattle were numerous. Two small barks were employed in fishing and trading along the coast. The supply of herrings, pilchards, mackerel, and salmon was plentiful, and would have been still more plentiful, had not the beach been, in the finest part of the year, covered by multitudes of seals, which preyed on the fish of the bay. Yet the seal was not an unwelcome visitor; his fur was valuable, and his oil supplied light through the long nights of winter. An attempt was made with great success to set up iron works. It was not yet the practice to employ coal for the purpose of smelting; and the manufacturers of Kent and Sussex had much difficulty in procuring timber at a reasonable price. The neighbourhood of Kenmare was then richly wooded; and Petty found it a gainful speculation to send ore thither. The lovers of the picturesque still regret the woods of oak and arbutus which were cut down to feed his furnaces. Another scheme had occurred to his active and intelligent mind. Some of the neighbouring islands abounded with variegated marble, red and white, purple and green. Petty well knew at what cost the ancient Romans had decorated their baths and temples with many coloured columns hewn from Laconian and

---

liam's reign Ireland was sometimes called by the nickname of Welfland. Thus in a poem on the battle of La Hogue, called Advice to a Painter, the terror of the Irish army is thus described:

"A chilling damp
And Welfland howl runs thro' the rising camp."

African quarries; and he seems to have indulged the hope that the rocks of his wild domain in Kerry might furnish embellishments to the mansions of Saint James's Square, and to the choir of Saint Paul's Cathedral.*

From the first, the settlers had found that they must be prepared to exercise the right of selfdefence to an extent which would have been unnecessary and unjustifiable in a well governed country. The law was altogether without force in the highlands which lie on the south of the vale of Tralee. No officer of justice willingly ventured into those parts. One pursuivant who in 1680 attempted to execute a warrant there was murdered. The people of Kenmare seem however to have been sufficiently secured by their union, their intelligence, and their spirit, till the close of the year 1688. Then at length the effects of the policy of Tyrconnel began to be felt even in that remote corner of Ireland. In the eyes of the peasantry of Munster the colonists were aliens and heretics. The buildings, the boats, the machines, the granaries, the dairies, the furnaces, were doubtless contemplated by the native race with that mingled envy and contempt with which the ignorant naturally regard the triumphs of knowledge. Nor is it at all improbable that the emigrants had been guilty of those faults from which civilised men who settle among an uncivilised people are rarely free. The power derived from superior intelligence had, we may easily believe, been sometimes displayed with insolence, and sometimes exerted with injustice. Now therefore, when the news spread from altar to altar, and from cabin to cabin, that the strangers were to be driven out, and that their houses and lands were to be given as a booty to the children of the soil, a predatory war commenced. Plunderers, thirty, forty, seventy in a troop, prowled round the town, some with firearms, some with pikes. The barns were robbed. The horses were stolen. In one forny a hundred and forty cattle were swept away and driven off through the ravines of Glenguriff. In one night six dwellings were broke open and pillaged. At last the colonists, driven to extremity, resolved to die like men rather than be murdered in their beds. The house built by Petty for his agent was the largest in the place. It stood on a rocky peninsula round which the waves of the bay broke. Here the whole population assembled, seventy-five fighting men, with about a hundred women and children.

* Smith's Ancient and Modern State of Kerry.

They had among them sixty firelocks, and as many pikes and swords. Round the agent's house they threw up with great speed a wall of turf fourteen feet in height and twelve in thickness. The space enclosed was about half an acre. Within this rampart all the arms, the ammunition, and the provisions of the settlement were collected, and several huts of thin plank were built. When these preparations were completed, the men of Kenmare began to make vigorous reprisals on their Irish neighbours, seized robbers, recovered stolen property, and continued during some weeks to act in all things as an independent commonwealth. The government was carried on by elective officers to whom every member of the society swore fidelity on the Holy Gospels.*

While the people of the small town of Kenmare were thus bestirring themselves, similar preparations for defence were made by larger communities on a larger scale. Great numbers of gentlemen and yeomen quitted the open country, and repaired to those towns which had been founded and incorporated for the purpose of bridling the native population, and which, though recently placed under the government of Roman Catholic magistrates, were still inhabited chiefly by Protestants. A considerable body of armed colonists mustered at Sligo, another at Charleville, a third at Mallow, a fourth still more formidable at Bandon.† But the principal strongholds of the Englishry during this evil time were Enniskillen and Londonderry.

Enniskillen, though the capital of the county of Fermanagh, was then merely a village. It was built on an island surrounded by the river which joins the two beautiful sheets of water known by the common name of Lough Erne. The stream and both the lakes were overhung on every side by natural forests. Enniskillen consisted of about eighty dwellings clustering round an ancient castle. The inhabitants were, with scarcely an exception, Protestants, and boasted that their town had been true to the Protestant cause through the terrible rebellion which broke out in 1641. Early in December they received from Dublin an intimation that two companies of Popish infantry were to be immediately quartered on them. The alarm of the little community was great, and the greater because it was known

* Exact Relation of the Persecutions, Robberies and Losses, sustained by the Protestants of Kilmare in Ireland, 1689; Smith's Ancient and Modern State of Kerry, 1756.
† Ireland's Lamentation, licensed May 18. 1689.

CHAP. XII.

that a preaching friar had been exerting himself to inflame the Irish population of the neighbourhood against the heretics. A daring resolution was taken. Come what might, the troops should not be admitted. Yet the means of defence were slender. Not ten pounds of powder, not twenty firelocks fit for use, could be collected within the walls. Messengers were sent with pressing letters to summon the Protestant gentry of the vicinage to the rescue: and the summons was gallantly obeyed. In a few hours two hundred foot and a hundred and fifty horse had assembled. Tyrconnel's soldiers were already at hand. They brought with them a considerable supply of arms to be distributed among the peasantry. The peasantry greeted the royal standard with delight, and accompanied the march in great numbers. The townsmen and their allies, instead of waiting to be attacked, came boldly forth to encounter the intruders. The officers of James had expected no resistance. They were confounded when they saw confronting them a column of foot, flanked by a large body of mounted gentlemen and yeomen. The crowd of camp followers ran away in terror. The soldiers made a retreat so precipitate that it might be called a flight, and scarcely halted till they were thirty miles off at Cavan.*

The Protestants, elated by this easy victory, proceeded to make arrangements for the government and defence of Enniskillen and of the surrounding country. Gustavus Hamilton, a gentleman who had served in the army, but who had recently been deprived of his commission by Tyrconnel, and had since been living on an estate in Fermanagh, was appointed Governor, and took up his residence in the castle. Trusty men were enlisted and armed with great expedition. As there was a scarcity of swords and pikes, smiths were employed to make weapons by fastening scythes on poles. All the country houses round Lough Erne were turned into garrisons. No Papist was suffered to be at large in the town; and the friar who was accused of exerting his eloquence against the Englishry was thrown into prison.†

Londonderry.

The other great fastness of Protestantism was a place of more importance. Eighty years before, during the troubles

* A True Relation of the Actions of the Inniskilling men, by Andrew Hamilton, Rector of Kilskerrie, and one of the Prebends of the Diocese of Clogher, an Eyewitness thereof and Actor therein, licensed Jan. 15. 16⁹¹/₉₀; A Further Impartial Account of the Actions of the Inniskilling men, by Captain William Mac Cormick, one of the first that took up Arms, 1691.
† Hamilton's True Relation; Mac Cormick's Further Impartial Account.

caused by the last struggle of the houses of O'Neil and O'Donnell against the authority of James the First, the ancient city of Derry had been surprised by one of the native chiefs: the inhabitants had been slaughtered, and the houses reduced to ashes. The insurgents were speedily put down and punished: the government resolved to restore the ruined town: the Lord Mayor, Aldermen, and Common Council of London were invited to assist in the work; and King James the First made over to them in their corporate capacity the ground covered by the ruins of the old Derry, and about six thousand acres in the neighbourhood.*

This country, then uncultivated and uninhabited, is now enriched by industry, embellished by taste, and pleasing even to eyes accustomed to the well tilled fields and stately manor houses of England. A new city soon arose which, on account of its connection with the capital of the empire, was called Londonderry. The buildings covered the summit and slope of a hill which overlooked the broad stream of the Foyle, then whitened by vast flocks of wild swans.† On the highest ground stood the Cathedral, a church which, though erected when the secret of Gothic architecture was lost, and though ill qualified to sustain a comparison with the awful temples of the middle ages, is not without grace and dignity. Near the Cathedral rose the Palace of the Bishop, whose see was one of the most valuable in Ireland. The city was in form nearly an ellipse; and the principal streets formed a cross, the arms of which met in a square called the Diamond. The original houses have been either rebuilt or so much repaired that their ancient character can no longer be traced; but many of them were standing within living memory. They were in general two stories in height; and some of them had stone staircases on the outside. The dwellings were encompassed by a wall of which the whole circumference was little less than a mile. On the bastions were planted culverins and sakers presented by the wealthy guilds of London to the colony. On some of these ancient guns, which have done memorable service to a great cause, the devices of the Fishmongers' Company, of the Vintners' Company, and of the Merchant Tailors' Company are still discernible.‡

* Concise View of the Irish Society. 1822; Mr. Heath's interesting Account of the Worshipful Company of Grocers, Appendix 17.
† The Interest of England in the Preservation of Ireland, licensed July 17. 1689.
‡ These things I observed or learned on the spot.

The inhabitants were Protestants of Anglosaxon blood. They were indeed not all of one country or of one church; but Englishmen and Scotchmen, Episcopalians and Presbyterians, seem to have generally lived together in friendship, a friendship which is sufficiently explained by their common antipathy to the Irish race and to the Popish religion. During the rebellion of 1641, Londonderry had resolutely held out against the native chieftains, and had been repeatedly besieged in vain.* Since the Restoration the city had prospered. The Foyle, when the tide was high, brought up ships of large burden to the quay. The fisheries throve greatly. The nets, it was said, were sometimes so full that it was necessary to fling back multitudes of fish into the waves. The quantity of salmon caught annually was estimated at eleven hundred thousand pounds' weight.†

Closing of the gates of Londonderry.

The people of Londonderry shared in the alarm which, towards the close of the year 1688, was general among the Protestants settled in Ireland. It was known that the aboriginal peasantry of the neighbourhood were laying in pikes and knives. Priests had been haranguing in a style of which, it must be owned, the Puritan part of the Anglosaxon colony had little right to complain, about the slaughter of the Amalekites, and the judgments which Saul had brought on himself by sparing one of the proscribed race. Rumours from various quarters and anonymous letters in various hands agreed in naming the ninth of December as the day fixed for the extirpation of the strangers. While the minds of the citizens were agitated by these reports, news came that a regiment of twelve hundred Papists, commanded by a Papist, Alexander Macdonnell, Earl of Antrim, had received orders from the Lord Deputy to occupy Londonderry, and was already on the march from Coleraine. The consternation was extreme. Some were for closing the gates and resisting; some for submitting; some for temporising. The corporation had, like the other corporations of Ireland, been remodelled. The magistrates were men of low station and character. Among them was only one person of Anglosaxon extraction; and he had turned Papist. In such rulers the inhabitants could place no confidence.‡ The Bishop, Ezekiel Hopkins,* resolutely

---

* The best account that I have seen of what passed in Londonderry during the war which began in 1641 is in Dr. Reid's History of the Presbyterian Church in Ireland.

† The Interest of England in the Preservation of Ireland; 1689.

‡ My authority for this unfavourable account of the corporation is an epic poem entitled the Londeriad. This extraordinary work must have been written very soon after the events to which it

adhered to the political doctrines which he had preached during many years, and exhorted his flock to go patiently to the slaughter rather than incur the guilt of disobeying the Lord's Anointed.* Antrim was meanwhile drawing nearer and nearer. At length the citizens saw from the walls his troops arrayed on the opposite shore of the Foyle. There was then no bridge: but there was a ferry which kept up a constant communication between the two banks of the river; and by this ferry a detachment from Antrim's regiment crossed. The officers presented themselves at the gate, produced a warrant directed to the Mayor and Sheriffs, and demanded admittance and quarters for His Majesty's soldiers.

Just at this moment thirteen young apprentices, most of whom appear, from their names, to have been of Scottish birth or descent, flew to the guard room, armed themselves, seized the keys of the city, rushed to the Ferry Gate, closed it in the face of the King's officers, and let down the portcullis. James Morison, a citizen more advanced in years, addressed the intruders from the top of the wall and advised them to be gone. They stood in consultation before the gate till they heard him cry, "Bring a great gun this way." They then thought it time to get beyond the range of shot. They retreated, reembarked, and rejoined their comrades on the other side of the river. The flame had already spread. The whole city was up. The other gates were secured. Sentinels paced the ramparts everywhere. The magazines were opened. Muskets and gunpowder were distributed. Messengers were sent, under cover of the following night, to the Protestant gentlemen of the neighbouring counties. The bishop expostulated in vain. It is indeed probable that the vehement and daring young Scotchmen who had taken the lead on this occasion had little respect for his office. One of them broke in on a discourse with which he interrupted the military preparations by exclaiming, "A good sermon, my lord; a very good sermon: but we have not time to hear it just now."†

---

relates; for it is dedicated to Robert Rochfort, Speaker of the House of Commons; and Rochfort was Speaker from 1695 to 1699. The poet had no invention: he had evidently a minute knowledge of the city which he celebrated; and his doggerel is consequently not without historical value. He says:

"For burgesses and freemen they had chosen Brogmakers, butchers, raps, and such as these:

In all the corporation not a man Of British parents, except Buchanan."

This Buchanan is afterwards described

"A braave old ole'er; For he had learned to tell his beads before."

* See a sermon preached by him at Dublin on Jan. 31, 1669. The text is "Submit yourselves to every ordinance of man for the Lord's sake."
† Walker's Account of the Siege of

CHAP. XII.

The Protestants of the neighbourhood promptly obeyed the summons of Londonderry. Within forty eight hours, hundreds of horse and foot came by various roads to the city. Antrim, not thinking himself strong enough to risk an attack, or not disposed to take on himself the responsibility of commencing a civil war without further orders, retired with his troops to Coleraine.

Mountjoy sent to pacify Ulster.

It might have been expected that the resistance of Enniskillen and Londonderry would have irritated Tyrconnel into taking some desperate step. And in truth his savage and imperious temper was at first inflamed by the news almost to madness. But, after wreaking his rage, as usual, on his wig, he became somewhat calmer. Tidings of a very sobering nature had just reached him. The Prince of Orange was marching unopposed to London. Almost every county and every great town in England had declared for him. James, deserted by his ablest captains and by his nearest relatives, had sent commissioners to treat with the invaders, and had issued writs convoking a Parliament. While the result of the negotiations which were pending in England was uncertain, the Viceroy could not venture to take a bloody revenge on the refractory Protestants of Ireland. He therefore thought it expedient to affect for a time a clemency and moderation which were by no means congenial to his disposition. The task of quieting the Englishry of Ulster was entrusted to William Stewart, Viscount Mountjoy. Mountjoy, a brave soldier, an accomplished scholar, a zealous Protestant, and yet a zealous Tory, was one of the very few members of the Established Church who still held office in Ireland. He was Master of the Ordnance in that kingdom, and was colonel of a regiment in which an uncommonly large proportion of the Englishry had been suffered to remain. At Dublin he was the centre of a small circle of learned and ingenious men who had, under his presidency, formed themselves into a Royal Society, the image, on a small scale, of the Royal Society of London. In Ulster, with which he was peculiarly connected, his name was held in high honour by the colonists.* He

Derry, 1689; Mackenzie's Narrative of the Siege of Londonderry, 1689; An Apology for the failures charged on the Reverend Mr. Walker's Account of the late Siege of Derry, 1689; A Light to the Blind. This last work, a manuscript in the possession of Lord Fingal, is the work of a zealous Roman Catholic and a mortal enemy of England. Large extracts from it are among the Mackintosh MSS. The date in the titlepage is 1711.

* As to Mountjoy's character and position, see Clarendon's letters from Ireland, particularly that to Lord Dartmouth of Feb. 6., and that to Evelyn of Feb. 14. 168⅚. "Bon officier, et homme d'esprit," says Avaux.

hastened with his regiment to Londonderry, and was well received there. For it was known that, though he was firmly attached to hereditary monarchy, he was not less firmly attached to the reformed religion. The citizens readily permitted him to leave within their walls a small garrison exclusively composed of Protestants, under the command of his lieutenant colonel, Robert Lundy, who took the title of Governor.*

CHAP. XII.

The news of Mountjoy's visit to Ulster was highly gratifying to the defenders of Enniskillen. Some gentlemen deputed by that town waited on him to request his good offices, but were disappointed by the reception which they found. "My advice to you is," he said, "to submit to the King's authority." "What, my Lord?" said one of the deputies; "Are we to sit still and let ourselves be butchered?" "The King," said Mountjoy, "will protect you." "If all that we hear be true," said the deputy, "His Majesty will find it hard enough to protect himself." The conference ended in this unsatisfactory manner. Enniskillen still kept its attitude of defiance; and Mountjoy returned to Dublin.†

By this time it had indeed become evident that James could not protect himself. It was known in Ireland that he had fled; that he had been stopped; that he had fled again; that the Prince of Orange had arrived at Westminster in triumph, had taken on himself the administration of the realm, and had issued letters summoning a Convention.

Those lords and gentlemen at whose request the Prince had assumed the government, had earnestly entreated him to take the state of Ireland into his immediate consideration; and he had in reply assured them that he would do his best to maintain the Protestant religion and the English interest in that kingdom. His enemies afterwards accused him of utterly disregarding this promise; nay, they alleged, that he purposely suffered Ireland to sink deeper and deeper in calamity. Halifax, they said, had, with cruel and perfidious ingenuity, devised this mode of placing the Convention under a species of duress; and the trick had succeeded but too well. The vote which called William to the throne would not have passed so easily but for the extreme dangers

William opens a negotiation with Tyrconnel.

* Walker's Account; Light to the Blind.   † Mac Cormick's Farther Impartial Account.

VOL. II.   L L

which threatened the state; and it was in consequence of his own dishonest inactivity that those dangers had become extreme.* As this accusation rests on no proof, those who repeat it are at least bound to show that some course clearly better than the course which William took was open to him; and this they will find a difficult task. If indeed he could, within a few weeks after his arrival in London, have sent a great expedition to Ireland, that kingdom might perhaps, after a short struggle, or without a struggle, have submitted to his authority; and a long series of crimes and calamities might have been averted. But the factious orators and pamphleteers, who, much at their ease, reproached him for not sending such an expedition, would have been perplexed if they had been required to find the men, the ships, and the funds. The English army had lately been arrayed against him: part of it was still ill disposed towards him; and the whole was utterly disorganised. Of the army which he had brought from Holland not a regiment could be spared. He had found the treasury empty and the pay of the navy in arrear. He had no power to hypothecate any part of the public revenue. Those who lent him money lent it on no security but his bare word. It was only by the patriotic liberality of the merchants of London that he was enabled to defray the ordinary charges of government till the meeting of the Convention. It is surely unjust to blame him for not instantly fitting out, in such circumstances, an armament sufficient to conquer a kingdom.

Perceiving that, till the government of England was settled, it would not be in his power to interfere effectually by arms in the affairs of Ireland, he determined to try what effect negotiation would produce. Those who judged after the event pronounced that he had not, on this occasion, shown his usual sagacity. He ought, they said, to have known that it was absurd to expect submission from Tyrconnel. Such however was not at the time the opinion of men who had the best means of information, and whose interest was a sufficient pledge for their sincerity. A great meeting of noblemen and gentlemen who had property in Ireland was held, during the interregnum, at the house of the Duke of Ormond in Saint James's Square. They advised the Prince

* Burnet, i. 807.; and the notes by Swift and Dartmouth. Tutchin, in the Observator, repeats this idle calumny.

to try whether the Lord Deputy might not be induced to capitulate on honourable and advantageous terms.* In truth there is strong reason to believe that Tyrconnel really wavered. For, fierce as were his passions, they never made him forgetful of his interest; and he might well doubt whether it were not for his interest, in declining years and health, to retire from business with full indemnity for all past offences, with high rank, and with an ample fortune, rather than to stake his life and property on the event of a war against the whole power of England. It is certain that he professed himself willing to yield. He opened a communication with the Prince of Orange, and affected to take counsel with Mountjoy, and with others who, though they had not thrown off their allegiance to James, were yet firmly attached to the Established Church and to the English connection.

In one quarter, a quarter from which William was justified in expecting the most judicious counsel, there was a strong conviction that the professions of Tyrconnel were sincere. No British statesman had then so high a reputation throughout Europe as Sir William Temple. His diplomatic skill had, twenty years before, arrested the progress of the French power. He had been a steady and an useful friend to the United Provinces and to the House of Nassau. He had long been on terms of friendly confidence with the Prince of Orange, and had negotiated that marriage to which England owed her recent deliverance. With the affairs of Ireland Temple was supposed to be peculiarly well acquainted. His family had considerable property there: he had himself resided there during several years: he had represented the county of Carlow in Parliament; and a large part of his income was derived from a lucrative Irish office. There was no height of power, of rank, or of opulence to which he might not have risen, if he would have consented to quit his retreat, and to lend his assistance and the weight of his name to the new government. But power, rank, and opulence had less attraction for his Epicurean temper than ease and security. He rejected the most tempting invitations, and continued to amuse himself with his books, his tulips, and his pineapples, in rural seclusion. With some hesitation, however, he consented to let his eldest son John enter into the service of William. During the vacancy of the throne, John Temple was employed in busi-

CHAP. XII.

The Temples consulted.

* The Orange Gazette, Jan. 10. 168

CHAP. XII.

ness of high importance; and, on subjects connected with Ireland, his opinion, which might reasonably be supposed to agree with his father's, had great weight. The young politician flattered himself that he had secured the services of an agent eminently qualified to bring the negotiation with Tyrconnel to a prosperous issue.

Richard Hamilton sent to Ireland on his parole.

This agent was one of a remarkable family which had sprung from a noble Scottish stock, but which had long been settled in Ireland, and which professed the Roman Catholic religion. In the gay crowd which thronged Whitehall, during those scandalous years of jubilee which immediately followed the Restoration, the Hamiltons were preeminently conspicuous. The long fair ringlets, the radiant bloom, and the languishing blue eyes of the lovely Elizabeth still charm us on the canvass of Lely. She had the glory of achieving no vulgar conquest. It was reserved for her voluptuous beauty and for her flippant wit to overcome the aversion which the coldhearted and scoffing Grammont felt for the indissoluble tie. One of her brothers, Anthony, became the chronicler of that brilliant and dissolute society of which he had been not the least brilliant nor the least dissolute member. He deserves the high praise of having, though not a Frenchman, written the book which is, of all books, the most exquisitely French, both in spirit and in manner. Another brother, named Richard, had, in foreign service, gained some military experience. His wit and politeness had distinguished him even in the splendid circle of Versailles. It was whispered that he had dared to lift his eyes to an exalted lady, the natural daughter of the Great King, the wife of a legitimate prince of the House of Bourbon, and that she had not seemed to be displeased by the attentions of her presumptuous admirer.* Richard had subsequently returned to his native country, had been appointed brigadier general in the Irish army, and had been sworn of the Irish Privy Council. When the Dutch invasion was expected, he came across Saint George's Channel with the troops which Tyrconnel sent to reinforce the royal army. After the flight of James, those troops submitted to the Prince of Orange. Richard Hamilton not only made his own peace with what was now the ruling power, but declared himself confident that, if he were sent to Dublin, he could conduct the negotiation which had been opened there to a happy close. If he failed, he pledged his word to return

* Mémoires de Madame de la Fayette.

to London in three weeks. His influence in Ireland was known to be great: his honour had never been questioned; and he was highly esteemed by John Temple. The young statesman declared that he would answer for his friend Richard as for himself. This guarantee was thought sufficient; and Hamilton set out for Ireland, proclaiming everywhere that he should soon bring Tyrconnel to reason. The offers which he was authorised to make to the Roman Catholics and personally to the Lord Deputy were most liberal.*

CHAP. XII.

It is not impossible that Hamilton may have really meant to keep his promise. But when he arrived at Dublin he found that he had undertaken a task which he could not perform. The hesitation of Tyrconnel, whether genuine or feigned, was at an end. He had found that he had no longer a choice. He had with little difficulty stimulated the ignorant and susceptible Irish to fury: To calm them was beyond his skill. Rumours were abroad that the Viceroy was corresponding with the English; and those rumours had set the nation on fire. The cry of the common people was that, if he dared to sell them for wealth and honours, they would burn the Castle and him in it, and would put themselves under the protection of France.† It was necessary for him to protest, truly or falsely, that he had never harboured any thought of submission, and that he had pretended to negotiate only for the purpose of gaining time. Yet, before he openly declared against the English settlers, and against England herself, what must be a war to the death, he wished to rid himself of Mountjoy, who had hitherto been true to the cause of James, but who, it was well known, would never consent to be a party to the spoliation and oppression of the colonists. Hypocritical professions of friendship and of pacific intentions were not spared. It was a sacred duty, Tyrconnel said, to avert the calamities which seemed to be impending. King James himself, if he understood the whole case, would not wish his Irish friends to engage at that moment in an enterprise which must be fatal to them and useless to him. He would permit them, he would command them, to submit to necessity, and to reserve themselves for better times. If any man of weight, any man loyal, able, and well informed, would repair to Saint Germains and explain the state of things, His Majesty would

Tyrconnel sends Mountjoy and Rice to France.

* Burnet, I. 808.; Life of James, II. 320.; Commons' Journals, July 29. 1689.
† Avaux to Lewis, May 2/April 4. 1689.

CHAP. XII.

easily be convinced. Would Mountjoy undertake this most honourable and important mission? Mountjoy hesitated, and suggested that some person more likely to be acceptable to the King should be the messenger. Tyrconnel swore, ranted, declared that, unless King James were well advised, Ireland would sink to the pit of hell, and insisted that Mountjoy should go as the representative of the loyal members of the Established Church, and should be accompanied by Chief Baron Rice, a Roman Catholic high in the royal favour. Mountjoy yielded. The two ambassadors departed together, but with very different commissions. Rice was charged to tell James that Mountjoy was a traitor at heart, and had been sent to France only that the Protestants of Ireland might be deprived of a favourite leader. The King was to be assured that he was impatiently expected in Ireland, and that, if he would show himself there with a French force, he might speedily retrieve his fallen fortunes.* The Chief Baron carried with him other instructions which were probably kept secret even from the Court of Saint Germains. If James should be unwilling to put himself at the head of the native population of Ireland, Rice was directed to request a private audience of Lewis, and to offer to make the island a province of France.†

Tyrconnel calls the Irish people to arms.

As soon as the two envoys had departed, Tyrconnel set himself to prepare for the conflict which had become inevitable; and he was strenuously assisted by the faithless Hamilton. The Irish nation was called to arms; and the call was obeyed with strange promptitude and enthusiasm. The flag on the Castle of Dublin was embroidered with the words, "Now or never! Now and for ever!" Those words resounded through the whole island.‡ Never in modern Europe has there been such a rising up of a whole people. The habits of the Celtic peasant were such that he made no sacrifice in quitting his potatoe ground for the camp. He loved excitement and adventure. He feared work far more than danger. His national and religious feelings had, during three years, been exasperated by the constant application of stimulants. At every fair and market he had heard that a good time was at hand, that the tyrants who spoke Saxon

* Clarke's Life of James, ii. 331.; Mountjoy's Circular Letter, dated Jan. 10. 1688; King, iv. 8. In light to the blind, Tyrconnel's "wise dissimulation" is commended.
† Avaux to Lewis, April 1¾. 1689.
‡ Printed Letter from Dublin, Feb. 24. 1689; Mephibosheth and Ziba, 1689.

and lived in slated houses were about to be swept away, and that the land would again belong to its own children. By the peat fires of a hundred thousand cabins had nightly been sung rude ballads which predicted the deliverance of the oppressed race. The priests, most of whom belonged to those old families which the Act of Settlement had ruined, but which were still revered by the native population, had, from a thousand altars, charged every Catholic to show his zeal for the true Church by providing weapons against the day when it might be necessary to try the chances of battle in her cause. The army, which, under Ormond, had consisted of only eight regiments, was now increased to forty-eight: and the ranks were soon full to overflowing. It was impossible to find at short notice one tenth of the number of good officers which was required. Commissions were scattered profusely among idle cosherers who claimed to be descended from good Irish families. Yet even thus the supply of captains and lieutenants fell short of the demand; and many companies were commanded by cobblers, tailors, and footmen.*

CHAP. XII.

The pay of the soldiers was very small. The private had no more than three pence a day. One half only of this pittance was ever given him in money; and that half was often in arrear. But a far more seductive bait than his miserable stipend was the prospect of boundless license. If the government allowed him less than sufficed for his wants, it was not extreme to mark the means by which he supplied the deficiency. Though four fifths of the population of Ireland were Celtic and Roman Catholic, more than four fifths of the property of Ireland belonged to the Protestant Englishry. The garners, the cellars, above all the flocks and herds of the minority, were abandoned to the majority. Whatever the regular troops spared was devoured by bands of marauders who overran almost every barony in the island. For the arming was now universal. No man dared to present himself at mass without some weapon, a pike, a long knife called a skean, or, at the very least, a strong ashen stake, pointed and hardened in the fire. The very women were exhorted by their spiritual directors to carry skeans. Every smith, every car-

Devastation of the country.

---

* The connection of the priests with the old Irish families is mentioned in Petty's Political Anatomy of Ireland. See the short view by a Clergyman lately escaped, 1689; Ireland's Lamentation, by an English Protestant that lately narrowly escaped with life from thence, 1689; A True Account of the State of Ireland, by a person who with Great Difficulty left Dublin, 1689; King. ii. 7. Avaux confirms all that these writers say about the Irish officers.

penter, every cutler, was at constant work on guns and blades. It was scarcely possible to get a horse shod. If any Protestant artisan refused to assist in the manufacture of implements which were to be used against his nation and his religion, he was flung into prison. It seems probable that, at the end of February, at least a hundred thousand Irishmen were in arms. Near fifty thousand of them were soldiers. The rest were banditti, whose violence and licentiousness the Government affected to disapprove, but did not really exert itself to suppress. The Protestants not only were not protected, but were not suffered to protect themselves. It was determined that they should be left unarmed in the midst of an armed and hostile population. A day was fixed on which they were to bring all their swords and firelocks to the parish churches; and it was notified that every Protestant house in which, after that day, a weapon should be found should be given up to be sacked by the soldiers. Bitter complaints were made that any knave might, by hiding a spearhead or an old gunbarrel in a corner of a mansion, bring utter ruin on the owner.*

Chief Justice Keating, himself a Protestant, and almost the only Protestant who still held a great place in Ireland, struggled courageously in the cause of justice and order against the united strength of the government and the populace. At the Wicklow assizes of that spring, he, from the seat of judgment, set forth with great strength of language the miserable state of the country. Whole counties, he said, were devastated by a rabble resembling the vultures and ravens which follow the march of an army. Most of these wretches were not soldiers. They acted under no authority known to the law. Yet it was, he owned, but too evident that they were encouraged and screened by some who were in high command. How else could it be that a market overt for plunder should be held within a short distance of the

* At the French War Office is a report on the State of Ireland in February 1689. In that report it is said that the Irish who had enlisted as soldiers were forty-five thousand, and that the number would have been a hundred thousand, if all who volunteered had been admitted. See the Sad and Lamentable Condition of the Protestants in Ireland, 1689; Hamilton's True Relation, 1690; The State of Papist and Protestant Properties in the Kingdom of Ireland, 1689; A True Representation to the King and People of England how Matters were carried on all along in Ireland, licensed Aug. 16. 1689; Letter from Dublin, 1689; Ireland's Lamentation, 1689; Compleat History of the Life and Military Actions of Richard, Earl of Tyrconnel, General-issimo of all the Irish forces now in arms, 1689.

capital? The stories which travellers told of the savage Hottentots near the Cape of Good Hope were realised in Leinster. Nothing was more common than for an honest man to lie down rich in flocks and herds acquired by the industry of a long life, and to wake a beggar. It was however to small purpose that Keating attempted, in the midst of that fearful anarchy, to uphold the supremacy of the law. Priests and military chiefs appeared on the bench for the purpose of overawing the judge and countenancing the robbers. One ruffian escaped because no prosecutor dared to appear. Another declared that he had armed himself in conformity to the orders of his spiritual guide, and to the example of many persons of higher station than himself, whom he saw at that moment in court. Two only of the Merry Boys, as they were called, were convicted: the worst criminals escaped; and the Chief Justice indignantly told the jurymen that the guilt of the public ruin lay at their door.*

When such disorder prevailed in Wicklow, it is easy to imagine what must have been the state of districts more barbarous and more remote from the seat of government. Keating appears to have been the only magistrate who strenuously exerted himself to put the law in force. Indeed Nugent, the Chief Justice of the highest criminal court of the realm, declared on the bench at Cork that, without violence and spoliation, the intentions of the government could not be carried into effect, and that robbery must at that conjuncture be tolerated as a necessary evil.†

The destruction of property which took place within a few weeks would be incredible, if it were not attested by witnesses unconnected with each other and attached to very different interests. There is a close, and sometimes almost a verbal, agreement between the descriptions given by Protestants, who, during that reign of terror, escaped, at the hazard of their lives, to England, and the descriptions given by the envoys, commissaries, and captains of Lewis. All agreed in declaring that it would take many years to repair the waste which had been wrought in a few weeks by the armed peasantry.‡ Some of the Saxon aristocracy had mansions richly furnished, and sideboards gorgeous with silver bowls and chargers. All

---

* See the proceedings in the State Trials.
† King. iii. 10.
‡ Ten years, says the French Ambassador; twenty years, says a Protestant fugitive.

this wealth disappeared. One house, in which there had been three thousand pounds' worth of plate, was left without a spoon.* But the chief riches of Ireland consisted in cattle. Innumerable flocks and herds covered that vast expanse of emerald meadow, saturated with the moisture of the Atlantic. More than one gentleman possessed twenty thousand sheep and four thousand oxen. The freebooters who now overspread the country belonged to a class which was accustomed to live on potatoes and sour whey, and which had always regarded meat as a luxury reserved for the rich. These men at first revelled in beef and mutton, as the savage invaders, who of old poured down from the forests of the north on Italy, revelled in Massic and Falernian wines. The Protestants described with contemptuous disgust the strange gluttony of their newly liberated slaves. Carcasses, half raw and half burned to cinders, sometimes still bleeding, sometimes in a state of loathsome decay, were torn to pieces, and swallowed without salt, bread, or herbs. Those marauders who preferred boiled meat, being often in want of kettles, contrived to cook the steer in his own skin. An absurd tragicomedy is still extant, which was acted in this and the following year at some low theatre for the amusement of the English populace. A crowd of half naked savages appeared on the stage, howling a Celtic song and dancing round an ox. They then proceeded to cut steaks out of the animal while still alive, and to fling the bleeding flesh on the coals. In truth the barbarity and filthiness of the banquets of the Rapparees was such as the dramatists of Grub Street could scarcely caricature. When Lent began, the plunderers generally ceased to devour, but continued to destroy. A peasant would kill a cow merely in order to get a pair of brogues. Often a whole flock of sheep, often a herd of fifty or sixty kine, were slaughtered; the beasts were flayed; the fleeces and hides were carried away; and the bodies were left to poison the air. The French ambassador reported to his master that, in six weeks, fifty thousand horned cattle had been slain in this manner, and were rotting on the ground all over the country. The number of sheep that were butchered during the same time was popularly said to have been three or four hundred thousand.†

* Animadversions on the proposal for sending back the nobility and gentry of Ireland, 1689.

† King. III. 10.; The Sad Estate and Condition of Ireland, as represented in a Letter from a Worthy Person who was

Any estimate which can now be framed of the value of the property destroyed during this fearful conflict of races must necessarily be very inexact. We are not however absolutely without materials for such an estimate. The Quakers were neither a very numerous nor a very opulent class. We can hardly suppose that they were more than a fiftieth part of the Protestant population of Ireland, or that they possessed more than a fiftieth part of the Protestant wealth of Ireland. They were undoubtedly better treated than any other Protestant sect. James had always been partial to them: they own that Tyrconnel did his best to protect them; and they seem to have found favour even in the sight of the Rapparees.* Yet the Quakers computed their pecuniary losses at a hundred thousand pounds.†

In Leinster, Munster, and Connaught, it was utterly impossible for the English settlers, few as they were and dispersed, to offer any effectual resistance to this terrible outbreak of the aboriginal population. Charleville, Mallow, Sligo, fell into the hands of the natives. Bandon, where the Protestants had mustered in considerable force, was reduced by Lieutenant General Macarthy, an Irish officer who was descended from one of the most illustrious Celtic houses, and who had long served, under a feigned name, in the French army.‡ The people of Kenmare held out in their little fastness till they were attacked by three thousand regular soldiers, and till it was known that several pieces of ordnance were coming to batter down the turf wall which surrounded the agent's house. Then at length a capitulation was concluded. The colonists were suffered to embark in a small vessel scantily supplied with food and water. They had no experienced navigator on board: but after a voyage of a fortnight, during which they were crowded together like slaves in a Guinea ship, and suffered the extremity of thirst and hunger, they reached Bristol in safety.* When such was the fate of the towns, it was evident that the country seats which the Protestant landowners had recently fortified in the three southern provinces could no longer be defended. Many families submitted, delivered up their arms, and thought themselves happy in escaping with life. But many resolute and highspirited gentlemen and yeomen were determined to perish rather than yield. They packed up such valuable property as could easily be carried away, burned whatever they could not remove, and, well armed and mounted, set out for those spots in Ulster which were the strongholds of their race and of their faith. The flower of the Protestant population of Munster and Connaught found shelter at Enniskillen. Whatever was bravest and most truehearted in Leinster took the road to Londonderry.†

Enniskillen and Londonderry hold out.

The spirit of Enniskillen and Londonderry rose higher and higher to meet the danger. At both places the tidings of what had been done by the Convention at Westminster were received with transports of joy. William and Mary were proclaimed at Enniskillen with unanimous enthusiasm, and with such pomp as the little town could furnish.‡ Lundy, who commanded at Londonderry, could not venture to oppose himself to the general sentiment of the citizens and of his own soldiers. He therefore gave in his adhesion to the new government, and signed a declaration by which he bound himself to stand by that government, on pain of being considered a coward and a traitor. A vessel from England soon brought

* Exact Relation of the Persecutions, Robberies and Losses sustained by the Protestants of Kilmare in Ireland, 1689.
† A true Representation to the King and People of England how Matters were carried on all along in Ireland by the late King James, licensed Aug. 10.

1689; A true Account of the Present State of Ireland by a Person that with Great Difficulty left Dublin, licensed June 8, 1689.
‡ Hamilton's Actions of the Inniskilling Men, 1689.

a commission from William and Mary which confirmed him in his office.*

To reduce the Protestants of Ulster to submission before aid could arrive from England was now the chief object of Tyrconnel. A great force was ordered to move northward, under the command of Richard Hamilton. This man had violated all the obligations which are held most sacred by gentlemen and soldiers, had broken faith with his most intimate friends, had forfeited his military parole, and was now not ashamed to take the field as a general against the government to which he was bound to render himself up as a prisoner. His march left on the face of the country traces which the most careless eye could not during many years fail to discern. His army was accompanied by a rabble, such as Keating had well compared to the unclean birds of prey which swarm wherever the scent of carrion is strong. The general professed himself anxious to save from ruin and outrage all Protestants who remained quietly at their homes; and he most readily gave them protections under his hand. But these protections proved of no avail; and he was forced to own that, whatever power he might be able to exercise over his soldiers, he could not keep order among the mob of camp followers. The country behind him was a wilderness; and soon the country before him became equally desolate. For, at the fame of his approach, the colonists burned their furniture, pulled down their houses, and retreated northward. Some of them attempted to make a stand at Dromore, but were broken and scattered. Then the flight became wild and tumultuous. The fugitives broke down the bridges and burned the ferryboats. Whole towns, the seats of the Protestant population, were left in ruins without one inhabitant. The people of Omagh destroyed their own dwellings so utterly that no roof was left to shelter the enemy from the rain and wind. The people of Cavan migrated in one body to Enniskillen. The day was wet and stormy. The road was deep in mire. It was a piteous sight to see, mingled with the armed men, the women and children weeping, famished, and toiling through the mud up to their knees. All Lisburn fled to Antrim; and, as the foes drew nearer, all Lisburn and Antrim together came pouring into Londonderry. Thirty thousand Protestants, of both sexes and of every age, were crowded behind the bulwarks of the City of Refuge. There, at length,

Richard Hamilton marches into Ulster with an army.

* Walker's Account, 1689.

on the verge of the ocean, hunted to the last asylum, and baited into a mood in which men may be destroyed, but will not easily be subjugated, the imperial race turned desperately to bay.*

James determines to go to Ireland.

Meanwhile Mountjoy and Rice had arrived in France. Mountjoy was instantly put under arrest and thrown into the Bastile. James determined to comply with the invitation which Rice had brought, and applied to Lewis for the help of a French army. But Lewis, though he showed, as to all things which concerned the personal dignity and comfort of his royal guests, a delicacy even romantic, and a liberality approaching to profusion, was unwilling to send a large body of troops to Ireland. He saw that France would have to maintain a long war on the Continent against a formidable coalition: her expenditure must be immense; and great as were her resources, he felt it to be important that nothing should be wasted. He doubtless regarded with sincere commiseration and good will the unfortunate exiles to whom he had given so princely a welcome. Yet neither commiseration nor good will could prevent him from speedily discovering that his brother of England was the dullest and most perverse of human beings. The folly of James, his incapacity to read the characters of men and the signs of the times, his obstinacy, always most offensively displayed when wisdom enjoined concession, his vacillation, always exhibited most pitiably in emergencies which required firmness, had made him an outcast from England and might, if his counsels were blindly followed, bring great calamities on France. As a legitimate sovereign expelled by rebels, as a confessor of the true faith persecuted by heretics, as a near kinsman of the house of Bourbon, who had seated himself on the hearth of that House, he was entitled to hospitality, to tenderness, to respect. It was fit that he should have a stately palace and a spacious forest, that the household troops should salute him with the highest military honours, that he should have at his command all the hounds of the Grand Huntsman and all the hawks of the Grand Falconer. But, when a prince, who, at the head of a great fleet and army, had lost an empire without striking a blow, undertook to furnish plans for naval and military expeditions; when a prince, who had been undone by his profound ignorance of the temper of his own country-

* Mackenzie's Narrative; MacCormick's Further Impartial Account; Story's Impartial History of the Affairs of Ireland, 1691; Apology for the Protestants of Ireland; Letter from Dublin of Feb. 25, 1689; Avaux to Lewis, April 1689.

men, of his own soldiers, of his own domestics, of his own children, undertook to answer for the zeal and fidelity of the Irish people, whose tongue he could not speak, and on whose land he had never set his foot; it was necessary to receive his suggestions with caution. Such were the sentiments of Lewis; and in these sentiments he was confirmed by his Minister of War Louvois, who, on private as well as on public grounds, was unwilling that James should be accompanied by a large military force. Louvois hated Lauzun. Lauzun was a favourite at Saint Germains. He wore the garter, a badge of honour which has very seldom been conferred on aliens who were not sovereign princes. It was believed indeed at the French Court that, in order to distinguish him from the other knights of the most illustrious of European orders, he had been decorated with that very George which Charles the First had, on the scaffold, put into the hands of Juxon.* Lauzun had been encouraged to hope that, if French forces were sent to Ireland, he should command them; and this ambitious hope Louvois was bent on disappointing.†

An army was therefore for the present refused: but everything else was granted. The Brest fleet was ordered to be in readiness to sail. Arms for ten thousand men and great quantities of ammunition were put on board. About four hundred captains, lieutenants, cadets, and gunners were selected for the important service of organising and disciplining the Irish levies. The chief command was held by a veteran warrior, the Count of Rosen. Under him were Maumont, who held the rank of lieutenant general, and a brigadier named Pusignan. Five hundred thousand crowns in gold, equivalent to about a hundred and twelve thousand pounds sterling, were sent to Brest.‡ For James's personal comforts provision was made with anxiety resembling that of a tender mother equipping her son for a first campaign. The cabin furniture, the camp furniture, the tents, the bedding, the plate, were luxurious and superb. Nothing which could be agreeable or useful to the exile was too costly for the munificence, or too trifling for the attention, of his gracious and splendid host. On the fifteenth of February, James paid a farewell visit to Versailles. He was conducted round the buildings and plantations with every mark of respect and

---

* Mémoires de Madame de la Fayette; Madame de Sévigné to Madame de Grignan, February 18. 1689.
† Barnet, II. 17.; Life of James II., II. 320, 321, 322.
‡ Maumont's Instructions.

kindness. The fountains played in his honour. It was the season of the Carnival: and never had the vast palace and the sumptuous gardens presented a gayer aspect. In the evening the two kings, after a long and earnest conference in private, made their appearance before a splendid circle of lords and ladies. "I hope," said Lewis, in his noblest and most winning manner, "that we are about to part, never to meet again in this world. That is the best wish I can form for you. But, if any evil chance should force you to return, be assured that you will find me to the last such as you have found me hitherto." On the seventeenth, Lewis paid in return a farewell visit to Saint Germains. At the moment of the parting embrace, he said, with his most amiable smile, "We have forgotten one thing, a cuirass for yourself. You shall have mine." The cuirass was brought, and suggested to the wits of the Court ingenious allusions to the Vulcanian panoply which Achilles lent to his feebler friend. James set out for Brest; and his wife, overcome with sickness and sorrow, shut herself up with her child to weep and pray.*

James was accompanied or speedily followed by several of his own subjects, among whom the most distinguished were his son Berwick, Cartwright Bishop of Chester, Powis, Dover, and Melfort. Of all the retinue, none was so odious to the people of Great Britain as Melfort. He was an apostate: he was believed by many to be an insincere apostate; and the insolent, arbitrary, and menacing language of his state papers disgusted even the Jacobites. He was therefore a favourite with his master: for to James unpopularity, obstinacy, and implacability were the greatest recommendations that a minister could have.

Choice of a French ambassador to accompany James.

What Frenchman should attend the King of England in the character of ambassador had been the subject of grave deliberation at Versailles. Barillon could not be passed over without a marked slight. But his selfindulgent habits, his want of energy, and, above all, the credulity with which he had listened to the professions of Sunderland, had made an unfavourable impression on the mind of Lewis. What was to be done in Ireland was not work for a trifler or a dupe. The agent of France in that kingdom must be equal to much more than the ordinary functions of an envoy. It would be his right and his duty to offer advice touching every part of the politi-

* Dangeau, Feb. 14. 17. 1689; Madame de Sévigné, Feb. 14. 25. ; Mémoires de Madame de la Fayette.

cal and military administration of the country in which he would represent the most powerful and the most beneficent of allies. Barillon was therefore suffered to retire into privacy. He affected to bear his disgrace with composure. His political career, though it had brought great calamities both on the House of Stuart and on the House of Bourbon, had been by no means unprofitable to himself. He was old, he said: he was fat: he did not envy younger men the honour of living on potatoes and whiskey among the Irish bogs: he would try to console himself with partridges, with Champagne, and with the society of the wittiest men and prettiest women of Paris. It was rumoured, however, that he was tortured by painful emotions which he was studious to conceal: his health and spirits failed; and he tried to find consolation in religious duties. Some people were much edified by the piety of the old voluptuary: but others attributed his death, which took place not long after his retreat from public life, to shame and vexation.*

CHAP. XII.

The Count of Avaux, whose sagacity had detected all the plans of William, and who had in vain recommended a policy which would probably have frustrated them, was the man on whom the choice of Lewis fell. In abilities Avaux had no superior among the numerous able diplomatists whom his country then possessed. His demeanour was singularly pleasing, his person handsome, his temper bland. His manners and conversation were those of a gentleman who had been bred in the most polite and magnificent of all Courts, who had represented that Court both in Roman Catholic and in Protestant countries, and who had acquired in his wanderings the art of catching the tone of any society into which chance might throw him. He was eminently vigilant and adroit, fertile in resources, and skilful in discovering the weak parts of a character. His own character, however, was not without its weak parts. The consciousness that he was of plebeian origin was the torment of his life. He pined for nobility with a pining at once pitiable and ludicrous. Able, experienced, and accomplished as he was, he sometimes, under the influence of this mental disease, descended to the level of Moliere's Jourdain, and entertained malicious observers with scenes

The Count of Avaux.

* Memoirs of La Fare and Saint Simon; Note of Renaudot on English affairs, 1697, in the French Archives; Madame de Sévigné, Feb. 5, March 14. 1689; Letter of Madame de Coulanges to M. de Coulanges, July 23. 1691.

almost as laughable as that in which the honest draper was made a Mamamouchi.* It would have been well if this had been the worst. But it is not too much to say that of the difference between right and wrong Avaux had no more notion than a brute. One sentiment was to him in the place of religion and morality, a superstitious and intolerant devotion to the Crown which he served. This sentiment pervades all his despatches, and gives a colour to all his thoughts and words. Nothing that tended to promote the interest of the French monarchy seemed to him a crime. Indeed he appears to have taken it for granted that not only Frenchmen, but all human beings, owed a natural allegiance to the House of Bourbon, and that whoever hesitated to sacrifice the happiness and freedom of his own native country to the glory of that House was a traitor. While he resided at the Hague, he always designated those Dutchmen who had sold themselves to France as the well intentioned party. In the letters which he wrote from Ireland, the same feeling appears still more strongly. He would have been a more sagacious politician if he had sympathised more with those feelings of moral approbation and disapprobation which prevail among the vulgar. For his own indifference to all considerations of justice and mercy was such that, in his schemes, he made no allowance for the consciences and sensibilities of his neighbours. More than once he deliberately recommended wickedness so horrible that wicked men recoiled from it with indignation. But they could not succeed even in making their scruples intelligible to him. To every remonstrance he listened with a cynical sneer, wondering within himself whether those who lectured him were such fools as they professed to be, or were only shamming.

Such was the man whom Lewis selected to be the companion and monitor of James. Avaux was charged to open, if possible, a communication with the malecontents in the English Parliament: and he was authorised to expend, if necessary, a hundred thousand crowns among them.

James arrived at Brest on the fifth of March, embarked there on board of a man of war called the Saint Michael, and sailed within forty-eight hours. He had ample time, however, before his departure, to exhibit some of the faults by which he

* See Saint Simon's account of the trick by which Avaux tried to pass himself off at Stockholm as a Knight of the Order of the Holy Ghost.

had lost England and Scotland, and by which he was about to lose Ireland. Avaux wrote from the harbour of Brest that it would not be easy to conduct any important business in concert with the King of England. His Majesty could not keep any secret from anybody. The very foremast men of the Saint Michael had already heard him say things which ought to have been reserved for the ears of his confidential advisers.*

The voyage was safely and quietly performed; and, on the afternoon of the twelfth of March, James landed in the harbour of Kinsale. By the Roman Catholic population he was received with shouts of unfeigned transport. The few Protestants who remained in that part of the country joined in greeting him, and perhaps not insincerely. For, though an enemy of their religion, he was not an enemy of their nation; and they might reasonably hope that the worst king would show somewhat more respect for law and property than had been shown by the Merry Boys and Rupparees. The Vicar of Kinsale was among those who went to pay their duty: he was presented by the Bishop of Chester, and was not ungraciously received.†

James learned that his cause was prospering. In the three southern provinces of Ireland the Protestants were disarmed, and were so effectually bowed down by terror that he had nothing to apprehend from them. In the North there was some show of resistance; but Hamilton was marching against the malecontents; and there was little doubt that they would easily be crushed. A day was spent at Kinsale in putting the arms and ammunition out of reach of danger. Horses sufficient to carry a few travellers were with some difficulty procured; and, on the fourteenth of March, James proceeded to Cork.‡

We should greatly err if we imagined that the road by which he entered that city bore any resemblance to the stately approach which strikes the traveller of the nineteenth century with admiration. At present Cork, though deformed by many miserable relics of a former age, holds no mean place among the ports of the empire. The shipping is more

---

* This letter, written to Lewis from the harbour of Brest, is in the Archives of the French Foreign Office, but is wanting in the very rare volume printed in Downing Street.

† A full and true account of the Landing and Reception of the late King James at Kinsale, in a letter from Bristol, licensed April 4, 1689; Leslie's Answer to King; Ireland's Lamentation; Avaux, March 14.

‡ Avaux, March 17, 1689; Life of James, ii. 327. Orig. Mem.

than half what the shipping of London was at the time of the Revolution. The customs exceed the whole revenue which the whole kingdom of Ireland, in the most peaceful and prosperous times, yielded to the Stuarts. The town is adorned by broad and well built streets, by fair gardens, by a Corinthian portico which would do honour to Palladio, and by a Gothic College worthy to stand in the High Street of Oxford. In 1689, the city extended over about one tenth part of the space which it now covers, and was intersected by muddy streams, which have long been concealed by arches and buildings. A desolate marsh, in which the sportsman who pursued the waterfowl sank deep in water and mire at every step, covered the area now occupied by stately buildings, the palaces of great commercial societies. There was only a single street in which two wheeled carriages could pass each other. From this street diverged to right and left alleys squalid and noisome beyond the belief of those who have formed their notions of misery from the most miserable parts of Saint Giles's and Whitechapel. One of these alleys, called, and, by comparison, justly called, Broad Lane, is about ten feet wide. From such places, now seats of hunger and pestilence, abandoned to the most wretched of mankind, the citizens poured forth to welcome James. He was received with military honours by Macarthy, who held the chief command in Munster.

It was impossible for the King to proceed immediately to Dublin; for the southern counties had been so completely laid waste by the banditti whom the priests had called to arms that the means of locomotion were not easily to be procured. Horses had become rarities: in a large district there were only two carts; and those Avaux pronounced good for nothing. Some days elapsed before the money which had been brought from France, though no very formidable mass, could be dragged over the few miles which separated Cork from Kinsale.*

While the King and his Council were employed in trying to procure carriages and beasts, Tyrconnel arrived from Dublin. He held encouraging language. The opposition of Enniskillen he seems to have thought deserving of little consideration. Londonderry, he said, was the only important post held by the Protestants; and even Londonderry would not, in his judgment, hold out many days.

* Avaux, March 1689.

At length James was able to leave Cork for the capital. On the road, the shrewd and observant Avaux made many remarks. The first part of the journey was through wild highlands, where it was not strange that there should be few traces of art and industry. But, from Kilkenny to the gates of Dublin the path of the travellers lay over gently undulating ground rich with natural verdure. That fertile district should have been covered with flocks and herds, orchards and cornfields: but it was an untilled and unpeopled desert. Even in the towns the artisans were very few. Manufactured articles were hardly to be found, and if found could be procured only at immense prices. The envoy at first attributed the desolation which he saw on every side to the tyranny of the English colonists. In a very short time he was forced to change his opinion.*

James received on his progress numerous marks of the goodwill of the peasantry; but marks such as, to men bred in the courts of France and England, had an uncouth and ominous appearance. Though very few labourers were seen at work in the fields, the road was lined by Rapparees armed with skeans, stakes, and half pikes, who crowded to look upon the deliverer of their race. The highway along which he travelled presented the aspect of a street in which a fair is held. Pipers came forth to play before him in a style which was not exactly that of the French opera; and the villagers danced wildly to the music. Long frieze mantles, resembling those which Spenser had, a century before, described as meet beds for rebels and apt cloaks for thieves, were spread along the path which the cavalcade was to tread; and garlands in which cabbage stalks supplied the place of laurels, were offered to the royal hand. The women insisted on kissing His Majesty; but it should seem that they bore little resemblance to their posterity; for this compliment was so distasteful to him that he ordered his retinue to keep them at a distance.†

On the twenty-fourth of March he entered Dublin. That city was then, in extent and population, the second in the British isles. It contained between six and seven thousand houses, and probably above thirty thousand inhabitants.‡

* Avaux, March 24. April 4. 1689. James; Ireland's Lamentation; Light to the Blind.
† A full and true Account of the Landing and Reception of the late King ‡ See the calculations of Petty, King, and Davenant. If the average number

In wealth and beauty, however, Dublin was inferior to many English towns. Of the graceful and stately public buildings which now adorn both sides of the Liffey scarcely one had been even projected. The College, a very different edifice from that which now stands on the same site, lay quite out of the city.* The ground which is at present occupied by Leinster House and Charlemont House, by Sackville Street and Merrion Square, was open meadow. Most of the dwellings were built of timber, and have long given place to more substantial edifices. The Castle had in 1686 been almost uninhabitable. Clarendon had complained that he knew of no gentleman in Pall Mall who was not more conveniently and handsomely lodged than the Lord Lieutenant of Ireland. No public ceremony could be performed in a becoming manner under the Viceregal roof. Nay, in spite of constant glazing and tiling, the rain perpetually drenched the apartments.† Tyrconnel, since he became Lord Deputy, had erected a new building somewhat more commodious. To this building the King was conducted in state through the southern part of the city. Every exertion had been made to give an air of festivity and splendour to the district which he was to traverse. The streets, which were generally deep in mud were strewn with gravel. Boughs and flowers were scattered over the path. Tapestry and arras hung from the windows of those who could afford to exhibit such finery. The poor supplied the place of rich stuffs with blankets and coverlids. In one place was stationed a troop of friars with a cross; in another a company of forty girls dressed in white, and carrying nosegays. Pipers and harpers played "The King shall enjoy his own again." The Lord Deputy carried the sword of state before his master. The Judges, the Heralds, the Lord Mayor and Aldermen, appeared in all the pomp of office. Soldiers were drawn up on the right and left to keep the passages clear. A procession of twenty coaches belonging to public functionaries was mustered. Before the Castle gate, the King was met by the host under a canopy borne by four bishops of his church. At the sight he fell on his knees, and passed some time in devotion. He then rose and was con-

of inhabitants to a house was the same in Dublin as in London, the population of Dublin would have been about thirty-four thousand.

* John Dunton speaks of College Green near Dublin. I have seen letters of that age directed to the College, by Dublin. There are some interesting old maps of Dublin in the British Museum.

† Clarendon to Rochester, Feb. 8. 168¾, April 20. Aug. 12., Nov. 30. 1686.

ducted to the chapel of his palace, once,—such are the vicissitudes of human things,—the riding house of Henry Cromwell. A Te Deum was performed in honour of His Majesty's arrival. The next morning he held a Privy Council, discharged Chief Justice Keating from any further attendance at the Board, ordered Avaux and Bishop Cartwright to be sworn in, and issued a proclamation convoking a Parliament to meet at Dublin on the seventh of May.*

CHAP. XII.

When the news that James had arrived in Ireland reached London, the sorrow and alarm were general, and were mingled with serious discontent. The multitude, not making sufficient allowance for the difficulties by which William was encompassed on every side, loudly blamed his neglect. To all the invectives of the ignorant and malicious he opposed, as was his wont, nothing but immutable gravity and the silence of profound disdain. But few minds had received from nature a temper so firm as his; and still fewer had undergone so long and so rigorous a discipline. The reproaches which had no power to shake his fortitude, tried from childhood upwards by both extremes of fortune, inflicted a deadly wound on a less resolute heart.

Discontent in England.

While all the coffeehouses were unanimously resolving that a fleet and army ought to have been long before sent to Dublin, and wondering how so renowned a politician as His Majesty could have been duped by Hamilton and Tyrconnel, a gentleman went down to the Temple Stairs, called a boat, and desired to be pulled to Greenwich. He took the cover of a letter from his pocket, scratched a few lines with a pencil, and laid the paper on the seat with some silver for his fare. As the boat passed under the dark central arch of London Bridge, he sprang into the water and disappeared. It was found that he had written these words: "My folly in undertaking what I could not execute hath done the King great prejudice which cannot be stopped—No easier way for me than this—May his undertaking prosper—May he have a blessing." There was no signature: but the body was soon found, and proved to be that of John Temple. He was young and highly accomplished: he was heir to an honourable name: he was united to an amiable woman: he was possessed of an ample fortune; and he had in prospect the greatest honours of the state. It does not appear that the public

* Life of James II. ii. 330.; Full and true Account of the Landing and Reception, &c.; Ireland's Lamentation.

CHAP. XII

had been at all aware to what an extent he was answerable for the policy which had brought so much obloquy on the government. The King, stern as he was, had far too great a heart to treat an error as a crime. He had just appointed the unfortunate young man Secretary at War; and the commission was actually preparing. It is not improbable that the cold magnanimity of the master was the very thing which made the remorse of the servant insupportable.*

Factions at Dublin Castle.

But, great as were the vexations which William had to undergo, those by which the temper of his father-in-law was at this time tried were greater still. No court in Europe was distracted by more quarrels and intrigues than were to be found within the walls of Dublin Castle. The numerous petty cabals which sprang from the cupidity, the jealousy, and the malevolence of individuals scarcely deserve mention. But there was one cause of discord which has been too little noticed, and which is the key to much that has been thought mysterious in the history of those times,

Between English Jacobitism and Irish Jacobitism there was nothing in common. The English Jacobite was animated by a strong enthusiasm for the family of Stuart; and in his zeal for the interests of that family he too often forgot the interests of the state. Victory, peace, prosperity, seemed evils to the stanch nonjuror of our island, if they tended to make usurpation popular and permanent. Defeat, bankruptcy, famine, invasion, were, in his view, public blessings, if they increased the chance of a restoration. He would rather have seen his country the last of the nations under James the Second or James the Third, than the mistress of the sea, the umpire between contending potentates, the seat of arts, the hive of industry, under a Prince of the House of Nassau or of Brunswick.

The sentiments of the Irish Jacobite were very different, and, it must in candour be acknowledged, were of a nobler character. The fallen dynasty was nothing to him. He had not, like a Cheshire or Shropshire cavalier, been taught from his cradle to consider loyalty to that dynasty as the first duty of a Christian and a gentleman. All his family traditions, all

---

* Clarendon's Diary; Reresby's Memoirs; Luttrell's Diary. I have followed Luttrell's version of Temple's last words. It agrees in substance with Clarendon's, but has more of the abruptness natural on such an occasion. If anything could make so tragical an event ridiculous, it would be the lamentation of the author of the Lansderiad.

"The wretched youth against his friend exclaims,
And in despair drowns himself in the Thames."

the lessons taught him by his foster mother and by his priests, had been of a very different tendency. He had been brought up to regard the foreign sovereigns of his native land with the feeling with which the Jew regarded Cæsar, with which the Scot regarded Edward the First, with which the Castilian regarded Joseph Bonaparte, with which the Pole regards the Autocrat of the Russias. It was the boast of the highborn Milesian that, from the twelfth century to the seventeenth, every generation of his family had been in arms against the English crown. His remote ancestors had contended with Fitzstephen and De Burgh. His greatgrandfather had cloven down the soldiers of Elizabeth in the battle of the Blackwater. His grandfather had conspired with O'Donnel against James the First. His father had fought under Sir Phelim O'Neil against Charles the First. The confiscation of the family estate had been ratified by an Act of Charles the Second. No Puritan, who had been cited before the High Commission by Laud, who had charged by the side of Cromwell at Naseby, who had been prosecuted under the Conventicle Act, and who had been in hiding on account of the Rye House plot, bore less affection to the House of Stuart than the O'Haras and Macmahons, on whose support the fortunes of that House now seemed to depend.

The fixed purpose of these men was to break the foreign yoke, to exterminate the Saxon colony, to sweep away the Protestant Church, and to restore the soil to its ancient proprietors. To obtain these ends they would without the smallest scruple have risen up against James; and to obtain these ends they rose up for him. The Irish Jacobites, therefore, were not at all desirous that he should again reign at Whitehall: for they were perfectly aware that a Sovereign of Ireland, who was also Sovereign of England, would not, and, even if he would, could not, long administer the government of the smaller and poorer kingdom in direct opposition to the feeling of the larger and richer. Their real wish was that the crowns might be completely separated, and that their island might, whether with James or without James they cared little, form a distinct state under the powerful protection of France.

While one party in the Council at Dublin regarded James merely as a tool to be employed for achieving the deliverance of Ireland, another party regarded Ireland merely as a tool to be employed for effecting the restoration of James. To the

English and Scotch lords and gentlemen who had accompanied him from Brest, the island in which they now sojourned was merely a stepping stone by which they were to reach Great Britain. They were still as much exiles as when they were at Saint Germains; and indeed they thought Saint Germains a far more pleasant place of exile than Dublin Castle. They had no sympathy with the native population of the remote and half barbarous region to which a strange chance had led them. Nay, they were bound by common extraction and by common language to that colony which it was the chief object of the native population to root out. They had indeed, like the great body of their countrymen, always regarded the aboriginal Irish with very unjust contempt, as inferior to other European nations, not only in acquired knowledge, but in natural intelligence and courage, as born Gibeonites who had been literally treated in being permitted to hew wood and to draw water for a wiser and mightier people. These politicians also thought,—and here they were undoubtedly in the right,—that, if their master's object was to recover the throne of England, it would be madness in him to give himself up to the guidance of the O's and the Macs who regarded England with mortal enmity. A law declaring the crown of Ireland independent, a law transferring mitres, glebes, and tithes from the Protestant to the Roman Catholic Church, a law transferring ten millions of acres from Saxons to Celts, would doubtless be loudly applauded in Clare and Tipperary. But what would be the effect of such laws at Westminster? What at Oxford? It would be poor policy to alienate such men as Clarendon and Beaufort, Ken and Sherlock, in order to obtain the applause of the Rapparees of the Bog of Allen.*

Thus the English and Irish factions in the Council at Dublin were engaged in a dispute which admitted of no compromise. Avaux meanwhile looked on that dispute from a point of view entirely his own. His object was neither the emancipation of Ireland nor the restoration of James, but the greatness of the French monarchy. In what way that object might be best attained was a very complicated problem. Undoubtedly a French statesman could not but wish for a counterrevolution in England. The effect of such a counterrevolution would be that the power which was the most for-

* Much light is thrown on the dispute between the English and Irish parties in James's council, by a remarkable letter of Bishop Maloney to Bishop Tyrrel, which will be found in the Appendix to King's State of the Protestants.

midable enemy of France would become her firmest ally, that William would sink into insignificance, and that the European coalition of which he was the chief would be dissolved. But what chance was there of such a counterrevolution? The English exiles indeed, after the fashion of exiles, confidently anticipated a speedy return to their country. James himself loudly boasted that his subjects on the other side of the water, though they had been misled for a moment by the specious names of religion, liberty, and property, were warmly attached to him, and would rally round him as soon as he appeared among them. But the wary envoy tried in vain to discover any foundation for these hopes. He could not find that they were warranted by any intelligence which had arrived from any part of Great Britain; and he was inclined to consider them as the mere daydreams of a feeble mind. He thought it unlikely that the usurper, whose ability and resolution he had, during an unintermitted conflict of ten years, learned to appreciate, would easily part with the great prize which had been won by such strenuous exertions and profound combinations. It was therefore necessary to consider what arrangements would be most beneficial to France, on the supposition that it proved impossible to dislodge William from England. And it was evident that, if William could not be dislodged from England, the arrangement most beneficial to France would be that which had been contemplated eighteen months before when James had no prospect of a male heir. Ireland must be severed from the English crown, purged of the English colonists, reunited to the Church of Rome, placed under the protection of the House of Bourbon, and made, in everything but name, a French province. In war, her resources would be absolutely at the command of her Lord Paramount. She would furnish his army with recruits. She would furnish his navy with fine harbours commanding all the great-western outlets of the English trade. The strong national and religious antipathy with which her aboriginal population regarded the inhabitants of the neighbouring island would be a sufficient guarantee for their fidelity to that government which could alone protect her against the Saxon.

On the whole, therefore, it appeared to Avaux that, of the two parties into which the Council at Dublin was divided, the Irish party was that which it was at present for the interest of France to support. He accordingly connected himself closely with the chiefs of that party, obtained from them the fullest avowals of all that they designed, and was soon able to report to his government that neither the gentry nor the common people were at all unwilling to become French.*

The views of Louvois, incomparably the greatest statesman that France had produced since Richelieu, seem to have entirely agreed with those of Avaux. The best thing, Louvois wrote, that King James could do would be to forget that he had reigned in Great Britain, and to think only of putting Ireland into a good condition, and of establishing himself firmly there. Whether this were the true interest of the House of Stuart may be doubted. But it was undoubtedly the true interest of the House of Bourbon.†

About the Scotch and English exiles, and especially about Melfort, Avaux constantly expressed himself with an asperity hardly to have been expected from a man of so much sense and so much knowledge of the world. Melfort was in a singularly unfortunate position. He was a renegade: he was a mortal enemy of the liberties of his country: he was of a bad and tyrannical nature; and yet he was, in some sense, a patriot. The consequence was that he was more universally detested than any man of his time. For, while his apostasy and his arbitrary maxims of government made him the abhorrence of England and Scotland, his anxiety for the dignity and integrity of the empire made him the abhorrence of the Irish and of the French.

The first question to be decided was whether James should remain at Dublin, or should put himself at the head of his army in Ulster. On this question the Irish and British factions joined battle. Reasons of no great weight were adduced on both sides; for neither party ventured to speak out. The point really in issue was whether the King should be in Irish or in British hands. If he remained at Dublin, it would be scarcely possible for him to withhold his assent from any bill presented to him by the Parliament which he had summoned to meet there. He would be forced to plunder, perhaps to attaint, innocent Protestant gentlemen and clergymen by hundreds; and he would thus do irreparable mischief to his

---

* Avaux, March 25/April 4, 1689, April 13/23. But it is less from any single letter, than from the whole tendency and spirit of the correspondence of Avaux, that I have formed my notion of his objects.

† "Il faut donc, oubliant qu'il a été Roy d'Angleterre et d'Ecosse, ne penser qu'à ce qui peut Loniser l'Irlande, et luy faciliter les moyens d'y subsister."— Louvois to Avaux, June 7/17, 1689.

cause on the other side of Saint George's Channel. If he repaired to Ulster, he would be within a few hours' sail of Great Britain. As soon as Londonderry had fallen, and it was universally supposed that the fall of Londonderry could not be long delayed, he might cross the sea with part of his forces, and land in Scotland, where his friends were supposed to be numerous. When he was once on British ground, and in the midst of British adherents, it would no longer be in the power of the Irish to extort his consent to their schemes of spoliation and revenge.

The discussions in the Council were long and warm. Tyrconnel, who had just been created a Duke, advised his master to stay at Dublin. Melfort exhorted His Majesty to set out for Ulster. Avaux exerted all his influence in support of Tyrconnel; but James, whose personal inclinations were naturally on the British side of the question, determined to follow the advice of Melfort.* Avaux was deeply mortified. In his official letters he expressed with great acrimony his contempt for the King's character and understanding. On Tyrconnel, who had said that he despaired of the fortunes of James, and that the real question was between the King of France and the Prince of Orange, the ambassador pronounced what was meant to be a warm eulogy, but may perhaps be more properly called an invective. "If he were a born Frenchman, he could not be more zealous for the interests of France."† The conduct of Melfort, on the other hand, was the subject of an invective which much resembles eulogy: "He is neither a good Irishman nor a good Frenchman. All his affections are set on his own country."‡

Since the King was determined to go northward, Avaux did not choose to be left behind. The royal party set out, leaving Tyrconnel in charge at Dublin, and arrived at Charlemont on the thirteenth of April. The journey was a strange one. The country all along the road had been completely deserted by the industrious population, and laid waste by bands of robbers. "This," said one of the French officers, "is like travelling through the deserts of Arabia."§ Whatever effects the colonists had been able to remove were at Londonderry or Enniskillen. The rest had been stolen or destroyed. Avaux informed his Court that he had not been

CHAP. XII.

James determines to go to Ulster.

Journey of James to Ulster.

---

* See the despatches written by Avaux during April 1689; Light to the Blind.
† Avaux, April 6/16, 1689.
‡ Avaux, May 2/12, 1689.
§ Pusignan to Avaux, March 30/April 9, 1689.

able to get one truss of hay for his horses without sending five or six miles. No labourer dared bring anything for sale lest some marauder should lay hands on it by the way. The ambassador was put one night into a miserable taproom full of soldiers smoking, another night into a dismantled house without windows or shutters to keep out the rain. At Charlemont, a bag of oatmeal was, with great difficulty, and as a matter of favour, procured for the French legation. There was no wheaten bread except at the table of the King, who had brought a little flour from Dublin, and to whom Avaux had lent a servant who knew how to bake. Those who were honoured with an invitation to the royal table had their bread and wine measured out to them. Everybody else, however high in rank, ate horsecorn, and drank water or detestable beer, made with oats instead of barley, and flavoured with some nameless herb as a substitute for hops.* Yet report said that the country between Charlemont and Strabane was even more desolate than the country between Dublin and Charlemont. It was impossible to carry a large stock of provisions. The roads were so bad, and the horses so weak, that the baggage waggons had all been left far behind. The chief officers of the army were consequently in want of necessaries; and the ill humour which was the natural effect of these privations was increased by the insensibility of James, who seemed not to be aware that everybody about him was not perfectly comfortable.†

On the fourteenth of April the King and his train proceeded to Omagh. The rain fell: the wind blew: the horses could scarcely make their way through the mud, and in the face of the storm; and the road was frequently intersected by torrents which might almost be called rivers. The travellers had to pass several fords where the water was breast high. Some of the party fainted from fatigue and hunger. All around lay a frightful wilderness. In a journey of forty miles Avaux counted only three miserable cabins. Everything else was rock, bog, and moor. When at length the travellers reached Omagh, they found it in ruins. The Protestants, who were the majority of the inhabitants, had abandoned it, leaving not a wisp of straw nor a cask of liquor. The windows had been broken: the chimneys had

* This lamentable account of the Irish beer is taken from a despatch which Desgrigny wrote from Cork to Louvois, and which is in the archives of the French War Office.   † Avaux, April 11. 1689; April 12.

been beaten in: the very locks and bolts of the doors had been carried away.*

Avaux had never ceased to press the King to return to Dublin: but these expostulations had hitherto produced no effect. The obstinacy of James, however, was an obstinacy which had nothing in common with manly resolution, and which, though proof to argument, was easily shaken by caprice. He received at Omagh, early on the sixteenth of April, letters which alarmed him. He learned that a strong body of Protestants was in arms at Strabane, and that English ships of war had been seen near the mouth of Lough Foyle. In one minute three messages were sent to summon Avaux to the ruinous chamber in which the royal bed had been prepared. There James, half dressed, and with the air of a man bewildered by some great shock, announced his resolution to hasten back instantly to Dublin. Avaux listened, wondered, and approved. Melfort seemed prostrated by despair. The travellers retraced their steps, and, late in the evening, got back to Charlemont. There the King received despatches very different from those which had terrified him a few hours before. The Protestants who had assembled near Strabane had been attacked by Hamilton. Under a truehearted leader they would doubtless have stood their ground. But Lundy, who commanded them, had told them that all was lost, had ordered them to shift for themselves, and had set them the example of flight.† They had accordingly retired in confusion to Londonderry. The King's correspondents pronounced it to be impossible that Londonderry should hold out. His Majesty had only to appear before the gates; and they would instantly fly open. James now changed his mind again, blamed himself for having been persuaded to turn his face southward, and, though it was late in the evening, called for his horses. The horses were in miserable plight; but, weary and half starved as they were, they were saddled. Melfort, completely victorious, carried off his master to the camp. Avaux, after remonstrating to no purpose, declared that he was resolved to return to Dublin. It may be suspected that the extreme discomfort which he had undergone had something to do with this resolution. For complaints of that discomfort make up a

* Avaux to Lewis, April 16. 1689, and to Louvois, of the same date.   † Commons' Journals, Aug. 12. 1689. Mackenzie's Narrative.

CHAP. XII.

large part of his letters; and, in truth, a life passed in the palaces of Italy, in the neat parlours and gardens of Holland, and in the luxurious pavilions which adorned the suburbs of Paris, was a bad preparation for the ruined hovels of Ulster. He gave, however, to his master a more weighty reason for refusing to proceed northward. The journey of James had been undertaken in opposition to the unanimous sense of the Irish, and had excited great alarm among them. They apprehended that he meant to quit them, and to make a descent on Scotland. They knew that, once landed in Great Britain, he would have neither the will nor the power to do those things which they most desired. Avaux, by refusing to proceed further, gave them an assurance that, whoever might betray them, France would be their constant friend.*

While Avaux was on his way to Dublin, James hastened towards Londonderry. He found his army concentrated a few miles south of the city. The French generals who had sailed with him from Brest were in his train; and two of them, Rosen and Maumont, were placed over the head of Richard Hamilton.† Rosen was a native of Livonia, who had in early youth become a soldier of fortune, who had fought his way to distinction, and who, though utterly destitute of the graces and accomplishments characteristic of the court of Versailles, was nevertheless high in favour there. His temper was savage: his manners were coarse: his language was a strange jargon compounded of various dialects of French and German. Even those who thought best of him, and who maintained that his rough exterior covered some good qualities, owned that his looks were against him, and that it would be unpleasant to meet such a figure in the dusk at the corner of a wood.‡ The little that is known of Maumont is to his honour.

The fall of Londonderry expected.

In the camp it was generally expected that Londonderry would fall without a blow. Rosen confidently predicted that the mere sight of the Irish army would terrify the garrison into submission. But Richard Hamilton, who knew the temper of the colonists better, had misgivings. The assail-

* Avaux, April 14. 1689. The story of these strange changes of purpose is told very disingenuously by James in his Life, ii. 320, 331, 322. Orig. Mem.
† Life of James, ii. 334, 335. Orig. Mem.
‡ Memoirs of Saint Simon.

English writers ignorantly speak of Rosen as having been, at this time, a Marshal of France. He did not become so till 1703. He had long been a Maréchal de Camp, which is a very different thing, and had been recently promoted to the rank of Lieutenant General. Same

ants were sure of one important ally within the walls. Lundy, the Governor, professed the Protestant religion, and had joined in proclaiming William and Mary; but he was in secret communication with the enemies of his Church and of the Sovereigns to whom he had sworn fealty. Some have suspected that he was a concealed Jacobite, and that he had affected to acquiesce in the Revolution only in order that he might be better able to assist in bringing about a Restoration: but it is probable that his conduct is rather to be attributed to faintheartedness and poverty of spirit than to zeal for any public cause. He seems to have thought resistance hopeless; and in truth, to a military eye, the defences of Londonderry appeared contemptible. The fortifications consisted of a simple wall overgrown with grass and weeds: there was no ditch even before the gates: the drawbridges had long been neglected: the chains were rusty and could scarcely be used: the parapets and towers were built after a fashion that might well move disciples of Vauban to laughter; and these feeble defences were on almost every side commanded by heights. Indeed those who laid out the city had never meant that it should be able to stand a regular siege, and had contented themselves with throwing up works sufficient to protect the inhabitants against a tumultuary attack of the Celtic peasantry. Avaux assured Louvois that a single French battalion would easily storm such a fastness. Even if the place should, notwithstanding all disadvantages, be able to repel a large army directed by the science and experience of generals who had served under Condé and Turenne, hunger must soon bring the contest to an end. The stock of provisions was small; and the population had been swollen to seven or eight times the ordinary number by a multitude of colonists flying from the rage of the natives.*

Lundy, therefore, from the time when the Irish army entered Ulster, seems to have given up all thought of serious resistance. He talked so despondingly that the citizens and his own soldiers murmured against him. He seemed, they said, to be bent on discouraging them. Meanwhile the enemy drew daily nearer and nearer; and it was known that James himself was coming to take the command of his forces.

* Avaux, April 4. 1689. Among the MSS. in the British Museum is a curious report on the defences of Londonderry, drawn up in 1705 for the Duke of Ormond by a French engineer named Thomas.

CHAP. XII.

Succours arrive from England.

Just at this moment a glimpse of hope appeared. On the fourteenth of April ships from England anchored in the bay. They had on board two regiments which had been sent, under the command of a Colonel named Cunningham, to reinforce the garrison. Cunningham and several of his officers went on shore and conferred with Lundy. Lundy dissuaded them from landing their men. The place, he said, could not hold out. To throw more troops into it would therefore be worse than useless: for the more numerous the garrison, the more prisoners would fall into the hands of the enemy. The best thing that the two regiments could do would be to sail back to England. He meant, he said, to withdraw himself privately; and the inhabitants must then try to make good terms for themselves.

Treachery of Lundy.

He went through the form of holding a council of war, but from this council he excluded all those officers of the garrison whose sentiments he knew to be different from his own. Some who had ordinarily been summoned on such occasions, and who now came uninvited, were thrust out of the room. Whatever the Governor said was echoed by his creatures. Cunningham and Cunningham's companions could scarcely venture to oppose their opinion to that of a person whose local knowledge was necessarily far superior to theirs, and whom they were by their instructions directed to obey. One brave soldier murmured. "Understand this," he said: "to give up Londonderry is to give up Ireland." But his objections were contemptuously overruled.* The meeting broke up. Cunningham and his officers returned to the ships, and made preparations for departing. Meanwhile Lundy privately sent a messenger to the head quarters of the enemy, with assurances that the city should be peaceably surrendered on the first summons.

The inhabitants of Londonderry resolve to defend themselves.

But as soon as what had passed in the council of war was whispered about the streets, the spirit of the soldiers and citizens swelled up high and fierce against the dastardly and perfidious chief who had betrayed them. Many of his own officers declared that they no longer thought themselves bound to obey him. Voices were heard threatening, some that his brains should be blown out, some that he should be hanged on the walls. A deputation was sent to Cunningham imploring him to assume the command. He excused himself on the plausible ground that his orders were to take direc-

* Commons' Journals, August 12. 1689.

tions in all things from the Governor.* Meanwhile it was rumoured that the persons most in Lundy's confidence were stealing out of the town one by one. Long after dusk on the evening of the seventeenth it was found that the gates were open and that the keys had disappeared. The officers who made the discovery took on themselves to change the passwords and to double the guards. The night, however, passed over without any assault.†

After some anxious hours the day broke. The Irish, with James at their head, were now within four miles of the city. A tumultuous council of the chief inhabitants was called. Some of them vehemently reproached the Governor to his face with his treachery. He had sold them, they cried, to their deadliest enemy: he had refused admission to the force which good King William had sent to defend them. While the altercation was at the height, the sentinels who paced the ramparts announced that the vanguard of the hostile army was in sight. Lundy had given orders that there should be no firing: but his authority was at an end. Two gallant soldiers, Major Henry Baker and Captain Adam Murray, called the people to arms. They were assisted by the eloquence of an aged clergyman, George Walker, rector of the parish of Donaghmore, who had, with many of his neighbours, taken refuge in Londonderry. The whole crowded city was moved by one impulse. Soldiers, gentlemen, yeomen, artisans, rushed to the walls and manned the guns. James, who, confident of success, had approached within a hundred yards of the southern gate, was received with a shout of "No surrender," and with a fire from the nearest bastion. An officer of his staff fell dead by his side. The King and his attendants made all haste to get out of reach of the cannon balls. Lundy, who was now in imminent danger of being torn limb from limb by those whom he had betrayed, hid himself in an inner chamber. There he lay during the day, and, with the generous and politic connivance of Murray and Walker, made his escape at night in the disguise of a porter.‡ The part of the wall from which he let himself down is still pointed out; and people still living talk of having tasted the fruit of a pear tree which assisted him in his descent. His name is, to this

---

* The best history of these transactions will be found in the Journals of the House of Commons, August 12, 1689. See also the narratives of Walker and Mackenzie. † Mackenzie's Narrative. ‡ Walker and Mackenzie.

CHAP. XII.

Their character.

day, held in execration by the Protestants of the North of Ireland; and his effigy is still annually hung and burned by them with marks of abhorrence similar to those which in England are appropriated to Guy Faux.

And now Londonderry was left destitute of all military and of all civil government. No man in the town had a right to command any other: the defences were weak: the provisions were scanty: an incensed tyrant and a great army were at the gates. But within was that which has often, in desperate extremities, retrieved the fallen fortunes of nations. Betrayed, deserted, disorganised, unprovided with resources, begirt with enemies, the noble city was still no easy conquest. Whatever an engineer might think of the strength of the ramparts, all that was most intelligent, most courageous, most highspirited among the Englishry of Leinster and of Northern Ulster was crowded behind them. The number of men capable of bearing arms within the walls was seven thousand; and the whole world could not have furnished seven thousand men better qualified to meet a terrible emergency with clear judgment, dauntless valour, and stubborn patience. They were all zealous Protestants; and the Protestantism of the majority was tinged with Puritanism. They had much in common with that sober, resolute, and Godfearing class out of which Cromwell had formed his unconquerable army. But the peculiar situation in which they had been placed had developed in them some qualities which, in the mother country, might possibly have remained latent. The English inhabitants of Ireland were an aristocratic caste, which had been enabled, by superior civilisation, by close union, by sleepless vigilance, by cool intrepidity, to keep in subjection a numerous and hostile population. Almost every one of them had been in some measure trained both to military and to political functions. Almost every one was familiar with the use of arms, and was accustomed to bear a part in the administration of justice. It was remarked by contemporary writers that the colonists had something of the Castilian haughtiness of manner, though none of the Castilian indolence, that they spoke English with remarkable purity and correctness, and that they were, both as militiamen and as jurymen, superior to their kindred in the mother country.* In all ages, men situated as the

* See the Character of the Protestants of Ireland, 1689, and the Interest of England in the Preservation of Ireland, 1689. The former pamphlet is the work of an enemy, the latter of a zealous friend.

Anglosaxons in Ireland were situated have had peculiar vices and peculiar virtues, the vices and virtues of masters, as opposed to the vices and virtues of slaves. The member of a dominant race is, in his dealings with the subject race, seldom indeed fraudulent,—for fraud is the resource of the weak,—but imperious, insolent, and cruel. Towards his brethren, on the other hand, his conduct is generally just, kind, and even noble. His selfrespect leads him to respect all who belong to his own order. His interest impels him to cultivate a good understanding with those whose prompt, strenuous, and courageous assistance may at any moment be necessary to preserve his property and life. It is a truth ever present to his mind that his own wellbeing depends on the ascendency of the class to which he belongs. His very selfishness therefore is sublimed into public spirit: and this public spirit is stimulated to fierce enthusiasm by sympathy, by the desire of applause, and by the dread of infamy. For the only opinion which he values is the opinion of his fellows; and in their opinion devotion to the common cause is the most sacred of duties. The character, thus formed, has two aspects. Seen on one side, it must be regarded by every well constituted mind with disapprobation. Seen on the other, it irresistibly extorts applause. The Spartan, smiting and spurning the wretched Helot, moves our disgust. But the same Spartan, calmly dressing his hair, and uttering his concise jests, on what he well knows to be his last day, in the pass of Thermopylæ, is not to be contemplated without admiration. To a superficial observer it may seem strange that so much evil and so much good should be found together. But in truth the good and the evil, which at first sight appear almost incompatible, are closely connected, and have a common origin. It was because the Spartan had been taught to revere himself as one of a race of sovereigns, and to look down on all that was not Spartan as of an inferior species, that he had no fellow feeling for the miserable serfs who crouched before him, and that the thought of submitting to a foreign master, or of turning his back before an enemy, never, even in the last extremity, crossed his mind. Something of the same character, compounded of tyrant and hero, has been found in all nations which have domineered over more numerous nations. But it has nowhere in modern Europe shown itself so conspicuously as in Ireland. With what contempt, with what antipathy, the ruling minority in that country long regarded the subject majority may be best learned from the hateful laws which, within the memory of men still living, disgraced the Irish statute book. Those laws were at length annulled: but the spirit which had dictated them survived them, and even at this day sometimes breaks out in excesses pernicious to the commonwealth and dishonourable to the Protestant religion. Nevertheless it is impossible to deny that the English colonists have had, with too many of the faults, all the noblest virtues of a sovereign caste. The faults have, as was natural, been most offensively exhibited in times of prosperity and security: the virtues have been most resplendent in times of distress and peril; and never were those virtues more signally displayed than by the defenders of Londonderry, when their Governor had abandoned them, and when the camp of their mortal enemy was pitched before their walls.

No sooner had the first burst of the rage excited by the perfidy of Lundy spent itself than those whom he had betrayed proceeded, with a gravity and prudence worthy of the most renowned senates, to provide for the order and defence of the city. Two governors were elected, Baker and Walker. Baker took the chief military command. Walker's especial business was to preserve internal tranquillity, and to dole out supplies from the magazines.* The inhabitants capable of bearing arms were distributed into eight regiments. Colonels, captains, and subordinate officers were appointed. In a few hours every man knew his post, and was ready to repair to it as soon as the beat of the drum was heard. That machinery, by which Oliver had, in the preceding generation, kept up among his soldiers so stern and so pertinacious an enthusiasm, was again employed with not less complete success. Preaching and praying occupied a large part of every day. Eighteen clergymen of the Established Church and seven or eight nonconformist ministers were within the walls. They all exerted themselves indefatigably to rouse and sustain the spirit of the people. Among themselves there was for the time entire harmony. All disputes about church government, postures, ceremonies, were forgotten. The Bishop, having found that his lectures on passive obedience were derided even by the Episcopalians, had withdrawn himself, first to Raphoe, and then to England,

* There was afterwards some idle dispute about the question whether Walker was properly Governor or not. To me it seems quite clear that he was so.

and was preaching in a chapel in London.* On the other hand, a Scotch fanatic named Hewson, who had exhorted the Presbyterians not to ally themselves with such as refused to subscribe the Covenant, had sunk under the well merited disgust and scorn of the whole Protestant community.† The aspect of the Cathedral was remarkable. Cannon were planted on the summit of the broad tower which has since given place to a tower of different proportions. Ammunition was stored in the vaults. In the choir the liturgy of the Anglican Church was read every morning. Every afternoon the Dissenters crowded to a simpler worship.‡

James had waited twenty-four hours, expecting, as it should seem, the performance of Lundy's promises; and in twenty-four hours the arrangements for the defence of Londonderry were complete. On the evening of the nineteenth of April, a trumpeter came to the southern gate, and asked whether the engagements into which the Governor had entered would be fulfilled. The answer was that the men who guarded these walls had nothing to do with the Governor's engagements, and were determined to resist to the last.

On the following day a messenger of higher rank was sent, Claude Hamilton, Lord Strabane, one of the few Roman Catholic peers of Ireland. Murray, who had been appointed to the command of one of the eight regiments into which the garrison was distributed, advanced from the gate to meet the flag of truce; and a short conference was held. Strabane had been authorised to make large promises. The citizens should have a free pardon for all that was past if they would submit to their lawful Sovereign. Murray himself should have a colonel's commission, and a thousand pounds in money. "The men of Londonderry," answered Murray, "have done nothing that requires a pardon, and own no Sovereign but King William and Queen Mary. It will not be safe for Your Lordship to stay longer, or to return on the same errand. Let me have the honour of seeing you through the lines."§

* Mackenzie's Narrative; Funeral Sermon on Bishop Hopkins, 1690.
† Walker's True Account, 1689. See also The Apology for the True Account, and the Vindication of the True Account, published in the same year. I have called this man by the name by which he was known in Ireland. But his real name was Houston. He is frequently mentioned in the strange volume entitled Faithful Contendings Displayed.
‡ A View of the Danger and Folly of being publicspirited, by William Hamill, 1721.
§ See Walker's True Account and Mackenzie's Narrative.

CHAP. XII.

James had been assured, and had fully expected, that the city would yield as soon as it was known that he was before the walls. Finding himself mistaken, he broke loose from the control of Melfort, and determined to return instantly to Dublin. Rosen accompanied the King. The direction of the siege was entrusted to Maumont. Richard Hamilton was second, and Pusignan third, in command.

Londonderry besieged.

The operations now commenced in earnest. The besiegers began by battering the town. It was soon on fire in several places. Roofs and upper stories of houses fell in, and crushed the inmates. During a short time the garrison, many of whom had never before seen the effect of a cannonade, seemed to be discomposed by the crash of chimneys, and by the heaps of ruin mingled with disfigured corpses. But familiarity with danger and horror produced in a few hours the natural effect. The spirit of the people rose so high that their chiefs thought it safe to act on the offensive. On the twenty-first of April a sally was made under the command of Murray. The Irish stood their ground resolutely; and a furious and bloody contest took place. Maumont, at the head of a body of cavalry, flew to the place where the fight was raging. He was struck in the head by a musket ball, and fell a corpse. The besiegers lost several other officers, and about two hundred men, before the colonists could be driven in. Murray escaped with difficulty. His horse was killed under him; and he was beset by enemies: but he was able to defend himself till some of his friends made a rush from the gate to his rescue, with old Walker at their head.*

In consequence of the death of Maumont, Richard Hamilton was once more commander of the Irish army. His exploits in that post did not raise his reputation. He was a fine gentleman and a brave soldier; but he had no pretensions to the character of a great general, and had never, in his life, seen a siege.† Pusignan had more science and energy. But Pusig-

* Walker; Mackenzie; Avaux, April 28/May 8, 1689. There is a tradition among the Protestants of Ulster that Maumont fell by the sword of Murray; but on this point the report made by the French ambassador to his master is decisive. The truth is that there are almost as many mythical stories about the siege of Londonderry as about the siege of Troy. The legend about Murray and Maumont dates from 1689. In the Royal Voyage, which was acted in that year, the combat between the heroes is described in these sonorous lines—

" They met; and Monsieur at the first encounter
Fell dead, blaspheming, on the dusty plain,
And dying, bit the ground."

† "Si c'est celuy qui est sorti de France le dernier, qui s'appelloit Richard, il n'a jamais veu de siège, ayant toujours servi en Rousillon."—Louvois to Avaux, June 14/24. 1689.

man survived Maumont little more than a fortnight. At four in the morning of the sixth of May, the garrison made another sally, took several flags, and killed many of the besiegers. Pusignan, fighting gallantly, was shot through the body. The wound was one which a skilful surgeon might have cured: but there was no such surgeon in the Irish camp, and the communication with Dublin was slow and irregular. The poor Frenchman died, complaining bitterly of the barbarous ignorance and negligence which had shortened his days. A medical man, who had been sent down express from the capital, arrived after the funeral. James, in consequence, as it should seem, of this disaster, established a daily post between Dublin Castle and Hamilton's head quarters. Even by this conveyance letters did not travel very expeditiously: for the couriers went on foot, and, from fear probably of the Enniskilleners, took a circuitous route from military post to military post.*

May passed away; June arrived; and still Londonderry held out. There had been many sallies and skirmishes with various success: but, on the whole, the advantage had been with the garrison. Several officers of note had been carried prisoners into the city; and two French banners, torn after hard fighting from the besiegers, had been hung as trophies in the chancel of the Cathedral. It seemed that the siege must be turned into a blockade. But before the hope of reducing the town by main force was relinquished, it was determined to make a great effort. The point selected for assault was an outwork called Windmill Hill, which was not far from the southern gate. Religious stimulants were employed to animate the courage of the forlorn hope. Many volunteers bound themselves by oath to make their way into the works or to perish in the attempt. Captain Butler, son of the Lord Mountgarret, undertook to lead the sworn men to the attack. On the walls the colonists were drawn up in three ranks. The office of those who were behind was to load the muskets of those who were in front. The Irish came on boldly and with a fearful uproar, but after long and hard fighting were

* Walker; Mackenzie; Avaux to Louvois, May 4/14, 1689; James to Hamilton, May 14, in the library of the Royal Irish Academy. Louvois wrote to Avaux in great indignation. "La mauvaise conduite que l'on a tenue devant Londonderry a coûté la vie à M. de Maumont et à M. de Pusignan. Il se fast pas que sa Majesté Britannique croye qu'en faisant tuer des officiers generaux comme des soldats, en paisse ne l'en point laisser manquer. Ces sortes de gens sont rares en tout pays, et doivent estre menagez."

driven back. The women of Londonderry were seen amidst the thickest fire serving out water and ammunition to their husbands and brothers. In one place, where the wall was only seven feet high, Butler and some of his sworn men succeeded in reaching the top; but they were all killed or made prisoners. At length, after four hundred of the Irish had fallen, their chiefs ordered a retreat to be sounded.*

The siege turned into a blockade.

Nothing was left but to try the effect of hunger. It was known that the stock of food in the city was but slender. Indeed it was thought strange that the supplies should have held out so long. Every precaution was now taken against the introduction of provisions. All the avenues leading to the city by land were closely guarded. On the south were encamped, along the left bank of the Foyle, the horsemen who had followed Lord Galmoy from the valley of the Barrow. Their chief was of all the Irish captains the most dreaded and the most abhorred by the Protestants. For he had disciplined his men with rare skill and care; and many frightful stories were told of his barbarity and perfidy. Long lines of tents, occupied by the infantry of Butler and O'Neil, of Lord Slane and Lord Gormanstown, by Nugent's Westmeath men, by Eustace's Kildare men, and by Cavanagh's Kerry men, extended northward till they again approached the water side.† The river was fringed with forts and batteries, which no vessel could pass without great peril. After some time it was determined to make the security still more complete by throwing a barricade across the stream, about a mile and a half below the city. Several boats full of stones were sunk. A row of stakes was driven into the bottom of the river. Large pieces of fir wood, strongly bound together, formed a boom which was more than a quarter of a mile in length, and which was firmly fastened to both shores by cables a foot thick.‡ A huge stone, to which the cable on the left bank was attached, was removed many years later, for the

---

* Walker; Mackenzie; Avaux, June 12. 1689.

† As to the discipline of Galmoy's Horse, see the letter of Avaux to Louvois, dated Sept. 12. Horrible stories of the cruelty, both of the colonel and of his men, are told in the Short View, by a Clergyman, printed in 1689, and in several other pamphlets of that year. For the distribution of the Irish forces, see the contemporary maps of the siege. A catalogue of the regiments, meant, I suppose, to rival the catalogue in the Second Book of the Iliad, will be found in the Londeriad.

‡ Life of Admiral Sir John Leake, by Stephen M. Leake, Clarencieux King at Arms, 1750. Of this book only ** copies were printed.

purpose of being polished and shaped into a column. But the intention was abandoned, and the rugged mass still lies, not many yards from its original site, amidst the shades which surround a pleasant country house named Boom Hall. Hard by is a well from which the besiegers drank. A little further off is a burial ground where they laid their slain, and where even in our own time the spade of the gardener has struck upon many skulls and thighbones at a short distance beneath the turf and flowers.

While these things were passing in the North, James was holding his court at Dublin. On his return thither from Londonderry he received intelligence that the French fleet, commanded by the Count of Chateau Renaud, had anchored in Bantry Bay, and had put on shore a large quantity of military stores and a supply of money. Herbert, who had just been sent to those seas with an English squadron for the purpose of intercepting the communications between Britanny and Ireland, learned where the enemy lay, and sailed into the bay with the intention of giving battle. But the wind was unfavourable to him: his force was greatly inferior to that which was opposed to him; and, after some firing, which caused no serious loss to either side, he thought it prudent to stand out to sea, while the French retired into the recesses of the harbour. He steered for Scilly, where he expected to find reinforcements; and Chateau Renaud, content with the credit which he had acquired, and afraid of losing it if he staid, hastened back to Brest, though earnestly entreated by James to come round to Dublin.

Both sides claimed the victory. The Commons at Westminster absurdly passed a vote of thanks to Herbert. James, not less absurdly, ordered bonfires to be lighted, and a Te Deum to be sung. But these marks of joy by no means satisfied Avaux, whose national vanity was too strong even for his characteristic prudence and politeness. He complained that James was so unjust and ungrateful as to attribute the result of the late action to the reluctance with which the English seamen fought against their rightful King and their old commander, and that His Majesty did not seem to be well pleased by being told that they were flying over the ocean pursued by the triumphant French. Dover, too, was a bad Frenchman. He seemed to take no pleasure in the defeat of his countrymen, and had been heard to say

CHAP. XII.

Naval skirmish in Bantry Bay.

that the affair in Bantry Bay did not deserve to be called a battle.*

On the day after the Te Deum had been sung at Dublin for this indecisive skirmish, the Parliament convoked by James assembled. The number of temporal peers of Ireland, when he arrived in that kingdom, was about a hundred. Of these only fourteen obeyed his summons. Of the fourteen, ten were Roman Catholics. By the reversing of old attainders, and by new creations, seventeen more Lords, all Roman Catholics, were introduced into the Upper House. The Protestant Bishops of Meath, Ossory, Cork, and Limerick, whether from a sincere conviction that they could not lawfully withhold their obedience even from a tyrant, or from a vain hope that the heart even of a tyrant might be softened by their patience, made their appearance in the midst of their mortal enemies.

The House of Commons consisted almost exclusively of Irishmen and Papists. With the writs the returning officers had received from Tyrconnel letters naming the persons whom he wished to see elected. Tho' largest constituent bodies in the kingdom were at this time very small. For scarcely any but Roman Catholics dared to show their faces; and the Roman Catholic freeholders were then very few, not more, it is said, in some counties, than ten or twelve. Even in cities so considerable as Cork, Limerick, and Galway, the number of persons who, under the new Charters, were entitled to vote did not exceed twenty-four. About two hundred and fifty members took their seats. Of these only six were Protestants.† The list of the names sufficiently indicates the religious and political temper of the assembly. Alone among the Irish parliaments of that age, this parliament was filled with Dermots and Geohegans, O'Neils and O'Donovans, Macmahons, Macnamaras, and Macgillicuddies. The lead was taken by a few men whose abilities had been improved by the study of the law, or by experience acquired in foreign countries. The Attorney General, Sir Richard Nagle, who represented the county of Cork, was allowed,

* Avaux, May 9/19 1689; London Gazette, May 9.; Life of James, ii 370.; Burchett's Naval Transactions; Commons' Journals, May 18. 21. From the Memoirs of Madame de la Fayette it appears that this paltry affair was correctly appreciated at Versailles.

† King, iii. 12.; Memoirs of Ireland from the Restoration, 1716. Lists of both Houses will be found in King's Appendix.

even by Protestants, to be an acute and learned jurist. Francis Plowden, the Commissioner of Revenue, who sate for Bannow, and acted as chief minister of finance, was an Englishman, and, as he had been a principal agent of the Order of Jesuits in money matters, must be supposed to have been an excellent man of business.* Colonel Henry Luttrell, member for the county of Carlow, had served long in France, and had brought back to his native Ireland a sharpened intellect and polished manners, a flattering tongue, some skill in war, and much more skill in intrigue. His elder brother, Colonel Simon Luttrell, who was member for the county of Dublin, and military governor of the capital, had also resided in France, and, though inferior to Henry in parts and activity, made a highly distinguished figure among the adherents of James. The other member for the county of Dublin was Colonel Patrick Sarsfield. This gallant officer was regarded by the natives as one of themselves: for his ancestors on the paternal side, though originally English, were among those early colonists who were proverbially said to have become more Irish than Irishmen. His mother was of noble Celtic blood; and he was firmly attached to the old religion. He had inherited an estate of about two thousand a year, and was therefore one of the wealthiest Roman Catholics in the kingdom. His knowledge of courts and camps was such as few of his countrymen possessed. He had long borne a commission in the English Life Guards, had lived much about Whitehall, and had fought bravely under Monmouth on the Continent, and against Monmouth at Sedgemoor. He had, Avaux wrote, more personal influence than any man in Ireland, and was indeed a gentleman of eminent merit, brave, upright, honourable, careful of his men in quarters, and certain to be always found at their head in the day of battle. His intrepidity, his frankness, his boundless good nature, his stature, which far exceeded that of ordinary men, and the strength which he exerted in personal conflict, gained for him the affectionate admiration of the populace. It is remarkable that the Englishry generally respected him as a valiant, skilful, and generous enemy, and that, even in the most ribald farces which were performed by mountebanks in Smithfield, he was always excepted from the

CHAP. XII.

* I found proof of Plowden's connection with the Jesuits in a Treasury Letter book, June 12, 1689.

disgraceful imputations which it was then the fashion to throw on the Irish nation.*

But men like these were rare in the House of Commons which had met at Dublin. It is no reproach to the Irish nation, a nation which has since furnished its full proportion of eloquent and accomplished senators, to say that, of all the parliaments which have met in the British islands, Barebone's parliament not excepted, the assembly convoked by James was the most deficient in all the qualities which a legislature should possess. The stern domination of a hostile class had blighted the faculties of the Irish gentleman. If he was so fortunate as to have lands, he had generally passed his life on them, shooting, fishing, carousing, and making love among his vassals. If his estate had been confiscated, he had wandered about from bawn to bawn and from cabin to cabin, levying small contributions, and living at the expense of other men. He had never sate in the House of Commons: he had never even taken an active part at an election: he had never been a magistrate: scarcely ever had he been on a grand jury. He had therefore absolutely no experience of public affairs. The English squire of that age, though assuredly not a very profound or enlightened politician, was a statesman and a philosopher when compared with the Roman Catholic squire of Munster or Connaught.

The parliaments of Ireland had then no fixed place of assembling. Indeed they met so seldom and broke up so speedily that it would hardly have been worth while to build and furnish a palace for their special use. It was not till the Hanoverian dynasty had been long on the throne, that a senate house which sustains a comparison with the finest compositions of Inigo Jones arose between the College and the Castle. In the seventeenth century there stood, on the spot where the portico and dome of the Four Courts now overlook the Liffey, an ancient building which had once been a convent of Dominican friars, but had, since the Reformation, been appropriated to the use of the legal profession, and

* "Sarsfield," Avaux wrote to Louvois, Oct. 11. 1689, "n'est pas un homme de la naissance de mylord Galloway" (Gislmoy, I suppose) " ny de Makarty: mais c'est un gentilhomme distingué par son mérite, qui a plus de crédit dans ce royaume qu'aucun homme que je connoisse. Il y a de la valeur, mais surtout de l'honneur et de la probité à toute épreuve . . . homme qui sera toujours à la tête de ses troupes, et qui en aura grand soin." Leslie, in his Answer to King, says that the Irish Protestants did justice to Sarsfield's integrity and honour. Indeed justice is done to Sarsfield even in such scurrilous pieces as the Royal Flight.

bore the name of the King's Inns. There accommodation had been provided for the parliament. On the seventh of May, James, dressed in royal robes and wearing a crown, took his seat on the throne in the House of Lords, and ordered the Commons to be summoned to the bar.*

He then expressed his gratitude to the natives of Ireland for having adhered to his cause when the people of his other kingdoms had deserted him. His resolution to abolish all religious disabilities in all his dominions he declared to be unalterable. He invited the houses to take the Act of Settlement into consideration, and to redress the injuries of which the old proprietors of the soil had reason to complain. He concluded by acknowledging in warm terms his obligations to the King of France.†

When the royal speech had been pronounced, the Chancellor directed the Commons to repair to their chamber and to elect a Speaker. They chose the Attorney General Nagle; and the choice was approved by the King.‡

The Commons next passed resolutions expressing warm gratitude both to James and to Lewis. Indeed it was proposed to send a deputation with an address to Avaux; but the Speaker pointed out the gross impropriety of such a step; and, on this occasion, his interference was successful.§ It was seldom however that the House was disposed to listen to reason. The debates were all rant and tumult. Judge Daly, a Roman Catholic, but an honest and able man, could not refrain from lamenting the indecency and folly with which the members of his Church carried on the work of legislation. Those gentlemen, he said, were not a parliament: they were a mere rabble: they resembled nothing so much as the mob of fishermen and market gardeners, who, at Naples, yelled and threw up their caps in honour of Massaniello. It was painful to hear member after member talking wild nonsense about his own losses, and clamouring for an estate, when the lives of all and the independence of their common country were in peril. These words were spoken in private; but some talebearer repeated them to the Commons. A violent storm broke forth. Daly was ordered to attend at the bar; and

---

* Journal of the Parliament in Ireland, 1689. The reader must not imagine that this journal has an official character. It is merely a compilation made by a Protestant pamphleteer, and printed in London.
† Life of James, ii. 355.
‡ Journal of the Parliament in Ireland.
§ Avaux, May 28/7, 1689.

there was little doubt that he would be severely dealt with. But, just when he was at the door, one of the members rushed in, shouting, "Good news: Londonderry is taken." The whole House rose. All the hats were flung into the air. Three loud huzzas were raised. Every heart was softened by the happy tidings. Nobody would hear of punishment at such a moment. The order for Daly's attendance was discharged amidst cries of "No submission: no submission: we pardon him." In a few hours it was known that Londonderry held out as obstinately as ever. This transaction, in itself unimportant, deserves to be recorded, as showing how destitute that House of Commons was of the qualities which ought to be found in the great council of a kingdom. And this assembly, without experience, without gravity, and without temper, was now to legislate on questions which would have tasked to the utmost the capacity of the greatest statesmen.*

A Toleration Act passed.

One Act James induced them to pass which would have been most honourable to him and to them, if there were not abundant proofs that it was meant to be a dead letter. It was an Act purporting to grant entire liberty of conscience to all Christian sects. On this occasion a proclamation was put forth announcing in boastful language to the English people that their rightful King had now signally refuted those slanderers who had accused him of affecting zeal for religious liberty merely in order to serve a turn. If he were at heart inclined to persecution, would he not have persecuted the Irish Protestants? He did not want power. He did not want provocation. Yet at Dublin, where the members of his Church were the majority, as at Westminster, where they were a minority, he had firmly adhered to the principles laid down in his much maligned Declaration of Indulgence.† Unfortunately for him, the same wind which carried his fair professions to England carried thither also evidence that his professions were insincere. A single law, worthy of Turgot or of Franklin, seemed ludicrously out of place in the midst of a crowd of laws which would have disgraced Gardiner or Alva.

* A True Account of the Present State of Ireland, by a Person that with Great Difficulty left Dublin, 1689; Letter from Dublin, dated June 12, 1689; Journal of the Parliament in Ireland.
† Life of James, ii. 361, 362, 363. In the Life it is said that the proclamation was put forth without the privity of James, but that he subsequently approved of it. See Welwood's Answer to the Declaration, 1689.

A necessary preliminary to the vast work of spoliation and slaughter on which the legislators of Dublin were bent, was an Act annulling the authority which the English Parliament, both as the supreme legislature and as the supreme Court of Appeal, had hitherto exercised over Ireland.* This Act was rapidly passed; and then followed, in quick succession, confiscations and proscriptions on a gigantic scale. The personal estates of absentees above the age of seventeen years were transferred to the King. When lay property was thus invaded, it was not likely that the endowments, which had been, in contravention of every sound principle, lavished on the Church of the minority, would be spared. To reduce those endowments, without prejudice to existing interests, would have been a reform worthy of a good prince and of a good parliament. But no such reform would satisfy the vindictive bigots who sate at the King's Inns. By one sweeping Act the greater part of the tithe was transferred from the Protestant to the Roman Catholic clergy; and the existing incumbents were left, without one farthing of compensation, to die of hunger.† A Bill repealing the Act of Settlement and transferring many thousands of square miles from Saxon to Celtic landlords was brought in and carried by acclamation.‡

Of legislation such as this it is impossible to speak too severely: but for the legislators there are excuses which it is the duty of the historian to notice. They acted unmercifully, unjustly, unwisely. But it would be absurd to expect mercy, justice, or wisdom from a class of men first abused by many years of oppression, and then maddened by the joy of a sudden deliverance, and armed with irresistible power. The representatives of the Irish nation were, with few exceptions, rude and ignorant. They had lived in a state of constant irritation. With aristocratical sentiments they had been in a servile position. With the highest pride of blood, they had been exposed to daily affronts, such as might well have roused the choler of the humblest plebeian. In sight of the fields and castles which they regarded as their own, they had been glad to be invited by a peasant to partake of his whey and his potatoes. Those violent emotions of

---

* Light to the Blind; An Act declaring that the Parliament of England cannot bind Ireland against Writs of Error and Appeals, printed in London, 1690.

† An Act concerning Appropriate Tythes and other Duties payable to Ecclesiastical Dignitaries. London, 1690.

‡ An Act for repealing the Acts of Settlement and Explanation, and all Grants, Patents, and Certificates pursuant to them or any of them. London, 1690.

hatred and cupidity which the situation of the native gentleman could scarcely fail to call forth appeared to him under the specious guise of patriotism and piety. For his enemies were the enemies of his nation; and the same tyranny which had robbed him of his patrimony had robbed his Church of vast wealth bestowed on her by the devotion of an earlier age. How was power likely to be used by an uneducated and inexperienced man, agitated by strong desires and resentments which he mistook for sacred duties? And, when two or three hundred such men were brought together in one assembly, what was to be expected but that the passions which each had long nursed in silence would be at once matured into fearful vigour by the influence of sympathy?

Between James and his parliament there was little in common, except hatred of the Protestant religion. He was an Englishman. Superstition had not utterly extinguished all national feeling in his mind; and he could not but be displeased by the malevolence with which his Celtic supporters regarded the race from which he sprang. The range of his intellectual vision was small. Yet it was impossible that, having reigned in England, and looking constantly forward to the day when he should reign in England once more, he should not take a wider view of politics than was taken by men who had no objects out of Ireland. The few Irish Protestants who still adhered to him, and the British nobles, both Protestant and Roman Catholic, who had followed him into exile, implored him to restrain the violence of the rapacious and vindictive senate which he had convoked. They with peculiar earnestness implored him not to consent to the repeal of the Act of Settlement. On what security, they asked, could any man invest his money or give a portion to his children, if he could not rely on positive laws and on the uninterrupted possession of many years? The military adventurers among whom Cromwell portioned out the soil might perhaps be regarded as wrongdoers. But how large a part of their estates had passed, by fair purchase, into other hands! How much money had proprietors borrowed on mortgage, on statute merchant, on statute staple! How many capitalists had, trusting to legislative acts and to royal promises, come over from England, and bought land in Ulster and Leinster, without the least misgiving as to the title! What a sum had those capitalists expended, during a quarter of a century, in building, draining, enclosing, planting! The terms of the compromise which Charles the Second had sanctioned might not be in all respects just. But was one injustice to be redressed by committing another injustice more monstrous still? And what effect was likely to be produced in England by the cry of thousands of innocent English families whom an English king had doomed to ruin? The complaints of such a body of sufferers might delay, might prevent, the Restoration to which all loyal subjects were eagerly looking forward; and, even if His Majesty should, in spite of those complaints, be happily restored, he would to the end of his life feel the pernicious effects of the injustice which evil advisers were now urging him to commit. He would find that, in trying to quiet one set of malecontents, he had created another. As surely as he yielded to the clamour raised at Dublin for a repeal of the Act of Settlement, he would, from the day on which he returned to Westminster, be assailed by as loud and pertinacious a clamour for a repeal of that repeal. He could not but be aware that no English Parliament, however loyal, would permit such laws as were now passing through the Irish parliament to stand. Had he made up his mind to take the part of Ireland against the universal sense of England? If so, to what could he look forward but another banishment and another deposition? Or would he, when he had recovered the greater kingdom, revoke the boons by which, in his distress, he had purchased the help of the smaller? It might seem an insult to him even to suggest that he could harbour the thought of such unprincely, of such unmanly, perfidy. Yet what other course would be left to him? And was it not better for him to refuse unreasonable concessions now than to retract those concessions hereafter in a manner which must bring on him reproaches insupportable to a noble mind? His situation was doubtless embarrassing. Yet in this case, as in other cases, it would be found that the path of justice was the path of wisdom.*

Though James had, in his speech at the opening of the session, declared against the Act of Settlement, he felt that these arguments were unanswerable. He held several conferences with the leading members of the House of Commons, and earnestly recommended moderation. But his exhortations irritated the passions which he wished to allay. Many of the native gentry held high and violent language. It was impudent, they said, to talk about the rights of purchasers.

* See the paper delivered to James King's appendix. Life of James, ii. 357 by Chief Justice Keating, and the speech —361. of the Bishop of Meath. Both are in

CHAP. XII.

How could right spring out of wrong? People who chose to buy property acquired by injustice must take the consequences of their folly and cupidity. It was clear that the Lower House was altogether impracticable. James had, four years before, refused to make the smallest concession to the most obsequious parliament that has ever sat in England; and it might have been expected that the obstinacy, which he had never wanted when it was a vice, would not have failed him now when it would have been a virtue. During a short time he seemed determined to act justly. He even talked of dissolving the parliament. The chiefs of the old Celtic families, on the other hand, said publicly that, if he did not give them back their inheritance, they would not fight for him. His very soldiers railed on him in the streets of Dublin. At length he determined to go down himself to the House of Peers, not in his robes and crown, but in the garb in which he had been used to attend debates at Westminster, and personally to solicit the Lords to put some check on the violence of the Commons. But just as he was getting into his coach for this purpose he was stopped by Avaux. Avaux was as zealous as any Irishman for the bills which the Commons were urging forward. It was enough for him that those bills seemed likely to make the enmity between England and Ireland irreconcileable. His remonstrances induced James to abstain from openly opposing the repeal of the Act of Settlement. Still the unfortunate Prince continued to cherish some faint hope that the law for which the Commons were so zealous would be rejected, or at least modified, by the Peers. Lord Granard, one of the few Protestant noblemen who sate in that parliament, exerted himself strenuously on the side of public faith and sound policy. The King sent him a message of thanks. "We Protestants," said Granard to Powis who brought the message, "are few in number. We can do little. His Majesty should try his influence with the Roman Catholics." "His Majesty," answered Powis with an oath, "dares not say what he thinks." A few days later James met Granard riding towards the parliament house. "Where are you going, my Lord?" said the King. "To enter my protest, Sir," answered Granard, "against the repeal of the Act of Settlement." "You are right," said the King; "but I am fallen into the hands of people who will ram that and much more down my throat." *

* Leslie's Answer to King; Avaux, $\frac{22}{12}$ 1689; Life of James, ii. 359.

James yielded to the will of the Commons: but the unfavourable impression which his short and feeble resistance had made upon them was not to be removed by his submission. They regarded him with profound distrust: they considered him as at heart an Englishman; and not a day passed without some indication of this feeling. They were in no haste to grant him a supply. One party among them planned an address urging him to dismiss Melfort as an enemy of their nation. Another party drew up a bill for deposing all the Protestant Bishops, even the four who were then actually sitting in Parliament. It was not without difficulty that Avaux and Tyrconnel, whose influence in the Lower House far exceeded the King's, could restrain the zeal of the majority.*

It is remarkable that, while the King was losing the confidence and good will of the Irish Commons by faintly defending against them, in one quarter, the institution of property, he was, himself, in another quarter, attacking that institution with a violence, if possible, more reckless than theirs. He soon found that no money came into his Exchequer. The cause was sufficiently obvious. Trade was at an end. Floating capital had been withdrawn in great masses from the island. Of the fixed capital much had been destroyed, and the rest was lying idle. Thousands of those Protestants who were the most industrious and intelligent part of the population had emigrated to England. Thousands had taken refuge in the places which still held out for William and Mary. Of the Roman Catholic peasantry who were in the vigour of life the majority had enlisted in the army or had joined gangs of plunderers. The poverty of the treasury was the necessary effect of the poverty of the country: public prosperity could be restored only by the restoration of private prosperity: and private prosperity could be restored only by years of peace and security. James was absurd enough to imagine that there was a more speedy and efficacious remedy. He could, he conceived, at once extricate himself from his financial difficulties by the simple process of calling a farthing a shilling. The right of coining was undoubtedly a flower of the prerogative: and, in his view, the right of coining included the right of debasing the coin. Pots, pans, knockers of doors, pieces of ordnance which had long been past use, were carried

Base of base money.

* Avaux, [dates illegible] 1689, and [illegible] to the Protestant Bishops who adhered to James. The author of Light to the Blind strongly condemns the indulgence shown

to the mint. In a short time lumps of base metal, nominally worth near a million sterling, intrinsically worth about a sixtieth part of that sum, were in circulation. A royal edict declared these pieces to be legal tender in all cases whatever. A mortgage for a thousand pounds was cleared off by a bag of counters made out of old kettles. The creditors who complained to the Court of Chancery were told by Fitton to take their money and be gone. But of all classes the tradesmen of Dublin, who were generally Protestants, were the greatest losers. At first, of course, they raised their demands: but the magistrates of the city took on themselves to meet this heretical machination by putting forth a tariff regulating prices. Any man who belonged to the caste now dominant might walk into a shop, lay on the counter a bit of brass worth three pence, and carry off goods to the value of half a guinea. Legal redress was out of the question. Indeed the sufferers thought themselves happy if, by the sacrifice of their stock in trade, they could redeem their limbs and their lives. There was not a baker's shop in the city round which twenty or thirty soldiers were not constantly prowling. Some persons who refused the base money were arrested by troopers and carried before the Provost Marshal, who cursed them, swore at them, locked them up in dark cells, and, by threatening to hang them at their own doors, soon overcame their resistance. Of all the plagues of that time none made a deeper or a more lasting impression on the minds of the Protestants of Dublin than the plague of the brass money.* To the recollection of the confusion and misery which had been produced by James's coin must be in part ascribed the strenuous opposition which, thirty five years later, large classes, firmly attached to the House of Hanover, offered to the government of George the First in the affair of Wood's patent.

There can be no question that James, in thus altering, by his own authority, the terms of all the contracts in the kingdom, assumed a power which belonged only to the whole legislature. Yet the Commons did not remonstrate. There was no power, however unconstitutional, which they were not willing to concede to him, as long as he used it to crush and plunder the English population. On the other hand, they respected no prerogative, however ancient, however legitimate,

* King, iii. 11.; Brief Memoirs by Haynes, Assay Master of the Mint, among the Lansdowne MSS. at the British Museum, No. 801. I have seen several specimens of this coin. The execution is surprisingly good, all circumstances considered.

however salutary, if they apprehended that he might use it to protect the race which they abhorred. They were not satisfied till they had extorted his reluctant consent to a portentous law, a law without a parallel in the history of civilised countries, the great Act of Attainder.

A list was framed containing between two and three thousand names. At the top was half the peerage of Ireland. Then came baronets, knights, clergymen, squires, merchants, yeomen, artisans, women, children. No investigation was made. Any member who wished to rid himself of a creditor, a rival, a private enemy, gave in the name to the clerk at the table, and it was generally inserted without discussion. The only debate of which any account has come down to us related to the Earl of Strafford. He had friends in the House who ventured to offer something in his favour. But a few words from Simon Luttrell settled the question. "I have," he said, "heard the King say some hard things of that Lord." This was thought sufficient, and the name of Strafford stands fifth in the long table of the proscribed.*

Days were fixed before which those whose names were on the list were required to surrender themselves to such justice as was then administered to English Protestants in Dublin. If a proscribed person was in Ireland, he must surrender himself by the tenth of August. If he had left Ireland since the fifth of November 1688, he must surrender himself by the first of September. If he had left Ireland before the fifth of November 1688, he must surrender himself by the first of October. If he failed to appear by the appointed day, he was to be hanged, drawn, and quartered without a trial, and his property was to be confiscated. It might be physically impossible for him to deliver himself up within the time fixed by the Act. He might be bedridden. He might be in the West Indies. He might be in prison. Indeed there notoriously were such cases. Among the attainted Lords was Mountjoy. He had been induced, by the villany of Tyrconnel, to trust himself at Saint Germains; he had been thrown into the Bastile: he was still lying there; and the Irish Parliament was not ashamed to enact that, unless he could, within a few weeks, make his escape from his cell, and present himself at Dublin, he should be put to death.†

As it was not even pretended that there had been any enquiry into the guilt of those who were thus proscribed, as

* King, iii. 12. † An Act for the Attainder of divers Rebels and for preserving the Interest of loyal Subjects, London, 1690.

not a single one among them had been heard in his own defence, and as it was certain that it would be physically impossible for many of them to surrender themselves in time, it was clear that nothing but a large exercise of the royal prerogative of mercy could prevent the perpetration of iniquities so horrible that no precedent could be found for them even in the lamentable history of the troubles of Ireland. The Commons therefore determined that the royal prerogative of mercy should be limited. Several regulations were devised for the purpose of making the passing of pardons difficult and costly; and finally it was enacted that every pardon granted by His Majesty, after the end of November 1689, to any of the many hundreds of persons who had been sentenced to death without a trial, should be absolutely void and of none effect. Sir Richard Nagle came in state to the bar of the Lords and presented the bill with a speech worthy of the occasion. "Many of the persons here attainted," said he, "have been proved traitors by such evidence as satisfies us. As to the rest we have followed common fame."*

With such reckless barbarity was the list framed that fanatical royalists, who were, at that very time, hazarding their property, their liberty, their lives, in the cause of James, were not secure from proscription. The most learned man of whom the Jacobite party could boast was Henry Dodwell, Camdenian Professor in the University of Oxford. In the cause of hereditary monarchy he shrank from no sacrifice and from no danger. It was about him that William uttered those memorable words: "He has set his heart on being a martyr; and I have set mine on disappointing him." But James was more cruel to friends than William to foes. Dodwell was a Protestant: he had some property in Connaught: these crimes were sufficient; and he was set down in the long roll of those who were doomed to the gallows and the quartering block.†

That James would give his assent to a bill which took from him the power of pardoning, seemed to many persons impossible. He had, four years before, quarrelled with the most loyal of parliaments rather than cede a prerogative which did not belong to him. It might, therefore, well be expected that he would now have struggled hard to retain a precious

* King, iii. 13.
† His name is in the first column of page 30. in that edition of the List which was licensed March 26, 1690. I should have thought that the proscribed person must have been some other Henry Dodwell. But Bishop Kennet's second letter to the Bishop of Carlisle, 1716, leaves no doubt about the matter.

prerogative which had been enjoyed by his predecessors ever since the origin of the monarchy, and which even the Whigs allowed to be a flower properly belonging to the Crown. The stern look and raised voice with which he had reprimanded the Tory gentlemen, who, in the language of profound reverence and fervent affection, implored him not to dispense with the laws, would now have been in place. He might also have seen that the right course was the wise course. Had he, on this great occasion, had the spirit to declare that he would not shed the blood of the innocent, and that, even as respected the guilty, he would not divest himself of the power of tempering judgment with mercy, he would have regained more hearts in England than he would have lost in Ireland. But it was over his fate to resist where he should have yielded, and to yield where he should have resisted. The most wicked of all laws received his sanction; and it is but a very small extenuation of his guilt that his sanction was somewhat reluctantly given.

That nothing might be wanting to the completeness of this great crime, extreme care was taken to prevent the persons who were attainted from knowing that they were attainted, till the day of grace fixed in the Act was passed. The roll of names was not published, but kept carefully locked up in Fitton's closet. Some Protestants, who still adhered to the cause of James, but who were anxious to know whether any of their friends or relations had been proscribed, tried hard to obtain a sight of the list: but solicitation, remonstrance, even bribery, proved vain. Not a single copy got abroad till it was too late for any of the thousands who had been condemned without a trial to obtain a pardon.*

Towards the close of July James prorogued the Houses. They had sate more than ten weeks; and in that space of time they had proved most fully that, great as have been the evils which Protestant ascendency has produced in Ireland, the evils produced by Popish ascendency would have been greater still. That the colonists, when they had won the victory, grossly abused it, that their legislation was, during many years, unjust and tyrannical, is most true. But it is not less true that they never quite came up to the atrocious

James prorogues his parliament.

---

* A list of most of the names of the Nobility, Gentry, and Commonalty of England and Ireland (amongst whom are several Women and Children) who are all, by an Act of a Pretended Parliament assembled in Dublin, attainted of High Treason, 1690; An Account of the Transactions of the late King James in Ireland, 1690; King, iii. 15.; Memoirs of Ireland, 1716.

example set by their vanquished enemy during his short tenure of power.

Indeed, while James was loudly boasting that he had passed an Act granting entire liberty of conscience to all sects, a persecution as cruel as that of Languedoc was raging through all the provinces which owned his authority. It was said by those who wished to find an excuse for him that almost all the Protestants, who still remained in Munster, Connaught, and Leinster, were his enemies, and that it was not as schismatics, but as rebels in heart, who wanted only opportunity to become rebels in act, that he gave them up to be oppressed and despoiled; and to this excuse some weight might have been allowed if he had strenuously exerted himself to protect those few colonists, who, though firmly attached to the reformed religion, were still true to the doctrines of nonresistance and of indefeasible hereditary right. But even those devoted royalists found that their heresy was in his view a crime for which no services or sacrifices would atone. Three or four noblemen, members of the Anglican Church, who had welcomed him to Ireland, and had sate in his parliament, represented to him that, if the rule which forbade any Protestant to possess any weapon were strictly enforced their country houses would be at the mercy of the Rapparees, and obtained from him permission to keep arms sufficient for a few servants. But Avaux remonstrated. The indulgence, he said, was grossly abused : these Protestant lords were not to be trusted : they were turning their houses into fortresses : His Majesty would soon have reason to repent his goodness. These representations prevailed ; and Roman Catholic troops were quartered in the suspected dwellings.*

Still harder was the lot of those Protestant clergymen who continued to cling, with desperate fidelity, to the cause of the Lord's Anointed. Of all the Anglican divines the one who had the largest share of James's good graces seems to have been Cartwright. Whether Cartwright could long have continued to be a favourite without being an apostate may be doubted. He died a few weeks after his arrival in Ireland; and thenceforward his Church had no one to plead her cause. Nevertheless a few of her prelates and priests continued for a time to teach what they had taught in the days of the Exclusion Bill. But it was at the peril of life and limb that they exercised their functions. Every wearer

* Avaux, 1689.

of a cassock was a mark for the insults and outrages of
soldiers and Rapparees. In the country his house was
robbed, and he was fortunate if it was not burned over his
head. He was hunted through the streets of Dublin with
cries of "There goes the devil of a heretic." Sometimes he
was knocked down; sometimes he was cudgelled.* The
rulers of the University of Dublin, trained in the Anglican
doctrine of passive obedience, had greeted James on his first
arrival at the Castle, and had been assured by him that he
would protect them in the enjoyment of their property and
their privileges. They were now, without any trial, without
any accusation, thrust out of their house. The communion
plate of the chapel, the books in the library, the very chairs
and beds of the collegians were seized. Part of the building
was turned into a magazine, part into a barrack, part into
a prison. Simon Luttrell, who was Governor of the capital, was, with great difficulty and by powerful intercession,
induced to let the ejected fellows and scholars depart in
safety. He at length permitted them to remain at large,
with this condition, that, on pain of death, no three of them
should meet together.† No Protestant divine suffered more
hardships than Doctor William King, Dean of Saint
Patrick's. He had been long distinguished by the fervour
with which he had inculcated the duty of passively obeying
even the worst rulers. At a later period, when he had published a defence of the revolution, and had accepted a mitre
from the new government, he was reminded that he had
invoked the divine vengeance on the usurpers, and had
declared himself willing to die a hundred deaths rather than
desert the cause of hereditary right. He had said that the
true religion had often been strengthened by persecution,
but could never be strengthened by rebellion; that it would
be a glorious day for the Church of England when a whole
cartload of her ministers should go to the gallows for the
doctrine of nonresistance; and that his highest ambition
was to be one of such a company.‡ It is not improbable
that, when he spoke thus, he felt as he spoke. But his
principles, though they might perhaps have held out against
the severities and the promises of William, were not proof
against the ingratitude of James. Human nature at last
asserted its rights. After King had been repeatedly imprisoned by the government to which he was devotedly attached,

* King's State of the Protestants in Ireland, iii. 10.
† Ibid. iii. 15.
‡ Leslie's Answer to King.

CHAP. XII.

after he had been insulted and threatened in his own choir by the soldiers, after he had been interdicted from burying in his own churchyard and from preaching in his own pulpit, after he had narrowly escaped with life from a musket-shot fired at him in the street, he began to think the Whig theory of government less unreasonable and unchristian than it had once appeared to him, and persuaded himself that the oppressed Church might lawfully accept deliverance, if God should be pleased, by whatever means, to send it to her.

Effect produced in England by the news from Ireland.

In no long time it appeared that James would have done well to hearken to those counsellors who had told him that the acts by which he was trying to make himself popular in one of his three kingdoms, would make him odious in the others. It was in some sense fortunate for England that, after he had ceased to reign here, he continued during more than a year to reign in Ireland. The Revolution had been followed by a reaction of public feeling in his favour. That reaction, if it had been suffered to proceed uninterrupted, might perhaps not have ceased till he was again King: but it was violently interrupted by himself. He would not suffer his people to forget: he would not suffer them to hope; while they were trying to find excuses for his past errors, and to persuade themselves that he would not repeat those errors, he forced upon them, in their own despite, the conviction that he was incorrigible, that the sharpest discipline of adversity had taught him nothing, and that, if they were weak enough to recall him, they would soon have to depose him again. It was in vain that the Jacobites put forth pamphlets about the cruelty with which he had been treated by those who were nearest to him in blood, about the imperious temper and uncourteous manners of William, about the favour shown to the Dutch, about the heavy taxes, about the suspension of the Habeas Corpus Act, about the dangers which threatened the Church from the enmity of Puritans and Latitudinarians. James refuted these pamphlets far more effectually than all the ablest and most eloquent Whig writers united could have done. Every week came the news that he had passed some new Act for robbing or murdering Protestants. Every colonist who succeeded in stealing across the sea from Leinster to Holyhead or Bristol, brought fearful reports of the tyranny under which his brethren groaned. What impression these reports made on the Protestants of our island may be easily inferred from the fact that they moved the indignation of Ronquillo, a Spaniard and a bigoted member of the Church of Rome. He informed his Court that, though the English laws against Popery might seem severe, they were so much mitigated by the prudence and humanity of the government, that they caused no annoyance to quiet people; and he took upon himself to assure the Holy See that what a Roman Catholic suffered in London was nothing when compared with what a Protestant suffered in Ireland.*

The fugitive Englishry found in England warm sympathy and munificent relief. Many were received into the houses of friends and kinsmen. Many were indebted for the means of subsistence to the liberality of strangers. Among those who bore a part in this work of mercy, none contributed more largely or less ostentatiously than the Queen. The House of Commons placed at the King's disposal fifteen thousand pounds for the relief of those refugees whose wants were most pressing, and requested him to give commissions in the army to those who were qualified for military employment.† An Act was also passed enabling beneficed clergymen who had fled from Ireland to hold preferment in England.‡ Yet the interest which the nation felt in these unfortunate guests was languid when compared with the interest excited by that portion of the Saxon colony which still maintained in Ulster a desperate conflict against overwhelming odds. On this subject scarcely one dissentient voice was to be heard in our island. Whigs, Tories, nay even those Jacobites in whom Jacobitism had not extinguished every patriotic sentiment, gloried in the glory of Enniskillen and Londonderry. The House of Commons was all of one mind. "This is no time to be counting cost," said honest Birch, who well remembered the way in which Oliver had made war on the Irish. "Are those brave fellows in Londonderry to be deserted? If we lose them will not all the world cry shame upon us? A boom across the river! Why have we not cut the boom in pieces? Are our brethren to perish almost in sight of England, within a few hours' voyage of our shores?"§ Howe, the most vehement man of one party, declared that the hearts of the people were set on Ireland. Seymour, the leader of the other party, declared

* "En comparacion de lo que se hace en Irlanda con los Protestantes, es nada." $\frac{April\ 2}{May\ 4}$ 1689; "Para que vea Su Santidad que aqui retan los Catolicos mas benignamente tratados que los Protestantes in Irlanda." June 11.

† Commons' Journals, June 15, 1689.
‡ Stat. 1 W. & M. sess. 1. c. 29.
§ Grey's Debates, June 19, 1689.

that, though he had not taken part in setting up the new government, he should cordially support it in all that might be necessary for the preservation of Ireland.* The Commons appointed a committee to enquire into the cause of the delays and miscarriages which had been all but fatal to the Englishry of Ulster. The officers to whose treachery or cowardice the public ascribed the calamities of Londonderry were put under arrest. Lundy was sent to the Tower, Cunningham to the Gate House. The agitation of the public mind was in some degree calmed by the announcement that, before the end of summer, an army powerful enough to reestablish the English ascendency in Ireland would be sent across Saint George's Channel, and that Schomberg would be the General. In the meantime an expedition which was thought to be sufficient for the relief of Londonderry was despatched from Liverpool under the command of Kirke. The dogged obstinacy with which this man had, in spite of royal solicitations, adhered to his religion, and the part which he had taken in the Revolution, had perhaps entitled him to an amnesty for past crimes. But it is difficult to understand why the Government should have selected for a post of the highest importance an officer who was generally and justly hated, who had never shown eminent talents for war, and who, both in Africa and in England, had notoriously tolerated among his soldiers a licentiousness, not only shocking to humanity, but also incompatible with discipline.

Actions of the Enniskilleners.

On the sixteenth of May, Kirke's troops embarked: on the twenty-second they sailed: but contrary winds made the passage slow, and forced the armament to stop long at the Isle of Man. Meanwhile the Protestants of Ulster were defending themselves with stubborn courage against a great superiority of force. The Enniskilleners had never ceased to wage a vigorous partisan war against the native population. Early in May they marched to encounter a large body of troops from Connaught, who had made an inroad into Donegal. The Irish were speedily routed, and fled to Sligo with the loss of a hundred and twenty men killed and sixty taken. Two small pieces of artillery and several horses fell into the hands of the conquerors. Elated by this success, the Enniskilleners soon invaded the county of Cavan, drove before them fifteen hundred of James's troops, took and destroyed the castle of Ballincarrig, reputed the strongest in that part of the kingdom, and carried off the pikes and mus-

* Grey's Debates, June 27. 1689.

kets of the garrison. The next incursion was into Meath.
Three thousand oxen and two thousand sheep were swept
away and brought safe to the little island in Lough Erne.
These daring exploits spread terror even to the gates of
Dublin. Colonel Hugh Sutherland was ordered to march
against Enniskillen with a regiment of dragoons and two
regiments of foot. He carried with him arms for the native
peasantry, and many repaired to his standard. The Enniskilleners did not wait till he came into their neighbourhood,
but advanced to encounter him. He declined an action, and
retreated, leaving his stores at Belturbet under the care of a
detachment of three hundred soldiers. The Protestants attacked Belturbet with vigour, made their way into a lofty
house which overlooked the town, and thence opened such a
fire that in two hours the garrison surrendered. Seven
hundred muskets, a great quantity of powder, many horses,
many sacks of biscuits, many barrels of meal, were taken,
and were sent to Enniskillen. The boats which brought
these precious spoils were joyfully welcomed. The fear of
hunger was removed. While the aboriginal population had,
in many counties, altogether neglected the cultivation of the
earth, in the expectation, it should seem, that marauding
would prove an inexhaustible resource, the colonists, true to
the provident and industrious character of their race, had, in
the midst of war, not omitted carefully to till the soil in the
neighbourhood of their strongholds. The harvest was now
not far remote; and, till the harvest, the food taken from the
enemy would be amply sufficient.*

Yet, in the midst of success and plenty, the Enniskilleners
were tortured by a cruel anxiety for Londonderry. They
were bound to the defenders of that city, not only by religious
and national sympathy, but by common interest. For there
could be no doubt that, if Londonderry fell, the whole Irish
army would instantly march in irresistible force upon Lough
Erne. Yet what could be done? Some brave men were for
making a desperate attempt to relieve the besieged city; but
the odds were too great. Detachments however were sent
which infested the rear of the blockading army, cut off supplies, and, on one occasion, carried away the horses of three
entire troops of cavalry.† Still the line of posts which sur-

---

* Hamilton's True Relation; Mac
Cormick's Further Account. Of the
island generally, Avaux says, " On n'attend rien de cette recolte cy, les paysans

ayant presque tous pris les armes."—
Letter to Louvois, March 1⁸⁄₁₁, 1689.
† Hamilton's True Relation.

rounded Londonderry by land remained unbroken. The river was still strictly closed and guarded. Within the walls the distress had become extreme. So early as the eighth of June horseflesh was almost the only meat which could be purchased; and of horseflesh the supply was scanty. It was necessary to make up the deficiency with tallow; and even tallow was doled out with a parsimonious hand.

Expedition under Kirke arrives in Lough Foyle.

On the fifteenth of June a gleam of hope appeared. The sentinels on the top of the Cathedral saw sails nine miles off in the bay of Lough Foyle. Thirty vessels of different sizes were counted. Signals were made from the steeples and returned from the mast heads, but were imperfectly understood on both sides. At last a messenger from the fleet eluded the Irish sentinels, dived under the boom, and informed the garrison that Kirke had arrived from England with troops, arms, ammunition, and provisions to relieve the city.*

In Londonderry expectation was at the height: but a few hours of feverish joy were followed by weeks of misery. Kirke thought it unsafe to make any attempt, either by land or by water, on the lines of the besiegers, and retired to the entrance of Lough Foyle, where, during several weeks, he lay inactive.

And now the pressure of famine became every day more severe. A strict search was made in all the recesses of all the houses of the city; and some provisions, which had been concealed in cellars by people who had since died or made their escape, were discovered and carried to the magazines. The stock of cannon balls was almost exhausted; and their place was supplied by brickbats coated with lead. Pestilence began, as usual, to make its appearance in the train of hunger. Fifteen officers died of fever in one day. The Governor Baker was among those who sank under the disease. His place was supplied by Colonel John Mitchelburne.†

Meanwhile it was known at Dublin that Kirke and his squadron were on the coast of Ulster. The alarm was great at the Castle. Even before this news arrived, Avaux had given it as his opinion that Richard Hamilton was unequal to the difficulties of the situation. It had therefore been resolved that Rosen should take the chief command. He was now sent down with all speed.‡

Cruelty of Rosen.

On the nineteenth of June he arrived at the head quarters of the besieging army. At first he attempted to undermine the walls; but his plan was discovered; and he was compelled to abandon it after a sharp fight, in which more than a hun-

* Walker.   † Walker; Mackenzie.   ‡ Avaux, June 19. 1689.

dred of his men were slain. Then his fury rose to a strange pitch. He, an old soldier, a Marshal of France in expectancy, trained in the school of the greatest generals, accustomed, during many years, to scientific war, to be baffled by a mob of country gentlemen, farmers, shopkeepers, who were protected only by a wall which any good engineer would at once have pronounced untenable! He raved, he blasphemed, in a language of his own, made up of all the dialects spoken from the Baltic to the Atlantic. He would raze the city to the ground; he would spare no living thing; no, not the young girls; not the babies at the breast. As to the leaders, death was too light a punishment for them: he would rack them: he would roast them alive. In his rage he ordered a shell to be flung into the town with a letter containing a horrible menace. He would, he said, gather into one body all the Protestants who had remained at their homes between Charlemont and the sea, old men, women, children, many of them near in blood and affection to the defenders of Londonderry. No protection, whatever might be the authority by which it had been given, should be respected. The multitude thus brought together should be driven under the walls of Londonderry, and should there be starved to death in the sight of their countrymen, their friends, their kinsmen. This was no idle threat. Parties were instantly sent out in all directions to collect victims. At dawn, on the morning of the second of July, hundreds of Protestants, who were charged with no crime, who were incapable of bearing arms, and many of whom had protections granted by James, were dragged to the gates of the city. It was imagined that the piteous sight would quell the spirit of the colonists. But the only effect was to rouse that spirit to still greater energy. An order was immediately put forth that no man should utter the word Surrender on pain of death; and no man uttered that word. Several prisoners of high rank were in the town. Hitherto they had been well treated, and had received as good rations as were measured out to the garrison. They were now closely confined. A gallows was erected on one of the bastions; and a message was conveyed to Rosen, requesting him to send a confessor instantly to prepare his friends for death. The prisoners in great dismay wrote to the savage Livonian, but received no answer. They then addressed themselves to their countryman, Richard Hamilton. They were willing, they said, to shed their blood for their King; but they thought it hard to die the ignominious death of thieves in consequence of the

CHAP. XII.

barbarity of their own companions in arms. Hamilton, though a man of lax principles, was not cruel. He had been disgusted by the inhumanity of Rosen, but, being only second in command, could not venture to express publicly all that he thought. He however remonstrated strongly. Some Irish officers felt on this occasion as it was natural that brave men should feel, and declared, weeping with pity and indignation, that they should never cease to have in their ears the cries of the poor women and children who had been driven at the point of the pike to die of famine between the camp and the city. Rosen persisted during forty-eight hours. In that time many unhappy creatures perished: but Londonderry held out as resolutely as ever; and he saw that his crime was likely to produce nothing but hatred and obloquy. He at length gave way, and suffered the survivors to withdraw. The garrison then took down the gallows which had been erected on the bastion.*

When the tidings of these events reached Dublin, James, though by no means prone to compassion, was startled by an atrocity of which the civil wars of England had furnished no example, and was displeased by learning that protections, given by his authority, and guaranteed by his honour, had been publicly declared to be nullities. He complained to the French ambassador, and said, with a warmth which the occasion fully justified, that Rosen was a barbarous Muscovite. Melfort could not refrain from adding that, if Rosen had been an Englishman, he would have been hanged. Avaux was utterly unable to understand this effeminate sensibility. In his opinion, nothing had been done that was at all reprehensible; and he had some difficulty in commanding himself when he heard the King and the secretary blame, in strong language, an act of wholesome severity.† In truth the French ambassador and the French general were well paired. There was a great difference, doubtless, in appearance and manner, between the handsome, graceful, and refined politician, whose dexterity and suavity had been renowned at the most polite courts of Europe, and the military adventurer, whose look and voice reminded all who came near him that he had been born in a half savage country, that he had risen from the ranks, and that he had once been sentenced to death for marauding.

* Walker; Mackenzie; Light to the Blind; King, iii. 14.; Leslie's Answer to King; Life of James, ii. 366. I ought to say that on this occasion King is unjust to James.

† Leslie's Answer to King; Avaux, July 17. 1689. "Je trouvay l'expression bien forte: mais je ne voulois rien répondre, car le Roy s'estoit desja fort emporté."

But the heart of the diplomatist was really even more callous than that of the soldier.

Rosen was recalled to Dublin; and Richard Hamilton was again left in the chief command. He tried gentler means than those which had brought so much reproach on his predecessor. No trick, no lie, which was thought likely to discourage the starving garrison was spared. One day a great shout was raised by the whole Irish camp. The defenders of Londonderry were soon informed that the army of James was rejoicing on account of the fall of Enniskillen. They were told that they had now no chance of being relieved, and were exhorted to save their lives by capitulating. They consented to negotiate. But what they asked was, that they should be permitted to depart armed and in military array, by land or by water at their choice. They demanded hostages for the exact fulfilment of these conditions, and insisted that the hostages should be sent on board of the fleet which lay in Lough Foyle. Such terms Hamilton durst not grant: the Governors would abate nothing; the treaty was broken off; and the conflict recommenced.*

By this time July was far advanced; and the state of the city was, hour by hour, becoming more frightful. The number of the inhabitants had been thinned more by famine and disease than by the fire of the enemy. Yet that fire was sharper and more constant than ever. One of the gates was beaten in: one of the bastions was laid in ruins; but the breaches made by day were repaired by night with indefatigable activity. Every attack was still repulsed. But the fighting men of the garrison were so much exhausted that they could scarcely keep their legs. Several of them, in the act of striking at the enemy, fell down from mere weakness. A very small quantity of grain remained, and was doled out by mouthfuls. The stock of salted hides was considerable, and by gnawing them the garrison appeased the rage of hunger. Dogs, fattened on the blood of the slain who lay unburied round the town, were luxuries which few could afford to purchase. The price of a whelp's paw was five shillings and sixpence. Nine horses were still alive, and but barely alive. They were so lean that little meat was likely to be found upon them. It was, however, determined to slaughter them for food. The people perished so fast, that it was impossible for the survivors to perform the rites of sepulture. There was scarcely a cellar in which some corpse was not

* Mackenzie.

decaying. Such was the extremity of distress that the rats who came to feast in those hideous dens were eagerly hunted and greedily devoured. A small fish, caught in the river, was not to be purchased with money. The only price for which such a treasure could be obtained was some handfuls of oatmeal. Leprosies, such as strange and unwholesome diet engenders, made existence a constant torment. The whole city was poisoned by the stench exhaled from the bodies of the dead and of the half dead. That there should be fits of discontent and insubordination among men enduring such misery was inevitable. At one moment it was suspected that Walker had laid up somewhere a secret store of food, and was revelling in private, while he exhorted others to suffer resolutely for the good cause. His house was strictly examined: his innocence was fully proved: he regained his popularity; and the garrison, with death in near prospect, thronged to the cathedral to hear him preach, drunk in his earnest eloquence with delight, and went forth from the house of God with haggard faces and tottering steps, but with spirit still unsubdued. There were, indeed, some secret plottings. A very few obscure traitors opened communications with the enemy. But it was necessary that all such dealings should be carefully concealed. None dared to utter publicly any words save words of defiance and stubborn resolution. Even in that extremity the general cry was, "No surrender." And there were not wanting voices which, in low tones, added, "First the horses and hides; and then the prisoners; and then each other." It was afterwards related, half in jest, yet not without a horrible mixture of earnest, that a corpulent citizen, whose bulk presented a strange contrast to the skeletons which surrounded him, thought it expedient to conceal himself from the numerous eyes which followed him with cannibal looks whenever he appeared in the streets.*

It was no slight aggravation of the sufferings of the garrison that all this time the English ships were seen far off in Lough Foyle. Communication between the fleet and the city was almost impossible. One diver who had attempted to pass the boom was drowned. Another was hanged. The language of signals was hardly intelligible. On the thirteenth of July, however, a piece of paper sewed up in a cloth button came to Walker's hands. It was a letter from Kirke, and

* Walker's Account. "The fat man in Londonderry" became a proverbial expression for a person whose prosperity excited the envy and cupidity of his less fortunate neighbours.

contained assurances of speedy relief. But more than a fortnight of intense misery had since elapsed; and the hearts of the most sanguine were sick with deferred hope. By no art could the provisions which were left be made to hold out two days more.*

Just at this time Kirke received from England a despatch, which contained positive orders that Londonderry should be relieved. He accordingly determined to make an attempt which, as far as appears, he might have made, with at least an equally fair prospect of success six weeks earlier.†

Among the merchant ships which had come to Lough Foyle under his convoy was one called the Mountjoy. The master, Micaiah Browning, a native of Londonderry, had brought from England a large cargo of provisions. He had, it is said, repeatedly remonstrated against the inaction of the armament. He now eagerly volunteered to take the first risk of succouring his fellow citizens; and his offer was accepted. Andrew Douglas, master of the Phœnix, who had on board a great quantity of meal from Scotland, was willing to share the danger and the honour. The two merchantmen were to be escorted by the Dartmouth, a frigate of thirty-six guns, commanded by Captain John Leake, afterwards an admiral of great fame.

It was the twenty-eighth of July. The sun had just set: the evening sermon in the cathedral was over; and the heartbroken congregation had separated; when the sentinels on the tower saw the sails of three vessels coming up the Foyle. Soon there was a stir in the Irish camp. The besiegers were on the alert for miles along both shores. The ships were in extreme peril: for the river was low; and the only navigable channel ran very near to the left bank, where the head quarters of the enemy had been fixed, and where the batteries were most numerous. Leake performed his duty with a skill and spirit worthy of his noble profession, exposed his frigate to cover the merchantmen, and used his guns with great

CHAP. XII.

Attack on the boom.

---

* This, according to Narcissus Luttrell, was the report made by Captain Withers, afterwards a highly distinguished officer, on whom Pope wrote an epitaph.

† The despatch, which positively commanded Kirke to attack the boom, was signed by Schomberg, who had already been appointed commander in chief of all the English forces in Ireland. A copy of it is among the Nairne MSS. in the Bodleian Library. Wodrow, on no better authority than the gossip of a country parish in Dumbartonshire, attributes the relief of Londonderry to the exhortations of a heroic Scotch preacher named Gordon. I am inclined to think that Kirke was more likely to be influenced by a peremptory order from Schomberg, than by the united eloquence of a whole synod of presbyterian divines.

effect. At length the little squadron came to the place of peril. Then the Mountjoy took the lead, and went right at the boom. The huge barricade cracked and gave way; but the shock was such that the Mountjoy rebounded, and stuck in the mud. A yell of triumph rose from the banks: the Irish rushed to their boats, and were preparing to board: but the Dartmouth poured on them a well directed broadside which threw them into disorder. Just then the Phoenix dashed at the breach which the Mountjoy had made, and was in a moment within the fence. Meantime the tide was rising fast. The Mountjoy began to move, and soon passed safe through the broken stakes and floating spars. But her brave master was no more. A shot from one of the batteries had struck him; and he died by the most enviable of all deaths, in sight of the city which was his birthplace, which was his home, and which had just been saved by his courage and selfdevotion from the most frightful form of destruction. The night had closed in before the conflict at the boom began: but the flash of the guns was seen, and the noise heard, by the lean and ghastly multitude which covered the walls of the city. When the Mountjoy grounded, and when the shout of triumph rose from the Irish on both sides of the river, the hearts of the besieged died within them. One who endured the unutterable anguish of that moment has told us that they looked fearfully livid in each other's eyes. Even after the barricade had been passed, there was a terrible half hour of suspense. It was ten o'clock before the ships arrived at the quay. The whole population was there to welcome them. A screen made of casks filled with earth was hastily thrown up to protect the landing place from the batteries on the other side of the river; and then the work of unloading began. First were rolled on shore barrels containing six thousand bushels of meal. Then came great cheeses, casks of beef, flitches of bacon, kegs of butter, sacks of pease and biscuit, ankers of brandy. Not many hours before, half a pound of tallow and three quarters of a pound of salted hide had been weighed out with niggardly care to every fighting man. The ration which each now received was three pounds of flour, two pounds of beef, and a pint of pease. It is easy to imagine with what tears grace was said over the suppers of that evening. There was little sleep on either side of the wall. The bonfires shone bright along the whole circuit of the ramparts. The Irish guns continued to roar all night; and all night the bells of the rescued city made answer to the Irish guns with a peal of joyous defiance. Through the three following days the batteries of the enemy continued to play. But, on the third night, flames were seen arising from the camp; and, when the first of August dawned, a line of smoking ruins marked the site lately occupied by the huts of the besiegers; and the citizens saw far off the long column of pikes and standards retreating up the left bank of the Foyle towards Strabane.*

So ended this great siege, the most memorable in the annals of the British Isles. It had lasted a hundred and five days. The garrison had been reduced from about seven thousand effective men to about three thousand. The loss of the besiegers cannot be precisely ascertained. Walker estimated it at eight thousand men. It is certain from the despatches of Avaux that the regiments which returned from the blockade had been so much thinned that many of them were not more than two hundred strong. Of thirty-six French gunners who had superintended the cannonading, thirty-one had been killed or disabled.† The means both of attack and of defence had undoubtedly been such as would have moved the great warriors of the Continent to laughter; and this is the very circumstance which gives so peculiar an interest to the history of the contest. It was a contest, not between engineers, but between nations; and the victory remained with the nation which, though inferior in number, was superior in civilisation, in capacity for selfgovernment, and in stubbornness of resolution.‡

As soon as it was known that the Irish army had retired, a deputation from the city hastened to Lough Foyle, and invited Kirke to take the command. He came accompanied by a long train of officers, and was received in state by the two Governors, who delivered up to him the authority which, under the pressure of necessity, they had assumed. He remained only a few days; but he had time to show enough of the incurable vices of his character to disgust a population

The siege of Londonderry raised.

---

* Walker; Mackenzie; Histoire de la Revolution d'Irlande, Amsterdam, 1691; London Gazette, Aug. 5, 12, 1689; Letter of Duchau among the Nairne MSS.; Life of Sir John Leake; The Londeriad; Observations on Mr. Walker's Account of the Siege of Londonderry, licensed Oct. 4. 1689.

† Avaux to Seignelay, July 12/22; to Lewis, Aug. 5/15.

‡ "You will see here, as you have all along, that the tradesmen of Londonderry had more skill in their defence than the great officers of the Irish Army in their attacks."—Light to the Blind. The author of this work is furious against the Irish gunners. The boom, he thinks, would never have been broken if they had done their duty. Were they drunk? Were they traitors? He does not determine the point. "Lord," he exclaims, "who secst the hearts of people, we leave the judgment of this affair to thy mercy. In the interim those gunners lost Ireland."

CHAP. XII.

distinguished by austere morals and ardent public spirit. There was, however, no outbreak. The city was in the highest good humour. Such quantities of provisions had been landed from the fleet that there was in every house a plenty never before known. A few days earlier a man had been glad to obtain for twenty pence a mouthful of carrion scraped from the bones of a starved horse. A pound of good beef was now sold for three halfpence. Meanwhile all hands were busied in removing corpses which had been thinly covered with earth, in filling up the holes which the shells had ploughed in the ground, and in repairing the battered roofs of the houses. The recollection of past dangers and privations, and the consciousness of having deserved well of the English nation and of all Protestant Churches, swelled the hearts of the townspeople with honest pride. That pride grew stronger when they received from William a letter, acknowledging, in the most affectionate language, the debt which he owed to the brave and trusty citizens of his good city. The whole population crowded to the Diamond to hear the royal epistle read. At the close all the guns on the ramparts sent forth a voice of joy: all the ships in the river made answer: barrels of ale were broken up; and the health of Their Majesties was drunk with shouts and volleys of musketry.

Five generations have since passed away; and still the wall of Londonderry is to the Protestants of Ulster what the trophy of Marathon was to the Athenians. A lofty pillar, rising from a bastion which bore during many weeks the heaviest fire of the enemy, is seen far up and far down the Foyle. On the summit is the statue of Walker, such as when, in the last and most terrible emergency, his eloquence roused the fainting courage of his brethren. In one hand he grasps a Bible. The other, pointing down the river, seems to direct the eyes of his famished audience to the English topmasts in the distant bay. Such a monument was well deserved: yet it was scarcely needed: for in truth the whole city is to this day a monument of the great deliverance. The wall is carefully preserved; nor would any plea of health or convenience be held by the inhabitants sufficient to justify the demolition of that sacred enclosure which, in the evil time, gave shelter to their race and their religion.* The summit of the ramparts forms a

* In a collection entitled "Deriana," published more than sixty years ago, is a curious letter on this subject.

pleasant walk. The bastions have been turned into little gardens. Here and there, among the shrubs and flowers, may be seen the old culverins which scattered bricks, cased with lead, among the Irish ranks. One antique gun, the gift of the Fishmongers of London, was distinguished, during the hundred and five memorable days, by the loudness of its report, and still bears the name of Roaring Meg. The cathedral is filled with relics and trophies. In the vestibule is a huge shell, one of many hundreds of shells which were thrown into the city. Over the altar are still seen the French flagstaves, taken by the garrison in a desperate sally. The white ensigns of the House of Bourbon have long been dust: but their place has been supplied by new banners, the work of the fairest hands of Ulster. The anniversary of the day on which the gates were closed, and the anniversary of the day on which the siege was raised, have been down to our own time celebrated by salutes, processions, banquets, and sermons: Lundy has been executed in effigy; and the sword, said by tradition to be that of Maumont, has, on great occasions, been carried in triumph. There is still a Walker Club and a Murray Club. The humble tombs of the Protestant captains have been carefully sought out, repaired, and embellished. It is impossible not to respect the sentiment which indicates itself by these tokens. It is a sentiment which belongs to the higher and purer part of human nature, and which adds not a little to the strength of states. A people which takes no pride in the noble achievements of remote ancestors will never achieve anything worthy to be remembered with pride by remote descendants. Yet it is impossible for the moralist or the statesman to look with unmixed complacency on the solemnities with which Londonderry commemorates her deliverance, and on the honours which she pays to those who saved her. Unhappily the animosities of her brave champions have descended with their glory. The faults which are ordinarily found in dominant castes and dominant sects have not seldom shown themselves without disguise at her festivities; and even with the expressions of pious gratitude which have resounded from her pulpits have too often been mingled words of wrath and defiance.

The Irish army which had retreated to Strabane remained there but a very short time. The spirit of the troops had been depressed by their recent failure, and was soon com-

CHAP. XII.

Operations against the Enniskilleners.

pletely cowed by the news of a great disaster in another quarter.

Three weeks before this time the Duke of Berwick had gained an advantage over a detachment of the Enniskilleners, and had, by their own confession, killed or taken more than fifty of them. They were in hopes of obtaining some assistance from Kirke, to whom they had sent a deputation; and they still persisted in rejecting all terms offered by the enemy. It was therefore determined at Dublin that an attack should be made upon them from several quarters at once. Macarthy, who had been rewarded for his services in Munster with the title of Viscount Mountcashel, marched towards Lough Erne from the east with three regiments of foot, two regiments of dragoons, and some troops of cavalry. A considerable force, which lay encamped near the mouth of the river Drowes, was at the same time to advance from the west. The Duke of Berwick was to come from the north, with such horse and dragoons as could be spared from the army which was besieging Londonderry. The Enniskilleners were not fully apprised of the whole plan which had been laid for their destruction: but they knew that Macarthy was on the road with a force exceeding any which they could bring into the field. Their anxiety was in some degree relieved by the return of the deputation which they had sent to Kirke. Kirke could spare no soldiers: but he had sent some arms, some ammunition, and some experienced officers, of whom the chief were Colonel Wolseley and Lieutenant Colonel Berry. These officers had come by sea round the coast of Donegal, and had run up the Erne. On Sunday, the twenty-ninth of July, it was known that their boat was approaching the island of Enniskillen. The whole population, male and female, came to the shore to greet them. It was with difficulty that they made their way to the Castle through the crowds which hung on them, blessing God that dear old England had not quite forgotten the Englishmen who were upholding her cause against great odds in the heart of Ireland.

Wolseley seems to have been in every respect well qualified for his post. He was a stanch Protestant, had distinguished himself among the Yorkshiremen who rose up for the Prince of Orange and a free Parliament, and had, even before the landing of the Dutch army, proved his zeal for liberty and pure religion, by causing the Mayor of Scarborough, who had made a speech in favour of King James, to be brought into the marketplace and well tossed there in a blanket.* This vehement hatred of Popery was, in the estimation of the men of Enniskillen, the first of all the qualifications of a leader; and Wolseley had other and more important qualifications. Though himself regularly bred to war, he seems to have had a peculiar aptitude for the management of irregular troops. He had scarcely taken on himself the chief command when he received notice that Mountcashel had laid siege to the Castle of Crum. Crum was the frontier garrison of the Protestants of Fermanagh. The ruins of the old fortifications are now among the attractions of a beautiful pleasureground, situated on a woody promontory which overlooks Lough Erne. Wolseley determined to raise the siege. He sent Berry forward with such troops as could be instantly put in motion, and promised to follow speedily with a larger force.

CHAP. XII.

Berry, after marching some miles, encountered thirteen companies of Macarthy's dragoons, commanded by Anthony, the most brilliant and accomplished of all who bore the name of Hamilton, but much less successful as a soldier than as a courtier, a lover, and a writer. Hamilton's dragoons ran at the first fire: he was severely wounded; and his second in command was shot dead. Macarthy soon came up to support Hamilton; and at the same time Wolseley came up to support Berry. The hostile armies were now in presence of each other. Macarthy had above five thousand men and several pieces of artillery. The Enniskilleners were under three thousand; and they had marched in such haste that they had brought only one day's provisions. It was therefore absolutely necessary for them either to fight instantly or to retreat. Wolseley determined to consult the men; and this determination, which, in ordinary circumstances, would have been most unworthy of a general, was fully justified by the peculiar composition and temper of the little army, an army made up of gentlemen and yeomen fighting, not for pay, but for their lands, their wives, their children, and their God. The ranks were drawn up under arms; and the question was put, "Advance or Retreat?" The answer was an universal shout of "Advance." Wolseley gave out the word "No Popery." It was received with loud applause. He instantly made his dispositions for an attack. As he approached, the enemy, to his great surprise, began to retire. The Enniskilleners were eager to pursue with all speed: but their

Battle of Newton Butler.

* Bernardi's Life of Himself, 1737. mentioned in one of the letters published Wolseley's exploit at Scarborough is by Sir Henry Ellis.

commander, suspecting a snare, restrained their ardour, and positively forbade them to break their ranks. Thus one army retreated and the other followed, in good order, through the little town of Newton Butler. About a mile from that town the Irish faced about, and made a stand. Their position was well chosen. They were drawn up on a hill at the foot of which lay a deep bog. A narrow paved causeway which ran across the bog was the only road by which the cavalry of the Enniskilleners could advance; for on the right and left were pools, turf pits, and quagmires, which afforded no footing to horses. Macarthy placed his cannon in such a manner as to sweep this causeway.

Wolseley ordered his infantry to the attack. They struggled through the bog, made their way to firm ground, and rushed on the guns. There was then a short and desperate fight. The Irish canoneers stood gallantly to their pieces till they were cut down to a man. The Enniskillen horse, no longer in danger of being mowed down by the fire of the artillery, came fast up the causeway. The Irish dragoons who had run away in the morning were smitten with another panic, and, without striking a blow, galloped from the field. The horse followed the example. Such was the terror of the fugitives that many of them spurred hard till their beasts fell down, and then continued to fly on foot, throwing away carbines, swords, and even coats, as incumbrances. The infantry, seeing themselves deserted, flung down their pikes and muskets and ran for their lives. The conquerors now gave loose to that ferocity which has seldom failed to disgrace the civil wars of Ireland. The butchery was terrible. Near fifteen hundred of the vanquished were put to the sword. About five hundred more, in ignorance of the country, took a road which led to Lough Erne. The lake was before them; the enemy behind: they plunged into the waters and perished there. Macarthy, abandoned by his troops, rushed into the midst of the pursuers, and very nearly found the death which he sought. He was wounded in several places; he was struck to the ground; and in another moment his brains would have been knocked out with the but end of a musket, when he was recognised and saved. The colonists lost only twenty men killed and fifty wounded. They took four hundred prisoners, seven pieces of cannon, fourteen barrels of powder, all the drums and all the colours of the vanquished enemy.*

* Hamilton's True Relation; Mac aerts, Aug. 22. 1689; Life of James; Cormick's Further Account; London Ga- ii. 368, 360.; Avaux to Lewis, Aug. ⁷⁄₁₇.

The battle of Newton Butler was won on the third day after the boom thrown over the Foyle was broken. At Strabane the news met the Celtic army which was retreating from Londonderry. All was terror and confusion: the tents were struck; the military stores were flung by waggon loads into the waters of the Mourne; and the dismayed Irish, leaving many sick and wounded to the mercy of the victorious Protestants, fled to Omagh, and thence to Charlemont. Sarsfield, who commanded at Sligo, found it necessary to abandon that town, which was instantly occupied by a detachment of Kirke's troops.* Dublin was in consternation. James dropped words which indicated an intention of flying to the Continent. Evil tidings indeed came fast upon him. Almost at the same time at which he learned that one of his armies had raised the siege of Londonderry, and that another had been routed at Newton Butler, he received intelligence scarcely less disheartening from Scotland.

It is now necessary to trace the progress of those events to which Scotland owes her political and her religious liberty, her prosperity, and her civilisation.

---

and to Louvois of the same date. Story mentions a report that the panic among the Irish was caused by the mistake of an officer who called out "Right about face" instead of "Right face." Neither Avaux nor James had heard any thing about this mistake. Indeed the dragoons who set the example of flight were not in the habit of waiting for orders to turn their backs on an enemy. They had run away once before on that very day. Avaux gives a very simple account of the defeat: "Ces mêmes dragons qui avoient fuy le matin lascherent le pied avec tout le reste de la cavalerie, sans tirer un coup de pistolet; et ils s'enfuirent tous avec une telle épouvante qu'ils jettérent mousquetons, pistolets, at espées; et la plupart d'eux, ayant crevé leurs chevaux, se déshabillerent pour aller plus viste à pied."

† Hamilton's True Relation.

END OF THE SECOND VOLUME.

www.ingramcontent.com/pod-product-compliance
Lightning Source LLC
Chambersburg PA
CBHW021228300426
44111CB00007B/470